T0330313

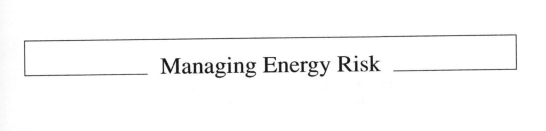

Managing Energy Risk

For other titles in the Wiley Finance series,
please see www.wiley.com/finance

Managing Energy Risk

A Practical Guide for Risk Management in Power, Gas and Other Energy Markets

Second Edition

Markus Burger
Bernhard Graeber
Gero Schindlmayr

This edition first published 2014
© 2014 Markus Burger, Bernhard Graeber & Gero Schindlmayr
First edition published 2007 by John Wiley & Sons, Ltd.

Registered office

John Wiley & Sons Ltd, The Atrium, Southern Gate, Chichester, West Sussex, PO19 8SQ, United Kingdom

For details of our global editorial offices, for customer services and for information about how to apply for
permission to reuse the copyright material in this book please see our website at www.wiley.com.

A catalogue record for this book is available from the Library of Congress

A catalogue record for this book is available from the British Library.

ISBN 978-1-118-61863-9 (hardback)   ISBN 978-1-118-61862-2 (ebk)
ISBN 978-1-118-61858-5 (ebk)   ISBN 978-1-118-61850-9 (obk)

Cover design: Wiley

Set in 10/12pt Times by Aptara Inc., New Delhi, India
Printed in Great Britain by CPI Group (UK) Ltd, Croydon, CR0 4YY

Contents

Preface   **xi**

Acknowledgements   **xiii**

1 Energy Markets   **1**
  1.1   Energy Trading   3
      1.1.1   Spot Market   3
      1.1.2   Forwards and Futures   4
      1.1.3   Commodity Swaps   6
      1.1.4   Options   6
      1.1.5   Delivery Terms   6
  1.2   The Oil Market   7
      1.2.1   Consumption, Production and Reserves   7
      1.2.2   Crude Oil Trading   10
      1.2.3   Refined Oil Products   11
  1.3   The Natural Gas Market   12
      1.3.1   Consumption, Production and Reserves   13
      1.3.2   Natural Gas Trading   15
      1.3.3   Liquefied Natural Gas   19
  1.4   The Coal Market   21
      1.4.1   Consumption, Production and Reserves   21
      1.4.2   Coal Trading   23
      1.4.3   Freight   26
  1.5   The Electricity Market   27
      1.5.1   Consumption and Production   27
      1.5.2   Electricity Trading   31
      1.5.3   Electricity Exchanges   38
  1.6   The Emissions Market   42
      1.6.1   Kyoto Protocol   42
      1.6.2   EU Emissions Trading Scheme   45
      1.6.3   Flexible Mechanisms   46
      1.6.4   Products and Marketplaces   48
      1.6.5   Other Emissions Trading Schemes   51

2   Renewable Energy   **55**
  2.1   The Role of Renewable Energy in Electricity Generation   55
        2.1.1   Historical Development   55
        2.1.2   Political Targets   58
        2.1.3   Forecasts   59
  2.2   The Role of Liquid Biofuels in the Transportation Sector   60
  2.3   Renewable Energy Technologies   61
        2.3.1   Hydropower   61
        2.3.2   Wind Power   66
        2.3.3   Solar Energy   69
        2.3.4   Geothermal Energy   71
        2.3.5   Bioenergy   73
        2.3.6   Not Widespread Renewable Energies   77
  2.4   Support Schemes for Renewable Energy   78
        2.4.1   Feed-In Tariffs   80
        2.4.2   Net Metering   83
        2.4.3   Electric Utility Quota Obligations and Tradable Certificates   83
        2.4.4   Auctions   85
        2.4.5   Subsidies, Investment Grants and Tax Benefits   86
  2.5   Key Economic Factors of Renewable Energy Projects   87
        2.5.1   The Project Developer's Perspective   87
        2.5.2   The Project Investor's Perspective   88
  2.6   Risks in Renewable Energy Projects and their Mitigation   90
        2.6.1   Project Development Risks   90
        2.6.2   Construction Risks   93
        2.6.3   Resource Risks   93
        2.6.4   Technical Risks   96
        2.6.5   Market Risks   97
        2.6.6   Regulatory Risks   99
        2.6.7   Other Operational Risks   100

3   Risk Management   **101**
  3.1   Governance Principles and Market Regulation   102
  3.2   Market Risk   104
        3.2.1   Delta Position   104
        3.2.2   Variance Minimising Hedging   110
        3.2.3   Value-at-Risk   111
        3.2.4   Estimating Volatilities and Correlations   120
        3.2.5   Backtesting   123
        3.2.6   Liquidity-Adjusted Value-at-Risk   123
        3.2.7   Profit-at-Risk and Further Risk Measures   127
  3.3   Legal Risk   130
  3.4   Credit Risk   134
        3.4.1   Credit Rating   137
        3.4.2   Quantifying Credit Risk   140
  3.5   Liquidity Risk   144
  3.6   Operational Risk   146

4   Retail Markets   **151**
  4.1   Interaction of Wholesale and Retail Markets   151
  4.2   Retail Products   155
        4.2.1   Fixed-Price Contracts   155
        4.2.2   Indexed Contracts   156
        4.2.3   Full Service Contracts   157
        4.2.4   Partial Delivery Contracts   157
        4.2.5   Portfolio Management   158
        4.2.6   Supplementary Products   159
  4.3   Sourcing   160
        4.3.1   Sourcing Fixed-Price Contracts   160
        4.3.2   Sourcing Indexed Contracts   161
        4.3.3   Sourcing B2C Contracts   162
  4.4   Load Forecasting   163
  4.5   Weather Risk in Gas Retail Markets   165
        4.5.1   Weather Derivatives   168
  4.6   Risk Premiums   172
        4.6.1   Risk-Adjusted Return on Capital   174
        4.6.2   Price Validity Period   174
        4.6.3   Structuring Fee and Balancing Energy   175
        4.6.4   Credit Risk   176
        4.6.5   Volume and Price Profile Risk   177
        4.6.6   Operational Risk   181
        4.6.7   Risk Premium Summary   182

5   Energy Derivatives   **185**
  5.1   Forwards, Futures and Swaps   186
        5.1.1   Forward Contracts   186
        5.1.2   Futures Contracts   189
        5.1.3   Swaps   191
  5.2   Commodity Forward Curves   192
        5.2.1   Investment Assets   194
        5.2.2   Consumption Assets and Convenience Yield   194
        5.2.3   The Market Price of Risk   196
  5.3   "Plain Vanilla" Options   197
        5.3.1   The Put–Call Parity and Option Strategies   198
        5.3.2   Black's Futures Price Model   200
        5.3.3   Option Pricing Formulas   200
        5.3.4   Hedging Options: The "Greeks"   202
        5.3.5   Implied Volatilities and the "Volatility Smile"   208
        5.3.6   Swaptions   210
  5.4   American, Bermudan and Asian Options   212
        5.4.1   American and Bermudan Options   212
        5.4.2   Asian Options   213
  5.5   Multi-Underlying Options   216
        5.5.1   Basket Options   216
        5.5.2   Spread Options   218
        5.5.3   Quanto and Composite Options   221

5.6   Modelling Spot Prices   224
      5.6.1   Pricing Spot Price Options   226
      5.6.2   Geometric Brownian Motion as Spot Price Model   231
      5.6.3   The One-Factor Schwartz Model   237
      5.6.4   The Schwartz–Smith Model   241
5.7   Stochastic Forward Curve Models   246
      5.7.1   One-Factor Forward Curve Models   247
      5.7.2   A Two-Factor Forward Curve Model   249
      5.7.3   A Multi-Factor Exponential Model   251

6 Stochastic Models for Electricity and Gas   **253**
6.1   Daily and Hourly Forward Curve Models   253
      6.1.1   Daily Price Forward Curve for Gas   255
      6.1.2   Hourly Price Forward Curve for Electricity   257
6.2   Structural Electricity Price Models   265
      6.2.1   The SMaPS Model   266
      6.2.2   The Multi-Commodity SMaPS model   269
      6.2.3   Regime-Switching Models   272
      6.2.4   Virtual Power Plants   278
6.3   Structural Gas Price Models   281
      6.3.1   Natural Gas Price Models   281
      6.3.2   Swing Options and Gas Storage   286
      6.3.3   Least-Squares Monte Carlo Method   291

7 Fundamental Market Models   **301**
7.1   Fundamental Price Drivers in Electricity Markets   301
      7.1.1   Demand Side   302
      7.1.2   Supply Side   306
      7.1.3   Interconnections   313
7.2   Economic Power Plant Dispatch   313
      7.2.1   Thermal Power Plants   315
      7.2.2   Hydropower Plants   322
      7.2.3   Optimisation Methods   325
7.3   Methodological Approaches   335
      7.3.1   Merit Order Curve   335
      7.3.2   Optimisation Models   347
      7.3.3   System Dynamics   353
      7.3.4   Game Theory   357
7.4   Relevant System Information for Electricity Market Modelling   366
      7.4.1   Demand Side   366
      7.4.2   Supply Side   367
      7.4.3   Transmission System   370
      7.4.4   Historical Data for Backtesting   371
      7.4.5   Information Sources   371
7.5   Application of Electricity Market Models   372
7.6   Gas Market Models   374
      7.6.1   Demand Side   375
      7.6.2   Supply Side   376

7.6.3	Transport	379
7.6.4	Storage	379
7.6.5	Portfolio Optimisation	382
7.6.6	Formulation of the Market Model	383
7.6.7	Application of Gas Market Models	385
7.7	Market Models for Oil, Coal and CO_2 Markets	386
7.8	Asset Investment Decisions	387
7.8.1	The Discounted Cashflow Method	387
7.8.2	Weighted Average Cost of Capital	389
7.8.3	The Capital Asset Pricing Model	390
Appendix: Mathematical Background		**393**
A.1	Econometric Methods	393
A.1.1	Linear Regression	393
A.1.2	Stationary Time Series and Unit Root Tests	395
A.1.3	Principal Component Analysis	397
A.1.4	Kalman Filtering Method	398
A.1.5	Regime-Switching Models	399
A.2	Stochastic Processes	402
A.2.1	Conditional Expectation and Martingales	402
A.2.2	Brownian Motion	402
A.2.3	Stochastic Integration and Itô's Lemma	403
A.3	Option Pricing Theory	405
A.3.1	Pricing Under the Risk-Neutral Measure	405
A.3.2	The Feynman–Kac Theorem	408
A.3.3	Monte Carlo Simulation	410
References		**413**
Index		**419**

Preface

Reliable energy supply is essential for our civilised society. With constantly growing worldwide energy demand it is one of the main challenges for the 21st century to secure sufficient energy supply at reasonable costs in alignment with environmental and climate protection targets. Incidents like increasing oil prices, climate change, the Fukushima nuclear accident or shale gas production have attracted a high degree of public, international media and political attention in the energy sector. However, suggested answers for safe future energy supply differ broadly in international comparison.

Until the mid-20th century, energy demand was almost exclusively met by domestic energy sources. Since then fossil fuels have become traded internationally and interconnected markets for electricity have evolved. Liberalisation of energy markets in many regions of the world led to new electricity and gas markets with increasing trading volumes. With the introduction of emissions trading for sulphur dioxide (SO_2) in the United States and for carbon dioxide (CO_2) in Europe, new markets with specific characteristics have been created.

Besides energy companies, large consumers and emitters, banks and other traders participate in growing energy markets. Commodities are also increasingly recognised as an important asset class in fund management that can improve the portfolio risk profile. However, energy and emissions markets are often described as unstable and erratic. They are characterised by a multitude of complex products, high price volatility and changing correlations between each other.

The financial crisis of 2007/8 has shown that for market participants, adequate risk management is essential. Risk management must cover all aspects – such as market, credit, liquidity and operational risk – and has to reflect the specifics of the relevant markets adequately. Such specifics also include the interaction between different energy markets. This book pursues a multi-commodity approach and addresses electricity, gas, coal, oil and CO_2 emissions.

Since the financial crisis, increased regulation of energy markets has broken the earlier trend of market liberalisation in many countries. On the one hand, this is caused by the interaction of financial markets and energy markets in terms of products and market participants. As a result, energy traders now have to comply with new regulatory requirements originally targeted at financial institutions. On the other hand, different political views on how to achieve ambitious renewable energy targets led to new market interventions and regulations. Furthermore, public concerns about the influence of speculators on commodity prices have fed discussions on further regulation. Increased regulation and market interventions provide new challenges for the energy industry that need to be taken into account in the risk management process.

One speciality of this book is to cover both energy economics approaches, including fundamental market models, and the financial engineering approaches commonly used in banks and other trading companies. One example of the combination of these approaches is the SMaPS electricity price model described in Chapter 6. This builds on stochastic price models similar to those used for financial markets but reflects the specific characteristics of electricity markets by using a merit order approach commonly found in fundamental electricity market models. As a consequence, this book addresses researchers and professionals from a technical background in energy economics as well as those with experience in financial mathematics or trading. Although the book introduces a wide range of theoretical concepts, its main focus is on applications within the energy business. As the best choice of model depends on the specific purpose, advantages and disadvantages of different modelling and risk management approaches are discussed throughout the book.

This second edition contains substantial new material to meet the requirements of the recent developments in energy markets. The main changes include:

- The structure of the book has been altered to offer a more intuitive approach for readers with different interests. Chapters 1 and 2 give an overview and explain the fundamental principles of energy markets. Chapters 3 and 4 describe risk management and customer-oriented retail processes for energy companies. These chapters are particularly focused on practical use. Chapters 5 and 6 cover the valuation of derivatives and structured energy products. They require basic knowledge of financial mathematics, some of which is summarised in the Appendix. An alternative for the valuation of real assets is the use of fundamental models as explained in Chapter 7.
- The growing influence of renewable energy is given much more space and a new and comprehensive chapter on renewable energy has been added (Chapter 2). This contains energy economic principles, value drivers and risks related to hydro, wind, solar, bio and further renewable energy sources.
- The growing gas markets and their modelling approaches are described in more detail. Specific topics added to this second edition are how to build a price forward curve for natural gas, stochastic modelling of gas prices and valuation of gas storage and swing options.
- The chapter on retail markets (Chapter 4) now contains a description of weather derivatives and their use for hedging gas retail contracts.
- To meet new requirements after the financial crisis, extended risk management processes are discussed in more detail.

Acknowledgements

The realisation of this second edition involved inspiring teamwork, which we really enjoyed. Besides the authors, a number of people provided valuable contributions to this book for which we want to express our gratitude. First of all, we thank Guido Hirsch for his contributions regarding gas price models and weather derivatives. Guido is Head of Market Risk and Valuation Models at EnBW and thanks to Guido's expertise the book could be expanded with respect to the recent developments in natural gas markets. Jan Müller has added a description of the multi-commodity SMaPS model, which formed part of his PhD thesis. Sven-Olaf Stoll has added refinements to the price forward curve for electricity. Both Jan and Sven-Olaf are experts in stochastic modelling at EnBW.

1

Energy Markets

Despite a global sustainability trend including climate protection and more efficient use of energy, worldwide energy consumption will continue to grow over the coming decades (see Figure 1.1). Besides future economic growth, an important driver of global energy demand is policy commitments, such as renewable energy or energy efficiency targets. Depending on scenario assumptions, the average annual growth rate in energy consumption is estimated to be between 0.5% and 1.5% (International Energy Agency, 2012) until 2035, with significant regional differences. Most of the energy demand growth is expected to come from non-OECD countries, with China and India being the largest single contributors.

The main primary energy source worldwide is oil, covering 32% of worldwide energy consumption (see Figure 1.2). Second are coal and natural gas, with a share of 27% (respectively 22%). Nuclear energy (6%) and renewables (13%) have a much smaller share. To meet the growing worldwide demand for energy, there will need to be an increase in energy supply from all primary energy sources. However, depending on the scenario, the share of oil and coal will diminish in favour of gas and renewable energy sources (Figure 1.2).

Not all of the primary sources of energy are used directly for consumption; they may first be transformed into secondary forms of energy, such as electricity or heat. Since part of the primary energy is used for the transformation process, the final consumption is below the primary energy demand. A breakdown of the final consumption into different sectors is given in Figure 1.3.

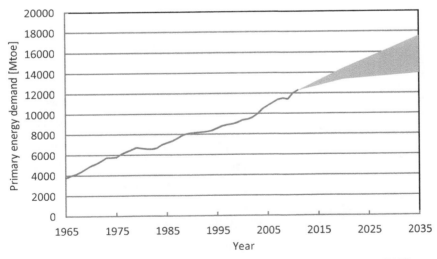

Figure 1.1 World energy demand. *Source*: International Energy Agency (2012).

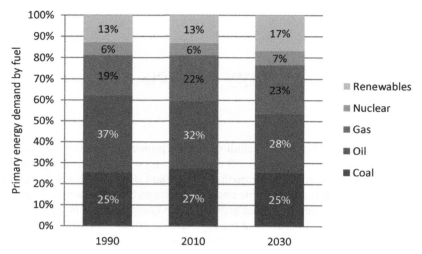

Figure 1.2   World primary energy sources. *Source*: International Energy Agency (2012).

The current trends by sector are as follows (International Energy Agency, 2012):

- *Industry:* The industrial sector accounts for 28% of the total energy consumption and has the highest growth rate among the sectors. The main energy sources are coal (28%), electricity (26%), gas (19%) and oil (13%). It is expected that electricity and gas will gain importance at the expense of coal and oil.
- *Transport:* The transport sector, which makes up 27% of the energy demand, is strongly dominated by oil (93%). On a worldwide scale, biofuels (2%) and electricity (1%) still play a minor role, but are expected to increase their share to 2% (respectively 6%) in the reference scenario. The actual development will be strongly influenced by future governmental policies.

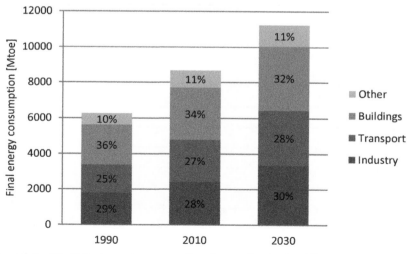

Figure 1.3   World final energy consumption. *Source*: International Energy Agency (2012).

- *Buildings:* This sector includes heating, air conditioning, cooking and lighting. It accounts for 34% of the total energy consumption. The energy is delivered mainly in the form of electricity (29%), bioenergy (29%), gas (21%) and oil (11%). There is a clear trend towards a higher share of electricity and gas at the expense of bioenergy and oil.

1.1   ENERGY TRADING

With the development of a global oil market in the 1980s, energy has become a tradable commodity. In the early 1990s, deregulation of the natural gas market in the United States led to a liquid and competitive gas market. In Europe, liberalisation of gas and electricity markets started in the UK in the late 1980s. In the late 1990s, the EU Commission adopted first directives making energy market liberalisation a mandatory target for EU member states along different steps of implementation. Whereas a wholesale market for electricity developed successfully in the early 2000s in some countries (e.g., Germany), a liquid gas wholesale market only existed in the UK. Gas markets in Continental Europe still remained fragmented and dominated by oil-indexed supply contracts. Further consolidation of market areas, easier market access and declining gas demand following the financial crisis in 2008 increased competition and finally led to growing market liquidity for gas markets in Continental Europe and a decoupling of gas and oil prices in the early 2010s.

Besides the commodities coal, oil, gas and electricity, which carry energy directly, the EU introduced carbon emission certificates (*European Emission Allowance* or *EUA*) in the year 2005 as part of the EU climate policy. The certificates were designed as tradable instruments for which a liquid market quickly developed. Since carbon certificates are closely related to energy commodities and electricity generation, they will be treated here along with the other energy commodities. Before describing the specific markets for each commodity, the general structure and basic products of commodity markets in general will be introduced. A more detailed description of commodity derivatives products will be given in Chapter 5.

We generally distinguish between *over-the-counter (OTC)* and exchange-traded markets. The OTC market consists of bilateral agreements, which are concluded over the phone or through Internet-based broker platforms. Such transactions are most flexible since the parties are free to agree individual contract terms. As a main disadvantage, OTC transactions may contain credit risk, meaning that one of the counterparties may not deliver on his contract (e.g., in case of insolvency). As a mitigation, collaterals may be defined to protect the counterparties from losses in such a case. Exchanges provide organised markets for commodities in the form of standardised contracts. In particular, they became popular for derivatives products (futures, options), where the exchange also eliminates credit risk for the market participants.

1.1.1   Spot Market

The *spot market* is the market for immediate (or nearby) delivery of the respective commodity in exchange for cash. The exact definition depends on the commodity. As an example, the spot market for electricity often refers to delivery on the next day or on the next working day. For coal markets, contracts delivering within the next several weeks ahead are typically still considered as spot transactions. Spot markets can either be bilateral OTC transactions or organised by exchanges. For electricity, gas and EUAs, energy exchanges typically offer spot market products.

A particular form of spot market is the *auction market*, where buyers submit their bids and sellers their offers at the same time. In most cases a uniform price, the *market clearing price*, is determined, which balances supply and demand. Such a uniform price auction is popular for electricity spot markets; traded products are typically single-hour (or even half-hour) deliveries.

Spot prices represent the final price of the "physical commodity" in the prevailing situation of supply and demand, and are therefore the *underlying* of the derivatives market, which is largely driven by expectations regarding the future situation on spot markets. There are various published spot price indices available for the different commodities that provide transparency for market participants and also serve as official references for the financial settlement of futures contracts.

1.1.2   Forwards and Futures

Forward and futures contracts are contractual agreements to purchase or sell a certain amount of commodity on a fixed future date (delivery date) at a predetermined contract price. The contract needs to be fulfilled regardless of the commodity price development between conclusion of the contract and delivery date. In case the spot price has increased, the seller needs to sell below the prevailing spot price at delivery and therefore incurs an opportunity loss, whereas the buyer makes an (opportunity) profit. In case prices decline, the situation is reversed. The buyer of a forward or future is said to hold a *long position* in the commodity (he profits from a price increase until delivery), the seller is said to hold a *short position* (he takes a loss from a price increase).

The final profit or loss for the buyer of a forward contract (long position) at delivery date T is the value of the commodity at delivery $S(T)$ minus the contract price K (i.e., $S(T) - K$), see Figure 1.4. Similarly, the profit or loss for the seller (short position) is $K - S(T)$.

Forward contracts are the most basic *hedging* instruments. If a producer of a commodity enters into a forward contract as a seller, he fixes his revenues and is indemnified from further

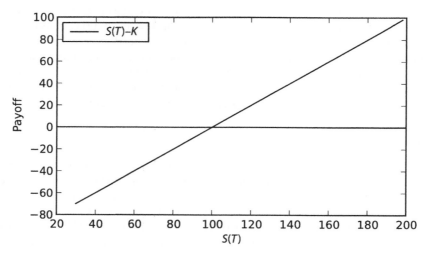

Figure 1.4   Profit or loss of a commodity forward contract.

price changes. On the contrary, a market participant who is dependent on the commodity for consumption may enter into a forward contract as a buyer to fix his purchasing costs for the commodity in advance.

The term "futures contract" is used for a standardised forward contract which is traded via an exchange. Often, futures contracts are financially settled, which means that only the value of the commodity at the delivery date is paid instead of a true physical delivery. Futures contracts open up the commodity market for participants who do not want to get involved in the physical handling of the commodity. Since the exchange serves as a *central counterparty* for futures contracts, market participants do not have to deal with multiple individual counterparties and their associated credit risk. This also makes it easier to unwind a position entered into previously.

The market size and liquidity of the futures market is often much higher than the actual physical (spot) market. A list of exchanges with global significance offering energy-related commodity derivatives products is given below.

- *CME Group (Chicago Mercantile Exchange):* The CME Group is the world's largest commodity futures exchange. The wide array of products offered by the CME Group includes futures and options contracts for energy (electricity, oil products, coal, natural gas), but also metals, agriculture, foreign exchange, equities and interest rates. The CME Group originated from a merger between the Chicago Mercantile Exchange (CME) and the Chicago Board of Trade (CBOT) in 2007. In 2008, the CME Group acquired the *New York Mercantile Exchange (NYMEX)*. The NYMEX light sweet crude oil futures contract introduced in 1983 and the NYMEX Henry Hub natural gas futures contract introduced in 1990 are the most popular energy benchmarks in the United States.
- *IntercontinentalExchange (ICE):* The ICE was founded in May 2000 with the objective of providing an electronic trading platform for OTC energy commodity trading. ICE expanded its business into futures trading by acquiring the International Petroleum Exchange (IPE) in 2001. ICE's products include derivative contracts based on the key energy commodities of crude oil, refined oil products, natural gas and electricity. The ICE Brent futures contract serves as an important international benchmark for pricing oil cargos (see Section 1.2) in Europe. In 2010, ICE acquired the European Climate Exchange (ECX), which is the leading exchange for emission certificates under the European Trading Scheme.
- *NASDAQ OMX Commodities Europe:* NASDAQ OMX Commodities Europe is part of the NASDAQ OMX Group and originates from the acquisition of the financial trading part of the Nord Pool exchange in 2008. Nord Pool was founded in 1993 in Norway and became the leading electricity market place for the Nordic and Baltic countries. Meanwhile, NASDAQ OMX Commodities Europe also offers electricity products for Continental European countries, electricity and gas contracts for the UK and emission certificates.
- *European Energy Exchange (EEX):* The EEX was founded at the beginning of the 2000s with origins in the German electricity market and has become one of the leading European energy exchanges with a focus on electricity, gas and emissions. EEX and the French energy exchange *Powernext* both hold a 50% share of the *EPEX Spot* exchange, which operates power spot markets for Germany, France, Austria and Switzerland.

There are several other energy exchanges with a focus on specific local markets for electricity or natural gas. Descriptions of these exchanges are included in the subsequent sections.

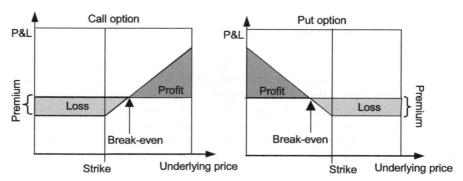

Figure 1.5   Profit or loss at maturity for an option holder.

1.1.3   Commodity Swaps

A *commodity swap* exchanges a fixed cashflow specified by a fixed commodity price against a varying cashflow calculated from a published commodity price index at the respective fixing dates. The risk profile of a commodity swap is similar to that of a financially settled forward (i.e., a forward paying the commodity price index instead of a physical delivery). Often, commodity swaps cover multiple payment periods, so that the swap is equivalent to a series of financially settled forward contracts with different delivery dates $T_1, \ldots, T_n$. On each payment date T_i, one counterparty (the holder of the long position) receives the *floating* price index $S(T_i)$ and pays the fixed price K whereas the other counterparty (the holder of the short position) pays the price index and receives the fixed price. The net amount the holder of the long position receives on the payment date T_i is therefore $S(T_i) - K$. For more details and examples, see Section 5.1.3.

1.1.4   Options

An *option* holder has the right but not the obligation to purchase (*call option*) or sell (*put option*) a certain commodity at a predetermined *strike price* from the option seller. See Figure 1.5. In exchange, the option holder pays an option premium to the seller of the option.

A call option will only be exercised at the option's *maturity date* T if the spot price at time T is above the strike price, as otherwise purchasing from the market is cheaper. If the option premium is P, then the profit or loss for the holder of a call option is $\max(S(T) - K, 0) - P$.

A put option will only be exercised if the spot price at time T is below the strike price, as otherwise selling in the market generates higher value. If the option premium is P, then the profit or loss for the holder of a put option is $\max(K - S(T), 0) - P$.

For more details and examples, see Section 5.3.

1.1.5   Delivery Terms

Unlike in financial markets, the point of delivery plays an important role in commodity trading, since transportation can be costly (coal, oil) or dependent on access to a grid (power, gas). Therefore, commodity prices are usually quoted with reference to the delivery point. Typical delivery points depend on the type of commodity, for example Richards Bay in South

Africa for coal or Amsterdam–Rotterdam–Antwerp (ARA) for oil or coal. Another important specification for physical commodity trades are the *Incoterms* (international commerce terms) dealing with the clearance responsibilities and transaction costs. The most important Incoterms for energy markets are as follows.

- *Free-On-Board (FOB):* The seller pays for transportation of the goods to the port of shipment and for loading costs. The buyer pays for freight, insurance, unloading costs and further transportation to the destination. The transfer of risk is at the ship's rail.
- *Cost, Insurance and Freight (CIF):* The selling price includes the cost of the goods, the freight or transport costs and also the cost of marine insurance. However, the transfer of risk takes place at the ship's rail.
- *Delivered-At-Place (DAP):* The seller pays for transport similar to CIF, but also assumes all risks up to the point that the vessel has arrived at the port and the goods are ready for unloading.
- *Delivered-ex-Ship (DES):* Similar to DAP (eliminated from Incoterms 2010).

1.2   THE OIL MARKET

The oil market is certainly the most prominent among the energy markets. *Crude oil* (or *petroleum*) is found in reserves spread across particular regions of the Earth, where it can be accessed from the surface. Even though petroleum has been known and used for thousands of years, it became increasingly important during the second half of the 19th century as a primary energy source and as a raw material for chemical products. The main advantages of oil as an energy carrier compared with other primary energy sources is its high energy density and the ease of handling for storage and transport. Today, crude oil is still the predominant source of energy in the transportation sector and is often taken as a benchmark for the price of energy in general. Chemically, crude oil is a mixture of *hydrocarbons* with different molecular weights. For actual usage, crude oil is transformed via a refinery process into different petroleum products, such as fuel oil or gasoline.

Because of oil's great economic importance historically, oil markets have always been subject to political regulations and interventions. Figure 1.6 shows the historical spot prices for Brent crude oil. Clearly, the oil price is influenced by political or military events (especially in oil-exporting countries), which explains, for example, the price spike during the First Gulf War of 1990/91. In addition, there are economic developments, such as the increase of energy demand in Asia or the financial crisis following the bankruptcy of Lehman Brothers in 2008, which have an impact on the oil price.

1.2.1   Consumption, Production and Reserves

Oil consumption and oil production are unevenly distributed accross the world. The majority of the world's oil consumption is located in North America, Europe & Eurasia and Asia & Pacific (see Figure 1.7), whereas the majority of the reserves are located in the Middle East and South & Central America (see Figure 1.8).

Historically, the OECD countries clearly dominated oil demand, but over the last decades the share of non-OECD countries increased to nearly 50% (see Figure 1.9), largely driven by

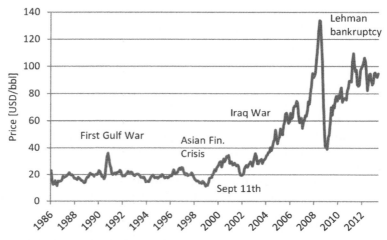

Figure 1.6   Brent historical spot prices. *Source*: Energy Information Administration.

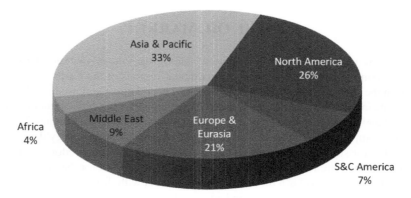

Total consumption: 90 million bbl per day

Figure 1.7   World oil consumption 2012 by region. *Source*: BP (2013).

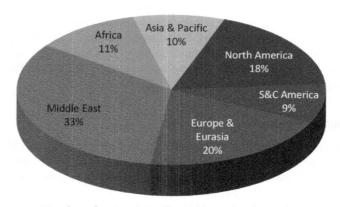

Total production: 86 million bbl per day (excl. biofuels)

Figure 1.8   World oil production 2012 by region. *Source*: BP (2013).

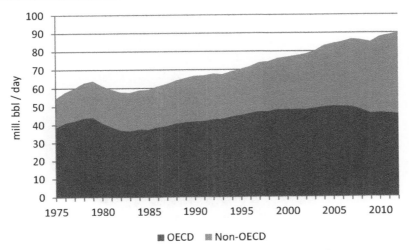

Figure 1.9 Historical oil demand. *Source*: BP (2013).

increased demand from China and India. The main driver for oil demand is the transport sector, accounting for more than 50% of the overall oil demand. Other drivers for oil demand include the buildings, industry and power generation sectors. Forecasts for oil demand over the next decades depend strongly on assumptions for the world's economic growth and government policies to curb oil demand. Different scenarios (see International Energy Agency, 2012) lead to an average annual growth rate between −0.5% and 1.80% in the period 2011 to 2035.

On the supply side, the OPEC member countries[1] control over 40% of the world's oil production and over 70% of all known conventional oil reserves (see Figure 1.10). An indication of the future production potential can be given by the *reserves-to-production ratio* describing the number of years that known reserves are estimated to last at the current rate of production. The worldwide reserves-to-production ratio as for 2012 was approximately 53 years, with great differences among the regions. For OPEC members the reserves-to-production ratio was 89 years, whereas for non-OPEC countries the ratio was only 26 years (see BP, 2013). However, this indication may be misleading due to changes in production, revised estimates for existing reserves and discoveries of new reserves. A major unknown is the future role of *unconventional oil*, which comprises extra heavy oils, oil sands, *kerogen oil* and *light tight oil*. Producing or extracting unconventional oil requires techniques that are usually more costly than conventional oil production and become profitable only if oil prices are sufficiently high. On the contrary, there may still be substantial "learning curve" effects leading to more efficient production processes. An example is the production of light tight oil, which only recently emerged with substantial production volumes using the same technology as for shale gas production (see Section 1.3).

Depending on its origin, oil can be of different quality. The main characteristics are viscosity and sulphur content. Fluid crude oils with low viscosity have a lower specific weight and are called *light* crudes. With increasing viscosity and specific weight the crudes are called *intermediate* and then *heavy*. Lighter crude oils are more valuable, since they yield more

---

[1] Iran, Iraq, Kuwait, Qatar, Saudi Arabia, United Arab Emirates, Algeria, Libya, Angola, Nigeria, Ecuador, Venezuela.

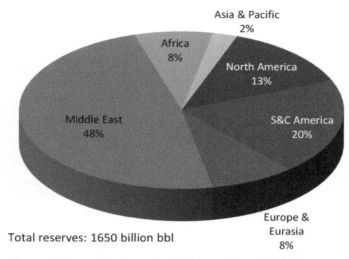

Figure 1.10   World oil reserves 2012 by region. *Source*: BP (2013).

marketable products. Crude oils with low sulphur content are called *sweet*, otherwise they are called *sour*. Since a high sulphur content causes additional costs in the refinery process, sweet crude oils are priced at a premium.

1.2.2   Crude Oil Trading

The physical crude oil market has to deal with a large variety of different oil qualities (viscosity, sulphur content) and with different means of transportation (pipeline, shipping). All of these characteristics influence the oil price. Nevertheless, a liquid oil market has developed, using reference oil qualities as benchmarks for pricing individual oil qualities. Depending on the quality, a certain price differential will be added to the benchmark price. Long-term supply contracts typically use such price formulas to price their individual cargos. The most popular benchmark oils are as follows.

- *West Texas Intermediate (WTI):* Quality sweet and light, main reference for the US market (delivery in Cushing/Oklahoma).
- *Brent:* Quality also sweet and light (slightly less than WTI), main reference for North Sea oil.
- *Dubai:* Reference for the Middle East and Far East with higher sulphur content ("sour").
- *ASCI:* Argus Sour Crude Index representing the price of medium sour crude oil of the US Gulf coast.

The benchmark price used in contracts is typically a spot price index for physical delivery published by an oil pricing reporting agency, such as Platts or Argus. Price assessments are carried out on the basis of information on concluded transactions or bids and offers in the market. The exact methodology varies between different reporting agencies. Also the benchmark itself may evolve over time, for example as the original Brent crude stream has declined over recent decades, the Brent benchmark now includes the North Sea streams Forties,

Oseberg and Ekofisk (BFOE). The benchmark prices above also serve as an underlying for the oil derivatives market, such as futures and swaps.

The structure of the physical market for BFOE crude oil is connected to its nomination procedure. In case of a 25-day[2] forward contract, the sellers are obliged to tell their counterparties 25 days in advance the first day of the three-day loading window when the cargo will actually be loaded. The final loading schedule is then published by the terminal operator. A contract with already nominated loading window less than 25 days ahead is called *Dated Brent*. The *25-day forward market* trades contracts for delivery up to multiple months ahead. A typical crude oil cargo has a size of about 600 000 bbl.

The need for producers and consumers to financially hedge oil price risks and the growing importance of oil derivatives for asset managers and speculators gave rise to a very large market of financial instruments related to oil. The most important commodity exchanges offering oil futures and options are the CME Group (formerly NYMEX) for WTI contracts and the ICE for Brent contracts. Both the WTI and the Brent contracts are monthly futures contracts quoted in USD per barrel with a contract size of 1000 bbl. The *Light Sweet Crude Oil (WTI) Futures* contract was introduced by NYMEX 1983 and soon became a global reference for the price of crude oil. The ICE Brent Crude Futures Contract was launched in 1988 by the former IPE (International Petroleum Exchange) and also reached global importance next to WTI as pricing reference.

	WTI Future	Brent Future
Exchange	CME Group	ICE
Contracts	monthly	monthly
Contract size	1000 bbl	1000 bbl
Price quotation	USD/bbl	USD/bbl
Expiration date	3rd business day prior to the 25th calendar day of the month preceding the delivery month	15th day before the first day of the delivery month
Settlement	physical	physical or financial

In addition to the futures contracts described above there is a wide range of related products for specific purposes, such as different option products, contracts-for-differences (CFDs) to manage the price differential between Dated Brent and forward contracts or spreads between different oil benchmarks (e.g., WTI vs. Brent).

The long-term forward market for crude oil (up to 10 years) is dominated by Brent and WTI swaps exchanging a fixed monthly payment against a floating payment, which is the monthly average of the front month futures price. Such swaps are typically traded OTC, but exchanges (e.g., CME Group and ICE) meanwhile offer a clearing service for swaps that is increasingly used by market participants.

1.2.3 Refined Oil Products

As mentioned earlier, crude oil can be of various qualities concerning its density and sulphur content. To become marketable to consumers, *refineries* convert crude oil into various products.

---

[2] Before 2012, a 21-day nomination period was typically used.

The refining process in its basic form is a distillation process, where crude oil is heated in a distillation column. The lightest components can now be extracted at the top of the column whereas the heaviest components come out of the bottom. To increase the yield of the more valuable lighter products, a *cracking* process is used to break up the longer hydrocarbon molecules. Other processes are needed to remove the sulphur content. Ordered by increasing density, the most important oil products are

- *Light distillates:* Liquefied petroleum gases (LPG), naphtha, gasoline.
- *Middle distillates:* Kerosine, gasoil or heating oil and diesel.
- *Fuel oil.*
- *Others*: For example, lubricating oils, paraffin wax, petroleum coke, bitumen.

LPG (propane or butane) are hydrocarbon gases that are liquid under pressure or low temperature. They are used mainly for heating appliances or vehicles. Naphtha is used mainly in the chemical industry. Middle distillates are the largest group of oil products, accounting for around 50% of refinery output. Besides its use for domestic heating, middle distillates (diesel) is used for transportation. Improvements in diesel engine technology and tax incentives have led to a strong growth of diesel consumption in Europe. Being more polluting and more difficult to process, fuel oil is less valuable and used mainly as bunker fuel in ships and to a limited extent for power generation (e.g., as a backup for gas).

Worldwide there are approximately 700 refineries to match the demand for the different oil distillates. Since building new refineries is a complex project involving very large investments, refining capacities react slowly to changes in demand. Owing to the combined production process, the prices of different oil products are usually tightly related to each other and can be expressed in terms of price spreads against crude oil. The lighter and more valuable products have higher spreads against crude oil than the heavier products. In special circumstances, such as a military crisis, prices for certain products (e.g., jet fuel) can spike upwards in relation to crude oil because of the limited refining capacities and the limited flexibility of refineries to change the production ratios among the different products.

The European market for refined oil products is divided into ARA and Mediterranean (Genova). Typical lot sizes for these contracts are barges that correspond to 1000 to 5000 (metric) tonnes.

Typical financial instruments for European gasoil are

1. *Gasoil swaps:* Gasoil swaps are traded OTC and typically refer to the monthly average gasoil price (ARA or Mediterranean) as published by Platts for setting the floating payments.
2. *ICE gasoil futures:* The ICE offers monthly gasoil futures contracts FOB Rotterdam.

In addition, there are local oil price indices available. In Germany, typical reference prices for HEL (gasoil) and HSL (fuel oil) are published monthly by the "Statistisches Bundesamt". They include certain taxes and transportation costs within Germany.

1.3   THE NATURAL GAS MARKET

Next to oil and coal, natural gas is one of the most important primary energy sources, covering about 22% of worldwide energy consumption. It is used primarily as a fuel for electricity generation, transportation and domestic heating. Natural gas consists mainly of methane (CH_4), which is the shortest and lightest in the family of hydrocarbon molecules. Other components are heavier hydrocarbons such as ethane, propane and butane and contaminants such as sulphur. Natural gas volume is usually measured in cubic metres or cubic feet (1 m^3 = 35.3 ft^3). For larger quantities of natural gas the units bcm (billion cubic metres) or bcf (billion cubic feet) are used. The combustion heat stored in one cubic metre of natural gas at normal atmospheric pressure is about 10.8 kWh (0.0368 mmBtu), but can vary depending on the specific quality. This section gives a general overview of the natural gas market. For economic modelling approaches, see Section 7.6.

1.3.1   Consumption, Production and Reserves

Among the fossil fuels there is a global trend in favour of natural gas. On the one hand, natural gas is the fossil fuel with lowest carbon intensity, therefore it is considered to contribute least to the greenhouse effect. On the other hand, due to the "shale gas boom" in the USA and an expanding infrastructure for *liquefied natural gas (LNG)*, there is a stable outlook for gas supply.

Natural gas and oil are often found in the same deposits. Depending on which of the two dominates, it is called either a natural gas or oil field. Unlike oil, because of its low density, gas is difficult to store and transport. In the past, gas found as a by-product in oil fields was therefore simply burned without any economic use. With growing demand for primary energy sources, gas prices have risen and large investments have been made to build up an infrastructure for gas transportation, either in the form of pipelines or in the form of LNG terminals (see Section 1.3.3). Because of the required transportation infrastructure, which historically was mainly pipelines, the regional distribution of natural gas consumption and production is more balanced between continents than the regional distribution for oil (see Figures 1.11 and 1.12). The countries with the highest gas production are the United States and Russia (between 600 and 650 bcm/a), followed by Canada, Iran and Qatar with around 150 bcm/a and Norway, Saudi Arabia and China with around 100 bcm/a.

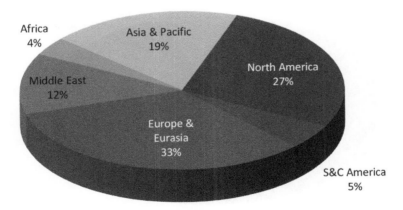

Total annual consumption: 3314 bcm

Figure 1.11   World gas consumption 2012 by regions. *Source*: BP (2013).

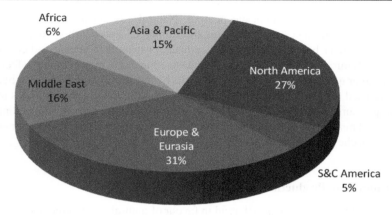

Total annual production: 3364 bcm

Figure 1.12   World gas production 2012 by regions. *Source*: BP (2013).

The distribution of natural gas reserves is less balanced, since gas production in many OECD countries (e.g., Europe) is in decline. Russia has a long history as a natural gas supplier to Western Europe and the reserves are well connected via pipelines. The large reserves in the Middle East (see Figure 1.13), however, could not be utilised fully in the past since efficient transportation to consumers was not available. Over the last decade a growing infrastructure for LNG has been established, allowing us to transport increasing volumes of natural gas between continents, leading to increased export volumes from the Middle East (e.g., Qatar). As of 2012, 90% of natural gas reserves are in non-OECD countries, mainly Russia and the Middle East.

At the current production rate, the proved natural gas reserves as of 2012 are estimated to last for 56 years (= reserves-to-production ratio). For OECD members, the reserves-to-production

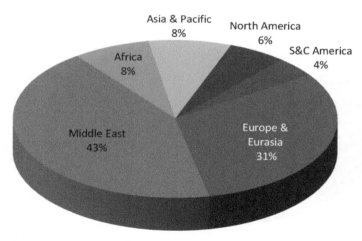

Total reserves: 187 trillion cm

Figure 1.13   World gas reserves 2012 by regions. *Source*: BP (2013).

ratio is only 15 years as of 2012, whereas for non-OECD countries the ratio is 78 years (see BP, 2013). As for oil, the future development of the reserves-to-production ratio will depend heavily on production growth and revised estimates for gas reserves.

A major role for the future of gas supply will be played by *unconventional gas*, which comprises *tight gas*, *shale gas* and *coalbed methane*. Extracting tight gas and shale gas requires *hydraulic fracturing*. Coalbed methane is gas extracted from coal beds, with significant reserves being in the USA, Canada and Australia. Tight gas and coalbed methane have been produced for many decades; the extraction of shale gas is technologically more intricate and began to become profitable only at the beginning of the 21st century. Since then a "shale gas boom" has emerged in the USA, able to overcompensate declining conventional gas production and leading to decreased gas prices in the USA (see Section 1.3.2). The global potential of shale gas is still disputed, since outside the USA there is uncertainty around resources and there are also environmental concerns in many countries regarding the hydraulic fracturing process, for example with respect to potential contamination of groundwater.

1.3.2 Natural Gas Trading

Compared with oil, the natural gas market is more regional due to the higher costs of gas transportation. The following main gas markets can be distinguished:

- North America
- Europe
- Asia-Pacific

Historically, those regional markets have had little interaction, since LNG played a significant role only for the Asian market. Owing to a growing LNG infrastructure, market interaction has increased significantly during recent years. However, due to the shale gas boom in the USA and increasing demand in Asia, the price differentials between gas prices in North America, Europe and Asia-Pacific have first of all increased substantially (see Figure 1.14). These price differentials may attract additional investments in LNG infrastructure, which could lead again to convergence of prices to some extent in the future.

The North American Market

The United States is an importer of natural gas, with the main imports via pipeline from Canada. Before the shale gas boom in the mid-2000s there was the expectation that substantial LNG imports would be required to replace declining conventional domestic gas production and therefore infrastructure for importing LNG was built. The additional shale gas supply has reversed this picture and the United States may even become an exporter of natural gas around 2020 (see Figure 1.15). The extent of exports will depend on infrastructure investments and also regulatory approval for export licences.

The US wholesale market for natural gas is liberalised and competitive. The highest liquidity is found at Henry Hub (Louisiana) in the Gulf of Mexico. Besides a liquid spot market there is also a very liquid futures market introduced by NYMEX (now the CME Group) in 1990. The range of products offered by NYMEX includes options on gas futures and spreads between Henry Hub and other US gas hubs. As can be seen from Figure 1.16, wholesale prices in the USA deteriorated after 2008 along with the financial crisis and increasing shale gas supply. A

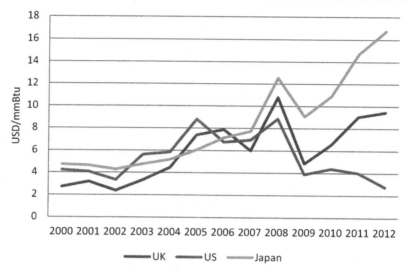

Figure 1.14   Global natural gas prices. *Source*: BP (2013).

recovery of prices will, among other factors, depend on future export volumes to higher-priced markets.

The monthly CME Natural Gas Futures contract has the following specification.

- *Trading unit:* 10 000 million British thermal units (mmBtu).
- *Price quotation:* USD and cents per mmBtu.
- *Trading months:* The current year and the following 12 years (Globex: 8 years).
- *Last trading day:* Three business days prior to the first calendar day of the delivery month.
- *Settlement type:* Physical delivery at Henry Hub.

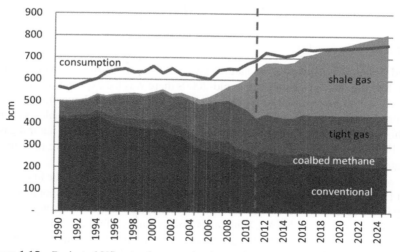

Figure 1.15   Projected US natural gas production and consumption. *Source*: EIA (2013).

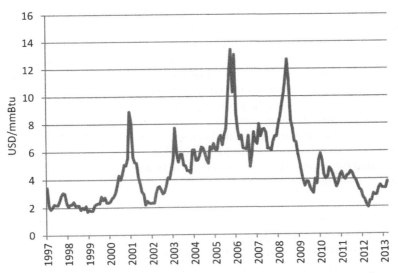

Figure 1.16   Natural gas US wholesale prices (Henry Hub, front-month contract). *Source*: EIA.

The European Market

As domestic gas production in Western Europe has been in decline for many years, an extensive infrastructure for gas imports was established. The main exporters to serve the Western European demand are Russia, Norway, the Netherlands, Algeria via pipelines and Qatar via LNG. The UK gas market was liberalised in 1996. The *National Balancing Point (NBP)* soon gained acceptance as a universal delivery point and "trading hub" in the UK. In 1997 the IPE (now ICE) launched a futures market for UK natural gas, which became the first liquid gas futures market in Europe. The natural gas market in Continental Europe was for a long time still dominated by long-term supply contracts indexed to oil prices. Fragmented market zones did not attract sufficient liquidity for a competitive wholesale gas market independent of oil-indexed supply contracts. This situation changed towards the end of the 2000s due to different developments:

- Downturn in gas demand caused by the global recession after 2008.
- Growth in global LNG supply.
- Consolidation of market zones, simplification of market access (e.g., in Germany).

Meanwhile, the liquidity of gas trading hubs has increased also in Continental Europe and corresponding futures markets were established. The most important natural gas hubs for trading in Europe are:

- National Balancing Point (NBP) in the UK;
- Title Transfer Facility (TTF) in the Netherlands;
- Zeebrugge Hub (ZEE) in Belgium;
- NetConnect Germany (NCG);
- Gaspool Hub (GPL) in Germany.

The Continental European market and the UK market are linked by the *Interconnector* pipeline that began operation in 1998. The Interconnector has a length of 235 km and connects Bacton, UK with Zeebrugge, Belgium. The pipline has a capacity of 20 billion cubic metres of gas per year to transport gas from Bacton to Zeebrugge (forward flow) and a capacity of 25.5 billion cubic metres in the reverse direction (reverse flow). Since the Interconnector enables arbitrage trading between the UK and Continental Europe (within the technical restrictions of the Interconnector), the gas spot prices at NBP and TTF are closely connected. However, the spread may become significant when the Interconnector is shut down due to maintenance work. The hubs in Continental Europe (TTF, ZEE, GPL, NCG) are well connected by pipelines, therefore prices are closely coupled.

The most liquid futures exchange for natural gas in Europe is the ICE. The ICE UK Natural Gas Futures have the following specifications.

- *Trading period:* 78–83 consecutive months, 11–12 quarters, 13–14 seasons and 6 years (however not all products are liquid).
- *Units of trading:* 1000 therms of natural gas per day.
- *Price quotation:* GB pence per therm.
- *Last trading day:* Two business days prior to the first calendar day of the delivery month, quarter, season or calendar year.
- *Settlement type:* Physical delivery at NBP, equal delivery during each day throughout the delivery period.

Further, there is a futures market for TTF natural gas at the ICE ENDEX and for NCG and GPL at the EEX. Liquidity on these exchanges has increased significantly since 2010.

Prior to hub-based pricing, long-term gas supply contracts were usually negotiated based on an oil price index formula. Since large investments were needed to build up a gas infrastructure, long-term contracts linked to oil prices guaranteed security of supply and a competitive pricing compared with oil. Contracts often contained a *take-or-pay* volume (i.e., a minimum off take) and flexibility components. Standard contract terms are as follows.

- *Take-or-pay volume:* Minimum annual off-take volume to be paid (even if not physically taken).
- *Maximum ACQ (annual contract quantity):* The maximum annual off-take.
- *Maximum and minimum DCQ (daily contract quantity):* The maximum and minimum daily gas off-take.
- *Make up:* Gas volumes below the take-or-pay volume that have been paid for, but can be taken in subsequent years.
- *Carry forward:* Gas volumes above the take-or-pay volume that can offset take-or-pay obligations in subsequent years.

A typical pricing formula for natural gas in Continental Europe is of the form

$$P = P_0 + A(X - X_0) + B(Y - Y_0), \tag{1.1}$$

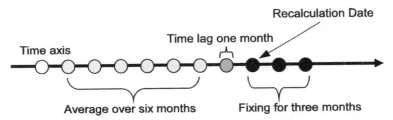

Figure 1.17   Calculation scheme of an oil price formula of type (6,1,3). On the recalculation date, the oil price is averaged over a period of six months ending one month prior to the recalculation date.

where A and B are constants and X and Y are monthly oil quotations such as gasoil or fuel oil. Typically, such formulas are characterised by a triple (n, l, m):

- n is the averaging period, e.g. 6 months ($n = 6$).
- l is the time lag of the price fixing, e.g. $l = 1$ means that to set a price for October the averaging period ends with August.
- m is the recalculation frequency, e.g. $m = 3$ means that the oil price formula is applied every 3 months to set a new price for the following quarter.

An example for a scheme of type (6,1,3) is shown in Figure 1.17. The new gas price is calculated on the recalculation date and is valid for a three-month period.

Long-term supply contracts typically contain price revision clauses, so that pricing parameters can be adjusted under certain conditions, for example if the market has changed structurally. At certain dates stipulated in the contract, either party can trigger such a price-revision procedure. In case the parties cannot agree on adjusted terms, an arbitration or court proceeding may follow. Such price revisions became an important topic when the end of the 2000s gas spot and futures prices fell substantially below oil-indexed prices.

The Asian Market

Japan and South Korea cover most of the gas demand through LNG, mainly from Indonesia, Malaysia, Australia and the Middle East. This market is dominated by long-term contracts linked to crude oil prices. A typical formula, used in Japan, is $P = A + B \times JCC$, where A and B are constants and JCC is the *Japan Customs-cleared Crude* (also known as *Japan Crude Cocktail*), a particular basket of crude oils. Instead of a linear dependence on the oil price, price formulas may be S-shaped, so that the slope is lower for very low or very high oil prices.

1.3.3   Liquefied Natural Gas

To transport natural gas over long distances where pipelines are not available, LNG can be used. LNG is natural gas condensed into a liquid at less than $-160°C$. The density is thereby increased by a factor of about 600 to approximately 0.46 kg/l. One (metric) tonne of LNG has a volume of 2.19 m^3, representing 1336 m^3 of natural gas with a heating value of 14.4 MWh. With a higher heating value of about 24 MJ/l, the energy density of LNG is around 70% of the energy density of crude oil (35 MJ/l). The LNG value chain is shown in Figure 1.18. In the *LNG plant*, which consists of one or more liquefaction units (*LNG trains*), the natural

Figure 1.18   LNG value chain.

gas is cooled down until it becomes liquid. Liquefaction gives rise to the largest costs in the LNG value chain. A modern LNG train has a capacity of up to 8 million t of LNG per year. After the liquefication process, the LNG can be loaded onto special insulated *LNG carriers*. Conventional LNG carriers have a capacity between 125 000 and 149 000 m^3. The capacity of more recent carriers is between 150 000 and 177 000 m^3. The largest LNG carriers (type Q-Flex or Q-Max as used by Qatar) have capacities up to 266 000 m^3. The next step in the value chain is the *regasification terminal*, where the LNG is unloaded, regasified and injected into pipelines. Besides land-based terminals, regasification units can be built on board an LNG carrier (*storage and regasification vessel*).

The main exporters for LNG are shown in Figure 1.19. The total LNG exports in 2012 amounted to 330 billion cubic metres.

The infrastructure needed for production, transport and regasification is capital intensive and the value chain is costly. Consequently, LNG has traditionally played a major role only in countries where pipelines are not available, such as Japan, South Korea or Taiwan. Most current LNG contracts are long-term contracts with prices linked to pipeline gas prices or oil prices. Take-or-pay clauses typically reduce the volume risk for the seller. However, an increasing number of short-term (spot) transactions could be observed over recent years. Directing spot LNG purchases to the market with highest gas prices can exploit arbitrage opportunities between regional markets.

In the future, more and more LNG will be needed to serve the growing worldwide gas demand and to replace the decreasing regional gas production in Western Europe. Therefore, the LNG trade is expected to grow substantially over the coming years.

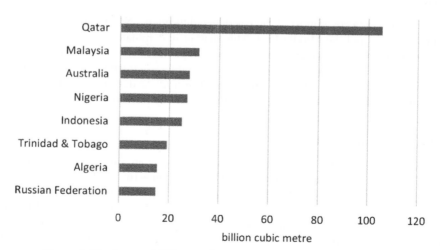

Figure 1.19   Largest LNG-exporting countries 2012. *Source*: BP (2013).

1.4   THE COAL MARKET

Coal is a fossil fuel, usually with the physical appearance of a black or brown rock, consisting of carbonised vegetal matter. It is formed from plant remains over geologic timescales under heat and pressure. Coal is a main source of fuel for the generation of electricity worldwide and for steel production. There exist a variety of different coal types which are distinguished by their physical and chemical characteristics. The characteristics defining coal quality are, for example, carbon, energy, sulphur, and ash content. The higher the carbon content of a coal, the higher its rank or quality. These characteristics determine the coal's price and suitability for various uses.

The three main categories of coal are (corresponding to their transformation process) *lignite*, *sub-bituminous coal* and *hard coal*. Lignite and sub-bituminous coal are also called *brown coal*. Hard coal has a high gross calorific value (GCV) greater than 23.9 MJ/kg (5700 kcal/kg). Lignite refers to coal with a GCV less than 17.4 MJ/kg (4165 kcal/kg), sub-bituminous coal includes coal with a GCV between those of hard coal and lignite. Depending on its usage, hard coal and sub-bituminous coal can be categorised as follows:

- *Coking coal* is a premium-grade hard coal used to manufacture coke for the steelmaking process.
- *Steam coal* is coal used for steam-raising and space-heating purposes. It includes all hard coals and sub-bituminous coals not classified as coking coal. As primary fuel for hard coal-fired power plants, steam coal with low moisture, ash and sulphur (less than 1%) is used.

Shipping of lower-quality coals is uneconomical, implying that they are not internationally traded. These low-rank coals are therefore not considered in more detail in this book. Since the energy content of coal determines the value to a large extent, coal volumes are often converted to energy units depending on their calorific value. Typical units are million tonnes of oil equivalents (Mtoe) or million tonnes of coal equivalents (Mtce), where 1 Mtce = 0.697 Mtoe. Measured in energy units, steam coal has a share of around 80% of overall coal production, coking coal a share of 15% and lignite a share of 5%.

1.4.1   Consumption, Production and Reserves

In 2010 coal accounted for 27% of total world energy consumption. In their International Energy Outlook 2012 (see International Energy Agency, 2012), the IEA forecasts a decreasing share of coal in total world energy consumption to slightly less than 25% by 2035. However, the future development of coal demand depends even more than that of other fossil fuels on environmental policies, since coal has a comparably high carbon intensity. Another driver is the competition with gas for electricity generation.

Total reserves of coal around the world are estimated at 861 billion tonnes according to BP (2013), half of which are hard coal and the other half lignite and sub-bituminous coal (see Figure 1.20). At the current consumption level those coal reserves should last approximately 109 years. There are, however, significant (unproven) resources, which may be developed. Even though many countries have access to coal reserves, the majority of reserves are located in the United States (28%), Russia (18%), China (13%) and India (7%). Other assessments

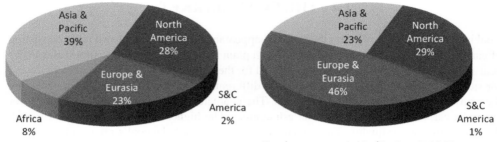

Total reserves hard coal : 405 billion t   Total reserves sub-bit./lignite: 456 billion t

Figure 1.20   Total world coal reserves 2012 by regions. *Source*: BP (2013).

result in higher reserve estimates for coal, especially in China. In BGR (2011), coal reserves are estimated as 1038 billion tonnes corresponding to a reserves-to-production ratio of more than 130 years. There are also significant reserves in Australia, South Africa, Ukraine and Kazakhstan.

Coal production is highest in China, with 1825 Mtoe in 2012, which is nearly 50% of worldwide coal production. Production and demand in China more than doubled in the period 2002 to 2012, contributing around 80% to the worldwide growth in coal demand and production during that period. The second largest coal producer is the United States with 516 Mtoe in 2012, followed by Australia, Indonesia, India, Russia and South Africa. Figure 1.21 shows coal production in 2012 by region in million tonnes oil equivalent.

As a general pattern, countries with high coal production also have high coal consumption. Consumption in 2012 in China was 1873 Mtoe and in the United States 438 Mtoe, followed by India with 298 Mtoe. The coal consumption in 2012 by region is illustrated in Figure 1.22. Of the coal consumption, around 65% is used for generating electricity and 27% for industry (mainly steel production). Other usages, such as buildings or coal liquefaction, play a minor role. Increasing electricity demand in non-OECD countries is the main driver for the current

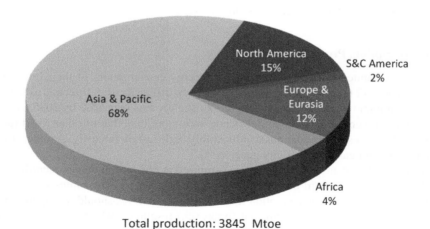

Total production: 3845 Mtoe

Figure 1.21   Total world coal production 2012 by regions. *Source*: BP (2013).

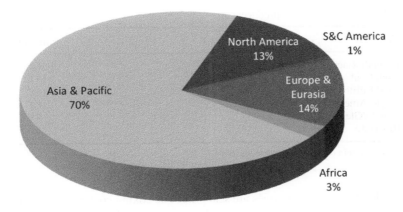

Total consumption: 3730 Mtoe

Figure 1.22   Total world coal consumption 2012 by regions. *Source*: BP (2013).

worldwide increase of coal demand. This is also the reason why the future growth of coal demand depends strongly on potential governmental interventions in the electricity generation sector to curb carbon emissions.

1.4.2   Coal Trading

Hard coal is traded worldwide as a commodity with increasing trade volumes over recent decades. Transport of lignite and other coal types with low energy density is uneconomic over large distances, therefore these coal types are mostly consumed near their production sites.

The volume of international physical coal exports in 2011 was 1080 million tonnes (source: BGR, 2011). Figure 1.23 shows the largest hard coal exporters. The largest coal importers were China, Japan, South Korea and India.

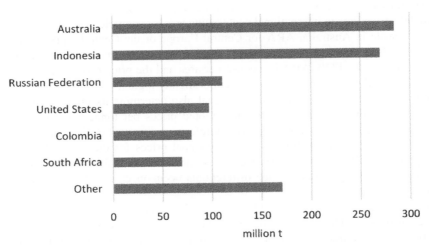

Figure 1.23   Largest hard coal exporters 2011. *Source*: BGR (2011).

Table 1.1 Largest coal producers 2011

Company	million t
Peabody Energy	268
Arch Coal	157
BHP Billiton	104
Anglo American	103
Xstrata/Glencore	85
Rio Tinto	49

Source: Verein der Kohlenimporteure (2012).

Most of the hard coal trade volumes are seaborne. The coking coal market (around 25% of trade volumes) is a premium-quality market with few suppliers, therefore a uniform worldwide market has been established. The steam coal market comprises the Atlantic and the Pacific region with different supply structures. South Africa, Columbia, Russia, and the United States are the main coal suppliers for the Atlantic region whereas Indonesia, Australia, South Africa, and Russia are the main suppliers for the Pacific region. There is also of course some exchange between the two regions, since especially Russia, South Africa, Indonesia and Australia supply both regions (see Verein der Kohlenimporteure, 2012).

Producers

Among the largest coal producers, several are state owned, for example, Coal India, Shenhua (China), China Coal and SUEK (Russia). The largest privately owned global coal producers are shown in Table 1.1.

Physical Coal Trading

Since coal transportation costs can be significant, coal prices depend on the point of delivery. Standard delivery points in international coal trading are, for example, Richards Bay in South Africa, Newcastle in Australia, ARA for Central Europe or the Central Appalachian in the United States. Both Richards Bay and the Central Appalachian are producing areas, so the price is usually quoted FOB. ARA is a consumer area and the price is often quoted as a CIF price. The FOB ARA price for further shipment is slightly higher.

The characteristics defining the quality of coal also determine its price. Energy content is the most price-relevant characteristic, and quoted prices per tonne (or per *short ton* in the USA, which equals around 907 kg) always refer to a specified quality and in particular to a specified energy content. Figure 1.24 shows coal prices for the years 2000–2012 for delivery points in NW Europe, the United States and Asia. Price differentials are naturally related to costs of freight. Large price differentials occur in cases where freight capacity is scarce.

Physical coal trading can be bilateral between producers and consumers or through trading companies or brokers. There are also online broker platforms available, for example *global-COAL*. To standardise trading, globalCOAL has introduced a special master agreement, the Standard Coal Trading Agreement (SCoTA).

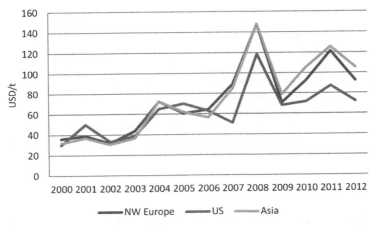

Figure 1.24 Coal prices for different NW Europe, United States and Asia delivery points. *Source*: BP (2013).

Price Indices

Price information for hard coal can be obtained either from exchanges, from brokers or from independent information service providers. These include Argus Media Ltd offering price information, market data and business intelligence for the global petroleum, natural gas, electricity and coal industries, and IHS McCloskey offering data, news and analysis focused on the coal industry. Price information published by information services is typically generated via telephone or e-mail survey covering sellers of physical coal, utility buyers, trading companies and broking companies. Market analysts then assess the price of the standard specified coal that conforms to the required specification. The mechanism of price assessment must eliminate the opportunity for gaming the mechanics of the index. In contrast to an exchange, an information service has no comprehensive secured information about the concluded trades.

The primary coal indices used as underlying for derivative contracts (e.g., swaps) are the API ("All Publication Index") indices published by the joint Argus/McCloskey Coal Price Index Service. The indices are calculated as averages of respective spot (i.e., delivery within the next 90 days) price assessments by Argus and McCloskey. There follows a list of API indices (see Section 1.1.5 for an explanation of the delivery Incoterms):

- API 2 is the index for the ARA region quoted as CIF ARA and is an important benchmark for NW Europe. It is calculated as an average of the Argus CIF ARA assessment and the McCloskey NW European steam coal marker. The energy content is specified at 6000 kcal/kg and the sulphur content must be less than 1%.
- API 4 is the index for the FOB Richards Bay, South Africa physical market. It is calculated as an average of the Argus FOB Richards Bay assessment and the McCloskey FOB Richards Bay marker. The energy content is specified at 6000 kcal/kg and the sulphur content must be less than 1%.
- API 5 is the index for the FOB Newcastle physical market in Australia, which is setting prices for delivery to China and South Korea. It is calculated from the Argus and McCloskey price assessments. The energy content is specified at 5500 kcal/kg and the sulphur content must be less than 1%.

Financial Derivatives for Coal

Financial swaps are the most common product for risk management for both coal producers and consumers. The swap market is particularly interesting for financial institutions, which are active market players. Financial swaps are traded usually up to three years in the future, while the time period for physical coal trading is usually shorter. Most swaps settle on the API indices described above. Coal swaps can be concluded OTC with banks or other traders or, for example, via the globalCOAL platform.

Exchanges also offer coal futures as trading product and offer clearing services for OTC trades. Both the CME Group and ICE have introduced coal futures for the main API coal indices.

1.4.3 Freight

The delivery price of coal is determined in part by ocean freight rates. They are an important factor for the price of coal in different regions and the competitiveness of coal against other fuels. The main factor that will affect the future movement of freight rates is the overall development of dry bulk trade.

Mainly Cape and Panamax-sized vessels are employed in international coal trading. Cape-sized vessels, used for example for the Richards Bay to ARA route, are also employed in the iron ore trade. As the shipping capacity is limited, the activity of the world's steel industry has an impact on coal freight rates. The other trade that can have an impact on coal freight rates is grain shipment, which is carried out predominantly in Panamax vessels. For both the export of grain and the import of iron ore, China's economy is an important factor.

A popular indicator for freight rates is the *Baltic Dry Index (BDI)* published by the Baltic Exchange. The BDI is an average of sub-indices for Cape, Panamax, Supramax and Handy-sized freight rates and considers different transportation routes. It is based on time-charter hire rates in USD per day. Figure 1.25 shows the considerable volatility of freight rates over recent years.

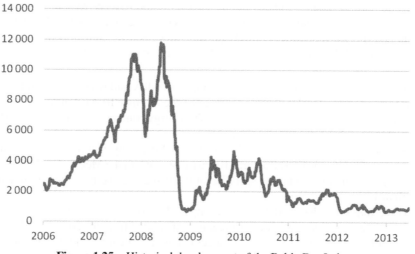

Figure 1.25   Historical development of the Baltic Dry Index.

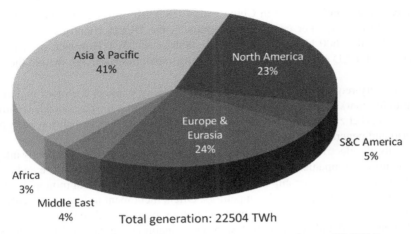

Figure 1.26 World electricity generation by country. *Source*: BP (2013).

1.5 THE ELECTRICITY MARKET

Electricity is a form of energy used for a very wide range of applications. It is easy to control, non-polluting at the location of its usage and convenient, used in the applications of heat, light and power. As a secondary energy source it is generated from the conversion of other energy sources, like coal, natural gas, oil, nuclear power, hydropower and other renewable sources. This implies that electricity markets and electricity prices are fundamentally linked to markets for primary fuels and environmental conditions. To understand electricity markets and price mechanisms, it is essential to consider the electricity generation process as well as the fuel markets. This section gives an introduction to the main marketplaces and wholesale products for electricity. Technical background information as well as energy economic modelling approaches can be found in Chapter 7.

1.5.1 Consumption and Production

Electricity is a growing market, even in proportion to the world energy market. The average growth rate of electricity consumption between 2002 and 2012 was 3.35%, whereas the average growth for primary energy demand was only 2.66%. This trend is likely to continue in the future, and most market projections assume higher growth rates for electricity compared with other forms of energy. In the year 2012, world electricity generation was 22 504 TWh.[3] According to the base scenario "New Policies" of the IEA (see International Energy Agency, 2012), electricity generation will grow to around 36 600 TWh by 2035. As for primary energy, the bulk of this growth is driven by increasing demand in non-OECD countries, with around 50% of worldwide growth originating from China and India. Figure 1.26 shows worldwide electricity generation by country. Between 1990 and 2012 the share of Asia & Pacific has grown from 20% to around 40%. China alone accounts for already 20% of worldwide electricity generation in 2012.

---

[3] 1 terawatt hour (TWh) = 1 billion kilowatt hour (kWh).

Electricity generation is highest in China with 4938 TWh, followed by the United States with 4256 TWh in 2012. Per capita consumption in the OECD countries was 7800 kWh compared with only 1600 kWh in non-OECD countries in 2010. However, per capita consumption in non-OECD countries is expected to grow much more strongly within the coming decades.

Since electricity requires a grid infrastructure, electricity markets are more regional than other commodity markets. However, efforts have been made over the past decades to integrate neighbouring market zones (e.g., in Europe) with the aim to foster competition and optimise usage of grid and generation infrastructure.

Traditionally, the electricity market in many countries was dominated by vertically integrated "incumbent" utility companies that owned generation assets, grid infrastructure and the retail business. Especially grid ownership has put those incumbents in a natural monopoly situation with high entry barriers for potential competitors. Often, incumbent utilities were state owned or at least regulated. Since the 1990s many countries have liberalised electricity markets to some degree. The details of market design and remaining regulation differ substantially between countries, but the main elements are common:

- Distinguish between natural monopoly areas (e.g., grid operation) and areas where competition shall be established. Monopoly areas need to be clearly separated ("unbundling") from competition areas, such that access to grid and other infrastructure is non-discriminatory for all market participants.
- Design wholesale markets to incentivise optimal economic usage of infrastructure, such as power plants and interconnections between market areas. Further, set sufficient incentives to build new generation capacity if required.
- Establish regulation to ensure security of supply and prevent market abuse.
- Incorporate mechanisms for environmental protection (e.g., carbon emissions).

European Union

Electricity market liberalisation started in the UK at the beginning of the 1990s, soon followed by Scandinavia. In 1996 and 2003 the European Commission issued Electricity Market Directives that defined steps for deregulated electricity markets on an EU-wide scale, which subsequently had to be implemented by the EU member states. Besides fostering competition in the generation and retail market, integration of the national electricity wholesale markets is seen as another important objective.

With the introduction of the European Trading System (EU ETS) for carbon emissions in 2005, the European electricity markets are closely connected to European environmental policy, since emission certificates (EUAs) have become an important driver for wholesale electricity prices. Another important driver is the increasing solar and wind generation fostered by national subsidy schemes, with ambitious growth targets (e.g., in Germany).

Electricity generation volumes for single European countries are shown in Figure 1.27. The generation structure differs substantially by country (see Figure 1.28). In most European countries electricity generation is dominated by conventional coal and natural gas plants. Exceptions are France with a 75% share of nuclear generation and Norway/Sweden with a high share (97%, respectively 48%) of hydro generation. In the EU-27 countries, nuclear, coal and natural gas each have a share of roughly 25% and renewables a share of slightly above 20%. Besides increasing renewable generation, there is generally a long-term trend

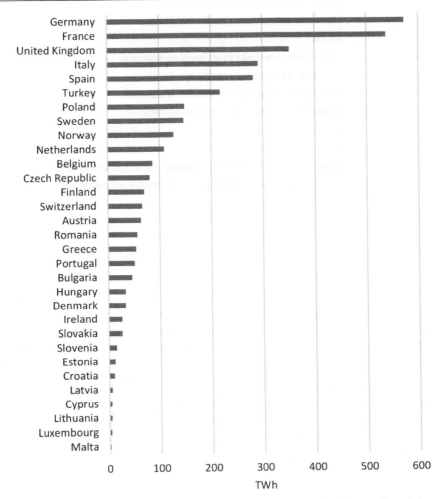

Figure 1.27 Electricity generation 2012 in European countries. *Source*: Eurostat.

towards a higher share of natural gas. However, due to low coal and carbon prices, this trend was at least temporarily broken from 2011 onwards, as generation volumes shifted from gas to coal.

Figure 1.29 shows historic wholesale spot prices (baseload) in Germany. In the period until 2008 frequent price spikes can be observed, which were caused by a tight supply situation. After 2008, prices generally dropped and even became negative on particular days. This change was caused on the one hand by increasing wind and solar generation volumes and decreasing power demand and decreasing EUA prices following the financial crisis on the other hand.

In several EU countries there is growing concern that lower wholesale electricity prices and the absence of price spikes do not sufficiently attract investments into conventional (non-intermittent) generation capacity to ensure security of supply. The background is that with

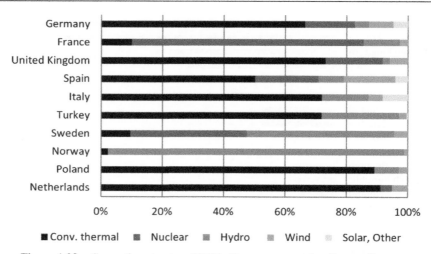

Figure 1.28   Generation structure 2012 in European countries. *Source*: Eurostat.

a growing share of intermittent renewable capacity, a larger part of conventional generation capacity is only required sporadically, when weather conditions lead to low renewable generation. In an "energy-only" market, investments in new conventional generation capacity would only be profitable in case of high price spikes on those selected days. However, such high price spikes may not be politically acceptable and would provide high volatility of earnings for investors. An alternative to the "energy-only" market is to introduce a *capacity market* that aims to provide a more stable revenue stream for conventional generation capacity – independent of actually generated electricity volumes. To some extent this can be seen as a premium to ensure security of supply at times of low renewable generation. Some countries have already introduced some form of capacity remuneration or are planning to do so. However, so far no unified mechanism across the European Union has emerged.

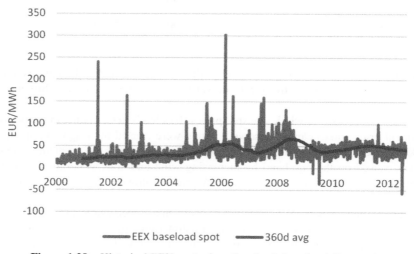

Figure 1.29   Historical EEX spot prices (baseload day-ahead Germany).

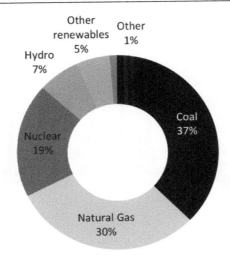

Figure 1.30   Electricity generation 2012 in the United States. *Source*: EIA.

United States

With overall electricity generation of around 4256 TWh in 2012, the United States is the second largest electricity producer behind China. Up to the beginning of the 2000s, generation was traditionally dominated by coal, followed by nuclear and gas. Driven by the shale gas boom, gas-fired generation has grown rapidly, reaching a higher share than nuclear generation. Coal-fired generation has decreased correspondingly, but still has the highest absolute share among the generation technologies. There is a trend towards increasing renewable generation, but further development will depend mainly on government regulation. The generation mix in 2012 is shown in Figure 1.30.

Deregulation of the United States electricity sector started with the Energy Policy Act of 1992 and developed unevenly amoung the states. A setback was caused by the California electricity crisis in 2000, where market manipulations caused shortages of supply. As a result, the market design had to be reviewed. Today, the US electricity market consists of a number of regional markets with different states of deregulation. In the deregulated regions, an independent system operator (ISO) or regional transmission organisation (RTO) operates the transmission system with non-discriminatory access for generators and suppliers. An example is PJM Interconnection covering all or parts of 13 states and the District of Columbia.

Also in the United States, wholesale electricity prices have decreased substantially in the years after 2008 following the financial crisis (see Figure 1.31). Low gas prices related to the shale gas boom contributed to this development.

1.5.2   Electricity Trading

For many commodities there is an intuitive answer to the question "What is the actual trading product?", but for electricity the answer to this question requires some more understanding of the technical background. Among all commodities electricity has the unique feature that it is hardly storable. An exception are hydro pumped storage power plants, but in most countries their capacity is small compared with total consumption. The second main feature is the necessity for a transmission network, which prevents a global market. These characteristics of

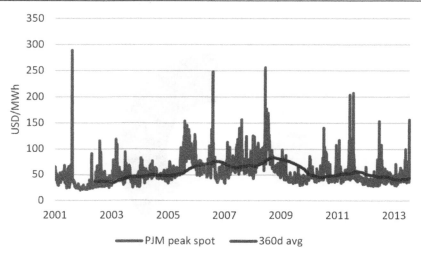

Figure 1.31   Historical US electricity spot peak prices (PJM Western Hub).

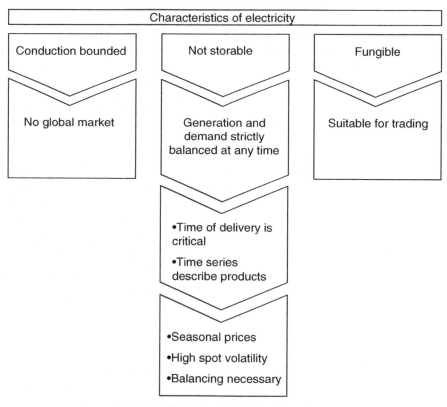

Figure 1.32   Characteristics of electricity.

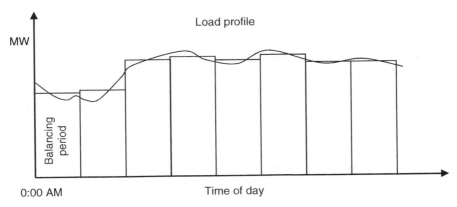

Figure 1.33   Balancing period.

electricity, shown in Figure 1.32, have strong implications for the trading products and their prices. An often discussed characteristic resulting from non-storability is the high volatility of power prices in the spot market in case of a tight or excessive supply situation. In the forward market the price movements are much smaller, because the availability of power plants and the weather-dependent demand are still unknown.

The lack of storability requires an exact matching of supply and demand at all times. Because a merchant cannot forecast the demand of his customers exactly, there must be someone responsible for balancing the system. This is the task of the transmission system operator (TSO), who charges the merchant directly or the retail customers via transmission fees for this service. The TSO defines a balancing period (e.g., 30 minutes in the UK, 15 minutes in Germany), which is the granularity of the measured electric energy supply. The continuously varying power requirements of retail customers are integrated over the balancing period and the average power is the size that is forecast and should be delivered by the supplying merchant. As a result, the merchant delivers energy as a discrete time series with time steps according to the balancing period and constant power during these time periods. Figure 1.33 illustrates the continuously varying power requirement (load profile) and the piecewise constant delivery of power during the balancing period.

The principal products in the electricity markets are delivery schedules in a granularity not finer than the balancing period. The usual granularity is one hour and this granularity is assumed in this book if not stated otherwise. The power balancing during the balancing period itself is the task of the TSO. Since the TSO usually has no own-generation capacities, it has to purchase products which allow the increase or decrease of production (including import and export) in its transmission system at short notice. In the following, the main features of products in the electricity market are described. As there is no global market for electricity, the products in regional markets may differ.

The electricity market can be divided into the following categories.

- *Forward and futures market:* The forward and futures market is the relevant market for risk management and serves the participants to hedge their positions. It is also the relevant market for traders who actively take positions and thereby also provide liquidity for hedgers. The agreed delivery period of these products may refer to specific weeks, calendar months or calendar years.

- *Day-ahead market:* In the day-ahead market products are traded which are delivered on the next day. If the next day is not a trading day, the day-ahead market also includes products delivered between the next day and the next trading day. Day-ahead products are common spot products and can be traded either on a power exchange or as bilateral agreement.
- *Intra-day market:* The intra-day market is for products with a delivery on the same day. This market allows the producers a short-term load-dependent optimisation of their generation and is typically not a market for pure trading purposes. Intra-day products are traded either on a power exchange or bilaterally.
- *Balancing and reserve market:* There are different definitions of the terms "balancing market" and "reserve market", because these markets depend on the regulator and are country specific. In the context of this book, the *reserve market* is the market allowing the TSO to purchase the products needed for compensating imbalances between supply and demand in the electricity system at short notice. The *balancing market* (also referred to as the real-time market) denotes the market where a merchant purchases or sells the additional energy for balancing his accounting grid. Since the balancing service is provided by the TSO, the TSO usually charges or reimburses the merchant for additional energy and only in some national markets does the merchant have the possibility to buy or sell this balancing energy from or to someone else. Therefore, the balancing market can be regarded as a market only in a broad sense. The different market categories and their time flow are described in Figure 1.34.

Outside the balancing and reserve market, products in the electricity market can be described by time series defining the delivery schedule. Usually the granularity of the time series is one hour and then each number of the time series specifies the constant power delivered in the corresponding hour. If the delivered power is constant over the delivery period $[T_1, T_2]$, the contract is called a *baseload contract*. If the delivered power is constant in those predefined hours of the delivery period when consumption is usually high, the contract is called a *peakload contract*. Peakload hours depend on the particular market. In Central Europe common peakload hours are the hours 8:00 AM to 8:00 PM on peakload days. Peakload days are usually Monday–Friday, including public holidays.

Forward Market

Forwards can be divided into standard forwards and individual power schedules. Standard contracts are baseload or peakload contracts whose delivery period is a day, week, month, quarter or year. Individual schedules are delivery schedules, whose power can vary every hour or even every balancing period (e.g., every 30 minutes in the UK). Figure 1.35 shows a baseload contract, a peakload contract, and an individual schedule, where the delivery period is one week.

Futures Market

Like other futures contracts, electricity futures are subject to daily margining (see Section 5.1.2). As electricity futures contracts do not have a single delivery date but a delivery period, the variation margin must also be calculated during the delivery period. Often, contracts with a long delivery period (e.g., a year or a quarter) are split into futures contracts with a shorter delivery period (e.g., a quarter or a month). This procedure is called cascading and is

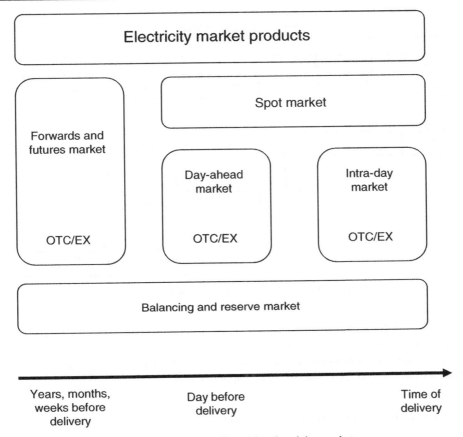

Figure 1.34   Categories of the electricity market.

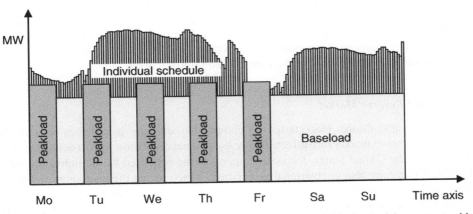

Figure 1.35   Delivery hours of a baseload, a peakload and an individual schedule contract with a delivery period of one week.

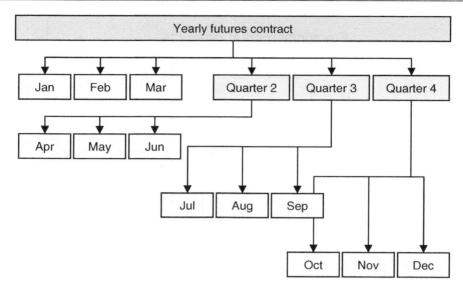

Figure 1.36   Cascading of a yearly futures contract.

shown in Figure 1.36. In this example the yearly futures contract cascades into three monthly futures contracts and into the three remaining quarterly futures contracts. Later, the quarterly contracts cascade into monthly contracts. The final settlement price of a monthly future is then established from the average of the associated spot market prices.

Spot Market (Day-Ahead and Intra-Day Market)

Spot products are traded OTC as well as on power exchanges. Standard products are baseload and peakload contracts with a delivery period of one day. In addition, there are usually hourly contracts and block contracts available. Contracts with a finer granularity (e.g., 30 or 15 minutes) can also be found in some markets. Hourly products are traded on the spot market only and are the basis for the pricing of many other products. In the case of block contracts, the delivery of electricity with a constant power over several delivery hours is traded. The spot market also serves as underlying for the forward and futures market.

Balancing and Reserve Market

While forwards and futures markets have a comparable structure in different regions, the balancing and reserve markets are affected more by national regulation, which defines the role of the TSO. In the United States, the system operators are regulated by the individual states and FERC.[4] There are also international associations which secure the interconnected power systems. In Europe, the *European Network of Transmission System Operators for Electricity (ENTSO-E)* is an association of 41 TSOs from 34 countries to coordinate overarching grid

---

[4] Federal Energy Regulatory Commission.

topics. It was established in 2008 as the successor of the European Transmission System Operators (ETSO).

One main task of a TSO is to ensure a constant power frequency in the transmission system. A change in frequency indicates to the TSO a shortage or a surplus of energy in the system. Physically, this means that there is a deceleration or acceleration of turbines because their kinetic energy balances consumption and generation. For such a case, there need to be rules and measures in place to stabilise the system.

For example, the ENTSO-E specifies control actions in its *Operation Handbook*. The frequency control actions are performed in different successive steps, each with different characteristics and qualities, and all depending on each other.

- *Primary reserve:* After a disturbance, the primary reserve (also called the primary control) starts within seconds as a joint action of all TSOs in the synchronised transmission system.
- *Secondary reserve:* The secondary reserve (also called the secondary control) replaces the primary reserve after a few minutes and is put into action by the responsible TSOs only.
- *Tertiary reserve:* The tertiary reserve (also called the tertiary control or minute reserve) frees secondary reserve by rescheduling generation and is put into action by the responsible TSOs.

The sequence of different control actions is displayed in Figure 1.37.

The products in the reserve market are derived from these control actions. The TSO tenders the required products to fulfil these functions. In contrast to forwards, futures or spot products, the reserve market products are more technical and refer to specified plants. These plants must be able to reduce or increase production at short notice. While for most other electricity products only energy delivered is paid for, reserve energy products often involve an additional payment for the availability of the reserved capacity.

The prices for balancing power are usually prices for the delivered energy only. For the merchant these are often additional costs, which are analysed in Section 4.6.3. Prices for balancing power differ widely and are only sometimes related to spot or futures market prices.

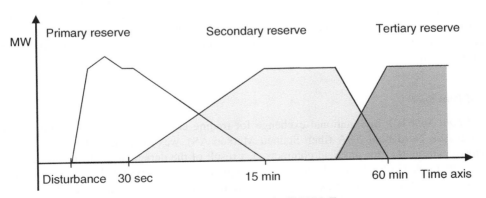

Figure 1.37   Control actions in the ENTSO-E system.

Market Coupling

In many cases, neighbouring local electricity markets are not completely disconnected but coupled via transmission capacities owned by the TSOs. An economically optimal usage of transmission capacities implies that in case of price differentials between two local markets, electricity would be transmitted from the higher-priced market A to the lower-priced market B. This would lower generation demand in B and increase generation demand in A, which in turn would push prices towards an equilibrium. Hence, a price differential between connected markets should only occur in case of congestions in transmission capacities.

One way of facilitating optimal usage of transmission capacities is to create an own-market for such capacities, for example via auctioning. The other way is to integrate allocation of transmission capacities in the price-finding algorithm of two or more collaborating spot exchanges via an *implicit auctioning*. This is generally considered more efficient because optimal allocation can be ensured by the exchanges and a separate auctioning of transmission capacities is no longer required. The result will be a single price in all participating markets unless there is a congestion of capacities.

In Europe, Nord Pool introduced a market coupling scheme in 1996 between Norway and Sweden, which later was expanded to other Nordic and Baltic countries. In 2006, Belgium, France and the Netherlands replaced explicit auctions of transmission capacities by implicit auctioning. This trilateral market coupling was expanded in 2010 by the Central Western Europe (CWE) initiative coupling Belgium, France, the Netherlands, Germany and Luxemburg. Further, the Interim Tight Volume Coupling (ITVC) provided an interim solution to include the connection between Germany and Denmark. The next step is the full integration of CWE with UK and the Nordic region (NWE) in 2014. Further integration is facilitated by the Price Coupling of Regions (PCR) initiative supported by different European power exchanges.

1.5.3   Electricity Exchanges

Energy exchanges are major marketplaces for electricity. In recent years more and more countries have founded exchanges for electricity. Some of them are only a marketplace for spot products, but the major exchanges are characterised by the existence of a derivatives market with a high trading volume. Most electricity exchanges are located in Europe and North America. Especially in Europe, the landscape of power exchanges has been changing rapidly over recent years. On the one hand, this is driven by a consolidation of derivatives trading platforms and related clearing services. On the other hand, further integration of electricity markets across Europe requires local power exchanges to cooperate more closely. Because of the large number of electricity exchanges, only a selection will be described further in this section.

Nord Pool Spot

Nord Pool Spot is a multinational exchange for trading electricity in Northern Europe. Its predecessor, Nord Pool ASA (then Statnett Marked AS), was founded in 1993 initially as a Norwegian market for physical contracts as a result of the deregulation of the Norwegian electricity market in 1991. In 1996 the joint Norwegian–Swedish power exchange commenced, the world's first multinational exchange for trade in power contracts. Subsequently, Finland and Denmark joined Nord Pool. In 2002, Nord Pool Spot was established as a separate company for short-term electricity trading. The derivatives trading business was sold in 2008 to *NASDAQ OMX Commodities*. In 2010, Nord Pool Spot and NASDAQ OMX Commodities jointly launched *N2EX*, which is a market for UK energy contracts. Overall, 432 TWh of electricity was traded through the Nord Pool Spot exchange in 2012.

Nord Pool Spot meanwhile comprises the Nordic countries of Denmark, Finland, Norway and Sweden and the Baltic countries of Estonia, Latvia and Lithuania. It operates a day-ahead market *Elspot* and an intra-day market *Elbas*.

The Elspot day-ahead market is based on an auction trade system. Bids for purchase and sale of power contracts of one-hour duration cover all 24 hours of the next day. As soon as the noon deadline for participants to submit bids has passed, all buy and sell orders are gathered into two curves for each power-delivery hour: an aggregate demand curve and an aggregate supply curve. The spot price for each hour is determined by the intersection of the aggregate supply and demand curves. This spot price is also called the *system price*. Since Nord Pool is a multinational exchange, possible grid congestions require a partition into separate bidding areas. Separate price areas occur if the contractual flow between bidding areas exceeds the capacity allocated by TSOs for spot contracts. If there are no such capacity constraints, the system price equals the spot price throughout the different bidding areas. The trading volume in the Elspot market was 334 TWh in 2012.

After publication of the Elspot results, trading continues in the physical intra-day market Elbas. The Elbas market is based on hourly contracts and provides continuous power trading 24 hours a day, up to one hour prior to delivery. Trading volume in the Elbas market was 3.2 TWh in 2012.

NASDAQ OMX Commodities Europe

The history of the NASDAQ OMX Commodities Europe financial market goes back to 1993, when the former Nord Pool AS began to establish a forward market in Norway with physical delivery. In 2008, Nord Pool's financial market business was acquired by NASDAQ OMX Commodities Europe. The market consists of futures, forwards, options and *contracts for differences (CfDs)*.

Futures contracts consist of standardised day and week contracts. Weeks are listed in a continuous rolling cycle of 6 weeks. The settlement of futures contracts involves a daily mark-to-market settlement and a final spot (system price) reference cash settlement after the contract reaches its due date.

Forward contracts are offered for the delivery periods of month, quarter and year. Months are listed in a continuous rolling cycle of 6 months. Years cascade into quarters, and quarters cascade into months. The term *forward contract* is used here also for an exchange-traded product. In the context of this book and consistent with the definition in many publications, the term "forward" is normally used for OTC trades, which implies that there is no mark-to-market settlement. The forward products offered by NASDAQ OMX Commodities Europe also have no mark-to-market settlement in the trading period prior to the due date. The mark-to-market value is accumulated as daily loss or profit but not realised throughout the trading period. During the delivery period the difference between the price when the contract was entered into and the spot reference price will be cleared.

Market participants who use financial market derivatives to hedge spot market prices remain exposed to the risk that the system price will differ from the actual area price of their spot purchases or sales. To overcome this potential price differential risk, NASDAQ OMX

Commodities Europe offers CfDs that settle on the difference between the system price and the area price. Thus, a perfect hedge can be obtained by a combination of a forward contract and a CfD.

Options contracts use standard forwards as the underlying contract. The option contracts are European-style, that is they can only be exercised at the exercise date. Options with new strike prices are automatically generated to reflect price movements of the underlying forward instrument.

In addition to products for the Nordic market, NASDAQ OMX Commodities Europe offers products for the German and Dutch market including CfDs to neighbouring countries. Further, futures for UK power are offered which are settled against the N2EX day-ahead index.

The NASDAQ OMX Commodities Clearinghouse provides a clearing service for contracts traded through the NASDAQ OMX Commodities Europe exchange as well as those traded OTC and registered for clearing. To be accepted for clearing, a bilateral market electricity contract must conform to the standardised products traded at the exchange. This clearinghouse guarantees the settlement of all cleared financial and physical derivative contracts.

N2EX

N2EX was established in 2010 jointly by Nord Pool Spot and NASDAQ OMX Commodities Europe. N2EX offers a day-ahead auction market for the UK and a continuously traded spot and *prompt* market. The prompt market covers the period 48 hours out up to 7 days out, afterwards the products are transferred to the spot market. The day-ahead prices are used as underlying for UK futures contracts offered by NASDAQ OMX Commodities Europe.

European Energy Exchange

The EEX is located in Leipzig, Germany and is one of the leading exchanges for electricity and gas in Central Europe. It was established in 2002 as a merger of the Leipzig Power Exchange founded in 2000 and the former European Energy Exchange founded in 2001. In 2008, the spot market operated by EEX was transferred into EPEX, a joint venture with the French exchange Powernext. In 2012 the total traded volume in the power derivatives market was 931 TWh.

The EEX Power Derivatives GmbH, which is owned 80% by EEX and 20% by Powernext, offers futures contracts for German and French power with delivery periods weekly, monthly, quarterly and yearly. For Germany, additional products for single days and weekends are available. The underlying of the financially settled futures contracts is the day-ahead auction results from the EPEX spot market. The settlement of futures contracts involves a daily mark-to-market settlement. Yearly and quarterly futures are fulfilled by cascading, and this process is displayed in Figure 1.36. At the end of a month the last payment for monthly futures is established on the basis of the difference between the final settlement price and the settlement price of the previous exchange trading day. The final settlement price is established from the average of the associated EPEX spot market prices.

In addition to futures, EEX offers European-style options for German electricity, that is the options can only be exercised on the last day of trading. The underlyings are the financially settled futures.

Through its subsidiary *European Commodity Clearing AG (ECC)*, EEX offers a well-accepted *clearing service* for OTC trades. OTC transactions corresponding to available products at the EEX or other partner exchanges can be registered by means of a so-called EFP trade (exchange futures for physical) for OTC clearing.

EPEX

In 2008, EEX together with the French energy exchange Powernext founded the electricity spot exchange EPEX based in Paris to jointly operate the electricity spot market for Germany, Austria, France and Switzerland. In 2012 the total traded volume was 339 TWh.

EPEX offers an auction day-ahead and a continuous intra-day market. Products are individual hours, baseload, peakload and other blocks of contiguous hours. The auction day-ahead market also contains *market coupling contracts* for deliveries between two market areas. The intra-day market is open 24 hours a day, 7 days a week and products can be traded until 45 minutes before delivery. For Germany, 15-minute periods can be traded in addition to hourly periods. Since 2010, EPEX has published the European Electricity Index ELIX, which represents a price level that would result in a physically unconstrained market environment.

APX

APX was founded in 1999 as Amsterdam Power Exchange. In the following years, APX expanded into the UK market under the name APX-UK (now APX Power UK). In 2008, APX acquired the exchange ENDEX, which was founded in 2002 and had a strong position in the derivatives market for Dutch and Belgian power and gas. The joint company, renamed APX-ENDEX, was again split in 2013 into a power spot exchange APX covering the Netherlands, Belgium and the UK and a derivatives exchange ICE ENDEX covering gas spot and power/gas derivatives. The traded volume of APX spot markets was 86 TWh in 2012.

The segments of APX are as follows.

- *APX Power NL:* Day-ahead auction and continuous intra-day market for Dutch electricity.
- *APX Power UK:* Day-ahead market (hourly), continuous spot market (half-hourly) and prompt market (block products up to 4 weeks out).
- *Belpex:* Day-ahead auction market and continuous intraday market for hourly periods.

ICE ENDEX

ICE ENDEX was split from APX-ENDEX in 2013 and provides gas spot products in the Netherlands, Belgium and the UK and power/gas derivatives in the Netherlands and Belgium. The majority shareholder of ICE ENDEX is the ICE, with a share of about 80%. The traded volume for the ENDEX futures market in the Netherlands and Belgium was 58 TWh in 2012. The ICE ENDEX electricity products comprise baseload and peakload futures in the Netherlands for weeks, months, quarters and calender years. For Belgium, only baseload futures for months, quarters and calender years are provided.

Intercontinental Exchange

UK electricity futures traded through ICE comprise products for weeks, months and seasons. A peculiarity of the UK power market was the use of the *EFA calendar* instead of the usual

Gregorian calendar as a convention for electricity futures. According to the EFA calendar, months by definition have either 4 or 5 weeks. However, a transition to the standard calendar is taking place in 2014.

For the United States the ICE offers financially settled monthly peak and off-peak futures and options for various delivery locations, for example PJM Western Hub. The underlying of these monthly futures is the arithmetic average of the PJM Western Hub real-time locational marginal price (LMP) for the peak hours, respectively off-peak hours, of each day provided by PJM Interconnection LLC. Alternative products are based on day-ahead prices instead of real-time prices.

CME Group

NYMEX, which was later acquired by the CME Group, launched the first electricity futures contracts in 1996. After a setback following the California electricity crisis in 2000/2001, NYMEX successfully launched financially settled electricity futures with settlement on PJM real-time Western Hub prices. The CME Group now provides financially settled monthly peak and off-peak futures and options for various delivery locations in the United States based on real-time prices and day-ahead prices.

1.6   THE EMISSIONS MARKET

Global warming caused by the greenhouse effect is one of the key environmental challenges of the 21st century. The greenhouse effect itself is caused by the property of certain gases in the atmosphere to absorb and reflect thermal radiation of the Earth's surface back to the Earth. The natural greenhouse effect is caused mainly by water vapour (H_2O), carbon dioxide (CO_2) ozone (O_3), nitrous oxide (N_2O) and methane (CH_4). Without the natural greenhouse effect, the average surface air temperature would be $-20°C$ instead of $+15°C$.

Increased concentrations of greenhouse gases in the atmosphere caused by human activities are responsible for the anthropogenic greenhouse effect. Since the beginning of the 20th century the average air surface temperature has increased by $0.6°C$ and the UN Intergovernmental Panel on Climate Change (IPCC) has projected a further increase by $1.4°C$ to $5.8°C$ by 2100. Climate change will have a severe impact on the environment, including rising sea levels, which will threaten coastal communities. The frequency of extreme weather events, storms, droughts and floods is expected to increase, thus causing the extinction of endangered species (European Commission, 2013).

1.6.1   Kyoto Protocol

Since the 1970s, climate change has been on the political agenda. The first World Climate Conference with scientific focus was organised in 1979 in Geneva. It issued a declaration calling on the world's governments "to foresee and prevent potential man-made changes in climate that might be adverse to the well-being of humanity". The declaration also identified increased atmospheric concentrations of carbon dioxide resulting from utilisation of fossil fuels, deforestation and changes in land use as a main cause of global warming. The conference led to the establishment of the World Climate Programme, a series of intergovernmental climate conferences and in 1988 to the establishment of the IPCC by the United Nations Environment

Programme (UNEP) and the World Meteorological Organization (WMO). Organised in three working groups, the IPCC prepares assessment reports on available scientific information on climate change, environmental and socio-economic impact of climate change and formulation of response strategies. Based on the first IPCC reports published in 1990, the United Nations General Assembly (UNGA) decided to initiate negotiations on an effective convention on climate change. The United Nations Framework Convention on Climate Change (UNFCCC) was opened for signature at the United Nations Conference on Environment and Development (UNCED) in Rio de Janeiro in 1992 and entered into force in 1994.[5] Signatories of the UNFCCC have different responsibilities.

- *Annex I countries:* Industrialised countries that have agreed to reduce their greenhouse gas emissions.
- *Annex II countries:* Developed countries that are responsible for bearing the costs of climate change mitigation in developing countries. The Annex II countries are a subset of the Annex I countries.
- *Developing countries:* These countries have no immediate responsibilities.

The UNFCCC sets a framework for climate change mitigation but does not contain greenhouse gas emission limits for individual countries. Since the UNFCCC entered into force, the parties meet annually in Conferences of the Parties (COP) to assess the progress in climate change mitigation and to negotiate legally binding targets.

The Kyoto Protocol to the UNFCCC was adopted at the 1997 COP 3 in Kyoto, Japan and entered into force in 2005. The Kyoto Protocol commits Annex I Parties to individual, legally binding targets to limit or reduce their greenhouse gas emissions. Only Parties to the Convention that have ratified the Kyoto Protocol will be bound by the Protocol's commitments; 191 countries and the EU had ratified the Protocol by the end of March 2013. Of these, 37 industrialised countries and the EU committed to reduce greenhouse gas emissions during 2008–2012 to individually designated levels (Annex B countries, which are almost identical with the Annex I countries of the UNFCCC). The Kyoto Protocol was not ratified by the USA. Canada withdrew from the Kyoto Protocol in December 2012. In total, the Annex B countries have committed to reduce their emissions by at least 5% from 1990 levels.

The global warming potential of different greenhouse gases is expressed in CO_2 equivalents. Annex A specifies which greenhouse gas emissions are subject to the Kyoto Protocol.

- Carbon dioxide (CO_2).
- Methane (CH_4), CO_2 equivalents: 23.
- Nitrous oxide (N_2O), CO_2 equivalents: 310.
- Hydrofluorocarbons (HFCs), CO_2 equivalents: 140–11 700.
- Perfluorocarbons (PFCs), CO_2 equivalents: 6500–9200.
- Sulphur hexafluoride (SF_6), CO_2 equivalents: 23 900.

The CO_2 equivalent figures above refer to the 100-year time horizon (International Panel on Climate Change, 2005). Furthermore, Annex A specifies sector and source categories for

---

[5] By 2013, the UNFCCC was ratified by 194 countries and the European Union.

emission covered by the Kyoto Protocol. The main categories are: energy, industrial processes, solvents and other product uses, agriculture and waste.

Quantified emission limits for the first commitment period, from 2008 to 2012, were specified in Annex B of the Kyoto Protocol. The base year was the year 1990. Instead of 1990, Parties may use 1995 as base year for HFCs, PFCs and SF_6. In addition to total emissions, the impact of Land-Use, Land-Use Change and Forestry (LULUCF) is considered. In 2012, the Doha Amendment to the Kyoto Protocol, was adopted. It includes new commitments of Annex I Parties to the Kyoto Protocol who agreed to take on commitments in a second period from 2013 to 2020. The scope of this extension is limited to only 15% of the global greenhouse gas emissions, due to lack of participation by major emitters, including Brazil, Canada, China (the world's largest emitter), India, the United States and Russia. Therefore, it is uncertain if and when a new international agreement with significant impact on the world's greenhouse gas emissions will be achieved.

Emission limits for the first and second commitment period under the Kyoto Protocol and changes in emissions between 1990 and 2010 are listed in Table 1.2. While the 8% EU target for the first commitment period was broken down to the EU Member States, so far no breakdown for the second period exists. The total greenhouse gas emissions from Annex I Parties declined by 8.9% between 1990 and 2010. In spite of significantly increasing emissions since 2009, the 5% reduction target for the Kyoto period 2008 to 2012 has most likely been achieved.

Table 1.2   Committed emission limits under the Kyoto Protocol

Country	1st P	2nd P	Change	Country	1st P	2nd P	Change
	Emission reduction targets for 1st and 2nd period (% of base year) and changes in emissions without LULUCF between 1990 and 2010 (%)						
Australia	+8	−0.5	+30.0	Liechtenstein	−8	−16	+1.1
Austria	−13	EU	+8.2	Lithuania	−8	EU	−56.9
Belarus	−	−	−35.7	Luxembourg	−28	EU	−5.9
Belgium	−7.5	EU	−7.6	Malta	−	EU	+49.1
Bulgaria	−8	EU	−52.0	Monaco	−8	−22	−18.7
Canada	−6	−	+17.4	Netherlands	−6	EU	−0.9
Croatia	−5	EU	−9.1	New Zealand	0	−	+19.8
Czech Rep.	−8	EU	−28.9	Norway	+1	−16	+8.2
Denmark	−21	EU	−10.5	Poland	−6	EU	−28.9
Estonia	−8	EU	−49.6	Portugal	+27	EU	+17.5
EU	−8	−20	−15.4	Romania	−8	EU	−57.6
Finland	0	EU	+6.0	Russian Federat.	0	−	−34.1
France	0	EU	−6.0	Slovakia	−8	EU	−35.9
Germany	−21	EU	−24.8	Slovenia	−8	EU	−3.5
Greece	+25	EU	+12.6	Spain	+15	EU	+25.8
Hungary	−6	EU	−40.9	Sweden	+4	EU	−9.0
Iceland	+10	−20	+29.7	Switzerland	−8	−15.8	+2.2
Ireland	+13	EU	+11.2	Turkey	−	−	+114.9
Italy	−6.5	EU	−3.5	Ukraine	0	−24	−58.8
Japan	−6	−	−0.7	UK	−12.5	EU	−22.6
Kazakhstan	−	−5		United States	−7	−	+10.4
Latvia	−8	EU	−54.5				

Source: Kyoto Protocol, Doha Amendment and UNFCCC (2012).

The decrease in emissions is mainly caused by the economic decline in Eastern European Countries and the global recession of 2009.

The Kyoto Protocol defines three types of "flexible mechanisms" to lower the overall costs of achieving its emissions targets: Joint Implementation (JI – Article 6), Clean Development Mechanism (CDM – Article 12) and International Emissions Trading (IET – Article 17). These mechanisms enable the Parties to access cost-effective opportunities to reduce emissions or to remove CO_2 from the atmosphere (e.g., by afforestation) in other countries. The establishment of these flexible mechanisms acknowledges that marginal emission reduction costs can vary considerably from region to region while the benefits for the atmosphere are the same, wherever the action is taken. Flexible mechanisms are explained in more detail in Section 1.6.3.

At annual climate conferences (COPs) following Kyoto, implementation rules for the Kyoto Protocol were negotiated.[6]

1.6.2 EU Emissions Trading Scheme

The member states of the European Union (EU-15) agreed in 1998 on a Burden Sharing Agreement. It redistributes among them the overall 8% reduction target under the Kyoto Protocol. The individual quantified emission limitation or reduction commitments for the Kyoto period 2008–2012 are listed in Table 1.2. Based on the latest available emission data for 2010, many, but not all, of the European countries will have achieved the emission targets for the Kyoto period.

At the end of the 1990s, only a few EU Member States were on good track to achieve their targets, while other countries were expected to have emissions that significantly exceeded these targets. Overall, it was realised by the European Commission that the EU commitment under the Kyoto Protocol would not be achieved without additional measures.

The European Commission considered the introduction of an emissions trading scheme on a company level as an appropriate measure for achieving the Kyoto target. In 2003, the European Council formally adopted the Emissions Trading Directive (Directive 2003/87/EC). The directive describes the framework for the EU ETS. The scheme limits the overall amount of CO_2 emissions of the participating sectors, introduces allowances for emissions and uses market mechanisms for the final allocation of these limited allowances to individual installations emitting CO_2. The EU ETS covers the electricity and heat sector as well as energy-intensive industrial sectors. All installations above certain size limits, for example rated thermal input exceeding 20 MW for combustion installations, have to participate. The EU ETS covers approximately 40% of all emissions under the Kyoto Protocol in the EU. So far, there are three trading periods under the EU ETS:

- 2005–2007: first trading period.
- 2008–2012: second trading period.
- 2013–2020: third trading period.

In the first two trading periods, only CO_2 emissions are covered by the EU ETS. In the third trading period, N_2O and PFC emissions formed by certain chemical processes are covered as well. While in the first trading period the EU ETS covered all 25 member countries of the

---

[6] Detailed information on the UNFCCC, the Kyoto Protocol and the COPs can be found on the UNFCCC Secretariat's homepage http://unfccc.int.

EU, it has been extended in the meantime to 27 member countries plus Liechtenstein, Iceland, Norway and Croatia. In total, more than 12 000 installations are covered.

All participating countries were responsible for the allocation of free emission allowances by means of national allocation plans (NAPs) for the first and second trading period. The NAPs had to be approved by the EU. Free EUAs were distributed to participating installations. The unit of the EUAs is 1 t CO_2 equivalent. For the first trading period, at least 95% of the EUAs have been allocated at no cost and for the second period, at least 90% of them. In the third trading period the allocation of EUAs was determined in accordance with EU community-wide harmonised rules based on national implementation measures (NIMs) submitted by each EU Member State. The NIMs contain lists setting out the proposed levels of free allocation in accordance with Article 11 of the revised ETS Directive (2009/29/EC). The overall emission limit for the EU ETS decreases by 1.75% per year during the third trading period. The free allocation decreases annually from 80% in 2013 to 30% in 2020. The remaining certificates are distributed to market participants through auctions. These auctions are executed by the Member States. For new installations or significant capacity increases of existing installations, EUAs have been set aside in new entrants reserves (NER).

All operators of installations participating in the EU ETS are required to compile annual emission reports to be verified by an independent auditor in accordance with EU regulation. Based on these emission reports, the operators must submit EUAs for their emissions to national emissions registries. EUAs can be traded freely. Therefore, installations with emissions above their allocation can buy EUAs to meet their demand and installations with emissions below their allocation can sell them. Transfer of certificates from one year to the next (banking) and for one year to the previous year (borrowing) is possible within a trading period. Banking or borrowing was not possible between the first and second trading periods, but banking was possible from the second to third trading period and will be possible for all subsequent trading periods. If the operator of an installation fails to deliver sufficient EUAs, a penalty of 40 EUR/t CO_2 for the first period as well as 100 EUR/t CO_2 for the second and third periods apply.

Each Member State has its own national registry containing accounts which hold the EUAs. These registries interlink with the European Union Transaction Log (EUTL) and the Community Independent Transaction Log (CITL), both operated by the Commission. These registries record and check every transaction. Apart from allocated EUAs for each installation, the EUTL and CITL also contain information on verified historic emissions for previous years for each installation. Figure 1.38 shows the distribution of historic emissions for the second trading period 2008–2012 by country. Four countries – Germany, the UK, Poland and Italy – are already responsible for more than 50% of all emissions covered by the EU ETS and half of the countries are responsible for approximately 90%.

CITL emission data allow the classification of emissions by activity. The most important category is combustion installations (72%), followed by mineral oil refineries (8%).

Unfortunately, the categories are not used in a consistent way for all countries. Therefore, for a detailed analysis it is necessary to consider the data on installation level.

1.6.3 Flexible Mechanisms

Under the Kyoto Protocol, countries may meet their emission targets through a combination of domestic activities and the use of flexible mechanisms. Besides allowing countries to meet their targets in a cost-effective way, flexible mechanisms aim to assist developing

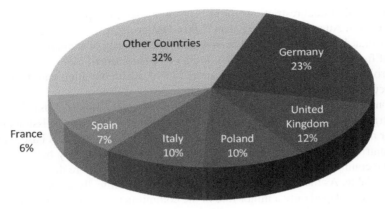

Total emissions 2008–2012: 7.84 billion t

Figure 1.38 CO_2 emissions 2008–2012 in the EU ETS by country. *Source*: CITL, June 2013.

countries in achieving sustainable development. The Kyoto Protocol includes three flexible mechanisms:

- Joint Implementation (JI)
- Clean Development Mechanism (CDM)
- International Emissions Trading (IET).

JI and CDM are project-based mechanisms. They involve developing and implementing measures that reduce greenhouse gas emissions in another country to generate emission credits. JI projects are carried out in industrialised countries with existing emission targets (Annex B countries under the Kyoto Protocol). CDM projects are carried out in developing countries without targets. JI projects generate Emission Reduction Units (ERUs) and CDM projects generate Certified Emission Reductions (CERs). Not only CO_2, but all greenhouse gases under the Kyoto Protocol are considered for JI and CDM projects. The unit of ERUs and CERs is t CO_2 equivalents. Sometimes these credits are also called Kyoto offsets.

JI projects have to be approved by the country in which they are implemented. One criterion is additionality; that is, the project would not have been implemented without the incentives created by JI. Therefore, measures covered by a company emissions trading scheme like the EU ETS are not eligible as JI projects. Until August 2013, almost 650 JI projects had been developed in 17 countries and submitted for approval to the UNFCCC.[7] With the expiration of the first Kyoto commitment period at the end of 2012, the future of JI is uncertain.

Under the CDM, investors from Annex I countries receive CERs for the actual amount of greenhouse gas emission reductions achieved. The issuing of CERs is subject to host and investor country agreement, third-party assessment and registration by the UNFCCC Clean Development Mechanism Executive Board (CDM EB). A key requirement for CDM projects is additionality: emissions reductions will only be recognised if the reduction of greenhouse gas emissions is in addition to any reduction that would have occured without the certified

---

[7] The UNFCCC Secretariat publishes detailed information on JI and on all submitted projects on the Internet under http://ji.unfccc.int.

project activity. Additional restrictions for projects apply, for example nuclear power projects are excluded. Until August 2013, more than 7100 CDM projects were registered by the CDM EB and more than 1.3 billion CERs had been issued. The majority of annually generated CERs are expected from projects in China (62%), India (10%) and Brazil (5%). The main areas of the CDM project activities are energy industries (75%), waste handling and disposal (11%) and manufacturing industries (4%).[8]

International Emissions Trading (IET) of Assigned Amount Units (AAUs) allow industrialised countries with emission targets (Annex B countries) to exchange emission allowances to meet their national Kyoto targets. Unlike CDM and JI, IET is not project based. Emissions in some countries, especially in Russia and Ukraine, were significantly below their Kyoto targets for the commitment period 2008–2012 (see Table 1.2) and more than sufficient AAUs have been available. As the use of this "hot air" is not really politically acceptable for meeting Kyoto targets, IET played only a minor role in the commitment period 2008–2012.

Besides AAUs, Annex B countries can also use CERs and ERUs for meeting their Kyoto targets. For instance, the Netherlands is aiming to do so through a state purchasing programme.

The Linking Directive (Directive 2009/27/EC), adopted by the EU Parliament in 2009, allows emission reduction units generated by project-based flexible mechanisms (JI and CDM) to be utilised for compliance by companies under the EU ETS. The rationale behind this linkage is to create additional potential for cost-effective measures and to reduce the overall costs for emission compliance for the participating companies. The Kyoto Protocol states that a significant portion of reductions should be achieved by domestic actions. Therefore, flexible mechanisms are considered supplementary to domestic measures and most NAPs have implemented limits for the use of JI and CDM. These limits are applied for each installation separately and not on a nationwide level. These limits are cumulative for all years of the second and third trading periods (e.g., 2008–2020). The Linking Directive allows the use of all ERUs or CERs that comply with the requirements established under the UNFCCC and which fulfil additional criteria set by the European Union. Only CERs and ERUs of projects registered before 2013 by the UNFCCC are eligible under the EU ETS, unless projects are located in Least Developed Countries (LDCs). The use of CERs and ERUs from projects involving the destruction of trifluoromethane (HFC-23) and N_2O from adipic acid production has been prohibited since 2013. Hydropower projects greater than 20 MW are required to be in line with criteria from the World Commission on Dams.

In addition to the EU ETS, the emission trading schemes in Australia and New Zealand allow the use of CERs and ERUs with certain restrictions. Furthermore, CERs are also used as voluntary emission offsets. But until August 2013 only 0.2 million CERs had been used for this purpose.

1.6.4 Products and Marketplaces

The main products on the market are EUAs and CERs eligible under the EU ETS. Common are spot, forward and futures trading of EUAs and CERs. In the case of spot trading, the certificates are transferred from the seller's account at a national registry to the buyer's account directly after the contract is concluded. Forward and futures trades generally settle in December of the specified year. Physical settlement by transferring certificates is common, but futures with

---

[8] The UNFCCC Secretariat publishes detailed CDM statistics on the Internet under http://cdm.unfccc.int/Statistics.

Table 1.3 Trading volumes of CO_2 emissions allowances

Certificate type	Volume (million t CO_2 equivalent)			Value (million EUR)		
	2010	2011	2012	2010	2011	2012
EUA	5172	6057	7478	71939	76162	54616
CER	1508	2012	2408	17993	17736	6120
ERU	59	101	574	507	713	906
AAU	63	69	119	460	404	151
North America	189	100	130	365	220	576
NZU	8	10	8	90	105	30
ACCU	–	–	0.3	–	–	6
Other	35	25	–	206	116	–
Total	7035	8373	10717	91559	95459	62404

Source: Talberg and Swoboda (2013).

financial settlement can be found as well. Standardised option contracts for EUAs and CERs also exist.

EUA and CER spot and forward contracts as well as options are traded bilaterally, either OTC or via brokers. Spot and futures trading of EUAs and CERs is possible at several exchanges. Futures contracts with settlement in December have the highest liquidity. Options are traded at exchanges as well, but the liquidity is very low. The main exchanges are:

- IntercontinentalExchange (ICE)[9]
- European Energy Exchange (EEX)
- NASDAQ OMX
- New York Mercantile Exchange (NYMEX)
- Commodity Exchange Bratislava (CEB).

As in other markets, the attractiveness of exchanges changes over time. One example in the emissions market is the BlueNext, which opened in 2007 and closed in 2012. It was considered the largest spot market for emissions certificates.

CERs are often bought in the form of bilateral Emission Reduction Purchase Agreements (ERPAs). Risks can be distributed differently between buyer and seller. In most cases, the seller commits to delivering all CERs generated from a specific project to the buyer, but the amount of CERs is not set. The buyer commits to buying all CERs delivered by the seller at a fixed price. In addition to participants in the EU ETS, also Annex B countries buy CERs in order to achieve their Kyoto targets.

In Table 1.3, trading volumes for EUAs, CERs and other types of CO_2 certificates are shown for the years 2010 to 2012. EUAs and CERs are the most important certificates in the emissions markets by far.

Figure 1.39 shows the development of CO_2 emission allowance prices in the EU ETS during the first trading period 2005–2007. The development is characterised by high volatility. While futures for the first period (settlement in December 2007) and for the second period (settlement

---

[9] The ICE acquired the ECX in 2010.

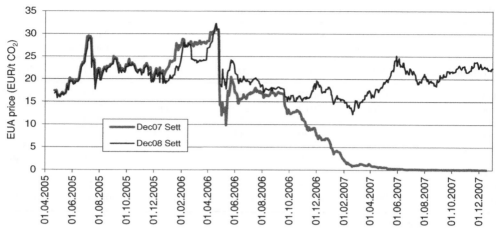

Figure 1.39 CO$_2$ emissions prices, EU ETS, first trading period. *Source*: ECX.

in December 2008) were priced more or less identically in the beginning, their prices became decoupled. The strong decline in prices for the 2007 futures can be explained by the excess of EUAs allocated by the NAPs for the first period. The futures for the second period (settlement in December 2008) remained at a level of 15 to 25 EUR/EUA, as no oversupply for the second trading period could be foreseen.

Fundamentally, the high volatility of CO$_2$ prices during the first trading period of the EU ETS can be explained by the price-inelastic supply of EUAs in the NAPs, and the low-demand elasticity in the short term. Most of the short-term demand elasticity exists in the electricity sector, where switching from coal-fired generation to gas-fired generation (fuel switching) is possible. Many other measures for emission reduction require investments with lead times too long to be effective within the first trading period. Furthermore, the demand is uncertain and depends on exogenous influences like wind and hydrological conditions that impact the demand for electricity generation from fossil fuels. Owing to the very small elasticity of the demand and the inherent demand uncertainty, fundamental prices are very uncertain and can decrease to zero.

One additional effect is the free allocation of EUAs via the NAPs. This resulted in most countries having an undersupply in the electricity sector and an oversupply in all other sectors. Electricity companies were the main actors in the first years. They intended to cover their short position (allocation below expected demand), but only a few other actors with a long position (allocation above expected demand) were willing to sell. Furthermore, no consistent and verified historical emission figures for participating installations were available for the years before 2005. Based on estimated historical emission figures, a significant shortage in the EU ETS was expected in a business-as-usual scenario. This led to high CO$_2$ prices until April 2006, with peak prices above 30 EUR/t CO$_2$. At the end of April 2006, certified emission figures for 2005 were published for several countries. They were significantly lower than expected. This led to a price collapse of more than 50% within one week.

The European Commission tried to improve the EU ETS by lengthening trading periods, allowing the possibility of banking EUAs from one period to the next, and by uniform allocation methods for all participating countries.

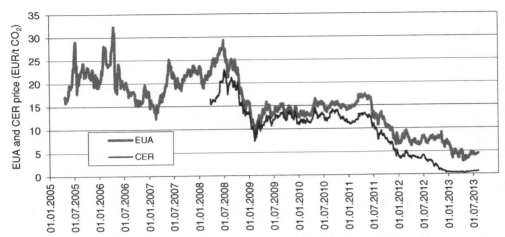

Figure 1.40 CO$_2$ emissions prices, EU ETS, second and third trading period. *Source*: ECX/ICE.

Figure 1.40 shows the price development of EUAs and CERs for the second and third trading periods. As the most liquid contracts are futures with settlement in December of the current or following year, these contracts have been selected for the figure. Until December 2008, the futures contract with settlement in 2008 is depicted as contracts with earlier settlement fell into the first trading period.

During the second trading period, the high price volatility continued. The sharp decline in prices between June 2008 and February 2009 can be explained by declining prices for oil, gas and coal, and by the economic recession in the European Union which led to a reduction in demand for allowances. After two years of relative stability, prices dropped further. The main reason was that it became apparent that there would be an oversupply of certificates during the third trading period 2008–2020. The European Commission considered several methods for reducing the amount of EUAs in the market, hence increasing the price, but nothing was implemented by the end of 2013. CERs were always traded with a discount to EUAs, as the quantity of CERs which can be used in the EU ETS is limited. Prices declined below 1 EUR per CER in 2013 due to the expectation that the number of CERs generated by 2020 would exceed the quantity restrictions for CERs in the EU ETS by far and the expectation that no new international agreement which could create additional demand for CERs would be in place until 2020. Prices for ERUs developed in a similar way to those of CERs.

1.6.5   Other Emissions Trading Schemes

As part of the Acid Rain Program, trading was introduced in the United States in the 1990s for sulfor dioxide (SO$_2$) emissions from fossil fuel power plants. This was the first emissions trading scheme. The so-called "cap-and-trade" method constrains overall emissions and allows certificate trading between participating generation units. In Phase I from 1995 to 1999, almost 500 generation units participated. In Phase II, which started in the year 2000, the number of participating units exceeded 2000. The Acid Rain Program is regarded as a success, as SO$_2$ emissions were reduced faster than anticipated. Figure 1.41 shows the development of the average prices for spot SO$_2$ emissions allowances at the annual Environmental Protection Agency

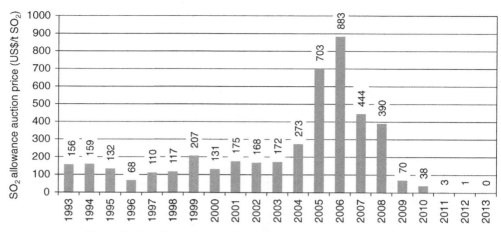

Figure 1.41   SO$_2$ emissions allowances auction prices. *Source*: EPA.

(EPA) auctions.[10] Similar to the EU ETS, this oldest emissions market is also characterised by high price volatility. While prices reached almost US$ 900 per tonne of SO$_2$ emissions in 2006, they dropped below US$ 1 in 2012 due to low demand caused by a shift from coal to natural gas as the main fuel in the electricity generation sector.

Regarding greenhouse gas emissions, there are several other smaller cap-and-trade systems implemented besides the EU ETS. Table 1.3 earlier gives an overview on traded volumes for different types of CO$_2$ emissions allowances and markets. The most important system is the EU ETS, in which EUAs, CERs and ERUs are traded.

The New Zealand Emissions Trading Scheme (NZ ETS) began in 2008 as a scheme covering only forestry activities. Land owners can generate certificates called New Zealand Units (NZUs) by afforestation and have to surrender NZUs for deforestation under certain conditions. In 2010, the NZ ETS was amended and expanded to cover also stationary energy, fishing, industrial processes and the liquid fossil fuels sectors. CERs and ERUs are accepted in the NZ ETS with some quality but without quantity restrictions. Therefore, with the decline in CER prices, the price for NZUs has fallen below NZ$ 2 in 2013. Plans for the New Zealand government to expand its emissions trading scheme to all sectors of the economy including agriculture, New Zealand's largest source of emissions, have been postponed. Therefore, it is unlikely that the NZ ETS will have a significant impact on greenhouse gas emissions in New Zealand in the near future.

Australia has introduced an emissions trading scheme called Carbon Price Mechanism (CPM). It is a mandatory scheme which covers all installations with annual emissions above 25 000 tonnes of CO$_2$ equivalents. In 2012, approximately 400 installations were covered. The emission certificates in the CPM are called Australian Carbon Credit Units (ACCUs). One ACCU is equivalent to one tonne of CO$_2$ emissions. The CPM is established in two phases. In the first phase from 2012 to 2014, a fixed price of A$ 23 applies. In the second phase from 2015 onward, a floating market price will be established under a cap-and-trade system. At this point there will be a unilateral link to the EU ETS. EUAs are accepted in the Australian

---

[10] Detailed information on the Acid Rain Program can be found on the US EPA's Acid Rain Program homepage http://www. epa.gov/airmarkets/progsregs/arp/.

system. And from 2018 onwards, a bilateral link is expected which will allow ACCUs to be used by European installations as well. As offset mechanisms, the CPM accepts CERs from the Clean Development Program under the Kyoto Protocol, with qualitative and quantitative restrictions, as well as offsets from national emission reduction measures from agriculture and landfill activities via the Carbon Farming Initiative (CFI).

Switzerland has introduced a carbon tax of CHF 36 per tonne of CO_2 in 2008. As Switzerland had not met its Kyoto targets, the tax was increased to CHF 60 per tonne of CO_2 in 2013. Large emitters were exempted from the carbon tax if they had participated in the Swiss Emissions Trading Scheme (Swiss ETS). Since 2013, participation in the Swiss ETS is compulsory for installations with an installed capacity above 20 MW, and voluntary for installations with an installed capacity between 10 MW and 20 MW in exchange for an exemption from the carbon tax. Approximately 400 installations participate in the Swiss ETS. Emission allowances are allocated for free based on benchmarks, and the remaining allowances are sold by auction. CERs and ERUs are accepted within the Swiss ETS with qualitative and quantitative restrictions. Switzerland plans to link its ETS to the EU ETS.

The Republic of Kazakhstan began a mandatory national emissions trading scheme in 2013. This scheme covers installations in the manufacturing, energy, mining, metallurgy, chemicals, agriculture and transport industries with emissions above 20 000 tonnes of CO_2 per year. It includes approximately 200 installations.

In North America several regional emissions trading schemes have been established. The oldest one is the Regional Greenhouse Gas Initiative (RGGI). It was established in 2009 and brings together nine states (Connecticut, Delaware, Maine, Maryland, Massachusetts, New Hampshire, New York, Rhode Island and Vermont). It is a mandatory scheme for fossil fuel power stations with an installed capacity above 25 MW, including approximately 200 installations. Certificates are sold by auction. The number of certificates available depends on certain price thresholds. RGGI accepts credits from five different types of offset projects in the participating states subject to quantitative and qualitative limits.

The Western Climate Initiative (WCI) started in 2007 with several states in the USA and provinces in Canada. But by 2013, only two trading schemes at state or provincial level have been implemented out of this initiative, the California Cap-and-Trade Program and the Quebec Cap-and-Trade System.

Since 2013, the Californian scheme is mandatory for installations with emissions above 25 000 tonnes of CO_2 equivalents per year. The number of participating installations is approximately 600. Initially, 90% of the permits have been allocated for free, the rest are sold by auction by the California Air Resources Board (CARB). For auctions, a floor price of US\$ 10 per certificate applies. And if market prices exceed certain thresholds, the quantity of certificates can be increased. Participants can use offset credits to cover up to 8% of their total obligation.

The Quebec Cap-and-Trade System is very similar to the California Cap-and-Trade Program. It has also been in operation since 2013 and includes approximately 100 installations. Plans exist to link these two programmes.

The Canadian province of Alberta introduced a Greenhouse Gas Reduction Program in 2007 which requires installations with emissions above 100 000 tonnes of CO_2 equivalents per year to reduce their emission intensity by 12%. Participating companies can meet this obligation by the following means: making improvements to their operations, purchasing Alberta-based offset credits, purchasing tradable Emission Performance Credits (EPCs) which are generated by reducing the emission intensity below the target, or paying a penalty of C\$ 15 per tonne to the Climate Change and Emissions Management Fund. Targets and the penalty for not meeting the targets are revised from time to time.

Two Japanese regions have operational mandatory emissions trading schemes in place: Tokyo and Saitama. The Tokyo metropolitan mandatory cap-and-trade scheme was launched in 2010. It covers approximately 1500 buildings and installations with a fuel, heat and electricity consumption above 1500 kilolitres of crude oil equivalent per year. Until 2014 the scheme only covered CO_2 emissions, but from 2015 all six Kyoto Protocol gases will be included. The region of Saitama launched a similar scheme in 2011 with approximately 600 participating installations. Both schemes are linked.

In addition, a national emissions trading scheme was in the implementation phase in South Korea in 2013. And in China, regional schemes were in the implementation phase in Beijing, Tianjin, Shanghai, Chongqing, Shenzhen, Hubei and Guangdong. Several other countries or regions worldwide are considering the implementation of a mandatory emissions trading scheme.[11]

In the long run, convergence of CO_2 prices in all trading schemes can be expected – either through a direct linkage of the schemes, or through an indirect linkage via CERs, ERUs or other certificates from offset projects which are accepted by more than one scheme.

---

[11] The homepage http://www.icapcarbonaction.com of the International Carbon Action Partnership (ICAP) gives a good overview on the development of regional and national emissions trading systems.

2

Renewable Energy

Renewable energy is energy from resources which are not depleted by utilisation but rather continually replenished. These resources include solar irradiation, wind, hydropower, tides, waves, geothermal heat and regrowing biomass utilised in a sustainable manner. Renewable energies have gained growing attention from the public in recent years. Many governments support renewable energies, and their share in energy consumption is constantly increasing. The main benefits of renewable energies are:

- A vast and inexhaustible energy supply.
- Little or no greenhouse gas emissions causing global warming.
- Little or no air pollution affecting public health and environmental quality.
- Job creation and other social benefits.
- Reduced dependency on imported energy resources.
- Higher resilience of the electricity system due to decentralised installations.
- Reduced volatility of energy prices.

In 2011, the estimated renewable energy share of global final energy consumption was 19% (Sawin, 2013). Almost half of this renewable energy share is traditional biomass used for cooking, heating and other applications, predominantly in developing countries. The remaining share is composed of renewable energies utilised by means of modern technologies developed in the last 120 years. This chapter covers only these modern renewables, focusing on electricity generation and some basic coverage of biofuels and heat.

The first section of this chapter covers the historical development of the utilisation of renewable energies, political goals and forecasts. Basic technical aspects are covered in Section 2.3. To understand the risks involved in renewable energy investments it is important to understand the regulatory framework of different support schemes (Section 2.4) and the key economic factors of renewable energy projects (Section 2.5). Finally, we conclude this chapter with a detailed discussion of the risks in the renewable energy sector and appropriate mitigation strategies.

2.1 THE ROLE OF RENEWABLE ENERGY IN ELECTRICITY GENERATION

In this section we will discuss the role of renewable energy in electricity generation with focus on the historical development, political targets and expected future development.

2.1.1 Historical Development

In the early times of electricity supply, hydropower was the predominant generation source and it still plays an important role with a share of approximately 16%. In recent years, wind, solar

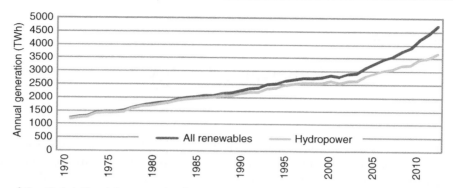

Figure 2.1   Global electricity generation from renewable sources. *Source*: BP (2013), EIA, OECD and own calculations.

and biomass have been developed as additional renewable energy sources with high growth rates. Geothermal energy is also utilised for electricity production, but growth rates are rather small. Figure 2.1 shows the development of worldwide electricity generation from renewable sources for the years 1971–2012. A constant growth over the years can be seen, but since the beginning of this century, growth rates have increased significantly. And in addition to hydropower as the predominant source for renewable electricity generation, other renewable energy sources have gained importance.

If one considers the share of renewable energy in electricity generation, the picture is slightly different (see Figure 2.2). The growth of generation from hydropower was not able to keep track with the total growth in electricity demand, and the share of renewables declined from 23.2% in 1971 to 17.6% in 2003. Only with the strong growth of electricity generation from other renewable sources (especially wind, solar and biomass) did the share of renewables increase again to 21% in 2012. This growth was accomplished by massive investments in the renewable energy sector, in most cases with governmental support.

The growth of renewables is quite different from country to country. For example, Germany has had strong support for renewable energy since the 1990s. The share of renewable electricity

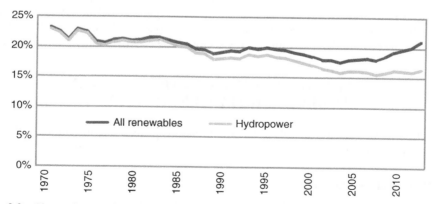

Figure 2.2   Share of renewables in global electricity generation. *Source*: BP (2013), EIA, OECD and own calculations.

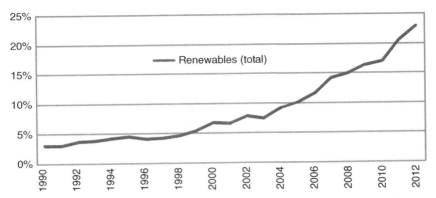

Figure 2.3   Share of renewable electricity in Germany. *Source*: BMU (2013).

increased from 3% in 1990 to 23% in 2012 (see Figure 2.3). Considering only the two years 2011 and 2012, renewable generation gained more than 5% additional market share within 48 months in the German electricity market. These are very rapid changes in an industry sector with long investment cycles and low growth rates. The average growth rate of renewable generation in TWh between 1990 and 2012 was approximately 10% per year.

The growth of renewable electricity generation since 2000 is caused to a large degree by new installations of wind farms and solar power plants with photovoltaics (PV). Figures 2.4 and 2.5 depict the development of the installed generation capacity from wind and PV, respectively. Europe played an important role in introducing these new technologies. But over time, the focus for new installed capacity has shifted to other regions, including Asia. In 2012, China was the country with the largest installed wind power capacity. A similar development can be expected for PV as well.

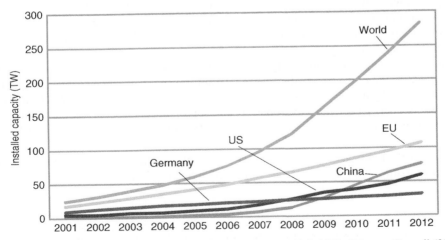

Figure 2.4   Installed wind energy generation capacity. *Source*: Global Wind Energy Council (2013).

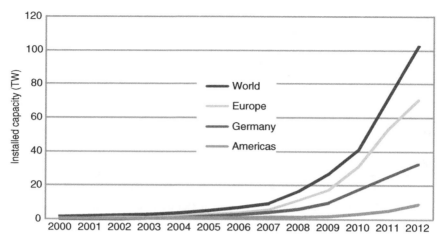

Figure 2.5   Installed PV generation capacity. *Source*: European Photovoltaic Industry Association (2013) and BSW-Solar.

2.1.2   Political Targets

Many governments have established political targets for renewable energy in general and for the electricity generation sector in particular. Political targets can change fast. Therefore, this section intends only to give a few examples of political targets. For details, up-to-date information has to be sought and evaluated.[1]

The European Union has a target of 20% for the share of energy from renewable sources in gross final energy consumption by 2020 (Directive 2009/28/EC). This overall goal is broken down into individual national targets, and all Member Countries of the European Union had to publish a National Renewable Energy Action Plan in 2010 defining sectors and measures for reaching their targets. In the case of Germany, the target for the share of energy from renewable sources in gross final consumption is 18% and Germany intends to reach this target (among other measures) with a 38.6% renewable energy share in the electricity sector. The UK has 15% as overall target and intends to meet this target with a 30% share of renewable energy in the electricity sector (compared with a share of 11% in 2012). Other European countries have similar, ambitious targets.

In the United States, no national targets for renewable energy exist. However, several states have decided on their own targets. For instance, California has a 33% renewable energy target (excluding large hydropower) in the electricity sector for the year 2020 (in 2012, the share of renewable energy excluding hydropower was approximately 15%). Another example is Colorado, which has a renewable energy target of 30% for investor-owned utilities for the year 2020.

To achieve the political targets, a large variety of support schemes have been implemented. The characteristics of these schemes are discussed in Section 2.4.

---

[1] The International Renewable Energy Agency (IRENA) publishes on its webpage http://www.irena.org renewable energy country profiles for many countries of the world which include renewable energy targets. Many national and regional governments publish their targets on the Internet as well.

2.1.3 Forecasts

The future development of renewable energy depends on many factors. On the one side there are commercial aspects, but there are also economical and political aspects and, in addition, specific investment barriers might have to be resolved. The development of the following key factors will have a strong influence on the future of renewable energy:

- Cost of renewable energy technology.
- Cost of fossil fuels.
- Political and public support for renewable energy.
- Local acceptance of renewable energy installations.
- Growth in electricity demand.
- Integration of renewable energy into the existing infrastructure.
- Integration of renewable energy into electricity markets.
- Development of decentralised energy systems.

A large number of forecasts for the future development of renewable energy in the electricity sector exist. These forecasts are updated from time to time and show a broad spectrum of possible future developments. Well-known forecasts are the annually published World Energy Outlook (WEO) of the International Energy Agency (IEA) and the International Energy Outlook (IEO) of the US Energy Information Agency (EIA). The Current Policies scenario of the WEO 2012 is similar to the reference scenario of the IEO 213. Figure 2.6 shows the average of these two scenarios for the worldwide development of different renewable energy technologies. The average annual growth rate between 2010 and 2035 for renewable energy is 3%. In 2035, the share of renewable energy in electricity generation should increase slightly to 24% (compared with 23% in 2012). The highest average growth rates are for solar energy (12% p.a.) and wind energy (7% p.a.). The lowest growth rate is for hydropower (2% p.a.),

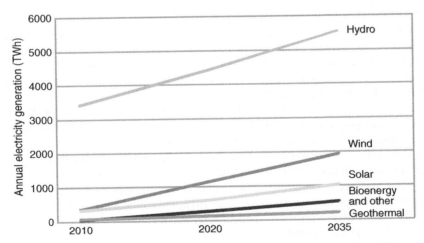

Figure 2.6   Renewable energy electricity generation forecast. *Source*: International Energy Agency (2012) and US Energy Information Agency (2013).

while the other technologies grow at 5% p.a. In 2035, the most important renewable energy technology remains hydropower, with a share of 60% in these scenarios.

The IEA publishes two additional scenarios in its World Energy Outlook:

- A New Policies scenario that takes account of broad policy commitments and plans to reduce greenhouse-gas emissions and phase out fossil-energy subsidies; this scenario can be considered the baseline scenario of the WEO.
- A 450 scenario that sets out an energy pathway consistent with the goal of limiting the global increase in temperature to 2°C by limiting concentration of greenhouse gases in the atmosphere to around 450 ppm of CO_2.

In these scenarios, renewable energy reaches a share of 31% and 48% in electricity generation, respectively, by 2035. The average growth rates of solar energy would be 15% and 18% p.a., respectively; and of wind energy 9% and 11% p.a., respectively. Also, the other renewable energy technologies would grow faster in these scenarios than in the Current Policies scenario.

The renewable energy industry is generally even more optimistic with respect to renewable energy growth rates. For instance the Global Wind Energy Council, the international trade association for the wind power industry, expected in the year 2013 growth rates of 14% p.a. for the global installed wind generation capacity over a 5-year horizon (Global Wind Energy Council, 2013).

2.2   THE ROLE OF LIQUID BIOFUELS IN THE TRANSPORTATION SECTOR

Liquid biofuels are made from different biomass sources and have qualities that are similar to fossil fuels used in the transportation sector. The two main liquid biofuels are bioethanol (approximately 80% market share) and biodiesel (20%). In 2012, the production of liquid biofuels was 1.2 million barrels per day of oil equivalents (bbl/doe). This production meets roughly 3% of the global transport fuel demand.

Bioethanol is produced from sugarcane, corn, sugar beets, wheat, potatoes, sorghum and cassava. In 2012, the largest producers of bioethanol were the United States, using corn, and Brazil, using sugarcane. Biodiesel is made from vegetable oils. The main feedstocks are rapeseed, soya beans, sunflowers, palm oil as well as waste oils. The largest producers of biodiesel are the European Union and the United States.

Figure 2.7 shows the development of liquid biofuel production since 1990. Brazil used to be the dominant player in the biofuel sector but between 2000 and 2010, liquid biofuel production increased by 500%, the main areas of growth being the United States and the European Union. In comparison to these regions, biofuel production in Brazil grew only moderately by approximately 100%. In Asian countries including China, a biofuel sector developed rapidly as well. The growth was mainly driven by support schemes for biofuels, including quota systems and tax incentives. In 2013, only bioethanol from sugarcane was economically competitive with fossil fuels. Therefore, the future development of biofuels depends strongly on governmental support and technological progress.

The main advantages of biofuels are a substantial reduction of greenhouse gas emissions in the transport sector and a reduction in reliance on oil imports. The disadvantages are that the

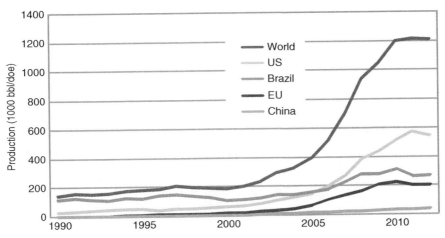

Figure 2.7   Liquid biofuel production. *Source*: BP (2013).

large-scale production of biofuels competes with food production for arable land and water as well as risks caused by land-use changes, including threats to biodiversity and rain forests.

The IEA projects that biofuels could provide up to 9% of total transportation fuels by 2030 and up to 27% by 2050 in a sustainable way (International Energy Agency, 2010). An annual increase in biofuel production of 30% would have to be achieved. However, this would require more than 100 million hectares of agricultural land being utilised for biofuels, in comparison with 30 million in 2010 (International Energy Agency, 2011). A large part of this additional agricultural land would be located in developing countries and significant yield improvements would have to be made.

The future of liquid biofuels depends on a number of key factors. The commercial viability will depend largely on the price of biomass, the price of crude oil and the governmental support for biofuels. An extended production of biofuels would increase biomass demand and prices. A global market for biofuels would develop, similar to those for crude oil or coal today. Technological progress in the production could make accessible a broader range of non-food biomass as feedstock for biofuels (e.g., forestry waste). This could reduce prices and address sustainability issues.

2.3   RENEWABLE ENERGY TECHNOLOGIES

This section gives a short overview of renewable energy technologies. Physical and technical principles are explained as well as current trends in technology development. For more details, specific textbooks are recommended including Kaltschmitt *et al.* (2007) and Sørensen (2010).

2.3.1   Hydropower

Hydropower is by far the most established and widely used renewable resource for electricity generation and a proven technology for more than 100 years. The first hydropower station was

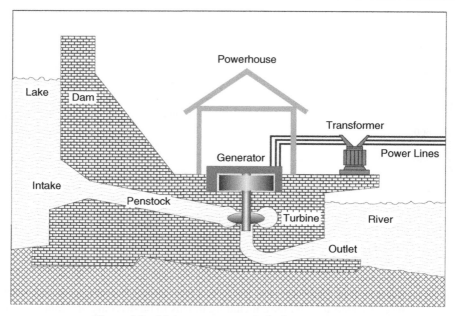

Figure 2.8   Main components of a hydropower station.

built in Northumberland (UK) in 1880. Before hydropower was used for electricity generation, it had been used at least since the third century BC for grinding grain, and later also for sawing wood and other applications.

Figure 2.8 shows the main components of a hydropower station. The principal idea of hydropower is to use the difference in potential energy of water at different elevations as mechanical energy, or for the generation of electricity. In fluid dynamics, Bernoulli's equation (2.1) describes the interrelation of speed, pressure and the fluid's potential energy for an inviscid flow of an incompressible fluid:

$$\frac{v^2}{2} + g \cdot h + \frac{p}{\rho} = \text{constant}, \tag{2.1}$$

where v is the fluid's flow speed at a point on a streamline, g is the acceleration due to gravity, h is the elevation of the point above a reference plane, p is the pressure at the chosen point and ρ is the density of the fluid at all points in the fluid.

The electrical power P_{el} of the schematic hydropower station in Figure 2.9 can be calculated:

$$P_{el} = \eta \cdot \dot{Q} \cdot \left(\rho \cdot g \cdot (h_1 - h_2) + (p_1 - p_2) + \frac{\rho}{2} \cdot \left(v_1^2 - v_2^2 \right) \right), \tag{2.2}$$

where η is the conversion efficiency and $\dot{Q}$ the flow rate.

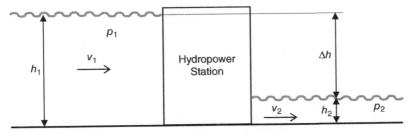

Figure 2.9   Schematic hydro power station.

In many cases, the differences in ambient pressure as well as the differences in flow speed before and after the power station can be neglected. In this case equation (2.2) can be simplified to

$$P_{el} = \eta \cdot \rho \cdot g \cdot \dot{Q} \cdot \Delta h, \qquad (2.3)$$

where $\Delta h = h_1 - h_2$ is the elevation difference or (hydraulic) head.

The two parameters, flow rate $\dot{Q}$ and head Δh, are the relevant parameters for selecting suitable sites for hydropower stations. Rivers with high flow rates and high elevation differences over a short geographical distance are likely to be suitable sites. The construction and operation costs of a hydropower station have to be recovered by the generated energy, which is proportional to the flow rate and the head.

For generating electrical energy out of the potential energy of water, several conversion steps are required. The potential energy of water is converted into pressure energy and kinetic energy at the site of the turbine. These forms of energy are converted in the turbine into mechanical energy, which is converted into electrical energy in the generator. In the transformer, the voltage level of the electrical current is increased to the high-voltage level of the connecting grid. During these different steps, conversion losses occur. Typical losses are:

- Losses caused by water not used, e.g. in case of seasonal high-water flows exceeding the capacity of the hydropower plant.
- Losses at the water catchment.
- Friction losses of the water on its way from the water catchment to the turbine outlet.
- Mechanical and electrical losses in the turbine, generator and transformer.
- Losses caused by the energy consumption of the hydropower station (internal consumption).

All together, these losses add up to approximately 10–20% of the design water flow, not considering any losses caused by water not used. The turbine losses depend strongly on the flow rate and on the turbine type. While, for instance, Pelton turbines typically still reach 80% efficiency at 15% of the design water flow, Francis turbines reach only 10–40% at these water flows. Therefore, it is often advisable to install several smaller turbines in one hydropower station instead of one with the same combined capacity to be able to operate the turbines with high efficiency at different water flow rates. An additional benefit is the partial redundancy during maintenance periods.

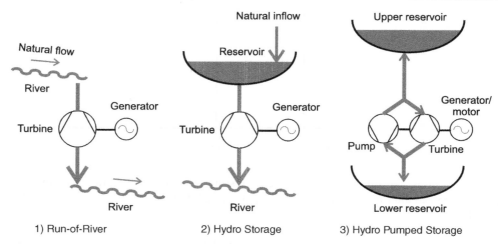

Figure 2.10   Design principles of hydropower stations.

There are three different design principles for hydropower stations (see Figure 2.10).

1. *Run-of-river hydropower plant:* A run-of-river hydropower plant is a hydropower plant without a reservoir. In most cases it utilises the difference in elevation of the water level above and below a weir in a river. Characteristic for this design type is the high design flow and a relatively low head, up to only 20 m. In rivers or streams with high gradients, run-of-river power stations can also be constructed by redirecting water at the location of the intake, transporting it through a channel or a tunnel and through a pressure pipe to the power house with the turbine and generator, and releasing it back into the river or stream. By this design, a high head can be achieved. The generation depends directly on the flow rate of the river, and only in some cases is a slight modulation of the generation possible by increasing or decreasing the water level above the weir for a short time (several hours). Thus, the generation output has substantial seasonal variations. With increasing flow rate of the river, the generation of the power plant increases until the design flow is reached. Any additional water cannot be utilised but flows over the weir. In the case of very high water flows, the generated power of the power station can decrease due to higher water levels behind the weir and thus decreasing head.
2. *Reservoir or storage hydropower plant:* A reservoir or storage hydropower plant utilises the head between an upper reservoir and the outlet into a river. The reservoir can be a natural or an artificial lake. The lake has natural water inflows. The key characteristic of a storage hydropower plant is that the generation is adjusted to the electricity demand. At times when the flow through the turbines exceeds the inflows, the lake level decreases and vica versa. Depending on the size of the reservoir, the storage is operated in daily, weekly or seasonal cycles. The hydraulic head depends on the reservoir level and thus the electricity generated per cubic metre of water. The average head of a storage hydropower plant is between 20 and several hundred metres.
3. *Pumped storage hydropower plants:* Pumped storage hydropower plants operate between two reservoirs. In addition to a turbine, they also have a pump to pump water from the lower

to the upper reservoir. The pump does not necessarily have to be a separate device. Some turbines are designed to be used as a pump as well, by operation in the reverse direction of rotation. And in most cases, the generator can be used as a motor to drive the pump. In times of low electricity demand, water is pumped from the lower to the upper reservoir. The electrical energy is thus converted into potential energy, which can be stored and reconverted into electrical energy by releasing the water through the turbine to the lower reservoir. The cycle efficiency of a pumped storage hydropower plant is approximately 75–80%. Depending on the size of the reservoirs and the turbines, the reservoirs can be designed to operate in daily, weekly or seasonal cycles. The hydraulic head is usually several hundred metres.

Pumped storage hydropower plants do not generate renewable energy unless the upper reservoir has a natural inflow, or electricity generated from renewable resources is used for pumping.

Different types of turbines are suitable for different heads. Further, there are differences in the suitability for part-load operation, maintenance costs and water quality requirements. Basically, there are two principle turbine designs.

- *Impulse turbines or constant-pressure turbines:* In the case of impulse turbines the potential and pressure energy of water is first converted completely into kinetic energy. Nozzles direct streams of water against the spoon-shaped buckets of a turbine. The impulse of the water is transmitted to the turbine, and the water flows out of the buckets with low velocity. Thus, the kinetic energy is converted into mechanical energy, which drives the generator. As the (typical atmospheric) pressure is the same before and after the turbine, this type of turbine is also called a "constant-pressure turbine". The most common impulse turbine is the Pelton turbine. It is used for sites with high heads (up to 2000 m) and low water flow rates. Its part-load efficiency is high in comparison with other turbines.
- *Reaction turbines:* In the case of reaction turbines, the potential energy of water is converted into pressure energy before it enters the turbine. Then the turbine blades transform the energy into mechanical energy. These turbines are called reaction turbines because the fluid pushes or reacts continuously against the turbine blades. In contrast to impulse turbines, reaction turbines are totally embedded in the fluid. The water loses most of its pressure while passing the turbine. Typical reaction turbines are Francis turbines, which are suitable for a head between 20 and 700 m, as well as Kaplan turbines, which are suitable for a head of up to 60 m and high water flows.

Hydropower plants have high investment costs of typically EUR 2000 to EUR 4000 per kW installed capacity. As every site has its own characteristics, every hydropower station has to be designed individually. Only some components, like generators or transformers, can be bought standardised. Therefore, the design phase is very long and complex. Hydropower stations have low operation costs, high availability and the technical lifetime can be 50 years or more. Storage and pumped storage hydropower plants have the advantage that the electricity generation can be scheduled independently of current water inflows following electricity demand.

Especially in the case of storage hydropower plants, the environmental and social impact of a hydropower station can be significant.

2.3.2 Wind Power

Wind power has been utilised to power sailing boats for thousands of years. Windmills were used for grinding grain, pumping water and other applications for centuries. But the use of wind power for electricity generation became widespread only two decades ago.

Wind energy is the kinetic energy of air in motion. The power P_w of wind can be calculated as

$$P_w = \frac{1}{2} \cdot \rho \cdot A \cdot v^3, \qquad (2.4)$$

where ρ is the density of the air, A is the area perpendicular to the wind direction the air is passing through (e.g., an area swept by the blades of a wind turbine) and v is the wind speed.

The velocity of the air cannot be reduced to zero by a wind turbine, as the air has to stay in motion to give way for additional air entering. Therefore, only a fraction of the wind power P_w can be utilised. Betz' law (2.5) describes the maximum power P_{max} which can be utilised theoretically:

$$P_{max} = \frac{1}{2} \cdot \rho \cdot c_{p.max} \cdot A \cdot v^3, \qquad (2.5)$$

where $c_{p.max}$ is the ideal power coefficient, which has a value of $c_{p.max} = \frac{16}{27} = 0.593$. Modern wind turbines reach 75–80% of this theoretical maximum and have power coefficients c_p in the range of 0.45 to 0.5 at the optimal point of operation.

Several designs for wind turbines have been developed. The most efficient wind turbines utilise the lift forces of the air in motion and not the drag forces. The aerodynamic principle is the same as that utilised by birds, insects or aeroplanes. The most common design is a wind turbine with a horizontal axis and three blades (see Figure 2.11). The speed of the rotor is controlled by adjusting the angle of the blades (pitch control). The rotational speed of the rotor is approximately 5 to 20 rotations per minute (rpm). Most generators operate at a higher speed. Therefore, a gearbox is required between the rotor hub and the generator. To avoid the gearbox, special generators with a large number of poles have been developed which can be operated at the same rotational speed as the rotor. The advantage of the gearless design, also called direct drive, is the avoidance of a gearbox and thus the reduction of elements which are prone to wear. The disadvantages are higher generator cost and weight.

The relation between electrical output and wind speed is described by the power curve of a wind turbine. Figure 2.12 shows a typical power curve. It can be divided into four phases. In phase 1, the wind speed is too low to generate enough power to compensate all losses in the system. As soon as the cut-in wind speed is reached, the wind turbine starts to generate electricity. The electrical power output increases until the rated wind speed is reached (phase 2). At that wind speed the power is equal to the rated power of the wind turbine. In phase 3, the power output stays constant. The control system of the wind turbine curtails the power to the rated power of the drive train to prevent overloading. If the wind speed exceeds the cut-out speed, the wind turbine is shut down to avoid damage to the turbine's structural components (phase 4).

Different wind power sites have different characteristics. The main criteria for wind turbine design are average wind speed at hub height, turbulence and extreme wind speeds (50-year maximum). The international standard IEC 61400-1 defines different design requirements for

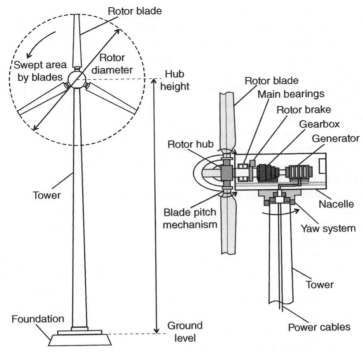

Figure 2.11   Key elements of a wind turbine.

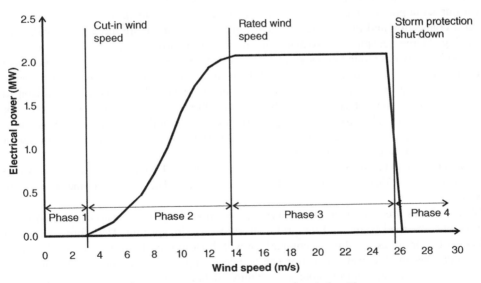

Figure 2.12   Typical power curve of a wind turbine.

the wind turbine generator classes Ia to IV. These classes are generally referred to as ICE wind classes. Class Ia has the highest wind speed and high turbulence, class IV the lowest wind speed. As the IEC 61400-1 does not cover all sites, in some cases additional site-specific requirements have to be considered by the turbine manufacturers.

To choose the correct type of turbine and for reliable wind yield predictions, site assessments are required. If no data from nearby wind measurements is available, a measurement campaign is necessary. Wind measurements should be taken at different heights. The highest anemometer should be located at a height above ground level which is equal to at least two-thirds of the planned hub height. The duration of the measurement campaign should be at least 12 months. The more complex the terrain, the more met masts are required and the higher the uncertainty of the wind yield assessment. A site layout of a wind farm is developed to select suitable sites for all wind turbines of the wind farm while maximising the overall wind yield of the wind farm. Interdependencies (wake effects) between the turbines have to be considered. In general, in the main wind direction, a distance of three to four rotor diameters between the wind turbines is required. Perpendicular to the main wind direction, distances of two to three rotor diameters can be sufficient.

The design of wind turbines has progressed rapidly in the last few decades. While in the 1980s a typical wind turbine had a rotor diameter of 17 m, 75 kW power and a hub height of 30 m, a typical size in the year 2000 was 70 m rotor diameter, 1.5 MW power and 80 m hub height. In 2013, turbines in series production with approximately 120 m rotor diameter, 3 MW power and 140 m hub height were available. These turbines are suitable for onshore sites with relatively low wind speeds. Wind turbines with hub heights of 120 m or more can even be installed in forests. For onshore sites with high wind speeds, turbines with up to 7.5 MW power and 130 m rotor diameter are available.

In addition to turbines for onshore sites, turbines for offshore sites have been developed and installed. The advantages of offshore sites are steadier winds, higher wind speeds and no visual impact in populated areas. The main challenges for offshore sites are the foundations, the grid connection and the maintenance concept. Most common are monopile foundations consisting of large steel pipes, 4 to 6 m in diameter, which are driven up to 60 m into the sea bed. Jacket and gravity base foundations are also used. Floating foundations are under development and being tested with prototypes. In spite of the better wind conditions offshore, the specific electricity generation costs are significantly higher at offshore locations in comparison to onshore locations. Wind turbines for offshore wind farms have fewer size restrictions for transport to the site. Therefore, even larger turbines have been developed for offshore sites. Turbines with more than 150 m rotor diameter and 6 MW power are available. Turbines with up to 10 MW power are under development.

Typical investment costs for onshore wind farms are 1000 to 1800 EUR/kW and for offshore wind farms 3000 to 5000 EUR/kW including grid connection. The design lifetime is generally 20 years.

Wind turbines are manufactured in series production. For most onshore sites, only the foundations, the road layout and the grid connection are site specific. Therefore, the design and construction times are short in comparison with hydropower. For offshore, the design of the foundations and the grid connection can be very complex and site specific. The logistics for installing the equipment offshore also requires detailed planning. In consequence, long design and construction times of several years are common for offshore wind projects.

The environmental impact of wind turbines is low in comparison with other electricity generation technologies. But in populated areas, the visual impact and noise emissions of wind turbines can be of concern. One disadvantage of wind power is the fluctuating generation. Wind farms generally reach load factors of only 20–50%. For phases with low wind speeds and thus no wind energy generation, other methods of generating electricity must be available to meet electricity demand.

2.3.3 Solar Energy

Solar power is the most plentiful energy source available on Earth. Renewable energy sources such as wind, hydro, and biomass energy are based indirectly on solar energy. The insolation of the Sun at the outer atmosphere has an intensity of 1.367 kW/m^2. This intensity is called the *solar constant*. While in the shorter term over days and weeks the insolation intensity can vary by up to 3%, the average over several years is very constant, with fluctuations below 0.1%. Only approximately 50% of the solar irradiation reaches the surface of the Earth. The remaining energy is either emitted to space as radiation or converted in other forms of energy within the atmosphere (inter alia into wind energy).

The average annual global radiation (direct solar insolation and reflected) on the Earth's surface varies outside the polar regions between approximately 800 and 2200 $W/(m^2 \cdot a)$. It depends on the geographic position and the climatic conditions. High insolation exists in deserts as well as in plateaus at high altitude, for example in the Rocky Mountains or the Andes. In Germany, it varies between 800 and 1300 $W/(m^2 \cdot a)$.

Traditionally, solar energy is utilised for heating, lighting, drying of crops, etc. But for grid-connected electricity generation, it has only been used since the 1980s. Electricity generation can either take place directly using solar cells, also called photovoltaics, or indirectly using concentrated solar power (CSP) technology.

Photovoltaics

Photovoltaics utilise the photovoltaic effect, which converts the energy of irradiation directly into electric energy. Photovoltaic cells consist of a semiconducting material like silicon, cadmium telluride or gallium arsenide. Photons with appropriate wavelength are absorbed by the solar cell and create electron–hole pairs in the semiconductor. These excited electrons and holes are swept into different directions by a built-in electric potential at the interface of an n-type and a p-type semiconductor. A voltage or electric current is created. Several solar cells are combined into a module. The generated DC is converted into AC by an inverter, which is connected to the grid. Figure 2.13 shows the principal setup of a solar cell. Modules can be installed on roof tops as small power generators with capacities between 5 kW and 10 MW, but also in open spaces as large-scale solar power stations with capacities of several hundred megawatts. In addition to grid-connected applications, solar cells are also utilised for off-grid power supply.

While in theory solar cells could reach an efficiency of 41%, the maximum efficiency under laboratory conditions is 25% and for normal applications efficiencies of 15–20% are common. In recent years, high production capacities for solar cells have been built and costs decreased dramatically. In 2013, solar cells were available for 500 to 1000 EUR/Wp, and complete installations including converter and grid connection for below 1000 EUR/Wp. In comparison, in 2005, prices around 5000 EUR/Wp were common. The technical lifetime of solar cells is 20 to 25 years. In areas with high insolation, electricity generation from PV can compete with fossil fuels without any subsidies.

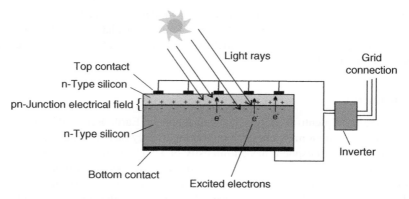

Figure 2.13   PV cell structure and operation schematic.

The advantages of PV cells are their modularity and the short construction time for instal-lations. The technological development in the PV sector has been very rapid. Further cost reductions and new applications, for example solar cells on curved surfaces, are expected from thin-film technology. Another tendency is to develop solar cells which are directly integrated into the outer shell of buildings. This could further reduce electricity generation costs from PV, as electricity generation becomes a by-product. The disadvantage of solar power is its dependency on insolation. Therefore, the production pattern of PV is very fluctuating. But in climatic zones where air conditioning is common, the production pattern of PV can match the demand pattern quite well. To overcome these fluctuations, battery-based energy storage can be applied. But the investment costs for battery storage are still too high to make these integrated systems financially attractive in areas with grid connection without subsidies. In areas without existing grid connection they can compete with diesel generation.

Concentrated Solar Power

Concentrated solar power (CSP) requires a fluid as intermediate energy carrier to generate electricity. Figure 2.14 depicts the main elements of a concentrated solar power station with parabolic reflectors. In the solar field, the reflectors concentrate the Sun's rays on receiver tubes in the centre of the mirrors. The orientation of the reflectors is adjusted continuously to follow the course of the Sun during the day. The tubes are filled with a heat transfer fluid like molten salt or synthetic oil. In a heat exchanger, the heat is transferred to a secondary steam–water cycle. The steam is expanded in a turbine and condensed to water in the condenser. A generator is driven by the turbine and produces electricity.

Another type of design is the solar power tower, where a field of plain reflectors concentrate the solar rays on a receiver located on top of a tower.

In some systems, a storage for hot salt is integrated. This allows heat to be stored for several hours and prolongs the daily energy production period. Also, a gas-heated boiler can be integrated into the system to produce heat at times without insolation.

In comparison with PV, CSP systems are relatively complex and require extensive main-tenance. As the price of solar cells has fallen, concentrated solar power plants are no longer competitive with PV, unless energy storage is essential.

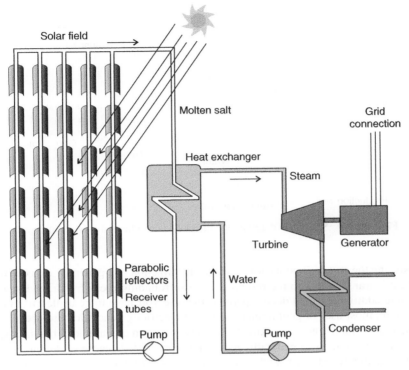

Figure 2.14 Concentrated solar power station (parabolic trough design).

2.3.4 Geothermal Energy

Below the surface of the Earth, the temperature increases with increasing depth. The average temperature gradient is approximately 0.03 K/m. In some areas, like South Africa, the temperature gradient is only 0.01 K/m; in areas with geothermal activity, the temperature gradient is higher, up to 0.2 K/m. In these areas, hot temperatures of 200°C or more can be found at a depth of only 1 km. In general, geothermally active areas are located in fault zones, and they are associated with above ground features like volcanoes, hot springs, geysers, etc.

For centuries, geothermal energy has been utilised for spas, heating and cooking. Since the beginning of the 20th century, it has also been used for electricity generation. The first electricity generation from geothermal steam took place in 1904 with a small piston engine and a 10-kW dynamo in Larderello, Italy. The first commercial geothermal power plant with a capacity of 0.25 MW was built at the same site in 1913.

Figure 2.15 depicts the setup of a geothermal power plant. In the simplest situation, hot fluids – generally a mixture of steam and water – can be extracted from the reservoir. In a separator, water and steam are separated. The water is discharged to surface water flows or reinjected to the reservoir. The steam is expanded in a steam turbine, which drives a generator. Geothermal fluids contain toxic substances like mercury. Therefore, for environmental protection it is generally required to reinject all geothermal fluids. Reinjection also helps to stabilise the pressure in the reservoir. By substraction of hot fluids, the reservoir pressure is reduced

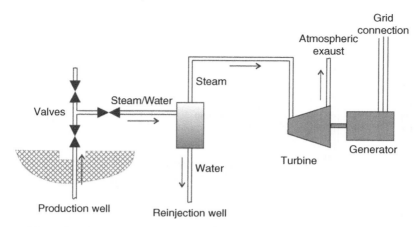

Figure 2.15   Schematic diagram of a direct cycle geothermal power station.

continuously and the reservoir cools down. The heat extraction rate generally exceeds the rate at which heat is transferred into the reservoir from surrounding rocks by far, and new wells for developing additional, often deeper parts of the reservoir have to be drilled from time to time. Therefore, most uses of geothermal energy for electricity generation are not renewable in the sense that no more energy is extracted than renewed on a continuous basis. In spite of this fact, geothermal energy is generally considered renewable because of the large quantity of geothermal energy resources available. Typically, a reservoir has a depth of 1000 to 5000 m and temperatures above 200°C.

If there are no, or not enough, hot fluids below the surface which can be extracted and directly fed through a steam turbine, the utilisation of geothermal heat for energy generation becomes more complex. To avoid corrosion in the turbine it might be necessary to introduce a closed secondary water–steam circuit which is heated by the geothermal fluids in a heat exchanger. If the temperature of the geothermal fluids is too low to operate a steam turbine, an Organic Rankine Cycle (ORC) can be chosen which utilises another organic fluid with a lower boiling point (e.g., propane), instead of water. In addition to electricity generation, geothermal reservoirs with lower temperature are even more suitable for district heating and industrial processes requiring heat.

If sufficient temperatures but no, or not enough, hot fluids are available in the reservoir, water can be injected into a well with high pressure and forced through small fissures in the rock. The water flows through the reservoir rock and extracts heat from it. The hot water is pumped back to the surface through a production well. Additional fissures are created artificially to increase the permeability of the rock. This type of geothermal utilisation is called *hot dry rock* technology.

The development of geothermal power stations is expensive in comparison with other power projects, as the drilling of several wells is required to explore a geothermal reservoir. This is a high barrier for the enhanced utilisation of geothermal energy resources.

Investment costs vary strongly from location to location, depending on reservoir conditions and the depth of the reservoir. Operation costs are moderate. Depending on the composition of the geothermal fluids, corrosion and deposition of minerals can affect operation costs and plant availability. In contrast to hydro, wind and solar energy, geothermal heat is continuously available and geothermal power stations have a constant, non-fluctuating production pattern.

2.3.5 Bioenergy

Bioenergy is renewable energy derived from biomass as an energy source. Biomass includes any carbon-based material with organic origin (from plants or animals) or from residues like manure. Wood, wood waste, straw, sugarcane and many other by-products from a variety of agricultural processes are utilised as bioenergy. Biomass contains solar energy stored as chemical energy. Fossil fuels like coal, mineral oil or natural gas, for which the conversion process has taken place in prehistoric times, are not considered as bioenergy.

Biomass was the first energy source utilised by humans for heating and cooking. And in many developing countries it is still the most important source of energy.

Bioenergy is a very heterogeneous product, which includes a large variety of energy carriers and final uses of energy. Often, there exists a long value chain from the feedstock to the final product: heat, power or solid, liquid or gaseous fuels. A large number of intermediate steps, including harvesting, conditioning, storage, transport, conversion or purification, may be required. Table 2.1 lists the main feedstocks, conversion routes and final bioenergy products.

The most important modern uses of bioenergy are the generation of electricity and the production of liquid biofuels, which have been substituted for fossil fuels in transportation. For electricity generation from biomass, there are three main processes:

- biomass power plant,
- anaerobic digester facility (biogas plant), and
- combined heat and power plants using liquid biofuels.

In the following sections we will describe these processes in more detail.

Table 2.1 Value chain of bioenergy conversion

Feedstock	Conversion routes	Final products

• Oil crops
  – rape, sunflower, soya, palm oil, etc.
• Sugar and starch crops
  – sugarcane, cassava, maize, etc.
• Lignocellulosic biomass
  – wood, straw, energy crops, wood pellets, etc.
• Biodegradable wastes
  – biomass fraction of municipal solid waste
  – sewage sludge
  – manure and other wet farm wastes
  – wet food wastes
  – waste oils, animal fats, etc.
• Photosynthetic microorganisms
  – e.g. microalgae and bacteria
	• Biomass pre-treatment
	  – drying
	  – pelletisation or briquetting
	• Thermochemical processes
	  – direct combustion
	  – pyrolysis (gasification, liquefaction, carbonisation)
	• Physical–chemical processes
	  – transesterification
	  – hydrogenation
	  – biorefineries
	• Biochemical processes
	  – anaerobic digestion
	  – aerobic digestion
	  – alcoholic fermentation
	  – biophotolysis
	• Agrochemical processes
	  – fuel extraction
	  – esterification
	• Bio-photochemical processes
		• Heat
		• Power
		• Solid biofuels
		  – wood chips
		  – wood pellets
		  – charcoal
		• Liquid biofuels
		  – vegetable oil
		  – biodiesel
		  – methanol, ethanol, butanol, hydrocarbons
		  – alcohols
		  – other fuels and fuel additives
		• Gaseous biofuels
		  – biomethane
		  – hydrogen
		  – dimethyl ether

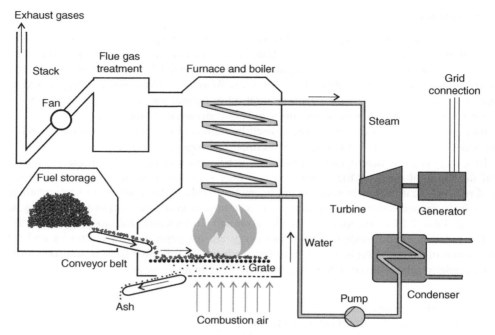

Figure 2.16   Biomass power plant.

Biomass Power Plants

A biomass power plant produces steam through combustion of solid biomass in a boiler. The steam is converted into electrical energy in a turbine and a generator in the same way as in a conventional coal power station. Alternatively, a co-fired biomass power plant could be fueled by coal or natural gas combined with biomass as a secondary fuel. A biomass power plant includes the following main components (see Figure 2.16):

- fuel delivery area (for road, rail or ship delivery),
- fuel storage area,
- on-site fuel transportation system,
- fuel preparation (e.g., chipper and grinder),
- boiler,
- furnace,
- turbine,
- generator,
- transformer and grid connection,
- condenser,
- pollution control devices, and
- smokestack.

Wood chips, wood waste or other solid biomass (like rice husks or straw) are delivered to the biomass power station by road, rail or ship and are stored on site. Typically, the capacity of the fuel storage is sufficient for several weeks of operation. Depending on the type of fuel, the fuel storage can be outdoor piles, covered piles or silos. In many cases, a fuel preparation like chopping or grinding and a mixing of several fuels is required before the fuel can be fed into the boiler. The most robust firing technology for biomass boilers is grate firing. Fluidised bed firing, where the fuel is suspended on high-pressure jets of air during the combustion process, is also common, but it is more complex and requires homogeneous fuels for reliable operation.

Combustion of the fuel produces steam in the boiler. The steam is fed into the turbine which drives the generator to generate electricity. The electricity produced is transformed to the voltage of the grid in a transformer which is connected to the medium or high-voltage grid. After expansion in the turbine, the steam is returned to the liquid state in the condenser. The condensed water is then recirculated to the boiler to again be converted into steam.

The condenser requires cooling water which is heated in the condenser and then either discharged directly to a receiving body of water or, more commonly, directed to a closed-loop cooling system where it can be cooled and recirculated back to the condenser. For biomass power plants, mechanical-draft wet cooling towers are common. The heated water is cooled by evaporation as the water drops from the top of the tower and passes through moving air produced by large fans.

A number of pollution control devices (flue gas treatment) are used at power plants: cyclone separators, baghouses, electrostatic precipitators and wet scrubbers.

Typical sizes for biomass power plants are 5 to 50 MW capacity. Efficiencies between 20% and 35% are achieved. Typical investment costs vary between EUR 1500 and EUR 4000 per MW installed capacity. Operation costs are mainly dominated by fuel costs. Fuel transport, storage and preparation are important cost items as well. The technical lifetime of a biomass power plant is 20 to 30 years.

Anaerobic Digester Facility (Biogas Plant)

Anaerobic digestion is the bacterial decomposition of organic material in the absence of oxygen. The two main products of anaerobic digestion are biogas and a solid residual material that can be used as fertiliser. A large variety of organic material can be used as feedstock for an anaerobic digestion facility: on the one side, waste material like manure, sewage, food scraps, biosolids, fats or oils and on the other side, energy crops like silage made from maize, sorghum, alfalfa or other crops. The biogas, a methane-rich gas, is used as fuel for a co-generation power plant with an internal combustion engine or it can be purified, compressed and fed into the natural gas grid. The purified biogas is also called biomethane. It can be used directly for heating, cooking or for industrial applications.

In Europe, anaerobic digester facilities are commonly called biogas plants. There are many different designs for anaerobic digester facilities depending on feedstock, environmental conditions and size. The simplest design is covered lagoons. But there are also much more complex systems where the anaerobic digestion takes place in several stages in different biogas reactors. Figure 2.17 depicts a typical setup of a single-stage anaerobic digestion facility utilising agricultural waste as feedstock. The initial step is the storage and pre-treatment of the feedstock. In some cases, grinding and mixing is required. Non-biodegradable components have to be removed before the substrate enters the biogas reactor where hydrolysis, acidogenesis, acetogenesis and methanogenesis take place. The content of the reactor is heated to approximately 30–35°C and it is mixed continuously. The biogas is burned in a gas engine to produce thermal

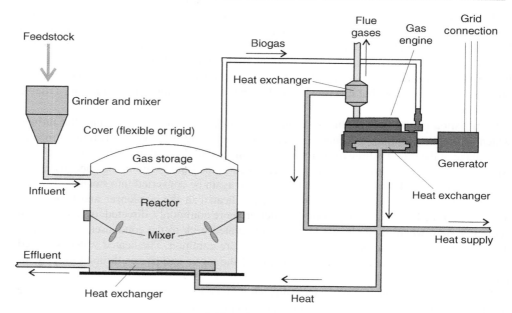

Figure 2.17   Biomass power plant.

and electrical energy, while the rest of the substrate is dewatered mechanically and used as fertiliser. Part of the heat generated by the gas engine is used to heat the reactor. Typical retention times of the substrate in the reactor are 2 to 4 weeks.

Typical sizes for anaerobic digestion facilities are 0.2 to 1.5 MW. Investment costs depend strongly on the type of technology applied and can vary between EUR 1000 and EUR 4000 per kW installed capacity. Anaerobic digestion facilities require extensive maintenance due to abrasive substances in the feedstock. Operation and maintenance costs depend mainly on the feedstock. The technical lifetime is approximately 20 years.

Another special type of anaerobic digester facility is a landfill gas power plant. In the landfill, an uncontrolled anaerobic digestion process takes place. The generated methane-rich gas is extracted from the landfill, purified and burned in an internal combustion engine or gas turbine, which drives a generator. Typical sizes are 0.5 to 5 MW, but at large landfill sites capacities of 100 MW or more can be installed. Typical investment costs are 1000 to 2000 EUR/kW installed capacity.

Combined Heat and Power Plants Using Liquid Biofuels

For electricity generation, liquid biofuels can be burned in a diesel engine driving a generator. Typical fuels are palm oil, rapeseed oil (canola), sunflower oil and other vegetable oils. The heat generated by the internal combustion engine can be used for district heating or as industrial process heat. In most cases, these combined heat and power (CHP) plants are operated according to heat demand. Small CHP plants can be installed in private houses with generation capacities up to 10 kW. Also in apartment buildings, public buildings, indoor swimming pools, industrial facilities, etc.

CHP plants with sizes up to 20 MW electrical capacity are available. Investment costs depend strongly on the sizes and vary between approximately EUR 1000 and EUR 5000 per kW electrical capacity. The electrical efficiency of a biofuel CHP plant varies between 30% and 48%.

Electricity generation from biomass has the advantage of continuous availability in comparison with hydro, wind or solar energy. Disadvantages are emissions, and in many cases, high energy demand for fuel transport and pre-treatment.

The production of biofuels for the substitution of fossil fuel is energy intensive and often involves intensive agriculture, destroying rain forests and other native landscapes. Furthermore, there is a debate in the public whether crops which could be used as food should be utilised for the production of biofuels.

2.3.6   Not Widespread Renewable Energies

Besides the main technologies covered in the previous sections, there are a number of other renewable energy technologies, most of them in the development phase. These technologies include the following.

- *Wave power:* Wave power utilises the energy of ocean surface waves. These waves are generated by wind passing over the surface of the sea. The machinery for utilising wave energy is called a *wave energy converter*. A large number of different designs are in the development or demonstration phase. They are based on different physical concepts, including floating buoys and oscillating water columns. The main challenges are the maritime environment, as well as storms.
- *Tidal power:* Tidal power is a form of hydropower that converts the energy of tides into electricity. It is a proven technology. The first tidal power plant has been in operation since 1966 at La Rance in France. It has 240 MW installed capacity. A plant with a similar size has been in operation in South Korea since 2011. These tidal power plants operate with tidal barrages placed at the mouth of a river or at a bay. They first allow water to flow into a bay or river during high tide, then return the water during low tide. Turbines are placed at sluices in the barrages to capture the energy as the water flows in and out.

  Another type of power plant is the tidal stream generator. These are similar to wind turbines submerged in the sea and driven by tidal streams. This technology is still in the development phase. Several demonstration projects with capacities of up to 1 MW are in operation.
- *Ocean thermal energy conversion (OTEC):* This technology utilises the temperature difference between cooler deep and warmer shallow ocean waters to run a heat engine and produce electricity. OTEC is still in the concept phase and it is not expected that it will be used for commercial applications in the near future.
- *Solar chimney power plant:* Sunshine heats the air beneath a large greenhouse-like collector structure surrounding a tall chimney tower. The hot air flows through the tower driven by the chimney effect, and this airflow drives wind turbines placed around the base of the chimney to produce electricity. The solar chimney technology is still in the development phase, with a 50-kW demonstration plant realised in Spain and a 200-kW plant in China. But it is unlikely that this technology can become competitive with photovoltaics or be applied widely.

2.4 SUPPORT SCHEMES FOR RENEWABLE ENERGY

Most governments across the globe have recognised the benefits of renewable energies and therefore have established targets for renewable energies. These targets are generally set for a specific year and include one or more performance indicators like the renewable energy share in final energy consumption, the renewable energy share in electricity generation, or installed capacity of photovoltaic generation capacity. In most cases investment barriers for renewable energies exist, hence support schemes are required to achieve political renewable energy targets.

As in any other technological field, the development of new technologies is cost intensive. Therefore, many governments support research and development in the renewable energy sector with the goal of enhancing the potential utilisation of limited existing renewable energy resources and reducing the specific costs per unit of useful energy. Demonstration projects are often supported by governments to prove and demonstrate the technical and economic feasibility of a new technology. One example is the wind energy demonstration project Growian, a wind turbine with 100 m rotor diameter, 100 m hub height and 3 MW capacity, which was erected in Germany in the year 1983. With its size it was well ahead of its time and stable operation was never achieved, but valuable experience was gained which supported the wind turbine development. Thirty years later, wind turbines with more than 100 m rotor diameter, more than 100 m hub height and several MW of capacity are proven technology. Other well-known examples of demonstration projects in renewable energy are the 60-MW offshore wind farm Alpha Ventus erected in the German North Sea in 2009 and the 11-MW solar power tower Planta Solar erected close to Seville, Spain in 2007. In the years 2009–2012, an annual average of EUR 3.6 billion was spent on research and development in the field of renewable energies by governments and another EUR 3.4 billion by private companies (FS – UNEP-Centre, 2013).

Once new renewable energy technologies have passed the demonstration phase, in most cases support is still required for the dissemination of these technologies, as the energy generation cost is higher in comparison with conventional energy technologies, or the existing or perceived risks are higher. The investment profile of most renewable energy technologies – with high upfront investment costs per unit installed capacity and low operation costs including fuel costs compared with conventional energy technologies – adds to the reluctance of investors. Governments address these issues with a variety of different support schemes for renewable energies.

Support schemes and other legislation addressing renewable energies have to balance the interests of a broad number of different stakeholders. The key stakeholders are as follows.

- *Project developers:* Project developers are organisations or individuals who invest capital or other resources in the development of renewable energy projects. The project development starts with the identification of a suitable site for a renewable energy generation facility, and includes securing the land rights and grid access, obtaining all permits required for building and operating the facility, as well as its technical design. The project development is successfully completed when it is ready to be built and the required equity and debt for funding the construction is in place. In most cases, project developers sell a renewable energy project at least partly to an investor before construction of the project. The development of a project generally takes several years and can cost up to 10% or more of the total investment cost of the project depending on project size and complexity. Project developers always bear the risk that a project fails to find sufficient funding due to not obtaining all required permits or grid access, or due to not achieving technical or economical feasibility.

The commercial success of a project developer is mainly determined by:
- the margin between the costs for the project development and the price at which a project is sold;
- the time lag between the expenditures for the project development and the successful sale of a project; and
- the development costs required for a project which turn out not to be feasible.

Therefore, project developers are interested in fast and predictable permitting procedures, support schemes which make projects financially feasible over longer periods of time, and high returns on investments into renewable energy projects. The price at which a renewable energy project is sold by a project developer is generally determined by the discounted future cashflows of an investor. Therefore, a project developer is interested in a regulatory framework which generates high revenues from the sale of renewable energy and low risks for the investor, which is reflected in a low discount rate.

Project development is often done by smaller companies with high risk appetite or by companies or individuals who have specific advantages in the access to attractive project sites or in the permitting procedures.

- *Investors:* Investors are organisations or individuals who contribute capital or other resources to the construction of a renewable energy project with the aim of generating a more than risk-adequate return on the investment with cashflows from operations. While for conventional energy facilities the project development and the investment are commonly done by the same company, renewable energy projects are often developed by a separate entity.

   Investors in renewable energy facilities include electrical utilities, private equity and venture capital organisations, banks, insurance companies, pension funds, wealthy individuals, ordinary private and industrial consumers, corporations, communities and public sector bodies. Each of these investor groups would typically have different risk and return appetites, investment horizons and evaluation criteria. Therefore, support schemes can be designed to attract or distract different groups of investors. In spite of the differences between investor groups, the following investment criteria will be preferred by most investors:
   - Low as possible risk around technical reliability and performance.
   - Low as possible risk concerning revenues from operation.
   - High as possible overall investment returns or cost savings in comparison with alternative energy supplies.

- *Manufacturers:* This stakeholder group includes manufacturers of hydro turbines, wind turbines, PV cells and other renewable energy equipment. In a broader sense it includes all companies participating in the supply chain from the design and manufacturing of components of renewable energy technologies until the final installation of a renewable energy project, including logistics. Manufacturers invest in research and development, manufacturing facilities and training of employees. Therefore, their main concern is a stable and predictable long-term growth in demand for renewable energy equipment. The support has to be adequate and has to reflect the actual costs of generating renewable energy. If the support is too low, the sector will not develop. If the support is too high, unsustainable over-investments in the supply chain can be expected, which ultimately leads to cut-throat competition.

- *Consumers:* The broader consumer body includes organisations and private households that consume energy or pay taxes. For these stakeholders the additional cost of supporting renewable energies is an important criterion. Depending on the way that these additional costs are distributed by taxes, additions to the energy bill or other levies, different consumer groups can be affected differently. Consumers may also be investors who benefit from a support scheme for renewable energies. In addition, it is also the consumers who ultimately benefit from renewable energies through environmental benefits. In summary, the key concerns of consumers are:
  - Total additional cost to consumer bills or additional taxes.
  - Efficiency and effectiveness of the support scheme (total cost per MWh renewable energy produced and transported to the final customer and progress in the dissemination of renewable energies).
  - Possibility to participate in renewable energy projects as investors.
  - Additional benefits of renewable energy support schemes (for example, environmental benefits, jobs or improved security of supply).
- *Affected local parties:* This group of stakeholders includes all land owners and citizens in the vicinity of renewable energy facilities. They are concerned about the visual impact of renewable energy installations, noise emission and other negative impacts that renewable energy installations might cause. But they are also concerned about benefits from land lease, local taxes, jobs, etc.
- *Regulators:* Renewable energy support schemes generally require substantial effort to be implemented and ongoing administrative support and oversight. This includes the initial design process, the legislative process including public consultation if applicable, scheme administration and any regular reviews regarding the scheme's efficiency and effectiveness. The term "regulator" is used here to cover all governmental or independent bodies that have a legislative, administrative or regulatory role in relation to support schemes for renewable energy. The success or failure of support schemes depends strongly on the performance of regulators. In many cases it takes several years until a support scheme is mature, efficient and effective. The required administrative efforts must not be underestimated. Regulators are mainly concerned about the following:
  - Efficiency and effectiveness of the support scheme.
  - Administrative costs of the scheme.
  - Achievement of political renewable energy targets.
  - Transparency.
  - Public perception.

The challenge for any support scheme for renewable energy is to keep an appropriate balance between the concerns of all stakeholders. In the following sections, the main characteristics of different support schemes will be described. As support schemes change quickly, only general aspects will be discussed. For up-to-date information the current legal and regulatory framework in any country of interest has to be studied in detail.

2.4.1   Feed-In Tariffs

The most common way to support electricity generation from renewable energy sources is via feed-in tariffs. In 2012, 71 countries had feed-in tariffs at national, state or province level (Sawin, 2013).

A renewable energy support scheme with feed-in tariffs generally includes the following components.

- *Guaranteed grid access:* This includes the obligation for distribution and transmission network operators to connect a renewable energy generation facility to the grid if certain criteria regarding power quality and network capacity are met. The cost for the connection of a facility to the existing distribution or transmission system is often borne by the renewable electricity generators, but sometimes also by the network operators. The guaranteed grid access includes normally the possibility to feed the generated power into the grid at any time and up to the rated power of the facility. In cases where the grid operator is not able to accept additional electricity, the operator of the renewable energy facility is compensated for the financial loss by the grid operator or regulator. Again, there might be restrictions linked to this obligation, for example the renewable energy facility might not be compensated in cases of planned and unplanned outages of the grid. The priority grid access generally prevails even after the period of guaranteed feed-in tariff.
- *Long-term guarantee for purchase prices:* The renewable energy generator receives a fixed price for the electricity produced by the grid operator or another party obliged to accept the renewable energy. The duration of this guaranteed price is in most cases between 15 and 20 years, with possible variations depending on the renewable energy technology. In many cases, almost the complete technical lifetime of the generation facility is covered. The price can be either a fixed nominal amount for the entire duration, a fixed adder to wholesale market electricity prices, or a floating price which is indexed to the consumer price index, electricity price index, currency exchange rates, labour costs or other indices. In some countries, the feed-in tariff is not guaranteed for a longer period of time, but rather adapted from time to time by the government.

  Furthermore, in some support schemes, the feed-in tariff is defined as a minimum tariff, and the generator can also opt to sell the generated energy to the market if market prices are above the feed-in tariff. While in some schemes the generator has the option to choose daily, monthly or annual rates in advance, or even retroactively between feed-in tariff and the market, in other schemes the operator does not have the option to return to a feed-in tariff once the market price is accepted.
- *Cost-based purchase prices:* The intention of a feed-in tariff is to guarantee an adequate return on investment in a renewable energy project. Therefore, it is calculated based on expected investment and operation costs. Often a feed-in tariff differentiates between different types of technologies and sizes of generation facilities. Furthermore, the feed-in tariff can reflect regional differences in wind speeds or solar irradiation. To reflect cost reduction by technological progress, a decrease in feed-in tariffs over time for new installations can be appropriate.

The first legislation to introduce some kind of feed-in tariff was the Public Utility Regulatory Policies Act (PURPA) in the United States in 1978 as part of the National Energy Act. It had the intention of promoting the greater use of renewable energy. Under PURPA, electric utilities were obliged to buy electricity from independent power producers at a price equivalent to their avoided costs for producing or purchasing this energy. Besides fuel costs, investment costs for meeting growing electricity demand were also considered part of the avoided costs.

PURPA's implementation was left to the individual states because of varying needs. Therefore, a variety of regulatory frameworks developed. Especially in California, where state authorities were more aggressive in their interpretation of PURPA, a notable renewable energy development took place. Beginning in the early 1980s, the first large wind energy projects in the USA were developed there.

In 1990, Germany adopted its Law on Feeding Electricity into the Grid (in German: *Stromeinspeisegesetz*). The Stromeinspeisegesetz required utilities to purchase electricity generated from renewable energy sources by independent power producers. For hydropower and landfill as well as sewage gas, only facilities with up to 5 MW generation capacity were eligible. The price was set at a percentage of the average retail price of electricity of the accepting utility. The percentage varied between 65% and 90%, depending on technology and size. Existing as well as new installations were eligible to receive this feed-in tariff for an unlimited duration.

The Stromeinspeisegesetz proved effective to encourage the development of wind farms in Germany. Until 1999, approximately 4500 MW of new wind capacity had been installed (Deutsche WindGuard, 2013). Similar percentage-based feed-in schemes were adopted in Spain, as well as in Denmark in the 1990s.

Germany's feed-in scheme underwent a major restructuring in 2000. The Stromeinspeisegesetz was replaced by a Renewable Energy Act (*Erneuerbare Energien Gesetz, EEG*). The EEG proved to be very effective in accelerating the development of renewable energy. The share of renewable energy generation in the final energy consumption increased from 5.4% in 1999 to 22.9% in 2012 (BMU, 2013). Important changes included:

- The feed-in tariffs were no longer based on retail prices of electricity, but fixed. Different tariffs apply for different technologies to reflect differences in generation costs. Efficiently operated projects are expected to yield a reasonable rate of return.
- The tariffs were guaranteed for 20 years.
- Differences in wind yield at different locations were reflected by different durations between 12 and 20 years of a higher initial tariff.
- An annual tariff degression was introduced for new installations based on anticipated cost reductions for renewable energy generation technology.
- Utilities were allowed to participate.

The EEG was amended in 2004, 2009 and twice in 2012. The amendments in 2012 were a response to the fast decline in prices for PV cells, which had led to more than 7000 MW of annual new installed capacity in the years 2010 to 2012 (BMU, 2013), and the adder for renewable energies for electricity customers increased from 2.047 EURct/kWh in 2012 to 5.277 EURct/kWh in 2013, a significant burden for consumers. The feed-in tariffs for PV were limited to installations with up to 10 MW capacity, the feed-in tariffs were reduced significantly and a monthly degression for new installations of the tariff was introduced. The tariff was reduced by 1% every month. An annual target corridor for newly installed PV capacity of 2500–3500 MW was introduced. If the new installations exceeded the target corridor, the monthly degression of the tariff was increased but if they fell below it, the monthly degression was decreased. An overall limit of 52 000 MW of installed PV capacity eligible for the feed-in tariff was introduced.

Many other countries followed the German approach and introduced feed-in tariffs for renewable energy similar to the EEG.

The key advantages of feed-in tariffs are:

- Low or no market risk for investors.
- Appropriate returns on investment for different technologies due to different tariffs.
- Low entrance barrier for small generators like private households.
- Low risk for project developers.

Disadvantages of feed-in tariffs are:

- No or limited integration of renewable energy into electricity markets.
- No or limited incentives to generate electricity where and when demand exists.
- No direct control of the quantity of capacity additions, and hence of the cost of renewable energy borne by the consumer.

2.4.2 Net Metering

Net metering, or net billing, is a renewable energy support scheme for consumers who own renewable energy facilities, such as small wind turbines and photovoltaic cells. The consumers offset electricity supplied by the grid with their own generation and feed excess generation back into the grid. Under a net metering scheme, customers are only billed for the difference between the amount of electricity they receive from the grid and the electricity they feed back into the grid. If customers feed more electricity back into the grid than they receive in any given billing period, specific tariffs for the excess production apply. In some cases a banking of excess generation is possible.

In the USA, all public electric utilities are required to offer net metering upon request by their customers. This scheme was introduced as part of the Energy Policy Act of 2005. Rules and regulations differ from state to state, and capacity as well as technological restrictions apply. By the end of 2012, approximately 220 000 customers in the USA utilised net metering for PV systems (SEIA, 2012). By the end of 2012, net metering had been introduced in 35 countries, including Canada, Denmark the UK, Italy and Japan (Sawin, 2013).

The key advantage of net metering is the simplicity of the system. In many cases, no additional electricity meter is required. The disadvantages of net metering are that the support does not reflect actual costs of renewable energy generation, electricity price risks for investors, and its restriction to small installations.

2.4.3 Electric Utility Quota Obligations and Tradable Certificates

Electric utility quote obligations are support schemes that require electricity supply companies to produce or purchase a certain percentage of their electricity from renewable energy sources. In the USA, this type of scheme is called a Renewable Portfolio Standard (RPS). In the UK, it is called a Renewable Obligation (RO).

The required percentage of renewable energy in a quota obligation scheme is generally increased annually by a regulator to meet longer-term political targets. If the quota obligation is not met by an electricity supply company, penalties apply. In the UK, these penalties are distributed to renewable energy generators. Most quota obligation schemes have introduced tradable certificates. Renewable energy generators which meet certain eligibility criteria receive one certificate for a specific unit, for example 1 MWh of renewable electricity produced. These certificates are called Renewable Energy Certificates (RECs) in the USA or Renewable Obligation Certificates (ROCs) in the UK.

As, in principle, a quote obligation scheme treats all renewable energy equally, the most cost-efficient sources for renewable energy – such as onshore wind or landfill gas – would be developed with priority. The disadvantage is that new and more costly technologies are difficult to develop under a quote obligation scheme. In consequence, this could lead to political targets not being met or to over-subsidies for cheaper technologies if REC prices increase to a level required for more cost-intensive technologies like offshore wind or PV. To overcome this shortcoming, two different approaches have been developed.

- *Multipliers:* One certificate is issued for different quantities of electricity depending on the type of technology. This approach has been chosen in the UK and is called banding. In 2013, the number of ROCs generated by 1 MWh of renewable energy ranged from 0.5 for co-firing of biomass and sewage gas to 5.0 for tidal and wave up to 30 MW capacity. Onshore wind above 5 MW generates 0.9 ROCs/MWh, offshore wind 2.0 ROCs/MWh (OFGEM, 2013).
- *Sub-targets:* In addition to the overall quota obligation, electricity supply companies have to show that they have generated or purchased a particular percentage of their electricity from a designated technology type. In the USA, these sub-targets are also called carve outs, set-asides or tears. Especially for solar, these sub-targets are established where electricity from solar irradiation generates specific RECs called Solar Renewable Energy Certificates (SRECs).

In addition to mandatory quota schemes, renewable energy certificates are also used in voluntary markets where electricity supply companies offer renewable energy as a premium product. In addition to renewable energy from proprietary sources, it is common to use tradable certificates for the generated environmental benefits of renewable energy which are traded independently from the electricity itself. A certifying body guarantees that the generation facilities meet specific standards and that the environmental benefits of the renewable electricity are not sold twice. Certificates are abandoned when electricity is delivered as renewable energy to retail customers. In Europe, the Renewable Energy Certificate System (RECS) is a voluntary certificate scheme in operation since 2002. In addition, the EU introduced in 2009 – with the Directive 2009/28/EC on the Promotion of the Use of Energy from Renewable Sources – a legal framework for certifying specific renewable qualities of electricity. It is called European Energy Certificate System – Guarantee of Origin (EECS-GoO), and will supersede the RECS. For each MWh of electricity, the EECS certificate certifies the quality of its source or the method of its production.

Electric utility quota obligations were introduced in the USA in many states on a state level with different rules in each state. In Europe, quota obligation schemes are in place in the UK (RO), Sweden (Elcert), Belgium (Groen Certificaat/Certificat Vert), Poland (linked to EECS), Italy (Certificati Verdi) and others. By the end of 2012, electric utility quota obligation schemes were used as renewable energy support schemes in 23 countries (Sawin, 2013). The UK plans to replace its RO system with a feed-in tariff system for new installations, and has already introduced a feed-in tariff for PV.

The key advantages of electric utility quota obligations are:

- Efficient in creating incentives to generate renewable energy at the lowest possible cost.
- No risk of excessive costs to customers due to exceeding renewable energy targets.

Disadvantages of electric utility quota obligations are:

- High market risks for investors and project developers.
- Low effectiveness in reaching political targets.
- Additional administrative costs and transaction costs for tradable certificates.
- High entrance barrier for small generators like private households.

2.4.4 Auctions

Renewable energy auctions or public tenders for renewable energy are support schemes whereby a regulator (or another public authority) issues a call for tenders to install a certain capacity of renewable energy-based electrical generation facilities. Project developers who participate in the auction submit a bid with a price per unit of electricity at which they are willing to sign a long-term power purchase agreement (PPA). The regulator evaluates the offers on the basis of the price and other criteria, and signs a PPA with all successful bidders. Typical durations for the PPA are 15 to 20 years, sometimes with the possibility for the investor to cancel the PPA earlier and sell the electricity on the free market. PPAs can have a fixed price in the local currency, but also indexation to US$ or other currencies; compensation for inflation is also common.

Based on regional or national energy plans and the maturity of the local renewable energy market, the design of auction schemes will reflect priorities in terms of technology, volume and location. Auctions can be tailored for a specific technology to promote certain technologies and a diversification of the generation portfolio. Often minimum and maximum sizes for projects apply. Alternatively, auctions can be technology-neutral and leave the selection of most economic technologies and sites to the participating project developers. In some cases, site-specific auctions also take place where the regulator has already selected a site and has completed the basic project development, including resource assessment and securing grid access. In these cases, the renewable auction is very similar to public tenders for other privately financed infrastructure projects in a build, own and operate (BOO) scheme.

Besides the aim to generate a certain quantity of renewable energy in a cost-efficient way, additional political aims can be reflected in the auction design. Common are minimum requirements or additional scoring points for local content in the supply chain, local job creation or local investment.

There are different types of auction designs. The most common type is the sealed-bid auction, where project developers simultaneously submit their bids with an undisclosed offer containing the bid price and other criteria relevant to ranking the bids. The regulator ranks and awards projects until the sum of the quantities they offer covers the volume of capacity being auctioned. Sometimes a prequalification of participants is required. A maximum price at which bids are accepted is common in sealed-bid auctions. In most cases this maximum price is not disclosed before the auction to avoid giving a price indication to the participants. Typically, successful participants are assigned PPAs with their bid prices (pay-as-bid), but awarding PPAs with the price of the highest successful bidding price (market clearing price) is also possible.

Another type of auction is the multi-round descending-clock auction, where in an initial round the regulator offers a price and developers bid the capacity they would be willing to provide at that PPA price. The regulator then reduces the price continuously in successive rounds until the capacity offered matches the capacity to be procured. These multi-round auctions give project developers the possibility to react to the competitive situation, hence reducing speculative elements.

Hybrid models have also been applied using the descending-clock auction in a first phase and the sealed-bid auction in a second phase.

One great risk of auction schemes is that projects awarded with a PPA are delayed, not implemented at all, or are of poor quality with respect to availability and lifetime. In some cases projects have been built with used equipment to lower the overall costs, but also the lifetime of the project. Therefore, it is very important that the design of auctions includes stringent bidding requirements (technical, financial, grid access, environmental, etc.) and strong compliance rules (penalties, bid bonds, project completion guarantees, etc.) that reduce the risk of participants bidding a price at which a project is not likely to be financially feasible (underbidding). Quality requirements like track records or financial strength of the project developer can also be part of the auction design. In many auctions, underbidding has led to a large number of awarded projects not being implemented at all. The disadvantage of stringent bidding requirements is that they impose a high barrier for smaller market participants and new players to participate, and thus reduce competition, potentially excluding local project developers from participating.

For the development of a local renewable energy industry, including a supply chain, it is crucial to have a continuous programme of auctions whose goal is the long-term continuous growth of the sector. Auctions should be scheduled at least once a year.

Renewable energy auctions, despite some difficulties of implementation in the past, have become a popular policy tool, especially in developing countries, as auctions have the potential to achieve deployment in a cost-efficient and regulated manner (IRENA, 2013). By the end of 2012, in 45 countries auctions were part of a renewable energy policy (Sawin, 2013). In many cases auctions were complementary to other support schemes. Examples of countries having successfully implemented auction schemes which led to significant renewable energy development are Brazil and South Africa.

The key advantages of auctions are:

- Cost efficiency due to price competition.
- Low risk for investors due to long-term PPAs.
- Establishment of a predictable development of renewable energy capacity to reach political goals (if auctions are well designed).

Disadvantages of auction schemes are:

- High risks for project developers of not winning a PPA, causing significant sunk costs for project development.
- High barriers to participate for small project developers.
- Risk of underbidding and consequent delays in the implementation of renewable energy capacity.
- Discontinuous market development in case of auctions being only a one-off event.

2.4.5   Subsidies, Investment Grants and Tax Benefits

A large variety of fiscal instruments and other incentives exist to support the development of renewable energy generation. Besides national schemes, often regional or local schemes exist

(KPMG, 2013). Often these subsidies, investment grants and tax benefits are in addition to other support schemes.

Common are:

- Investment grants.
- Project development grants.
- Interest-free or interest-subidised loans.
- Government guarantees for commercial loans.
- Accelerated depreciation rules.
- Investment or production tax credits.
- Tax holidays for corporate taxes.
- Exception from import taxes.
- Accelerated value added tax (VAT) recovery.
- VAT or other tax refunds.

In the USA, the federal renewable electricity production tax credit (PTC) is an important instrument for supporting renewable energy. The PTC is a per-kilowatt-hour tax credit for electricity generated by qualified renewable energy resources and sold by the taxpayer. In 2013, it had a level of 2.3 USct/kWh for wind, geothermal and biomass and 1.1 USct/kWh for other eligible technologies. It generally applies to the first 10 years of operation. Unused credits may be carried forward for up to 20 years. Originally, the PTC expired in 1999, but it has been expanded several times. The extensions often took place at short notice or only after an expiration which exposed project developers to high uncertainty.

2.5 KEY ECONOMIC FACTORS OF RENEWABLE ENERGY PROJECTS

Before discussing renewable energy project risks, it is necessary to have a look at the key economic factors of renewable energy projects. These key factors vary depending on technology, country, regulatory regime and the involvement a player has in a project. Figure 2.18 depicts the key elements of the renewable energy value chain. For biomass projects, fuel supply would be an additional element of the value chain.

In this section we will concentrate on a project developer's and investor's perspective. For debt financing, a project will be evaluated in a similar way as for equity investment. Equipment manufacturing, construction, and operation and maintenance are quite distinct from the other perspectives, and are not covered in this book.

2.5.1 The Project Developer's Perspective

A project developer invests capital and other resources in the development of a renewable energy project with the aim of selling it to an investor at financial close. For a project

Figure 2.18   Value chain of renewable energy projects.

developer the key economic factors are:

- Required investment for the project development.
- Duration of the project development.
- Success rate of the project development.
- Implementation costs for the project.
- Realised price at which the project can be sold.

Project development is risky and unpredictable. Obtaining all required permits and licences might prove difficult or impossible. Resources might be different from expected. Grid access can delay projects, and regulatory schemes are likely to change between the start of project development and the start of operation. While small PV projects can be planned and implemented within several months, 5 to 10 years or more between the identification of a site and the start of operation is typical for large-scale wind and hydro projects. Many projects fail to obtain financing for different reasons. Therefore, a key skill of a project developer is to keep sunk costs for failing project developments low.

The realised price at which a project is sold depends mainly on the future cashflows a project investor can expect, and on the risks to which these cashflows are exposed. Therefore, a project developer always has to consider the investor's perspective as well.

2.5.2   The Project Investor's Perspective

The project investor buys a renewable energy project generally in a ready developed stage before the start of construction. The construction risks can be borne either by the project developer who sells the project as a turn-key project or by the investor. Typically, an investor considers a renewable energy project as a long-term investment in which he prefers to remain invested until the end of the technical lifetime of the project. While typically in the case of conventional power stations and large hydropower stations an investor also does the project development, for renewable energy projects, and especially for wind energy projects and PV projects, it is common that different companies do the project development and investment. But with the exception of equipment manufacturing, many investors are also active in other parts of the value chain. In this section we consider an investor who is only active in the equity investment for a specific project.

The key economic factors from an investor's perspective are:

- Purchase price for the project, including equipment and construction costs.
- Construction risk, if applicable.
- Land lease.
- Resource availability (i.e., hydrology, wind yield, solar irradiation).
- Fuel costs, if applicable.
- Price risks associated with fuel costs, if applicable.
- Technical availability of the generation facility.
- Revenues from the sale of electricity.
- Electricity market risks.
- Interest rate and other debt finance conditions.
- Regulatory and country risks.
- Operation and maintenance costs.

- Insurance costs.
- Taxes.
- Technical lifetime of the generation facility.

For any investment, an investor will analyse all these factors thoroughly, often with the help of external consultants. The risks involved in a project will determine the minimum rate of return an investor can expect from his investment.

For the analysis of a project, financial models are used. First an investor will make base-case assumptions for all uncertain parameters in the model, and then perform a sensitivity and scenario analysis to evaluate the impact on the cashflows and rate of return if one takes a rather optimistic or pessimistic view on uncertain parameters. In the next section, we will discuss these uncertainties in more detail.

Figure 2.19 depicts an example of a simple financial model for a wind energy project with fixed revenues from a feed-in tariff scheme. In practice, more details will be required, and differences in tax and regulatory schemes have to be considered.

The equity investor is mainly interested in the internal rate of return (IRR) and the net present value (NPV) of the project. In a risk analysis he might reduce the wind yields by

		Year	0	1	2	3	19	20	21
		Capital Expenditures							
R1		Project Cost	10 000 000						
R2		Decommissioning							350 000
R3	=R3(Y-1)+R28	Liquidity Reserve	200 000	230 000	250 000	250 000	80 000	60 000	0
R4	=R4(Y-1)-R27	Debt	8 000 000	7 466 667	6 933 333	6 400 000	0	0	
R5	=R1+R2-R4	Equity	2 200 000						
		Revenues							
R4	declining availability	Generation (MWh)		18 000	18 000	18 000	16 780	16 696	0
R5		Feed-in Tariff (EUR/MWh)		90	90	90	90	90	
R6	=R4*R5	Electricity Sales		1 620 000	1 620 000	1 620 000	1 510 213	1 502 662	0
R7	interest on (R3+R18)	Interest on Credit		5 000	5 800	6 200	9 200	9 200	7 000
R8	R6+R7	Total Annual Revenues		1 625 000	1 625 800	1 626 200	1 519 413	1 511 862	7 000
		Operating Expenses							
R9		Operation & Maintenance		306 000	318 240	330 970	619 900	644 696	0
R10		Land Lease Payments		48 600	48 600	48 600	45 306	45 080	0
R11		Project Management		15 000	15 300	15 606	21 424	21 852	22 289
R12		Insurance		55 000	56 100	57 222	78 554	80 125	5 000
R13		Accounting and Audits		13 000	13 260	13 525	18 567	18 939	19 317
R14	=R9+R10+R11+R12+R13	Total Operation Expenses		437 600	451 500	465 923	783 751	810 691	46 607
R15	=R8-R14-R7	EBITDA		1 182 400	1 168 500	1 154 077	726 462	691 971	-39 607
		Other Taxable Expenses							
R16	taxation rules	Depreciation		2 000 000	1 600 000	1 280 000	70 369	70 369	0
R17		Provisions for Decommissioning		20 000	20 000	20 000	20 000	20 000	-50 000
R18	=R18(Y-1)+R17	Procisions (cumulative)		20 000					
R19	interest on R4	Interest		400 000	373 333	346 667	0	0	0
R20	=R14+R16+R18+R18	Total Annual Expenses		2 857 600	2 444 833	2 112 589	874 119	901 060	-3 393
R21	=R8-R20	Taxable Income		-1 232 600	-819 033	-486 389	645 293	610 802	10 393
		Taxes							
R22	taxation rules	Tax Credit (cumulative)		357 454	594 974	736 027	0	0	0
R23	taxation rules	Corporate Tax (at 29%)		0	0	0	187 135	177 133	3 014
R24	taxation rules	Local Tax (on electr. sales)		9 720	9 720	9 720	9 061	9 016	0
R25	=R23+R24	Total Tax		9 720	9 720	9 720	196 196	186 149	3 014
		After-Tax Cash flows							
R26	=R16	Depreciation (added back)		2 000 000	1 600 000	1 280 000	70 369	70 369	0
R27	here: 15 years linear	Dept Principal Payment		533 333	533 333	533 333	0	0	0
R28	=R21-R25+R26+R27	Net After-Tax Project Cash flow		224 347	237 913	250 557	519 466	495 022	7 379
R29	loan requirements	Change in Liquidity Reserve		30 000	20 000	0	-20 000	-20 000	-60 000
R30	=-R5+R28-R29	Equity Investor Return	-2 200 000	194 347	217 913	250 557	539 466	515 022	67 379
R30	=IRR(Row 30)	Equity IRR	10.2%						
R31	=NPV(Row 30)	Equity NPV (at 8%)	430 145						
R32	=R15/(R19+R26)	Debt Service Coverage Ratio		1.27	1.29	1.31			

Figure 2.19 Example of a simple cashflow model for a wind energy project.

5% for all years. In our example, the IRR drops from 10.2% to 7.7% and the NPV becomes negative.

The project developer will also use a financial model to determine a price at which he can expect to sell the project. He can expect to sell the project at a price at which the NPV for an investor is close to zero, assuming competition among investors.

A bank which provides the debt financing is mainly interested in the ability of the project to pay interest and to repay the loan as scheduled. The most important figure for the bank is the debt service coverage ratio (DSCR). If the DSCR is negative, the project is not able to pay the interest and repay the loan. Also the bank will consider conservative scenarios in which the DSCR still has to meet certain thresholds.

2.6   RISKS IN RENEWABLE ENERGY PROJECTS AND THEIR MITIGATION

Investments in renewable energy projects are generally considered low-risk investments but as for any investment, a thorough risk assessment is advisable before an investment decision is made. In this section, we will discuss the main risks from a project developer's and investor's perspective.

2.6.1   Project Development Risks

Project development is certainly the most risky part of the renewable energy value chain. But on the other side, returns can be very high. From a single project perspective, the key risk is that the project never reaches a status at which it can be sold, or that the price at which it can be sold does not cover the costs of the project development, including an adequate return on investment. Project development costs depend strongly on technology, country and many project-specific aspects. Often for small-scale rooftop photovoltaic plants, no permits are required, grid access is guaranteed and the equipment is completely standardised. In this case, the project development can be accomplished within a few days at no significant cost, except for labour. And after a project of this category has passed an initial assessment including principal agreement with an investor and with the rooftop owner, the risks for project failure are small. In contrast, the development of a large hydro project with 1000 MW capacity, for example, can easily take 10 years to complete and can cost more than EUR 50 million. And within 10 years, market conditions and regulatory schemes are likely to change, which exposes the economic viability of such a project to significant risk.

Typical project development costs for medium-sized onshore wind energy projects with 10 to 50 MW capacity are EUR 200 000 to 1 000 000. The project development costs depend only to a small degree on the size of the project. Therefore, specific project development costs per MW capacity are significantly lower for larger projects. Photovoltaic projects of the same size generally require fewer permits, environmental impact studies, road planning and geotechnical investigation. This significantly reduces the typical cost to EUR 100 000 to 500 000. Hydropower stations are more complex and have to be designed site specific. Therefore, typical project development costs for small hydropower stations of 10 to 100 MW are in the range of EUR 1 to 5 million. Biomass projects are less standardised than wind energy projects, but not as complex as hydropower stations. Therefore, the project development costs are somewhere between those of wind energy and hydropower. Offshore wind energy projects with sizes of 300 MW or more have typical project development costs of EUR 10 to 30 million. The development of geothermal power stations generally requires extensive investigation of the geothermal reservoir, which involves deep drilling. Therefore, development costs for geothermal power stations are above those for hydropower. For the reduction of development risk, government grants for drilling costs or other subsidies are often available.

There are many reasons for which a project development fails. And if a project has to be abandoned, all development costs spent until this decision has been made are sunk costs. As support schemes for renewable energy, permitting procedures as well as rules for grid access differ strongly from country to country and sometimes even from region to region, it is not possible to generalise reasons for failure. However, typical reasons are:

- Failure to secure land rights.
- Resources (e.g., wind, irradiation or biomass) prove not to be sufficient.
- Failure to obtain all required permits and licences.
- Opposition of local affected parties.
- Failure to obtain grid access.
- Environmental restrictions (e.g., due to the discovery of endangered species).
- The project proves technically or financially infeasible.
- The project loses eligibility for support schemes due to regulatory changes or its participation in auctions of renewable energy is without success.

To mitigate project development risk, a systematic risk management approach applied to any project is substantial. This approach includes the following elements:

- *Initial screening process:* A project developer develops a large number of project ideas, and often is approached with such ideas. This creativity is essential for the growth of his business. In this situation, it is necessary to have a quick and efficient initial screening process to distinguish between attractive and unattractive project ideas. The initial screening process should address at least the following elements: resource availability, grid access, applicability of support schemes, financial feasibility, technical feasibility, availability of experience within the organisation or externally, environmental constraints and the expected level of opposition of local affected parties. The initial screening process can be based on a scoring model. It should be designed not to take more than a few hours. And ideally, the initial screening is performed by two experienced persons independently. For many projects which never reach the funding stage, the reasons for failure could have been identified in a simple initial screening process.
- *Assessment of risks and opportunities:* Once a project has passed an initial screening process and more relevant information has been gathered, an assessment of risks and opportunities should be performed. At least all potential risks listed above should be addressed. Key risks and opportunities should be identified and their probabilities of occurrence should be estimated. In addition, an estimate for detailed project development costs and for the price at which the project can be sold should be made. With this approach, a scenario tree with 10 to 20 scenarios should be developed. The next step is the calculation and estimation of cost run-ups, revenues from project sales and probabilities for each scenario. Based on this information, an expected return on the investment in the development of a project can be calculated. If this return does not meet expectations and if there are no possibilities for risk

reduction, the project should be discarded at this stage. And in the case of limited resources, several attractive projects can be prioritised accordingly.

- *Definition of budgets and milestones:* Based on the assessment of risks and opportunities, a project schedule with separate budgets for all tasks and clear milestones should be defined. Furthermore, clear responsibilities for single tasks and for the project management should be assigned.
- *Regular and irregular reassessments:* Based on the project plan, a reassessment of risks and opportunities should be performed at regular intervals, for example every six months, and if one of the following events occurs:
  - A milestone was not met.
  - The budget for one task has been exceeded by a defined threshold, e.g. 10%.
  - An external event increasing the project risk has occurred, for example a change in the feed-in tariff or a decision on additional environmental requirements.
- *Risk-conscious prioritisation of tasks:* The project schedule should be designed with potential risks and the risk of sunk costs in mind. For example, if obtaining a required environmental licence has been identified as a key risk, then if possible, all other tasks should be started only after this environmental licence is obtained. This approach is likely to take more time and might be more expensive as well, but as it reduces sunk costs in case of project failure, it can be the more economic approach. Of course, the higher probability of changes in the regulatory framework in the case of a longer duration project development has to be kept in mind as well. As it is often difficult to balance advantages and disadvantages of the two different approaches, it is advisable to calculate an expected return for these approaches using estimated probabilities for uncertain parameters.

Besides a systematic risk management approach, strategic means for risk mitigation are as follows.

- *Cost efficiency:* It is always important to be cost efficient in project development. This increases competitiveness and reduces the potential loss in the case of a failed project. Besides direct project development costs, overhead costs have to be reviewed constantly with respect to efficiency.
- *Strategic partnerships and risk sharing agreements:* Especially in new markets, it is advisable to engage in strategic partnerships with local companies that have experience with permitting procedures. Also, partnerships with investors who are willing to participate in the project development risk can be of strategic value. Furthermore, some project developers have strategic partnerships with equipment manufacturers, which can increase their competitiveness in the market. In some cases, development finance institutions are willing to fund project development in emerging markets. Other governmental support for project development is sometimes available as well. If project risks exceed the risk-bearing ability of a company, for example in the case of large-scale offshore wind farms, risk-sharing agreements with other project developers are an option to consider.
- *Diversification:* From a risk perspective, diversification is a good strategy as well. Increasing the number of different projects automatically creates portfolio effects. This diversification can have the following dimensions:
  - geographical
  - technological
  - value chain related.

While diversification is positive from a risk perspective, the challenges of diversification must be kept in mind. Among the key challenges are complexity and limited experience. Therefore, it can also be of strategic advantage to stick to one's key competence.

- *Flexibility:* In the renewable energy sector, regulatory frameworks and market conditions change rapidly. Therefore, flexibility is one of the key success factors of a project developer. The project developer's employees must be flexible to work for different projects and in different areas. Also, it might be necessary to increase or decrease staff size at short notice. Furthermore, if an opportunity arises, it can be a better choice to sell a project at an early stage than to develop it until it is funded. The same is true for entering into projects. Besides starting greenfield development, opportunities to buy projects at an early stage should be considered as well.

A systematic risk-aware approach is certainly an important element of successful project development, but it is advisable not to become too academic in this aspect. It is important to realise that besides systematic considerations, successful project development also requires a good portion of experience, endurance, intuition and good luck.

2.6.2   Construction Risks

While every renewable energy project involves construction risk, the extent varies strongly from technology to technology. It depends mainly on the complexity of the project, the extent of structural work below ground level and the extent of non-standardised equipment. From an economic point of view, construction risks can result in cost overruns and delays for the commercial operation date (COD). Projects with extensive construction risks are wind offshore projects, hydropower stations – especially if the design includes tunnels – and geothermal projects. PV projects and wind onshore are low in risk.

Construction risks can be reduced by choosing experienced contractors with good track records, reducing the number of interfaces between tasks, and applying adequate contingencies for the budget and the construction time. It is always possible to transfer the construction risk at least partly to another company, whereby in general a risk premium has to be paid. Risk transfer in the case of a turn-key contract is straightforward. The contractor guarantees the completion of the project until a defined COD at a fixed budget. For some risks, insurance is available; an investor can try to pass on the risk to the project developer, as well. Most difficult is the transfer of geological risk, for example tunnels as part of hydropower plants.

2.6.3   Resource Risks

Wind speeds, solar irradiation and water flows in rivers are weather dependent. Natural fluctuations apply. Therefore, it is crucial to assess the resource availability for any project thoroughly. It is common to hire external consultants for resource assessments. If not enough data are available, measurements of wind speeds, irradiation or water flows are required. Every investor should be aware of the fact that resource assessments always contain uncertainties. Consequently, ordering more than one resource assessment can be advisable. Most wind resource assessments include estimates of the uncertainty in the form of confidence intervals. The expected value of the wind yield is called P50. This yield is exceeded with a probability of 50%. The yield which is exceeded with 75% probability is called P75. Besides these two values, the calculation of a P90 value is common. Banks often use the P75, P90 or even a P95

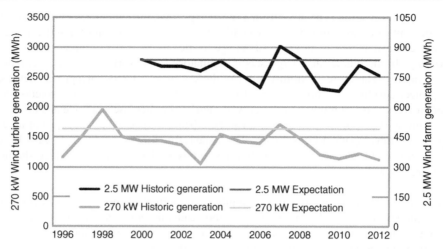

Figure 2.20   Historical and expected yields of a 270-kW wind turbine and a 2.5-MW wind farm in Eastern Germany. *Source*: www.windfang-sachsen.de and own data.

value in their financial models. It is important to know that these values are not calculated based on proper statistical methods, but rather contain many rough assumptions and estimates. This also explains why expected wind yield and uncertainties can differ significantly among different resource assessments for one project. Some consultants tend to be systematically more optimistic than others.

Figure 2.20 shows the expected yields and the historical yields of a 270-kW wind turbine in operation since 1995 and a 2.5-MW wind farm in operation since 1999 – both located in Eastern Germany. Apart from the fact that the average historic wind yield is on average 15% and 6% below the expected yield, respectively, significant differences from year to year become quite obvious. In our example, the difference from year to year was up to 30%. While one might expect that the quality of wind yield assessments has improved since the 1990s, wind yield assessments will always have an inherent uncertainty and there is no guarantee that the confidence intervals in an assessment are correct. Often there is not enough statistical data available, nor long historic time series of wind measurements. Moreover, the quality of these measurements is uncertain; the surface roughness in the area surrounding meteorological stations might have changed over several decades, which influences the measurements. Wind patterns might also be influenced in the longer term by climate change.

Figure 2.21 shows the expected and historical yields of a small 5-kW PV system in operation since 2002, located in Germany. Yield assessments for PV systems will always be of limited accuracy. Furthermore, longer-term changes in cloudiness might be caused by climate change or by changes in land use. Therefore, besides purely statistical effects, systematic changes in yield might occur.

For hydropower, there are longer historical time series available than for wind or PV. A good proxy for annual generation is the annual discharge of a river. Figure 2.22 depicts the annual discharge of the River Rhone in Switzerland at the station Brig for a 20-year period. Deviations of almost 20% from the long-term annual average discharge can be seen.

In many rivers, long-term historical discharge data are available but often the quality of these data has to be questioned, as measurement equipment and station location might have

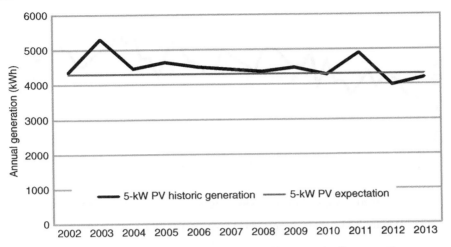

Figure 2.21   Historical and expected yields of a 5-kW PV system in Germany. *Source*: www.pv-log.com.

changed. Therefore, it is advisable to base the calculations of expected discharge not just on the data of one station, but also on several stations of rivers nearby. In cases where no discharge data are available, hydrological studies based on precipitation data in the catchment area of the river are required. The uncertainty of these results is obviously higher than in cases where direct discharge data are available.

Besides statistical effects, changes in land use and especially the use of water for irrigation upstream of the power station might cause systematic changes in available water flows for electricity generation. Climate change could also have an impact. On the one hand, precipitation patterns might be affected and on the other hand, global warming can cause melting of glaciers.

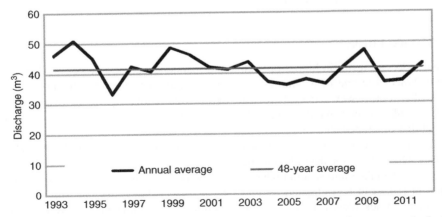

Figure 2.22   Historical discharge of the River Rhone at the station Brig. *Source*: www.hydrodaten.admin.ch.

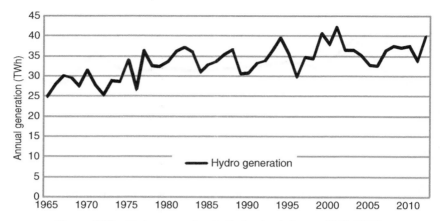

Figure 2.23   Hydro generation in Switzerland. *Source*: BFE (2013).

Not only for a single power station, but also for whole regions, significant annual variations in hydropower generation exist. Figure 2.23 shows the annual hydropower generation in Switzerland since 1960. Until the 1980s, the increasing hydropower generation was caused mainly by the addition of new hydropower stations. Since then, the increase has partly been caused by additional water flows in the rivers due to melting of the glaciers in the Swiss Alps. This will have only a temporary effect until the glaciers are completely melted, or have reached a new stable size.

The risk mitigation potential is limited with respect to resource risk. An investor will have to live with the inherent risk of resource-dependent energy yields. One should be aware of these risks and not rely on a single resource assessment, but rather on several, and use scenario analysis to study the robustness of a project with respect to resource risks. Furthermore, diversification of investments in different regions and technologies reduces the risk of a portfolio of investments in renewable energies.

Another aspect of resource risk is the availability of biomass for both biomass and biogas power generation. This will be discussed in Section 2.6.5.

2.6.4   Technical Risks

Technical risks can result in higher operation and maintenance costs, lower availability and shorter technical lifetime of a renewable energy generation facility. While for older technologies like hydropower and onshore wind power, long-term experience exists, for later technologies like offshore wind power or PV, the historical experience is limited. In general, the availability of a renewable energy generation facility decreases slightly over the years, and the maintenance costs increase. In the case of PV systems, a degradation of the PV cells also takes place. On average, the degradation rate is 0.5% per year (Jordan and Kurtz, 2012). These effects have to be taken into account when evaluating projects and modelling cashflows.

Technical risks can be mitigated by choosing proven technologies and suppliers with a proven positive track record. It is common that equipment manufacturers give performance guarantees for two years. Sometimes longer guarantees are available, in the case of PV even up to 20 years for the PV cells. The value of long-term guarantees obviously depends on the probability that the manufacturer giving the guarantee still exists when the guarantee is needed. Some equipment suppliers also offer long-term operation and maintenance contracts at fixed prices and with guaranteed availability levels. Machinery breakdown insurance can cover not only repair and replacement costs in case of damage, but also the loss of income from electricity sales due to outages caused by technical defects.

2.6.5   Market Risks

A renewable energy investment which utilises free resources like wind or irradiation and receives a fixed feed-in tariff for the complete technical lifetime of the project is not exposed to any market risk. In contrast, a biomass project in an electric utility quota obligation scheme with renewable energy certificates is exposed to market risks on the fuel side, the electricity side and the certificate side. These risks will be discussed in the following sections.

Fuel Market Risks

Biomass and biogas power stations rely on the supply of biomass as feedstock. The availability and price of the feedstock is crucial for any biomass project. Owing to the low calorific value of biomass in comparison with other fuels, transportation of biomass to the power station is an important cost element. Storage of biomass at the power station site has to be considered as well, as it can affect fuel availability and fuel cost. As sources of biomass vary strongly from project to project, this section can cover only general aspects. Detailed fuel availability, fuel price and fuel logistics studies will be required for any biomass project.

The idea for a biomass or biogas project is developed based on the demand for electricity or heat, or on the availability of the fuel in a specific region. In the first case, appropriate sources of biomass have to be identified; in the second case, the demand for electricity and heat as well as the possibility for grid connection have to be identified.

Regarding the supply of biomass, it is very important to identify the relevant fuel market. While a large biomass power station with 100 MW capacity or more located at the sea and near a harbour has access to international biomass markets, a small biomass power station located inland with only road access will be restricted to local markets. Typical road transport distances are generally restricted to 100 to 200 km due to high transportation costs. Supply and demand for biomass have to be studied in detail in these markets – in the first case, worldwide and in the second case, in the region of the site location. It is important to notice that the demand for biomass is not only driven by the energy sector. Wood and wood waste are also used in the pulp and paper industry as well as in the chipboard industry. In the case of corn as typical feedstock for biogas plants, alternative uses of the crop in the food industry have to be considered. In general, there is competition for agricultural land and therefore increasing prices for agricultural products like wheat will influence the availability and price for biomass grown for biogas plants.

It is crucial not only to consider the current situation in a fuel market, but also to anticipate changes. For example, in Germany many biomass power stations have been built since 2000 with wood waste as the main fuel. In the beginning, the operators of these biomass power stations were paid for the disposal of wood waste which previously had been dumped on landfill sites. However, with the increasing number of biomass power stations in operation, this situation has quickly changed and wood waste has become a scarce resource the operators have to pay for.

The means for mitigating fuel market risks are as follows.

- *Site selection:* Besides grid access and heat demand, the fuel logistics and the local fuel market are important considerations when selecting a site for a biomass or biogas plant. It is important to ensure a robust fuel chain for the fuel to the power station by road, rail, barge or ship. To access international fuel markets, a location at the sea near a harbour is advisable. For sites inland, it is necessary to analyse both supply and demand for the fuel carefully. All present and future alternative uses for the fuel have to be considered. The supply in the relevant region should exceed the demand, including the projected biomass power station, by at least 50%. The risk of increasing competition for the fuel due to additional biomass power stations being constructed in the relevant region has to be taken seriously. Ideally, limits exist due to environmental restrictions, grid capacity or logistical bottle necks.
- *Fuel flexibility:* Biomass power plants and biogas reactors are designed for a specific fuel spectrum. In order to reduce construction costs or to increase efficiency, often biomass power plants are designed for a relatively narrow fuel spectrum. As demand patterns for biomass change over time, it is advisable to design a biomass power station flexible enough to handle a broad range of fuels available in the region. For example, it could be advisable to consider agricultural residues as secondary fuel to wood chips as primary fuel. Of course, the power plant design has to be adapted and construction costs will increase, but the reduced reliance on one fuel is likely to pay out over time as it allows the operator of a biomass power plant to react to changes in the fuel market to a certain degree.
- *Long-term fuel supply contracts:* If possible, fuel price and quantity risk should be mitigated by long-term fuel supply contracts. However, in general, it is not possible to obtain contracts for the complete technical lifetime of a biomass power plant or a biogas reactor of approximately 20 years. Moreover, often long-term contracts can be cancelled or renegotiated when market conditions change. Therefore, it is good to have long-term fuel supply contracts, but one should not rely solely on them.
- *Fuel storage:* For increasing flexibility, a fuel storage facility should be erected at the site of the power station with a capacity of at least 2 to 4 weeks' usage. This gives flexibility in the fuel supply as well as the potential to utilise short-term market opportunities and to bridge interruptions in the supply chain. However, it is important to notice that the biomass feedstock can only be stored for a limited amount of time without adverse effects on its quality. For example, the calorific value of the biomass in the storage can decrease over time.

Many biomass and biogas projects are CHP plants. Besides electricity, heat is generated and sold. The price for heat depends in most cases on the price of alternative fuels – often gas, coal or oil. Common are contracts for the delivery of heat, which are indexed to these alternative fuels. In consequence, many biomass projects are also exposed to fossil fuel price risks. These risks can be modelled and addressed as described in Chapters 6 and 7.

Electricity Market Risks

In cases where no fixed feed-in tariff or long-term state-guaranteed off-take contracts for renewable electricity exist, a renewable energy project is exposed to market risks like any other generation facility. These risks can be modelled and addressed as described in Chapters 6 and 7. To mitigate market risks, the following alternatives should be considered:

- long-term fixed-price off-take contracts with a utility company, an electricity trading company or a consumer, ideally with a premium for the renewable quality of the electricity;
- forward contracts for standardised market products with physical fulfilment; and
- the use of financial instruments like forward contracts with financial settlement or option contracts.

Certificate Market Risks

If a support scheme for renewable energy with utility quota obligations and tradable certificates (see Section 2.4.3) exists, a renewable energy project is exposed to certificate market risks. In comparison with electricity markets, these certificate markets are relatively small, with low liquidity and only a limited number of standardised products, if any. Furthermore, they are strongly influenced by regulatory changes, which are difficult to foresee and model. If revenues from certificates are crucial for the success of a renewable energy project, it is advisable to mitigate this risk with an off-take contract for the certificates generated (e.g., with a utility company that requires these certificates to fulfil its quota obligations).

2.6.6 Regulatory Risks

Every business is exposed to regulatory risks to a certain degree. Taxes might change, new taxes can be introduced, environmental standards can be increased, subsidies can influence market prices, the introduction of minimum wages can increase labour costs, etc. In this respect, the renewable energy sector is no exception. However, the main and important differences from other sectors are the long amortisation periods of renewable energy projects and the limited potential for compensation of regulatory changes. With the investment decision for a renewable energy project which utilises free resources like hydropower or wind, most of the lifecycle costs are fixed. Furthermore, there is generally no significant potential for performance improvements. Therefore, renewable energy projects are especially vulnerable to regulatory changes.

One can differentiate between retroactive and prospective regulatory changes.

- *Retroactive regulatory changes:* Retroactive changes affect the performance of existing renewable energy investments in ways that an investor could not have expected at the time of the investment decision. One example is the reduction of a fixed feed-in tariff which is guaranteed for the first 20 years of operation for renewable energy – not only for new power plants but also for plants already in operation. Another example is the introduction of a specific tax for electricity generation from PV. Spain is probably the most prominent example of a country having introduced several retroactive changes for renewable energy. Since 2010 a limit on the number of full-load hours has been introduced, which limits the quantity of annual generation eligible to receive the feed-in tariff; also, an electricity production tax has been introduced and the feed-in tariff has been reduced. The profitability – especially of PV investments – has been affected severely, and many projects will not be able to repay their loans. Spanish and international courts will have to decide if these changes are in line with national and international law.

- *Prospective regulatory changes:* Prospective changes mainly affect the profitability of projects under development. One example is the decision in Germany in 2011 and 2012 to reduce the feed-in tariff for PV installations which start operation in the future. The notice time was long enough to reasonably ensure that projects for which an investment decision had already been made when the change was announced would be unaffected. Only projects under development were affected. More difficult is the case of an introduction of a 7% tax on electricity generation which was introduced in Spain for all types of electricity generation. Most likely this would rather be considered a retroactive change as it only affects the profitability of renewable energy generation receiving a fixed feed-in tariff, not any other generation sold in the wholesale market as the generation tax will lead to increasing wholesale market prices compensating or even overcompensating the tax. A clearly prospective change would be a general change in the company tax affecting all companies in a country. Also the introduction of additional safety standards, for example in the operation of existing and new wind farms, would rather be considered a prospective change as these changes are common in any industry and can therefore be expected when an investment decision is made.

Not only the risk of retroactive changes but also the risk of prospective changes has to be taken seriously when making investment decisions.

Political risks are hard to mitigate. Therefore, it is important to analyse historical regulatory changes in a country, not only in the field of renewable energy but in general. If these changes in a country had significant adverse financial effects for a specific industrial sector, regulatory risks have to be taken very seriously. Investors might require additional government guarantees, or should expect appropriate risk premia in these cases.

For international investments, insurances against political risks are available. For example, the Multilateral Investment Guarantee Agency – a member of the World Bank Group – offers this kind of insurance.

Another strategy is to have one's interests in line with important political stakeholders. For example, investors in German PV installations have common interest with more than one million German private investors and voters, most likely including a large number of members of the parliament. This reduces the risk of retroactive regulatory changes for PV generation in Germany. Also, influential co-investors can reduce political risks. An example in the conventional generation sector is the coal power station Iskenderun in Turkey. It was built by a German utility company and is partly owned by the pension fund of the Turkish Armed Forces.

Lobbying activities should also be considered as a means of mitigating regulatory risks.

2.6.7 Other Operational Risks

Besides resource, technical, market and regulatory risks, a large number of other operational risks can affect renewable energy projects. These risks include operational errors, availability of an adequate workforce, theft of components (e.g., solar panels or transformers), interruption of the grid connection and natural hazards. Some of these risks can be covered by insurance policies. Other risks can be mitigated by appropriate design of the equipment or anticipatory, risk-aware management.

3

Risk Management

In this chapter the main features of a risk management process in the energy industry will be described, with the focus on practical applications. We start with the basic definitions of *risk* and *risk management* according to ISO 31000 (see International Organization for Standardization (2009)) used throughout this book.

- *Risk* is defined as the effect of uncertainty on objectives. An effect is a positive or negative deviation from the expected, so according to this ISO definition risk also includes uncertain positive outcomes. Objectives can have different aspects, such as financial, health and safety, and environmental goals. In this book mainly financial aspects are regarded.
- *Risk management* is defined as the set of activities to direct and control an organisation with regard to risk.

Risk management includes the methodical identification, assessment and prioritisation of risks followed by coordinated and economical application of resources to minimise, monitor and control the probability and/or impact of unfortunate events. The main focus of this book is the financial risk management process of an energy company. Other risk management processes can be risk management processes of projects, natural disasters or technical operations.

The strategies to manage risk typically include *avoiding, reducing, transferring* or even *accepting* the risk. *Avoiding* the risk means choosing an alternative without the given risk exposure, but this often implies also eliminating business opportunities. *Reducing* the risk can be achieved either by minimising the probability of occurrence of the unwanted outcome or by reducing the negative impact. *Transferring* the risk to another party can be reached for example using derivatives contracts (hedging) or closing an insurance contract.

From a legal aspect, effective risk management is a common requirement for stock corporations in the respective national legislation. Also, the global regulatory standard of the Basel Committee on Banking Supervision is put into national legislation by defining standards for effective risk management. This is necessary to secure standards on bank capital adequacy, stress testing and market liquidity risk agreed upon by the members of the Basel Committee.

The basis of an effective risk management is the business strategy and the corresponding risk strategy. Securing the adequacy of risk capital is a central task of the risk management process.

Risk Identification

The risk management process starts with the methodical identification of risks. The usual method is a regular risk inventory and evaluation process including interviews with potential risk owners. The result can be illustrated in a risk map. This risk map should contain the main risks of the company. Figure 3.1 illustrates such a risk map for a utility on the first level. The risk identification is a basic but essential task and demands a deep knowledge of the

Figure 3.1   Risk map.

business processes of the company. From a practical point of view it makes no sense going into sophisticated risk models like Value-at-Risk, Profit-at-Risk or similar methods if the risk identification process and the effects of uncertain outcomes on the profit of the company have not been described carefully.

Further steps of the risk management process are risk assessment, risk monitoring and evaluation of mitigation measures, which depend on the specific risk type. After a short description of governance principles, the remaining chapter is therefore subdivided into market risk, legal risk, credit risk, liquidity risk and operational risk.

3.1   GOVERNANCE PRINCIPLES AND MARKET REGULATION

Sound corporate governance that defines clear responsibilities and avoids conflicts of interest is an essential prerequisite for effective risk management and ensuring compliance with relevant regulatory requirements. As a consequence of the financial market crisis following the bankruptcy of Lehman Brothers in 2008, a number of new market regulation initiatives were launched that on the one hand address corporate governance directly and on the other hand introduce various new requirements for documentation, transparency and processes that lead to significantly more complex compliance requirements.

For energy companies only some of the legal requirements for financial institutions are legally binding, depending on the business model and the extent of trading activities. However, many principles applicable for banks can be considered as the best practice approach also for non-banks involved in energy trading. Besides financial market regulation, there are various specific regulatory requirements for energy markets in place that need to be considered by energy companies. Also, the energy market regulation has become more extensive over recent years.

For banks, the Basel Committee on Banking Supervision (see Basel Committee on Banking Supervision (2010a)) has defined governance principles that explicitly cover responsibilities for risk management. Most of the basic principles are in some form also part of national legislation for financial institutions. Typical recommended roles and responsibilities related to risk management are:

- *The board* has overall responsibility for the company and the business. Regarding risk management, the board needs to approve and oversee the company's risk strategy and organisationally establish robust and independent risk and control functions. As part of the risk strategy, the board needs to approve the risk tolerance, which is the amount of risk the company is willing to take.

- *Risk management or risk control* is responsible for identifying risks, assessing and measuring risk and monitoring risk exposures. They further assess decisions regarding risk acceptance or risk mitigation measures and whether decisions are in line with the risk strategy or given risk policy. Further, risk management is responsible for reporting relevant risk topics to the senior management and to the board.
- *The Chief Risk Officer (CRO)* is a senior executive with distinct responsibility for the risk management function. To ensure independency, the CRO should not have any management responsibility for the operational business.
- *The risk committee* may be established to advise the board on risk strategy or risk tolerance and to oversee the implementation of the risk strategy by senior management. If a risk committee is established, its mandate and responsibilities should be clearly defined.

Further to the above, independent audit and compliance functions need to be established as part of the overall corporate governance structure.

A topic that came into public focus following the financial crisis after 2008 is the compensation scheme in banks. Since compensation schemes have a strong impact on risk-taking by business units, they need to be seen as part of the risk management and governance framework. In general, compensation schemes should be aligned with prudent risk-taking and be symmetric towards risk outcomes. Further, they should take a multi-year perspective, ensuring that wrong incentives are not given for short-term revenues whilst ignoring the long-term risks that might be involved.

It is beyond the scope of this book to provide a comprehensive description of regulatory frameworks relevant for energy trading. Further, the discussion around the appropriate extent of regulation and legislative procedures is still ongoing in many countries. For the European market, important initiatives are the following.

- *MiFID (Markets in Financial Instruments Directive):* This directive, implemented in 2007, provides a unified regulatory framework for the European Union with the aim of fostering competition and protecting consumers. Commodity traders and energy trading units of utility companies can make use of certain exemptions, so that they are not directly affected by MiFID. Consultations on an updated directive (MiFID II) started in 2010. Current proposals extend the scope of traded instruments and remove exemptions, so that the relevance for energy markets will increase. Relevant areas of regulation include supervisory power, increased transparency and potential position limits for market participants.
- *EMIR (European Market Infrastructure Regulation):* The EMIR directive regulates OTC transactions to provide more market transparency and better protection for counterparties. The measures include additional reporting requirements, central clearing obligations for eligible OTC products and obligations to reduce credit risk via collaterals. There are exemptions in place for market participants with transaction volumes below certain thresholds.
- *REMIT (Regulation on wholesale Energy Market Integrity and Transparency):* REMIT is a special directive for the energy market to prohibit insider trading and market manipulation and to increase market transparency. It is relevant not only for energy trading units but also for electricity generators, TSOs and large consumers. According to REMIT, market participants are obliged to publish insider information and report energy market transactions to the Agency for the Cooperation of Energy Regulators (ACER).

In the United States, the *Dodd–Frank Act* was introduced in 2010 as a response to the financial crisis. Among other market regulations it contains clearing obligation and transparency measures for OTC derivatives similar to EMIR. In addition, the *Commodity Futures Trading Commission (CFTC)* has been authorised to set position limits per market participant for certain commodity contracts.

3.2 MARKET RISK

Considering the financial risk management of an energy company, the main business risk is the exposure against market prices for commodities. The quantification of market risk is therefore a major objective of this chapter. Market risk always arises if a portfolio is not balanced between purchased and sold contracts, and therefore has an *open position* that at some point in time needs to be closed in the market. Such an imbalance can arise because purchased and sold volumes do not match, but it can also arise in more complex ways when contracts have different price formulas.

We therefore start with a more general definition of the portfolio position that can be considered as the equivalent for an energy trader to the inventory of a traditional merchant. A first natural approach for the definition of the portfolio position is given by the energy net total. The total quantity of physical purchases, production and sales volumes results in the *energetic portfolio position*. For logistic and technical reasons the energetic portfolio position is essential, but for most portfolios it is not adequate for determination of the market risk. As an example, financially settled futures are not included in an energetic position but they affect market price risk, while vice versa price-indexed forward contracts do not necessarily affect market price risk but are included in the energetic position. For small companies with a strong physical background, a pragmatic approach for determining the (financial) portfolio position is an extension of the energetic portfolio position by financial components. Financially settled futures contracts have to be included, contracts with an indexation on the market price of the delivered commodity have to be excluded. Depending on the portfolio composition, this *modified energetic position* can then be used as a basic approach to determine the market risk. However, the usability of a modified energetic position is limited to specific products and does not provide a general concept to assess market risk for complex energy portfolios. For example, adequately including the oil price risks of oil-indexed natural gas contracts would need further modifications of the energetic position.

From a financial point of view, the common definition of the portfolio position is the *delta position* defined in Section 3.2.1. The concept of the delta position allows the determination of market risk in a very general way. It is suitable for contracts with any price formula, and it takes into account payment dates and interest rates. The alternative definitions of the portfolio position and their main applications are summarised in Figure 3.2. Throughout this book "portfolio position" always means the delta position of the portfolio.

3.2.1 Delta Position

The delta position is defined as the sensitivity of the portfolio value against a market price change. More technically, if $V(t, F(t))$ denotes the value of a portfolio at t depending on

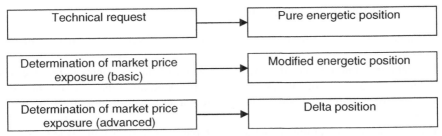

Technical request		Pure energetic position
Determination of market price exposure (basic)		Modified energetic position
Determination of market price exposure (advanced)		Delta position

Figure 3.2   Determination of the position of an energy portfolio.

the market prices $F(t)$ of some traded product, the delta position Δ_F is defined as (for fixed t)

$$\Delta_F = \frac{\partial V(F)}{\partial F} \approx \frac{V(F + \Delta F) - V(F - \Delta F)}{2\Delta F}.$$

As an approximation, the delta position can be considered as the change of the portfolio value if the selected market price $F(t)$ increases or decreases by one monetary unit (the same unit as F), that is,

$$\Delta_F = V(F + 1) - V(F),$$

which is exact if the portfolio contains only forward contracts. As a "Greek", the delta is known from option price theory and in this context it is explained in Section 5.3.4. In energy trading the delta position is important for many forward contracts, for example oil price-indexed gas price formulas or hedging power schedules. A position which loses value for a price increase of F ($\Delta_F < 0$) is called a *short position*, the opposite case $\Delta_F > 0$, a *long position*. A position with $\Delta_F = 0$ is called a *delta-neutral position*. A delta-neutral position does not change value for small changes of F.

The delta position can be computed from many risk management systems numerically. Evaluating the portfolio should be a basic function of every risk management system and for an approximation of the delta position only a simulation of the portfolio value is needed, if the price F increases by one monetary unit. Note that in this simulation the price of every other trading product remains unchanged. In practice, the first step for calculating the delta position is the determination of the relevant market risk drivers, which are typically forward/futures prices for different commodities and maturity dates. Then the delta position of the portfolio with respect to each market risk driver can be determined.

The determination of the market risk drivers has to be complete but not overlapping. If, for example, baseload and peakload electricity contracts are chosen as market risk drivers, the delta position with respect to an electricity baseload contract means simulating the portfolio value if the baseload contract increases (decreases) about one monetary unit and the peakload contract remains unchanged. Since peakload delivery is included in a baseload contract, peakload contracts and off-peakload contracts are more suitable as specified market risk drivers calculating a delta position.

Elementary properties of the delta position are as follows:

1. The delta position of a portfolio can be interpreted as the equivalent quantity of futures contracts.
   (a) The delta position indicates the required quantity of futures contracts for an effective hedge. If the quantity of futures contracts corresponding to the delta position is sold or respectively purchased, small changes in market prices do not affect the portfolio value.
   (b) The delta position of a futures contracts with physical delivery equates to the energetic position.
2. The unit of the delta position is equal to the unit of the quantity of the trading product. Particularly if F belongs to an energy product with the unit MWh, then the delta position Δ_F also has the unit MWh.
3. The delta position of a forward contract equates the discounted energetic position.
4. As a derivative, the delta position is linear with respect to the quantity of the trading product.
5. The delta position of an option is the common option delta defined in Section 5.3.4.

Example: Delta Position of an Oil-Indexed Gas Supply Contract

As a practical example, consider the purchase of a 100MW natural gas baseload contract, which is oil price indexed. The delivery periods are the gas years 2015/2016 and 2016/2017, which means the delivery starts on 01 October 2015 and ends on 30 September 2017. The price formula for the natural gas price $P(t_0)$ (per MWh) for delivery at month t_0 is

$$P(t_0) = P_0 + bGO_a(t_0) + cFO_a(t_0),$$

where P_0 denotes the fixed-price component per MWh, $GO_a(t_0)$ the average gasoil price and $FO_a(t_0)$ the average fuel oil price per tonne. The coefficients $b = 0.035$ t/MWh and $c = 0.0175$ t/MWh are constants. The recalculation date of GO_a is at the beginning of each quarter, the recalculation date of FO_a at the beginning of each month. The average gasoil price $GO_a(t_0)$ at the beginning of each quarter, respectively the average fuel oil price at the beginning of each month, is given by

$$GO_a(t_0) = \frac{1}{8} \sum_{k=1}^{8} GO(t_0 - k - 1), \qquad FO_a(t_0) = \frac{1}{3} \sum_{k=1}^{3} FO(t_0 - k),$$

where $GO(t_0 - k - 1), FO(t_0 - k)$ denotes published price indices for gasoil/fuel oil $k + 1$ months, respectively k months, before the month t_0. The pricing scheme for gasoil is illustrated in Figure 3.3 and for fuel oil in Figure 3.4.

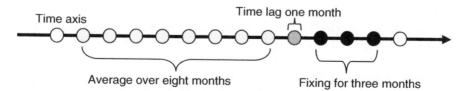

Figure 3.3   Gasoil price component.

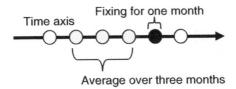

Figure 3.4   Fuel oil price component.

Now, the sensitivities against a change of market prices (i.e., the delta positions) shall be analysed. The relevant market prices against which sensitivities are calculated are gas, gasoil and fuel oil prices for different maturities.

We denote by $P(t, t_0), P(t, t_0 + 1), \ldots, P(t, t_0 + 23)$ the natural gas forward prices at t for the next 24 delivery months. $GO(t, t_0 - 9), GO(t, t_0 - 8), \ldots, GO(t, t_0 + 18), GO(t, t_0 + 19)$ denote the forward gasoil prices at t for delivery months January 2015 until May 2017 and $FO(t, t_0 - 3), FO(t, t_0 - 2), \ldots, FO(t, t_0 + 21), FO(t, t_0 + 22)$ denote the forward fuel oil prices at t for delivery months July 2015 until August 2017.

If the price for the natural gas forward $P(t, t_0)$ with delivery in October 2015 rises by 1 USD/MWh, the profit will rise by the discounted value of

$$1 \times 100\,\text{MW} \times 31 \times 24\,\text{h} \times 1\,\text{USD/MWh} = 74\,400\,\text{USD}.$$

This means that the delta position of natural gas in October 2015 is, except for discounting, equal to the energetic position of 74 400 MWh (see property 3 of the delta position).

Now consider the case that the gasoil forward price for January 2015 rises by 1 USD/t. This price increase will enter with weight 1/8 into the gasoil averaging formula which is relevant for the gas price calculation for the third quarter 2015 with monthly payment dates t_1, t_2, t_3. Except for discounting, the profit will change by

$$-\frac{1}{8} \times b \times 100\,\text{MW} \times (31 + 30 + 31) \times 24\,\text{h} \times 1\,\text{USD/t} = -966\,\text{USD}.$$

Therefore the delta position of gasoil with delivery in January 2015 is the discounted value of -966 tonnes. Note that the energetic gasoil position is zero and we have only a financial sensitivity against a change of gasoil prices.

Calculating the delta position of fuel oil with delivery in July 2015 is very similar. If the fuel oil price rises by 1 USD/t the profit will change by the discounted value of

$$-\frac{1}{3} \times c \times 100\,\text{MW} \times 31 \times 24\,\text{h} \times 1\,\text{USD/t} = -434\,\text{USD}.$$

Therefore, except for discounting, the delta position of fuel oil with delivery in July 2015 is -434 tonnes, while the energetic fuel oil position is zero.

Figure 3.5 shows the delta positions for all relevant monthly natural gas, gasoil and fuel oil products (except for discounting). The delta position for gasoil oscillates, which results from the eight months' averaging period for the gasoil price in combination with the quarterly price fixing. Depending on the specific monthly contract, the gasoil forward price has an impact on the natural gas price for either two or three months. These oscillations may cause hedge inefficiencies if the contract is hedged with a yearly gasoil swap instead of monthly products.

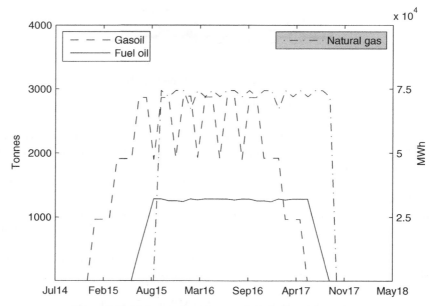

Figure 3.5   Delta position for gasoil, fuel oil and natural gas.

The Delta Position of Power Schedules

For an electricity supplier, calculating the delta position of a power schedule is an important task, which is required for hedging sales contracts or power generation. It will first be explained how to apply the delta position of power schedules, followed by an example for its calculation.

An electricity supplier often delivers the required load $L(t)$ to its retail customers in the form of a flexible contract, since the exact consumption in each hour is unknown in advance. For hedging purposes the supplier therefore uses the forecasted (expected) customer load $\hat{L}(t)$. This is the short position the supplier wants to hedge at the market. Since forward or futures contracts are not available in hourly granularity, the usual hedging products are baseload and peakload contracts for years and, closer to delivery, quarters or months. The problem for the supplier is therefore to determine optimal quantities of standard trading products for hedging a portfolio containing non-standard products. These quantities can be determined as the delta position with respect to those standard contracts. Note that calculating the delta position of a power schedule requires and depends on a pricing model for the hourly forward curve. Usually the hourly forward curve is obtained by scaling the observable forward contract prices with hourly "shaping" factors. Such a model is introduced in Section 6.1.2. Based on that model, the calculation of the delta position of a power schedule is described.

The power schedule is denoted by $\hat{L}(T_i)$, where $T_i, i = 1, \ldots, N$ denotes the delivery hours. The value $V(t)$ of the power schedule is given by

$$V(t) = \sum_{i=1}^{N} e^{-r(T_i - t)} \hat{L}(T_i) F(t, T_i),$$

with the hourly forward curve $F(t, \cdot)$ and the (continuously compounded) interest rate r.

The hourly forward curve is determined so that it is consistent with the prices of the traded forward contracts (see Section 6.1.2 for details). Let us assume as a simple case that the forward curve is determined by applying hourly shaping factors s_i to a baseload forward contract,

$$F(t, T_i) = s_i F^b.$$

Consistency with forward prices means that the hourly forward curve correctly prices the baseload forward contract. In this case it means that the shaping factors have a mean of one,

$$\frac{1}{N} \sum_{i=1}^{N} s_i = 1.$$

By definition, the delta position with respect to the forward price F^b is given by

$$\Delta_{F^b} = \sum_{i=1}^{N} e^{-r(T_i-t)} \hat{L}(T_i) \left(\tilde{F}(t, T_i) - F(t, T_i) \right), \tag{3.1}$$

where $\tilde{F}(t, \cdot)$ denotes the forward curve consistent with a forward price shifted by one monetary unit,

$$\tilde{F}(t, T_i) = s_i(F^b + 1).$$

Substituting the expression for $\tilde{F}$ into (3.1) yields

$$\Delta_{F^b} = \sum_{i=1}^{N} e^{-r(T_i-t)} \hat{L}(T_i) s_i = \frac{V(t)}{F^b}. \tag{3.2}$$

In other words, the delta position times the forward price F^b has the same value as the power schedule ($\Delta_{F^b} \times F^b = V(t)$). Hedging this position is therefore also referred to as *value-equivalent hedging*.

This approach can be generalised to hourly forward curves based on multiple forward contracts for more than one delivery period and peak/off-peak. In this case the above value condition (equation (3.2)) will apply to the delivery hours of the respective forward contract for which the delta position is calculated.

In summary, the energetic position of the power schedule is $\sum_{i=1}^{N} \hat{L}(T_i)$, while we have seen that the delta position is a discounted and value-weighted sum of the $\hat{L}(T_i)$. The principal differences between the delta position and the energetic position are:

- The energy of the power schedule at T_i is weighted with the price-scaling factor s_i. Power delivered at times of high prices affects the delta position more than the same energy amount delivered at times of low prices.
- As a financial sensitivity, the delta position is discounted. As a consequence, the delta position of comparable futures and forward contracts is different.

As a last extreme example assume that the delivery hours of the power schedule L are the expensive morning hours $T_i \in M$ on weekdays 8:00 AM–9:00 AM and the energy price at these hours is 1.5 times the peakload price F^p:

$$\hat{L}(T_i) = \begin{cases} 1, & i \in M \\ 0, & \text{otherwise;} \end{cases}$$

$$F(t, T_i) = 1.5 F^p, \quad i \in M.$$

Ignoring the discounting effect, equation (3.2) gives

$$\Delta_F = 1.5 |M|,$$

which is 1.5 times the energetic position.

This example shows that the difference between the delta and the energetic position can be remarkable. Delta hedging such a power schedule with a peakload contract F^p means that the hedge contains 150% of the energy of the delivery schedule. Using an hourly forward curve with scaling factors like those introduced in Section 6.1.2 implies that a price change of the baseload or peakload contracts changes the hourly prices proportional to their value. Using the delta position as a hedge ratio is consistent with this fact. Using the energetic position as hedge ratio would instead implicitly assume that a price shift of the baseload or peakload contract changes all hourly prices by the same absolute value, for which market observations give less evidence.

3.2.2 Variance Minimising Hedging

We have seen that the delta position indicates the required quantity of futures contracts for an effective hedge against changing market prices. However, in case of a retail portfolio, the supplier has to deliver an uncertain load $L(t)$ to its customers, so that additional to a pure market price risk he also has to manage stochastic load processes. The uncertainty of the load process makes the delta hedge less effective. Instead of a delta hedge it is also possible to minimise the volatility of the hedged stochastic portfolio value.

As an example, we consider a retail portfolio P with a sold aggregated delivery schedule $L(T_i)$, $T_i, i = 1, 2, \ldots, N$. To source the sold energy, the supplier has purchased adequate standard baseload and peakload contracts F_k^b, F_k^p with contract volumes μ_k and v_k. In case the deliveries from the purchased baseload and peakload contracts do not exactly match the delivery schedule $L(T_i)$, we assume that the supplier can purchase or sell shortage (respectively excess) energy at the spot price $S(T_i)$. This leads to additional stochastic spot market expenses or revenues V_P.

Let $J_k^b, J_k^p \subseteq \{1, \ldots, N\}$ denote the set of delivery hours for the kth purchased baseload respectively peakload contract. Then the purchased energy in the hour T_i is

$$\sum_k \left(\mu_k e_{ki} + v_k f_{mi} \right),$$

where

$$e_{ki} = \begin{cases} 1, & \text{for } T_i \in J_k^b \\ 0, & \text{otherwise} \end{cases} \; ; \qquad f_{ki} = \begin{cases} 1, & \text{for } T_i \in J_k^p \\ 0, & \text{otherwise} \end{cases} .$$

Summation over all delivery hours and multiplying by the spot price $S(T_i)$ yields

$$V_P = \sum_{i=1}^{N} \left(\sum_{k} \left(\mu_k e_{ki} + v_k f_{mi} \right) - L(T_i) \right) S(T_i). \tag{3.3}$$

The idea is to choose the quantities μ_k, v_k such that the variance σ^2 of V_P is as small as possible, that is the market and volume risk of the portfolio is minimal. To minimise σ^2 a combined stochastic model for spot prices and load is needed. As a starting point, the SMaPS model introduced in Section 6.2.1 can be used, which models spot prices and the total system (grid) load. Using this model for modelling the stochastic load of specific retail customers is explained in Chapter 4. As an initial value of the optimisation problem the delta hedge ratios can be used.

In the example illustrated in Figure 3.6, P contains a deterministic load and one baseload respectively peakload forward with the energetic hedge ratios μ, v. In contrast to an energetic hedging, the variance minimising hedging demands purchasing more standard products (typically between 3% and 6%). The standard deviation of $V_{P,t}$ can then be reduced by 10% to 40%.

3.2.3   Value-at-Risk

The market risk exposure introduced in Section 3.2 shows the effect of changing market prices (risk factors) on the portfolio value. However, these exposures or sensitivities do not include

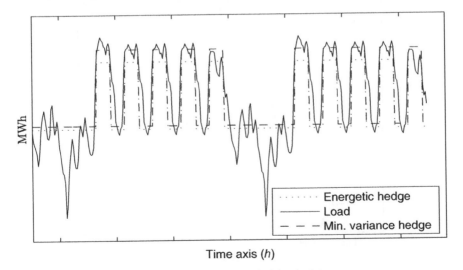

Time axis (h)

Figure 3.6   Variance minimising hedging.

any information about the probability of changing market prices. The Value-at-Risk (VaR) or other risk measures considered later in this chapter take into account the stochastic behaviour of market prices and answer the question "How bad can things get with which likelihood?"

Definition of Value-at-Risk

VaR is a risk measure widely used by financial institutions, fund managers or corporate treasurers. The acceptance is demonstrated by the fact that even bank regulators use VaR for determining the bank's capital requirements for their market risk exposure. The popularity of VaR began with the publication of JP Morgan's RiskMetrics Technical Document (cf. Guldimann (1995)).

Today there is a comprehensive literature on VaR, such as Jorion (2006) or Holton (2009). An application-oriented introduction to the VaR concept can also be found in Hull (2011). We will restrict our considerations about VaR to the principle methods and their practical usage in the energy business.

VaR, as illustrated in Figure 3.7, is a specified quantile of the profit or loss distribution of a given portfolio over a specified holding period. In other words, VaR specifies a "worst case", which will not be exceeded with a given high probability, of the performance of the given portfolio over the holding period. More technically, if $X[t_1, t_0]$ is the random variable of the market value change of a given portfolio during the time period $[t_1, t_0]$ with probability distribution P, then $VaR(\alpha, t_1 - t_0)$ with holding period $t_1 - t_0$ and confidence level α is defined as the infimum of all real numbers x with

$$P\big(X[t_1, t_0] \leq x\big) \geq 1 - \alpha . \tag{3.4}$$

As a possible loss VaR is technically a negative number, but often the absolute value is noted. In our examples we also use the absolute value of this possible negative performance as

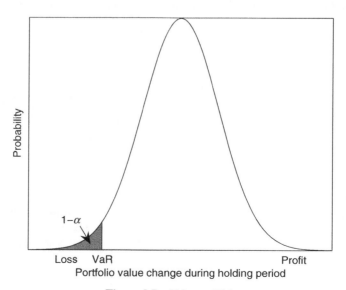

Figure 3.7   Value-at-Risk.

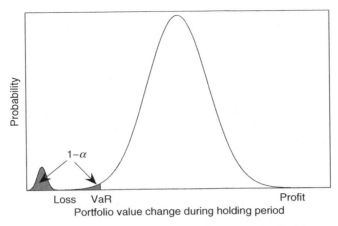

Portfolio value change during holding period

Figure 3.8   Portfolio with a low VaR compared with risk.

the VaR number. Note that the VaR only makes a statement about which loss is not exceeded with a given probability of α, but it does not give any information about what may happen in the remaining cases with a probability of $1 - \alpha$. As an example, Figure 3.8 shows a portfolio which has more risk in the tails of the distribution compared with Figure 3.7, but has the same VaR. For this reason the VaR can be substituted or complemented by the *conditional VaR*, defined as the loss expectation during the holding period conditional on being in the left tail of the distribution not belonging to the confidence level α.

Parameters of the Value-at-Risk

The two parameters of VaR are time horizon (or holding period) and confidence level. Assuming that the changes in the value of the portfolio on successive days have independent identical distributed normal distributions with mean zero, we have

$$\text{VaR}(\alpha, N) = \sqrt{N}\text{VaR}(\alpha, 1). \tag{3.5}$$

Therefore, a VaR with a given time horizon can easily be converted to any other time horizon by scaling with $\sqrt{N}$. Often, the VaR is calculated with a time horizon of one day and is afterwards converted into a VaR with the requested time horizon. In practice, equation (3.5) is used as an approximation, even if the assumption on the probability distributions above is not strictly true. A special case where care needs to be taken is for products with delivery during the time horizon. One solution is to split the energy portfolio into one part with no delivery during the time horizon and a remaining part for which other risk measures are used, for example a Profit-at-Risk approach.

How to choose the time horizon: In the revisions to the Basel II market risk framework (cf. Basel Committee on Banking Supervision (2010b)), calculation of capital for the trading book uses the VaR measure with a time horizon $N = 10$ and a confidence level $\alpha = 99\%$. So, from a formal point of view these are preferred parameters at least for a proprietary trading portfolio. Another possible criterion for the choice of time horizon is market liquidity. The idea is to choose the holding period in such a way that all positions can be closed until the end of the

Table 3.1   Quantiles of a centred normal distribution quoted as multiples of the standard deviation

Confidence level (quantile) α	99%	98%	95%	90%	84%
Probability	1%	2%	5%	10%	16%
Multiplier m_α	−2.33	−2.05	−1.64	−1.28	−1.00

holding period. Then the VaR specifies the total market risk of the portfolio which is consistent with the notion of risk capital. For portfolios in illiquid markets or containing large positions compared with market liquidity, this can mean that the holding period is chosen longer than for portfolios only containing highly liquid positions.

Confidence level: Usually, a confidence level between 95% and 99% is chosen. If the change in portfolio value is normally distributed, the VaR for a given confidence level can easily be converted to another confidence level using a certain factor. Table 3.1 shows the conversion factors for some common confidence levels.

For example, the VaR at 99% confidence level is $2.33/1.64 = 1.4$ times the VaR at 95% level in the normally distributed case. If a VaR model is used to determine risk capital, which should also cover extreme events, a confidence level even beyond 99% would in principle be required. However, methods for calculating the VaR and the implied distribution assumptions have significant inaccuracies in those extreme tails of the distribution. Statistical tests (backtesting) for commodity portfolios show that the tails of the normal or log-normal distribution are not sufficiently accurate for this problem. Choosing more realistic stochastic models often causes problems with available data for the parameter estimation or structural breaks in the data history. In practice, a VaR with confidence level above 99% can hardly be justified to represent a quantile for a real risk distribution. Regulatory frameworks therefore typically work with a conservative "rule of thumb" scaling factor to translate VaR at 99% confidence level into risk capital.

Computational Methods

Several approaches are available to calculate the VaR of a portfolio numerically. They all share the first step of identifying the main risk factors affecting the value of the portfolio. In a large energy portfolio several different commodities have to be taken into account. For each commodity, there may be a variety of different contracts with daily, weekly, monthly, quarterly and yearly delivery periods. Further, risk factors like foreign exchange, interest rates or implied volatilities may be relevant. To be able to apply statistical methods, a comprehensive database for historical prices covering all relevant risk factors is required. After a brief survey of the different computational methods, the most common delta–normal approach will be explained in more detail.

- *Historical simulation method:* Historical data is used directly for the determination of risk scenarios. Assuming that k historical prices are available, observed percentage changes in market prices (returns) between the observation days i and $i + 1$ with $i \in 1, 2, \ldots, k - 1$ are applied to today's market prices to generate $k - 1$ price scenarios for tomorrow. The price scenarios include observed correlations between different trading products. For each scenario the value of the portfolio will be determined and the $(1 - \alpha)$ quantile of all portfolio values yields the VaR. As an example, for $k = 1000$ and $\alpha = 0.98$ the VaR(0.98, 1 day) is the 20th highest loss in the portfolio value. To this point the historical simulation method does not require any assumption about the distribution of price changes, but the observation

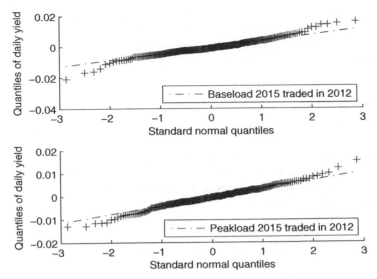

Figure 3.9   QQ-Plot of the yield baseload/peakload 2015 traded in 2012 versus standard normal.

grid then needs to match the holding period. For a holding period of N days, historical returns over N days would need to be evaluated, which reduces the number of data points compared with daily returns. However, it is often taken that the assumptions of equation (3.5) are at least approximately fulfilled, which allows us to calculate a VaR with a longer holding period using daily return as input data. The advantage of the historical simulation method is that it is robust, easy to understand and implement. Disadvantages are that it is computationally slow and only considers market price changes that have already occurred in the past.

- *Analytical method:* The analytical method is fast and the most common method for calculating VaR. Assuming a probability distribution for market prices, the resulting portfolio values are approximated using market price sensitivities of the portfolio. Subsequently, an analytic or semi-analytic formula for the VaR is derived. The most common assumption is that market prices are log-normally distributed, implying that the returns of the trading products are normally distributed. In practice, this assumption can be justified only to a limited extent, as the QQ-plot for power baseload and peakload products in Figure 3.9 demonstrates. If the returns were normally distributed, the QQ-plot of the returns would be linear, but the fat tails are clearly visible. Nevertheless, calculating the VaR with the log-normal assumption for a large diversified portfolio performs better than expected, since the portfolio distribution is closer to a normal distribution than the distribution of individual products. The analytical method can be differentiated in the way the portfolio value is approximated while there is a shift in market prices (see subsequent sections for more details).

- *Delta-normal method:* First-order approximation using only the portfolio delta, which is inaccurate if the portfolio contains significant non-linear positions like options.
- *Delta-gamma method:* Second-order approximation using the portfolio delta and gamma.

- *Structured Monte Carlo method:* The structured Monte Carlo method requires a stochastic model for the risk factors to generate price samples. With these price samples the possible changes in portfolio value can be simulated and the VaR can be determined as a quantile of the associated probability distribution.

Delta–Normal Approach

The impact of a change in market prices on the change in portfolio value is not always linear. If a portfolio contains options, the interrelation described in Section 5.3.4 is complex. The delta–normal method is a linear approximation of the change in portfolio value, which is adequate if the portfolio contains basically linear instruments like forward or futures contracts. Determining the VaR with the delta–normal method means a linear approximation of the change in portfolio value ΔV, that is

$$\Delta V(F_1, F_2, \ldots, F_n) = \sum_{i=1}^{n} \frac{\partial V}{\partial F_i} \Delta F_i. \tag{3.6}$$

The partial derivative $\frac{\partial V}{\partial F_i}$ is the delta position Δ_{F_i} with respect to F_i. To avoid confusion between the delta position Δ_{F_i} and the change ΔF_i, we denote in the following Δ_{F_i} as q_i.

We start with the simplest case that the portfolio contains only one futures contract F as risk factor (i.e., one tradable product). In this case the VaR calculation is straightforward. Analogous to option price theory (see, for example, Black's Futures Price Model described in Section 5.3.2) we assume that market prices follow a geometric Brownian motion with drift μ. The change in logarithms of the futures prices is normally distributed and can be written as

$$\ln(F(t)) - \ln(F(t_0)) = \left(\mu - \frac{\sigma^2}{2} \right)(t - t_0) + \sigma\sqrt{t - t_0}\, X,$$

where X denotes a standard normally distributed random variable and σ the annualised volatility of F. With the requested confidence level α and the belonging multiplier m_α (see Table 3.1) we have, with a probability of α,

$$F(t) - F(t_0) \geq F(t_0) \left(\exp\left(\left(\mu - \frac{\sigma^2}{2} \right)(t - t_0) - m_\alpha \sigma \sqrt{t - t_0} \right) - 1 \right).$$

The VaR with confidence level α and holding period $t - t_0$ is therefore

$$\text{VaR}(\alpha, t - t_0) = F(t_0) \left(\exp\left(\left(\mu - \frac{\sigma^2}{2} \right)(t - t_0) - m_\alpha \sigma \sqrt{t - t_0} \right) - 1 \right).$$

Considering a portfolio of different trading products, the change in portfolio value is the sum of log-normally distributed random variables. Since this sum is not log-normally distributed itself, determining the VaR (i.e., a specified quantile) is more complex. One possibility is to use a Monte Carlo simulation for the log-normally distributed prices F_i. An alternative is to use approximations for the distributions, which will be elaborated now.

We denote the continuously compounding return between t_0 and t as

$$\bar{r}_i[t_0, t] = \ln\left(\frac{F_i(t)}{F_i(t_0)}\right)$$

and the discrete return between t_0 and t as

$$r_i[t_0, t] = \frac{F_i(t) - F_i(t_0)}{F_i(t_0)}.$$

As a difference from option price theory, the focus of VaR calculations is usually short time periods (change in the portfolio over a short time period), while in option theory longer periods (maturities up to a year or longer) are also regarded. For a small discrete return (i.e., a small $\Delta t = t - t_0$) the linear approximation

$$\ln(1 + r_i[t_0, t]) \approx r_i[t_0, t]$$

gives

$$\bar{r}_i[t_0, t] = \ln\left(1 + \frac{F_i(t) - F_i(t_0)}{F_i(t_0)}\right) \approx r_i[t_0, t].$$

Even though this is a deterministic consideration only, it is an indication that with a normally distributed continuously compounded return $\bar{r}_i[t_0, t]$ the discrete return $r_i[t_0, t]$ is approximately normally distributed for a small time interval $[t_0, t]$. Figure 3.10 shows the small difference in

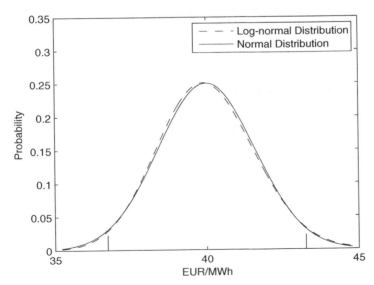

Figure 3.10   Comparison of the density of a log-normal and a normal distribution with 20% volatility (annualised) converted for a holding period of 10 days.

distribution functions for the example of a baseload power contract and a holding period of 10 days.

The procedure for calculating the VaR is as follows. By equation (3.6), the change in portfolio value can be expressed as

$$\Delta V(F_1, F_2, \ldots, F_n) = \sum_{i=1}^{n} q_i F_i(t_0) \frac{F_i(t_0+1) - F_i(t_0)}{F_i(t_0)} = \sum_{i=1}^{n} q_i F_i(t_0) r_i[t_0, t_0+1].$$

Consistent with standard option price theory, we assume that market prices follow a geometric Brownian motion. Then the VaR is calculated for a one-day period and scaled to the requested holding period by equation (3.5), which is an approximation. The discrete return $r_i[t_0, t_0+1]$ of F_i for a small holding period of one day is approximately normally distributed and additionally it is assumed that the mean of the discrete return is zero. Since ΔV can be expressed as a weighted sum of normally distributed variables $r_i[t_0, t_0+1]$ with a mean of zero, ΔV is also normally distributed with mean zero. Only the standard deviation $\sigma_{\Delta V}$ still has to be determined. If σ_i denotes the standard deviation of $r_i[t_0, t_0+1]$ (approximately the daily volatility), $(\mathbf{C_{i,j}})$ the correlation matrix of the r_i and $\mathbf{v}$ the column vector

$$\mathbf{v} = (q_1 F_1(t_0)\sigma_1, \ldots, q_n F_n(t_0)\sigma_n),$$

we have

$$\sigma_{\Delta V} = \sqrt{\mathbf{v}^T(\mathbf{C_{i,j}})\mathbf{v}}. \tag{3.7}$$

Once the standard deviation $\sigma_{\Delta V}$ is determined, the VaR$(\alpha, \Delta t)$ can easily be calculated using the multiplier m_α corresponding to confidence level α (Table 3.1):

$$\text{VaR}(\alpha, \Delta t) = \sigma_{\Delta V} m_\alpha \sqrt{\Delta t}. \tag{3.8}$$

Example: Value-at-Risk Calculation Using the Delta–Normal Method

As a practical example, the VaR(98%, 10d) of the energy portfolio described in Table 3.2 will be calculated using the delta–normal method. The assumed correlation matrix is shown in Table 3.3.

Table 3.2   Assumed energy portfolio

Product	Delta position	Market price	Volatility 1d
Power baseload 2017	10 000 000 MWh	40 EUR/MWh	1%
Power peakload 2017	5 000 000 MWh	45 EUR/MWh	0.8%
Coal 2017	−1 000 000 tonnes	70 EUR/t	0.8%
USD 2017	−91 000 000 USD	0.77 EUR/USD	0.6%
CO$_2$-EUA 2017	−1 000 000 tonnes	3 EUR/t	3.5%

Table 3.3   Market price correlations

	Baseload 2017	Peakload 2017	Coal	USD	CO$_2$
Baseload 2017	1.0	0.9	0.2	0.0	0.5
Peakload 2017	0.9	1.0	0.2	0.0	0.4
Coal 2017	0.2	0.2	1.0	0.0	0.1
USD 2017	0.0	0.0	0.0	1.0	0.0
CO$_2$-EUA 2017	0.5	0.4	0.1	0.0	1.0

Following equation (3.7), the standard deviation of the change in portfolio value is determined by the matrix multiplication

$$\sigma_{\Delta V}^2 = \begin{pmatrix} 4\,000\,000 \\ 1\,800\,000 \\ -560\,000 \\ -420\,420 \\ -105\,000 \end{pmatrix}^T \begin{pmatrix} 1.0 & 0.9 & 0.2 & 0.0 & 0.5 \\ 0.9 & 1.0 & 0.2 & 0.0 & 0.4 \\ 0.2 & 0.2 & 1.0 & 0.0 & 0.1 \\ 0.0 & 0.0 & 0.0 & 1.0 & 0.0 \\ 0.5 & 0.4 & 0.1 & 0.0 & 1.0 \end{pmatrix} \begin{pmatrix} 4\,000\,000 \\ 1\,800\,000 \\ -560\,000 \\ -420\,420 \\ -105\,000 \end{pmatrix},$$

which yields

$$\sigma_{\Delta V} = 5\,553\,624.$$

From equation (3.8) the VaR with holding period of 10 days and confidence level 98% is

$$VaR(98\%, 10d) = \sigma_{\Delta V} \times 2.05 \times \sqrt{10} = 36\,002\,306 \text{ EUR}.$$

Now we want to interpret this result. The portfolio described in Table 3.2 may be the generation portfolio of a utility. The utility has a long position in power (they can generate power) and they need fuel and emission allowances to run their plants. The market price risk for the production in 2017 is measured in euros. Because coal is traded in USD, but risk will be measured in euros, the risk drivers must be chosen carefully. In our example we choose coal denoted in USD and USD forwards priced in EUR as risk drivers and for these risk drivers, correlations and volatilities are measured. For the VaR calculation the USD amounts are converted into euros using the actual USD spot price. This approach can be used generally if different currencies are used for pricing.

Alternatively, the risk driver coal priced in euros can be used, which means using correlations and volatilities from a virtual coal price in euro time series. In this case the VaR calculation does not use USD as a risk driver. This alternative makes it easier to work out properly the correlation between electricity and coal and may be recommended for a portfolio dominated by the European electricity market.

Delta–Gamma Approach

For option portfolios with significant non-linear positions, the linear approximation for the portfolio value (3.6) used in the delta–normal approach may not be sufficient. Instead, a quadratic approximation can be used to determine the VaR. If a portfolio P has the market prices $F_1, F_2, \ldots, F_n$ as risk factors, then the Taylor series expansion for $V(F_1, F_2, \ldots, F_n)$ can be written as

$$\Delta V(F_1, F_2, \ldots, F_n) = \sum_{i=1}^{n} \frac{\partial V}{\partial F_i} \Delta F_i + \frac{1}{2} \sum_{i=1}^{n} \sum_{j=1}^{n} \frac{\partial^2 V}{\partial F_i \partial F_j} \Delta F_i \Delta F_j + R(\Delta(F_1, F_2, \ldots, F_n)), \quad (3.9)$$

where $R(\cdot)$ denotes a higher-order residual term.

In a first step of the delta–gamma approach, the moments of ΔV are calculated. Subsequently, the Cornish–Fisher expansion (see for example Holton (2009)) can be used to estimate quantiles of the probability distribution from these moments.

Qualitatively, a portfolio with a positive gamma (e.g., including a long call option) reduces its market price sensitivity (i.e., its delta position) in the case of decreasing market prices. If market prices are increasing there is a positive effect from an increasing delta. A VaR calculated with the delta–normal method is therefore too high. Vice versa, the calculated VaR will be too low if the portfolio has a negative gamma.

3.2.4 Estimating Volatilities and Correlations

The analytical method for calculating VaR requires the volatilities σ_i for the daily returns $r_i[t, t+1]$ of the trading products F_i as input parameters. To simplify notation, the following discussion considers a single trading product F and therefore omits the associated subscript i. The estimation of the daily volatility σ of F estimated at the end of day t_{n-1} is denoted by σ_n. To calculate σ_n, the most recent m ($m < n$) observations of the continuously compounded returns

$$r(t_{n-j}) := r[t_{n-j-1}, t_{n-j}] = \ln\left(\frac{F(t_{n-j})}{F(t_{n-j-1})}\right), \quad j \in \{1, 2, \ldots, m\}$$

are used. Often, as an approximation, the percentage changes in market prices instead of the continuously compounded returns are applied, that is

$$r(t_{n-j}) = \left(\frac{F(t_{n-j}) - F(t_{n-j-1})}{F(t_{n-j-1})}\right), \quad j \in \{1, 2, \ldots, m\}.$$

The estimation for σ at the end of day t_{n-1} is given by

$$\sigma_n^2 = \frac{1}{m-1} \sum_{j=1}^{m} \left(r(t_{n-j}) - \bar{r}\right)^2,$$

where

$$\bar{r} = \frac{1}{m} \sum_{j=1}^{m} r(t_{n-j})$$

denotes the mean of $r(t_{n-j})$ over the last m observations. Using the assumption that the mean of the returns is zero,[1] we have approximately

$$\sigma_n^2 = \frac{1}{m} \sum_{j=1}^{m} r^2(t_{n-j}). \qquad (3.10)$$

Using equation (3.10) is the simplest method for estimating the volatility σ. All observations have the same weight, which is consistent with the idea of a constant volatility. However, in practice, market volatilities are changing and therefore weighting recent data higher than older observations is a reasonable improvement on estimating volatilities and correlations.

The Exponentially Weighted Moving Average Model (EWMA)

Introducing weights α_i in equation (3.10) gives

$$\sigma^2(t_n) = \sum_{j=1}^{m} \alpha_j r^2(t_{n-j}). \qquad (3.11)$$

The weights are assumed to be normalised, that is

$$\sum_{j=1}^{m} \alpha_j = 1.$$

The EWMA approach uses exponentially decreasing weights for the estimation of $\sigma(t_n)$ of the form

$$\sigma^2(t_n) = (1 - \lambda) \sum_{j=1}^{m} \lambda^{j-1} r^2(t_{n-j}) + \lambda^m r^2(t_{n-m}). \qquad (3.12)$$

For the sum of the weights we have

$$(1 - \lambda) \sum_{j=1}^{m} \lambda^{j-1} + \lambda^m = 1.$$

In practice, there are two common approaches for a calculation of $\sigma(t_n)$.

1. If m is large, λ^m is small and the term $\lambda^m r^2(t_{n-m})$ can be ignored. Equation (3.12) results in approximately

$$\sigma^2(t_n) = (1 - \lambda) \sum_{j=1}^{m} \lambda^{j-1} r^2(t_{n-j}). \qquad (3.13)$$

---

[1] For unbiasedness, $m - 1$ is replaced by m because of the assumption that the mean is known and not estimated.

2. $\sigma^2(t_n)$ is calculated recursively from the previous value $\sigma^2(t_{n-1})$ as

$$\sigma^2(t_n) = (1 - \lambda)r^2(t_{n-1}) + \lambda\sigma^2(t_{n-1}). \qquad (3.14)$$

After m iterations of this formula we get

$$\sigma^2(t_n) = (1 - \lambda)\sum_{j=1}^{m} \lambda^{j-1}r^2(t_{n-j}) + \lambda^m\sigma^2(t_{n-m}),$$

which converges to equation (3.12) for large m.

If the EWMA approach is used to estimate the volatility, the parameter $\lambda \in (0, 1)$ has to be specified. If λ is close to 1, a long history is used to estimate $\sigma(t_n)$. The estimation is stable but new market information is slowly integrated. Such a λ is adequate if the VaR for a large asset portfolio has to be calculated, which typically cannot be closed within a short period of time. If λ is lower, the volatility itself is more volatile. For a proprietary trading portfolio a fast adaptation to the actual market volatility is useful. One way to specify λ is by defining a "half-life period", that is a period after which the observation of the return is weighted half as much as the most recent observation. Equation (3.12) shows that the weight of an observation made j trading days ago is half reduced if λ fulfils $\lambda^{j-1} = \frac{1}{2}$. J.P. Morgan (see J.P. Morgan (1995)) uses a parameter $\lambda = 0.94$ for their RiskMetrics database. This corresponds to a half-life period of approximately 10 days. This can be used as a first setting for λ in the energy markets as well.

GARCH Models

Another useful method for estimating volatilities is via the GARCH models proposed by Bollerslev (1986). With the GARCH(1,1) model the volatility can be estimated with a recursion formula similar to equation (3.14):

$$\sigma^2(t_n) = \lambda_1\bar{\sigma} + \lambda_2r^2(t_{n-1}) + \lambda_3\sigma^2(t_{n-1}),$$

where the non-negative weights λ_i sum to one and $\bar{\sigma}$ is a long-run average volatility. The GARCH(1,1) model tends to get pulled back to the long-run average volatility $\bar{\sigma}$. GARCH(1,1) allows us to model a wide range of volatility behaviour. In energy markets, volatilities can change very fast so using GARCH models seems adequate. However, in some cases GARCH models can produce extreme scenarios which seem unrealistic and are not as robust as the EWMA model. A careful estimation of the parameters and permanent backtesting is therefore essential.

Estimating Correlations

Methods for estimating volatilities can be adapted to estimate correlations. If F_1, F_2 are trading products with daily returns r_1, r_2 and daily volatilities σ_1, σ_2, the correlation between the returns is

$$\text{Corr}(r_1, r_2) = \frac{\text{Cov}(r_1, r_2)}{\sigma_1\sigma_2} = \frac{\mathbb{E}[(r_1 - \mathbb{E}[r_1])(r_2 - \mathbb{E}[r_2])]}{\sigma_1\sigma_2}. \qquad (3.15)$$

Analogous to equation (3.10), the covariance and therefore the correlation at t_n can be estimated by

$$\text{Cov}_{t_n}(r_1, r_2) = \frac{1}{m} \sum_{j=1}^{m} r_1(t_{n-j}) r_2(t_{n-j}).$$

The EWMA approach can also be used to estimate the covariance. The recursion formula analogous to (3.14) is

$$\text{Cov}_{t_n}(r_1, r_2) = (1 - \lambda) r_1(t_{n-1}) r_2(t_{n-1}) + \lambda \text{Cov}_{t_{n-1}}(r_1, r_2).$$

3.2.5 Backtesting

Backtesting is an important task because VaR and other risk measures require extensive assumptions on the stochastic process representing market prices. There are many influencing factors which are critical to the VaR calculation. If the backtesting rejects the appointed VaR model, the reason is often inadequate model parameters and this does not always mean that the VaR concept itself is not adequate for the specific problem. Critical factors concerning VaR are the following.

- *Choice of risk drivers:* One usual assumption is that delivery periods are considered in relation to today, for example month ahead, year ahead, etc., and there is a roll-over in the time series. It needs to be decided if it is adequate to ignore potential seasonal patterns for volatilities and correlations.
- *Risk for non-standard products (e.g., power schedules):* The price of standard contracts is often the basis for the valuation of other non-standard contracts and shifting standard contract prices should reflect the risk of non-standard products.
- *Stability:* Estimation of volatilities and correlations may not be stable; large market shifts can cause unrealistic parameters and therefore an unrealistic VaR. Therefore, outliers in the data need to be identified.

Figure 3.11 shows the daily change of a larger energy portfolio versus the calculated 98% confidence interval. There are 2% outliers (i.e., losses exceeding the VaR) expected. If the probability distribution of the daily value change is symmetric (e.g., normally distributed), outliers belonging to a positive value change also provide information concerning the adequateness of the implied VaR method. Because the holding period is 1 day and the backtesting involves 200 trading days, there are 8 expected outliers (4 higher and 4 lower values). In the backtested portfolio there are fewer outliers (but not too few) and the backtesting supports the selected model.

3.2.6 Liquidity-Adjusted Value-at-Risk

The VaR model in its basic form assumes that a given portfolio position is held constant over a fixed and typically short holding period. The holding period is chosen in such a way that the position can be closed within that period. For very large positions relative to market liquidity, it may take a long time (e.g., multiple months) to close all positions, for example a large utility

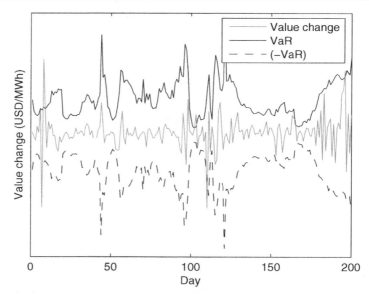

Figure 3.11   Backtesting – VaR(98%, 1 day) versus daily change of an energy portfolio's value.

company may need multiple months to fully hedge positions from their generation assets. Simply applying the VaR model with a long holding period would neglect that the position will already be stepwise reduced during the holding period, which reduces market risk.

The liquidity-adjusted Value-at-Risk (LVaR) extends the VaR concept to positions that change during the holding period. One application is to establish a stop-loss strategy which reduces the VaR in the same degree as losses occur while taking into account liquidity constraints. In this way the portfolio losses can be limited to the VaR within the confidence level. If no such stop-loss strategy exists, the information content of VaR is strictly limited to the holding period and it can be used as a relative risk measure to compare today's price risk with yesterday's price risk. The LVaR concept merges elements from the VaR concept with the central idea of Profit-at-Risk (measuring market risk until the position is closed) introduced in Section 3.2.7.

LVaR was developed to quantify market risk for large portfolios. A typical example is the asset book of an energy supplier containing its primary activities, such as production, generation or sales. Often, the asset book is too large to close the open position in a time horizon of a few days. The price risk of the asset portfolio is an important indicator for the management of energy companies to anticipate potential negative deviations from the financial plan. Measuring market risk simply by extending the holding period of a standard VaR is not adequate, because it ignores the successive reduction of the position over time or at least the possibility of such a reduction.

Calculating the LVaR implies that there is an estimation about the necessary time horizon to close the position. We regard the case where there is a strategy with defined quantities to close the position, for example a strategy with continuous selling of the generation volumes in line with available market liquidity.

At first the portfolio is approximated by tradable standard contracts $F_1, \ldots, F_n$ with the quantities (delta positions) $q_1, \ldots, q_n$. Then, depending on market liquidity, for each trading product the number β_i of contracts which can be sold (respectively purchased) in a given short time period Δt (e.g., one trading day) without any significant impact on market prices is determined. This means that the open position q_i can be reduced to $q_i - k\beta_i$ after the period $k\Delta t$. We define $p := \max\{q_i/\beta_i : i \in \{1, \ldots, n\}\}$ as the number of time periods required to close all positions and a_{ik} as an indication whether the total number of contracts has been reached:

$$a_{ik} = \begin{cases} 1, & \text{if } k\beta_i \leq q_i \\ 0, & \text{otherwise} \end{cases} ; \quad i \in \{1, \ldots, n\}, k \in \{1, \ldots, p\}.$$

Thus, the assumed portfolio at period k consists of the trading products $F_i, i \in \{1, \ldots, n\}$ with quantities $a_{ik}(q_i - k\beta_i)$ and the standard deviation of their changes σ_i. At period p all positions have been closed. The variance $\sigma^2(k)$ of the change in market value for the portfolio at period k over the period Δt is

$$\sigma^2(k) = \Delta t \, \mathbf{v_k}^T (\mathbf{C_{i,j}}) \mathbf{v_k}, \quad k \in \{1, \ldots, p\}, \tag{3.16}$$

where $(\mathbf{C_{i,j}})$ denotes the correlation matrix of the daily returns r_i and $\mathbf{v_k}$ denotes the column vector

$$\mathbf{v_k} = \left(a_{1k}(q_1 - k\beta_1)F_1(t_0)\sigma_1, \ldots, a_{nk}(q_n - k\beta_n)F_n(t_0)\sigma_n\right).$$

Assuming that market price changes over the successive time periods are independent and normally distributed with mean zero and variance σ_i^2, the change in total asset portfolio as a sum of independent normally distributed random variables is also normally distributed with mean zero and variance

$$\sigma^2 = \sum_{k=1}^{p} \sigma^2(k) = \sum_{k=1}^{p} \Delta t \, \mathbf{v_k}^T (\mathbf{C_{i,j}}) \mathbf{v_k}. \tag{3.17}$$

Using the multiplier m_α belonging to the requested confidence level α indicated in Table 3.1, the LVaR(α) for the portfolio is

$$\text{LVaR}(\alpha) = m_\alpha \sigma.$$

A special case is the uniform reduction of an asset portfolio, in which case the LVaR calculation can be simplified further. A natural strategy is to close the long position of the production output (e.g., power generation) to the same degree as closing the short position of the input commodities (e.g., fuels). With p as defined above, the quantity β_i is replaced by the smaller quantity $\bar{\beta}_i = q_i/p$, forcing a uniform closing of all positions without violating any liquidity restrictions. Then we have $a_{ik} = 1$ for all $i = 1, \ldots, n, k = 1, \ldots, p$ and

$$q_i - k\bar{\beta}_i = (p - k)\bar{\beta}_i.$$

Equation (3.17) yields

$$\sigma^2 = \Delta t \ \mathbf{v}^T (\mathbf{C_{i,j}}) \mathbf{v} \sum_{k=1}^{p} (p - k)^2, \tag{3.18}$$

where $\mathbf{v}$ denotes the column vector

$$\mathbf{v} = \left(\bar{\beta}_1 F_1(t_0)\sigma_1, \ldots, \bar{\beta}_n F_n(t_0)\sigma_n \right).$$

The sum can be reduced to

$$\sum_{k=1}^{p} (p - k)^2 = \sum_{k=1}^{p-1} k^2 = \frac{(p-1)p(2p-1)}{6}.$$

Example: As an example, the portfolio described in Table 3.2 is reconsidered. We assume that the closing of the position requires 100 trading days because of the limited market liquidity, so that $\Delta t = 1$ and $p = 100$. It is assumed that all trading products will always be reduced uniformly as described above. The position that can be closed during one trading day contains one-hundredth of the initial portfolio and equation (3.18) gives

$$\sigma^2 = \frac{99 \times 100 \times 199}{6} \begin{pmatrix} 40\,000 \\ 18\,000 \\ -5\,600 \\ -4\,204 \\ -1\,050 \end{pmatrix}^T \begin{pmatrix} 1.0 & 0.9 & 0.2 & 0.0 & 0.5 \\ 0.9 & 1.0 & 0.2 & 0.0 & 0.4 \\ 0.2 & 0.2 & 1.0 & 0.0 & 0.1 \\ 0.0 & 0.0 & 0.0 & 1.0 & 0.0 \\ 0.5 & 0.4 & 0.1 & 0.0 & 1.0 \end{pmatrix} \begin{pmatrix} 40\,000 \\ 18\,000 \\ -5\,600 \\ -4\,204 \\ -1\,050 \end{pmatrix}$$

$$= 1\,012\,721\,301\,455\,090.$$

The LVaR with confidence level of 98% is therefore

$$\text{LVaR}(98\%) = 2.05 \ \sigma = 2.05 \times 31.823.282 = 65.237.728 \text{ EUR}.$$

How can this quantification of the market risk be interpreted? A utility that owns generation capacities may have a portfolio as described in Table 3.2. If the utility has a risk management strategy allowing the reduction of the open position restricted only by the market liquidity, the risk against the actual portfolio value is EUR 65 million.

   Extension: For the calculation and to achieve a closed-form solution, the assumption of independent and normally distributed changes in market price was made. If market prices for the traded commodities do not meet these assumptions, a Monte Carlo simulation for the market prices can be used. This allows us to calculate market risk for more complex strategies to close open positions.

3.2.7   Profit-at-Risk and Further Risk Measures

VaR is by far the most popular risk measure, even though it has a number of disadvantages, most of which have already been discussed. In brief, VaR is a risk measure which is adequate for short holding periods and for price risks concerning the forward market. For large portfolios, where market risks cannot be eliminated in a short holding period, LVaR is useful.

In energy markets there are positions which cannot be traded liquidly on the forward market and therefore a market risk persists until delivery. As an example, hourly profiles in the power market can be traded on the spot market, but there is no forward market for power delivered for one hour only. Spot prices are found to be much more volatile than forward prices, especially for commodities which can hardly be stored. Because the distribution of spot prices is often heavy-tailed, the assumption of a log-normal distribution is not adequate. There are risk measures like Profit-at-Risk (PaR), Earnings-at-Risk (EaR) or Cashflow-at-Risk (CFaR), which integrate spot market risks and therefore give an additional view on market risk. We start with a short overview of further risk measures in the energy business, followed by a calculation example for PaR, the most popular risk measure for energy besides VaR.

- *Cashflow-at-Risk:* The considered random variable is the cashflow of a company until a specified date. The CFaR is the difference between the expected cashflow and the cashflow corresponding to the given confidence level α, that is the $(1 - \alpha)$ quantile of the distribution of the cashflow. CFaR reflects whether a company has adequate cash reserves and can be used to help companies assess their capital structure and creditworthiness.
- *Earnings-at-Risk:* The considered random variable is the earnings of a company until a specified date. For energy companies this includes spot price revenues generated by the assets less all production costs plus all related trading and hedging transactions. EaR is the difference between the expected earnings and the earnings corresponding to the given confidence level.
- *Profit-at-Risk:* This is related to EaR and was designed for the energy markets to include volatile spot prices in the market risk consideration. Usually, costs like production costs are not included, so PaR is focused on the market value of the portfolio. With a given confidence level α, PaR is the $(1 - \alpha)$ quantile of the change in value of a given portfolio until delivery. Using PaR requires an effective spot market model such as those introduced in Chapter 6.

Note that PaR, EaR and CFaR are expressions used to mean several slightly different things by different segments of the industry, and there exists no standard calculation concepts. The most used risk measure besides VaR is PaR, and following example shows the advantages and area of application of PaR.

Example: Assume an electricity supplier has acquired at t_0 a customer for the next calender year with the delivery hours $T_i, i \in \{1, 2, \dots, 8760\}$. At t_0 the estimated load is $\hat{L}(t_0, T_i)$, and the hourly price forward curve $F(t_0, T_i)$. The supplier immediately hedges the sold estimated load by purchasing a baseload contract with the same energy amount; the corresponding capacity of the contract is denoted by β. In this example we are only interested in the market price risk of the unhedged hourly profile of the retail customer. So we do not consider other risk, for example volume risk or a changing load profile. Consequently, the regarded portfolio

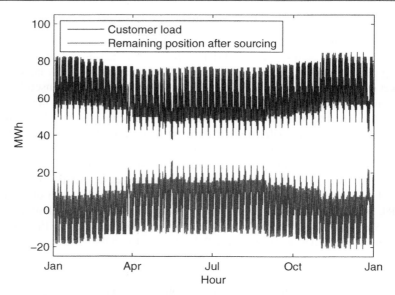

Figure 3.12   Estimated customer load, before and after hedging.

consists of the sold estimated load and the purchased baseload contract. The resulting power schedule is denoted as

$$\hat{L}_H(t_0, T_i) = \beta - \hat{L}(t_0, T_i), \quad i \in \{1, 2, \ldots, 8760\}.$$

A numerical example for the estimated load $\hat{L}$ and the remaining position after sourcing $\hat{L}_H$ is shown in Figure 3.12. In this example (see also Table 3.4) the total load is 556 GWh/a and the purchased baseload contract has a capacity of 64 MW.

Table 3.4   Profit-at-Risk calculation using electricity spot price scenarios for the 8760 single hours of the front year

Hour i	Position MWh $\hat{L}_H$	Forward EUR/MWh $F(t_0, T_i)$	Simulated price in scenario (EUR/MWh)			Value EUR $V(t_0)$	Value change in scenario (EUR/MWh)		
			no. 37	no. 94	no. 1		no. 37	no. 94	no. 1
1	12.21	30.45	28.84	35.62	36.62	371.73	−19.56	59.82	75.36
2	13.81	28.59	29.39	39.41	32.16	394.92	11.02	149.50	49.33
3	15.46	27.96	30.05	26.40	31.08	432.09	32.38	−24.00	48.22
4	16.74	27.30	26.04	21.35	30.25	456.88	−21.03	−99.51	49.45
5	12.21	30.45	28.84	35.62	36.62	371.73	−19.56	59.82	75.36
...	...	...	...	...	...	...	...	...	...
8759	8.49	44.94	65.68	53.98	43.05	381.33	176.00	76.72	−16.04
8760	9.66	41.87	49.91	48.29	44.77	404.35	77.64	61.99	28.06
	MWh					kEUR	kEUR	kEUR	kEUR
Sum	4237					−273	−228	−161	−160

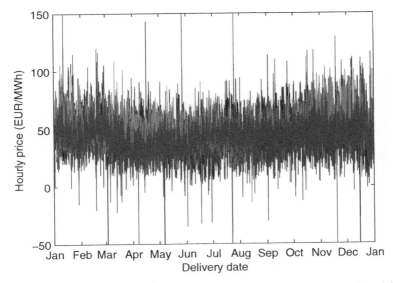

Figure 3.13   Hourly prices for the front year, simulated using the SMaPS model.

The value $V(t_0)$ of the considered portfolio position $\hat{L}_H$ at t_0 is

$$V(t_0) = \sum_{i=1}^{8760} e^{-r(T_i - t_0)} \hat{L}_H(t_0, T_i) F(t_0, T_i),$$

with the (continuously compounded) interest rate r. In our numerical example the value of the remaining power schedule $\hat{L}_H$ is −273 350 EUR. This means that at the date of concluding the retail contract there are expected costs of 273 350 EUR additional to the costs of the baseload contract. These costs are uncertain at t_0 since $\hat{L}_H$ can hardly be hedged at the forward market and the remaining power schedule $\hat{L}_H$ has to be purchased/sold successively at the spot market. Our aim is to calculate this risk using the PaR measure. The most sophisticated part of the calculation is the construction of an electricity spot price model. For our example, the SMaPS model is used (see Section 6.2.1). Figure 3.13 illustrates some price paths for the front year generated with SMaPS. These price paths are consistent with the actual market prices; they meet on average the baseload and peakload prices for the front months, quarters and front year.

Zooming in on Figure 3.13 results in the more detailed Figure 3.14, where daily and weekly patterns of electricity prices for the first week of the front year are visible.

In the next step we evaluate $\hat{L}_H$ for each SMaPS scenario. For our numerical example we simulate $n = 100$ spot price paths for the front year, that is we generate spot price scenarios

$$S_k(t_0, T_i), \quad i \in \{1, 2, \dots, 8760\}, \; k \in \{1, \dots, n\}.$$

For scenario k the change in value of the considered portfolio is

$$\Delta_k V = \sum_{i=1}^{8760} e^{-r(T_i - t_0)} \hat{L}_H(t_0, T_i)(S_k(t_0, T_i) - F(t_0, T_i)).$$

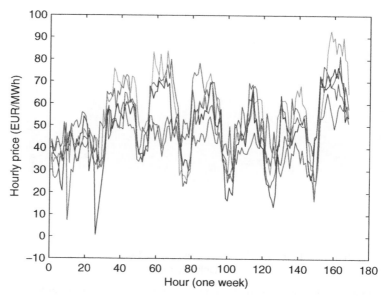

Figure 3.14 Hourly prices for the first week of the front year, simulated with the spot price model SMaPS.

In the next step the $\Delta_k V$ are ranked in increasing order. The results of this ranking for our numerical example are displayed in Table 3.4, for simplification discounting is ignored.

The highest loss in value of the portfolio occurs in scenario 37, followed by scenarios 94 and 1. In the last step, to determine PaR with a confidence level of α, the $(1 - \alpha)n$ lowest scenarios are ignored. The lowest remaining scenario u yields

$$\text{PaR}(\alpha) = \Delta_u V.$$

In our numerical example we calculate the PaR with a confidence level of 98%. The lowest 2% of the scenarios (scenario 37 and scenario 94) are ignored. Scenario 1 yields

$$\text{PaR}(98\%) = \Delta_1 V = 160\,000\,\text{EUR}.$$

This means that the market price risk of the hedged customer load is still 160 000 EUR because of the hourly profile, which can be balanced one day before delivery only. Note that the change in value between the lowest scenario 37 and the second lowest scenario 94 is large. As a consequence, 100 scenarios for calculating PaR with a confidence level of 98% are too little. In practice, 1 000 or even more scenarios are needed for sufficient accuracy.

3.3 LEGAL RISK

Each market transaction needs to have a reliable contractual basis, which also determines the future credit risk management possibilities. For single, complex products individual

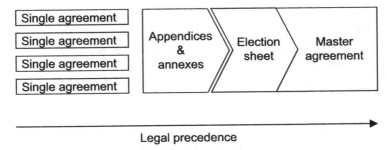

Figure 3.15   Contract structure.

agreements are reasonable. However, for a regular and efficient trading of standard products, master agreements between the counterparties are necessary. After signing a master agreement each subsequent individual transaction refers to this master agreement and therefore requires only a brief individual trade confirmation. To allow individual specifications, the master agreement includes an election sheet where alternatives of a certain clause can be selected. Usually, master agreements can be extended with annexes and appendices (e.g., for credit risk management). Figure 3.15 illustrates the contractual structure of trading contracts.

Master agreements: Master agreements are developed from different organisations with the intention of setting a standard. These organisations offer legal opinions from reputable law firms concerning their master agreements. For each trading company a standardised contractual basis has the vital advantage of a reduction in back-to-back risks (i.e., rights and liabilities of supply contracts match those of corresponding delivery contracts).

This standardisation should also include the election sheet. Because the election sheet is the result of negotiations, a perfect standardisation is not possible. An example for a contractual back-to-back risk is a far-ranging *Force Majeure* clause in a sourcing contract, whereas the corresponding sales contract has only a very limiting Force Majeure clause. In this case an interruption of the delivery cannot be passed on to the buyer.

Organisations providing common master agreements are:

ISDA – International Swaps and Derivatives Association
   ISDA is a large global trade association with over 800 member institutions from 60 countries. The ISDA master agreement is widely used for products with a financial settlement (e.g., swaps). ISDA also provides a credit support annex which further permits parties to mitigate their credit risk via exchanging collaterals.

EFET – European Federation of Energy Traders
   EFET is a group of more than 100 energy trading companies from 27 European countries and is designed to improve conditions for energy trading in Europe. EFET offers concerted general agreements, appendices and annexes for electricity, natural gas, LNG, CO_2 allowances and coal (based on SCoTA). An advantage of the EFET general agreements are the manifold appendices that regularise the individual trading activities. As an example, for natural gas trading there are specific appendices for the hubs NBP, TTF, GasPool, VTP and Zeebrugge. Regarding credit risk there are credit support and netting agreements available. Electronic confirmation agreements are the basis for efficient

back-office processes. The most significant general agreements published by EFET are the following.

- EFET Power: Master agreement for power with physical delivery.
- EFET Gas: Master agreement for gas with physical delivery.
- EFET Allowance Appendix: Appendix for CO_2 emission trading with physical delivery of the allowances.

globalCOAL

globalCOAL is a provider of an important online trading platform for physical and financial coal. The introduction of globalCOAL's Standard Coal Trading Agreement (SCoTA) in 2001 has set the standard for the contractual basis in seaborne thermal coal trading. SCoTA has over 1500 licensed users worldwide.

IETA – International Emissions Trading Association

IETA is an organisation dedicated to the establishment of effective systems for trading in greenhouse gas emissions. The IETA master agreement is therefore designed for CO_2 emission trading with physical delivery of the allowances.

EBF – European Banking Federation

EBF has published the European Master Agreement (EMA), which is supported in particular by German and French banks with the aim of establishing a European standard. On a national level there are master agreements like the Deutsche Rahmenvertrag, published by the Association of German Banks (Bundesverband deutscher Banken).

The legal aspects regulated by master agreements are manifold, depending on the commodity, the market area, the individual product, the governing law and individual risk management decisions. For a detailed discussion there is specialised literature for master agreements, like the ISDA master agreement (see Harding (2010)). A detailed treatment of legal aspects of derivative trading can be found, for example, in Franzen (2001). In the following we give a brief overview of some important legal aspects requiring regulation in the master agreements.

Liabilities and obligations

- *Obligations for delivery and acceptence of the commodity:* Obligations and responsibility concerning the network operator, transportation, storage or insurance must be determined.
- *Force Majeure:* Defined as an occurrence beyond the reasonable control of a party that prevents the party from fulfilling its obligations. Such an event can be war, strike, riot, crime or natural disasters and it must have a materially adverse effect on the ability of such party to perform its obligations. Sometimes technical problems or a drop-out of preceding sourcing is also defined as Force Majeure. Applicable Force Majeure events have to be defined in the master agreement. Managing Force Majeure is a risk management task. If sourcing fails because of Force Majeure, a downstream clause which allows the interruption to be passed on to the buyer eliminates or reduces back-to-back risks.
- *Remedies for failure to deliver and accept:* Failures to deliver or accept not excused by an event of Force Majeure constitute the right to receive a compensation amount from the failing party.
- *Limitation of liability:* A usual limitation is to exclude the liability for indirect or consequential damages. This may include technical damages for power plants in case of the delivery of off-grade fuels. Excluding back-to-back risks related to liabilities is also a risk management target.

- *Governing law:* The agreement is construed and governed by the chosen law. Referring a possible dispute to an arbitral tribunal can also be agreed. An advantage of an arbitral tribunal is to achieve a faster decision at lower costs.

Processes and invoicing

- *Confirming individual contracts:* Trading companies conclude hundreds or thousands of deals per day. These deals must be entered into the database of the risk management system. An obligation of sending a written confirmation decreases operational risk and misunderstanding.
- *Standardised payment dates:* Payment dates must be specified. A standardisation of payment dates is a precondition for payment netting and reduces fluctuations of liquidity.

Credit risk and netting

- *Early termination:* Material reasons for an early termination must be defined. This is usually non-performance, especially non-payment. An important reason for early termination is the insolvency of the counterparty. Even if a counterparty institutes against it a proceeding, seeking a judgement of insolvency under a bankruptcy or insolvency law, a material reason for early termination is founded.
- *Termination amount:* In case of early termination a termination amount equal to the present value of the contracts must be paid by the counterparties.
- *Netting:* Payment netting allows to aggregate payments and reduce settlement risks. Close-out netting is the aggregation of all liabilities and claims as a termination amount by one single payment "one logical second" before the insolvency of a counterparty. Close-out netting is an important component of credit risk management and is explained later in this section in more detail.
- *Right to require performance assurance:* In case of a material adverse change in respect of the other party, a right to require performance assurance is often agreed. Such a material change can be an adverse change in the credit rating or financial covenants. A performance assurance can be a letter of credit, cash or other securities.

In case of the bankruptcy of a counterparty, the master agreement regulates the further process mainly in two steps. The first step uses the early termination clause and terminates all contracts. This step is important to keep a calculable position and market risk exposure. For commodities, where supply is critical (e.g., electricity), the termination also increases the security of supply. Without termination the position would contain trades, where the performance is vague. The second step is the so-called close-out netting. Gains, losses and costs of all trades in the commodity are added and establish the termination amount. If the termination amount is for the benefit of the insolvency party it has to be paid, if not it has to be claimed in the insolvency proceedings. Sometimes these claims can be sold to companies bundling claims to increase bargaining power.

This general process in case of insolvency of a counterparty is supported by additional agreements. If several commodities are traded with a counterparty, a cross-product master agreement expands close-out netting on specified commodities. If there are several master agreements with a counterparty, material reasons for an early termination are harmonised in a master netting agreement. Such an agreement allows a simultaneous termination of all trades, even if they are concluded under different master agreements. An extension of the close-out

Counterparty default in the case of applicable close-out netting

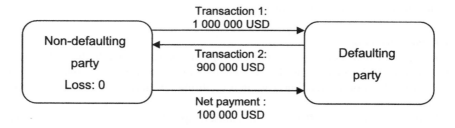

Counterparty default in the case of not enforceable close-out netting

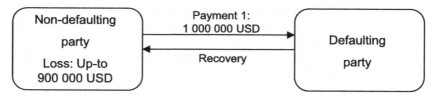

Figure 3.16   Close-out netting reduces credit risk.

netting on specified affiliates of a counterparty can be regulated in a cross-affiliate master netting agreement.

Particularly for trading companies, close-out netting is important and reduces credit risk significantly; for an example, see Figure 3.16. Therefore, close-out netting is part of most master agreements. However, close-out netting is sensitive with respect to the governing law. There are legal opinions which regard close-out netting as not always enforceable in some countries. In these countries there are requirements like margining, cash settlement or a financial institution as a counterparty for the applicability of close-out netting. The impact of a possibly not enforceable close-out netting is discussed, for example, by the International Swaps and Derivatives Association (ISDA), see Mengle (2010) or, by the Bank for International Settlements (BIS), see Bank for International Settlements (2002).

Credit support annex: A credit support agreement is the legal basis for the most effective credit risk management activity. If the Risk-at-Default exceeds a specified threshold, an eligible credit support (generally cash margins) has to be transferred.

3.4   CREDIT RISK

The importance of credit risk management for the energy sector has grown since the liberalisation of energy markets. In many countries, energy companies started as public sector institutions. So traditionally, many energy companies had a high degree of creditworthiness with valuable assets and stable cashflows. At such times credit risk was mainly regarded as the risk that customers could not pay for the energy obtained. Nowadays, in most industrial nations energy markets are fully liberalised and highly competitive, so that the financial strength of energy companies is varying strongly. Further, the availability of wholesale markets allows companies to be active only in parts of the value chain instead of being fully integrated. As a consequence, contractual agreements between companies have become an essential part of the companies' business models.

An important milestone for the improvement of credit risk management in the energy industry was the bankruptcy of Enron on December 2, 2001. Enron was one of the world's major electricity and natural gas companies based in Houston, TX. Enron employed approximately 20 000 staff and claimed revenues of nearly \$101 billion during 2000, while hiding losses in offshore accounts. Enron operated their own web-based transaction system EnronOnline for trading commodity products globally. Enron was acting as a market maker, the counterparty at EnronOnline was always Enron. Therefore, users had a credit risk with respect to Enron, which became evident during the Enron collapse.

Another milestone reforming credit risk management was caused by Lehman Brothers Holdings Inc., which filed for Chapter 11 bankruptcy protection on September 15, 2008. Traditionally, Lehman Brothers was involved in the commodity and energy business financing Murphy Oil and the TransCanada pipeline, as well as supporting the oil service business of Halliburton and the development of Kerr–McGee's oil and gas exploration and production business. Until their bankruptcy, Lehman Brothers was an active counterparty in commodity and energy trading. The bankruptcy of Lehman Brothers had a high impact on the financial sector and made the importance of margining agreements more prominent.

Nowadays, credit risk is one of the major risks being monitored and managed by energy companies. Utilities use growing wholesale markets to hedge their primary market risk from their asset positions. However, this requires instruments for limiting credit risk to achieve the overall hedge objectives.

Credit risk is an asymmetric risk when concluding forward contracts with financially weaker counterparties and therefore needs to be treated with special care. Entering into a forward contract does not require any capital, so there is no "natural" selection of creditworthy counterparties. If an energy company A concludes forward contracts with a financially weak counterparty B, A will lose money in the sense of an expectation value. If, at the settlement date, the forward contract has a negative value for A it has to be fulfilled. If the value is positive for A and therefore negative for B, there is a noteworthy probability that B becomes bankrupt and the positive value cannot be realised. While market risk always implies a chance, this is usually not the case for credit risk.

Credit risk is defined as the risk that a counterparty cannot fulfil its contractual obligations. The main obligations are the payment and agreed physical delivery or acceptance. So, credit risk always occurs, concluding OTC trades, while exchange-cleared trades bear no noteworthy credit risk. Credit risk can be classified as follows.

- *Settlement risk:* The settlement risk is defined as the possibility that a counterparty cannot pay the obtained benefits, for example the delivered energy amount. The settlement risk exists in nearly every business, therefore most companies have a credit risk management regarding settlement risk. The acceptance of claims in the case of insolvency is high. When entering a fixed-price contract, the development of settlement risk is predictable for the future.
- *Replacement risk:* The replacement risk is defined as the possibility that a counterparty will be unable to meet the terms of a contract even for the future and thus a new replacement

contract will have to be entered into. The new replacement contract can only be concluded under the actual market conditions and prices may differ negatively compared with the original contract. The replacement risk is the major risk for trading companies and depends on the development of market prices. Therefore, the development of replacement risk is not predictable for the future. Regarding retail contracts, the acceptance of claims in the case of insolvency usually fails.

Example: A utility A sells 12 000 tonnes of coal in Amsterdam (API#2) to counterparty B for 120 USD/t in January 2015 for delivery at January 2018 and the continuously compounding interest rate for USD is 1% p.a. Assume that in January 2016 the price for coal is 100 USD/t. In case of bankruptcy of B in January 2016 the settlement risk is zero, because A still has not delivered the coal to B. However, A has a loss caused by the replacement risk, because reselling the coal to another counterparty in January 2016 can be done for the actual market price of 100 USD/t only. The settlement risk is therefore

$$12\,000 \text{ tonnes} \times 20 \text{ USD/t} \times \exp(-0.01 * 2) = 235\,248 \text{ USD}.$$

Credit risk exposure is defined as the sum of the settlement and the replacement risk.

Credit risk management has several components, as described in the next sections. An overview is given in Figure 3.17. After the contractual preparation, credit risk management

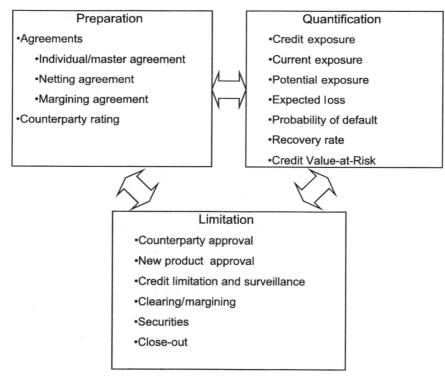

Figure 3.17   Credit risk components.

starts with counterparty analysis, followed by credit risk quantification and surveillance. Subsequently, the credit risk limitation includes credit risk-reducing activities like operational margining or security management.

3.4.1   Credit Rating

Besides the contractual basis, the counterparty analysis is the second most important step to prepare an OTC trading relationship with a counterparty. The counterparty analysis itself consists of several steps, where analysing the financial strength is perhaps the most complex task. Other steps of the counterparty analysis – like due diligence activities – are described in the operational risk section.

The simplest way to check the financial strength of a counterparty is by using a rating agency or a business information service. The international rating agencies Moody's, Standard & Poor's (S&P) and Fitch provide detailed credit analyses for most large companies. These international rating agencies have a broad database and a wide experience and can deliver widely accepted ratings which are adjusted continuously. The relevant counterparties can be observed with little effort using a watchlist. Actual rating-relevant information about the counterparties marked in the watchlist will then be sent to the rating agencies' customers. In contrast, large corporate rating agencies have been criticised, particularly after the 2007–2009 financial crisis. Errors of judgement in rating structured products have become evident. Another allegation is that rating agencies do not downgrade companies promptly enough and they are accused of being too close to their clients. Agencies are also accused of being oligopolistic. Nevertheless, the judgement of the rating agencies is still essential for issuers of debt instruments and generally for the valuation of the financial strength of a company. The methodology and judgement of these large rating agencies will be explained later in more detail.

Besides these large international rating agencies there are several smaller agencies and business information services like Dun and Bradstreet, Coface, Creditreform or Euler Hermes. Often these smaller agencies offer credit insurances, which have the possibility of reducing credit risks. Smaller counterparties not rated by an international rating agency are often analysed by these business information services. This is a reasonable and simple possibility for valuing the financial strength of a counterparty. However, because of the differing amount of available data of a counterparty, the quality of the credit judgement varies and the used data and methodology to achieve a credit opinion is not always transparent. For companies with higher requirements on the credit risk management process, an internal analysis of a counterparty's creditworthiness is therefore necessary.

We start with a consideration of the rating system of the large international rating agencies, before explaining the basic features of an internal rating process. More detailed descriptions can be found in comprehensive publications concerning credit analysis, like Laurentis *et al.* (2010).

External Ratings

The definitions for long-term ratings of the international rating agencies are similar, and, as an example, Moody's rating definition is explained in Table 3.5. Table 3.6 shows, how these ratings can be transferred.

A rating can be considered as an estimated classification of probabilities of default for the future. If the rating and credit exposure are known, an expected loss or the credit VaR

Table 3.5   Moody's long-term ratings definitions

Rating	Definition
Aaa	Highest quality, minimal credit risk
Aa	High quality, subject to very low credit risk
A	Upper–medium grade, subject to low credit risk
Baa	Medium grade, subject to moderate credit risk
Ba	Speculative elements, subject to substantial credit risk
B	Speculative, subject to high credit risk
Caa	Poor standing, subject to very high credit risk
Ca	Highly speculative and likely in, or very near, default
C	Lowest rated class and typically in default

Note: Moody's appends numerical modifiers 1, 2 and 3 to each generic rating classification from Aa through Caa. Modifier 1 indicates that the rank is at the higher end of its generic rating category, modifier 2 indicates a mid-range ranking and modifier 3 a ranking at the lower end of that generic rating category.

Table 3.6   Long-term rating scales comparison

Moody's	Aaa	Aa1	Aa2	Aa3	A1	A2	A3	
S&P	AAA	AA+	AA	AA−	A+	A	A−	
Fitch	AAA	AA+	AA	AA−	A+	A	A−	
Baa1	Baa2	Baa3	Ba1	Ba2	Ba3	B1	B1	B3
BBB+	BBB	BBB−	BB+	BB	BB−	B+	B	B−
BBB+	BBB	BBB−	BB+	BB	BB−	B+	B	B−
Caa1	Caa2	Caa3	Ca	C				
CCC+	CCC	CCC−	CC	C	D			
CCC+	CCC	CCC−	CC	C	D			

can be determined. So, knowing these probabilities is essential for determining credit risk. Rating agencies and some banks have a broad database and offer probabilities of default for the different rating categories. These probabilities are estimated from statistical data. For the highest-ranking categories there are only a few events of default, which makes estimating the probability of default difficult. Also, empirically determined default probabilities may not have the desired properties of an increasing probability of default for lower rating categories or longer time horizons. Therefore, the default probability tables are sometimes smoothed to offer the desired properties. Table 3.7 shows default probabilities published by Moody's Investors Service, inc. S&P also publishes default probabilities in its *Annual Global Corporate Default Study and Rating Transitions* report, for example.

In the event of default, there is a fraction of the exposure (*recovery rate*) which may be recovered through bankruptcy proceedings or some other form of settlement. Estimating the recovery rate is difficult, but there are also published rates. For example, Moody's has used a recovery rate of 45% for the generation of their idealised expected loss table.

Internal Ratings

Even if internal ratings are used, the structure should be matchable to those of rating agencies. If there is a mapping from an internal rating to a rating category of a rating agency, default probabilities and recovery rates can be used which are otherwise difficult to obtain.

Table 3.7   European issuer-weighted cumulative default rates, 1985–2012

Moody's Rating	Year					
	1	2	3	4	5	10
Aaa	0.0%	0.0%	0.0%	0.0%	0.0%	0.0%
Aa	0.0%	0.1%	0.2%	0.3%	0.4%	1.0%
A	0.2%	0.4%	0.9%	1.3%	1.9%	5.4%
Baa	0.2%	0.6%	1.0%	1.3%	1.7%	5.6%
Ba	1.1%	2.9%	4.2%	5.3%	5.8%	12.7%
B	2.6%	7.1%	12.0%	16.6%	20.8%	27.6%
Caa–C	15.1%	25.6%	34.1%	40.3%	45.2%	56.3%

Source: Adapted from European Corporate Default and Recovery Rates, 1985–2012. © Moody's Investors Service, Inc. and/or its affiliates. Reprinted with permission. All rights reserved.

An internal rating is usually based on specified criteria which will be evaluated in a scoring approach. There are evaluation categories for each of the rating criteria. The number of these evaluation categories should be sufficient to avoid volatile results.

The factors for the determination of an internal rating can be differentiated into quantitative and qualitative criteria. The quantitative criteria can be obtained from business reports, financial statements, etc. and refer to the past. Qualitative criteria are appraisals referring to the future of a company. Usually, the qualitative factors have a weighting of 40–60%. If the internal rating is used only in the context of the credit risk of the trading activities, the fraction of the qualitative factors can be lower. The reason for this is that the business sectors of the counterparties are similar and rating criteria based on the sector do not result in a differentiation of the rating. The applied factors and their weights are the decision of the responsible rating unit and cannot be generalised, but some frequently used criteria are listed below.

Common *quantitative factors* for an internal rating are as follows.

- *Size of the company:* The size of the company measured by its balance sheet total.
- *Company's owners:* The structure and financial strength of the company's owners.
- *Tangible net worth:* The tangible net worth is a measure of the physical worth of a company. Tangible net worth is calculated by taking a firm's total assets and subtracting the value of all liabilities and the value of all intangible assets (e.g., copyrights, patents and intellectual property).
- *Revenue reserves:* Trends of increase or decrease in revenue reserves.
- Criteria based on debt and repayment are as follows.
  - *Funds from operations to total debt:* The amount of cash generated or employed by the company in its operating activities in proportion to its total debt.
  - *Funds from operations to interests:* The amount of cash generated or employed by the company in its operating activities in proportion to its interest payments.
  - *Total debt to total capitalisation:* Total debt in proportion to equity and long-term debt.
  - *EBIT to interests:* Earnings before interest and taxes in proportion to the paid interests.
- Criteria concerning maturity matching are as follows.
  - *Current assets:* Current assets in proportion to current liabilities.
  - *Equity/assets ratio:* Equity and long-term debt in proportion to the asset capital.
- *Return on equity:* The return on equity (ROE) is a measure of a company's profitability, revealing how much profit it generates with the money shareholders have invested.

- Criteria concerning the development of the business ratios are as follows.
  - *Development of sales:* Annual percentage change of sales.
  - *Development of the operative margin:* Annual percentage change of the operative margin.

The quantitative factors must be adapted to the applied accounting standard (IFRS, US-GAAP, etc.). While the quantitative factors can be analysed more or less mechanically, most qualitative factors require an estimation by an analyst with good knowledge of the business sector.

Common *qualitative factors* for an internal rating are as follows.

- *Market position of a company:* Is the company among the leading companies in its sector?
- *Sector characteristics:* Are there high market entry barriers? Are there substitute products?
- *Economic situation of the sector:* Is there a boom, a stable cycle or a recession?
- *Duration of the business connection:* How long has the business connection existed with the counterparty?
- *Payment history:* Did the company exceed the terms of payment in the history of the relationship?
- *Seasonality of cashflow:* Are there substantial seasonal fluctuations of the cashflow?
- *Place of business:* Where is the registered office of the company located?

A calibration of an internal rating method with external ratings is useful. For this purpose some companies with an external rating are chosen and after applying the internal rating method the result is compared with the external rating. For substantial differences there should be an obvious reason, otherwise the weights or the rating criteria should be re-evaluated.

3.4.2   Quantifying Credit Risk

The preceding subsections explained the preparatory steps of the credit risk management process. Now, the quantification and surveillance of credit risk will be described. There are several risk figures available to quantify credit risk, depending on their intended usage. We start with an explanation of the most important credit risk measures, followed by a numerical example.

- *Risk-at-Default:* The Risk-at-Default figure specifies how much the company will lose as a result of the default of a specified counterparty. The loss is contingent upon the amount to which the firm was exposed at the time of default. A recovery rate may be assumed (the amount that a creditor would receive in final satisfaction of his claims).
- *Expected loss:* The expected loss is the product of the calculated credit exposure (Risk-at-Default) and the estimated probability of default.
- *Potential exposure:* Analogous to the market risk metric of VaR, the potential exposure is the maximal likely credit exposure at a given confidence level (e.g., 98%), while market prices are shifted. This means that market price scenarios are used to generate scenarios for the credit risk exposure. For fixed-price contracts the settlement risk is predictable and the scenarios concern the replacement risk only, but for indexed contracts scenarios for the settlement risk must be generated as well. The potential exposure answers the question: "What is the most I could lose to this counterparty with some degree of confidence?" and is useful for limit setting and stress testing.
- *Credit VaR:* Credit VaR can be defined similarly to the way VaR is defined for market risk. With a given confidence level α and a holding period according to the duration of the

contracts, the credit VaR is the $(1 - \alpha)$ quantile of the loss as a consequence of a default. In contrast to potential exposure, market prices are usually kept constant and the default of the counterparties in the portfolio is the relevant and simulated random variable. Given a large number of counterparties, defaults can be simulated with a Monte Carlo simulation and probabilities of default can be found in Table 3.7. For banks, where credit risk is the main risk, the confidence level is often deduced from their own target rating. The probability of non-default of this target rating can be used as a confidence level. Events beyond this confidence level are as seldom as the insolvency of their own rating category and the credit risk calculated in this way can be compared, for example, with the equity capital. An approach for obtaining the joint distribution function of the risk caused by default of one or more counterparties is the Gaussian copula model of time to default. For banks, models for credit rating changes are also necessary, because of their influence on bond prices. If credit risk is only used to manage the default risk of trading counterparties, modelling the credit rating changes is less important.

Example: We assume that an energy supplier Z with a Moody's rating Aa sells the portfolio described in Table 3.2 on the OTC market in December 2014. Counterparty X with a Moody's rating Aa purchases the total power position and counterparty Y with a Moody's rating Baa sells the total coal position, the required USD and CO_2 certificates. The transaction price is always the market price as indicated in Table 3.2. One year after, the transaction credit risk should be determined and it is assumed that market prices have changed as specified in Table 3.8.

For a simplification of the following explanations, discounting effects are ignored.
   Risk-at-Default: A calculation of the mark-to-market value V_X, V_Y of all transactions with counterparty X (respectively Y) yields (quoted in million EUR)

$$V_X = 40 + 25 = 65, \quad V_Y = 20 + 2.73 - 1 = 21.73.$$

In case of immediate insolvency of counterparty X (respectively Y), the positive mark-to-market value cannot be realised. The replacement risk is therefore EUR 65 million for counterparty X and EUR 21.73 million for counterparty Y. Because there has been no energy delivered until now, the settlement risk is zero and the Risk-at-Default is also EUR 65 (respectively EUR 21.73) million. Assuming a recovery rate of 45% as implied by Moody's Idealised Expected Loss Table, the Risk-at-Default reduces to EUR 35.75 (respectively EUR 11.95 million).
   Expected loss: For the calculation of the expected loss, again a recovery rate of 45% is used. The first payments start in one year, and all payments end in 25 months. So, we choose

Table 3.8   Market prices one year after OTC transaction

Product	Transaction price	Actual market price
Baseload 2017	40 EUR/MWh	36 EUR/MWh
Peakload 2017	45 EUR/MWh	40 EUR/MWh
Coal 2017	70 EUR/t	90 EUR/t
USD 2017	0.77 EUR/USD	0.8 EUR/USD
CO_2-EUA 2017	3 EUR/t	2 EUR/t

a conservative holding period of two years and using Table 3.7 we get the expected loss rate of 0.055% for X (respectively 0.33% for Y). This results in an expected loss of EUR 35 750 for X and EUR 71 709 for Y.

Potential exposure: In Section 3.2.3 the Value-at-Risk of the portfolio in December 2014 was calculated. Recalculating the Value-at-Risk with December 2015 prices (but unchanged correlations and volatilities) gives a market risk VaR of EUR 32.98 million for the portfolio sold to X and EUR 5.52 million for the portfolio sold to Y. Selling this position to a counterparty means that the credit risk rises in the case of a negative mark-to-market value of the original portfolio positions. Therefore, during a holding period of 10 days and with a given confidence level of 98%, the credit exposure does not exceed the:

$$\text{potential exposure for } X = V_X + 32.98 = 97.98,$$

$$\text{potential exposure for } Y = V_Y + 5.52 = 27.25.$$

If requested, a recovery rate can additionally be assumed. Further, instead of a 10-day holding period, the full transaction tenor can be considered. Generally, the potential future exposure increases with a longer time horizon. However, when entering the delivery period, the potential future exposure declines again, because the outstanding volume decreases.

Credit VaR: Following the idea of deducing the confidence level from the own (assumed as target) rating, and using the fact that the supplier Z has a probability of default of 0.1%, the confidence level of the credit VaR is chosen as 99.9%. The probability of default of the counterparties X and Y is 0.1% (respectively 0.6%). Assume that a possible insolvency of X and Y is independent. There is no data available for estimating a probability distribution of a recovery rate. Because of the high confidence level, we assume a recovery rate of zero. So, there are the four possible credit event losses EUR 86.73, EUR 65, EUR 21.73 and EUR 0 million. Referring to the VaR in equation (3.4), the credit VaR is the highest loss (lowest performance) with a probability of occurrence higher than or equal to 0.1%. Since the simultaneous insolvency of X and Y is not probable enough, the insolvency of X can cause the highest loss with a sufficient probability of occurrence of 0.1% and therefore the credit VaR is EUR 65 million.

Credit Risk-Reducing Activities

Reducing credit risk is a key task of credit risk management. While market risk can be reduced easily by closing an open position, reducing credit risk is not straightforward. If utility A buys a forward from a counterparty B and the price for this forward increases, the credit risk increases as well. If there is no other agreement, A has no possibility to control the credit risk without cooperation from B. The credit risk is market price driven only. For an effective credit risk management, most risk-reducing arrangements must be made before concluding contracts. Common credit risk-reducing methods are listed below.

- *Margining agreement.* The most powerful instruments for limiting credit risk are margining agreements. As described in Section 3.3, the legal basis is a credit support annex, such as published by ISDA or EFET. Both parties agree on a credit limit (normally a bilateral limit) and, if the credit exposure of one of the parties exceeds their limit, this party needs to provide a margin payment as collateral to the other party. This implies that the values of all derivatives between each of the parties are periodically (often daily) marked-to-market, which excludes illiquid products from the margining process. In contrast to the variation margin on an exchange, the OTC margin is an eligible credit support and not a regular cashflow of the derivative. Consequently, these cash securities are interest-bearing. The interest rate is often a short-rate index defined in the credit support annex. An obligation of a margining process for clearing OTC derivatives may be an element of market regulations like the European Market Infrastructure Regulation (EMIR) or the United States Dodd–Frank Wall Street Reform and Consumer Protection Act, at least for the major counterparties.

- *Credit sleeve.* A common credit risk management instrument is credit sleeves, particularly for OTC trades via a broker. Sleeving a trade will come into consideration if counterparty X wants to conclude a trade with counterparty Y but cannot accept the related credit risk. In this case a third party Z will be identified (for example by the involved broker) that is acceptable as a counterparty for X and Y. This third party sleeves the trade for X and Y, that is he buys (respectively sells) a specified product from X and resells it to (or buys it from) Y for the same price or with a small additional margin.

- *Portfolio compression.* Energy traders that buy and sell energy on the forward market can reduce their gross credit risk significantly by a portfolio compression. A regular portfolio compression is a risk management method required by market regulations like the EMIR or the United States Dodd–Frank Wall Street Reform and Consumer Protection Act. With a portfolio compression, existing trades are terminated or replaced by a smaller number of new trades with substantially smaller notionals that carry the same risk profile and cashflows as the initial portfolio. A portfolio compression also reduces operational burdens and operational risks. There are providers offering a portfolio compression service. From a named set of trades they identify the trades suitable for a compression. While bilateral trades can be identified easily, this can be more complex if multiple counterparties are involved. Figure 3.18 illustrates the effect of a portfolio compression. The mark-to-market value must be cleared with additional cashflows or with price adjustments.

- *Exchange of futures for physicals.* If counterparties have concluded an OTC transaction there are exchanges (e.g., the EEX) which offer to transfer the transaction in a regular

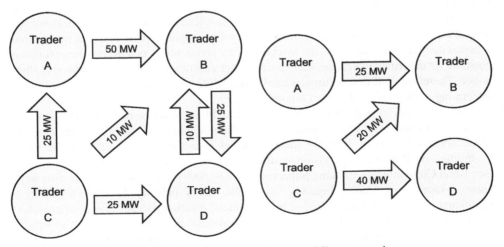

Figure 3.18   Deals before and after a portfolio compression.

futures position. Because of the margining, credit risk can be reduced immediately. As a disadvantage there are exchange fees, modified cashflows and perhaps implications on the accounting treatment.

- *Additional collateralisation.* The party on the downside of the transactions may collateralise their transactions additionally. The collateralisation can be included in the credit risk calculation or increase the allocated credit risk.
- *Countertrade.* If there is a netting agreement, the conclusion of a countertrade with the same counterparty reduces the settlement risk of sold forward contracts and locks the actual replacement risk. The arising market position can be closed with another counterparty or on an exchange. Since the countertrade is concluded at the actual market price, the replacement risk is not reduced immediately. A subsequent portfolio compression and payment of the mark-to-market value also eliminates the replacement risk.
- *Price adjustment.* The price of transactions with high replacement risk can be adjusted on the actual market price. The present value of the price adjustment will be paid directly. The modified cashflow may have implications for accounting treatment.

3.5 LIQUIDITY RISK

For a definition of liquidity risk we distinguish between market liquidity risk and funding liquidity risk.

- *Market liquidity risk* is defined as the lack of marketability of a commodity or a derivative. Market liquidity risk is typically reflected in wide bid–offer spreads or low open interest. Another indication of a significant market liquidity risk is an expanding bid–offer spread while executing a large order on the market. As a consequence, stop-loss orders can result in high losses, and significant positions can be difficult to close or require a long time period to close. Some popular examples where excessive positions led to large losses are connected to hedge funds. An example is Amaranth Advisors LLC, who in 2006 held a position representing around 10% of the global market in natural gas futures resulting in a loss of USD 6 billion. Another popular example is the loss of Long-Term Capital Management L.P. (LTCM) with its former principals Myron S. Scholes and Robert C. Merton. However, market liquidity risk can also be significant for energy suppliers, particularly in fragmented regional markets. An example is the asset book of a power utility containing the generation position. As described in Section 3.2.6, a significant generation cannot be liquidated at short notice. Therefore, VaR underestimates market risk while LVaR is designed as a risk measure integrating market risk and market liquidity risk.
- *Funding liquidity risk* is defined as the risk that liabilities cannot be met when they fall due or can only be met at an uneconomic price. Funding liquidity risk was a key characteristic of the financial crisis in 2008 for many financial institutions. As a reaction, the Basel Committee on Banking Supervision issued a framework for liquidity risk measurement (see Basel Committee on Banking Supervision 2008, 2009). There are, however, also well-known examples of funding liquidity risk in the energy industry. In 2002, following a significant and sustained deterioration in its financial position, British Energy approached the UK Department of Trade and Industry for financial assistance because it otherwise risked falling into administration. The Department agreed to support a plan for restructuring British Energy. Another example is the 1993 Metallgesellschaft debacle. Futures contracts

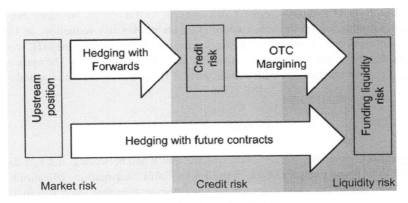

Figure 3.19   Transformation of risk type.

were used to hedge an OTC finance obligation. A liquidity crisis caused by staggering margin calls on the futures forced Metallgesellschaft to unwind the positions, resulting in a loss of USD 1.3 billion. Nowadays, the extended clearing of OTC derivatives, which successfully reduces credit risk, may increase funding liquidity risk due to margin payments. In particular, energy companies with a significant upstream position like power generation, oil or natural gas fields or coal mines want to reduce market risk. Selling the energy on the forward market reduces market risk but creates credit risk with OTC counterparties. An OTC margin agreement reduces credit risk but results in a funding liquidity risk. This interrelation is shown in Figure 3.19.

The Basel Committee on Banking Supervision has developed two standards for supervisors to use in funding liquidity risk supervision (see Basel Committee on Banking Supervision (2009)). Even though these standards are designed for financial institutions, they are a useful basis for liquidity risk management for energy companies. The first standard, the *liquidity coverage ratio*, addresses the sufficiency of a stock of high-quality liquid assets to meet short-term liquidity needs under a specified acute stress scenario. The second standard, the *net stable funding ratio*, addresses longer-term liquidity mismatches.

The liquidity coverage ratio and the corresponding minimal requirement are defined as

$$\frac{\text{stock of high-quality liquid assets}}{\text{net cash outflows over a 30-day time period}} \geq 100\%.$$

In this definition the stock of high-quality liquid assets must be unencumbered, clearly convertible into cash and sufficient to cover cumulative net cash outflows. Ideally these assets are central bank eligible, which secures that a company's bank accepts these assets without difficulty. The net cash outflow over a 30-day period is determined under an acute liquidity stress scenario. For financial institutions, the Basel Committee on Banking Supervision has defined basic assumptions for the stress scenario. These include a credit rating downgrade, a loss of secured and unsecured assets and an increase in market volatilities, accompanied by larger variation margins. The basic points of the stress scenario must be completed by individual stress tests adapted to the specific business activities.

The following brief examples transfer this concept to the energy business. For a utility, selling power production on the wholesale market for market risk reduction, an increase in variation margins is part of an individual stress scenario. We reconsider the OTC transactions between the supplier Z and the counterparties X, Y according to Table 3.8. The mark-to-market values V_X, V_Y of all transactions with counterparty X (respectively Y) was (quoted in million EUR)

$$V_X = 65, \quad V_Y = 21.73.$$

Assuming an OTC margining agreement between Z and X and between Z and Y, X and Y need EUR 65 million (respectively EUR 21.73 million) to fulfil their margin obligations. A stress test before concluding the margin agreement must demonstrate that the respective company is prepared for such a potential decrease of liquidity. Vice versa, Z must have the financial strength to fulfil their obligations under opposite market conditions. Generating risk scenarios with respect to funding liquidity risk includes the impact of margin scenarios on the net cash outflow.

The *net stable funding ratio* and the corresponding minimal requirement are defined as

$$\frac{\text{available amount of stable funding}}{\text{required amount of stable funding}} > 100\%.$$

For the net stable funding ratio the definitions of the available amount of stable funding (respectively the required amount of stable funding) are crucial. There is a detailed regulation for financial institutions published by the Basel Committee. The available amount of stable funding consists of several components weighted by a factor. 100% eligible is the total amount of capital, including both Tier 1 and Tier 2 as defined in the standards of the Basel Committee. Also, the total amount of secured and unsecured borrowings and liabilities with effective maturities of one year or greater is 100% eligible. Excluded are instruments with explicit or embedded options that can reduce the expected maturity to less than one year. Less eligible are, for example, stable wholesale fundings or retail deposits. The required amount of stable funding is calculated as the sum of the value of the assets held and funded by the financial institution, multiplied by a specific required stable funding factor. This factor is, for example, 85% for loans to retail clients, 50% for unencumbered equity securities, 20% for unencumbered corporate bonds (rated at least AA) with an effective maturity of more than a year and zero for cash.

3.6 OPERATIONAL RISK

Following the definition of the Basel Committee on Banking Supervision (cf. Basel Committee on Banking Supervision (2011)), *operational risk* is defined as the risk of loss resulting from inadequate or failed internal processes, people and systems or from external events. In the committee's definition, legal risk is included, strategic and reputational risk are excluded. In this book, legal risk is discussed separately, because of the specific context in the energy trading business. Operational risk differs from other types of risk, because it is not used to generate profit. While market risk is typically exploited by traders and fund managers and credit risk is exploited by lending institutions to create a profit, operational risk should always be as low as possible.

The Basel Committee elaborates the principles of sound operational risk management. These principles include the establishment of a strong risk management culture, development and regular review of an integrated framework for operational risk management, approval of the risk appetite and tolerance statement, establishment of identification, monitoring and reporting processes for operational risk and enforcement of adequate approval processes for all new products, activities and processes. Even though these principles are developed to manage the operational risk of financial institutions, they can be transferred to the energy industry. The practical adaption of operational risk management tasks to the energy industry is explained in more detail below. This concerns identification, monitoring and reporting processes for operational risk and the approval processes for new products and counterparties.

Risk identification concerning operational risk starts with a workshop or interviews with key experts or respectively process owners about the risks of all relevant processes. As a basis, the operational business process framework, which provides information on the main tasks and activities of the organisation, can be used. The risks can be classified according to the frequency of their occurrence and the amount of potential damage. They can also be categorised with respect to risk types (e.g., fraud, system failures and business disruption, damage to physical assets, failures of the execution and delivery process or failures caused by data errors). These potential risk scenarios should be complemented with a loss data collection on actual loss events. In a first step, actual losses of materialised historical operational risks of the own organisation shall be collected. This requires a reporting process of losses and an appropriate corporate culture. In a second step, these internal data can be complemented with external data. External data are available only in particular cases (e.g., fraud events are sometimes published), but they support the identification of hidden risks. For the risk management of operational risk, key risk indicators for the identified operational risks are useful. In energy trading this can be IT-related performance indicators, adherence to implemented trading limits, outstanding or not confirmed trading confirmations, employee turnover or indicators for market turbulence.

Operational risk can subsequently be aggregated using an operational VaR (cf. Böcker and Klüppelberg (2005)). This requires additional assumptions about the distributions and correlations between the different sources of operational risk. Because empirical data show heavy-tailed distributions for operational risks, the choice of the distribution is critical. For approval of a risk appetite statement, a calculation of operational VaR is useful. However, the practical risk management concerning operational risk depends on the specific source of risk.

Trading new products is such a common source of operational risk that an established approval process should be an essential part of operational risk management. The approval process clarifies processes and respective roles and the responsibilities of the parties involved. The usual topics to be addressed during the approval process are listed below. The results of the assessment can be documented in a product approval form, which provides the basis for the final sign-off by senior management.

- *Business plan:* A business plan starts with a detailed description of the product and the development plan. The expected scale (e.g., trading volume, sales quantities, etc.) of the new business opportunity must be included. It also contains investments, expected costs, efforts, gains and a description of the advantages of the new product. A description of risks is also an essential part of the business plan.

- *Risk management and valuation:* An absolutely essential requirement is an agreed product valuation method. Products with unknown value must not be traded. Also, the risks involved must be known and appropriate procedures should be put in place to monitor and manage these risks.
- *Legal, compliance and taxation:* The approval process shall ensure that the necessary legal and regulatory inquiries and checks have been made and the outcomes are satisfactory. The consideration of reputational risk is also essential.
- *Accounting:* Before approval of new products is given, their accounting treatment needs to be clarified. Sometimes manual processes are necessary, and therefore the volume of these new products must be restricted.
- *Operations and IT systems:* The systems requirements necessary to support the product should be assessed and the necessary measures put in place to support the new product. For substantially new or modified products, closing a test deal is reasonable. Such a deal allows testing, the systems and processes with limited operational risks.
- *Post-implementation:* A review of the new product approval is advisable for several reasons.
  - Supervision of volume of the new product: Processes are designed for a specified volume. For new products this trading volume is uncertain. In the case of extraordinary success of the product, operations must be enforced. Vice versa, in the case of low acceptance, processes can be reduced or disposed of.
  - Supervision of pre-conditions: The product approval is often subject to pre-conditions. Pre-conditions can be an upgrade of the IT systems, contractual limitations or the traded volume.
  - Controlling of the business plan: Costs and gains must be controlled and supervised.

The importance of the approval process of new counterparties has grown rapidly during recent years. Credit risk and legal risk aspects are described in Section 3.4. However, special focus should also be put on compliance and reputational risk aspects. The requirements and responsibilities transferred from public authorities to private companies are diverse and increasing. Like financial institutions, energy companies need to be very careful not to get even indirectly linked with tax fraud, money laundering or corruption. Further, compliance with antitrust regulation and unbundling requirements is critical. These requirements often concern OTC trading and counterparty selection. Therefore, a regular, documented *know your customer (KYC)* process containing all relevant information about the counterparty is essential. Analogous to the responsibility of banks, the objective of KYC guidelines is to prevent commodity traders from being used for criminal purposes. Elements of the KYC process are as follows.

- *Questionnaire:* Potential counterparties have to fillout a questionnaire with the relevant information about their company. EFET has developed and published such a standard-ised questionnaire. Besides contact and identification details, information about authorised executives, classification and registration according to European or American regulation, memberships, auditors and owners are requested.
- *Combating threats:* Checking consolidated lists of financial sanctions targets or of ineligible firms published by the European Union, Worldbank or US authorities is a step in combating terrorist financing and other threats.

- *Verification:* Extracts of the commercial register, proof of authority, owners and business knowledge, checking of public information (Internet based) and business data (including address data) verify the data of the potential counterparty.

In the next step, the information about the intended counterparty must be evaluated. This leads to a final decision about the acceptance of the counterparty. Probably, this is the most delicate step of the approval process. Additional information like size, age, public awareness level, legal form and objective of the company are helpful to filter out eligible counterparties.

4

Retail Markets

This chapter describes the retail markets for electricity and natural gas. The two markets are similarly structured and many risk management processes are identical. Nevertheless, there are some technical differences that will be explained first. A core task both for supply of electricity and gas is balancing delivery and consumption volumes. However, in contrast to natural gas, electricity can hardly be stored, whereas storages (including storage capacity of pipelines) for natural gas are an important part of the gas logistics. As a consequence, electricity production must cover consumption even for short time periods. If we regard delivery volumes with electricity or gas as constant during each time period at a certain granularity, this granularity is usually finer for electricity than for gas. The (market-dependent) settlement period for electricity imposed by the grid operator is, for example, a quarter of an hour in Germany and half an hour in the UK, while the settlement period for natural gas is, for example, one hour or even one day. Consequently, traded products for electricity cover shorter time periods compared with natural gas (see also Sections 1.3 and 1.5). As an example, the electricity wholesale market typically offers peakload contracts in the forward and spot markets and single hours or even 15-minute contracts in the spot market. For natural gas, daily baseload contracts are typically the products with the finest granularity available. Another difference between electricity and gas supply is the stronger dependency of gas consumption on the daily temperature (see Section 4.5).

This chapter starts with the basic risk management processes for retail portfolios. Then, the most common types of retail contracts and their sourcing processes are explained. A further key topic of this chapter is the determination of adequate risk premia for retail products, which are included in the pricing for taking over the particular retail risks.

4.1 INTERACTION OF WHOLESALE AND RETAIL MARKETS

After the deregulation of the natural gas and electricity markets in many countries, the supply of gas and electricity was open to competition, that is, end-use customers can choose their supplier among competing retailers. For utilities, the role of the retail business changed from an embedded function tightly linked to electricity generation to a separate business unit competing with other retail companies and requiring their own risk management. Neither sales quantities nor sales prices are deduced from own upstream or generation facilities (respectively own costs) anymore. Instead, retail prices are deduced from wholesale prices, which provides an alternative channel for selling own upstream or generation volumes.

The actual opportunity may be restricted by market liquidity. However, even in markets with rather low trading activities, the market opportunity exists at least in a marginal consideration. That means, instead of selling natural gas or electricity to a specific customer, there is always the alternative of pushing this incremental energy to the wholesale market. Hence, for this

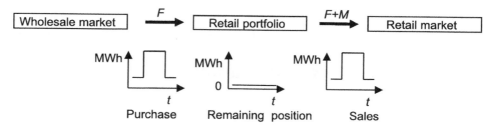

Figure 4.1   Portfolio of a utility with distribution only, idealised.

specific customer the retail price is still deduced from the wholesale price. Because this argument is also true for the next retail offer, prices for trading products will determine prices for end customers. These marginal considerations can also be found in other markets, for example, acquisition costs for a company are often based on actual stock prices, even though the trading volume is often significantly less than the acquisition volume.

As a basic scenario to explain the pricing process, we consider a utility selling a retail product that exactly matches a certain wholesale product. To minimise market risk, the utility covers its short position immediately after selling the energy to the end customer. The risk management process concerning price risk is as follows. First, the market price F of the corresponding trading product is determined. Subsequently, a price quotation to the end customer with the selected margin M can be made, which is $F + M$. If the customer accepts the offer, the short position in the portfolio can be covered with the corresponding trading product. So far, the risk management process is simple and does not differ from other markets. Figure 4.1 shows this idealised situation, where the retail portfolio contains the purchase of a forward contract with price F and the sale of the same forward contract with price $F + M$, and is not exposed to market risk.

The next step takes into account the difference between retail and traded products in the forward market. In this step a retail contract is regarded as an individual energy schedule resulting from the consumption forecast. Supplementary costs resulting from consumption uncertainty or from the demand of balancing energy are subsequently considered in Section 4.6.

As discussed in Chapter 1, predominantly baseload contracts for days, weeks, months, quarters, years and seasons are traded. In some electricity markets *peakload* contracts are also common. For all of these products, the delivered energy is constant over the delivery period. Since the utility is obliged to deliver the individual energy schedule resulting from the consumption forecast, wholesale forward contracts may only be used to purchase an approximate profile. Additional products with a finer granularity can be purchased only on the spot market. Because of the typically shorter settlement period for electricity compared with gas, the remaining spot market risk is usually higher on electricity markets compared with gas markets.

There are several approaches to identify standard forward contracts that are purchased in order to minimise the remaining price risk on the spot market. As a first idea, the remaining energetic position can be minimised, which means that the energy amount of the purchased forward contracts matches the consumption forecast. Other methods, such as hedging the delta position or minimising the variance of the profit and loss function, have been discussed in Section 3.2.

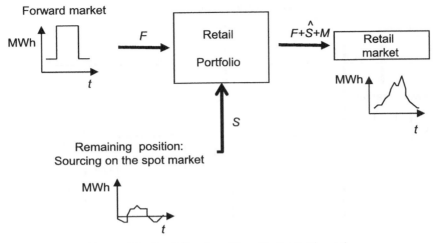

Figure 4.2 Portfolio of a utility with distribution only.

After hedging with standard forward contracts, the remaining position can be interpreted as a non-standard forward contract or energy schedule that can be covered at the spot market for a presently unknown price S. The retail customer will be charged with $F + \hat{S}$, where $\hat{S}$ denotes the presently expected value of S, but there remains a price risk. This yields the situation shown in Figure 4.2 and, in contrast to the idealised situation in Figure 4.1, the final margin is not fixed until the time of delivery.

The last consideration is the situation of a utility which also owns generation assets or upstream facilities. There is always the opportunity to sell the upstream energy into the wholesale market. This would require that some or all of the energy required for supplying end customers has to be purchased on the wholesale market. To be able to separate the profit or losses from the upstream (or generation) business from the retail (downstream) business, two separate portfolios can be created. The transaction price between the upstream and the downstream portfolio should be the price which can be obtained at the wholesale market. In this way, hedging of the upstream portfolio can be handled separately from retail hedging and follows a separate risk management strategy imposed by the utility. This process is shown in Figure 4.3, where an additional risk premium R is introduced to cover the remaining risks from the retail sales. This risk premium will be discussed in Section 4.6.

Concerning the retail pricing process, there is no significant difference between utilities owning upstream capabilities and utilities without any upstream portfolio. Wholesale markets for natural gas and electricity can be used to sell upstream capabilities (even optionalities) and purchase the required energy for the retail contracts. Subtle differences do, however, occur when risk premiums are considered. The position in the downstream portfolio is an energy schedule which can be covered by an internal transaction from the upstream portfolio. Electricity generation and natural gas upstream portfolios contain energy schedules and flexibilities in a fine granularity. This can (partly) mitigate the problem of high bid–offer spreads for individual energy schedules. The lower remaining price risk in the retail portfolio requires a smaller retail risk premium and the *price profile risk* in the upstream portfolio is reduced. Optionality and the Vega risk (see Section 5.3.4) can also be hedged by internal transactions. Such

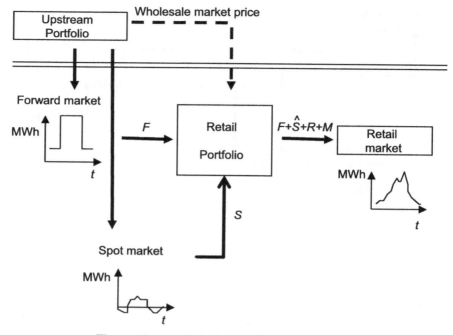

Figure 4.3   Portfolio of a utility with own generation.

transactions reduce the risk of both portfolios and provide integration benefits of integrated utilities.

This section concludes with a portfolio concept that supports the described processes. The profit of the upstream unit and the profit of the sales and distribution activity are shown separately as two essential portfolios. Transfer prices are always deduced from the wholesale price. Table 4.1 shows this portfolio concept for electricity.

The *downstream portfolio* contains all sales activities and the associated sourcing. The *upstream portfolio* includes assets, production, fuels and all transfers for retail sourcing and

Table 4.1   Portfolio concept

Generation portfolio (upstream)	Retail portfolio (downstream)

• Expected power generation and the resultant
  – Coal position
  – Gas position
  – Oil position
  – Nuclear-fuel position
  – Emission allowances position
  – FX position
• Asset-related contracts
• Transfers to the retail portfolio
• Sales and purchases on the wholesale market for hedging and optimisation purposes
	• Retail sales
	• Transfers from the generation portfolio
	• Purchases from the wholesale market

all energy sold on the wholesale market. The separate retail portfolio allows the utility to verify the adequacy of the risk premiums. The target value for the profit in the retail portfolio is the retail margin and the additionally aspired price for taking over the risk.

4.2 RETAIL PRODUCTS

In this section, the most common types of retail contracts are classified. Starting with the customers, we classify retail customers as follows.

- *Business-to-business customer (B2B)*: These are business customers with a consumption metered according to the settlement period of the TSO (e.g., 15-minute metering period). Such a metering will also be denoted as continuous metering.
- *Business-to-consumer customer (B2C)*: These are end customers where the consumption is metered as an energy amount of a time period significantly longer than the settlement period of the TSO (e.g., a yearly metering period). So, in particular, private households are B2C customers.

A classification of the types of retail contracts can be done with respect to the price formula or with respect to the quantity. Before describing in the following sections the different types of retail contracts, we introduce some notation used throughout this chapter. Time t is regarded as a discrete variable. The granularity of the time series corresponds to the granularity of the traded products or the settlement period of the TSO. As an example, this may be one hour for electricity and one day for natural gas. In this case, summing over t with $t \in [T_1, T_2]$ means summing over all single hours (respectively all single days) between date T_1 and T_2. $F(t_0, t)$ denotes the price of a forward contract valid at t_0 with delivery at t. Note that because of the fine granularity, $F(t_0, t)$ is usually not a trading product but calculated as an hourly (or daily) price forward contract, see Section 6.1.2. $\hat{L}(t_0, t)$ denotes the consumption forecast for the consumption at t forecasted at t_0. If t_0 is fixed, the notations $F(t)$ and $\hat{L}(t)$ are used.

4.2.1 Fixed-Price Contracts

Fixed-price contracts are supply contracts, with a previously agreed fixed price for a specified delivery period. In the simplest form the fixed price is a pure price $P + M + R$ per energy unit (e.g., kWh or MWh), where P denotes the pure commodity price, M the retail margin and R the risk premium. The pricing process requires forecasting the consumption of the customer $L(t), t \in [T_1, T_2]$, where $[T_1, T_2]$ is the delivery period. Then, the price component P per MWh for the expected consumption $\hat{L}(t)$ is

$$P = \frac{\sum_{t=T_1}^{T_2} \hat{L}(t)F(t)}{\sum_{t=T_1}^{T_2} \hat{L}(t)}. \tag{4.1}$$

While the fixed price P is calculated with a consumption forecast, the billing is based on the real consumption. P will be referred to as the *basic price* in the following.

As an alternative to pricing with a single fixed price per energy unit, time-dependent tariffs may be used. For example, the energy price can be composed of a *high tariff price* P_{HT} and a *low tariff price* P_{LT}, which is common for electricity retail products. The HT and LT tariffs can be aligned to peak and off-peak specifications of wholesale markets. Time-dependent tariffs reduce the risk that more energy than expected is used at times when energy prices are above average.

An alternative to a pure price per energy unit is to split P into a price for the energy P_L and a *demand charge* P_C for the maximum capacity used by the customer during the delivery period. The expected price to be paid by the customer needs to be the same in both cases, therefore the sum

$$P = P_{\hat{L}} + P_{\hat{C}} \frac{\hat{C}}{\hat{L}}$$

has to fulfil equation (4.1), where $\hat{L}$ denotes the accumulated expected consumption in $[T_1, T_2]$ and $\hat{C}$ is the expected maximal capacity. The advantage of a demand charge for the capacity is that the risk of higher sourcing prices caused by changing demand is reduced. If an industrial customer extends production during time periods when energy prices are typically high, this will increase the required capacity and the customer will pay a higher demand charge. In return, the supplier can reduce his risk premium as an advantage for the retail customer.

4.2.2 Indexed Contracts

Indexed contracts are an alternative for customers who want to be closer to the market development instead of fixing a price at the time the contract is signed. The main advantage for the purchaser is risk diversification, since it reduces the risk of buying the energy at the wrong moment when prices are near a local maximum. This is important when energy prices are relevant for the purchaser to be competitive in the market. Index-linked contracts are also interesting for resellers (e.g., municipalities) if the price can be fixed in parts. Then, the reseller can hedge its own sales contracts by fixing a corresponding part of the sourcing price. Let $I(t)$ denote the value of the index at t, T_0 the closing date of the contract, P the commodity price determined in equation (4.1), R the risk premium, M the retail margin and n the number of possible fixings, then a typical form of indexed price formula P_x is given by

$$P_x = (P + R + M)\frac{\sum_{k=1}^{n} I(t_k)}{nI(T_0)}, t_k \in [T_0, T_1]. \tag{4.2}$$

The buyer has the possibility to fix the energy price n times for a fraction $1/n$ of the total quantity. An example with four fixings is displayed in Figure 4.4.

If the purchaser does not actively fix the energy price, there is usually an automatic fixing at a specified date prior to delivery.

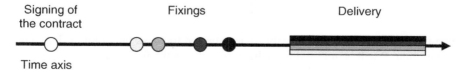

Figure 4.4   Fixing of indexed contracts.

The index can be a weighted average of two or more forward or futures contracts. As an example, for an electricity supply contract, let F_B, F_P denote the prices of a baseload respectively peakload contract. Then, a price index $I(t)$ that corresponds to a load profile with baseload and peakload components can be defined as

$$I(t) = (1 - a)F_B(t, T_1, T_2) + aF_P(t, T_1, T_2), a \in [0, 1].$$

The index is not necessarily the price of the commodity to be delivered. As an example, natural gas supply contracts in Europe have regularly been indexed to oil prices in the past (see Section 1.3.2). Further, electricity supply contracts can be indexed to a fuel price or the product of an energy-intensive industry (e.g., a price for metals). As an example, we consider an indexation to the coal API#2 index. Such a contract can be considered as a virtual power plant, since it involves similar commodity positions. Consider a EUR-based power supply contract indexed to coal prices with a monthly adjusted power price P_m valid for delivery month m. Let the positive number c be the coal price ratio, C_m the monthly average of the coal index for the month m, C_0 the initial value of the coal price index, X_m the average value of 1 USD in EUR for the month m, and $m = 0$ the initial month when the contract and P are fixed. Then, in our example, the power price P_m is

$$P_m = (P + M + R) \left[1 + c \left(\frac{X_m}{X_0} \frac{C_m}{C_0} - 1 \right) \right].$$

The coal price ratio c determines the influence of coal prices on the power supply price. If 1 t of coal is required to generate 3 MWh of electricity, this would yield a ratio of $c = 33\%$. The contract does not consider emission prices, which would also be relevant for a coal-fired plant in Europe, however the formula could be extended accordingly.

4.2.3   Full Service Contracts

Historically, almost all delivery contracts were *full service contracts*, where the customer purchases all consumption from one provider. The provider cares about the transmission and the customer has full flexibility in terms of how much energy he uses at any time. Because of this flexibility, the utility bears a *volume risk*. To limit this risk, a range of tolerance for the delivered energy can be agreed. In supply contracts for natural gas there is usually a clause defining such a tolerance band referring to the annual energy amount. In electricity supply contracts, such risk management arrangements are also gaining importance. Another risk caused by the flexibility of delivery is the *price profile risk*, that the actual consumption differs from the forecasted profile and causes higher costs. This is the case if consumption is higher than forecasted when energy is expensive and lower than forecasted when energy prices are low.

4.2.4   Partial Delivery Contracts

Since retail customers can change their supplier, *partial delivery contracts* have appeared to allow energy consumers to purchase their energy demand from more than one supplier at different points in time. Customers with partial delivery contracts can manage their energy portfolio without necessarily setting up a trading department. To avoid the risk of high prices

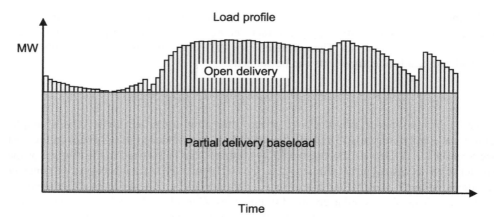

Figure 4.5 Partial delivery contract.

for balancing power, there is one specified supplier who owns the remaining *open contract*. This supplier must know the quantities of energy purchased from third parties by the customer and agree to deliver the remaining volumes. The supplier's risk in relation to the sold energy is higher compared with a full service contract, yielding a higher risk premium R. Figure 4.5 shows the general setup of partial delivery contracts.

The sourcing process of the supplier owning the open contract starts with forecasting the customer's consumption. Then the partial delivery volumes are defined, usually as a combination of standardised baseload contract quantities, and the price for the open contract and the risk premium can be determined. Purchasing the partial deliveries is the responsibility of the retail customer. In case the customer fails to purchase all partial deliveries there needs to be a fall-back arrangement such as an automatic price fixing by the supplier holding the open contract.

4.2.5   Portfolio Management

Portfolio management contracts provide even more flexibility for a retail customer to determine and manage the energy price risk they are prepared to take. With the described partial delivery contracts they have some of these possibilities, but restricted by predefined partial delivery products and using the services of the open contract provider. These possibilities can be expanded if the customer has a delivery contract which allows portfolio management by the customer's order. In this way the supplying utility acts more like a broker than a traditional supplier. The retail customer is responsible for determining exactly the points of time $k, k \in 1, \ldots, n$ when they want to buy standardised wholesale products $F(t_k, \cdot, \cdot)$. Energy not covered by the purchased wholesale products $F(t_k, \cdot, \cdot)$ will be complemented by purchasing spot products. The principle of these contracts is displayed in Figure 4.6.

The consumption forecast is the responsibility of the retail customer and deviations between the true consumption and the forecast are charged to the customer as balancing energy. This means that the customer needs to be able to forecast consumption as exactly as possible. The main risks for the customer are unpredictable prices for spot products and balancing energy. For an individual customer, prices for balancing energy can be significant. As part of a larger

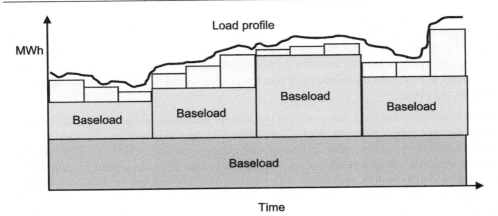

Figure 4.6   Portfolio management by customer order.

portfolio there is a risk diversification and therefore the premium for balancing energy can be lower.

4.2.6 Supplementary Products

In the gas and electricity industry flexible delivery is an essential requirement for many customers. A selection of energy products that provide a certain type of flexibility are described in the following.

Reserve contracts for electricity: Customers with electricity generation capabilities have to manage the outage risk of their own power plants. With reserve contracts they can transfer the risk of an outage to a supplier. To separate regular supply from the reserve contract (e.g., for billing purposes), a fixed maximum capacity for the regular supply can be agreed. In the case of an outage of the customer's generation units, the maximum capacity will be exceeded. The consumption of reserve energy can be determined as the energy exceeding the maximum capacity. In this way information about the customer's power plant dispatch is not necessarily used.

For pricing reserve contracts a differentiation between scheduled outages (e.g., for maintenance) and unscheduled outages (e.g., a breakdown) is common. A *scheduled outage* can simply be priced at the time of announcement at current forward prices as described in equation (4.1). As a disadvantage for the retail customer, the price is still uncertain when the supply contract is concluded. The prices for reserve energy are not fixed until the times of maintenance are defined and announced. If a retail customer wants a fixed price for reserve energy at the time when the contract is signed, the selling utility can only hedge this with an option. Therefore, a natural approach is to use option price theory for calculating the reserve contract. However, reserve contracts are options restricted to technical events, while option price theory assumes that the option is exercised to optimise value against market prices. Also, an upfront payment for the option premium is an unusual price component for retail customers. Thus, an approach which prices only the risk of a reserve contract, like the RAROC approach discussed further in equation (4.17), is a good alternative.

Pricing reserve contracts for an *unscheduled outage* is not covered by the usual option pricing approaches. A breakdown of a retail customer's generation unit can only be absorbed with own generation units. So, the full costs of own reserve capacities (under utilisation of a portfolio effect) can be an indication for the pricing. Alternatively, the unexpected demand can be regarded as an option on balancing power but pricing would then require a market model for balancing power.

Interruptible retail contracts: Because spot markets for electricity and gas are highly volatile, options on spot products are particularly valuable. The previous section discussed reserve contracts, where the utility sells additional optionality to a retail customer. Consider the contrary situation, where a retail customer accepts a market price-dependent interruption of his gas or electricity supply, effectively selling an option to his supplier. In practice, a one-day notice period for the supply interruption can be agreed and the option premium can be included in a reduced energy price. As a customer-oriented alternative, it can also be agreed that each individual interruption requires the customer's acceptance and instead of a reduced energy price the customer receives a premium for each accepted interruption.

Right of cancellation: Selling a right of cancellation of the supply contract is another alternative for a retail customer to obtain a reduced energy price. In such an arrangement the supplier has the option to terminate the contract after a certain period. The option premium is used to reduce the energy price for the period of the supply contract where no cancellation is possible. Instead of a contract cancellation, the retail customer can sell the right, not the obligation, of a price adjustment. As an example, a retail customer signs a full service contract in 2013 for delivery in the gas business years 2016/2017 and 2017/2018. The calculated energy price for 2016/2017 is 27 EUR/MWh and for 2017/2018 it is 28 EUR/MWh. The retail customer can reduce the energy price in 2016/2017 by the option premium (e.g., 1 EUR/MWh) by granting the supplier the right of a price alignment at the end of the gas business year 2016/2017 for delivery in 2017/2018. A retail customer who signs such a contract has to take into account that their energy price will follow the wholesale price according to equation (4.2) if, and only if, wholesale prices are increasing. If wholesale markets are decreasing, the supplier will not exercise the right to adjust prices and therefore the customer will not participate in the price reduction for the delivery period 2017/2018.

4.3 SOURCING

From a risk management perspective, sourcing retail contracts should be clearly separated from speculative market expectations. This makes it much easier to manage the total risk and control the financial performances of the retail business as well as potential trading activities. A key factor in the sourcing process is to minimise unwanted market price risk. Since in recent years price volatility in energy markets on an annual basis was a multiple of the retail margin, ineffective risk management may lead to operating profits being dominated by random market price movements.

4.3.1 Sourcing Fixed-Price Contracts

For B2B customers the short position of a fixed-price full service contract is simply the delta position resulting from the load forecast. The load forecast should therefore be included in

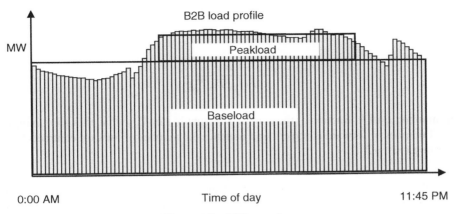

Figure 4.7   B2B sourcing.

the risk management system. The delta position can then be hedged with available trading products. An example for electricity contracts is illustrated in Figure 4.7. The electricity position can be divided into off-peak and peak components consistent with available trading products (e.g., monthly contracts).

4.3.2   Sourcing Indexed Contracts

The delta position of an indexed contract changes with each price fixing. Therefore, a regular position update needs to ensure that the correct market price exposure is indicated by the risk management system. This subsection describes how the consecutive fixings can be handled within the risk management process.

For simplification, the index in the contract with the price formula (4.2) is assumed to be a traded forward or futures contract with delivery period starting at T_1 and ending at T_2. For the index we use the notation $I(t) = F(t, T_1, T_2)$ and T_0 denotes the time when the retail contract is concluded. However, the consideration can easily be adjusted to more general cases, for example where $I(t)$ is a combination of two or more forward or futures contracts.

The basic idea is to decompose the considered retail contract into a physical leg (energy supply obligation) and a financial leg (payments to be received). The physical leg of an indexed contract does not differ from the physical leg of a fixed-price contract. The financial leg of the indexed contract represents the equivalent amount of the forward contract F on a value basis. More precisely, the sold indexed contract can be decomposed into:

1. Selling a full service contract with a fixed price P calculated according to equation (4.1) at T_0. As mentioned before, the physical leg of this contract represents the physical leg of the indexed contract.
2. Buying a specific amount of forward contract $F(T_0, T_1, T_2)$ at T_0 corresponding to the price formula (4.2). If $\hat{L}$ denotes the accumulated expected customers' load, the required number of forward contracts is

$$\frac{(P + R + M)\hat{L}}{F(T_0, T_1, T_2)}.$$

3. For each fixing date $t_k, k \in \{1, \dots, n\}$, selling the following number of forward contracts at price $F(t_k, T_1, T_2)$:

$$\frac{1}{n} \frac{(P + R + M)\hat{L}}{F(T_0, T_1, T_2)}.$$

This number is a $1/n$ fraction of the contracts bought in step 2, so that after all n fixings the overall number of forward contracts sold matches the number of forward contracts bought according to step 2.

Within the sourcing process, contracts 1 and 2 should be entered into the risk management system after concluding the retail contract. With each fixing one additional contract according to step 3 will be added.

4.3.3 Sourcing B2C Contracts

In principle, a back-to-back sourcing as described for B2B customers can also be used for B2C customers with a fixed-price full service contract. However, because of the large number of customers, B2C contracts are often not concluded with individual price and contract period, but follow tariffs that are valid for all customers with the same product. Typically, contracts are evergreen contracts without predetermined duration. The contracts are automatically renewed until the customer explicitly terminates the contract after a certain notice period. To respond to changing market developments, the utility may adjust tariffs from time to time with a given notice period.

As a consequence, the required energy to supply the B2C customer base is often purchased in tranches instead of contract by contract. Thereby, the following targets should be taken into account:

- The intention of pricing B2C contracts is to absorb volatile price movements. In some regional markets price adjustments for B2C customers must be approved by the authorities. Targeting an average price by purchasing the required energy in multiple tranches avoids strong price movements, which may be difficult to justify.
- Customer turnovers are less frequent in the B2C segment and building up a B2C customer base can take years. A sourcing strategy that leads to non-competitive retail prices can hardly be compensated. Therefore, a second target is not to deviate too much from the sourcing of the main competitors in the same market.

More formally, sourcing in multiple tranches means that the required energy for delivery period $[T_1, T_2]$ is purchased at n different dates $t_1, t_2, \dots, t_n$. The adequate n and $t_1, t_2, \dots, t_n$ are chosen such that the targets of the sourcing strategy are achieved. The choice of these parameters defines the own sourcing strategy and depends on the market and the assumed strategy of the competitors as benchmark. A long time period $[T_1, T_2]$ increases the averaging effect, but leads to sourcing prices that may differ significantly from actual market prices.

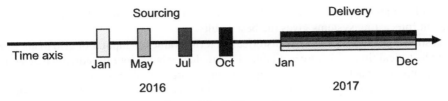

Figure 4.8   B2C sourcing.

As an example, consider the sourcing of B2C customers where the delivery period is the entire year 2017 and the sourcing will be done in four parts ($n = 4$) at the beginning of each quarter in the year 2016 (Figure 4.8).

If the utility adjusts tariffs for B2C customers in the fourth quarter they can align tariffs with the sourcing price.

4.4   LOAD FORECASTING

Load forecasting plays an important role in electricity system operation. For integrated utilities forming regional monopolies, the main focus is forecasting of grid loads in their transmission or distribution areas. Grid loads are identical with the cumulative load of all consumers connected to the grid. In liberalised energy markets suppliers need to forecast their own customers.

In terms of forecasting horizon, load forecasting applications can be divided into four categories.

- *Long-term forecasting* with horizons of several years or decades: The main focus is on annual peak loads and annual average load as input for system expansion planning. The main influencing factors are population and economic growth rates.
- *Medium-term forecasting* with horizons up to one or two years: The main characteristics are daily, weekly and seasonal patterns. For most applications hourly time resolution is required. Medium-term load forecasts are required to price full service contracts or partial delivery contracts (see Section 4.2) and for portfolio management.
- *Short-term load forecasting* with horizons up to one week: Besides characteristic daily, weekly and seasonal patterns, weather forecasts are used as influencing factors. Hourly or quarter-hourly time resolution is common. Applications are also power plant and transmission system operation planning. For retailers, load forecasts for aggregates of customers are required. If the composition of customers changes significantly over time, as is generally the case in liberalised markets, forecasts should be based on forecasts for individual customers.
- *Ultra-short-term load forecasting* with horizons up to several hours: Quarter-hourly or higher time resolution is common. Load forecasts for these time horizons are mainly used for power plant dispatch and grid operation. Forecasts are based on short-term historical load data as well as on historical load curves of similar days.

There are many well-established techniques for grid load forecasting. Common are end-use and econometric approaches for long-term forecasts. For short- and ultra-short-term forecasts, so-called similar-day approaches, regression models, time series models, artificial neural networks (ANN), expert systems and statistic learning algorithms are used. For medium-term forecasts all of these approaches can be found. Often, a combination of different approaches or different forecasting systems gives the best results.

Forecasting algorithms always use historical metering values as input. For grid loads generally, long historical time series are available. The stochastic behaviour of individual customers has only a minor impact on grid loads representing a large number of individual customers. Therefore, high forecasting accuracy can be achieved. Load forecasts for individual customers are more difficult as often less historical data is available, stochastic impacts are not well diversified and significant changes in consumption patterns may occur, for example in case of a change from two-shift to three-shift production. Therefore, robustness and flexibility are important characteristics of load forecasting algorithms for individual customers.

The following similar-day approach is suitable for medium-term load forecasts for individual customers. The basic principle of a similar-day approach is to select historical days for which metering data are available and that are similar to the day for which the forecast has to be made and use the average of these days as forecast. It is also possible to use a weighted average where the weight of historical days depends on the similarity. Similarity can be defined by the following criteria.

- *Season:* Load patterns show typical seasonal behaviour. Similarity can be defined as seasonal distance between days. For example, historical days which have a seasonal distance of plus or minus three weeks to the day the forecast is made might be considered as similar. Also, days in spring might be similar to days in autumn and vice versa.
- *Day of the week:* While Tuesdays, Wednesdays and Thursdays have similar load patterns in most countries, all other weekdays are distinct.
- *Irregular sectoral non-work or limited activity days:* These include public holidays, school holidays, days between public holidays and weekends. These days are most difficult to forecast as there are often only a small number of similar historical days available. Similarity between these days and normal days has to be considered, for example load patterns on public holidays can be similar to those on Sundays.
- *Historical distance:* Historical load data which is several years old might not be as suitable as more recent data.
- *Structural change:* Often structural changes in load patterns can be observed. It is important to realise these structural changes and not to use historical load profiles for similar days without adjustments for compensating structural changes. General trends, for example average load growth, can be considered as well by scaling historical load profiles.
- *Exceptional load patterns:* If a significant number of similar days, for example 10 days, with historical data have been identified, the load patterns for these days can be compared. If load patterns of single days deviate strongly from the load patterns of all other days, these days should not be considered in the weighted average. Reasons can be exceptional events like strikes or data errors.

A similar-day approach typically contains many parameters which can be modified. Intensive backtesting with many historical time series is required to derive appropriate values of all parameters. It is also important to repeat this backtesting regularly, for example annually, to adjust the forecasting algorithm to systematic changes and trends (e.g., faster availability of historical metering data or changes in customer groups).

Short-term forecasts for individual customers required for scheduling can be based on the same similar-day approach as medium-term forecasts. Weather forecasts can be considered either by giving more weight to historical days with similar weather conditions or by linear regression. It might be appropriate to assign higher weights to more recent historical values than in medium-term forecasts to capture shorter-term structural changes.

4.5   WEATHER RISK IN GAS RETAIL MARKETS

Retail contracts in electricity and gas markets typically allow for demand variations caused by individual customer behaviour or by weather conditions, such as temperature. Unlike individual customer behaviour, weather conditions affect larger geographical regions. Therefore, demand variations driven by weather conditions are not diversified in larger retail portfolios. Weather risk for retail portfolios is the financial risk resulting from weather-driven consumption variations.

Weather conditions relevant for retail consumption include temperature, solar irradiation, precipitation and wind speed. This section focuses on temperature as the most important driver of weather risk in retail portfolios. Weather risk exists in natural gas and in electricity markets. However, gas consumption is much more influenced by the daily temperature compared with electricity consumption, so in this section weather risk is regarded with respect to gas markets only. Nevertheless, the basic concepts can also be applied to electricity markets. Weather risk can be reduced by hedging with weather derivatives. The efficiency of such hedging and the pricing of weather derivatives is examined in this section.

Among retail customers, process gas and heating gas form the two extremes regarding weather dependency. While load profiles of process gas customers are temperature independent, profiles for heating gas customers are strongly temperature dependent. Cold temperatures during winter increase the demand for space heating in commercial as well as residential buildings and thereby gas consumption also increases. Nevertheless, space heating is only required if the average daily air temperature is below a certain limit temperature. Otherwise, heating is not necessary due to the insulation of buildings. Heating degree days (HDD) have been introduced to reflect the dependence of energy demand for space heating on the daily average air temperature $\bar{T}_t$:

$$\text{HDD}(\bar{T}_t) = \max(T_0 - \bar{T}_t, 0). \tag{4.3}$$

Above a base temperature T_0, a particular building needs no heating; for HDD often 16°C or 18°C is used, which are appropriate approximations for average buildings. Cumulated heating degree days (CHDD) for a time period $[T_1, T_2]$

$$\text{CHDD}(T_1, T_2) = \sum_{t=T_1}^{T_2} \text{HDD}(\bar{T}_t) \tag{4.4}$$

reflect the need for heating during this time period. To describe the heating degree days for a longer period, the notation $\text{HDD}(d, w)$ instead of $\text{HDD}(t)$ is used where t is day number d of winter w. In line with the definitions of winter in the gas year, the term "winter" describes the period 1st October to 31st March. With this notation, cumulated heating degree days for day d of winter w can be written as

$$CHDD(d, w) = \sum_{k=1}^{d} HDD(k, w) \text{ for } 1 \leq d \leq 182. \tag{4.5}$$

Sometimes it is more interesting how cold the winter has been so far in comparison with an average winter. For this purpose, normalised cumulated heating degree days (NCHDD) are defined as

$$NCHDD(d, w) = CHDD(d, w) - \frac{1}{w-1} \sum_{\ell=1}^{w-1} CHDD(d, \ell) \text{ for } 1 \leq d \leq 182. \tag{4.6}$$

In many countries like the United States, hot temperatures during summer increase the demand for air conditioning, which in turn results in a larger natural gas demand, as power for air conditioning is generated by gas-fired power plants. For this reason, cooling degree days (CDD) have also been introduced to reflect the energy demand for cooling a commercial or residential building:

$$CDD(\bar{T}_t) = \max(\bar{T}_t - T_0, 0). \tag{4.7}$$

Quite often a base temperature of 18°C is used. Cumulated cooling degree days

$$CCDD(T_1, T_2) = \sum_{t=T_1}^{T_2} HDD(\bar{T}_t) \tag{4.8}$$

in turn reflect the energy demand for cooling within the time period $[T_1, T_2]$.

In Europe, natural gas consumption peaks during the coldest winter months (December–February) and the lowest consumption occurs during the summer months (June–August). In the United States the gas demand peaks also during the winter months but it increases again during the warmest summer months (July–August) due to air conditioning and is lowest during the transition months (May–June and September–November).

Heating degree days are still a simplification of the temperature dependence of gas demand. If temperatures are very low, gas consumption is limited by the capacity of the installed heating and in summer, when temperatures are high, gas is still used for hot water preparation and therefore gas consumption is low but not zero and independent of temperature. Between these two extremes there is typically an almost linear relationship between temperature and gas consumption. One possibility to model this temperature dependence of the gas consumption $h(\cdot)$ of a customer or a portfolio of customers is using a piecewise linear function. Nevertheless, from economic sciences it is well known that a sigmoid function is able to describe this behaviour with a single continuous function:

$$h(\bar{T}_t) = \frac{A}{1 + \left(\frac{B}{\bar{T}_t - 40}\right)^C} + D. \tag{4.9}$$

The four parameters A, B, C and D define shape of the sigmoid function illustrated in Figure 4.9.

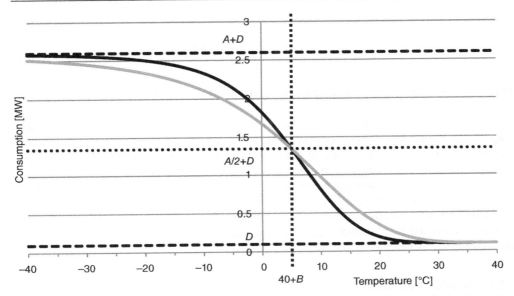

Figure 4.9 Sigmoid function for a typical parameter set $A = 2.5, B = -35, D = 0.1$ with $C = 6$ (black) and $C = 4$ (grey). High and low-temperature asymptotes are shown as dashed lines and consumption $A/2 + D$ for normal temperature $40 + B$ is plotted as a dotted line.

D is the high-temperature asymptote of gas consumption and $A + D$ the low temperature asymptote, that is, the maximum consumption in very cold winters. Furthermore, B defines the normal temperature. For example, $B = -35$ means that for a normal temperature of $\bar{T}_t = 40°C + B = 5°C$ the consumption is the average between minimum and maximum. Around this normal temperature the temperature dependence of gas consumption is more or less linear. The parameter C determines the slope of the sigmoid function around the normal temperature, that is the larger C the larger the gradient around the normal temperature.

While the consumption of households is largely independent of weekday, business customers often show a strong dependence. For most business customers a reduced consumption at weekends can be observed. Therefore, daily factors are introduced:

$$h(\bar{T}_t, d) = F(d) \cdot \left(\frac{A}{1 + \left(\frac{B}{\bar{T}_t - 40} \right)^C} + D \right). \tag{4.10}$$

Owing to the thermal storage capacity of solid buildings, the gas consumption does not react immediately to temperature changes but shows a certain inertia. For this reason the temperature of some past days is included to get a better prognosis of the actual gas consumption. Often, an unweighted average of two

$$\bar{T}_t = \frac{T_t + T_{t-1}}{2} \tag{4.11}$$

or a weighted average of four days is used:

$$\bar{T}_t = \frac{8 \cdot T_t + 4 \cdot T_{t-1} + 2 \cdot T_{t-2} + 1 \cdot T_{t-3}}{15}. \tag{4.12}$$

Here, exponentially decreasing weights are used, that is the weight for older data is much lower.

Overall, the gas consumption varies depending on temperature and this variance is a challenge for energy utilities. Whenever a prognosis based on historical consumption data is done, the temperature dependence of the historical data should be determined (e.g., by fitting a sigmoid function). Afterwards, the prognosis can be done using an average weather year. This reduces the long and medium-term prognosis error. Furthermore, the quality of the temperature prognosis is essential to minimise the short-term prognosis error and thereby the balancing costs. Nevertheless, all efforts to minimise prognosis errors can only reduce the weather risk to some extent and help to understand the exact dependencies. The remaining risk can be reduced further by hedging with weather derivatives.

4.5.1 Weather Derivatives

The market for weather derivatives makes it possible to manage weather risk via risk-transfer instruments based on a given weather variable, deduced for example from temperature, rainfall, snowfall or wind. The company giving away risk pays the risk-taker a predefined premium and in turn gets paid depending on the deviation of the weather variable from its expected value.

In July 1996 the first weather derivative transaction was contracted, when Aquila Energy and Consolidated Edison Co. embedded a weather clause into a power transaction. By this clause Aquila committed to pay Consolidated Edison a discount on the fixed power price if temperatures in August turned out to be cooler than expected. CCDDs were used to measure the deviation from the expectation. If CCDDs were more than 10% below the expectation, the company received a discount and the discount levels increased with the deviation from expectation. At that time, several energy companies in the United States realised that temperature is one of the key drivers for profit and loss in the energy business. As a consequence, an OTC market started to develop in 1997 with Enron as a major participant and driver of the market. As the market for these products grew, the CME introduced the first exchange-traded weather futures contracts as well as options written on these futures in 1999. Since that time this new derivatives market has developed, first in the United States and then gradually expanding around the globe. At the CME, weather derivatives for 41 locations around the world are traded – for 24 cities in the United States, six in Canada, nine in Europe and two in Japan. The contracts with the largest trading volume depend on temperature indices, namely heating and cooling degree days. In 2006 the market reached a size of more than USD 45 billion measured in terms of the total notional value of all contracts traded per year including both OTC and CME transactions.

Owing to the financial crisis starting in 2008, the weather derivatives market shrank and remained according to the Weather Risk Management Association (WRMA) at a size of USD 11.8 billion in 2011. Many major players at the exchange side, like banks and natural gas-focused hedge funds, have reduced their activity or even completely left the stage. Most of the collapse has been on the exchange-traded side, while the OTC weather market has grown from year to year as more and more large energy companies, among others, have transferred significant risks using this market. Several years ago, the first quantity-adjusting options (quantos) were introduced on the OTC weather derivatives markets and have now become a standard product offered by energy traders as well as reinsurance companies. The payoff of these derivatives depends on two variables, typically temperature and the price of a commodity such as natural gas or electricity. Thereby, energy companies are able to hedge price and volume risk at the same time.

Today, futures contracts on cumulated HDD as well as CDD are traded at the CME for 41 locations around the world for individual months October to April as well as seasonal strips (minimum of two up to maximum of seven consecutive months) a couple of years out. The minimum contract value is 20 USD (for European locations 20 EUR) for each HDD (or CDD) throughout the period. For a single month starting at T_1 and ending at T_2, the settlement price of the futures contract is

$$F = 20\,\text{USD} \cdot \text{CHDD}(T_1, T_2).\qquad(4.13)$$

The buyer of this futures contract gains a profit if the CHDD is larger and a loss if the CHDD is smaller than expected. The situation is reversed for the seller of this futures contract.

At the CME, European-style options written on degree days futures contracts as an underlying are also traded. Strike prices K for these put and call options are at intervals of 1 index point in a range of 0 to 7500 index points for the CDD season and a range of 0 to 16 000 index points for the HDD season:

$$p_{\text{call}} = 20\,\text{USD} \cdot \max(\text{CHDD}(T_1, T_2) - K)\qquad(4.14)$$
$$p_{\text{put}} = 20\,\text{USD} \cdot \max(K - \text{CHDD}(T_1, T_2))\qquad(4.15)$$

In recent years the use of quanto options, which are tailormade for hedging price and weather risk at the same time, has increased (see Benth *et al.* (2012)). The payoff of these double options depends on two variables, for example the average gas price $\bar{G}(T_1, T_2)$ and the cumulated heating degree days. For both variables, strikes K_G and K_{CHDD} have to be defined and γ determines the contract size:

$$p_{\text{quanto, call}} = \gamma \cdot \max\left(\text{CHDD}(T_1, T_2) - K_{\text{CHDD}}\right) \cdot \max(\bar{G}(T_1, T_2) - K_G).\qquad(4.16)$$

A challenge about weather derivatives is the pricing, as the underlying itself (e.g., cumulative heating degree days) is not tradable. Only the options written on weather futures contracts are comparable with the usual energy derivatives, since in this case the futures contract is a tradable underlying for the option. For this reason other pricing methods are used for basic weather derivatives.

Pricing of Weather Derivatives

There exist different methods for the pricing of weather futures contracts and European-style options. The following three methods are often used.

1. *Historical pricing* (known as "burn analysis", see Müller and Grandi (2000)): This method answers the question "What would have been the average payoff in the past?" and it proceeds as follows:
   (a) In a first step, a number of years with historical weather data has to be chosen and degree days are calculated for each day in this period.
   (b) Using these degree days, the derivative payoff for each year of the historical data is calculated.
   (c) In the next step the payoffs are discounted.
   (d) Finally, the so-called burning cost premium is calculated as the average discounted payoff plus a percentage of the standard deviation of the discounted payoffs as a risk premium.

   The biggest advantage of this method is that it is easy to implement if reliable historical weather data is available. The downside of this approach is that long-term trends like increasing temperature due to climate change or extreme weather situations like El Niño in America are not included.

   As an example, historical temperature data for Berlin are available since 1953. The average CHDD for all winters (October to March) for Berlin is 2 588. Without risk premium this would result in a historical price of 51 760 EUR for a futures contract on the CHDD for this seasonal strip. Including a risk premium of 20% of the standard deviation, a price for selling this futures contract would instead be 52 688 EUR.

2. *Actuarial approach:* A methodology (Hamisultane, 2008) that is popular in the insurance sector is the actuarial approach, which calculates the price of a weather derivative as the expected payoff plus a risk-dependent margin via the following steps.
   (a) First a joint stochastic model of the dynamic of energy prices and temperature based on historical prices, as well as measured temperature, has to be built. Using this model, paths for energy prices and temperature are simulated.
   (b) For each simulation path the payoff for the weather derivative is calculated.
   (c) In a next step, the expected payoff is calculated as the average of simulated payoffs and increased by a risk-dependent margin. This margin is computed using a hurdle rate (e.g., 15%) times the VaR at a certain confidence level (e.g., 98%).
   (d) Finally, this value is discounted.

   Besides modelling assumptions, this method is based on historical data only. It does not include additional information from market prices of traded weather contracts available to market participants.

3. *Arbitrage-free approach:* In contrast to the actuarial approach, a risk-neutral measure is used to calculate the fair value of the derivative (see Benth *et al.* (2012), Hamisultane, (2008)).
   (a) First a joint stochastic model of the dynamic of energy prices and temperature, including the market price of risk, has to be built. Using this model, simulation paths for energy prices and temperature are calculated.
   (b) As in the actuarial approach, the payoff for the weather derivative is calculated for each path and the expected payoff is calculated as the average.
   (c) Finally, this value is discounted.

   In this approach all market data like prices of futures contracts are included, but calculating the market price of risk is a challenge. In contrast to the actuarial approach this market price of risk is a common risk premium fixed by market participants, while an individual risk premium consistent with the risk appetite of the company is used in the actuarial approach. An example for the calculation of this market price of risk for quanto options is given by Benth *et al.* (2012), but this is still work in progress.

Hedge Effectiveness

To compare the effectiveness of different weather derivatives for hedging weather risk resulting from gas retail business, backtesting is important. We consider an example and choose a typical profile for households (sigmoid parameters $A = 3.047, B = -37.1833, C = 5.673, D = 0.0962$) scaled to a consumption of 100 GWh. With the gas spot price model described in Section 6.3.1, the profit and loss distribution for a set of spot price scenarios can be calculated.

Starting with temperature scenarios, gas consumption scenarios have been calculated for the gas year 2013/14 (October 2013–September 2014) via a sigmoid function with given parameters A, B, C, D and hedged with seasonal products (summer and winter). The profits and losses (losses are shown with a positive sign) in the spot scenarios resulting from TTF prices as of May 2013 are shown in Figure 4.10; a profit at risk of 92.8 thousand euros (TEUR) results at a confidence level of 98%. In the same figure the profits and losses of a weather futures contract, weather option and a quanto option are shown (the profits have a positive sign in these cases). For these derivatives the volume has been chosen to reproduce the 98% quantile of the profit and loss of the consumption scenarios (15.9 futures contracts, 19.6 options, 4.3 quantos). Thereby the basic price P defined in equation (4.1) is used as the retail price paid by

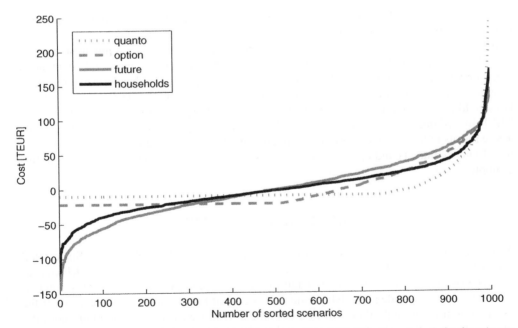

Figure 4.10   Risk profile for household customers (cost positive sign) and weather derivatives (cost negative sign). The volumes of the weather derivatives have been chosen to reproduce the 98% quantile of the household customers' profit distribution.

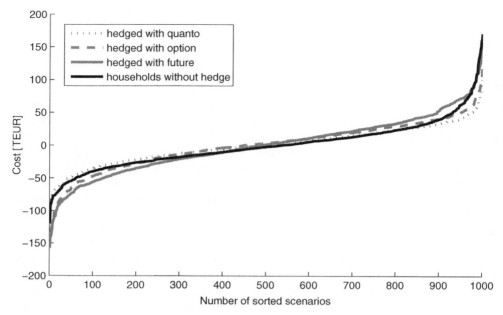

Figure 4.11   Risk profile for household customers (cost positive sign) standalone and hedged with weather derivatives. The largest risk reduction results from hedging with quanto options.

the customer. If the risk profile of the derivative and the household profile were the same, the risk in the portfolio combining the profile and the derivative would be zero.

As the spot price model not only consists of temperature as an extrinsic component, but also of an independent stochastic component as well as an independent stochastic oil component, risk is only reduced but not perfectly compensated by hedging with weather derivatives (futures contract, option as well as quanto). Without any hedge a risk of 92.8 TEUR results for the household profile; this risk reduces to 89.9 TEUR by hedging with futures contracts, to 63.4 TEUR by hedging with options and to 51.3 TEUR by hedging with quantos (cf. Figure 4.11). These results indicate that quantos are more effective for hedging the weather risk of utilities than futures contracts and options, but still a residual risk of more than 50% remains in this example.

4.6   RISK PREMIUMS

As discussed in Section 4.1, retail prices are deduced from wholesale prices. Since retail contracts bear additional risks and supplementary costs, a retail-based business model requires adequate risk premiums. Because the retail market in the energy business is highly competitive, determining an adequate risk premium is a critical task for an energy company. If the risk premium is too high, they will lose customers. However, if the risk premium does not adequately cover the risks, the company will not be profitable. Allocating adequate risk premiums to different types of retail customers is a vital risk management process and provides a balanced risk profile. Underpriced risks can easily attract customers with unfavourable risk profile, shifting these risks to the supplier.

We divide risk premiums into *strict risk premiums* and *expected additional costs*. Strict risk premiums correspond to risk factors that have a zero mean, that is the expected loss in a mathematical sense is zero. Strict risk premiums can be regarded as the required return for allocating risk capital. The return of taking these risks has to be adequate in view of the financial policy of the company and therefore there is no established standard for the determination of strict risk premiums. Expected additional costs correspond to risk factors whose stochastic behaviour causes additional costs on average, for example due to non-linear payoffs or certain correlations. These hidden costs are costs not visible in a purely deterministic pricing framework and are therefore not covered by the basic price defined in equation (4.1).

Another distinction can be made by dividing risk factors into *systematic* and *unsystematic* risks. Systematic risks affect a whole portfolio of customers so there is no risk diversification for large portfolios. Unsystematic risks are risks corresponding to individual customers. Such risks can be diversified if individual customers are small relative to the retail portfolio.

In this section we describe how to quantify risk premiums with the focus on B2B customers with fixed-price contracts. The risk map and the determination of risk premiums must be adapted to the specific market and contract types. This quantification is interesting for suppliers and also for retail customers with large energy costs who should understand how their energy costs are composed. If a customer purchases a structured contract there may be a risk transfer from the supplier to the customer compared with a full service contract. These risks have to be managed and additional costs may need to be taken into account.

The following risk premium types are discussed in more detail.

- *Price validity period:* A binding price quotation valid for a determined period can be considered as an option free of charge for the retail customer. The supplying utility will have hidden costs from this granted option.
- *Structuring fee and balancing energy:* Fees and costs demanded by the TSO for structuring and balancing power or gas in the relevant grid. The basic price defined in equation (4.1) does not include these costs.
- *Credit risk:* Selling energy to a retail customer will cause credit risk. In case of insolvency of the customer the supplying utility will suffer a loss if the delivered energy cannot be paid for. Additionally, there is the risk that the energy already purchased for the remaining contract period cannot be sold for the same price in case of decreased market prices.
- *Price profile risk:* For calculation of the basic price, the price forward curve $P(\cdot)$ in the finest available granularity (e.g., hourly or daily) was used. Because of the absence of a forward market in this granularity, $P(\cdot)$ has to be partly estimated from historical data (see Section 6.1 for details). The estimated price profile can change until delivery. On average, there should be no additional costs but there remains a risk for which a strict risk premium can be calculated.
- *Volume risk:* Systematic volume risk leading to additional expected costs results from the correlation between spot price and the energy consumed by the customer. In addition, there is the risk of unsystematic change in the load of an individual retail customer.
- *Operational risk:* There are further risks which are not considered in the categories above. These include the duration of the sourcing process described in Section 4.1, bid–offer spreads (which increase the basic price calculated on a mid-market basis), or inaccuracy of load and volume forecasts. If these risks can be kept small this can be an important competitive advantage for the supplying utility.

4.6.1   Risk-Adjusted Return on Capital

Before discussing individual retail risks, a general approach for determining strict risk premiums is considered. The aim is the determination of an adequate risk premium for the allocation of risk capital according to the financial policy of the company. The simplest approach for determining a strict risk premium is to define it as a specified ratio of the risk. The risk is usually quantified via a standard risk measure such as VaR or PaR as introduced in Section 3.2.

This approach can be enhanced to the risk-adjusted return on capital (RAROC) approach originally developed for banks. The idea is that potential losses need to be covered by economic capital for which the cost of equity applies. Because economic capital is limited for the company, a business is only realised if the return on the required economic capital exceeds a specified hurdle rate. RAROC was applied to the power market, for example by Prokopczuk *et al.* (2007).

We define RAROC as

$$\text{RAROC} = \frac{\text{expected return}}{\text{economic capital}}. \qquad (4.17)$$

The economic capital is the capital needed to cover heavy shocks in the value of the considered contracts or portfolio and corresponds to the risk measured usually as VaR or PaR.

RAROC can be used as an indicator of the profitability of a business activity in the sense of the capital policy of the utility. For this, an internal hurdle rate μ will be specified, which reflects the cost of equity capital. If this hurdle rate is reached, the investment or the transaction can be carried out.

In our considerations, PaR(α) with a confidence level of α is used as a risk measure because it includes all market risks until delivery. The risk premium R is calculated as the smallest premium so that RAROC exceeds the hurdle rate μ, that is

$$R = \mu \text{PaR}(\alpha). \qquad (4.18)$$

4.6.2   Price Validity Period

Suppose a customer in need of a supply contract asks for a price quote. Assume that the customer receives an offer at time t_0 and at a fixed price P valid for a limited period of time, say until time t_1. The date t_1 results from the time the customer needs for his purchase decision. As the quotation is an obligation only for the supplier, the retail customer gets at t_0 a call option with the strike price P and maturity t_1. If market prices decrease before the offer expires, the customer can request a new quote at a reduced price, potentially from another supplier. Vice versa, if market prices increase, the customer probably will close the contracts at the lower offer P.

Theoretically the risk can be covered by asking for an upfront option premium for the obliging offer. Since this is unusual and hardly accepted by a retail customer, the most promising way of lowering this risk for the supplier is to shorten the time period $t_1 - t_0$ as far as possible. The remaining risk can be covered partly by a risk premium which increases the price for the energy. Because this is not an upfront premium and only paid if the contract is concluded, the risk premium cannot avoid a loss to the supplying utility. It only increases

Table 4.2 Premium for the price validity period

Maturity	Premium for off-peakload (EUR/MWh)	Premium for peakload (EUR/MWh)
1 day	0.12	0.18
1 week	0.27	0.39
2 weeks	0.37	0.55
1 month	0.55	0.81

the strike price and makes the option less valuable, although the option is still free of charge. Furthermore, a high risk premium may threaten the success of the retail acquisition.

Asking for a risk premium is therefore a compromise between market conditions and the theoretical valuation. The option premium for a call with strike price P and maturity t_1 can be calculated with the Black–Scholes formula using implied volatility of traded options as parameter. This option premium can be used as an indication to derive the risk premium to be added to the energy price even though a payment of an upfront premium cannot be achieved.

As an example, Table 4.2 shows the size of the risk premium for different option maturities of an electricity contract. We assume that the peakload price is 47 EUR/MWh, the off-peak price is 32 EUR/MWh and the estimated annualised volatility is 15%.

In practice, to avoid a noteworthy risk premium for larger retail customers, offers are usually valid less than a day. An indexed contract with a specified fixing according to actual market prices fully avoids a premium for a price validity period.

4.6.3 Structuring Fee and Balancing Energy

The costs for balancing and structuring the grid are charged directly by the TSO and are subject to the conditions of grid access. Therefore, the following considerations explain general aspects which have to be adapted to the specific product and market conditions. Some components of costs for balancing the grid are charged indirectly and included in the TSO's grid access fees. These components are not in the focus of this section.

Market Practices

For customers without continuous metering (generally B2C customers), standard load profiles are used to determine the load profile that has to be delivered by the supplier. Deviations are balanced by the TSO who usually demands a fixed charge, sometimes included in the grid access fee. To balance the energy quantity over a longer time horizon (settlement period), there is an excess (respectively shortfall) billing. Because of the large number of B2C customers with individually low consumption, the volatility of balancing costs is low and can be estimated from past values with a high degree of accuracy.

For customers with continuous metering (generally B2B customers), the load profile is forecast in a granularity according to the settlement period of the TSO (e.g., hourly, quarter-hourly) and delivered by the supplier. But there are exceptions. At some natural gas hubs a daily baseload profile can be delivered to supply B2B customers not exceeding a specified consumption. For this service to obtain a defined tolerance band for the customers' daily profile, a *structuring fee* is charged by the TSO.

Balancing energy can be charged with or without a price spread for excess (respectively shortfall) of the delivered energy. As an example, in the German electricity market balancing energy is charged without price spread. A supplier delivering less energy than their customers' consumption at the time t (precisely a 15-minute time period) will be charged the balancing energy at a price $B(t)$ per MWh. The same price $B(t)$ per MWh is applied to compensate suppliers delivering a surplus of energy at time t. If the TSO needs additional energy at short notice because there is not enough energy in total for their grid, $B(t)$ is high. If, however, there is an energy surplus in the grid, $B(t)$ will be low and the supplier will receive only a small amount for the surplus energy. Even a negative price $B(t)$ is possible. An example of a market with a price spread for balancing energy is the gas hub Net Connect Germany (NCG). Here, excess (respectively shortfall) of delivered energy is reimbursed (respectively charged) with a (virtual) spot price multiplied by a factor less than (respectively greater than) 100%.

Pricing

The expected costs of balancing energy can be derived from past values. If the retail portfolio was significantly modified, a calculation with virtual costs is also possible. For this purpose, at the actual date t_0 dates in the past $T_1 < T_2 < T_3 < t_0$ are defined. Load data (for the aggregated portfolio or for individual customers) for the period $[T_1, T_2]$ are used for a load forecast in $[T_2, T_3]$. A comparison of the actual load with this forecast determines the forecasting error and therefore the required virtual balancing energy. Using historical balancing power prices for $[T_2, T_3]$ results in an estimation of balancing costs. This approach requires historic load data and published balancing power prices.

In a first step, calculating balancing energy costs for the total portfolio is reasonable. Therefore, load and load forecast refer to the aggregated portfolio load. For the calculation of costs for individual customers, a single customer can be added to the portfolio. Executing the calculation twice, once for the portfolio with the additional customer and once without the customer, yields the additional balancing costs for this customer taking portfolio effects into account.

So far we have calculated the expected costs resulting from the usage of balancing energy. But there is also a risk of much higher costs than estimated in this calculation. If a distribution of the costs can be estimated, it is possible to calculate a strict risk premium additional to the expected costs using the RAROC approach described above.

4.6.4   Credit Risk

Credit risk, that a retail customer cannot fulfil his contractual obligation, can be classified into settlement risk and replacement risk (see Section 3.4). Settlement risk is the risk that the customer defaults before payment of the delivered energy. Replacement risk occurs, because the supplier has sourced the energy based on a load forecast and therefore needs to sell the purchased energy on the market in case of the customer's default. In case of decreasing market prices, the supplier is in this case unable to meet his sourcing price. In a liquidation proceeding, the claims resulting from the settlement risk are usually accepted and are satisfied with a calculated recovery rate. In contrast, claims resulting from replacement risk are usually not accepted. This is different to claims from replacement risk in pure trading contracts according to a standard master agreement.

On average, credit risk causes expected additional costs. For settlement risk this is evident, because a potential payment after the liquidation process will not exceed the contractual obligation. For replacement risk there is a theoretical possibility of selling energy not needed by the insolvent customer at a higher price if market prices have increased since the defaulting contract was concluded. But in this case the purchased energy is very competitive for the defaulting customer and the liquidator has a higher chance of continuing the energy-consuming production process.

Using historical data of losses caused by credit events is the simplest way of determining expected additional costs. This can be justified for a large number of small retail customers. For large B2B customers, expected additional costs for settlement risk can be calculated by multiplying outstanding payments (on average) by the probability of default (PD), which can then be used as a risk premium for settlement risk. For replacement risk, a strict risk premium is calculated using a RAROC approach with the potential exposure (see Section 3.4.2) as risk measure. The determination of potential exposure uses the assumption that the default of a customer is independent of a change in market prices since the original supply contract was concluded.

4.6.5   Volume and Price Profile Risk

In this section risks caused by the uncertain retail volume and the hourly price profile are considered.

- *Price–volume correlation risk* is the systematic risk portion of volume risk. In electricity and gas markets there exists a positive correlation between spot price and total system load. This implies a correlation between spot price and the load of an average customer. As a consequence, additional expected costs arise because, in cases of higher than expected customer load (e.g., due to cold weather), additional energy has to be bought on average at higher prices. Vice versa, if the customer load is lower than expected then surplus energy needs to be sold on average at lower prices. This effect is illustrated as a basic example in Table 4.3, where additional costs of a retail gas customer are calculated whose load depends on the outside temperature and is correlated with spot prices. In electricity markets with a fluctuating weather-dependent production the correlation is weaker than in markets with a large thermal production.
- *Unsystematic volume risk* is the risk in unsystematic change in load of an individual customer or the retail portfolio. Because the supplier purchases the expected sold retail volume in the forward market when concluding the retail contract, the expected load may differ until

Table 4.3   Costs for the price-volume correlation

Temperature	Load MWh	Price EUR/MWh	Total costs EUR
Cold day	120	30	3600
Warm day	80	24	1920
Average	100	27	2700
Total average costs for two days			5400
Total costs for a warm and a cold day			5520

delivery. The deviation is balanced in the spot market and leads to additional costs or revenues.

- *Price profile risk* is the risk of a changing price structure until delivery. The retail contract can only be hedged on the forward market with standard contracts. Products with the required finer granularity are traded on the spot market only, and their costs (or revenues) can differ from the expectation used to price the retail contract.

We start with a calculation of the risk premium for the price–volume correlation risk. Two different methods are introduced, a basic calculation without the requirement of a market model and a more advanced analytical method using the SMaPS model (see Section 6.2.1). Finally, a more complex model is introduced that can be used for an integrated calculation of a risk premium for the price–volume correlation risk, the unsystematic volume risk and the price profile risk in a single step.

Basic calculation for the price–volume correlation: The first suggested method determines an adequate price–volume correlation premium R_c by calculating the covariance between spot price and load directly. This does not require a market model and can be used for electricity and gas markets. The load used in the following considerations can either be the retail customers' load or the total grid load. For the total grid load there exists sufficient historical data, and the calculations are stable. As a disadvantage, every retail customer is charged with the same average risk premium.

More formally, we consider a fixed-price contract with delivery period $[T_1, T_2]$ and basic price P concluded at t_0 and remember that the basic price P according to equation (4.1) is calculated using a load forecast for the retail customer. As usual, $L(\cdot)$ denotes the customers' load in the granularity specified by the TSO (daily, hourly, . . .) and $S(\cdot)$ the spot price. The forecast $\hat{L}(t)$ is the expected value $\mathbb{E}[L(t)]$ of the load as seen at time t_0.

The price–volume correlation premium R_c is given by the difference of the expected costs and the basic price:

$$
R_c = \frac{\sum_{t=T_1}^{T_2} \mathbb{E}[L(t)S(t)] - \sum_{t=T_1}^{T_2} \mathbb{E}[L(t)]\mathbb{E}[S(t)]}{\sum_{t=T_1}^{T_2} \mathbb{E}[L(t)]}
$$

$$
= \frac{\sum_{t=T_1}^{T_2} \mathrm{Cov}(L(t)S(t))}{\sum_{t=T_1}^{T_2} \hat{L}(t)}. \tag{4.19}
$$

The price–volume correlation premium R_c per MWh was calculated using the forecast energy amount. The billing is then based on the real load. An estimation of the covariance between load and spot price using historical data at $t_1, t_2, \ldots, t_n$ is given by

$$
\hat{\mathrm{cov}}(LS) = \frac{1}{n-1} \sum_{t=t_1}^{t_n} (S(t) - F(t, \bar{t}))(L(t) - \hat{L}(t, \bar{t})),
$$

with the price forward curve $F(t, \bar{t})$ and the load forecast $\hat{L}(t, \bar{t})$ estimated at $\bar{t}$ for delivery date t. Note that for this estimation $S(t), L(t)$ are regarded as samples of a random variable S, L and not as stochastic processes.

Analytical calculation for the price–volume correlation: There is also the possibility of an analytical determination of R_c for electricity using the SMaPS model. Using the notation of Section 6.2.1, the stochastic spot price in the SMaPS model is given by

$$S(t) = \exp(f(t, L(t)/v(t)) \exp(X(t)) \exp(Y(t)),$$

with the average relative availability of power plants $v(t)$ (a deterministic variable), and the time series $X(t)$ and $Y(t)$ representing short and long-term variations. The correlation between grid load and spot price is completely reflected by the function f. The remaining normally distributed load noise

$$l(t) := L(t) - \hat{L}(t)$$

and the remaining price noises $X(t)$ and $Y(t)$ are independent.

Calculating R_c using equation (4.19) requires, for each fixed $t \in [T_1, T_2]$, evaluation of

$$\mathbb{E}[L(t)S(t)] - \mathbb{E}[L(t)]\mathbb{E}[S(t)] = \mathbb{E}[(L(t) - \hat{L}(t))S(t)]$$
$$= \mathbb{E}\left[l(t)\exp\left(f\left(\frac{\hat{L}(t) + l(t)}{v(t)}\right)\right)\right]\mathbb{E}\left[\exp(X(t))\right]\mathbb{E}\left[\exp(Y(t))\right]$$
$$= \mathbb{E}\left[l(t)\exp\left(f\left(\frac{\hat{L}(t) + l(t)}{v(t)}\right)\right)\right]\exp\left(\frac{\text{Var}[X(t)]}{2}\right)\exp\left(\frac{\text{Var}[Y(t)]}{2}\right). \quad (4.20)$$

Because $l(t)$ is normally distributed, the term

$$\mathbb{E}\left[l(t)\exp\left(f\left(\frac{\hat{L}(t) + l(t)}{v(t)}\right)\right)\right]$$

can be calculated as an integral over the density of a normal distribution. Thus, equations (4.19) and (4.20) determine the price–volume correlation premium R_c.

Integrated calculation: Now we consider a more complex method for calculation of the price–volume correlation risk, the unsystematic volume risk and the price profile risk. In the first step we regard a sold retail contract that is sourced purely on the spot market. The return of the contract (without discounting) is then given by

$$\text{return} = \sum_{t=T_1}^{T_2} (P - S(t))L(t). \quad (4.21)$$

As a next step, we take sourcing with baseload and (if available) peakload futures contracts into account. In the following $F_B(\cdot, T_1, T_2)$, $F_P(\cdot, T_1, T_2)$ denote the prices of baseload and peakload futures contracts with delivery period $[T_1, T_2]$ and γ_B, γ_P (set $\gamma_P = 0$ if peakload contracts are not available) the corresponding baseload and peakload hedge ratios based on the load forecast $\hat{L}(t)$. It is assumed that the baseload and peakload futures contracts are standardised with a capacity of 1 MW. Finally, $\mathbf{1}_A(t)$ denotes the indicator function so that

$$\mathbf{1}_A(t) = \begin{cases} 1, \text{ if } t \in A \\ 0, \text{ otherwise} \end{cases}.$$

If the set "peak" denotes the peak hours, the absolute return of the contract apart from discounting is given by

$$\begin{aligned}
\text{return} &= \text{revenues} - \text{costs} \\
&= \sum_{t=T_1}^{T_2} \Big(PL(t) - \gamma_B F_B(t_0, T_1, T_2) \\
&\quad - \gamma_P F_P(t_0, T_1, T_2)\mathbf{1}_{\text{peak}}(t) - \big(L(t) - \gamma_B - \gamma_P\mathbf{1}_{\text{peak}}(t)\big)S(t) \Big).
\end{aligned} \qquad (4.22)$$

The return depends on the spot prices $S(t)$ and the load $L(t)$ for the dates $t \in [T_1, T_2]$, which are unknown at date t_0, when the contract is priced and concluded. Using a combined load and spot price model, the expected return and the risk measured as PaR(α) at a given confidence level α can be calculated. Subsequently, equation (4.18) can be used to calculate a strict risk premium for volume and hourly price profile risk. The difference between expected return and basic price P yields the price-volume correlation premium. So, the main task is the development of an adequate combined load and spot price model. Using the models described in this book, we distinguish between gas and electricity markets.

Combined load and spot price model for natural gas: In the spot price model for gas introduced in Section 6.3.1, temperature is an exogenous factor influencing the gas spot price via the normalised cumulated heating degree days. Thus, in a first step temperature scenarios are simulated and in a second step corresponding spot price scenarios are obtained. The temperature dependency of a customer consumption can be fitted using a sigmoid function (see Section 4.5). Applying this sigmoid function to the temperature scenarios results in customer load scenarios that are correlated with the corresponding spot price scenarios. In case of customers with standard load profiles, the load behaviour is perfectly described by a sigmoid function. In case of continuously measured customer load, the resulting sigmoid function is an approximation. The additional prognosis error can be modelled via an additional autoregressive component (e.g., an AR(1) or higher-order autoregressive AR(n) process). This component can be fitted to the residuals resulting from the fit of the sigmoid function.

Combined load and spot price model for electricity: For electricity, we introduced the SMaPS model in Section 6.2.1 for creating consistent total system load and spot price scenarios. This model simulates the total grid load and can be used to calculate R_c and a strict risk premium for the volume and the hourly price profile risk for a customer on average. To calculate risk premiums for individual customers, the SMaPS model will be extended to be able to generate consistent customer load scenarios, as published in Burger and Müller (2011). The SMaPS model generates electricity spot price scenarios $S(t)$ and load scenarios $L(t)$ for the total system load. These system load scenarios are used to generate load scenarios $C(t)$ for an individual customer reflecting the correlation between total system load and individual customer load. In a first step, clusters $D_i, i \in 1, 2, \dots, k$ of day types are defined (see Section 6.1.2 for a similar

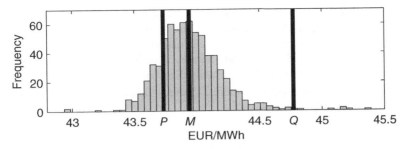

Figure 4.12   Simulated sourcing costs.

approach), taking into account yearly season, weekdays or holidays. Using historical customer data a regression with coefficients α, α_i and noise $X^{(C)}(t)$ yields

$$\ln C(t) = \alpha \ln L(t) + \sum_{i=1}^{k} \alpha_i \mathbf{1}_{D_i}(t) + X^{(C)}(t).$$ (4.23)

In a second step, a model for the short-term process $X^{(C)}(t)$ is fitted. In practice, a SARIMA process with a seasonality of 24 hours produces satisfying results. Student's t-distribution with scale parameter for the innovations of $X^{(C)}(t)$ has proved suitable. Note that the customer load $C(t)$ according to the retail SMaPS model is always positive. Retail customers with significant own generation that may exceed consumption have to be priced separately.

The following example for electricity shows the application of the retail SMaPS model for calculating strict risk premiums for volume risk and price–volume correlation costs. Assume that the deterministic load schedule of a retail customer has a price $P = 43.73$ EUR/MWh and is hedged with baseload and peakload forward contracts. Using the retail SMaPS model, price and load scenarios are calculated. The corresponding simulated costs are shown in Figure 4.12. The expected costs M are 43.94 EUR/MWh, resulting in a strict risk premium of 0.21 EUR/MWh for price–volume correlation. The 99% quantile Q of the expected costs of the hedged retail contract is 44.77 EUR/MWh in our example. Assuming a hurdle rate μ of 15%, the risk premium for volume risk is

$$15\% \times (44.77 \text{ EUR/MWh} - 43.94 \text{ EUR/MWh}) = 0.12 \text{ EUR/MWh}.$$

4.6.6   Operational Risk

The sourcing process described in Section 4.3 is complex, especially for a large number of customers, and therefore sensitive to errors. Operational risk appears to be one of the most significant risks which can cause high losses. A precise quantification of operational risk is impossible. However, identification of key tasks that are sensitive with respect to the risk management process helps us to understand operational risk. These are:

1. determination of load profiles and load volumes,
2. time-critical sourcing and
3. settlement of the grid access.

The risk of delayed sourcing can be quantified if it is assumed that the forward prices follow a geometric Brownian motion. In this case, VaR can be used as a risk measure and using a RAROC approach a strict risk premium can be calculated.

If a retail contract is concluded at t_0 and sourcing is delayed by N trading days, then the volatility for the time period N of the log-normally distributed forward price $F(t_0 + N, T_1, T_2)$ with annualised volatility σ is $\sigma\sqrt{N/T}$, where T denotes the number of trading days per year. The VaR with confidence level α is

$$\text{VaR}(\alpha, N) = q_\alpha[F(t_0 + N, T_1, T_2) - F(t_0, T_1, T_2)],$$

where q_α denotes the α quantile.

Based on a period of one year, the risk is lower. As an example, assume that there are T/N consecutive, non-overlapping process delays within a year (assumed to be an integer), then the risk for T/N delays with a confidence level α can be calculated as

$$q_\alpha \left[\sum_{i=1}^{T/N} \left(F(t_0 + iN, T_1, T_2) - F(t_0 + (i-1)N, T_1, T_2) \right) \right]$$
$$= q_\alpha \left[F(t_0 + T, T_1, T_2) \right] - F(t_0, T_1, T_2).$$

Consider an example with $\sigma = 25\%$ using a normal distribution as an approximation and a current forward price $F(t_0, T_1, T_2) = 40$ EUR/MWh. Then the risk of a single sourcing delay of $N = 5$ trading days measured as VaR with 98% confidence level is

$$\text{VaR}(98\%, 5 \text{ days}) = q_{0.98} \left[F(t_0 + 5, T_1, T_2) \right] - F(t_0, T_1, T_2) = 2.90 \text{ EUR/MWh}.$$

The apparent risk seems high, but as a yearly average with the assumptions above the risk is substantially smaller. In this example it is

$$\frac{1}{50} q_{0.98} \left[F(t_0 + 50N, T_1, T_2) \right] - F(t_0, T_1, T_2) = 0.41 \text{ EUR/MWh}.$$

Using a hurdle rate of 15%, for example, results in a risk premium of 0.06 EUR/MWh.

4.6.7 Risk Premium Summary

Delivering energy to retail customers involves hidden costs and additional risks. A utility can cover these risks with adequate risk premiums. Understanding these hidden costs and risks is important for the customer as well as for the supplier. A retail customer purchasing a structured product must be aware that depending on the type of structured product, a part of these additional costs may be transferred to him. These additional costs should be included in the customer's calculation and the purchased structured product must still be competitive compared with a full service contract. This is not always the case, and sometimes a full

Table 4.4   Risk components by retail contract type

Type of risk	Full service contract	Indexed contract	Portfolio management	B2C (standard load profile)
Price validity period	Supplier	None	None	None
Balancing power	Supplier	Supplier	Customer	TSO
Credit risk	Supp., Cust.	Supp., Cust.	Supp., Cust.	Supp., Cust.
Price–volume correlation	Supplier	Supplier	Customer	TSO
Hourly price profile	Supplier	Supplier	Customer	Supplier
Volume risk	Supplier	Supplier	Customer	Supplier

service contract is the most economical choice for a retail customer. Purchasing a structured product requires awareness of the involved risk. This is particularly the case for contracts with embedded options such as a right of cancellation.

Table 4.4 shows the types of risk for some retail products and identifies the party likely to bear the costs. The costs accepted by the TSO are market dependent and the table must be adapted to each specific market.

5

Energy Derivatives

An *energy derivative* is a contract that is derived from an underlying energy-related commodity. Such a contract may be an agreement to trade a commodity at some future date or to exchange cashflows based on energy prices at future dates. A basic classification of energy derivatives is given in Figure 5.1. We distinguish between options and contracts without optionality, such as forwards, futures or swaps. Options in energy markets have a long history. Before the formation of liberalised energy markets, optionality was needed to react to fluctuations in consumption, interruptions in transmissions or power plant outages. Power plants or gas storage facilities provided flexibility that was historically used to balance the system load and is presently being used to optimise the profit against market prices (see Section 7.2). Many options on a daily or hourly basis can be seen as an abstract model of a certain type of power plant, also spoken of as a *virtual power plant*.

Besides describing different types of energy derivatives, this chapter introduces methods to determine their *fair value*. The fair value of a contract is defined as the price at which a rational market participant would be indifferent whether to buy or sell the contract. When deriving fair values, we make the general assumption that the market is *arbitrage*-free, that is, making a profit without taking any risk is not possible, although there may occasionally be such *arbitrage opportunities* in real markets. If, for a given product, market prices can be determined on a regular basis one also speaks of a *mark-to-market valuation* of a product or portfolio. A more theoretical account of derivatives pricing is given in Section A.3 of the appendix.

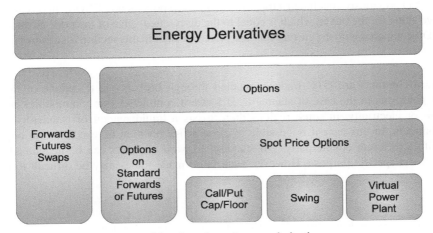

Figure 5.1 Overview of energy derivatives.

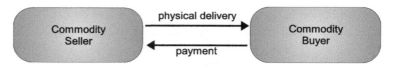

Figure 5.2   Commodity forward contract.

5.1   FORWARDS, FUTURES AND SWAPS

Forwards, futures and swaps are hedging instruments that have no optionality. For a given commodity, they are typically the most liquid type of derivatives. Compared with options, they are much easier to use and to price.

5.1.1   Forward Contracts

Forward contracts are bilateral agreements to purchase or sell a certain amount of a commodity on a fixed future date (delivery date) at a predetermined contract price. The seller of the forward contract has the obligation to deliver the commodity on the delivery date (see Figure 5.2), whereas the buyer has the obligation to receive the commodity and pay the specified contract price. The payment date specified in the contract is usually at (or near) the delivery date, so that no cashflow happens until delivery. The current *forward price* $F(t, T)$ at time t for a given delivery date T is the contract price at which a forward contract has a fair value of zero, that is the price at which forward contracts are currently transacted in the market. If a forward contract has been concluded in the past at a different contract price K, the forward contract has a positive or negative fair value. The forward price can therefore be understood as the current market price of the commodity for a given delivery date.

Example: The forward price for gasoil with delivery in December is quoted at 1000 USD/t, meaning that market participants can buy or sell gasoil for December at 1000 USD/t. If someone had previously concluded a forward contract at a price of 900 USD/t, this contract has a positive value for the buyer, which is equal to the discounted value of the price advantage of 100 USD/t compared with the current forward price (see later in this section for a more rigorous valuation).

Forward contracts are OTC trades, executed through brokers via telephone or through Internet platforms in the case of standardised forward contracts.[1] For commodities such as crude oil or electricity, in some regions there exists a liquid market of standardised forward contracts. In this case it is possible to close a risk position by executing an opposite trade with a different counterparty. Off-standard forward contracts can be negotiated individually for a specific purpose. However, such tailor made trades may be difficult to revise later.

---

[1] Different from our definition, the term *forward contract* is sometimes also used for certain exchange-traded products (e.g., at Nord Pool, see Section 1.5.2).

One of the most severe disadvantages of forward contracts is the credit risk involved, where one of the counterparties does not, or cannot, fulfil his obligation to deliver or pay the commodity (see Section 3.4).

The main uses of forward contracts are to:

- hedge the obligation to deliver or purchase a commodity at a future date;
- secure a sales profit from a commodity production;
- speculate on rising or falling commodity prices.

If forward contracts are valued against market prices (mark-to-market valuation), then the buyer of the forward contract (holder of the "long" position) makes a profit if the commodity price rises and makes a loss if the commodity price falls. The value of the forward contract (long position) at delivery date is the value of the commodity that is being delivered minus the contract price that has to be paid. The value of the commodity is given by the *spot price* $S(T)$, such that the payoff for a long forward contract with contract price K can be written as $S(T) - K$ (see Figure 5.3). Similarly, the payoff for a short position is $K - S(T)$.

Where the forward market is sufficiently liquid, calculating the fair value of a forward contract is model independent and follows immediately from the no-arbitrage assumption. Assume a customer is long on a forward contract for delivery date T at contract price K. By selling another forward contract at the current market price $F = F(t, T)$, the physical deliveries of both forward contracts in the portfolio cancel and there is a fixed net cashflow of $F - K$ at delivery T. The fair value of the forward contract equals the value of this cashflow at today's time t, which is just the discounted value of the difference between the current forward price F and the contract price K, that is $e^{-r(T-t)}(F - K)$.

For this example we carry out the arbitrage argument to determine the fair value explicitly. Let $U_{K,T}$ denote the fair value of a forward contract with contract price K and delivery date T.

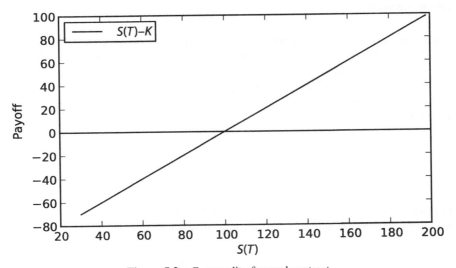

Figure 5.3   Commodity forward contract.

If $U_{K,T}$ were less than $e^{-r(T-t)}(F-K)$, a market participant could purchase the forward contract with contract price K (paying the fair value $U_{K,T}$ in exchange) and at the same time sell another forward contract at the current market price $F(t,T)$. Both contracts together yield a fixed cashflow with a higher value $e^{-r(T-t)}(F-K)$ compared with the premium paid, that is an arbitrage profit is generated. Conversely, if $U_{K,T}$ were larger than $e^{-r(T-t)}(F-K)$, one would sell the forward contract with contract price K (receiving the fair value $U_{K,T}$ in exchange), and buy another forward contract at the current market price $F(t,T)$ and again gain an arbitrage profit. This shows that the fair value of a forward contract with contract price K is uniquely given by

$$U_{K,T} = e^{-r(T-t)}(F-K),\qquad(5.1)$$

where $e^{-r(T-t)}$ is the discount factor to the delivery date T. If we have $K=F$, then the value of the forward contract is exactly zero.

Example: An electricity producer buys $10\,000$ t coal at time t_0 to be delivered two years later at time $T = t_0 + 2$ at a price $K = 100$ USD/t. One year later at time $t_1 = t_0 + 1$ the forward price for coal to be delivered at time T has risen to $F(t_1, T) = 110$ USD/t. The interest rate for one year at time t_1 is assumed as $R = 4\%$, which gives a discount factor of $1/(1+R) = 0.96154$. The fair value of the forward contract is

$$U_{K,T} = \frac{1}{1+R} \times 10\,000 \times (110 - 100) \text{ USD} = 96\,154 \text{ USD}.$$

This value $U_{K,T}$ is the price a neutral market participant would be willing to pay to enter into this contract as a buyer. If the seller counterparty defaults on the contract, this is also the loss the buyer suffers having to buy the coal at the current more expensive market price from a different counterparty.

Forward contracts for some commodities typically do not have a single delivery date but either a sequence of delivery dates (e.g., coal) or a continuous delivery schedule (e.g., gas or electricity). If we have a sequence of delivery dates $T_1, \ldots, T_n$, we can decompose the forward contract into n forward contracts that each have a single delivery date. Let K be the fixed price of the forward contract with delivery dates $T_1, \ldots, T_n$. Then the present fair value of the contract is given by

$$U_{K,\{T_1,\ldots,T_n\}} = \sum_{i=1}^{n} e^{-r(T_i-t)}(F(t, T_i) - K).\qquad(5.2)$$

The fair price of the forward contract is the price K for which the fair value of the contract is zero. Setting the expression above to zero, we can solve for K:

$$K = \frac{\sum_{i=1}^{n} e^{-r(T_i-t)}F(t, T_i)}{\sum_{i=1}^{n} e^{-r(T_i-t)}}.\qquad(5.3)$$

Example: The example forward contract for coal specifies four quarterly deliveries of coal for a given year each with a volume of 30 000 t. The forward prices and discount factors ($r = 4.5\%$) for the four quarters are given by

Date	Price (USD/t)	Discount factor
Q1	69.50	0.956
Q2	69.70	0.945
Q3	70.40	0.935
Q4	71.20	0.924

The fair foward price from equation (5.3) is $K = 70.19$ USD/t. In this case the fair forward price is very close to the arithmetic average of the quarterly prices, 70.20 USD/t.

For delivery over a continuous period $T_1 \leq t \leq T_2$, the value of a forward contract at fixed price K is given by the integral expression

$$U_{K,T_1,T_2} = \int_{T_1}^{T_2} e^{-r(T-t)} \left(F(t,T) - K\right) dT.$$

Solving $U_{K,T_1,T_2} = 0$ for K we get the fair price of the forward contract as

$$K = \frac{\int_{T_1}^{T_2} e^{-r(T-t)} F(t,T) \, dT}{\int_{T_1}^{T_2} e^{-r(T-t)} \, dT}.$$

We will denote the fair price of a forward contract with delivery period $T_1 \leq t \leq T_2$ as $F(t, T_1, T_2)$.

5.1.2 Futures Contracts

Futures contracts can be defined as standardised forward contracts traded at commodity exchanges where a clearinghouse serves as *central counterparty* for all transactions (see Figure 5.4). This eliminates the counterparty risk present in OTC forward contracts. The commodity exchange sets rules to protect the clearinghouse from possible losses. Trading participants usually pay an initial margin as guarantee to the exchange. Each trading day a

Figure 5.4   Commodity futures contract.

settlement price for the futures contract is determined and gains or losses are immediately realised via a margin account. In this way, no unrealised losses may occur that could impose a substantial credit risk.

Futures contracts often do not lead to physical delivery but are settled financially. This is especially in favour of speculators who neither have the capability nor the interest to handle a physical delivery of the commodity. A market participant using a financially settled futures contract to hedge a planned physical buy or sell bears a "basis risk" that the actual price for the physical transaction differs from the final settlement price for the contract. Since futures contracts are standardised and traded against a central counterparty, it is easy to close out a futures position by executing a trade opposite to the first one. In this case, those two trades cancel each other out. Most futures contracts are not held until maturity but closed out in advance.

Example: On January 14 a trader enters into a long yearly baseload futures contract for electricity at a price of 54.20 EUR/MWh. The contract size is 1 MW, resulting in a contract volume of 8760 MWh since the delivery year has 8760 hours. On January 19 the trader closes his long position at a price of 52.97 EUR/MWh. His total loss is 1.23 EUR/MWh, or 10 775 EUR in total. Leaving aside the initial margin payment and interest payments, the market price-dependent daily cashflows (*variation margin*) are as follows:

Date	Settlement price	Cashflow (EUR/MWh)	Total cashflow (EUR)
Jan 14	54.25	0.05	438
Jan 15	54.70	0.45	3 942
Jan 16	53.53	−1.17	−10 249
Jan 17	53.20	−0.33	−2 891
Jan 18	53.25	0.05	438
Jan 19	52.97	−0.28	−2 453
Total		**−1.23**	**−10 775**

The immediate realisation of daily profits and losses via a margin account may lead to subtle differences of forward and futures prices. One reason is that forward contracts may imply credit risk (see Section 3.4), the other reason is that the P&L of forward contracts is only realised at the time of delivery and therefore the present value is still subject to interest rate risk. The latter effect can be disregarded from a theoretical point of view if interest rates are assumed independent of the underlying price, in particular if interest rates are considered deterministic (see Cox *et al.* (1981) for more details). For practical purposes, in commodity markets both prices can often be considered as equivalent.

If used for hedging purposes, there is indeed an important difference between forward and futures contracts concerning the hedge ratio, that is the optimal number of contracts offsetting a certain market price risk. Suppose the underlying forward price F changes by ΔF. Then the change in fair value of a forward contract is given by the discounted price shift

$$\Delta U_{K,T} = e^{-r(T-t)} \Delta F.$$

For a futures position the price difference ΔF is immediately realised as a margin payment, which can be put to a riskless money market account. This means that even though forward

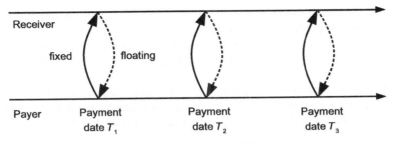

Figure 5.5   Commodity swap agreement.

and futures prices coincide, we have different sensitivities with respect to changes of the underlying forward price (Section 3.2.1).

5.1.3 Swaps

Commodity swaps are mid- and long-term risk management instruments used to lock in a fixed price for a commodity over a specific time period. These OTC-traded products are financially settled and for that purpose refer to a published commodity price index. A swap agreement defines a number of payment (or settlement) dates. In its basic form ("plain vanilla" fixed-for-floating swap), one counterparty (payer) pays on each of the payment dates a stipulated fixed price (swap price) whereas the other counterparty (receiver) pays the variable price given by the commodity index (Figure 5.5). In practice, only net amounts are paid, that is if the fixed price exceeds the variable price the payer pays the difference, in the opposite case the payer receives the difference.

Consider a swap contract with payment dates $T_1, \ldots, T_n$ where at each payment date T_i the holder pays a fixed payment K and receives a floating payment $S(T_i)$, where $S(T_i)$ is a given commodity (spot) price index. Receiving a payment $S(T_i)$ at time T_i has the same value as receiving the commodity at time T_i. This swap contract is equivalent to a forward contract with delivery dates $T_1, \ldots, T_n$, except that the settlement is purely financial. The fair value of a swap is given by equation (5.2). The fair swap rate (*par rate*) K that leads to a present value of zero is the same as for the forward contract:

$$K = \frac{\sum_{i=1}^n e^{-r(T_i-t)} F(t, T_i)}{\sum_{i=1}^n e^{-r(T_i-t)}}. \tag{5.4}$$

A swap holder paying the fixed and receiving the floating cashflows is said to hold a *payer swap*, in the opposite case the swap holder is said to hold a *receiver swap*. The swap contract can be decomposed into two *legs*: the fixed payments and the floating payments. The fixed payments are called the *fixed leg* of the swap, the floating payments are called the *floating leg* of the swap.

Example: An oil producer wants to hedge his revenues against declining oil prices. For this purpose he enters into a (receiver) swap agreement in January for the calendar months May, June and July at a price of 100 USD/bbl, which is the current forward price at this time. For each calender month the swap refers to a monthly price index, which is available at the beginning of the following month. If the oil settlement price for a given month is below the swap price, then the oil producer receives a payment equivalent to the price difference. This payment should offset the lower revenues (compared with the swap price) from selling the oil production within the respective month at the prevailing lower prices. In case the oil settlement price is above the swap price the oil producer has to pay the price difference, for which he can use the higher revenues from selling the oil to the market. In reality, the prices the oil producer achieves for his oil production will of course not match exactly the published price index, therefore the hedge will never be perfect but subject to a certain basis risk.

Calender month	Payment date	Settlement price	Cashflow (USD)
May	Jun 7	110.34	−10.34
June	Jul 6	95.16	+4.84
July	Aug 7	102.62	−2.62

Swaps are very popular OTC risk management instruments for energy market participants. They are easy to structure to the specific needs of a counterparty and offered by banks with high liquidity for many commodities. If a swap is used to hedge the price risk of production or demand of a physical commodity, then the underlying index should obviously be chosen to have a small basis risk between the index value and the actual price of the physical commodity. However, a second important criterion may be the liquidity of the index, so that transaction costs are low and positions can be closed later if required. Other important aspects are transparency in terms of how the index is determined and reliability of the index publication.

Instead of basic fixed-for-floating swaps, a swap can also refer to a second commodity price index, that is a different oil product, so the net payment depends on the price differential between two oil products. Such a swap could be used by a refinery as a hedge instrument.

Similar to OTC forward contracts, swap agreements contain credit risk that one counterparty cannot fulfil the payments he is obliged to make. To mitigate this risk, exchanges offer clearing services for certain swap types, so that a central counterparty guarantees contract performance.

5.2 COMMODITY FORWARD CURVES

As defined in Section 5.1.1, the *forward price* $F(t, T)$ at time t of a commodity for delivery date T is defined as the price of a forward contract that yields a contract fair value of zero. Typically, forward prices of a commodity are quoted by brokers or exchanges for a set of different standardised delivery dates T, for example, monthly delivery dates for the next 12 calendar months. Depending on the expected future demand and availability of the commodity, the forward prices can differ substantially between two different delivery dates. This dependence is called the *forward curve* of a commodity. In mathematical notation, the forward curve is the price $F(t, T)$ interpreted as a function of T for fixed t.

As an example, Figure 5.6 shows historical forward curves for crude oil. Not only does the level of the oil price change substantially, but the shape of the forward curve also varies between upward and downward sloping. A downward-sloping forward curve is called a *backwardation*, an upward-sloping curve a *contango*. According to the classical theory, a backwardation occurs when demand for the commodity is high and inventory levels are low. If demand for the commodity decreases and inventory levels increase, the shape will switch to contango. This

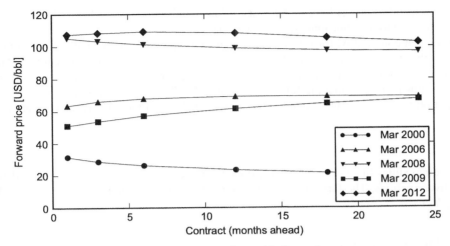

Figure 5.6   WTI crude oil monthly forward curve.

behaviour can be observed in Figure 5.6 looking at the forward curves from the years 2008 and 2009. Following the bankruptcy of Lehman Brothers in 2008, demand for oil decreased and deteriorating spot prices pulled the forward curve into contango.

Depending on the commodity, forward curves can have more complex shapes than just contango or backwardation. Figure 5.7 shows a forward curve for natural gas in the UK. The curve has a seasonal shape, since demand is seasonal and storage capacity is limited. The price spread between summer and winter is an important characteristic of the forward curve and may change over time. It determines the value of gas storage used to inject gas in summer when demand and prices are low and withdraw in winter to be able to sell the gas at higher prices. Conversely, as storage increases demand in summer (to inject gas) and decreases demand in

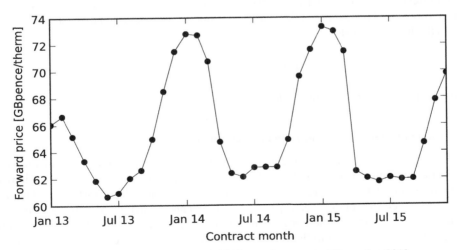

Figure 5.7   Natural gas UK monthly forward curve as of December 2012.

winter (by withdrawal), as long as the costs to inject and withdraw are lower than the price spread, storage has a dampening effect on seasonal spreads.

For a given commodity, forward market quotes are typically only available for a number of standardised delivery dates (e.g., the exchange-traded futures contracts). For delivery dates in between, interpolation can be used. When modelling forward curves mathematically, we therefore mostly assume that the full forward curve $F(t, T)$ for all $t < T < T_{max}$ is available. The spot price $S(t)$ can be interpreted as the limit case $T \to t$ of the forward curve, that is

$$S(t) = F(t, t) = \lim_{T \to t} F(t, T).$$

For commodities like gas or electricity, traded contracts do not have single delivery dates, but delivery periods. The forward price at time t for a delivery period $[T_1, T_2]$ is denoted by $F(t, T_1, T_2)$.

5.2.1 Investment Assets

Investment assets are assets such as gold, which are mainly held for investment purposes. For this purpose they have to be easily storable and standardised. Pricing models for such commodities come closest to those of financial assets. The relationship between spot price $S(t)$ and forward price $F(t, T)$ can be derived from cash-and-carry arbitrage arguments. Let $C(t, T)$ denote the present value of the storage costs to store one unit of the commodity from today (time t) until the forward expiry T. Then the arbitrage-free forward price is given by

$$F(t, T) = (S(t) + C(t, T))\, e^{r(T-t)},$$

where r is the (instantaneous) continuously compounded interest rate (Hull, 2011). If there is an income from storing the commodity, it can be included in $C(t, T)$ with a negative value. The methodology is completely analogous when calculating forward prices for financial assets, such as foreign currencies or stocks, where $C(t, T)$ represents the interest payments of the foreign currency or the dividend payments of the stock. If storage costs in any time period are proportional to the asset price, they can be considered as an additional negative yield and added to the financing costs:

$$F(t, T) = S(t)e^{(r+c)(T-t)},$$

where c is the continuously compounded rate for storage costs.

5.2.2 Consumption Assets and Convenience Yield

Many commodities, such as oil or gas, are not traded primarily for investment purposes but for consumption. There is a steady flow from sources (production or exploration) to sinks (consumption). Often, there are limited storage facilities to balance differences between production and consumption over a period of time. This behaviour has strong effects on forward prices. For longer time horizons it is too costly to hedge a short forward position by storing the commodity up to the forward expiration date. To understand where the usual arbitrage argument fails, the hedge strategy will be investigated in more detail.

In a market situation where $F(t, T) > (S(t) + C(t, T)) e^{r(T-t)}$, an arbitrage strategy would be to

- short the forward contract,
- borrow the amount of $S(t) + C(t, T)$ cash at the risk-free rate, and
- buy the commodity at price $S(t)$.

The borrowed cash would cover exactly the purchase of the commodity at the spot price $S(t)$ plus storage costs. At time T the loan would have to be paid back with interest payments, which amounts to $(S(t) + C(t, T))e^{r(T-t)}$. The cashflow at time T from settling the forward contract is $F(t, T)$. Thus, there would be a riskless profit at time T of $F(t, T) - (S(t) + C(t, T)) e^{r(T-t)}$. In an efficient market without arbitrage, an upper limit for the forward price is therefore

$$F(t, T) \leq (S(t) + C(t, T)) e^{r(T-t)}.$$

The inverse inequality, however, does not necessarily hold. Let us assume a market situation where $F(t, T) < (S(t) + C(t, T)) e^{r(T-t)}$ (strict inequality). If a market participant is already in possession of the commodity, a possible trading strategy would be to buy the forward contract and sell one unit of the commodity at price $S(t)$. At the forward expiry date he gets back the commodity and makes more profit compared with holding the commodity until the expiry date and paying storage costs for the whole period. However, this is in most cases not an attractive alternative for the holder of the commodity, since he typically requires the commodity for consumption and does not plan to hold the commodity until expiry of the forward contract. Since the strategy requires to be already in possession of the commodity, it cannot be considered as an arbitrage strategy. Simply short-selling the physical commodity (similar to a stock) is typically not possible, as this would require borrowing the commodity which is likely not feasible for consumption assets.

Let $Y(t, T)$ be the sum of the additional benefits for owners of the physical commodity within the time period from t to T compared with just being long a forward contract. Then the forward price inequality can be replaced by the equality

$$F(t, T) = (S(t) + C(t, T) - Y(t, T)) e^{r(T-t)}.$$

If benefits and storage costs are written as yields y and c, this equation becomes

$$F(t, T) = S(t)e^{(r+c-y)(T-t)}.$$

The yield y is then called the *convenience yield*. The convenience yield plays the same role that dividends play for stocks. Often, the storage cost is by convention included in the convenience yield, such that the convenience yield is the benefit from holding the commodity minus the storage costs. In this case, the forward price formula simply becomes

$$F(t, T) = S(t)e^{(r-y)(T-t)}, \tag{5.5}$$

where the convenience yield can be positive or negative.

Financing and storage costs lead to a natural upward slope of the forward curve, that is contango, whereas the convenience yield leads to a backwardation. In the terminology of

Pindyck (2001), a *strong backwardation* means that $F(t, T) < S(t)$, that is the convenience yield overcompensates for storage costs and financing costs, so that the forward curve is downward sloping. A *weak backwardation* means that the forward curve is upward sloping, but the convenience yield overcompensates for storage costs, that is $F(t, T) < S(t)e^{r(T-t)}$.

The value of the forward price depends to a large extent on market expectations about the future availability of the commodity. It may change over time even if storage costs do not change. The convenience yield is responsible for the fact that the forward prices of commodities have an independent stochastic behaviour that is not explained by spot prices. Using a more fundamental approach, commodity price dynamics can be understood by taking into account inventories and the market for storage (Pindyck, 2001, 2002). Electricity prices can be seen as a limit case. Since electricity is hardly storable, forward prices are determined completely by the expectations about future availability and production costs and not by the current spot price. Therefore, electricity forward curves have strong seasonal patterns, which can also be observed in historical spot prices.

In practice, the convenience yield itself is not directly observable, but rather a concept which can explain the shape of the observed forward curve. In other words, formula (5.5) *implies* a certain convenience yield, which reproduces the observed forward prices. This convenience yield will of course change from day to day, reflecting changing market views on the future availability of the commodity.

5.2.3   The Market Price of Risk

For commodities with limited storage capacities the relationship between spot and forward prices depends on the convenience yield and on expectations of the future availability of the commodity (see Section 5.2.2). Thus, there is a relationship between forward prices $F(t, T)$ and the expected spot price $\mathbb{E}_t[S_T]$ at the forward expiry date. Ultimately, the futures prices must converge to the spot price (up to basis risks) when approaching the futures delivery date $(S(t) = \lim_{T \to t} F(t, T))$. Figure 5.8 shows the Brent futures price and the spot price starting

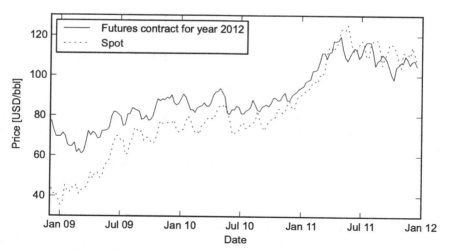

Figure 5.8   Brent spot and futures (contract expiry 2012) prices.

end of 2008 when the forward curve had a very pronounced contango shape. Over time, both prices converged, but at a higher price level compared with 2008.

A systematic difference between forward prices and expected spot prices does not lead to arbitrage opportunities, but may generate profits on average for a speculator. For example, if $F(t, T) > \mathbb{E}_t[S(T)]$ then a speculator could sell a forward contract at price $F = F(t, T)$ in hope that the spot price at maturity will be below F, which it is on average. The profit or loss at time T is then $F - S(T)$. However, such a trading strategy is risky and speculators will use it if they expect sufficient profit as compensation for the risk taken. But how can a situation, such as $F(t, T) > \mathbb{E}_t[S(T)]$, occur in the first place? No speculator would be willing to buy a forward contract above the expected spot price, that is take a risk with negative expected return, unless the forward contract offsets risk he already has in his portfolio. However, apart from speculators there may also be hedgers as a group of market participants who are prepared to buy forward contracts at a premium to reduce the market risk of their company. There may further be other hedgers who need to sell forward contracts to reduce their market risk and therefore would drive forward prices down. Since this may equally be true, there is no general rule for the relation between forward prices and expected spot prices. Whether the risk premium is positive or negative depends very much on the structure of the market participants and their particular interests. Only when the risk premium in either direction becomes too large is there an incentive for speculators to take the risk in exchange for the premium. In equilibrium conditions the premium paid for a given "unit" of risk is called the *market price of risk*. The classical theory dating back to Keynes in 1930 concludes that future prices should generally be below spot prices (*normal backwardation*), since there is a higher hedging pressure for producers who are long the commodity whereas speculators as risk takers would require a risk premium. More recent work (e.g., Bessembinder (1992)) distinguishes the following origins of potential risk premiums:

- The "hedging pressure" of market participants (producers and consumers).
- Asset pricing theory predicting a linear relation between expected return and risk that cannot be diversified in a large portfolio (*systematic risk*).

For an analysis of risk premia in the US electricity market, see Geman and Vasicek (2001) or Bessembinder and Lemmon (2002).

5.3 "PLAIN VANILLA" OPTIONS

A *call (put) option* contract gives the option holder the right, but not the obligation, to purchase (sell) a certain commodity at a predetermined strike price. The option seller has the obligation to deliver (purchase) the commodity upon exercise by the option holder. Typically, the option seller receives an option premium at the time the contract is signed (upfront). Options can be traded as OTC products or via commodity exchanges. Exchange-traded options often do not give the right to physical delivery of the commodity but are financially settled, with the option holder receiving a cash payment equivalent to the value of the commodity according to a published commodity index. In some cases the option holder receives a futures contract on exercise that finally will be financially settled.

If at the option's *maturity* (or *expiration*) date T the commodity price $S(T)$ exceeds the strike price K, then the holder of a call option will exercise the option to buy the commodity

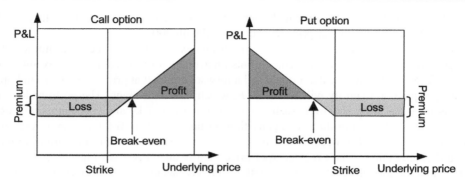

Figure 5.9   Gains and losses at maturity for an option holder.

for the price K. In this case his payoff (value at maturity) is $S(T) - K$. In the opposite case $(S(T) < K)$, the holder of a call option will not exercise the option, because the value of the commodity is lower than the price K he would have to pay upon option exercise. Therefore, the payoff for the call option at maturity is

$$C_{K,T} = \begin{cases} S(T) - K & \text{if } S(T) > K \\ 0 & \text{otherwise.} \end{cases} \tag{5.6}$$

This can be written more concisely as $C_{K,T} = \max(S(T) - K, 0)$. Similarly, a put option is only exercised if at maturity the commodity price is below the strike price. In this case the payoff is $K - S(T)$, because the option holder receives the strike price K and has to deliver the commodity, which has the lower value $S(T)$. If $S(T) > K$, then the put option will not be exercised since the commodity could be sold at the market for a higher price. The payoff for a put option at maturity is

$$P_{K,T} = \begin{cases} K - S(T) & \text{if } S(T) < K \\ 0 & \text{otherwise.} \end{cases} \tag{5.7}$$

Or in short, $P_{K,T} = \max(K - S(T), 0)$. Figure 5.9 shows the financial results for the holder of a call option as a function of the underlying price at maturity. The financial result at maturity is the option payoff minus the option premium paid. At the break-even point, the option payoff equals the option premium. The option premium is also the maximum loss for the option holder, which he incurs if he does not exercise the option, that is the option expires worthless. For the option seller, however, the maximum loss may be unlimited, for example if he has written a call option without being in possession of the commodity. Analogous to financial markets, options can be *European* style (i.e., exercisable only at the maturity date) or *American* style (i.e., exercisable any time until maturity).

5.3.1   The Put–Call Parity and Option Strategies

Options together with futures and forward contracts can be used as hedging instruments or to implement more sophisticated trading strategies. One important relation between the different instruments is the *put–call parity*. Let $C_{K,T}$ and $P_{K,T}$ denote the fair value of a call and respectively a put option with strike K and maturity T and let F denote the current underlying forward price for maturity T. Then, regardless of any assumptions on stochastic models, the following identity holds in an arbitrage-free market:

$$C_{K,T} - P_{K,T} = e^{-r(T-t)}(F - K). \tag{5.8}$$

To prove the identity, consider a portfolio consisting of a long call option and a short put option. At maturity T, the following cases can occur.

1. $S(T) \geq K$: The call option is exercised and the put option expires worthless. The total payoff is $S(T) - K$.
2. $S(T) < K$: The put option is exercised by the counterparty and the call option expires worthless. The payoff of the short put is $-(K - S(T)) = S(T) - K$.

In both cases the payoff is $S(T) - K$, which is also the payoff of a forward contract with strike K and by equation (5.1) the value is equal to the right-hand side of the identity.

An important consequence of the put–call parity is that a call option can be replicated by a put option and a forward contract as

$$C_{K,T} = P_{K,T} + e^{-r(T-t)}(F - K).$$

Therefore, knowing the price of a put option implies knowing the price of the corresponding call option and vice versa.

Two examples of useful trading strategies involving options are shown in Figure 5.10. A holder of a long forward or futures position can buy a put option (*protective put*) as an insurance against declining commodity prices. If the commodity price falls below the strike price, the put option can be exercised and the commodity is sold at the strike price. Therefore, the put option secures a minimum price for selling the commodity without losing the upside potential of rising commodity prices. The *covered call* strategy can be employed to increase profits if the market is expected to stay near the current price level. If a market participant with a

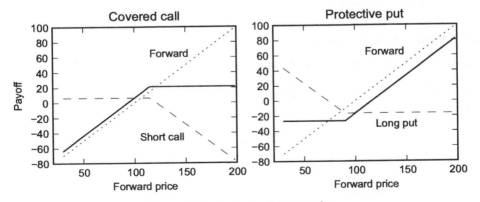

Figure 5.10   Typical option strategies.

long futures or forward position sells a (out-of-the-money) call option, he receives the option premium and in return loses the upside potential above the strike level.

5.3.2 Black's Futures Price Model

The Black model (Black, 1976) defines the "market standard" for pricing options on future contracts. It models a single futures contract for a given maturity in a similar way to the Black–Scholes model for a stock option (Black and Scholes, 1973). For a single futures contract with a given fixed maturity date, we denote the futures price by $F(t)$ instead of $F(t, T)$, leaving out explicit reference to the maturity date. By making no distinction between forward price and futures price, the model can also be used to model a forward price. The Black model assumes that the futures price $F(t)$ follows a geometric Brownian motion

$$\frac{dF(t)}{F(t)} = \mu \, dt + \sigma \, dW(t).$$

Since we are interested in option pricing, we can switch to risk-neutral parameters (discussed further in Section A.3 of the Appendix). In a risk-neutral world, a futures contract has no drift term, that is $\mu = 0$. This is different compared with a stock price, whose (risk-neutral) drift (ignoring dividends) is the riskless rate r. In contrast to a stock, a futures contract refers to a payment in the future, therefore no capital is bound at $t = 0$. Therefore, in a risk-neutral world, concluding a futures contract cannot be expected to earn a positive return. In fact, as explained in Section A.3 in more detail, the expected futures price at maturity T equals the current futures price $F(t)$ (*martingale* property) in a risk-neutral world:

$$F(t) = \mathbb{E}_t[F(T)].$$

Referring to the discussion in Section 5.2.3, the *market price of risk* is zero in the risk-neutral world, that is there is no risk premium contained in forward (or futures) prices.

The resulting Black model equation is

$$dF(t) = \sigma(t)F(t) \, dW(t), \tag{5.9}$$

where we assume a deterministic volatility function $\sigma(t)$.

5.3.3 Option Pricing Formulas

To derive analytical formulas for European-style options on futures, let $F(t) = F(t, T_1)$ denote a futures price for expiration date T_1 and let $C_{K,T}(t, F)$ and $P_{K,T}(t, F)$ denote the fair value of a call and respectively a put option with strike K and maturity T. The option maturity T may be earlier or equal to the futures expiry T_1. At maturity of the option, the payoffs are

$$C_{K,T}(T, F) = \max(F(T) - K, 0),$$
$$P_{K,T}(T, F) = \max(K - F(T), 0).$$

Evaluated at time t, the payoff formulas $\max(F(t) - K, 0)$ for the call option and $\max(K - F(t), 0)$ for the put option are also called the *intrinsic value* of the options. They define the payoff received if the option were exercised now (which is, however, only possible for

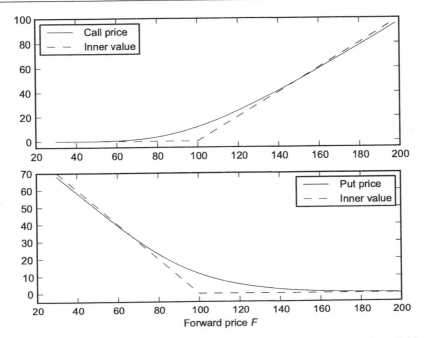

Figure 5.11   European-style option prices for $K = 100$, $T = 1$, $\sigma = 0.3$ and $r = 0.03$.

American-style options) or if the underlying price $F(t)$ will not change any more until maturity. Even if the *intrinsic value* is zero, so that the option would not be exercised at the current price $F(t)$ (i.e., the option is *out-of-the-money*), the option may have a positive fair price. This is due to the fact that $F(t)$ may move until maturity and the option may still generate a positive payoff (i.e., the option will be *in-the-money*) with a certain probability. Figure 5.11 shows an example of option prices for a call and a put option as a function of the futures price F.

For a futures contract with the same expiry date as the option $T = T_1$, the payoffs are $\max(S(T) - K, 0)$ and $\max(K - S(T), 0)$, since at expiry the futures price is equal to the spot price $(F(T, T) = S(T))$. In this way, options can also be priced on the spot price rather than the futures price using the same formulas.

By general option pricing theory (see Section A.3), the fair option price is the expectation of the discounted payoff under the risk-neutral parameters (5.9):

$$C_{K,T}(t, F) = e^{-r(T-t)}\mathbb{E}_t\left[\max(F(T) - K, 0)\right],$$
$$P_{K,T}(t, F) = e^{-r(T-t)}\mathbb{E}_t\left[\max(K - F(T), 0)\right].$$

For the model assumptions (5.9), the expectation values can be calculated analytically. Since $F(t)$ has the same dynamics as a stock price under the Black–Scholes model when the dividend yield d is equal to the risk-free rate r, the analytical formulas available for the Black–Scholes model can be used by setting $d = r$. This gives the following results for European-style call and put options:

$$C_{K,T}(t, F) = e^{-r(T-t)}(FN(d_1) - KN(d_2)), \tag{5.10}$$
$$P_{K,T}(t, F) = e^{-r(T-t)}(KN(-d_2) - FN(-d_1)), \tag{5.11}$$

evaluated at the current futures price $F = F(t)$ where

$$d_1 = \frac{\ln(F/K) + V/2}{\sqrt{V}}, \quad d_2 = d_1 - \sqrt{V}.$$

The expression $e^{-r(T-t)}$ is the discount factor until maturity and $N(x)$ denotes the *cumulative normal distribution function*

$$N(x) = \frac{1}{\sqrt{2\pi}} \int_{-\infty}^{x} e^{-u^2/2} \, du.$$

V denotes the variance

$$V = \mathrm{Var}_t[\ln F(T)] = \int_t^T \sigma^2(s) \, ds.$$

If the volatility σ is constant, the variance is given simply by $V = \sigma^2(T - t)$.

The cumulative normal distribution function $N(x)$ requires numerical approximation and is available in numerical libraries as well as in spreadsheet applications. Otherwise, implementation of Black's formula only involves standard mathematical operations.

5.3.4   Hedging Options: The "Greeks"

The option price within the Black–Scholes theory is an *arbitrage price*, meaning that any other price would lead to an arbitrage opportunity by replicating the option with a dynamic portfolio strategy of the underlying commodity. The replicating strategy can be used to eliminate (*hedge*) the market price risk of the option. From the derivation of the Black–Scholes formulas, the hedging strategy can be constructed explicitly. For this purpose it is important to look at the sensitivities of an option or portfolio value with respect to changes in the market parameters. These sensitivities of an option or portfolio are traditionally denoted by Greek letters and are called the "Greeks".

Hedging an Option

Let $U(t, F)$ be the price of a European option on a futures contract. Assume that in a small time period dt the futures price changes by dF. By Itô's formula (see Section A.2.3 in the Appendix) applied to (5.9) we get

$$dU = \left(\frac{\partial U}{\partial t} + \frac{1}{2}\sigma^2 \frac{\partial^2 U}{\partial F^2} \right) dt + \sigma \frac{\partial U}{\partial F} \, dW(t).$$

Consider now a portfolio Π consisting of a written option with value $-U(t, F)$ and a number ϕ of futures contracts F. The value from the futures contracts will be accrued on a margin account G, which is part of the portfolio. The futures contracts themselves have no value, so that $\Pi = -U + G$. Within the small time period dt, the margin account will receive (or pay) a risk-free interest payment $rG\,dt$ and margin calls $\phi\,dF$. The overall portfolio value will therefore change by

$$d\Pi = -dU + rG\,dt + \phi\,dF$$
$$= \left(-\frac{\partial U}{\partial t} - \frac{1}{2}\sigma^2\frac{\partial^2 U}{\partial F^2} + rG\right)dt + \left(\phi - \frac{\partial U}{\partial F}\right)\sigma F\,dW(t).$$

By choosing exactly $\phi = \frac{\partial U}{\partial F}$ at each point of time, the random term involving $W(t)$ can be eliminated and the portfolio evolves deterministically. In an arbitrage-free market, any riskless portfolio cannot have a profit greater than the risk-free rate r. Since a reverse portfolio can be constructed by buying the option and holding $-\phi$ futures contracts, one can show that the profit of Π cannot be less than the risk-free rate. Hence, we conclude that $d\Pi = r\Pi\,dt$. Applying the expression for $d\Pi$ derived above and $\Pi = -U + G$, this leads to the partial differential equation

$$\frac{\partial U}{\partial t} + \frac{1}{2}\sigma^2\frac{\partial^2 U}{\partial F^2} = rU. \tag{5.12}$$

The Delta

We have seen that the hedging strategy is defined by the number $\frac{\partial U}{\partial F}$ specifying the number of futures contracts in the hedging portfolio. This number is called the *delta* of the option,

$$\Delta = \frac{\partial U}{\partial F} \tag{5.13}$$

and the hedging strategy is called *delta hedging*. The delta can be defined for any security as the first derivative of its value with respect to the underlying price. It measures the sensitivity of the portfolio value with respect to small changes in the underlying price F. The delta can either be calculated analytically as a derivative or it can be calculated numerically as

$$\Delta \approx \frac{U(t, F + \Delta F) - U(t, F - \Delta F)}{2\Delta F},$$

where ΔF is a small change of F.

The delta position is often specified in units of the underlying commodity. This also results naturally from looking at the units in equation (5.13). If, for example, the futures price F is denoted in USD/bbl and the option value U in USD, then the quotient in (5.13) yields the unit barrel.

Example: Let $F = 100$ EUR/MWh be the price of an electricity futures contract. Now assume a portfolio consisting of various forwards and futures positions with portfolio value $U = 5$ million EUR and delta $\Delta = 1\,000\,000$ MWh. If F changes by $\Delta F = 0.5$ EUR/MWh to 100.5 EUR/MWh, then the portfolio value will change to $\tilde{U} \approx U + \Delta \times \Delta F = 5.5$ million EUR. The change of the portfolio value per 0.01 EUR/MWh change of F is 10 000 EUR.

A futures contract has a delta of 1, since a price shift of dF in the underlying price leads to a margin payment dF. This means that the delta exactly matches the futures contract size in the

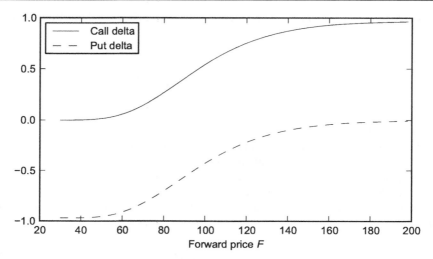

Figure 5.12 European option deltas ($K = 100$, $T = 1$, $\sigma = 0.3$ and $r = 0.03$).

respective units, for example a futures contract over 1000 bbl crude oil has a delta of 1000 bbl. A forward contract with strike K and maturity T by (5.1) has a value of $F_{K,T} = e^{-r(T-t)}(F - K)$ and a delta of

$$\frac{\partial \left(e^{-r(T-t)}(F - K)\right)}{\partial F} = e^{-r(T-t)},$$

which is the discount factor until the contract expiry. Therefore, the deltas of a futures and a forward contract are different although the fair prices are the same. If one wants to hedge a long forward contract using short futures contracts, the number of futures contracts required is slightly lower (multiplied by the discount factor).

In a portfolio consisting of multiple derivatives with the same underlying F, the net delta of the whole portfolio can be considered for hedging purposes. The delta hedging strategy would then offset the portfolio delta by an appropriate derivative, such as a futures or forward contract, so that the hedged portfolio has a net delta of zero. In this case the portfolio is said to be *delta neutral*.

For European-style call and put options the deltas can be computed explicitly as (see Figure 5.12 for a graphical representation)

$$\Delta_C = e^{-r(T-t)}N(d_1),$$
$$\Delta_P = e^{-r(T-t)}(N(d_1) - 1).$$

The Theta

The difference between the option price and the intrinsic value is often called the *time value* of the option and measures the value of the optionality in addition to the payoff if the option were exercised immediately. The time value decreases when approaching the expiry of the

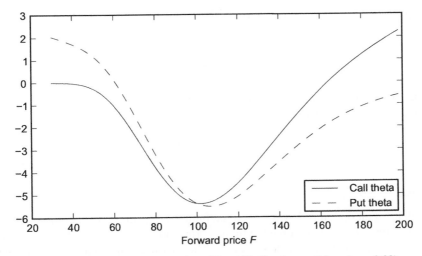

Figure 5.13   European option theta ($K = 100$, $T = 1$, $\sigma = 0.3$ and $r = 0.03$).

option. This dependency is described by the *theta* (Θ) of an option, defined as the derivative of the option price with respect to time, keeping the futures price and all other parameters fixed:

$$\Theta = \frac{\partial U}{\partial t}.$$

Figure 5.13 shows theta as a function of the futures price. Theta measures the sensitivity of the option price (or more generally of a portfolio) with respect to time as market prices are kept constant.

Example: For the call option in Figure 5.11 the loss in value per trading day shall be derived if market prices do not change. For the given market prices, assume $\Theta = -5$ EUR/year. A trading day is given by $\Delta t = 1/252$ if we have 252 trading days per year. Then the change in value per trading day is

$$\Delta U = \Theta \times \Delta t \approx 0.02 \text{ EUR per trading day.}$$

This loss is caused by the decreased lifetime of the option reducing the optionality.
The analytical formulas for the theta of European-style call and put options are

$$\Theta_C = e^{-r(T-t)} \left(-\frac{FN'(d_1)\sqrt{V}}{2(T-t)} + rFN(d_1) - rKN(d_2) \right),$$

$$\Theta_P = e^{-r(T-t)} \left(-\frac{FN'(d_1)\sqrt{V}}{2(T-t)} - rFN(-d_1) + rKN(-d_2) \right).$$

In these equations N' denotes the derivative of the cumulative normal distribution N, which is the normal density function

$$N'(x) = \frac{1}{\sqrt{2\pi}} e^{-x^2/2}.$$

Often, when used in reports, the theta is already normalised to the change in value per 1 trading day. It can then be approximated numerically as

$$\Theta_{1d} = U(t + \Delta t, F) - U(t, F).$$

The Gamma

Since the delta of an option is dependent on the futures price, the delta hedging strategy is a *dynamic hedging strategy*. Each time the futures price moves up or down, the hedge must be rebalanced by the amount the delta has changed. The measure of how much the delta changes according to a change in the underlying futures price is called the *gamma* of the option. It is defined as the first derivative of the option delta or the second derivative of the option price with respect to the futures price:

$$\Gamma = \frac{\partial \Delta}{\partial F} = \frac{\partial^2 U}{\partial F^2}.$$

The unit of gamma is less intuitive, for example, if U is measured in USD and F in USD/bbl, then the unit of gamma is $(bbl)^2/USD$.

European-style call and put options with the same strike and maturity have the same gamma, given by

$$\Gamma_C = \Gamma_P = \frac{N'(d_1)e^{-r(T-t)}}{F\sqrt{V}}.$$

The gamma as a function of the underlying price is shown in Figure 5.14. The gamma is highest if the futures price is near the strike (*at-the-money*).

Example: Assume we have a delta-neutral electricity option portfolio with a gamma value of $\Gamma = 100\,000$ MWh²/EUR. If the underlying price changes by $\Delta F = 1$ EUR/MWh, then the new delta value will be

$$\Delta(t, F + \Delta F) \approx \Gamma \times \Delta F = 100\,000\,\text{MWh}.$$

To keep the portfolio delta-neutral we have to rebalance the portfolio and sell future contracts with a contract size (equal to delta) of 100 000 MWh.

The Vega

Finally, consider the price sensitivity with respect to the option volatility. For European-style call and put options the price increases with increasing volatility. Since estimates about volatility may change over the lifetime of the option, it is important to know the effect a change

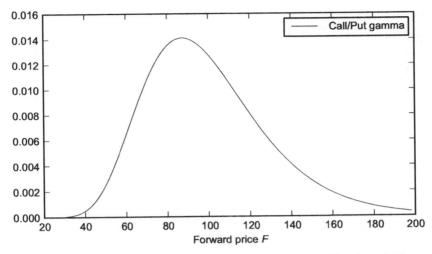

Figure 5.14   European option gamma ($K = 100$, $T = 1$, $\sigma = 0.3$ and $r = 0.03$).

in volatility has on the option price. The *vega* of an option is defined as the derivative of the option price with respect to the volatility parameter:

$$\mathcal{V} = \frac{\partial U}{\partial \sigma}.$$

As a result of the put–call parity, European-style call and put options with identical strike and maturity have the same vega. The analytical formula is:

$$\mathcal{V}_C = \mathcal{V}_P = FN'(d_1)\, e^{-r(T-t)} \sqrt{T - t}.$$

An example is shown in Figure 5.15.

Example: Assume the option in Figure 5.15 has a vega of 25 for an underlying price $F = 80$. If the volatility changes from 30% ($\sigma = 0.3$) by one point ($\Delta\sigma = 0.01$) to 31%, then the option price changes by

$$\Delta U \approx \mathcal{V} \times \Delta\sigma = 0.25.$$

Usually the vega is already normalised to the change in value per 1% change in volatility. Then the effect on the portfolio of a change in volatility by 1% is just the vega of the portfolio. A portfolio that only consists of forwards and futures has a vega of zero, which implies that it is not possible to hedge the vega of a portfolio using forwards or futures. The vega can only be reduced using other options.

Hedging the Greeks

The Greeks were defined as the sensitivities of an option value with respect to changes in the market parameters. If the assumptions of Black's model were exactly true, then delta

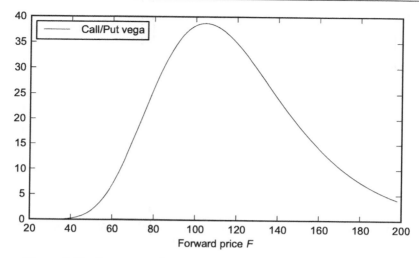

Figure 5.15 European option vega ($K = 100$, $T = 1$, $\sigma = 0.3$ and $r = 0.03$).

hedging would give a perfect hedge. However, there are at least two problems with the model assumptions:

1. The estimate on the model parameters (most importantly the σ) change, altering the valuation of the option or portfolio.
2. A continuous dynamic hedging is not possible. There will always be a finite, but not infinitesimal, change (ΔS) in the underlying price until the hedge can be rebalanced. Rebalancing too often would also lead to unacceptable transaction costs.

To identify how the option price changes with the market parameters, we use a Taylor series expansion:

$$\Delta U = \frac{\partial U}{\partial F} \Delta F + \frac{\partial U}{\partial \sigma} \Delta \sigma + \frac{\partial U}{\partial t} \Delta t + \frac{\partial^2 U}{\partial F^2} \Delta F^2 + \text{higher-order terms}$$

and after replacing the derivatives by the corresponding Greeks, we get

$$\Delta U = \Delta \left(\Delta F \right) + \mathcal{V} \Delta \sigma + \Theta \Delta t + \Gamma \Delta F^2 + \text{higher-order terms}.$$

If a portfolio is hedged in such a way that Δ, Γ and $\mathcal{V}$ are all close to zero, the portfolio is insensitive (to some degree) against changes in the underlying price F and the volatility parameter σ. Hedging the delta of the portfolio can be done using forward or futures contracts, whereas hedging the gamma or vega involves trading options.

5.3.5 Implied Volatilities and the "Volatility Smile"

The Black model defines the market standard for most futures options and thus plays a similar role to the Black–Scholes model for stock options. Market prices for futures options are often

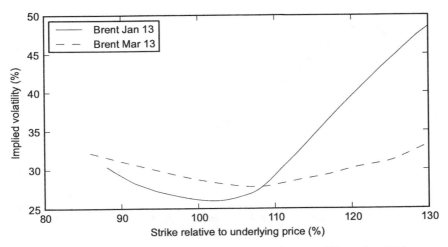

Figure 5.16   Volatility smile of Brent futures options as of November 2012.

quoted as *implied volatilities* with respect to the Black model. The implied volatility for a given option price is the (constant) volatility $\hat{\sigma}$ that has to be used in (5.10) or (5.11) to reproduce the given market price. If the market priced options exactly according to the Black model, there would be the same implied volatility for options with different strikes. The market is aware, however, that large price movements are more likely in reality than predicted by a log-normal probability distribution assumed in the Black model. Therefore, it is often the case that call options with high strike price protecting commodity buyers against extreme price movements tend to have a higher market price than calculated compared with Black's model using the same volatility as for at-the-money options. As a consequence, implied volatility is higher for options with a high strike price. Similarly, the implied volatility may differ for low strike prices.

Figure 5.16 shows an example of the implied volatilities for Brent options with two different expiry dates. The horizontal axis is the strike divided by the underlying price, so that 100% represents the "at-the-money" level. A non-constant implied volatility curve, as shown in the figure, is also called a *volatility smile*. The term refers to the convex shape of the implied volatility curve. In one-sided sloped curves, the term *volatility skew* is frequently used.

The Black model used with one set of parameters is insufficient to explain the volatility smile, consequently various extensions of the model have been developed. One possibility is to include jumps of random size in the underlying dynamics. This *jump-diffusion model* approach has been identified by Merton (1976). The additional parameters included in the model, jump size and jump frequency, can be calibrated so that option prices give a close fit to the market price and reproduce the volatility smile. Modelling volatility as a stochastic process rather than as a constant is a second approach. Heston (1993) introduces a *stochastic-volatility model* with mean-reverting volatility that leads to option pricing formulas which are analytically treatable. Additional parameters for the volatility process (e.g., volatility of volatility, mean-reversion speed, mean-reversion constant, correlation of volatility to underlying) can be fitted to the volatility smile observed in the market.

Implied volatilities typically increase with proximity to expiry of the underlying futures contract. Futures contracts with a short time to expiry are often more volatile since they are

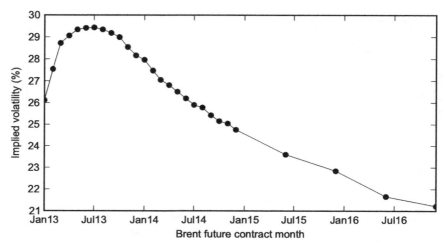

Figure 5.17   Brent implied volatility term structure as of November 2012.

more liquidly traded and market participants receive more information concerning demand and availability of the commodity during the delivery period. An example of such a term structure of implied volatilities for Brent is shown in Figure 5.17. In this example the implied volatility term structure is actually "hump shaped", that is the implied volatility first increases and then decreases again for longer option maturities. Such a shape may occur if a tight market is not expected in the short term.

5.3.6   Swaptions

A *swaption* is an option to enter into a swap contract (see Section 5.1.3) at a pre-fixed price (strike) for the fixed payments. The following data specifies a swaption (see Figure 5.18):

- The swap payment dates $T_1, \ldots, T_n$.
- The swap type, i.e. payer swap or receiver swap.
- The strike K_0 of the swaption, i.e. the fixed price of the swap.
- The option's maturity date T_S, where $T_S < T_1$, i.e. the option is exercised before the swap payments.

A swaption granting the right to enter into a payer swap is called a *call swaption* or *payer swaption*, in the other case the swaption is called a *put swaption* or *receiver swaption*.

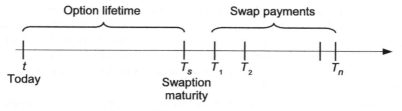

Figure 5.18   Scheme of a swaption.

Many commodity options with physical delivery can be treated as swaptions when deriving pricing models. The floating leg of the swap is then interpreted as the physical delivery of the option. An option on a yearly baseload electricity delivery can be seen as a swaption where the swap has 12 monthly payment dates. At each payment date the fixed payment is the monthly energy times the strike price and the floating payment is the value of the delivered electricity given by the respective electricity price index.

To derive the payoff of a payer (call) swaption, let $K(t)$ be the fair swap rate at time t given by equation (5.4). At maturity T_S the value of the swaption is either the value of the underlying swap at time T_S if the value is positive or zero otherwise. The value of the swap at time T_S is

$$U_{swap}(T_S) = \sum_{i=1}^{n} e^{-r(T_i-T_S)}(F(T_S, T_i) - K_0),$$

where $F(T_S, T_i)$ is the forward price for delivery date T_i at the option's maturity date T_S. Since, for the fair swap rate $K(T_S)$ at time T_S, by definition the value of the fixed leg is equal to the value of the floating leg we have

$$\sum_{i=1}^{n} e^{-r(T_i-T_S)}K(T_S) = \sum_{i=1}^{n} e^{-r(T_i-T_S)}F(T_S, T_i).$$

Substituting the last equation into the expression for $U_{swap}(T_S)$, the swap value can be expressed as

$$U_{swap}(T_S) = \sum_{i=1}^{n} e^{-r(T_i-T_S)}(K(T_S) - K_0).$$

Using the definition $P = \sum_{i=1}^{n} e^{-r(T_i-T_S)}$ for the average discount factor from the maturity date to the payment dates, we get the swaption payoff

$$U_{swaption}(T_S) = P \times \max(K(T_S) - K_0, 0). \tag{5.14}$$

Black's Formula for Swaptions

Making additional assumptions on the stochastics of the fair swap rate $K(t)$, a variant of Black's formula (5.10) can be used to price European-style swaptions. By general option pricing theory, the option price is given as the expectation of the discounted payoff (5.14) under the risk-neutral measure

$$U_{swaption}(t) = e^{-r(T_S-t)}\mathbb{E}_t[P \times \max(K(T_S) - K_0, 0)].$$

Now we make the assumption that the fair swap rate $K(t)$ follows a geometric Brownian motion with volatility σ. Then we are in the same situation as in Section 5.3.3, where option price formulas for Black's future price model were given, only now there is an additional discount factor P to take into account. Accordingly, the option price formula for a payer (call) swaption is

$$U_{swaption}(t, F) = e^{-r(T-t)} P \times (K(t)N(d_1) - K_0 N(d_2)),$$ (5.15)

where

$$d_1 = \frac{\ln(K(t)/K_0) + V/2}{\sqrt{V}},$$

$$d_2 = d_1 - \sqrt{V},$$

$$V = \sigma^2(T_S - t).$$

5.4   AMERICAN, BERMUDAN AND ASIAN OPTIONS

American and Asian options belong to the class of *path-dependent options*. Unlike European options, their payoff does not depend only on the underlying price at maturity but on the whole price path from purchase date until maturity. Since analytical formulas for path-dependent options are often not available, option prices have to be calculated using numerical methods, such as Monte Carlo simulation, trinomial trees or PDE solvers. Throughout this section, let the underlying price be denoted by $S(t)$, which could be a spot price of a commodity or a futures price.

5.4.1   American and Bermudan Options

An American-style option grants the holder the right to exercise the option any time τ during the lifetime $[t, T]$ of the option. At the exercise time τ, the option holder receives the payoff $S(\tau) - K$ for a call option or $K - S(\tau)$ for a put option. In case of a physical settlement of the option, the price $S(\tau)$ represents the value of the commodity being delivered. Calculating the fair price for an American option requires finding the optimal *exercise strategy*, that is finding the optimal decision for each market price situation whether to exercise or not to exercise.

The standard methods to calculate American option prices are as follows.

- *Binomial/trinomial trees:* The continuous-time model for $S(t)$ based on a Brownian motion is approximated by a discrete-time model. To compute the optimal exercise strategy a backwards iteration similar to a dynamic-programming approach is used.
- *Finite-difference methods:* Finite-differences methods are used to calculate numerical approximations of the partial differential equation satisfied by the option price (see Section A.3.2).

Details about these numerical methods can be found in standard textbooks on option pricing (e.g., Wilmott (2007)). Standard Monte Carlo methods are not suitable for American options, since they give no solution of the optimal exercise strategy. An extension to the Monte Carlo approach for American options is given in Longstaff and Schwartz (2001).

A Bermudan-style option is intermediate between a European-style option with an exercise right at only one point in time and an American-style option with exercise right over the whole lifetime of the option. The Bermudan option grants the holder the right to exercise at a given set of dates $T_1, \ldots, T_n$. Numerical methods to price Bermudan options are similar to those for American options, that is binomial/trinomial trees, finite differences or Longstaff–Schwartz-type Monte Carlo approaches.

5.4.2 Asian Options

Asian options differ from European options in that the payoff is not a function of the underlying price at maturity but a function of the arithmetic mean of the underlying price over a number of fixing dates $T_1, \ldots, T_n$. An Asian call option with maturity date $T \geq T_n$ and strike K has the payoff

$$\text{payoff} = \max(A(T) - K, 0),$$

where $A(T)$ is the arithmetic mean

$$A(T) = \frac{1}{n} \sum_{i=1}^{n} S(T_i).$$

Asian options are less expensive than European options because the arithmetic mean has a lower volatility compared with the underlying at a single point in time. Asian options are common in energy markets, since energy is usually delivered over a period of time and the price risk for the whole period needs to be hedged.

If a Black–Scholes framework is assumed, that is $S(t)$ follows a geometric Brownian motion, then $S(T_i)$ is log-normally distributed for each fixing date T_i. The arithmetic mean $A(T)$, however, is no longer log-normally distributed and consequently there is no simple option price formula similar to the Black–Scholes formula available. One possibility to price Asian options is by means of a Monte Carlo simulation (see Section A.3.3), where each simulation path needs to contain the prices at the fixing dates. Such a Monte Carlo simulation can be used for all types of stochastic models that can be simulated, but often the computations are very slow. There are, however, several approximations to the option price available that can be evaluated very efficiently. Two popular methods, the *Vorst method* and the *log-normal approximation*, are described in the following sections. Example results are shown in Table 5.1. When using Monte Carlo simulations it is advisable to use the geometric-mean approximation (5.16) as a *control variate* (see Section A.3.3).

Table 5.1 Approximation results for an Asian option with 12 monthly fixings $T_1 = 1, T_2 = 1 + 1/12, \ldots, T_{12} = 1 + 11/12$ and parameters $S(t) = 100, K = 100, \sigma = 0.3, \mu = r = 0.03$

Pricing method	Result
Exact price	15.30
Vorst method	15.19
Log-normal approximation	15.32

The Vorst Method

We assume that $S(t)$ is a geometric Brownian motion (see Section 5.6.2) of the form

$$dS(t) = \mu S(t)\,dt + \sigma S(t)\,dW(t),$$

with respect to the risk-neutral measure. For the logarithm the process equation is

$$d\ln S(t) = \left(\mu - \tfrac{1}{2}\sigma^2\right)dt + \sigma\,dW(t).$$

The Vorst method (see Vorst (1992)) approximates the arithmetic mean by a geometric mean

$$G(T) = \sqrt[n]{\prod_{i=1}^{n} S(T_i)}, \qquad (5.16)$$

that is again log-normally distributed. This can be seen by looking at the logarithm of $G(T)$:

$$\ln G(T) = \frac{1}{n}\sum_{i=1}^{n}\ln S(T_i),$$

that is a sum of normally distributed random variables and is therefore also normally distributed. To simplify the notation, let $T_0 = t$ and we get

$$\ln G(T) = \frac{1}{n}\sum_{i=1}^{n}\ln S(T_i)$$

$$= \ln S(t) + \frac{1}{n}\sum_{i=1}^{n}\sum_{j=1}^{i}(\ln S(T_j) - \ln S(T_{j-1}))$$

$$= \ln S(t) + \sum_{i=1}^{n}\frac{n-i+1}{n}(\ln S(T_i) - \ln S(T_{i-1})).$$

Since the increments $\left(\ln S(T_i) - \ln S(T_{i-1})\right)$ are independent, the mean and variance of $\ln G(T)$ are given by

$$\mathbb{E}[\ln G] = \ln S(t) + \left(\mu - \tfrac{1}{2}\sigma^2\right)\sum_{i=1}^{n}\frac{n-i+1}{n}(T_i - T_{i-1}),$$

$$\mathrm{Var}[\ln G] = \sigma^2\sum_{i=1}^{n}\left(\frac{n-i+1}{n}\right)^2(T_i - T_{i-1}).$$

To price Asian call or put options, we can now use Black's option price formulas (5.10) and (5.11) setting $F = \mathbb{E}[G] = \exp(\mathbb{E}[\ln G] + \tfrac{1}{2}\mathrm{Var}[\ln G])$ and $V = \mathrm{Var}[\ln G]$. However, there is a systematic bias in the option price since the geometric mean is always lower than the arithmetic mean:

$$G(T) \leq A(T).$$

In the Vorst approximation this bias is compensated by adjusting the strike of the option accordingly to

$$K' = K - (\mathbb{E}[A(T)] - \mathbb{E}[G(T)]).$$

The Log-Normal Approximation

Another approach is to approximate the arithmetic average $A(T)$ by a log-normal distribution $\tilde{A}(T)$ that coincides with $A(T)$ in the first two moments, that is they have the same mean and variance. The mean of $A(T)$ is given by

$$\mathbb{E}[A(T)] = \frac{1}{n} \sum_{i=1}^{n} F(t, T_i) \tag{5.17}$$

and shall be denoted by F_A. Since by assumption $\tilde{A}(T)$ is a log-normally distributed random variable with mean F_A, it must be of the form

$$\tilde{A}(T) = F_A \exp\left(-\tfrac{1}{2}\beta^2 + \beta N\right),$$

for some parameter β, where N is a standard Gaussian random variable. The second moment of $\tilde{A}(T)$ is given by

$$\mathbb{E}[\tilde{A}^2(T)] = F_A^2 \, \mathbb{E}[\exp(-\beta^2 + 2\beta N)] = F_A^2 \, \exp(\beta^2).$$

By definition of the variance $\mathrm{Var}[A(T)] = \mathbb{E}[A^2(T)] - \mathbb{E}[A(T)]^2$ and by definition $\mathbb{E}[A(T)] = F_A$, the moment matching condition is

$$F_A^2 \exp\left(\beta^2\right) = \mathbb{E}[A^2(T)] = \mathrm{Var}[A(T)] + F_A^2.$$

Solving for β^2 yields

$$\beta^2 = \ln\left(\frac{\mathbb{E}[A^2(T)]}{F_A^2}\right) = \ln\left(1 + \frac{\mathrm{Var}[A(T)]}{F_A^2}\right).$$

Thus, to calculate a value for β, either $\mathbb{E}[A^2(T)]$ or $\mathrm{Var}[A(T)]$ has to be known. An explicit calculation of $\mathbb{E}[A^2(T)]$ yields

$$\mathbb{E}[A^2(T)] = \frac{1}{n^2} \sum_{i,j=1}^{n} F(t, T_i)F(t, T_j) \exp(\sigma^2(\min(T_i, T_j) - t)).$$

Knowing F_A and β, Black's option pricing formulas (5.10) and (5.11) can again be used with $F = F_A$ and $V = \beta^2$.

5.5 MULTI-UNDERLYING OPTIONS

Often, market participants have a risk exposure not with respect to a single underlying, but with respect to a combination of multiple underlyings. As an example, the owner of a coal-fired power plant has a risk exposure to the price spread between coal and power (*dark spread*). To hedge such risk exposures, options with multiple underlyings can be constructed. The price of such options depends not only on the volatilities of the underlyings, but also on their correlation structure.

Let $S_1(t), \dots, S_n(t)$ denote the different underlyings. The multiple-underlying extension of the Black–Scholes framework (using risk-neutral parameters) is given by the following system of stochastic differential equations:

$$dS_i(t) = \mu_i S_i(t)\,dt + \sigma_i S_i(t)\,dW_i(t), \tag{5.18}$$

where $W_1(t), \dots, W_n(t)$ are Brownian motions correlated by

$$dW_i(t)\,dW_j(t) = \rho_{ij}\,dt.$$

The forward prices of the n underlyings are denoted by

$$F_i(t, T) = \mathbb{E}_t[S_i(T)], \quad i = 1, \dots, n.$$

5.5.1 Basket Options

A *basket option* is an option with not a single commodity as underlying but a basket $B(t)$, that is calculated as a weighted sum of multiple commodities

$$B(t) = \sum_{i=1}^{n} w_i S_i(t). \tag{5.19}$$

A prominent example is a *commodity index*, which is calculated as a weighted average of different commodity notations.

Example: A basket of energy prices related to power production could be defined as

$$B(t) = 100 \times \left(30\% \frac{\text{oil}(t)}{\text{oil}(0)} + 30\% \frac{\text{coal}(t)}{\text{coal}(0)} + 40\% \frac{CO_2(t)}{CO_2(0)} \right).$$

At time 0 the basket value is normalised to 100. If the oil price increases by 100% and the prices of coal and CO_2 emission allowances stay constant, then the basket value $B(t)$ increases by 30% to a value of 130.

A basket option is an option with a basket B as underlying. As an example, the payoff of a European call option on the basket $B(t)$ is

$$\text{payoff} = \max{(B(T) - K, 0)}. \tag{5.20}$$

The forward price F_B of a basket is simply the weighted sum of the corresponding forward prices of the constituents,

$$F_B(t, T) = \mathbb{E}_t[B(T)] = \sum_{i=1}^{n} w_i F_i(t, T). \tag{5.21}$$

Pricing basket options in the Black–Scholes framework is not straightforward, since a weighted sum of log-normally distributed random variables is no longer log-normally distributed. The same problem arises when pricing Asian options (see Section 5.4.2). Using a similar approach as for Asian options, the price of a basket option can be approximated using a log-normal approximation of the basket underlying (5.19).

Let the log-normal approximation of the basket B be given by

$$\tilde{B}(T) = F_B \exp{\left(-\tfrac{1}{2}\beta^2 + \beta N\right)},$$

where N is a standard Gaussian random variable. The first two moments of B are given by

$$\mathbb{E}[B(T)] = \sum_{i=1}^{n} w_i F_i(t, T),$$

$$\mathbb{E}[B^2(T)] = \sum_{i,j=1}^{n} w_i w_j F_i(t, T) F_j(t, T) \exp(\rho_{ij} \sigma_i \sigma_j).$$

Whereas the first two moments of $\tilde{B}$ are given by

$$\mathbb{E}[\tilde{B}] = F_B,$$
$$\mathbb{E}[\tilde{B}^2] = F_B^2 \exp(\beta^2).$$

Setting the first two moments of B and $\tilde{B}$ equal yields

$$F_B = \sum_{i=1}^{n} w_i F_i(t, T),$$

$$\beta^2 = \ln{\left(\frac{\sum_{i,j=1}^{n} w_i w_j F_i(t, T) F_j(t, T) \exp(\rho_{ij} \sigma_i \sigma_j)}{F_B^2} \right)}.$$

Now Black's option pricing formulas (5.10) and (5.11) can again be used with $F = F_B$ and $V = \beta^2$.

Example: Continuing the example earlier in this section, consider the following basket of oil, coal and CO_2 allowances, where the forward prices are all normalised to zero:

Commodity	Weight (%)	Forward price	Volatility (%)
Oil	30	100	30
Coal	30	100	20
CO_2	40	100	40

The correlation matrix of these three commodities is assumed as

	Oil	Coal	CO_2
Oil	1.0	0.1	0.6
Coal	0.1	1.0	−0.2
CO_2	0.6	−0.2	1.0

The following table compares the log-normal approximation of a one-year at-the-money call option to the exact result calculated via a sufficient number of Monte Carlo simulations:

Computation method	Price	Implied volatility (%)
Monte Carlo	8.81	22.85
Log-normal approximation	8.95	23.16

The approximation error in this example is small but noticable. However, often the uncertainties about correlations and volatility skew are larger than the approximation errors from a log-normal approximation, making this method suitable for a day-to-day valuation and for the calculation of Greeks.

A more sophisticated problem is how to derive the volatility skew or smile for a basket based on the implied volatilities of the constituents. Typically, a basket has a less pronounced volatility skew or smile compared with the single underlyings, especially if correlations are not high. A modelling approach based on copulas is described in Qu (2010).

5.5.2 Spread Options

Market participants in energy markets are often not exposed outright to commodity prices but rather to the difference of two or more commodity prices involved in a production or transformation process. Examples are given below:

- The *dark spread* or *spark spread* between power and coal (respectively gas) modelling a coal or gas-fired power plant

$$S_{el}(t) - H\,S_{fuel}(t),$$

where S_{el} is the electricity price, S_{fuel} is the coal (respectively gas) price and H the *heat rate* (or efficiency factor), that is the amount of fuel required to produce one unit of electricity.

- The *clean dark spread* or *clean spark spread* modelling a power plant with emission cost

$$S_{el}(t) - H S_{fuel}(t) - E S_{CO_2},$$

where S_{CO_2} is the price for emission of one unit of CO_2 and E is the *emission factor*, that is the emission volume per one unit of electricity production.
- The *crack spread* between different refinement levels of oil modelling a refinement process, for example

$$S_{ho}(t) - S_{co}(t),$$

where S_{ho} is the price of heating oil and S_{co} the price of crude oil.
- *Location spreads* denoting the price differential between two delivery locations modelling a potential transportation facility

$$S_A(t) - S_B(t),$$

where S_A and S_B are the prices of one commodity at locations A and B, for example the price differential of coal between Richards Bay coal terminal in South Africa and ARA in Europe.
- *Time spreads* denoting the price differential between two delivery dates modelling a potential storage facility

$$S(T_2) - S(T_1),$$

where T_1 and T_2 are different delivery dates, for example the dates where gas is injected (respectively withdrawn) from a storage facility.

Spread option models are required on the one hand to determine the value of a corresponding production, transportation or storage facility and on the other hand to determine suitable hedge strategies for such facilities. Hedge strategies may be based on futures contracts on the individual underlyings of the corresponding spread or they may target selling a spread option product offsetting risks of the facility.

When exercised, a two-underlying spread option pays the option holder at maturity T the difference of two underlying prices minus the strike price K. Denoting the underlying prices by $S_1(t)$ and $S_2(t)$, the payoff formula is

$$\text{payoff} = \max(S_1(T) - S_2(T) - K, 0).$$

Unlike basket options, a log-normal approximation of the spread is usually not recommended since a spread can be positive or negative.

The case $K = 0$ (*exchange option*) is treated analytically in Margrabe (1978). It turns out that the pricing formula is identical to Black's formulas (5.10) and (5.11) setting the strike equal to the second forward price $F_2(t, T)$ and the volatility to $\tilde{\sigma} = \sqrt{\sigma_1^2 - 2\rho\sigma_1\sigma_2 + \sigma_2^2}$, where ρ is the correlation between the two underlyings. For a call option we have the *Margrabe formula*

$$U = e^{-r(T-t)}(F_1 N(d_1) - F_2 N(d_2))$$

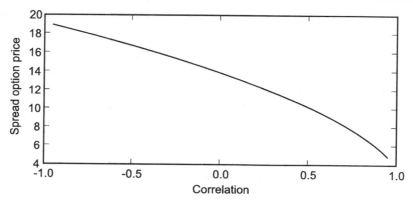

Figure 5.19   Value of a spread option as a function of the correlation for $F_1 = F_2 = 100, T = 1, \sigma_1 = 0.3$ and $\sigma_2 = 0.2$.

evaluated at the current futures prices $F_1 = F_1(t, T), F_2 = F_2(t, T)$, where

$$d_1 = \frac{\ln(F_1/F_2) + V/2}{\sqrt{V}}, \quad d_2 = d_1 - \sqrt{V}$$

and $V = \tilde{\sigma}^2(T - t)$.

The value of a spread option depends strongly on the correlation between the two underlyings (see Figure 5.19). The higher the correlation between the two underlyings the lower is the value of the spread option. This is intuitively right, since the volatility of the spread is lower for positively correlated underlyings. In practical applications (see examples above), the correlation between the underlyings of a spread is typically positive since one underlying is the input and the other underlying the output of a production or transformation process and to a certain extent a cost increase of the input factor passes through to the output factor. As an example, if gas prices rise then we are likely to see higher electricity prices since the marginal cost of electricity production increases (see Chapter 7).

The general case $K \neq 0$ has no direct analytical solution. Option prices can be calculated using either Monte Carlo simulations for the two underlyings or semi-analytical techniques that involve numerical integration (Pearson 1995). A problem with such numerical techniques is that they may be expensive in terms of computing time and they may not be suitable to extract stable sensitivities (Greeks) required for hedging. Therefore, some effort has been made to derive analytical approximations for the case $K \neq 0$.

Kirk's approximation (see Kirk (1995)) is similar to the Margrabe formula, but replaces F_2 by $F_2 + K$ and σ_2 by $\sigma_2 F_1/(F_2 + K)$. For a spread call option with strike K the resulting formula is

$$U = e^{-r(T-t)} \left(F_1 N(d_1) - (F_2 + K)N(d_2) \right) \tag{5.22}$$

evaluated at the current futures prices $F_1 = F_1(t, T), F_2 = F_2(t, T)$, where

$$d_1 = \frac{\ln(F_1/(F_2 + K)) + V/2}{\sqrt{V}}, \quad d_2 = d_1 - \sqrt{V},$$

$$V = \left(\sigma_1^2 - 2\frac{F_2}{F_2 + K}\rho\sigma_1\sigma_2 + \left(\frac{F_2}{F_2 + K}\right)^2 \sigma_2^2 \right)(T - t).$$

There are other closed-form pricing formulas available. One possibility is to model the spread as an arithmetic Brownian motion instead of a geometric Brownian motion

$$dS(t) = \mu S\, dt + \sigma\, dW(t),$$

for constants μ, σ. Such a model is justified by the fact that the spread, in contrast to a single underlying, can become either positive or negative. Details of this approach can be found in Poitras (1998). For more elaborate approximation formulas and surveys see, for example, Carmona and Durrleman (2003) and Deng et al. (2006).

5.5.3   Quanto and Composite Options

Often, commodities are traded in a currency different from a market participant's home currency. To simplify the notation, let USD be the currency the commodity is traded in (the foreign currency) and EUR be the home currency of the market participant. We call a trader in the USD market the USD trader and a trader in the EUR market a EUR trader. Let $X(t)$ be the exchange rate from EUR to USD, that is the value of one EUR in USD. There are three ways to structure an option specifically for EUR traders.

1. *Plain conversion:* Take an ordinary option in USD (with strike K in USD) and convert the payoff into EUR at maturity. The payoff in EUR is then

$$P = \max(S(T) - K, 0)/X(T) \quad \text{(in EUR)}.$$

2. *Composite option:* Construct a synthetic underlying $Z(t) = S(t)/X(t)$ traded in EUR by converting at each time t the underlying price $S(t)$ from USD into EUR. An option written on this synthetic underlying with strike $\tilde{K}$ (in EUR) has the payoff

$$P = \max(S(T)/X(T) - \tilde{K}, 0) \quad \text{(in EUR)}.$$

3. *Quanto option:* Take the USD payoff (with strike K in USD) and convert it at a fixed exchange rate X_0 into EUR without applying the exchange rate at the maturity date. In contrast to the plain conversion described above, the payoff in EUR does not explicitly depend any more on the exchange rate $X(t)$:

$$P = \max(S(T) - K, 0)/X_0 \quad \text{(in EUR)}.$$

In case 1 (plain conversion), the value of the option at time t is just the usual option price in USD converted to EUR at the current exchange rate. In fact, buying the option in USD in the foreign market and converting the payoff at maturity yields the same payoff.

The other two cases are more complicated but can both be treated analytically. To fix some notation, let r_{USD} and r_{EUR} be the (continuously compounded) interest rates for USD and EUR. The model for $S(t)$ (in USD) with respect to the risk-neutral measure is assumed as

$$\frac{dS(t)}{S(t)} = (r_{USD} - y)\, dt + \sigma_S\, dW_S(t),$$

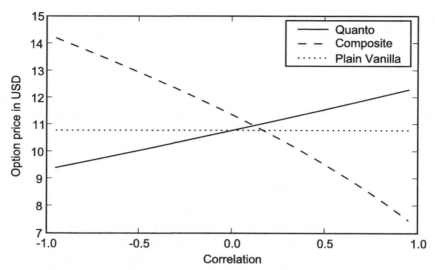

Figure 5.20   Value of quanto and composite options as a function of the correlation for $F = K = 100$, $T = 1$, $\sigma_S = 30\%$ and $\sigma_X = 10\%$.

where y is the convenience yield. The model for the corresponding futures price $F(t)$ is

$$\frac{dF(t)}{F(t)} = \sigma_S \, dW_S(t).$$

The stochastic differential equation for the exchange rate $X(t)$ with respect to the risk-neutral measure is

$$\frac{dX(t)}{X(t)} = (r_{USD} - r_{EUR}) \, dt + \sigma_X \, dW_X(t).$$

The risk-neutral drift must be $r_{USD} - r_{EUR}$ since one EUR can be seen as a traded asset in the USD-based market, where the interest rate r_{EUR} plays the role of the (dividend) yield. The forward price for one EUR is

$$F_X(t) = F_X(t, T) = e^{(r_{USD} - r_{EUR})(T-t)}.$$

Let ρ be the correlation between the two risk factors $W_S(t)$ and $W_X(t)$. The dependence of quanto and composite options on ρ is shown in Figure 5.20.

Composite Options

A composite option can be priced using the Black–Scholes framework applied to the synthetic underlying $Z(t) = S(t)/X(t)$. Using Itô's formula (see Section A.2.3), one gets

$$\frac{dZ(t)}{Z} = \left(r_{EUR} - y + \sigma_x^2 - \rho\sigma_S\sigma_X\right) dt + \sigma_S \, dW_S(t) - \sigma_X \, dW_X(t).$$

From the perspective of the EUR market, the underlying Z is a tradable asset (it is just the value of $S(t)$ converted to EUR). Therefore, with respect to the risk-neutral measure in the EUR market, the drift must be $r_{EUR} - y$ and a change of measure yields the stochastic differential equation

$$\frac{dZ(t)}{Z} = (r_{EUR} - y)\, dt + \sigma_S\, dW_S(t) - \sigma_X\, dW_X(t).$$

The stochastic term $\sigma_S\, dW_S(t) + \sigma_X\, dW_X(t)$ can be written as $\sigma_Z\, dW_Z(t)$ using a single Brownian motion $W_Z(t)$ and the volatility

$$\sigma_Z = \sqrt{\sigma_S^2 - 2\rho\sigma_S\sigma_X + \sigma_X^2}.$$

Now the Black–Scholes formula can be applied to the underlying Z:

$$U = e^{-r_{EUR}(T-t)}\left(F_Z N(d_1) - \tilde{K} N(d_2)\right)$$

evaluated at the synthetic futures price for Z

$$F_Z(t) = F_S(t)/F_X(t)$$

with

$$d_1 = \frac{\ln(F_Z/\tilde{K}) + V/2}{\sqrt{V}}, \quad d_2 = d_1 - \sqrt{V} \quad \text{and} \quad V = \sigma_Z^2(T - t).$$

Quanto Options

We first derive the value of the quanto option in USD. For the USD trader the payoff is just the EUR payoff coverted to USD at the exchange rate $X(T)$ at maturity:

$$P_{USD} = \max(S(T) - K, 0)\, X(T)/X_0 \quad \text{(in USD)}.$$

To price the option, a *change of numeraire* technique can be used. Details about this technique can be found in Musiela and Rutkowski (2004). As numeraire we use the USD value of one EUR including the accumulated interest payments (at rate r_{EUR})

$$\beta(t) = e^{r_{EUR}t}X(t),$$

which can be considered as a tradable asset in USD which pays no dividend (since interest is accumulated). Now we consider all values relative to the numeraire $\beta(t)$. Instead of the usual risk-neutral measure one now chooses a measure $\tilde{Q}$ under which all prices of non-dividend-paying assets relative to the numeraire $\beta(t)$ are martingales. Then the option price (in USD) is given by

$$U = \beta(t)\, \mathbb{E}_t^{\tilde{Q}} \left[\frac{P_{USD}}{\beta(T)} \right] = e^{-r_{EUR}(T-t)}(X(t)/X_0)\, \mathbb{E}_t^{\tilde{Q}} \left[\max(S(T) - K, 0) \right].$$

Note that dividing the payoff $P_{USD}(T)$ by $\beta(T)$ cancels out $X(T)$ in the expectation value, which leaves us with only one remaining stochastic factor. It can be shown that under $\tilde{Q}$ the stochastic differential equation for $S(t)$ has an additional drift term $\rho\sigma_X\sigma_S\, dt$:

$$\frac{dS(t)}{S(t)} = \left(r_{USD} - y + \rho\sigma_X\sigma_S \right) dt + \sigma_S\, dW_S(t),$$

Applying the Black–Scholes formula, the option price formula is

$$U = e^{-r_{EUR}(T-t)} \left(X(t)/X_0 \right) \left(\tilde{F}_S N(d_1) - KN(d_2) \right)$$

evaluated at the quanto forward price under $\tilde{Q}$

$$\tilde{F}_S(t) = e^{\rho\sigma_X\sigma_S(T-t)} F_S(t)$$

with

$$d_1 = \frac{\ln(\tilde{F}_S/K) + V/2}{\sqrt{V}}, \quad d_2 = d_1 - \sqrt{V} \quad \text{and} \quad V = \sigma_S^2(T - t).$$

5.6 MODELLING SPOT PRICES

Black's model (see Section 5.3) deals with options on forwards or futures contracts, where we have one exercise opportunity before the start of delivery. In fact, for many commodities the forward and futures markets are more liquid than the actual physical spot market and the proximity to financial markets is closest. However, it is ultimately the physical spot market that determines much of the characteristics of a particular commodity market, such as the following.

- *Mean reversion:* In many commodity markets prices fluctuate around some equilibrium price that is stable over the medium term. In the long term, the equilibrium price may also change.
- *Seasonality:* For many commodities, including energy, the demand follows a seasonal pattern. Owing to storage limitations, seasonality is also seen in the prices.
- *Price spikes:* The demand for commodities is often inelastic to prices. If there is limited storage capacity available, constraints in availability may lead to extremely high spot prices.

Market participants with a natural position in the physical commodity (either as producer or consumer) most likely have exposure to the spot market, since typically both production and consumption have short-term fluctuations that cannot be anticipated in the forward market. However, production or storage assets have certain flexibilities that can be used deliberately as options to react to volatility in price or demand. Especially for flow commodities, such as power or gas, there is a demand for optionality on a short-term basis, since storage capacities are limited and demand varies from day to day due to weather conditions not known much in advance.

As an example, consider a power distribution company that procures its energy demand partly via standard forward contracts and partly on the spot market. The delivery obligation from the company's full service contracts is an hourly load schedule that depends on weather conditions and customer behaviour. The company needs to rely on the spot market for two reasons:

1. There is no liquid forward market for hourly load schedules and the distribution company does not want to pay a high premium for such individual products. The distribution company therefore buys baseload and peakload products on the forward market. The exact hourly profile is then bought on the spot market.
2. The weather conditions determining the load can be forecast reliably only shortly before the delivery day, so balancing the portfolio has to be done on the spot market.

Since spot market prices are extremely volatile, the company wants to secure a certain price for additional energy it may need. One possible product that serves this purpose is a strip of call options for a certain capacity on an hourly basis. Whenever the spot price is high (above the option's strike level), the distribution company can exercise the option and pays only the strike price. Since the strike price can be seen as the maximum price paid for the energy, the product is also called a *cap* on the electricity price. There are variants to the simple strip of call options, such as swing options, with additional restrictions on the optionality. Such products may lead to reduced option premiums or give a better match to optionalities granted by physical assets.

Modelling spot prices is important in two different contexts.

1. *Risk analysis:* If a portfolio value depends on future spot prices, a stochastic model can simulate price scenarios to evaluate the corresponding profits and losses for the portfolio. For this application we need the stochastic process under the statistical probability measure and a model which closely represents the actual spot price behaviour.
2. *Derivatives pricing:* As already mentioned, in energy markets an important class of options can be exercised short term against the volatility of the spot market. For this purpose, according to Section A.3, the stochastic process generally needs to be considered under the risk-neutral measure. Especially for commodities that cannot be efficiently stored (e.g., electricity), a complete hedging of the option using forward or futures contracts is not possible, so that further assumptions compared with classical option pricing theory need to be made (see Section 5.6.1).

The statistical properties of spot prices for energy are much different from underlyings considered in standard option pricing theory. Further, the (discounted) spot price process – unlike a forward price – does not have to be a martingale under the risk-neutral measure (see Section A.3.1), that is the current spot price does not have to be equal to the expected (discounted) spot price at a future date. Modelling spot prices with geometric Brownian motion will be analysed in Section 5.6.2. However, in many cases this model is not appropriate, mainly because the mean-reversion property of spot prices for many commodities is not reflected in a geometric Brownian motion. Therefore, Sections 5.6.3 and 5.6.4 introduce a one-factor and a two-factor model for a mean-reverting spot price process. For each of the spot price models, calibration of parameters from historical price data and from market prices for derivatives will be examined. Further, basic formulas for option pricing will be given.

More specialised models for electricity, taking into account price spikes and seasonalities, are described in Chapter 6.

5.6.1 Pricing Spot Price Options

Often, options on spot prices have not just one single exercise date but can be exercised at multiple dates during the option lifetime. As an example, the owner of a (virtual) power plant can decide each day or even each hour whether to generate electricity or not. In this general setup, let $t_1, \dots, t_N$ be the exercise dates and $h_1(S(t_1)), \dots, h_N(S(t_N))$ the payoffs in case the option is exercised. An exercise strategy $\phi_k \in \{0, 1\}$ indicates whether to exercise the option or let the option expire. Given an appropriate model for the spot price $S(t)$, according to Section A.3 the option price is given as the discounted expectation of the option's payoff under the risk-neutral measure assuming an optimal (i.e., value maximising) exercise strategy:

$$U(t) = \max_{\phi} \mathbb{E}_t^Q \left[\sum_{i=1}^N e^{-r(t_i - t)} \phi_i \, h_i(S(t_i)) \right], \tag{5.23}$$

where the optimisation is done over all exercise strategies $\phi = (\phi_1, \dots, \phi_m)$. However, the decision on ϕ_i may be based only on information up to t_i, the time of decision.

Example 5.1: Caps and floors

The basic example is a *cap*, where the option holder has the right (but not the obligation) to buy a certain amount of energy at stipulated times $t_1, \dots, t_N$ during the delivery period at a fixed strike price K. The option exercise typically has to be nominated a certain time in advance. The strike price K secures a maximum price for buying the energy, since in all cases where the spot price is above the strike price the option holder can exercise the option and buy the energy at price K. In this way, the cap is used to protect a short position against increasing market prices (see Figure 5.21). Using the notation introduced above, the payoff depending on the exercise strategy ϕ is

$$h_i(S(t_i)) = \phi_i(S(t_i) - K), \quad \phi_i \in \{0, 1\}.$$

Of course, the value-maximising (optimal) exercise strategy is to choose $\phi_i = 1$ (exercise) if $S(t_i) - K \geq 0$ and $\phi_i = 0$ (not exercise) if $S(t_i) - K < 0$, so that the overall payoff at time t_i is the well-known option payoff $\max(S(t_i) - K, 0)$. The cap can therefore be considered as a strip of independent call options.

By equation (5.23), the fair value of the option is given by the discounted expected payoff under the (risk-neutral) stochastic model. The cap price may be divided by the number of

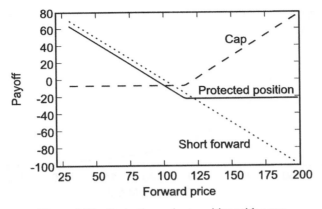

Figure 5.21   Protecting a short position with a cap.

delivery hours to make different delivery periods comparable. In this case we get a price per MWh. The formula for the cap is

$$U(t) = \frac{1}{N} \sum_{i=1}^{N} e^{-r(t_i-t)} \mathbb{E}[\max(S(t_i) - K, 0)].$$

Figure 5.22 shows the price per MWh of a one-year cap as a function of the strike price. For high strike prices there are few opportunities to exercise the option and the value is determined more and more by the price spikes within the delivery period. In the example for strike prices greater than about 140 EUR/MWh the intrinsic value is zero, that is all forward prices are below the strike price. The average number of exercised hours over all simulation paths is given in Figure 5.23. For a strike price of 140 EUR/MWh there are on average still about 200 exercises per year that generate an average profit of about 1 EUR/MWh or about 8760 EUR per year.

Similar to a cap, a *floor* grants the option buyer the right (but not the obligation) to sell a certain amount of energy at stipulated times $t_1, \ldots, t_N$ during the delivery period at a fixed strike price K. The strike price K secures a minimum price for the energy, since in all cases

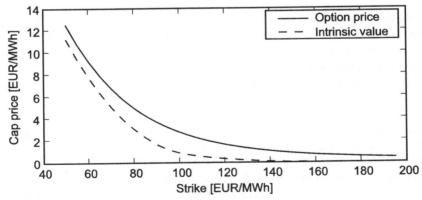

Figure 5.22   Price and intrinsic value of a cap as a function of the strike price. The delivery period is one year.

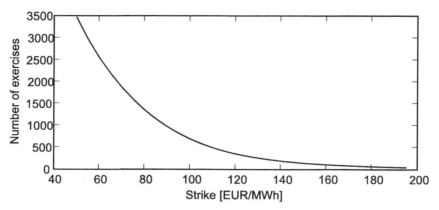

Figure 5.23 Average number of hours the cap is exercised for a given strike price (one year delivery period = 8760 hours).

where the spot price is below the strike price, the option holder can exercise the option and sell the energy at price K. In this way, the cap is used to protect a long position against decreasing market prices. This *protective put* strategy was shown in Figure 5.10. The floor can be considered as a strip of independent put options and the fair value is given by

$$U(t) = \sum_{i=1}^{N} e^{-r(t_i-t)} \mathbb{E}[\max(K - S(t_i), 0)].$$

Practical Issues Pricing Spot Price Options

In more complex examples, for example swing options (see Example 5.2 below), there may be additional restrictions on the number of exercise opportunities:

$$E_{min} \le \sum_{i=1}^{N} \phi_k \le E_{max}.$$

Since, for the more complicated models, analytical formulas are no longer available, one has to employ numerical methods to evaluate the option price. In many cases, Monte Carlo schemes have to be used. A least-squares Monte Carlo technique for dealing with exercise strategies can be found in Longstaff and Schwartz (2001), where American options are studied.

To interpret the theoretical option value given by equation (5.23), the following remarks may be helpful:

- The price is not strictly an arbitrage price in the sense that there exists a complete hedging strategy. One reason is market *incompleteness* due to a lacking forward market for all single delivery times t_i.
- The option price is model dependent. For options getting their value from a few extreme market events (e.g., spikes), the values derived from two stochastic models may differ substantially.

- In equation (5.23) it is assumed that the option can be exercised optimally against spot prices. In real-world examples, one often has to nominate the exercise before the spot auction where the spot prices are determined.
- An optimal exercise strategy is often very complicated to calculate and may be difficult to implement in daily business.

Because of these uncertainties it is useful to calculate the *intrinsic value* of an option. This is defined as the value against the forward curve instead of the stochastic paths:

$$IV(t) = \max_{\phi} \sum_{i=1}^{N} e^{-r(t_i-t)} \phi_i \, h_i(F(t, t_i)). \qquad (5.24)$$

Since today's forward prices are used, the problem is deterministic and the expectation value is not needed. Equation (5.24) describes a deterministic linear optimisation problem. The intrinsic value reflects the option value if one had to nominate the complete exercise schedule today based on the information in today's forward curve. Thus, the intrinsic value gives a lower bound on the option value.

An upper bound on the option price is found by dropping the restriction that the exercise decision can only be based on the information up to the time of decision. Then the decisions can use all the information on the future spot prices and optimise the value *ex post* over the whole spot price path. Under this assumption the optimisation is done pathwise and the pricing equation can be reformulated as

$$U^*(t) = \mathbb{E}_t^Q \left[\max_{\phi} \sum_{i=1}^{N} e^{-r(t_i-t)} \phi_i \, h_i(S(t_i)) \right]. \qquad (5.25)$$

If $S^k(t)$ for $k = 1, \ldots, n$ are simulation paths, the Monte Carlo approximation of the upper option value is

$$U^*(t) = \frac{1}{n} \sum_{k=1}^{n} U_k^*.$$

where

$$U_k^* = \max_{\phi} \sum_{i=1}^{N} e^{-r(t_i-t)} \phi_i \, h_i(S^k(t_i)).$$

For each path a linear optimisation problem needs to be solved.

Example 5.2: Swing options

A *swing* option is similar to a cap or floor except that we have additional restrictions on the number of option exercises. As above, let $\phi_i \in \{0, 1\}$ be the decision whether to exercise ($\phi_i = 1$) or not exercise ($\phi_i = 0$) the option at time t_i. The option's payoff at time t_i is then given by $\phi_i \left(S(t_i) - K \right)$ for a call and $\phi_i \left(K - S(t_i) \right)$ for a put option. We now require that the

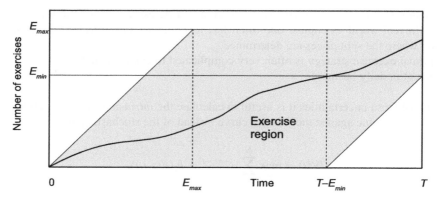

Figure 5.24   Example exercise path for a swing option.

number of exercises is between E_{min} and E_{max}. This restriction imposes a constraint on the energy that is received or delivered by exercising the option. Figure 5.24 shows graphically the possible exercise paths over time. If the option holder exercises all hours right from the start of the exercise period, he follows the left boundary of the exercise region. If he delays exercising, he follows the time axis until he is forced to start exercising all hours at time $T - E_{min}$ to end up with E_{min} exercises at time T (right boundary). By deciding from time to time which hours to exercise, the option holder might follow some path similar to the example in Figure 5.24. Since the option holder has to exercise a certain number of hours, it is in general possible that he has to exercise at times where the spot price is below the strike price and therefore the payoff is negative. In cases where the strike price is high, it may even happen that the value of the swing option is negative for the option holder.

To determine the option value, we have to find an optimal exercise strategy $\Phi = (\phi_1, \dots, \phi_N)$ maximising the expected payoff (see Section 5.6.1)

$$\sum_{i=1}^{N} e^{-r(t_i - t)} \mathbb{E} \left[\phi_i(S(t_i) - K) \right] \rightarrow \max \tag{5.26}$$

subject to the restrictions

$$E_{min} \leq \sum_{i=1}^{N} \phi_i \leq E_{max}.$$

If the spot prices were deterministic and known in advance, we would have a linear optimisation problem. It can easily be seen that the condition $\phi_i \in \{0, 1\}$ can be relaxed to $0 \leq \phi_i \leq 1$ without changing the solution, such that we have no integer conditions. The steps to solve the deterministic case are:

1. Calculate the discounted payoffs $P(t_i) = e^{-r(t_i - t)}(S(t_i) - K)$.
2. Sort the discounted payoffs $P(t_i)$ in descending order.
3. Take the first E_{min} payoffs regardless of their value and subsequent payoffs up to E_{max} until their sign become negative.

The exercise strategy for stochastic spot prices is more complicated than in the deterministic case. The decision at time t_i, whether to exercise or not, can only be based on the history of spot prices $S(t_1), \ldots, S(t_i)$ and on the assumptions of the stochastic properties of the future spot prices $S(t_{i+1}), \ldots, S(t_N)$. Without regarding the complexity of finding an optimal exercise strategy, we can calculate lower and upper bounds on the swing value. As a lower bound we can take the intrinsic value of the option. As an upper bound we can calculate the expected value assuming that we knew each spot price path in advance (see Section 5.6.1). Using a Monte Carlo approach we generate n simulation paths $S^k(t_1), \ldots, S^k(t_N)$ for $k = 1, \ldots, n$. For each path S^k we solve the linear optimisation problem for $\phi_1, \ldots, \phi_n$

$$\sum_{i=1}^{N} e^{-r(t_i - t)} \phi_i \left(S^k(t_i) - K \right) \to \max$$

subject to the energy constraints

$$E_{min} \leq \sum_{i=1}^{N} \phi_i \leq E_{max}.$$

Since the path $S^k(t_i)$ is assumed to be known in advance, the algorithm based on sorting the payoffs can be used here. Let the maximum be attained at U_k^*, which is then the optimal value from path S^k. The expected value over all paths is given by the average

$$U^* = \frac{1}{n} \sum_{k=1}^{n} U_k^*.$$

A strategy based only on the available information at the time of the decision cannot in general attain the maximum value for each path. Therefore, the true option value must fall between the intrinsic value and the upper bound U^*:

$$IV(t) \leq U(t) \leq U^*(t).$$

Figure 5.25 shows the intrinsic value, option price and upper bound for an example swing option as a function of the strike price. For high strike prices above 120 EUR/MWh the option value becomes negative. The average number of exercises for a given strike price is shown in Figure 5.26. Below a strike price of around 50 EUR/MWh it is optimal to exercise the maximum number of 2000 hours because there are enough hours available above the strike price. Increasing the strike price, there are on average not enough hours with prices above the strike price available, so the number of exercises decreases. Above a strike price of around 110 EUR/MWh the average number of exercises approaches the minimum number of 1000 hours, since most paths then contain less than 1000 hours with prices above the strike level.

5.6.2   Geometric Brownian Motion as Spot Price Model

Geometric Brownian motion was introduced in Section 5.3.2 as the underlying stochastic model for Black's futures price model (equation (5.9)). Applying GBM to spot prices, a drift

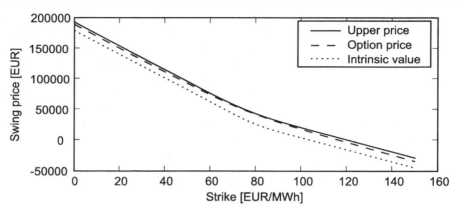

Figure 5.25 Price and intrinsic value of a swing option as a function of the strike price. The delivery period is one year and $E_{min} = 1000$, $E_{max} = 2000$.

term also needs to be considered under the risk-neutral measure. This is different from Black's model, since spot prices under the risk-neutral measure in general are not martingales. It should be noted that GBM has to be used with care for commodity spot prices, since many commodity spot prices are considered mean reverting, so that other models described in this section are preferable.

GBM is described by the following stochastic differential equation:

$$\frac{dS(t)}{S(t)} = \mu \, dt + \sigma \, dW(t), \tag{5.27}$$

where μ and σ are constant. As usual, $W(t)$ denotes a standard Brownian motion. Using Itô's lemma it is easily shown that the natural logarithm of $S(t)$ satisfies the equation

$$d \ln S(t) = \left(\mu - \tfrac{1}{2}\sigma^2 \right) dt + \sigma \, dW(t).$$

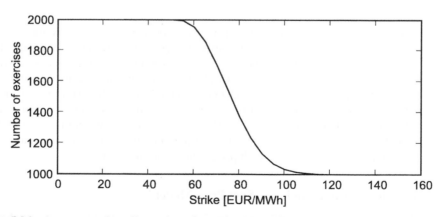

Figure 5.26 Average number of hours the swing option is exercised for a given strike price. $E_{min} = 1000$, $E_{max} = 2000$.

Integrating this equation yields

$$S(t) = S(0) \exp\left(\left(\mu - \tfrac{1}{2}\sigma^2\right)t + \sigma W(t)\right).$$ (5.28)

Model Characteristics

The most important characteristics of GBM are:

- The asset price $S(t)$ is positive for all t.
- For $t_1 < t_2 < t_3$ the asset returns $\frac{S(t_2)-S(t_1)}{S(t_1)}$ and $\frac{S(t_3)-S(t_2)}{S(t_2)}$, or equivalently the logarithmic increments $\ln S(t_2) - \ln S(t_1)$ and $\ln S(t_3) - \ln S(t_2)$, are independent.
- At today's spot price $S(0)$, the logarithm of the spot price $\ln S(t)$ is normally distributed with mean $\ln S(0) + \mu t - \tfrac{1}{2}\sigma^2 t$ and variance $\sigma^2 t$.
- At today's spot price $S(0)$ the expectation of $S(t)$ is given by

$$\mathbb{E}[S(t)] = S(0)e^{\mu t}.$$

As already mentioned, GBM is applicable for price processes without mean reversion. Typical sample paths are shown in Figure 5.27. Numerical calculation is discussed later in this section. The dashed line indicates the corridor of one standard deviation

$$S(0)\exp((\mu - \sigma^2/2)t - \sigma\sqrt{t}) < S(t) < S(0)\exp((\mu - \sigma^2/2)t + \sigma\sqrt{t}).$$

The corridor of one standard deviation of $\ln S(t)$ increases with $\sigma\sqrt{t}$ and the variance $\mathrm{Var}[\ln S(t)] = \sigma^2 t$ increases linearly with t. This means that the longer the time horizon the larger the price uncertainty.

A straightforward generalisation of the model in equation (5.27) is obtained using time-dependent but deterministic functions for μ and σ. Then the logarithm $\ln S(t)$ is still normally distributed with mean $\int_0^t \mu(s) - \tfrac{1}{2}\sigma^2(s)\,ds$ and variance $\int_0^t \sigma^2(s)\,ds$.

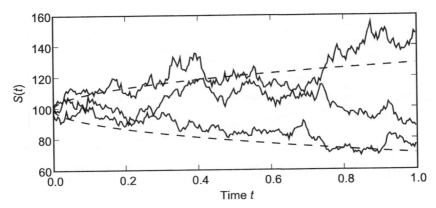

Figure 5.27   GBM sample paths for one year ($\sigma = 0.3$, $\mu = 0$).

Forward and Option Price Formulas

In Section A.3 the forward price was given by the expectation under the risk-neutral measure Q. Under Q, the process follows the stochastic model equation

$$\frac{dS(t)}{S(t)} = \mu^* \, dt + \sigma \, d\tilde{W}(t). \tag{5.29}$$

Using risk-neutral parameters we derive the forward prices as

$$F(t, T) = \mathbb{E}_t^Q[S(T)] = S(t)e^{\mu^*(T-t)}. \tag{5.30}$$

For non-constant risk-neutral drift μ^* this generalises to $F(t, T) = S(t) \exp(\int_t^T \mu^*(s) \, ds)$.

Depending on the sign of μ^*, the forward curve can be in contango or backwardation. Note that, in contrast to modelling stock prices, the risk-neutral μ^* is not given *a priori* as it contains the convenience yield. Figure 5.28 shows the possible forward curve shapes for the GBM model with constant μ^*. More general shapes can be obtained using non-constant values for the drift parameter μ^*.

In equation (5.30) the forward curve changes stochastically with $S(t)$. The dynamics of the forward curve are easily calculated using Itô's lemma:

$$\begin{aligned} dF(t, T) &= e^{\mu^*(T-t)}dS(t) - \mu^* S(t)e^{\mu^*(T-t)} \, dt \\ &= \sigma e^{\mu^*(T-t)}dS(t) \, d\tilde{W}(t) \\ &= \sigma F(t, T) \, d\tilde{W}(t), \end{aligned}$$

giving Black's model for futures prices (cf. Section 5.3.2):

$$\frac{dF(t, T)}{F(t, T)} = \sigma \, d\tilde{W}(t). \tag{5.31}$$

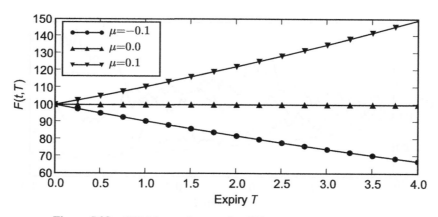

Figure 5.28   GBM forward curves for different constant values of μ.

For European-style call and put options on the spot price index $S(t)$ we use the Black–Scholes formula

$$C_{K,T}(t,F) = e^{-r(T-t)}\mathbb{E}_t^Q[\max(S(T)-K,0)]$$
$$= e^{-r(T-t)}(FN(d_1) - KN(d_2)),$$
$$P_{K,T}(t,F) = e^{-r(T-t)}\mathbb{E}_t^Q[\max(K-S(T),0)]$$
$$= e^{-r(T-t)}(KN(-d_2) - FN(-d_1)),$$

where

$$F = F(t,T) = S(t)e^{\mu^*(T-t)},$$
$$d_1 = \frac{\ln(F/K) + \frac{1}{2}\sigma^2(T-t)}{\sigma\sqrt{T-t}},$$
$$d_2 = d_1 - \sigma\sqrt{T-t}.$$

For non-constant volatility $\sigma(t)$, the same formulas can be used if σ is replaced by $\bar{\sigma}$, which is defined as

$$\bar{\sigma}^2 = \frac{1}{T-t}\int_t^T \sigma^2(s)\,ds.$$

Calibration to Historical Data

Model parameters are commonly given as annualised quantities with the time variable t measured in years. Let $S_0, \ldots, S_N$ be observed market prices at times $t_0, \ldots, t_N$. As discussed earlier, logarithmic returns $\ln S_{t_i} - \ln S_{t_{i-1}}$ are independent and normally distributed with standard deviation $\sigma\sqrt{t_i - t_{i-1}}$. Setting

$$X_i = \frac{\ln S(t_i) - \ln S(t_{i-1})}{\sqrt{t_i - t_{i-1}}}$$

we can estimate the volatility as

$$\hat{\sigma}^2 = \frac{1}{N-1}\sum_{i=1}^N (X_i - \bar{X})^2$$

where $\bar{X} = \frac{1}{N}\sum_{i=1}^N X_i$. To evaluate $t_i - t_{i-1}$ as a year fraction in the formulas above we can either take the actual number of days and divide by 365 or we can take the number of trading days between t_i and t_{i-1} and divide by the total number of trading days per year, which may be about 250. In market practice, total annual trading days is usually set by convention to a certain number, regardless of the actual number of trading days in that year.

Using historical price data, volatility is not constant but depends on the time period and granularity of the data used for the parameter estimation. A moving time window of a certain period length, for example 20 trading days, can be used to obtain a graphical representation

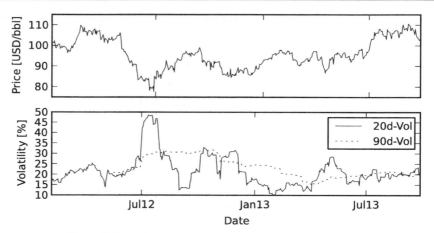

Figure 5.29   Historical volatility for WTI front-month prices.

of historical volatility behaviour. An example is shown in Figure 5.29. The longer the moving time window for the volatility calculation, the smoother the curve.

Calibration Under the Risk-Neutral Measure

Historical spot market prices do not reveal any information about the market price of risk. Additional market information is used to calibrate the risk-neutral parameters. Such additional market data can be futures or forward price data which is available for most commodities. Assuming known market prices for a number of futures contracts $F(t, T_1), \ldots, F(t, T_n)$ with maturities $t \equiv T_0 < T_1 < T_2 < \ldots < T_n$ we must have under the risk-neutral measure Q

$$\mathbb{E}^Q_t[S(T_i)] = F(t, T_i), \quad i = 1, \ldots, n.$$

We can choose a piecewise constant risk-neutral drift μ^* such that the above identities hold and all given futures prices are correctly priced. Let

$$\mu^*(t) = \sum_{i=1}^n \mu_i^* \mathbf{1}_{[T_{i-1}, T_i)}(t).$$

Then formula (5.30) for the forward price becomes

$$F(t, T_k) = S(t) \exp\left(\sum_{i=1}^k \mu_i^*(T_i - T_{i-1}) \right).$$

Given the market prices $F(t, T_i)$ we can extract all μ_i^* iteratively as

$$\mu_1^* = \frac{1}{T_1 - t}\left(\ln \frac{F(t, T_1)}{S(t)} \right),$$

$$\mu_i^* = \frac{1}{T_i - T_{i-1}}\left(\ln \frac{F(t, T_i)}{F(t, T_{i-1})} \right), \quad i = 2, \ldots, k.$$

The volatility is not changed under the risk-neutral measure, therefore it can be estimated from historical data. If market prices for options are available, one can use implied volatilities as a model parameter. This is explained in more detail in Section 5.3.5.

Generating Simulation Paths

For option pricing via Monte Carlo techniques or for risk analysis there is a need to numerically generate simulation paths according to the stochastic model. Simulating GBM follows immediately from equation (5.28). Letting $t_1, \ldots, t_n$ be the points of time and $\Delta t_i = t_i - t_{i-1}$ we generate a path taking the following steps:

1. Generate standard normally distributed random numbers $\epsilon_1, \ldots, \epsilon_n$.
2. Starting with today's spot price $S(t_0)$ we iteratively calculate

$$S(t_i) = S(t_{i-1}) \exp\left((\mu - \sigma^2/2)\Delta t_i + \sigma\sqrt{\Delta t_i}\epsilon_i \right).$$

5.6.3   The One-Factor Schwartz Model

The one-factor Schwartz model (Schwartz, 1997) or logarithmic Vasicek model is used to model prices that have a mean-reversion property, which is the case for many commodity markets. The stochastic differential equation is the following:

$$d \ln S(t) = \kappa \left(\theta(t) - \ln S(t) \right) dt + \sigma(t) \, dW(t), \tag{5.32}$$

where κ describes the mean-reversion speed, $\theta(t)$ the (logarithmic) mean-reversion level and $\sigma(t)$ the (instantaneous) volatility. Figure 5.30 shows a sample path for an example set of model parameters.

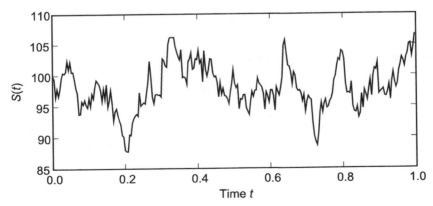

Figure 5.30   Schwartz model sample path for one year ($\sigma = 0.3$, $\theta = \ln 100$, $\kappa = 12$).

Using Itô's formula, the model equation (5.32) can alternatively be written in the following form:

$$\frac{dS(t)}{S(t)} = \kappa \left(\tilde{\theta}(t) - \ln S(t) \right) dt + \sigma(t) dW(t),$$

with $\tilde{\theta}(t) = \theta(t) + \frac{\sigma^2}{4\kappa}$.

In the general case, all parameters may be deterministic functions of time. However, for notational convenience, we assume κ is always constant. If constancy is not assumed, the term $e^{-(T-t)}$ is replaced by $\exp(-\int_t^T \kappa(s) ds)$ in all formulas. In the following discussion θ and σ are assumed to be constant to get explicit formulas.

Model Characteristics

GBM (see Section 5.6.2) has no "mean" level around which the price fluctuates. Regardless of how high or low the price is, the probabilities for the price increasing or decreasing in the next time period do not change. Commodity prices often have a mean-reversion property so that if prices are already above or below a long-term mean level they tend to be drawn back towards the mean. In a chart (e.g., Figure 5.30), we see fluctuations around a mean level. In financial markets a similar behaviour can be observed for interest rates. The Vasicek model

$$dX(t) = \kappa \left(\theta - X(t) \right) dt + \sigma dW(t)$$

is popular and well studied for the short-term interest rate. It incorporates mean reversion to a long-term mean level while allowing for efficient numerical methods. Using the Vasicek model directly for commodity prices has the disadvantage that, with a certain probability, prices may become negative. For modelling commodity prices the Vasicek model is typically applied to the logarithm of the price instead of the price itself.

The mean-reversion speed κ can be evaluated as follows. If there were no stochastic fluctuations ($\sigma = 0$) then instead of the stochastic differential equation (5.32) we have an ordinary differential equation for $y(t) = \ln S(t)$ of the form

$$\frac{dy(t)}{dt} = \kappa \left(\theta - y(t) \right),$$

where the solution can easily be calculated as

$$y(t) = y(0)e^{-\kappa t} + \theta(1 - e^{-\kappa t}),$$

so that an exponential convergence occurs from $y(0)$ to θ with a "half-life" of $\tau = \frac{\ln 2}{\kappa}$.

Applying Itô's lemma, the solution to the stochastic differential equation (5.32) can be derived as

$$S(t) = \exp \left(e^{-\kappa t} \ln S(0) + \int_0^t \kappa \theta e^{-\kappa(t-s)} ds + \int_0^t \sigma(s) e^{-\kappa(t-s)} dW(s) \right). \qquad (5.33)$$

For the special case of constant parameters the first integral can be computed explicitly as

$$S(t) = \exp\left(e^{-\kappa t}\ln S(0) + \theta\left(1 - e^{-\kappa t}\right) + \sigma\int_0^t e^{-\kappa(t-s)}\,dW(s)\right).$$

From equation (5.33) and Theorem A.1 it can be seen that $\ln S(t)$ is normally distributed with

$$\mathbb{E}[\ln S(t)] = e^{-\kappa t}\ln S(0) + \int_0^t \kappa\theta e^{-\kappa(t-s)}\,ds \qquad \text{and}$$

$$\text{Var}[\ln S(t)] = \int_0^t \sigma^2(s)e^{-2\kappa(t-s)}\,ds.$$

Thus, the spot price $S(t)$ is log-normally distributed. Applying the general identity

$$\mathbb{E}\left[e^X\right] = e^{\mathbb{E}[X] + \text{Var}[X]/2}$$

for an arbitrary normally distributed random variable to $X = \ln S(t)$, the expectation of $S(t)$ can be calculated as

$$\mathbb{E}[S(t)] = \exp\left(\mathbb{E}[\ln S(t)] + \frac{1}{2}\text{Var}[\ln S(t)]\right). \tag{5.34}$$

Forward and Option Price Formulas

To calculate forward and option prices we need the price process under the risk-neutral measure. Previously it was identified that switching to the risk-neutral measure changes the drift of the process. Therefore, the risk-neutral process can be written as

$$d\ln S(t) = \kappa\left(\theta^* - \ln S_t\right)dt + \sigma\,d\tilde{W}_t, \tag{5.35}$$

where $\theta^* = \theta - \lambda/\kappa$ and λ is the market price of risk. To simplify the notation we now assume that all parameters are constant. The integrals in equation (5.34) applied to the risk-neutral process can be computed explicitly to derive the following expression for the forward price $F(t, T)$:

$$F(t, T) = \exp\left(e^{-\kappa(T-t)}\ln S(t) + \theta^*\left(1 - e^{-\kappa(T-t)}\right) + \frac{\sigma^2}{4\kappa}\left(1 - e^{-2\kappa(T-t)}\right)\right). \tag{5.36}$$

Regardless of the current spot price, for the long-term limit as $T \to \infty$ this devolves to $F(t, T) \to \exp(\theta^* + \frac{\sigma^2}{4\kappa})$. The mean-reversion constant κ determines the convergence speed. If the current spot price $S(0)$ is below the long-term limit the forward curve is upward sloping (contango) and if the current spot price is above the long-term limit the forward curve is downward sloping (backwardation). Figure 5.31 shows these different cases and can be compared with the forward curve shapes for GBM previously shown in Figure 5.28.

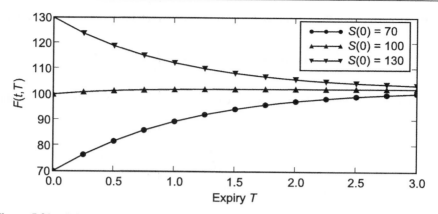

Figure 5.31 Schwartz model forward curves ($\kappa = 1, \theta = \ln 100$) for different values of $S(0)$.

For option prices, since $S(t)$ is log-normally distributed, the prices for European-style call and put options can be calculated analytically via the Black–Scholes formula

$$C_{K,T}(t, F) = e^{-r(T-t)} \left(FN(d_1) - KN(d_2) \right),$$
$$P_{K,T}(t, F) = e^{-r(T-t)} \left(KN(-d_2) - FN(-d_1) \right),$$

where

$$F = F(t, T),$$
$$V = \frac{\sigma^2}{2\kappa} \left(1 - e^{-2\kappa(T-t)} \right),$$
$$d_1 = \frac{\ln(F/K) + \frac{1}{2}V}{\sqrt{V}} \qquad d_2 = d_1 - \sqrt{V}.$$

Calibration to Historical Data

The simplest method for calibrating the one-factor Schwartz model to historical data is by linear regression. Let $S_0, \ldots, S_N$ be a series of historical prices and Δt the time between two observations. The Euler discretisation of the model equation (5.32) is

$$\ln S_i - \ln S_{i-1} = \kappa(\theta - \ln S_{i-1})\Delta t + \epsilon_i,$$

where ϵ_i are independent normally distributed random numbers with mean zero and standard deviation $\sigma\sqrt{\Delta t}$. Substituting $a = 1 - \kappa\Delta t$, $b = \kappa\theta\Delta t$ and $y_i = \ln S_i$ this is equivalent to

$$y_i = ay_{i-1} + b + \epsilon_i.$$

Thus, a least-squares algorithm yields values for a and b minimising the variance of ϵ_i. The model parameters can then be recovered as

$$\theta = \frac{b}{1-a}, \quad \kappa = \frac{1-a}{\Delta t}, \quad \sigma^2 = \frac{\text{Var}[\epsilon_i]}{\Delta t}.$$

For a more accurate calibration one can use a maximum likelihood method.

Generating Simulation Paths

Let $t_0, \ldots, t_N$ be the path dates, $\Delta t_i = t_i - t_{i-1}$ and assume constant parameters. Using equation (5.33) with $S(t_{i-1})$ instead of $S(0)$ and $S(t_i)$ instead of $S(t)$, we get

$$S(t_i) = \exp\left(e^{-\kappa \Delta t_i} \ln S(t_{i-1}) + \theta \left(1 - e^{-\kappa \Delta t_i}\right) + \sigma \int_{t_{i-1}}^{t_i} e^{-\kappa(t_i - s)} dW(s) \right).$$

The integral $\sigma \int_{t_{i-1}}^{t_i} e^{-\kappa(t_i - s)} dW(s)$ is normally distributed with mean zero and variance

$$V_i = \frac{\sigma^2}{2\kappa} \left(1 - e^{-2\kappa \Delta t_i}\right).$$

Therefore, we can proceed similarly as in Section 5.6.2 for the GBM:

1. Generate standard normally distributed random numbers $\epsilon_1, \ldots, \epsilon_N$.
2. Starting with today's spot price $S(t_0)$, iteratively calculate

$$S(t_i) = \exp\left(e^{-\kappa \Delta t_i} \ln S(t_{i-1}) + \theta \left(1 - e^{-\kappa \Delta t_i}\right) + \sqrt{V_i}\epsilon_i \right).$$

5.6.4 The Schwartz–Smith Model

Even though mean-reverting behaviour is observable in many commodity markets, simple mean-reverting models such as the one-factor Schwartz model (5.32) have the drawback of requiring a predefined fixed mean-reverting level that is not known and may change in the long term. Schwartz and Smith (2000) propose a model combining mean-reverting behaviour on a short time scale with non-mean-reverting behaviour on a long time scale. The commodity price S_t is modelled by

$$\ln S(t) = \chi(t) + \xi(t). \tag{5.37}$$

The first factor $\chi(t)$ represents the short-term variations and follows a mean-reverting (*Ornstein–Uhlenbeck*) process

$$d\chi(t) = -\kappa \chi(t)\, dt + \sigma_\chi dW_\chi(t). \tag{5.38}$$

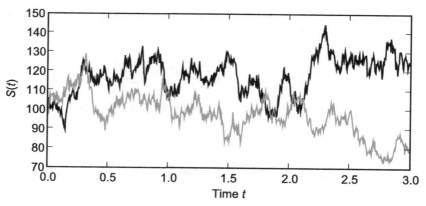

Figure 5.32 Sample paths for the Schwartz–Smith model ($\sigma_\chi = 0.3, \sigma_\xi = 0.1, \kappa = 4, \mu_\xi = 0.02, \rho = 0$).

The second factor $\xi(t)$ represents the long-term dynamics and is given by a Brownian motion with drift

$$d\xi(t) = \mu_\xi \, dt + \sigma_\xi dW_\xi(t), \tag{5.39}$$

where $dW_\chi(t)$ and $dW_\xi(t)$ are standard Brownian motions with correlation ρ. Two sample paths from a Schwartz–Smith model are shown in Figure 5.32.

Model Characteristics

This two-factor model can be seen as an extension to the mean-reverting model (5.32) so that the "mean" level is also stochastic. Setting $X(t) = \ln S(t)$, $\theta(t) = \xi(t) + \mu_\xi/\kappa$, $\sigma_X^2 = \sigma_\chi^2 + \sigma_\xi^2 + 2\rho\sigma_\chi\sigma_\xi$ and $W_X(t) = \sigma_X^{-1}(\sigma_\chi W_\chi(t) + \sigma_\xi W_\xi(t))$ gives

$$dX(t) = \kappa \, (\theta(t) - X(t)) \, dt + \sigma_X \, dW_X(t),$$
$$d\theta(t) = \mu_\xi \, dt + \sigma_\xi dW_\xi(t).$$

The first equation defines a mean-reverting process for $X(t)$ to the mean level $\theta(t)$. In the second equation the mean reversion level $\theta(t)$ follows a Brownian motion with drift.

Integrating the stochastic differential equation for $\ln S(t)$ we get, compared with equation (5.33) for the one-factor Schwartz model,

$$\ln S(t) = \xi(0) + \mu t + e^{-\kappa t}\chi(0) + \sigma_\chi \int_0^t e^{-\kappa(t-s)}dW_\chi(s) + \sigma_\xi W_\xi(t).$$

From this identity we see that $\ln S(t)$ is normally distributed with mean

$$\mathbb{E}[\ln S(t)] = \xi(0) + \mu t + e^{-\kappa t}\chi(0) \tag{5.40}$$

and variance

$$\text{Var}[\ln S(t)] = \frac{\sigma_\chi^2}{2\kappa} \left(1 - e^{-2\kappa t}\right) + \sigma_\xi^2 t + \frac{2\rho\sigma_\chi\sigma_\xi}{\kappa} \left(1 - e^{-\kappa t}\right). \tag{5.41}$$

The spot price $S(t)$ itself is log-normally distributed with

$$\mathbb{E}[S(t)] = \exp\left(\mathbb{E}[X(t)] + \frac{1}{2}\text{Var}[X(t)]\right).$$

Forward and Option Price Formulas

To derive a formula for futures prices we need to switch to the risk-neutral measure. From Section A.3 the futures price is given by

$$F(t, T) = \mathbb{E}_t^Q[S(T)],$$

where Q is the risk-neutral measure. The processes $\chi(t)$ and $\xi(t)$ under Q follow the stochastic differential equations

$$d\chi(t) = \left(-\kappa\chi(t) - \lambda_\chi\right) dt + \sigma_\chi d\tilde{W}_\chi(t),$$
$$d\xi(t) = \mu_\xi^* dt + \sigma_\xi d\tilde{W}_\xi(t),$$

where $\mu^* = mu_\xi - \lambda_\xi$ and λ_χ, λ_ξ represent the market prices of risk corresponding to the respective risk factors which are assumed to be constant. The futures prices can be calculated as follows:

$$\ln F(t, T) = \mathbb{E}_t^Q[X(T)] + \frac{1}{2}\text{Var}^Q[X(T)]$$

$$= e^{-\kappa(T-t)}\chi(t) + \xi(t) + \left(\mu_\xi^* + \sigma_\xi^2/2\right)(T - t) \tag{5.42}$$

$$- \left(1 - e^{-\kappa(T-t)}\right)\frac{\lambda_\chi}{\kappa} + \frac{\sigma_\chi^2}{4\kappa}\left(1 - e^{-2\kappa(T-t)}\right) + \frac{\rho\sigma_\chi\sigma_\xi}{\kappa}\left(1 - e^{-\kappa(T-t)}\right).$$

Compared with the one-factor Schwartz model, the additional parameters give more flexibility to the possible shapes of forward curves that can be modelled. A range of curve shapes are shown in Figure 5.33. The asymptotics of $\ln F(t, T)$ for large T are determined by the long-term process $\xi(t)$, which is a GBM. If we have $T - t \gg 1/\kappa$, such that $e^{-\kappa(T-t)} \approx 0$, we derive

$$\ln F(t, T) \sim \xi(t) + C + \left(\mu_\xi^* + \sigma_\xi^2/2\right)(T - t) \qquad \text{for } T \to \infty$$

with $C = -\frac{\lambda_\chi}{\kappa} + \frac{\sigma_\chi^2}{4\kappa} + \frac{\rho\sigma_\chi\sigma_\xi}{\kappa}$.

As was the case for the one-factor Schwartz model, we still have the property that $S(t)$ is log-normally distributed. Prices for European-style call and put options can be calculated

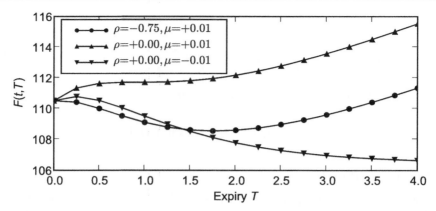

Figure 5.33   Different forward curves for the Schwartz–Smith model with $\kappa = 1$, $\sigma_\chi = 0.5$, $\sigma_\xi = 0.1$, $\chi(0) = 0.1$, $\xi(0) = \ln 100$ and variations of ρ and μ_ξ^*.

analytically via the Black–Scholes formula

$$C_{K,T}(t, F) = e^{-r(T-t)} \left(FN(d_1) - KN(d_2) \right),$$
$$P_{K,T}(t, F) = e^{-r(T-t)} \left(KN(-d_2) - FN(-d_1) \right),$$

where

$$F = F(t, T),$$
$$V = \frac{\sigma_\chi^2}{2\kappa} \left(1 - e^{-2\kappa(T-t)} \right) + \sigma_\xi^2 (T - t) + \frac{2\rho\sigma_\chi\sigma_\xi}{\kappa} \left(1 - e^{-\kappa(T-t)} \right),$$
$$d_1 = \frac{\ln(F/K) + \frac{1}{2}V}{\sqrt{V}} \qquad d_2 = d_1 - \sqrt{V}.$$

Calibration to Historical Data

Calibrating the Schwartz two-factor model to historical data is more difficult than calibrating the one-factor models since the stochastic factors $\chi(t)$ and $\xi(t)$ are not directly observable. Observable data usually consists of

- spot prices $S_i = S(t_i) = \exp(\chi(t_i) + \xi(t_i))$, $i = 0, \dots, N$ and
- forward prices $F_{i,j} = F(t_i, T_j)$ for different maturity dates $T_j, j = 1, \dots, n$.

To overcome the problem that the stochastic process is not observable, we make use of the Kalman filter described in the Appendix A.1.4. To derive a state-space representation, integrate the model differential equations (5.38) and (5.39) to get

$$\chi_{i+1} = e^{-\kappa\Delta t} \chi_i + \epsilon_i^\chi,$$
$$\xi_{i+1} = \xi_i + \mu\Delta t + \epsilon_i^\xi,$$

where $\chi_i = \chi(t_i)$, $\xi_i = \xi(t_i)$ and ϵ_i^χ, ϵ_i^ξ are normally distributed random numbers with covariance matrix

$$\mathrm{Cov}\left[(\epsilon_i^\chi, \epsilon_i^\xi)\right] = \begin{pmatrix} \frac{\sigma_\chi^2}{2\kappa}\left(1 - e^{-2\kappa\Delta t}\right) & \frac{\rho\sigma_\chi\sigma_\xi}{\kappa}\left(1 - e^{-\kappa\Delta t}\right) \\ \frac{\rho\sigma_\chi\sigma_\xi}{\kappa}\left(1 - e^{-\kappa\Delta t}\right) & \sigma_\xi^2\Delta t \end{pmatrix}. \tag{5.43}$$

In matrix notation the discretised equations become

$$\begin{pmatrix} \chi_{i+1} \\ \xi_{i+1} \end{pmatrix} = \begin{pmatrix} e^{-\kappa\Delta t} & 0 \\ 0 & 1 \end{pmatrix}\begin{pmatrix} \chi_i \\ \xi_i \end{pmatrix} + \begin{pmatrix} 0 \\ \mu_\xi \end{pmatrix} + \begin{pmatrix} \epsilon_i^\chi \\ \epsilon_i^\xi \end{pmatrix}. \tag{5.44}$$

The observable factors include the logarithm of the spot price

$$\ln S_i = \chi_i + \xi_i$$

and logarithms of futures prices $f_{i,j} = \ln F(t_i, T_j)$. Note that the state-space representation is taken with respect to the statistical measure and not the risk-neutral measure, since the model is calibrated to historical spot price data. The risk-neutral measure is only needed to derive futures prices. From the futures price formula (5.42), the measurement equations are

$$\begin{pmatrix} \ln S_i \\ f_{i,1} \\ \vdots \\ f_{i,n} \end{pmatrix} = \begin{pmatrix} 1 & 1 \\ e^{-\kappa(T_1 - t)} & 1 \\ \vdots & \vdots \\ e^{-\kappa(T_n - t)} & 1 \end{pmatrix} \cdot \begin{pmatrix} \chi_i \\ \xi_i \end{pmatrix} + \begin{pmatrix} 0 \\ A(T_1) \\ \vdots \\ A(T_n) \end{pmatrix} \tag{5.45}$$

with

$$A(T) = \left(\mu_\xi^* + \sigma_\xi^2/2\right)(T - t) - \left(1 - e^{-\kappa(T-t)}\right)\frac{\lambda_\chi}{\kappa}$$

$$+ \frac{\sigma_\chi^2}{4\kappa}\left(1 - e^{-2\kappa(T-t)}\right) + \frac{\rho\sigma_\chi\sigma_\xi}{\kappa}\left(1 - e^{-\kappa(T-t)}\right).$$

Generating Simulation Paths

For simulation, let $t_0, \ldots, t_N$ be the path dates, $\Delta t = t_i - t_{i-1}$ and assume constant parameters. The sample path values $S_i = S(t_i)$ can be generated using the iteration scheme from equation (5.44) as follows:

1. Generate two-dimensional random vectors $(\epsilon_0^\chi, \epsilon_0^\xi), \ldots, (\epsilon_N^\chi, \epsilon_N^\xi)$ where each random vector $(\epsilon_i^\chi, \epsilon_i^\xi)$ is drawn from a bivariate normal distribution with mean zero and covariance matrix given by equation (5.43).
2. Starting with today's state variables χ_0 and ξ_0, iteratively calculate χ_{i+1} and ξ_{i+1} from equation (5.44).
3. Calculate $S(t_i) = \exp(\chi_i + \xi_i)$.

5.7 STOCHASTIC FORWARD CURVE MODELS

In Section 5.3.2 a single futures price was modelled by a geometric Brownian motion. Looking at implied volatilities of different futures contracts of the same commodity it was shown (Figure 5.17) that the implied volatility depends on the time to expiry of the futures contract. Typically, implied volatility decreases with increasing time to expiry, explained by futures with longer time to expiry having less new information available. Often, the dynamics of not only single futures contracts but also the whole forward or futures curves $F(t, T)$ are modelled. In this case, regard must be given to the volatility structure of the forward curve and the covariance structure of futures contracts with different expiry dates. The situation is similar to the Heath–Jarrow–Morton (HJM) theory for interest rates (Heath et al., 1992), where the dynamics of the interest rate term structure are modelled.

A general model for the dynamics of the forward curve is

$$dF(t, T) = \alpha(t, T)\, dt + \sum_{i=1}^{n} \sigma_i(t, T)\, dW_i(t), \tag{5.46}$$

where $W_1, \ldots, W_n$ are standard Brownian motion processes and $\sigma_1(t, T), \ldots, \sigma_n(t, T)$ are the volatilities. In its general form, the volatility functions $\sigma_i(t, T)$ can be stochastic processes. This section considers special cases for this general multi-dimensional model and examines its specific characteristics.

Assuming that the market allows no arbitrage, there exists an equivalent martingale (risk-neutral) measure Q under which all forward prices are martingales. If the process in equation (5.46) is written with respect to Q, the drift term $\alpha(t, T)$ becomes zero for all t and T. Since we are interested in the dynamics under the risk-neutral measure, we assume zero drift:

$$dF(t, T) = \sum_{i=1}^{n} \sigma_i(t, T)\, dW_i(t). \tag{5.47}$$

Using the identity $S(t) = F(t, t)$, each model for the forward curve $F(t, T)$ also contains a model for the spot price $S(t)$ that can be derived as follows:

$$dS(t) = \left. \frac{\partial F(t, T)}{\partial T} \right|_{T=t} dt + dF(t, T)|_{T=t}. \tag{5.48}$$

The first term can be calculated more explicitly using the integration of equation (5.47) and taking the derivative with respect to T. In this way we get the following model equation for the spot price:

$$dS(t) = \int_0^t \left(\sum_{i=1}^{n} \frac{\partial \sigma_i(s, t)}{\partial T}\, dW_i(s) \right) dt + \sum_{i=1}^{n} \sigma_i(t, t)\, dW_i(t). \tag{5.49}$$

Since the drift term depends on the realised path of the Brownian motion, the process $S(t)$ is in general non-Markovian.

The model equations (5.47) and (5.49) so far are general and rather theoretical. In the following, examples of models that can be fitted to real market data are presented.

5.7.1 One-Factor Forward Curve Models

The simplest case of model (5.47) occurs where $n = 1$ and the forward curve dynamic depends on only one Brownian motion. With a volatility specification

$$\sigma_1(t, T) = e^{-\kappa(T-t)}\sigma,$$

where κ is a positive constant modelling the volatility dependence on the time to expiry, the model equation becomes

$$\frac{dF(t, T)}{F(t, T)} = e^{-\kappa(T-t)}\sigma \, dW(t). \tag{5.50}$$

An explicit solution is given by

$$F(t, T) = F(0, T) \exp\left(-\int_0^t \tfrac{1}{2}\sigma^2 e^{-2\kappa(T-s)} \, ds + \int_0^t \sigma e^{-\kappa(T-s)} \, dW(s)\right). \tag{5.51}$$

The implied spot price model can be calculated using equation (5.49) by applying the simple chain rule to get

$$\frac{\partial F(t, T)}{\partial T} = F(t, T)\frac{\partial \ln F(t, T)}{\partial T}$$

and by taking the derivative of the logarithm of (5.51) with respect to T:

$$\frac{\partial \ln F(t, T)}{\partial T} = \frac{\partial \ln F(0, T)}{\partial T} + \kappa\left(\ln F(0, T) - \ln F(t, T) + \frac{\sigma^2}{2}\int_0^t e^{-2\kappa(T-s)} \, ds\right).$$

Setting $T = t$ and applying the result to equation (5.49), we derive

$$\frac{dS(t)}{S(t)} = \kappa\left(\mu(t) - \ln S(t)\right) dt + \sigma \, dW(t) \tag{5.52}$$

where

$$\mu(t) = \frac{1}{\kappa}\frac{\partial \ln F(0, t)}{\partial t} + \ln F(0, T) + \frac{\sigma^2}{4\kappa}(1 - e^{-2\kappa t}).$$

The forward curve model applied to a particular futures contract is a special case of the Black model (Section 5.3.2) and all option pricing formulas derived for the Black model can be employed. The implied volatility $\bar{\sigma}_{t,T_1,T}$ for an option expiring in T_1 written on a futures contract $F_{t,T}$ is

$$\bar{\sigma}^2_{t,T_1,T} = \frac{1}{T_1 - t} \int_t^{T_1} e^{-2\kappa(T-s)}\sigma^2\, ds$$

$$= \frac{\sigma^2}{2\kappa(T_1 - t)} \left(e^{-2\kappa(T-T_1)} - e^{-2\kappa(T-t)}\right). \tag{5.53}$$

This identity can also be used to calibrate the forward curve model to a given implied volatility term structure observed in the market. The calibration works as follows. Let T_1^i, T^i, $\bar{\sigma}^i$ ($i = 1, \ldots, N$) be a set of option expiries, the underlying futures expiries and the corresponding market implied volatilities. For each set of model parameters $\Phi = (\kappa, \sigma)$ we can calculate the model implied volatilities $\bar{\sigma}^i_\Phi = \bar{\sigma}_{t,T_1^i,T^i}$ by substitution. The optimal parameters are found by solving an optimisation problem

$$\min_\Phi \sum_{i=1}^N \left|\bar{\sigma}^i - \bar{\sigma}^i_\Phi\right|^2.$$

Calibration of a model to implied volatility data is shown in Figure 5.34.

A second example of a one-factor forward curve model corresponds to the Cox–Ingersoll–Ross model for short interest rates (Cox et al., 1985). The model equation is

$$dF(t, T) = e^{-\kappa(T-t)}\sigma\sqrt{F(t,t)}\, dW(t). \tag{5.54}$$

Heath and Jara (2000) note that the futures curve dynamic depends only on the current spot price $S_t = F_{t,t}$ and that futures prices can become negative. Integrating yields

$$F_{t,T} = F_{0,T} + \int_0^t e^{-\kappa(T-s)}\sigma_s\sqrt{F_{s,s}}\, dW_s$$

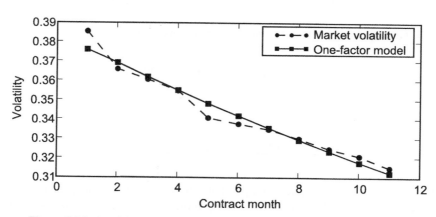

Figure 5.34 Model calibration to implied volatility data ($\kappa = 0.48$, $\sigma = 0.38$).

and one can derive the implied spot price dynamics as:

$$dS_t = \left(\frac{\partial F_{0,t}}{\partial t} - \kappa S_t \right) dt + \sigma_t \sqrt{S_t}\, dW_t.$$

In most cases model (5.50) seems more appropriate for commodity prices than model (5.54).

5.7.2   A Two-Factor Forward Curve Model

The one-factor model equation (5.50) has the disadvantage that with only a single source of randomness, futures contracts of different expiry dates are all perfectly correlated and cannot explain changes in the shape of the forward curve. Further, the volatility approaches zero exponentially for increasing time to expiry. For modelling a more realistic dynamic of the forward curve, multiple sources of randomness are considered. As previously stated, not all volatility functions $\sigma(t, T)$ yield a simple Markovian spot price dynamic.

A two-factor model with good analytical tractability is given by

$$\frac{dF(t,T)}{F(t,T)} = e^{-\kappa(T-t)}\sigma_1\, dW_1(t) + \sigma_2\, dW_2(t), \tag{5.55}$$

where $W_1(t)$ and $W_2(t)$ are Brownian motions with correlation $dW_1(t)\, dW_2(t) = \rho\, dt$.

The implied spot price model $S(t) = F(t, t)$ is derived as in Section 5.7.1:

$$\frac{dS(t)}{S(t)} = \kappa\,(\alpha(t) + \xi(t) - \ln S(t))\, dt + \sigma_1 dW_1(t) + \sigma_2 dW_2(t), \tag{5.56}$$

where $\alpha(t)$ is the deterministic function

$$\alpha(t) = \frac{\partial F(0,t)}{\partial t} + \kappa \ln F(0,t) - \frac{1}{2} \int_0^t \frac{\partial \sigma^2(s,t)}{\partial t} + \kappa \sigma^2(s,t)\, ds,$$

$$\sigma^2(s,t) = \sigma_1^2 e^{-2\kappa(t-s)} + 2\rho\sigma_1\sigma_2 e^{-\kappa(t-s)} + \sigma_2^2$$

and $\xi(t)$ is a Brownian motion given by the stochastic differential equation

$$d\xi(t) = \sigma_2\, dW_2(t).$$

The calculation uses the integrated logarithmic forward price

$$\ln F(t,T) = \ln F(0,T) - \frac{1}{2} \int_0^t \sigma^2(s,T)\, ds + \chi(t,T) + \xi(t), \tag{5.57}$$

where $\chi(t,T) = \int_0^t e^{-\kappa(T-s)}\sigma_1\, dW_1(s)$ and $\xi(t) = \int_0^t \sigma_2\, dW_2(s)$.

The model gives back the two-factor Schwartz spot price model presented in (5.37)–(5.39) with time-dependent parameters. Setting $T = t$ in (5.57) and $\chi(t) = \chi(t,t)$, we get

$$\ln S(t) = A(t) + \chi(t) + \xi(t),$$

where

$$A(t) = \ln F(0, t) - \frac{1}{2} \int_0^t \sigma^2(s, t) \, ds$$

$$= \ln F(0, t) - \left(\frac{\sigma_1^2}{4\kappa} \left(1 - e^{-2\kappa t} \right) + \frac{\rho \sigma_1 \sigma_2}{\kappa} \left(1 - e^{\kappa t} \right) + \frac{\sigma_2^2 t}{2} \right).$$

The processes $\chi(t)$ and $\xi(t)$ satisfy the stochastic differential equations

$$d\chi(t) = -\kappa \chi(t) + \sigma_1 \, dW_1(t),$$
$$d\xi(t) = \sigma_2 \, dW_2(t).$$

As for the one-factor model, the implied volatility $\bar{\sigma}(t, T_1, T)$ for an option expiring in T_1 written on a futures contract $F(t, T)$ is calculated as

$$\bar{\sigma}^2(t, T_1, T) = \frac{\sigma_1^2}{2\kappa(T_1 - t)} \left(e^{-2\kappa(T - T_1)} - e^{-2\kappa(T - t)} \right) + \sigma_2^2$$

$$+ \frac{2\rho \sigma_1 \sigma_2}{\kappa(T_1 - t)} \left(e^{-\kappa(T - T_1)} - e^{-\kappa(T - t)} \right). \tag{5.58}$$

This formula can be used to price European-style options. Figure 5.35 shows calibration results for the two-factor model using the same data set as for the one-factor model in Figure 5.34. The two-factor model fits closer to the shape of the market implied volatility curve. There is additional complexity if the implied volatilities refer to futures contracts with different time periods, for example months, quarters and years. For more details about the model calibration, see Kiesel *et al.* (2009).

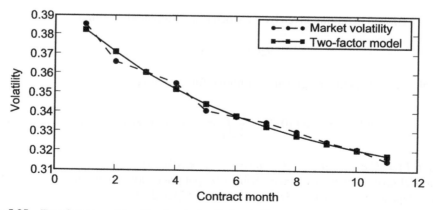

Figure 5.35   Two-factor model calibration to implied volatility data ($\kappa = 1.87$, $\sigma_1 = 0.26$, $\sigma_2 = 0.28$, $\rho = 0$).

5.7.3   A Multi-Factor Exponential Model

Heath and Jara (2000) describe an analytically tractable n-factor model. Taking the general forward curve model from equation (5.47) with the volatility functions

$$\sigma_i(t, T) = F(t, T) \sum_{j=1}^{m} \beta_{i,j} \exp\left(-\lambda_j(T - t)\right), \quad \lambda_j \geq 0,$$

we derive the model equation

$$\frac{dF(t, T)}{F(t, T)} = \sum_{i=1}^{n} \sum_{j=1}^{m} \beta_{i,j} e^{-\lambda_j(T-t)} \, dW_i(t).$$

This stochastic differential equation is solved explicitly by assuming the technical condition $\lambda_j + \lambda_k \neq 0$ for all pairs j, k to give

$$\frac{F(t, T)}{F(0, T)} = \exp\left\{ \int_0^t \sum_{i=1}^{n} \sum_{j=1}^{m} \beta_{i,j} e^{-\lambda_j(T-s)} \, dW_i(s) - \frac{1}{2} \int_0^t \sum_{i=1}^{n} \left(\sum_{j=1}^{m} \beta_{i,j} e^{-\lambda_j(T-s)} \right)^2 ds \right\}$$

$$= \exp\left\{ \sum_{j=1}^{m} e^{-\lambda_j(T-t)} Z_j(t) - \frac{1}{2} \sum_{i=1}^{n} \sum_{j,k=1}^{m} \frac{\beta_{i,j}\beta_{i,k}}{\lambda_j + \lambda_k} \left(e^{-(\lambda_j+\lambda_k)(T-t)} - e^{-(\lambda_j+\lambda_k)T} \right) \right\},$$

where

$$Z_j(t) = \int_0^t \sum_{i=1}^{n} \beta_{i,j} e^{-\lambda_j(t-s)} \, dW_i(s).$$

The auxiliary processes $Z_j(t)$ are Ornstein–Uhlenbeck processes satisfying

$$dZ_j(t) = -\lambda_j Z_j(t) \, dt + \sum_{i=1}^{n} \beta_{i,j} dW_i(t).$$

From here we get the derived spot price $S(t) = F(t, t)$ as

$$S(t) = F(0, t) \exp\left\{ \sum_{j=1}^{m} Z_j(t) - \frac{1}{2} \sum_{i=1}^{n} \sum_{j,k=1}^{m} \frac{\beta_{i,j}\beta_{i,k}}{\lambda_j + \lambda_k} \left(1 - e^{-(\lambda_j+\lambda_k)t} \right) \right\}.$$

6

Stochastic Models for Electricity and Gas

Compared with financial assets, commodities are more closely linked to the "physical" world, so the supply and demand situation has a direct impact on prices. This is especially true for the spot market when supply shortages or oversupply become transparent. The spot price models introduced in Section 5.6 have their origins in models used for financial markets and were extended to include typical features of commodity prices, such as mean reversion or seasonality. To be able to derive analytical solutions or efficient numerical solutions for option pricing, these models (also called *reduced-form models*) are restricted in complexity and are not aimed at capturing all statistical characteristics of real commodity prices.

Especially for electricity and other commodities with limited storability, these reduced-form models may not be sufficient for all applications. To capture features like extreme price spikes, *structural models* were developed that combine stochastic models known from financial markets with elements from fundamental modelling (see Chapter 7), but without the full complexity of fundamental models.

Also, the forward curve models considered in Section 5.2 are not sufficient for electricity and gas markets. Dedicated models of hourly and daily electricity and gas forward curves are therefore described in the following section.

6.1 DAILY AND HOURLY FORWARD CURVE MODELS

In most electricity and gas markets there is a liquid market for a set of standardised contracts with certain delivery periods (monthly, quarterly and yearly) and certain delivery products (e.g., baseload and peakload for electricity). As an example, Figure 6.1 shows the curve of monthly future prices for gas in Continental Europe. Sometimes, the resolution of traded contracts is finer for the near future (e.g., monthly products) compared with a period further ahead, where often only yearly contracts are traded. Figure 6.2 shows available futures prices for electricity at the EEX.

Generation assets and retail products, however, involve individual delivery schedules with daily, hourly or even finer resolution, for example to match the demand pattern of a customer (see Chapter 4). As this resolution is only available on the spot market and not on the standardised forward market, pricing such products requires modelling of a daily price forward curve (DPFC) or even an hourly price forward curve (HPFC). Assume that at current time t we have such a forward curve $F(t, T_i)$ available for all delivery hours (or days) T_i $(i = 1, \ldots, N)$. Then the value of a supply contract with hourly delivery schedule $L(T_i)$ and fixed price K is given by

$$V(t) = \sum_{i=1}^{N} e^{-r(T_i - t)} L(T_i) \left(F(t, T_i) - K \right). \tag{6.1}$$

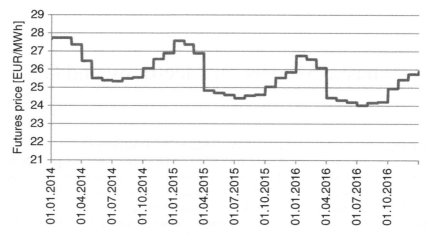

Figure 6.1   ICE European gas futures quotes with monthly granularity as of October 2013.

The "fair price" is the price K for which the value $V(t)$ becomes zero,

$$K = \frac{\sum_{i=1}^{N} e^{-r(T_i - t)} L(T_i) F(t, T_i)}{\sum_{i=1}^{N} e^{-r(T_i - t)} L(T_i)}.$$

In practice, the payment dates of the supply contract do not match exactly the delivery dates, for example they could be monthly. In this case the denominator needs to be adjusted according to the payment dates. Since electricity is hardly storable even intra-day, there are significant intra-day patterns observable for spot prices, for example prices at night are much lower than prices during the day. Therefore, the settlement period defined by the grid operator for balancing purposes is usually below one hour. For gas markets intra-day effects can often be

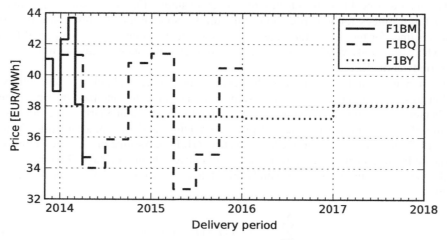

Figure 6.2   EEX prices for monthly (F1BM), quarterly (F1BQ) and yearly (F1BY) baseload futures contracts.

neglected since short-term storage is less restricted and the pipline grid itself serves as storage to some extent. Therefore a daily balancing regime is often sufficient.

How can a daily or hourly forward curve $F(t, T_i)$ be derived? Since there are no market prices for single days or hours directly observable in the forward market (beyond a few days ahead), the forward curve must be mathematically modelled to represent the value of a single delivery day or hour in the future. In a derivatives valuation framework, the forward price would be the expected spot price under the pricing measure:

$$F(t, T_i) = \mathbb{E}_t[S(T_i)].$$

Since daily or hourly forward contracts are not tradable in the market, the market is incomplete so there is no unique (risk-neutral) pricing measure (see Section A.3). However, the pricing measure ensures that there are no arbitrage opportunities. In this context it means that daily or hourly forward prices must be consistent with observed market prices for standardised forward or futures contracts. In other words, for a standard baseload or peakload contract, the valuation using the hourly forward curve according to equation (6.1) must match the valuation using market quotes from exchanges or broker platforms.

Let F_b be the price of a standard baseload contract (e.g., a certain calendar year) and J_b the set of hours within the delivery year. Then the consistency condition is

$$\frac{1}{|J^b|} \sum_{i \in J^b} F(t, T_i) = F^b,$$

where $|J^b|$ is the number of hours within the delivery period ($|J^b| = 8760$ for non-leap years).

A typical approach to construct daily or hourly forward curves is to evaluate statistical patterns (hourly, daily, weekly, seasonal shape) from historical spot prices and apply those patterns to quoted forward prices. There is extensive literature available on the construction of daily or hourly forward curves, for example Fleten et al. (2013) or Hildemann et al. (2011). A basic approach is:

1. Model the weekly and yearly shape of average daily prices, that is calculate daily shape factors from historical spot prices.
2. Model the (hourly) intra-day shape for different profile types depending on weekday and season (not required for daily forward curves).
3. Apply the yearly and intra-day shape factors to quoted forward prices.

In the following sections, the construction of a daily forward curve for gas and an hourly forward curve for electricity will be explained in more detail.

6.1.1 Daily Price Forward Curve for Gas

Gas spot prices contain seasonalities due to variations in gas consumption. Cold temperatures during winter increase demand for space heating in commercial as well as residential buildings and, as a consequence, gas consumption. In many countries like the United States hot temperatures during summer increase demand for air conditioning, which in turn results in larger natural gas demand, as power for air conditioning is generated by gas-fired power plants. While consumption of households is less dependent on the weekday, business customers often have a reduced gas consumption on weekends. Because of this variation in gas consumption, a weekly as well as a yearly seasonality can be observed for gas spot prices. Weekend prices are on average lower than working day prices and summer prices are on average lower than winter prices – at least in Europe.

To construct a DPFC reflecting these seasonalities we follow the basic approach described above. Since intra-day shape is not required, the calculation consists of the following two steps:

Step 1 (yearly and weekly shape). For many gas markets monthly futures prices are available sufficiently far out, therefore the yearly shape will automatically result from the alignment with monthly market prices in step 2. Historical spot prices $y(t)$ in this step will therefore only be used to extract the weekly shape. First a running 7-day average $\bar{y}(t)$ is subtracted from the spot price:

$$\Delta y(t) = y(t) - \bar{y}(t) = y(t) - \frac{1}{7} \sum_{i=0}^{6} y(t - i). \tag{6.2}$$

The resulting difference $\Delta y(t)$ reflects the deviation of the daily spot price from the weekly average and therefore contains only the weekly seasonalities but no longer the yearly seasonalities.

Now dummy variables for different day types are introduced, which cluster all days by weekday and season (summer/winter). We use the indicator function to evaluate whether a certain day t belongs to a given set A:

$$\mathbf{1}_A(t) = \begin{cases} 1 & t \in A, \\ 0 & \text{otherwise.} \end{cases}$$

The set of all Sundays will be denoted by D_1, all Mondays by D_2 and so forth. All days in winter (October to March) are denoted by D^w, all days in summer by D^s. We further use the notation $D_i^s = D_i \cap D^s$ for a certain weekday in summer and analogously D_i^w for a certain weekday in winter.

The weekly shape factors then result from the following regression:

$$\Delta y(t) = \sum_{i=1}^{7} \beta_i^w (1 - w_t) \mathbf{1}_{D_i^w}(t) + \beta_8^w w_t \mathbf{1}_{D^w}(t)$$

$$+ \sum_{i=1}^{7} \beta_i^s (1 - w_t) \mathbf{1}_{D_i^s}(t) + \beta_8^s w_t \mathbf{1}_{D^s}(t) + \epsilon(t). \tag{6.3}$$

Here, $\beta_i^{w/s}$ are the regression parameters with index either w or s for winter (respectively summer), w_t is the holiday weight of day t:

$$w_t = \begin{cases} 0, & \text{if } t \text{ is neither a holiday nor a bridge day} \\ p, & \text{if } t \text{ is a holiday } (p \text{ is the part of the population that has a holiday}) \\ g \cdot p, & \text{if } t \text{ is a bridge day and } p \text{ the population weight.} \end{cases} \tag{6.4}$$

For the regression a weighting of the historical spot prices can be used. For example, with a half-life of two years an exponential weight of

$$\lambda = \sqrt{\exp(0.5\log(0.5)\,\text{floor}\,((T-t)/365))} \tag{6.5}$$

and a spot history for multiple years can be used. Here T denotes the last day of the spot history. A choice of $g = 0.4$ for bridge days (working days between holidays and weekends) can be interpreted such that around 40% of the population who have a holiday are also on holiday on the associated bridge day. Altogether, 16 coefficients $\beta_1^s, \ldots, \beta_8^s, \beta_1^w, \ldots, \beta_8^w$ have to be fitted using least-squares regression.

Step 2 (align to forward prices). First, the weekly shape $\Delta y(t)$ resulting from step 1 is rolled out to the future period setting $\epsilon = 0$ in equation (6.3). Let us assume that monthly futures prices are available. Then the weekly shape is additively shifted to reproduce the monthly futures prices as the average of the daily price over the corresponding month. If instead of monthly forward prices a combination of overlapping monthly, quarterly and yearly prices is used, applying the shapes in such a way as to be consistent with all forward prices is slightly more complex. This situation will be considered below for the hourly price forward curve for electricity.

An example for futures prices, weekly pattern and the resulting DPFC is shown in Figure 6.3. The resulting DPFC reflects the spot price expectation as far as level and structure are concerned over a longer time period – for example a year. It is not a spot price forecast for the next day – to gain such a forecast, methods have to be applied using more recent information such as current weather forecasts. Furthermore, the DPFC does not contain any information about volatility of the spot or futures market. Therefore, valuation of flexibility requires spot price scenarios that reflect possible variations of the spot price around the DPFC.

6.1.2 Hourly Price Forward Curve for Electricity

Similar to gas, electricity spot prices exhibit strong seasonalities that are driven by corresponding seasonalities in electricity demand and electricity generation:

- Temperature and daylight depending on the yearly season and the time of the day drive electricity demand for heating, air conditioning and electric lighting. Further, renewable generation output is determined by weather conditions, such as wind speed, solar irradiation or precipitation (water reservoir levels).
- Residential and industrial electricity demand depend on the weekday and holidays, for example industrial demand is much lower on weekends and holidays compared with working days. Within each day, demand depends strongly on time of the day, for example demand is much lower during night hours.

To construct the hourly forward curve we follow the basic approach from the beginning of this chapter, where historical price data is used to statistically evaluate shape factors that can be applied to forward prices. Compared with the gas forward curve we need all three steps, since for electricity the intra-day shape is also relevant.

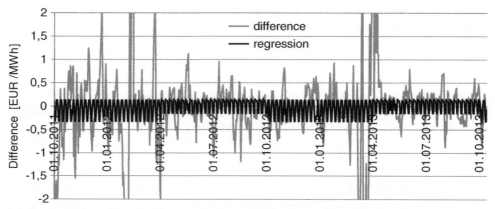

(a) Fit of weekly pattern to difference between spot price and weekly average

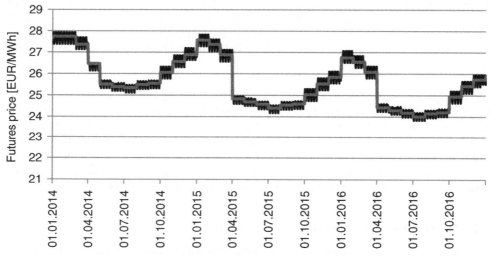

(b) Gas PFC resulting from shift of weekly pattern to futures prices with monthly granularity

Figure 6.3   Steps for the generation of a daily price forward curve for gas spot prices.

Step 1 (yearly and weekly shape). In principle, deriving the daily shape for electricity can be done analogously to gas (see previous section). However, when deriving the DPFC for gas it was assumed that a monthly forward curve is available from the market, which makes modelling a yearly shape obsolete. If market prices are only available on a quarterly or even yearly basis, the yearly shape also has to be calibrated from historical spot prices. We consider here this more general case.

Let $y(t)$ be normalised daily spot prices, that is the daily baseload spot price at day t divided by the average spot price in the year in which t lies. The normalised spot price for the kth hour of day t ($k = 1, \ldots, 24$) that will be used in step 2 is denoted as $y_k(t)$. Using the same idea as for the construction of the gas forward curve, we define suitable clusters for yearly season, weekdays and holidays, for example by month and weekday, where Tuesday, Wednesday and Thursday can be combined into one cluster:

Cluster	Months	Weekdays
1	Jan	Mo
2	Jan	Tu–Th
3	Jan	Fr
4	Jan	Sa
5	Jan	Su
⋮		
$N-1$	Dec	Sa
N	Dec	Su

As an alternative, months with similar price expectations can be combined to get more stable results, for example January and February could be defined as one cluster. The set of all days within cluster j is denoted by D_j. Again, the indicator function is used as a dummy variable in the following basic regression model:

$$y(t) = \sum_{j=1}^{N} \beta_j \mathbf{1}_{D_j}(t) + \epsilon(t).$$ (6.6)

Each resulting regression coefficient β_j corresponds to a shape factor for cluster j. Applying the regression model to a given day in the future yields the expected shape factor $\hat{y}(t)$ reflecting both yearly and weekly shape. In the simple regression model (6.6) exactly one indicator function yields value 1 for any given day t and all others 0, so that $y(t) = \beta_j + \epsilon(t)$ for exactly one index j. Instead of solving a regression, β_j can in this case also be determined as the average value of all daily prices within cluster D_j:

$$\beta_j = \frac{1}{|D_j|} \sum_{t \in D_j} y(t).$$

However, in practical applications, the regression approach should be refined at least by including holidays and bridge days (see previous section on DPFC). Further, refinements could take into account trends or add temperature as an explanatory variable in the regression model. Solving a regression model is therefore a general approach that can easily be adjusted to more complex situations. If the data contains price spikes, these can significantly distort results, therefore outliers should be treated with care or eliminated.

Figure 6.4 shows an example for a yearly shape in Germany, which is composed of a weekly and a yearly pattern including holiday adjustments. As can be seen in the figure, holiday adjustments are especially important around Christmas and New Year, where prices are typically much lower than on other days during winter.

Step 2 (intra-day shape). To calculate intra-day shape factors we use historical data for the normalised hourly shape $h_k(t) = y_k(t)/y(t)$, that is the normalised hourly spot price divided by the average daily price on day t. The intra-day shape depends on the season within the year and on weekday and holidays. Therefore a similar clustering as in step 1 can be chosen. The

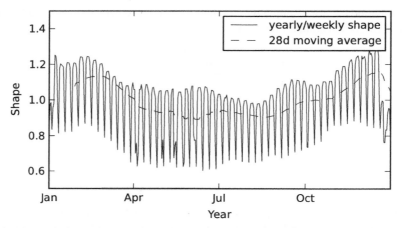

Figure 6.4   Yearly and weekly shape for electricity prices in Germany (including holiday adjustments). The 28-day moving average indicates the yearly shape only.

expected shape factor $\hat{h}_k(t)$ can be calculated as the average of all historical intra-day shapes $h_k(t)$ within the relevant cluster (see Figure 6.5 for an example). Since outliers may have a large effect on intra-day patterns, the number of clusters should be chosen carefully so that the data history is large enough for each cluster. Months with similar patterns should be integrated into the same cluster. Again, the approach can be refined by using a more complex regression model instead of an average value to derive $\hat{h}_k(t)$.

Calculating intra-day shapes for a larger number of day-type clusters requires a multiple-year history of price data to give stable results. If the shapes are used to calculate a forward curve for multiple years ahead, one needs to be careful to identify structural breaks or trends. One prominent example is the electricity market in Germany, where within a few years a rapid expansion of photovoltaic generation capacity significantly changed the intra-day shape of

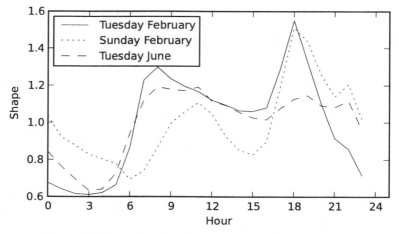

Figure 6.5   Intra-day shape in Germany for different day types.

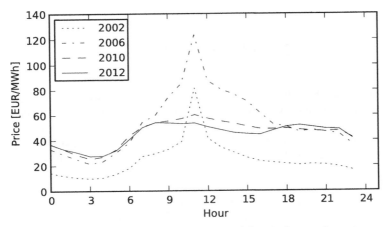

Figure 6.6   Average hourly prices on weekdays in June to August.

power prices (see Figure 6.6). An approach to incorporate this structural trend is described later in this section (under refinements).

Step 3 (align to forward prices). In this step the shape factors are applied in such a way that the resulting hourly forward curve is consistent with quoted forward prices. As a simple example, assume that there is only a yearly baseload forward price F available. Then the hourly forward curve for the kth hour of day t (denoted by T) can be defined as

$$F(t_0, T) = \hat{y}(t)\hat{h}_k(t)F.$$

Since by construction the intra-day shape factors $\hat{h}_k(t)$ have mean 1 over all hours k of each day t and the yearly shape factors $\hat{y}(t)$ have mean 1 over all days within a year, the hourly forward curve is consistent with the yearly price F. If instead of one market forward price there are several non-overlapping market forward prices, then the shape factors can be normalised to mean 1 during each contract period and the same method can be used.

As a particular case, the shape factors $\hat{h}_k(t)$ can be normalised to mean 1 separately for peak and off-peak hours and applied to the corresponding peak or off-peak forward price. Since in this case peak and off-peak hours are scaled by different shape factors it may happen that a discontinuity arises at the intersection between peak and off-peak which may require an additional smoothing procedure.

In reality, forward contracts for electricity may overlap, for example quarters are traded that overlap with a simultaneously traded yearly contract. In such a general situation, let F_k^b and F_k^p denote all traded baseload and peakload forward contracts. Let J_k^b (respectively J_k^p) denote the set of hours corresponding to the delivery period of F_k^b (baseload) [respectively F_k^p (peakload)].

Consistency of the hourly foward curve $F(t_0, T_i)$ with all baseload and peak forward prices can then be written as

$$\frac{1}{|J_k^b|} \sum_{i \in J_k^b} F(t_0, T_i) = F_k^b \quad \text{for all } k = 1, \ldots, N_b \tag{6.7}$$

and

$$\frac{1}{|J_k^p|} \sum_{i\in J_k^p} F(t_0, T_i) = F_k^p \quad \text{for all } k = 1, \dots, N_p. \tag{6.8}$$

Now we assume that shape factors s_i for each hour T_i have been derived (e.g., by multiplication of intra-day shape $\hat{h}_k$ and yearly/weekly shape factor $\hat{y}$) that do not have to be normalised during each forward period. The idea is to apply additional scaling factors α_m and β_m which are effective during the delivery period of the forward contracts F_l^b (respectively F_l^p) to ensure consistency with all given market prices. The model for the hourly forward curve is

$$F(t, T_i) = \left(\sum_{m=1}^{N_b} \alpha_m e_{mi} + \sum_{m=1}^{N_p} \beta_m f_{mi} \right) s_i,$$

where

$$e_{mi} = \mathbf{1}_{J_m^b}(i), \qquad f_{mi} = \mathbf{1}_{J_m^p}(i).$$

The consistency condition becomes

$$\frac{1}{|J_k^b|} \sum_{i\in J_k^b} \left(\sum_{m=1}^{N_b} \alpha_m e_{mi} + \sum_{m=1}^{N_p} \beta_m f_{mi} \right) s_i = F_k^b \quad \text{for all } k = 1, \dots, N_b.$$

Rearranging terms, these equations can be written as

$$\sum_{m=1}^{N_b} A_{km}^b \alpha_m + \sum_{m=1}^{N_p} B_{km}^b \beta_m = F_k^b |J_k^b| \quad \text{for all } k = 1, \dots, N_b \tag{6.9}$$

where

$$A_{km}^b = \sum_{i\in J_k^b} e_{mi} s_i = \sum_{i\in J_k^b \cap J_m^b} s_i \quad \text{and} \quad B_{km}^b = \sum_{i\in J_k^b} f_{mi} s_i = \sum_{i\in J_k^b \cap J_m^p} s_i.$$

The analogous equations for the peakload contracts are

$$\sum_{m=1}^{N_b} A_{km}^p \alpha_m + \sum_{m=1}^{N_p} B_{km}^p \beta_m = F_k^p |J_k^p| \quad \text{for all } k = 1, \dots, N_p \tag{6.10}$$

where

$$A_{km}^p = \sum_{i\in J_k^p \cap J_m^b} s_i \quad \text{and} \quad B_{km}^p = \sum_{i\in J_k^p \cap J_m^p} s_i.$$

Equations (6.9) and (6.10) define a linear system of $N_b + N_p$ equations for the same number of variables α_m and β_m. If there are no arbitrage opportunities in the forward prices then there is a unique solution for the scaling factors α_m and β_m. Sometimes forward prices are not totally arbitrage-free, for example where a yearly contract is slightly inconsistent with the quarterly contracts covering the same delivery year. In these situations, we can remove redundant forward prices or solve a least-squares problem instead of trying to solve a linear system exactly.

Refinements: The methodology above can be refined in various ways to improve calibration results.

1. *Off-standard contracts:* Instead of calibrating the forward curve only to standard forward and futures prices, additional quotes for off-standard contracts can be included. As an example, there is an OTC market for block contracts:

Delivery period	Delivery days	Delivery hours
Cal 14	Mon–Sun	00–06
Cal 14	Mon–Fri	06–22
Q1 14	Sat–Sun	00–24
⋮		

This additional market information can be used to recalibrate the structure of the hourly price forward curve within step 3. However, liquidity of the non-standard products is typically not very high.

2. *Bid–offer prices and smoothing:* So far it has been assumed that there is exactly one market price for a given product. For very liquid products with low bid-offer spreads this may be a reasonable assumption, otherwise a price range between the bid and offer prices can be considered instead of one price. Especially when using off-standard products this approach may yield more realistic results. The calibration method suggested by Fleten and Lemming (2003) requires that the forward curve is in between bid and offer price. Further, the forward curve should be as smooth as possible, which results in the following optimisation problem for the forward curve $f(t)$:

$$\min \sum_{t=1}^{T} (f(t) - s(t))^2 + \lambda \sum_{t=2}^{T-1} (f(t-1) - 2f(t) + f(t+1))^2$$

subject to

$$F(T_{1i}, T_{2i})_{\text{bid}} \leq \frac{1}{\sum_{t=T_{1i}}^{T_{2i}} e^{-rt}} \sum_{t=T_{1i}}^{T_{2i}} e^{-rt} f(t); \forall i \in \mathcal{F},$$

$$F(T_{1i}, T_{2i})_{\text{offer}} \geq \frac{1}{\sum_{t=T_{1i}}^{T_{2i}} e^{-rt}} \sum_{t=T_{1i}}^{T_{2i}} e^{-rt} f(t); \forall i \in \mathcal{F}$$

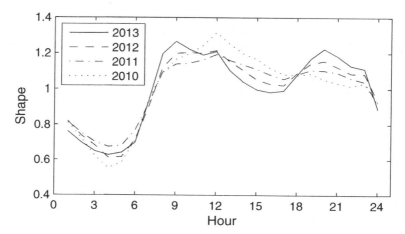

Figure 6.7   Development of average shape of summer profiles.

with $\mathcal{F}$ being the set of observed market prices, T_{1i}, T_{2i} the beginning and end of the delivery period, s_t the candidate for the forward curve, $F(T_{1i}, T_{2i})_{\text{bid}}$, $F(T_{1i}, T_{2i})_{\text{offer}}$ the bid and offer prices for product i and λ a weighting factor for smoothing the curve.

3. *Structural trends:* As already mentioned, we have to take care of structural breaks or trends. Figure 6.7 shows the shape of the German EPEX market clearing prices on summer weekdays. We observe a downward trend in the sunshine hours and an upward trend in the early morning and late evening hours. Owing to the German renewable energy support regime, electricity generation from wind, solar, biomass and run-of-river production has higher priority than conventional power plants. This means that the merit order curve (see Section 7.3.1) is shifted to the right. Figure 6.8 shows the increase in solar production in Germany during the summer months over recent years. To take this trend into account, the

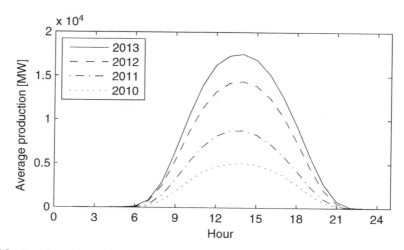

Figure 6.8   Development of average daily solar production during summer. *Source*: http://www.transparency.eex.com.

development and future expectations of renewable generation should be considered in the construction of an hourly price forward curve. A hybrid approach suggested in de Jong *et al.* (2013) filters out the impact of solar and wind production via a regression

$$\Delta s(t) = -\beta_1 s(t - 24) - \beta_2 \Delta p_{solar}(t) - \beta_3 \Delta p_{wind}(t) + \epsilon(t),$$

with $s(t)$ being the spot price for hour t, Δ being a lag operator with period 24, $p_{wind}(t), p_{solar}(t)$ being wind and solar production at time t. Of course the correct day types should be considered in this approach. The estimation is more stable than a direct regression of the prices against a day-type scheme extended by solar and wind production because of different price levels caused by fuel prices.

6.2 STRUCTURAL ELECTRICITY PRICE MODELS

Owing to the non-storability of electricity, electricity generation needs to match demand at every point in time. In a competitive market, the spot price is determined by the marginal cost of production (see Chapter 7). If all available power plants are ordered by their variable costs of production (mostly fuel and emission costs), then the marginal plant is the last (most expensive) plant still required to match demand. The ordered variable costs are also called the *merit order curve* (see Section 7.3.1).

Many structural electricity price models have a merit order curve built into the stochastic model. As a basic approach, the spot price is represented as

$$S(t) = f(D(t)), \tag{6.11}$$

where f is a non-linear merit order function and $D(t)$ a mean-reverting stochastic process modelling demand fluctuation. If f is sufficiently steep for high demand, such a model is appropriate to model price spikes.

One of the first models following this idea was the model introduced in Barlow (2002). It uses a merit order curve of the form

$$f(x) = (a + \alpha x)^{1/\alpha}, \quad \alpha < 0$$

and an Ornstein–Uhlenbeck process for $X(t)$:

$$dX(t) = -\lambda(X(t) - a) \, dt + \sigma dW(t).$$

A model for the European market is described in Section 6.2.1 and extended to multiple commodities in Section 6.2.2.

A different conceptual approach to model price spikes in electricity markets is presented in Section 6.2.3. Here, a tight supply situation is modelled by a regime-switching process where a Markov chain switches between a low-volatile and a high-volatile market situation. Because this model does not use a merit order curve, it is not a structural model in the narrow sense.

6.2.1 The SMaPS Model

The spot market price simulation (SMaPS) model (Burger *et al.* 2004) described in this section belongs to the category of structural models, since it models the system load as a fundamental driver for the electricity spot price. System load and a second stochastic price driver are modelled as discrete time series. The model can be used in situations where load and prices are considered stochastic, for example full service electricity contracts (see Section 4.6).

Model Overview

In the SMaPS model the spot market price is described by a discrete stochastic process $S(t)$, $t = 0, 1, \ldots$ with hours as time units. The full model can be considered as a three-factor model, based on the following stochastic processes:

- Total system load (electricity demand) $L(t)$, $t \geq 0$.
- Short-term price variations $X(t)$, $t \geq 0$.
- Long-term price variations $Y(t)$, $t \geq 0$.

as well as the following additional quantities:

- (Logarithmic) empirical merit order curve $f(t, L)$.
- Average relative availability of power plants $v(t)$.

The fundamental equation of the SMaPS model is

$$S(t) = \exp(f(t, L(t)/v(t)) + X(t) + Y(t)). \tag{6.12}$$

The two stochastic factors $L(t)$ and $X(t)$ produce the short-term price variations, while factor $Y(t)$ is responsible for the long-term stochastic behaviour. All three factors are assumed to be stochastically independent. The process $L(t)$ describes the total system (grid) load. In many markets the total system load is published on a regular basis, so the process parameters can be estimated directly from load data, independent of the spot market prices. To eliminate the seasonality of the system load, we set

$$L(t) = \hat{L}(t) + l(t),$$

where $\hat{L}(t)$ is a deterministic load forecast and $l(t)$ is a SARIMA (see below) time series model with 24-hour seasonality. The deterministic function $v(t)$ specifies the expected relative availability of power plants in the system. Usually, regular maintenance of power plants is scheduled during periods when the average load is comparably low. For example, during summer in European countries. Consequently, the availability of power plants in European countries is typically higher in winter than in summer. The highest availability is normalised to one and the expression $L(t)/v(t)$ will be called the adjusted load.

Many governments strongly support renewables by guaranteeing fixed prices for their generation. Thus, these generation volumes are available independent of the spot price. Only the remaining quantity, that is grid load less generation of renewables, is relevant for the spot price auction. This quantity is denoted as residual load by Wagner (2012). As generation of

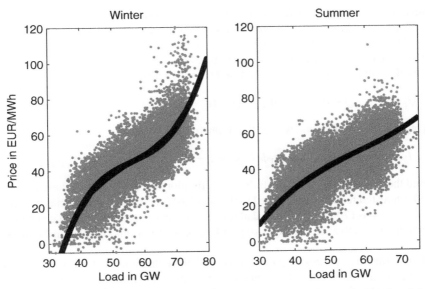

Figure 6.9 SMaPS empirical merit order curve, calibrated to EEX prices January 2010 to July 2013.

nuclear power plants is not subject to significant price fluctuations we reduce the grid load not only by generation of renewables, $R(t)$, but also by generation of nuclear power plants, $N(t)$:

$$L_{th}(t) = L(t) - R(t) - N(t).$$

We refer to this variable as the thermal residual load. Instead of using $L(t)$, the thermal residual load can be used for spot price modelling to include the effects of renewables in such a model. An example of a model using thermal residual load is given in Section 6.2.2.

The relationship between price and load described by the so-called *merit order curve* (see Section 7.3.1) is typically highly non-linear and can be very steep when generation capacity is scarce. Since the merit order curve at a future point in time t depends on various uncertain parameters such as fuel costs, economic situation and availability of power plants, the model does not include a merit order curve derived from fundamental technical data, but instead uses an empirical function estimated from hourly price and load data, called the *empirical merit order curve*. The empirical merit order curve depends to some extent on weekday and daytime, such that f is time dependent. Different empirical curves are used for different weekdays and daytimes. In practice, only a few different curves are used, differentiating between workdays and holidays and between peak hours and off-peak hours (see Figure 6.9 for an example).

Model Selection and Calibration

Since electricity prices may show different behaviour in different markets, the specification of the time series model depends on the market. We look here at EEX spot prices as an example, but similar results hold for other markets. The analysis of the load process uses only load data. To build the residual process $l(t) = L(t) - \hat{L}(t)$ we need the deterministic component $\hat{L}(t)$ which can be found by regression using techniques from Section 4.4. Statistical analysis of the load residual $l(t)$ reveals a strong autocorrelation for a 24-hour time lag. A family of stochastic time-series models taking into account such seasonal behaviour is the family of SARIMA processes. The simplest model that gives a satisfactory fit is a SARIMA$(1, 0, 1) \times (1, 0, 1)_{24}$ model. This is defined by composing an ARMA$(1, 1)$ rule for differences with a 24-hour time lag. The model equation (writing l_t instead of $l(t)$ for better readability) is

$$(l_t - \Phi_1 l_{t-24}) - \phi_1(l_{t-1} - \Phi_1 l_{t-25}) = (\epsilon_t - \Theta_1 \epsilon_{t-24}) - \theta_1(\epsilon_{t-1} - \Theta_1 \epsilon_{t-25}).$$

Multiplying out the coefficients, we get the iterative rule

$$l_t = \phi_1 l_{t-1} + \Phi_1 l_{t-24} - \Phi_1 \phi_1 l_{t-25} + \epsilon_t - \theta_1 \epsilon_{t-1} - \Theta_1 \epsilon_{t-24} + \Theta_1 \theta_1 \epsilon_{t-25}.$$

It is beyond the scope of this book to study the calibration and properties of these processes in detail, and interested readers are directed to the standard literature on time-series models (e.g., Brockwell and Davis (2002)). Numerical algorithms for parameter calibration can be found in many mathematical software packages (e.g., Matlab, S-PLUS) and numerical libraries (e.g., NAG).

The short-term price process $X(t)$ explains market fluctuations that are not explained by the load. Again, a significant autocorrelation for a 24-hour time lag can be observed (see Figure 6.10), also leading to the choice of a SARIMA$(1, 0, 1) \times (1, 0, 1)_{24}$ model with different parameters.

The long-term price process $Y(t)$ is modelled by a random walk, which can be seen as the discrete version of a Brownian motion. The model equation is

$$Y(t + 1) = Y(t) + \left(\mu(t) - \tfrac{1}{2}\sigma_Y^2 \right) + \sigma_Y \epsilon^Y(t).$$

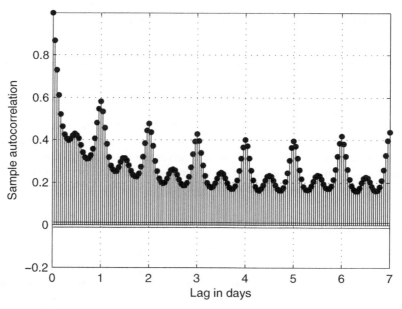

Figure 6.10   Autocorrelation function for the price process $X(t)$.

The short-term processes $l(t)$ and $X(t)$ model very short-term fluctuations around 0. For a point of time $T \gg t$ far enough in the future, the values $l(t)$ or $X(t)$ at time t have hardly any influence on the expected values $\mathbb{E}_t[l(T)]$ and $\mathbb{E}_t[X(T)]$ at the later time T. Typically this will be the case for time differences greater than one month. As a consequence, the futures price $F(t, T) = \mathbb{E}_t[S(T)]$ for $T \gg t$ depends, as an approximation, only on the long-term process $Y(t)$ and not on $X(t)$ or $l(t)$. Burger $et~al.$ (2004) show that

$$F(t, T) = \hat{S}(T)e^{Y(t) + \mu(T - t)},$$

where $\hat{S}(T)$ is a (non-stochastic) technical price given by

$$\hat{S}(T) = e^{\text{Var}[X(T)]/2}\mathbb{E}[\exp\left(f(T, L(T)/v(T))\right)].$$

Since $Y(t)$ follows a Brownian motion, the forward price follows a discrete version of GBM of the form

$$\frac{dF(t, T)}{F(t, T)} = \sigma^Y \, dW(t).$$

In the long-term approximation the model reduces to Black's model for futures prices. To calibrate the model parameters, we can choose forward or futures prices with a long time to expiry and calibrate the parameters of Black's model using the methods of Section 5.3.2.

6.2.2   The Multi-Commodity SMaPS model

After presentation of a structural spot price model for electricity in the previous section we will present an extension to a multi-commodity model in this section. This extended model was introduced by Müller (2013).

Within the general representation (6.11) of a structural electricity price model the function f is an approximation of the merit order curve depending on demand fluctuations $D(t)$. As the spot price of electricity depends not only on the grid load but also on generation of renewables, capacities of nuclear power plants, prices of emission allowances and prices of all fuels in the market, these dependencies are added to the function f. The model equation (6.12) is therefore extended, so that f depends on the thermal residual load $l_{th}(t)$, price of natural gas $G(t)$, price of coal $C(t)$ and price of emission allowances $E(t)$:

$$S(t) = f(l_{th}(t), G(t), C(t), E(t), t) + X(t).$$

In detail, the function f is given by

$$
\begin{aligned}
f(l_{th}(t), G(t), C(t), E(t), t) = {} & a_0 + a_1 \mathbf{1}_{\text{Sat}}(t) + a_2 \mathbf{1}_{\text{Sun}}(t) \\
& + a_4 G(t)\mathbf{1}_A(t) + a_5 C(t) + a_6 E(t) \\
& + l_{th}(t)(a_3 + a_7 G(t) + a_8 C(t) + a_9 E(t)).
\end{aligned}
$$

Using absolute prices instead of log prices allows for modelling direct influences of commodity price changes within this model. Furthermore, negative spot prices which are becoming more common in several markets can be simulated using such a model structure.

The parameters $a_0, \dots, a_9$ within this approach can be estimated via ordinary least-squares regression as the model is linear in these parameters. The indicator function $1_A(t)$ describes the hours from 7 a.m. to midnight as the statistical significance of the gas price is only given in these hours. The model describes a weighted average price $a_3 + a_7 G(t) + a_8 C(t) + a_9 E(t)$ multiplied by the thermal residual load $l_{th}(t)$. This is the average electricity price determined by the model. The other terms describe further influences by weekday (a_1, a_2) and commodity price influences (a_4, a_5, a_6). If the oil price is considered to be an important influence factor as well it can be included in the model in the same way as the other commodities.

Calibration of the above model is based on historical prices. In case of $S(t)$ historical spot prices of electricity, for example from the EEX, can be used. Historical grid load data as well as generation of renewables and capacities of nuclear power plants can be used to derive a time series for the thermal residual load $l_{th}(t)$. Day-ahead prices for natural gas can be obtained from the EEX as well. In contrast to electricity and gas where the spot market implies delivery on the next day, there is a spot market for coal (and oil) implying delivery within the next few weeks. As fuel prices are supposed to explain the spot price of electricity, we use fuel prices for those products closest to spot delivery. This means we use prices of the first monthly futures contract traded on the ICE. Emission allowances can be bought on the spot market but since emission allowances are storable, only the cost of carry is responsible for price differences between spot and forward contracts. As the December contract is the most liquidly traded contract on the ICE, these prices are used instead of spot prices. Based on the data described above, the model can be calibrated via ordinary least-squares regression. The resulting model fit can be seen in Figure 6.11.

The basis for calibration of $X(t)$ is the deviation of the model price $f(\cdot)$ from the historical price $S(t)$:

$$S(t) - f(l_{th}(t), G(t), C(t), E(t), t).$$

In analogy with the SMaPS model, this time series exhibits strong seasonal autocorrelations (see Figure 6.12). Again, a SARIMA process provides a good fit for this situation. Analysis of autocorrelations leads to a SARIMA $(1, 0, 0) \times (1, 0, 1)_{24}$ process. The innovations of this

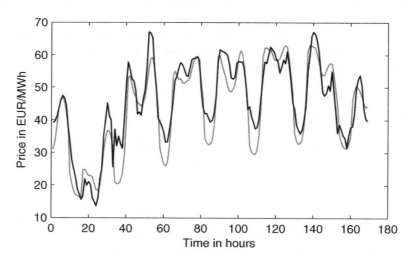

Figure 6.11   Fit of the model by Müller (2013) (grey) to historical spot prices (black) for one week in 2012.

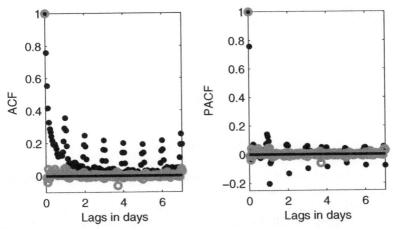

Figure 6.12   ACF (left) and PACF (right) of residuals (black) and innovations (grey) of the price process.

process are uncorrelated but not normally distributed. Owing to the heavy-tailed empirical distribution, the use of a Student's t-distribution with scale parameter provides an adequate fit (see Figure 6.13). Both the process and its distribution can be calibrated using maximum likelihood methods.

Having specified estimation procedures of both major model components we need to set up models for the four factors of $f(\cdot)$. An approach for the thermal load is to set up distinct models for grid load, generation of renewables and capacities of nuclear power plants. Then, the thermal residual load can be recomposed from these models. As a simplification, grid load instead of thermal residual load can be used.

The other three factors need to be considered in a combined model. The prices of gas, coal and emission certificates (and oil) exhibit strong dependencies. As a basic approach to model

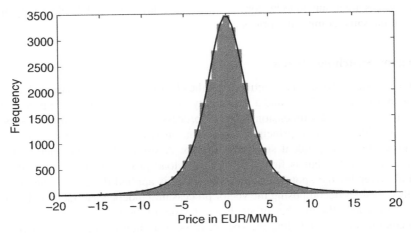

Figure 6.13   Student's t-distribution with scale parameter (black) fitted to innovations (grey).

a non-stationary time series we use a GBM (compare with Section 5.6.2) where log-returns follow a normal distribution. In the multivariate case the GBM is given by

$$\frac{dS^i(t)}{S^i(t)} = \mu_i \, dt + \sigma_i \, dW^i(t)$$

for component $i = 1, \ldots, m$ of the multivariate process. The standard Brownian motion processes $W^i(t)$ in this formulation are correlated:

$$E(dW^i(t)dW^j(t)) = \rho_{ij}dt,$$

where $\rho_{ii} = 1$. This formulation means that distinct GBMs with drift μ_i and volatility σ_i can be combined using correlated Brownian motions.

This pure stochastic approach can be combined with the structural gas price model presented in Section 6.3.1. We apply the GBM to the prices of oil, coal and emission certificates. The gas price is derived from the oil price as it is an exogenous factor in the gas price model. Thus, the dependencies between gas and the other commodities are reflected within this framework. Instead of using a multivariate one-factor model like GBM, the well-known two-factor model by Schwartz and Smith (2000) can be applied to these prices as well. This increases complexity but is commonly seen as a more appropriate commodity price model. Though originally introduced as a univariate model it can easily be extended to a multivariate model incorporating correlations.

Both alternatives rely on the concept of (linear) correlation. In case of non-stationary time series there is the concept of cointegration to model stronger dependencies. In the framework of vector-error-correction models the idea of cointegration can be applied to the multi-commodity situation. A discussion of these three approaches and the different thermal residual load models is also given by Müller (2013).

The choice of the commodity price model in this framework is an important issue with respect to the valuation of assets. Modelling the dependencies between electricity and coal prices is crucial for the evaluation of a coal-fired power plant (compare Section 6.2.4). A set of corresponding scenarios for electricity, natural gas and coal is shown in Figure 6.14. The commodity prices are assumed to be constant within the day so that all 24 electricity prices in a day rely on the same commodity prices.

6.2.3 Regime-Switching Models

In the SMaPS model introduced in Section 6.2.1 the electricity spot price is modelled as a time series with an hourly granularity and a seasonality of time lag 24. Another approach, regime switching, uses a daily 24-dimensional vector process instead of the 24-hour seasonality (Schindlmayr, 2005). Using a principal component analysis (PCA) the vector process can be decomposed into independent stochastic factors. A similar PCA approach is also used in Skantze et al. (2000), but is first applied to the load process which is considered as a fundamental driver for the spot price. Here, the PCA is applied directly to the hourly spot price profiles. Besides decomposing the vector process into independent factors, the PCA can also be used to reduce the number of stochastic factors to the most significant ones, which speeds up computations. Modelling the spot process as an hourly vector on a daily basis is also closer to the actual trading schedule, where spot prices are usually the result of an auction

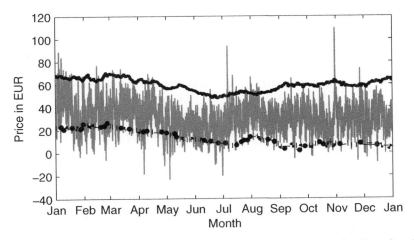

Figure 6.14   Corresponding scenarios for the electricity price (grey), the gas price (dotted) and the coal price (solid).

for the day (or weekend) ahead. A regime-switching approach in a continuous time setup with applications to option pricing is considered in Deng (2000).

The following notation is used:

- $S(t) = (S^1(t), \ldots, S^{24}(t))$, the vector of hourly spot prices on day t.
- $s(t) = \ln S(t)$, the vector of logarithmic hourly spot prices.
- $s(t) = \frac{1}{24} \sum_{i=1}^{24} s^i(t)$, the mean logarithmic price.

Hourly spot prices are modelled at a logarithmic scale decomposed into the mean level and the hourly profile:

$$s(t) = s(t) + \mathbf{h}(t), \quad \sum_{i=1}^{24} h^i(t) = 0. \tag{6.13}$$

For the scalar process $s(t)$ and the vector process $\mathbf{h}(t)$, the following time series models are used:

1. The non-seasonal component of $s(t)$ is an AR(1) model with regime switching.
2. The stochastic component of $\mathbf{h}(t)$ is decomposed via PCA into factor loads $u^i(t)$ ($i = 1, \ldots, 24$) which are then modelled as independent ARMA processes.

It is often advisable to treat business days and non-business days as separate processes since they have a different behaviour regarding volatility and spikes. Fitting a single process to both business and non-business days generally gives poor results. In the simplest case, one can neglect the correlation between price on business and non-business days and take independent processes.

The Daily Price Process

The (logarithmic) daily price process $s(t)$ has a yearly seasonality and is sensitive to weekdays and holidays. To account for price spikes in the daily prices a regime-switching approach is used.

First the seasonal component of $s(t)$ is identified using a regression model:

$$s(t) = \sum_{j=1}^{N_d} \mathbf{1}_{D_j}(t)\beta_j^A + \mathbf{1}_{D_j}(t)\cos\left(\frac{2\pi t}{365}\right)\beta_j^B + \mathbf{1}_{D_j}(t)\sin\left(\frac{2\pi t}{365}\right)\beta_j^C + \mathbf{1}_{D_j}(t)t\beta_j^D + y(t),$$

where $y(t)$ is the residual and D_j, $j = 1, \ldots, N_d$ define a partition into day types (e.g., Mo, Tu–Th, Fr, Sa, Su, Holidays). The indicator functions $\mathbf{1}_{D_j}(t)$ are dummy variables, similar to the approach used for the HPFC construction in Section 6.1.2. The regression coefficients $\beta_j^A, \ldots, \beta_j^E$ have the following meaning:

Coefficient	Description
β_j^A	mean level
β_j^B, β_j^C	amplitudes for yearly seasonality
β_j^D	deterministic drift

Next, a regime-switching ARMA process is calibrated to the $y(t)$ data with the process divided into business and non-business days:

$$y(t) = \mathbf{1}_{J^B}(t)y^B(t) + \mathbf{1}_{J^H}(t)y^H(t),$$

where J^B denotes the business and J^H the non-business days.

The following description of model and calibration for either of the processes $y^B(t)$ or $y^H(t)$ is simplified by leaving out the superscript B (respectively H, and working with a time series y_k, $k = 1, \ldots, N$ observed at times t_k.

To account for price spikes, an AR(1) model with regime switching is chosen, where the regime change is modelled via a discrete Markov chain. The model equation is given by

$$y_k - \mu_{r_k} = \phi_{r_k}(y_{k-1} - \mu_{r_{k-1}}) + \sigma_{r_k}\epsilon_k, \tag{6.14}$$

where $r_k \in \{1, 2\}$ denotes the current regime at time t_k and $\epsilon_k \sim N(0, 1)$. The Markov chain is characterised by the transition probability matrix

$$P = \begin{pmatrix} p_{11} & p_{21} \\ p_{12} & p_{22} \end{pmatrix}$$

with $p_{ij} = P(r_k = j \mid r_{k-1} = i)$.

Example: We consider the following set of parameters:

	μ	ϕ	σ	
Regime #1	−0.004	0.74	0.11	$P = \begin{pmatrix} 0.94\ 0.28 \\ 0.06\ 0.72 \end{pmatrix}.$
Regime #2	−0.02	0.68	0.30	

In this case regime #2 is the spike regime with a much higher volatility ($\sigma_2 = 0.3$) compared to the normal regime ($\sigma_1 = 0.11$). Being in the normal regime, the probability is 94% to stay in the normal regime and 6% to switch to the spike regime. Once in the spike regime, the probability is 72% to stay in the spike regime and 28% to switch back to the normal regime.

Since the regime state is not observable, we use a Hamilton filter (see Section A.1.5). The Hamilton filter requires that transition probabilities depend only on the current state. The two-state model is transformed into a four-state model (Hamilton, 1994, p. 691) with states $\tilde{r}_k \in \{1, 2, 3, 4\}$, such that

$$
\begin{aligned}
\tilde{r}_k = 1 &\quad \text{if } r_k = 1 \text{ and } r_{k-1} = 1. \\
\tilde{r}_k = 2 &\quad \text{if } r_k = 2 \text{ and } r_{k-1} = 1. \\
\tilde{r}_k = 3 &\quad \text{if } r_k = 1 \text{ and } r_{k-1} = 2. \\
\tilde{r}_k = 4 &\quad \text{if } r_k = 2 \text{ and } r_{k-1} = 2.
\end{aligned}
$$

The transition probability matrix becomes

$$
\tilde{P} = \begin{pmatrix}
p_{11} & 0 & p_{11} & 0 \\
p_{12} & 0 & p_{12} & 0 \\
0 & p_{21} & 0 & p_{21} \\
0 & p_{22} & 0 & p_{22}
\end{pmatrix}.
$$

The conditional probability densities are

$$
f(y_k \mid y_{k-1}, \tilde{r}_k = 1) = \frac{1}{\sqrt{2\pi}\sigma_1} \exp\left(\frac{-[(y_k - \mu_1) - \phi_1(y_{k-1} - \mu_1)]^2}{2\sigma_1^2} \right),
$$

$$
f(y_k \mid y_{k-1}, \tilde{r}_k = 2) = \frac{1}{\sqrt{2\pi}\sigma_2} \exp\left(\frac{-[(y_k - \mu_2) - \phi_2(y_{k-1} - \mu_1)]^2}{2\sigma_2^2} \right),
$$

$$
f(y_k \mid y_{k-1}, \tilde{r}_k = 3) = \frac{1}{\sqrt{2\pi}\sigma_1} \exp\left(\frac{-[(y_k - \mu_1) - \phi_1(y_{k-1} - \mu_2)]^2}{2\sigma_1^2} \right),
$$

$$
f(y_k \mid y_{k-1}, \tilde{r}_k = 4) = \frac{1}{\sqrt{2\pi}\sigma_2} \exp\left(\frac{-[(y_k - \mu_2) - \phi_2(y_{k-1} - \mu_2)]^2}{2\sigma_2^2} \right).
$$

In this way, the model is of the general form

$$
y_k = \tilde{\mu}_{\tilde{r}_k} + \tilde{\phi}_{\tilde{r}_k} y_{k-1} + \tilde{\sigma}_{\tilde{r}_k} \epsilon_k. \tag{6.15}
$$

The Hamilton filter produces estimates $\hat{\xi}^i_{k|k}$ for the probability $P(\tilde{r}_k = i \mid y_k, y_{k-1}, \ldots)$ that the observation was generated by regime i based on observations up to time k. The vector of all those estimates is denoted by $\hat{\xi}_{k|k}$. The forecast of the probability that the process is in a certain regime at the next time step, $P(\tilde{r}_{k+1} = i \mid y_k, y_{k-1}, \ldots)$, is denoted by $\hat{\xi}^i_{k+1|k}$ or $\hat{\xi}_{k+1|k}$ for the vector. Adapting the general Hamilton iteration equations to the current situation we get the following algorithm.

1. **Start:** For $\hat{\xi}_{1|0}$ choose the unconditional probabilities of the Markov chain generated by P.
2. **Calculate** $\hat{\xi}_{k|k}$:

$$\hat{\xi}^i_{k|k} = \frac{\hat{\xi}^i_{k|k-1}\eta^i_k}{\sum_{i=1}^{4}\hat{\xi}^i_{k|k-1}\eta^i_k},\tag{6.16}$$

where $\eta^i_k = f(y_k \mid y_{k-1}, \tilde{r}_k = i)$ denotes the conditional probability density.
3. **Calculate** $\hat{\xi}_{k+1|k}$:

$$\hat{\xi}^i_{k+1|k} = P \cdot \hat{\xi}^i_{k|k}.\tag{6.17}$$

4. **Iterate:** Repeat from step 2 with k increased by one.

Figure 6.15 shows the regime probability $\hat{\xi}^i_{k|k}$ for the spike regime for example spot price data. In periods of high volatility the probability for the spike regime increases.

A by-product of the Hamilton filter is the log maximum likelihood function, calculated as

$$L = \sum_{k=1}^{N_k} \ln\left(\sum_{i=1}^{4}\hat{\xi}^i_{k|k}\eta^i_k\right).\tag{6.18}$$

The optimal parameters can be found by numerically maximising the function L.

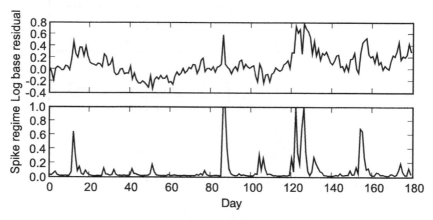

Figure 6.15   Regime inspection returned by the Hamilton filter.

The Hourly Profile Process

The hourly profile process is defined as the logarithmic spot process normalised to mean zero:

$$\mathbf{h}(t) = \mathbf{s}(t) - s(t).$$

The steps for modelling the profile dynamics are:

1. De-seasonalise the profile for each hour.
2. Use PCA to decompose the vector process into factor loads.
3. Model each factor load as an ARMA process.

Daily spot price profiles have a pronounced yearly and weekly seasonality due to different temperature and light conditions. De-seasonalising the profiles for each single hour utilises a similar technique to that for the daily process $s(t)$. The profiles can be written as

$$\mathbf{h}(t) = \hat{\mathbf{h}}(t) + \Delta\mathbf{h}(t),$$

where $\hat{\mathbf{h}}(t)$ is the deterministic seasonal component and $\Delta\mathbf{h}(t)$ is the stochastic residual from the regression.

The residuals $\Delta\mathbf{h}(t)$ form a vector process with a covariance structure reflecting the different volatilities of each single hour and the correlations between the hourly profile values. As before, the process $\Delta\mathbf{h}(t)$ is divided into business days and non-business days:

$$\Delta\mathbf{h}(t) = \mathbf{1}_{JB}(t)\Delta\mathbf{h}^B(t) + \mathbf{1}_{JH}(t)\Delta\mathbf{h}^H(t).$$

The two processes $\Delta\mathbf{h}^B(t)$ and $\Delta\mathbf{h}^H(t)$ are treated separately. For notational convenience we consider only one of these processes and denote it by $\Delta\mathbf{h}_k$, $k = 1, \ldots, N$. By PCA the vector process $\Delta\mathbf{h}_k$ is now decomposed into independent factor loads (see Section A.1.3). Let $\mathbf{p}_1, \ldots, \mathbf{p}_{24}$ be the principal component factors of $\Delta\mathbf{h}_k$ after column-wise normalisation to standard deviation 1, that is the eigenvectors of the matrix $(\Delta\mathbf{h})^T \Delta\mathbf{h}/N$, where $\Delta\mathbf{h}$ is an $N \times 24$ matrix. It is assumed that the corresponding eigenvalues are in descending order $\lambda_1 > \ldots > \lambda_{24}$. The 24×24 matrix $(\mathbf{p}_1, \ldots, \mathbf{p}_{24})$ containing the eigenvectors as columns is denoted by Q. The $N \times 24$ matrix of factor loads is then given by $W = (\Delta\mathbf{h})Q$.

The ith eigenvalue λ_i represents the variance contributed by the ith principal component. In typical cases, a large number of principal components is needed to explain most of the variance.

For stochastic modelling of the factor loads, let $w_k^i = W_{ki}$, $i = i, \ldots, 24$, $k = 1, \ldots, N$ be the time series of the ith factor load, which is the ith column of the matrix W. The series w_k^i is modelled as independent ARMA processes. From the simulated factor loads W the process $\Delta\mathbf{h}(t)$ can be calculated as $\Delta\mathbf{h}(t) = WQ^T$.

A more careful study of the profile dynamics reveals that on days with extremely high daily price the profiles behave differently, since those prices are often the result of spikes at single hours. To get a more realistic price behaviour on days when the regime is in a volatile state, we can randomly draw historical profiles according to the day type, season and regime state.

6.2.4 Virtual Power Plants

A coal-fired power plant is commonly seen as a real option on the clean dark spread and a gas-fired power plant as a real option on the clean spark spread. The owner decides from day to day, even from hour to hour whether the power plant comes into operation. This decision is not only influenced by the clean dark spread but also by technical constraints, such as costs for starting the power plant, minimum up- and downtimes and ramp-up rates. These constraints increase the complexity of pricing the option.

A virtual power plant (VPP) separates technical operation and maintenance of the real asset from its economic optimisation in energy markets. Power plant operators may use virtual power plants as hedging instruments and traders may be interested in VPPs to use their market expertise without becoming involved in technical operation. Even though VPPs contain less complex constraints and are therefore a simplification of real power plants, they are still complex derivatives on a spread as underlying. There is a variety of arrangements for VPPs, but there are a few common elements:

- The buyer of the VPP pays the option premium to obtain the right to the output or share of the output of a power plant or a pool of power plants during a specified time period. Often, the option premium is paid in the form of a fixed monthly or yearly capacity price.
- For each nominated MWh, the buyer has to pay an energy price, that is the strike price (e.g., in EUR/MWh). This strike price can be fixed, or it can depend on other commodity prices, such as emission certificates, coal or gas prices.
- The duration of the contract is specified and may range from a few months to some years.
- Typically, the buyer nominates generation volumes on a day-ahead basis between zero and a maximum capacity (in MW).
- Depending on the product specification, different nominations for each hour of the day are possible.
- Only in complex cases are maximum rates for ramping up and down power production or other technical restrictions specified.

VPP auctions were also used to promote the development of a wholesale electricity market and to provide easier market access for potential investors. Buyers of these options had a drawing right on generation capacity at a predefined fixed as well as variable cost, without being exposed to all of the engineering and operational risk of plant ownership. As an example, France introduced such auctions in 2001, forcing EDF (Electricité de France) to sell part of its generation capacity to entrants into the French power market. Later, auctions of a similar kind were introduced in Belgium, the Netherlands, Denmark, Germany and Spain as well as in the United States. The specifications in France and Denmark were as follows:

- The VPP contracts offered by EDF were designed as baseload and peakload products with durations of 3, 6, 12, 24 and 36 months. In addition, the baseload VPP was available with a duration of 48 months. In total, EDF made 4400 MW of baseload VPP and 1000 MW of peakload VPP available. EDF sold the VPPs in the form of contracts specifying both an energy price and a capacity price. The energy price was fixed in advance and remained fixed for the duration of the contract. This strike price was higher for the peak than for the base product. The capacity price was determined in an auction and was to be paid every month for each MW purchased during the duration of the contract.

- The VPP offered in Denmark by Dong Energy can be nominated up to 14 days ahead on an hourly basis. For day-ahead nominations until 11:00 no ramping restrictions apply, whereas for later nominations until 14:00 hourly deviations are restricted to 40% of the maximum capacity. In 2007 Dong made 500 MW of VPP capacity with supply periods of 3, 12 and 36 months available and from 2008 onwards even 600 MW. Nomination is made to an independent nomination aggregator, who informs Dong Energy of the aggregated hourly power deliveries.

In case there are no ramping constraints and the option can be exercised independently for each hour during the nomination period, the VPP can be decomposed into a strip of European options on the clean dark spread. Consequently, analytical methods for spread options based on the Black valuation framework (e.g., Kirk's approximation, see Section 5.5.2) can be applied.

Example: The clean dark spread for Germany is calculated by ICIS Heren (cf. Heren) using a fuel efficiency factor of 35% for the coal conversion and an energy conversion factor of 7.1 for converting tonnes of coal into MWh of electricity assuming that coal has a standard quality of 5800 kcal/kg. As other variable costs for power production a typical value $K = 4$ EUR/MWh (cf. Wissel *et al.*) is assumed. For different types of coal with different energy values or coal-fired plants with different efficiencies, adjustments need to be made. Let $F_P(t, T)$ denote the price of the power futures contract at time t for maturity T, $F_C(t, T)$ the coal and $F_E(t, T)$ the emissions futures contract price. Then the forward price for the clean dark spread value is given by

$$F_{CDS} = F_P(t, T) - h_C F_C(t, T) - h_E F_E(t, T),$$

with $h_C = \frac{1}{0.35}$t Coal/MWh and $h_E = 0.96$tCO_2/MWh.

Kirk's formula (5.22) for a clean dark spread call option with strike price K, interest rate r and maturity at T yields

$$C(t, T, K) = e^{-r(T-t)}(F_P(t, T)N(d_1) - F_{CE}(t, T, K)N(d_2)), \qquad (6.19)$$

where

$$F_{CE}(t, T, K) = h_C F_C(t, T) + h_E F_E(t, T) + K,$$

$$d_1 = \frac{\ln\left(\frac{F_P(t,T)}{F_{CE}(t,T,K)}\right) + \frac{1}{2}\sigma^2(T - t)}{\sigma\sqrt{T - t}},$$

$$d_2 = d_1 - \sigma\sqrt{T - t}$$

and

$$
\begin{aligned}
\sigma^2 = {} & \sigma_P^2 + \sigma_C^2 \left(\frac{h_C F_C(t, T)}{F_{CE}(t, T, K)}\right)^2 + \sigma_E^2 \left(\frac{h_E F_E(t, T)}{F_{CE}(t, T, K)}\right)^2 \\
& - 2\rho_{PC}\sigma_P\sigma_C \frac{h_C F_C(t, T)}{F_{CE}(t, T, K)} - 2\rho_{PE}\sigma_P\sigma_E \frac{h_E F_E(t, T)}{F_{CE}(t, T, K)} \\
& + 2\rho_{CE}\sigma_C\sigma_E \frac{h_C F_C(t, T)}{F_{CE}(t, T, K)} \frac{h_E F_E(t, T)}{F_{CE}(t, T, K)}.
\end{aligned}
$$

Calibration to historical price data for 125 days during June–December 2013 results in the following parameters:

- Correlations: $\rho_{PC} = 47\%, \rho_{PE} = 61\%, \rho_{CE} = 23\%$.
- Volatilities: $\sigma_P = 36\%, \sigma_C = 14\%, \sigma_E = 50\%$.
- Prices: $F_P = 37.3$ EUR/MWh, $F_C = 67$ EUR/t, $F_E = 4.9$ EUR/t.

With these values an intrinsic value of 7.6 EUR/MWh results. For time to maturity of 1 year, a fair value of 8.7 EUR/MWh is obtained from the Kirk formula, that is the extrinsic value resulting from the optionality is 1.1 EUR/MWh. For a time to maturity of 2 years, this value increases to 10 EUR/MWh. For the seller of the VPP, the option premium also needs to cover the fixed costs of the power plant. For a typical power plant the fixed production costs amount to 4.6 EUR/MWh (calculated with 7500 utilisation hours, cf. Wissel *et al.*). Subtracting these costs from the fair value of 8.7 EUR/MWh for 1 year time to maturity results in a value of 4.1 EUR/MWh, which may be used by the VPP seller to cover the costs of capital. However, according to Wissel *et al.* capital costs amount to 16.6 EUR/MWh for a typical power plant, so that only a fraction of this can be covered from the fair option premium in this example.

In reality, the spot volatility is much higher than the volatility derived from monthly power contracts, which increases the value of the VPP. However, spot prices are mean reverting. Especially for longer times to maturity this mean reversion decreases the fair value compared with Kirk's formula. These limitations of the analytical price formulas can be overcome using Monte Carlo simulations based on a more realistic spot price model like the multi-commodity SMaPS model (cf. Section 6.2.2).

VPPs structured closer to real power plants may incorporate the following technical constraints.

- *Ramping rates:* The VPP can be switched on or off not instantaneously but only at a given maximum hourly change of production.
- *Minimum up- and downtimes:* If the VPP is switched off, it must stay switched off at least for a given number of hours. If it is switched on, it has to produce for a minimum number of hours before it can be switched off again.
- *Minimum power output:* If the VPP is switched on, a minimum power output applies.

Under such constraints the option exercise can no longer be optimised for each hour independently. The general case of such options was described in Section 5.6.1, where the intrinsic value as a lower bound and the ex-post value as an upper bound of the option value were derived. For complex VPPs, finding an optimal exercise strategy may already be a complex optimisation problem for one price scenario. The modelling approaches for the optimal dispatch of power plants are explained in detail in Section 7.2. A short comparison of the most relevant solution methods for the VPP option value is as follows.

1. *Mixed integer linear programming (MILP):* This is the most flexible approach to cover various technical constraints. However, even the most powerful solvers like Cplex need a long calculation time to find the optimal solution for typical power plant optimisation problems. The calculations may even take several hours and they are done for each scenario as a whole. For this reason, unrealistic perfect foresight on future price levels is included in the value of the VPP. For VPPs based on coal or gas-fired power plants, this approximation error is often negligible, but it is inaccurate for virtual pumped storage hydropower plants.

2. *Dynamic programming (DP):* For this method all potential states of the asset have to be specified and must be finite. The main challenge is to keep the number of states within reasonable bounds (but 10 000 or more states may still be feasible to solve), while the main advantage of DP is that it can be many times faster than MILP. Nevertheless, perfect foresight is assumed as in MILP.

3. *Least-squares Monte Carlo (LSMC):* As described in detail for optimisation of gas assets, this method is very similar to DP. However, perfect foresight is avoided as the continuation values are estimated using a least-squares regression of the future cashflows on the actual spot prices. With this methodology the fair value of pumped storage hydropower plants can be estimated correctly under uncertainty.

From all three methods option deltas can also be calculated and a dynamic delta hedge can be implemented to reduce the exposure to changes of the spread.

6.3   STRUCTURAL GAS PRICE MODELS

Customer consumption varies stochastically as it depends on temperature as well as the economic environment. Before the liberalisation of the energy markets, flexible assets like storage or long-term gas supply contracts (LTC) were used to balance these variations. With an existing liquid gas market, customer consumption can be covered without such assets via forward and spot markets. In reverse, the profit of these assets can be maximised as well as stabilised by hedging the assets on the forward markets and optimally exercising them in the spot market. Because of that, the focus has moved from customer load coverage to an optimal hedging strategy and the profit that can be achieved. This illustrates the need for reliable pricing methods. Both options – storage as well as swing options – rely on non-trivial trading strategies where exercise decisions are taken under uncertainty. Given the complexity of such options, analytic pricing formulas cannot be expected. The identification of an optimal trading strategy under uncertainty is a typical problem of stochastic dynamic programming, where even numerical solutions are difficult to obtain due to the curse of dimensionality. Therefore, simulation-based approximation algorithms have been applied successfully in this area. Longstaff and Schwartz (2001) introduced the LSMC method for the valuation of American options, Meinshausen and Hambly (2004) extended the idea to swing options, Boogert and de Jong (2006) applied it to the valuation of gas storage and Holden *et al.* (2011) extended the method to cover carry-forward and make-up rights found in long-term contracts (see Section 1.3.2). The LSMC algorithm is based on gas price scenarios that have to result from an adequate stochastic price model for the daily gas spot prices. The advantage of this approach in comparison with methods using scenario trees or finite elements is that it is independent of the underlying price process. In the following subsections a daily price forward curve that depicts the daily spot price expectation, a possible price process for the daily gas spot price as well as the LSMC algorithm are introduced.

6.3.1   Natural Gas Price Models

Oil has a longer history as a traded commodity than natural gas. As a consequence, modelling issues for oil prices came about earlier. As oil and gas share a common usage for heating and often common reservoirs, the modelling issues of gas were considered to be the same as for oil. Therefore, models initially proposed for oil prices were also applied to gas prices. This practice made use of the considerable history of setting up oil price models but neglected the distinct features of gas prices. As oil is easily storable – in contrast to gas – oil prices do not show seasonality. After giving a brief overview of the literature, we present two specific gas price models.

Commodity price models such as the one-factor Schwartz model (see Section 5.6.3) and the two-factor Schwartz–Smith model (see Section 5.6.4) are general approaches applicable to many commodities. Nevertheless, these models were applied to oil prices first. Another stochastic price model is presented by Cortazar and Schwartz (2003). Their three-factor model is introduced as a model for the term structure of oil prices but applied to gas prices as well. The various factors represent short- and long-term influences on the price.

These models are extended for the application to gas prices by Jaillet *et al.* (2004) and Xu (2004). Their focus is on the inclusion of deterministic functions covering the seasonality of gas prices into the existing stochastic modelling approaches. A specific gas price model is proposed by Cartea and Williams (2008). The focus of their two-factor model with a function for the seasonality is the market price of risk in British gas markets.

As the issue of valuation of gas storage came up, further gas price models were proposed. Various regime-switching approaches incorporating mean-reverting processes as well as random walks has been analysed by Chen and Forsyth (2010). Boogert and de Jong (2011) introduced a three-factor model representing short and long-term fluctuations as well as random behaviour of the winter–summer spread.

The models mentioned above are pure stochastic approaches applicable to gas prices. Stoll and Wiebauer (2010) take a different approach based on a temperature component and a deterministic seasonality as major influence factors on the gas price:

$$G(t) = s(t) + \alpha \text{NCHDD}(t) + X(t) + Y(t). \tag{6.20}$$

$X(t)$ is a stochastic process that describes the short-term deviations from the temperature as well as a deterministic component, while the long-term uncertainty is included via the stochastic component $Y(t)$. The temperature component NCHDD (*normalised cumulated heating degree days*, see definition in Section 4.5, equation (4.6)) is considered to be an approximation of the filling level of gas storage responsible for the gas price behaviour in winter. Until the financial crisis this model performed very well, but is not able to explain the drop in gas prices of winter 2008/9. For this reason Hirsch *et al.* (2013) extended the model by substituting the long-term component $Y(t)$ with an oil price component Oil(t) as a second exogenous factor:

$$G(t) = s(t) + \alpha_1 \text{NCHDD}(t) + \alpha_2 \text{Oil}(t) + X(t). \tag{6.21}$$

Both models, with their specific components, are described in more detail in the following subsections.

Deterministic Components

In both models, the deterministic components (constant, trend, indicator variables and sine function) are included in $s(t)$. This term covers seasonalities caused by consumers as well as a statistically significant trend. It is an extension of the components used for the DPFC (see Section 6.1.1) by yearly seasonality as well as trend:

$$
\bar{s}(t) = \sum_{i=1}^{7} \beta_i^w (1 - w_t) \mathbf{1}_{D_i^w}(t) + \beta_8^w w_t \mathbf{1}_{D^w}(t)
$$

$$
+ \sum_{i=1}^{7} \beta_i^s (1 - w_t) \mathbf{1}_{D_i^s}(t) + \beta_8^s w_t \mathbf{1}_{D^s}(t) \qquad (6.22)
$$

$$
+ \beta_9 t + \beta_{10} \sin \left(\frac{2\pi t}{365.25} \right) + \beta_{11} \cos \left(\frac{2\pi t}{365.25} \right).
$$

Here $D^{s/w}$ denotes again the set of all days in summer/winter and $D_i^{s/w}$ the respective subset with weekday number i (starting with 1 for Sunday). w_t is again the holiday weight of day t (cf. equation (6.4)). The regression is performed separately for summer and winter. Altogether $\bar{s}(t)$ is linear with respect to the 19 parameters $\beta_1^s, \ldots, \beta_8^s, \beta_1^w, \ldots, \beta_8^w, \beta_9, \beta_{10}, \beta_{11}$.

Temperature Component

Besides the average temperature-driven seasonality covered by the sine and cosine function in $s(t)$, there is a more complex, asymmetric influence from gas storage. Capacities of import pipelines are exceeded by gas demand in winter so that gas storage is needed to cover a considerable part of the demand. Thus, gas storage is filled when prices are low (usually in summer) and emptied when prices are high. Thus, the filling level is low at the end of a long cold winter. Another cold day in such a situation has a stronger impact on the price compared with a cold day at the end of a warm winter when storage levels are still high.

As the information about filling levels of all gas storage in a market is not available, an approximation is required. Stoll and Wiebauer (2010) use NCHDD to describe the temperature-dependent price influence of gas storage. This is based on the observation that heating systems operate below a certain base temperature T_0 underlying the definition of HDD, for example $T_0 = 15\,°C$. Under the assumption of a constant filling rate of gas storage during summer, it is reasonable to complement the definition of NCHDD(t) in winter by a linear return to zero during summer.

Using such a component, the gas price behaviour due to colder or warmer winters can successfully be described. Nevertheless, changes of the gas price for economic reasons cannot be reflected by deterministic functions or a temperature-driven component such as the NCHDD. This drawback is eliminated by Hirsch et al. (2013). They propose an extension by another fundamental factor to account for dependency on the economy and the oil price.

Oil Price Component

Caused by the economic crisis of 2008/9, gas demand in Central Europe dropped by approximately 10% within a short period, leading to a pronounced decrease in the price level. Similar behaviour was observed in the oil market at that time. Despite speculations on the oil market, the economy is still the main driver for remarkable changes in the oil price level. As the oil market is global, the oil price can be seen as an indicator of the state of the world economy. Short-term oil price movements influence the gas price to a lesser extent than long-term changes do. Considering a moving average of the oil price over 180 days removes short-term price effects and results in a variable describing economic influences. Hirsch *et al.* (2013) incorporate this variable in their model (cf. equation (6.21) in comparison with equation 6.20).

Another argument for the choice of such an oil price component valid for Central European gas markets is that prices for gas imports via long-term contracts were mostly oil price indexed in the past – even though this coupling to oil prices has recently lost its importance due to increasing competition in the gas market (see Section 1.3.2). The moving average of 180 days can be considered as a smoothed version of a 6-0-1 oil price formula.

Hirsch *et al.* (2013) show that this 180-day moving average of the Brent front-month oil price is able to explain the gas price behaviour in recent years and include this moving average Oil(t) as an exogenous component in their model.

Estimation of Deterministic and Exogenous Components

For parameter estimation of the models, day-ahead gas prices from TTF are used, which has a longer data history (starting 2003) than neighbouring markets. The corresponding temperature data from Eindhoven, Netherlands is available for a much longer time period. To estimate the oil price component, front-month prices of Brent traded on the ICE are used.

Using this data, outliers are removed from the gas price time series $G(t)$ in a preprocessing step. Detection of outliers can be achieved by running a median method (see Weron (2006)) as follows:

- First a 180-day running median $G^m(t)$ of the unfiltered series $G(t)$ is computed.
- Then filter bands around the running median with a multiple (for example $3 \cdot \sigma$) of the variance of the difference between the median and the original time series are constructed: $F^{\pm}(t) = G^m(t) \pm 3 \cdot \sigma(G(t) - G^m(t))$.
- All prices $G(t)$ above $F^+(t)$ and below $F^-(t)$ are detected as outliers and replaced by prices following a normal distribution with expectation $G^m(t)$ and variance $\sigma(G(t) - G^m(t))$. In case of a positive outlier a price above $G^m(t)$ and in case of a negative outlier a price below $G^m(t)$ is used.

Using the definition (6.22) of the seasonal component $s(t)$, the parameters $\beta_1^s, \ldots,$ $\beta_8^s, \beta_1^w, \ldots, \beta_8^w, \beta_9, \beta_{10}, \beta_{11}$ as well as α (model (6.20)) or α_1, α_2 (model (6.21)) are calibrated via least-squares regression to historical gas prices. The resulting fit is shown in Figure 6.16. Including the oil price component dramatically improves the goodness of fit for the calibration period until 2011. For this reason the model with an additional oil component is preferable.

Altogether, the model components fitted so far give fundamental explanations in terms of exogeneous factors for the historical day-ahead price behaviour. Nevertheless, short-term deviations from this fundamentally explained gas price remain and have to be described by a stochastic process. Long-term uncertainty in the gas price due to the uncertain development of the oil price is included in the oil price process.

Stochastic Processes

The fit of NCHDD, oil price formula and deterministic components to the gas price via ordinary least-squares regression results in a residual time series. These residuals contain all unexplained "random" deviations from the usual price behaviour. The residuals exhibit a strong autocorrelation to the first lag. Therefore, an AR(1) process provides a good fit. The resulting innovations are not normally distributed, but show a higher density around the mean as well

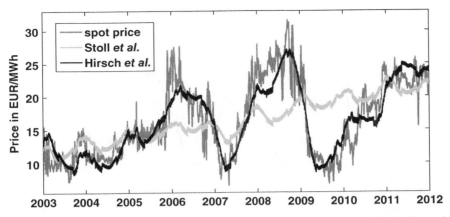

Figure 6.16   Fit of deterministic function and exogenous components for model by Stoll *et. al* (light gray) in comparison with the model by Hirsch *et. al* (black) to TTF prices (dark gray).

as in the tails than the normal distribution. A normal-inverse Gaussian (NIG) distribution is able to reproduce the innovations. This distribution with four parameters is a special case of the generalised hyperbolic distributions introduced by Barndorff-Nielsen (1978). Overall, the stochastic process $X(t)$ is specified as an AR(1) process with innovations following a NIG distribution. Both the distribution of the innovations and the parameters of autoregressive processes can be estimated using maximum likelihood estimation.

In the model of Stoll and Wiebauer (2010), instead of the oil component, a long-term process $Y(t)$ is used to reflect the long-term volatilities of the futures markets, which can be derived from implied volatilities of options. The long-term process $Y(t)$ is modelled by a geometric Brownian motion given by

$$Y(t) = Y_0 \exp\left(\left(\mu - \tfrac{1}{2}\sigma_Y^2\right)t + \sigma_Y \varepsilon_t^Y\right),$$

where the innovations ε_t^Y are normally distributed. The long-term process is calibrated to the futures market.

Since the oil price lacks seasonality, it can be modelled without a deterministic function or fundamental component. A standard oil price model is the Schwartz–Smith model calibrated to oil forward prices (see Section 5.6.4).

Temperature Model

For simulation of gas spot price paths, a temperature model is required. The process $NCHDD(t)$ is derived from the daily average temperature $T(t)$. When modelling this daily average temperature, a long history of temperature data is usually available. Here, a yearly seasonality and a linear trend can be identified:

$$T(t) = a_1 + a_2 t + a_3 \sin\left(\frac{2\pi t}{365.25}\right) + a_4 \cos\left(\frac{2\pi t}{365.25}\right) + X(t),$$

with an AR(3) process $X(t)$. A similar model is given by Benth and Benth (2007). Again, ordinary least-squares regression can be used to estimate the parameters $a_1, \dots, a_4$. The fit to historical data from Eindhoven, Netherlands is shown in Figure 6.17.

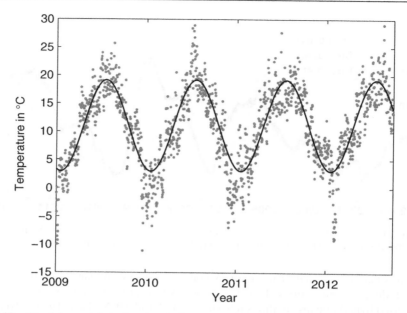

Figure 6.17   Fit of deterministic function (solid) to daily average temperatures in Eindhoven, Nether-lands (dashed).

Simulation of Gas Spot Price Scenarios

Spot price scenarios for a given time interval $[T_1, T_2]$ can be simulated as follows:

1. Calculate the deterministic component for the period $[T_1, T_2]$.
2. Simulate Brent front-month scenarios for a period $[T_1 - 180, T_2]$ and derive the 180-day average.
3. Simulate temperature scenarios and calculate the NCHDD.
4. Simulate scenarios for the short-term component $X(t)$ and add up all scenarios to obtain the final gas spot price scenarios.

Figure 6.18 shows four gas scenarios for a year resulting from a simulation of the model including the oil component. Based on these gas spot price scenarios, valuation methods for gas flexibility can be introduced.

6.3.2   Swing Options and Gas Storage

Flexibility is contained in swing options and gas storage. A virtual gas storage contract is characterised by the following restrictions:

- The initial volume can be chosen between a minimum volume $v_{\min}(0)$ and a maximum volume $v_{\max}(0)$.
- The final volume can be chosen between a minimum volume $v_{\min}(T + 1)$ and a maximum volume $v_{\max}(T + 1)$.

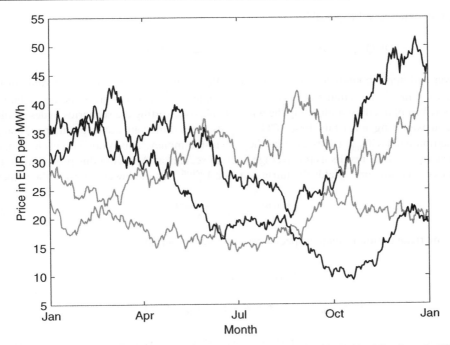

Figure 6.18 Four gas price scenarios for one year resulting from the model by Hirsch *et al.* (2013).

- The filling level must lie between given minimum and maximum volumes: $v_{min}(t) \leq v(t) \leq v_{max}(t)$.
- For each day, volume changes are limited by withdrawal and injection rate: $\Delta v_{min}(t, v(t)) \leq \Delta v(t) \leq \Delta v_{max}(t, v(t))$.

A swing option is a special case of a virtual storage contract. During the delivery period a daily nomination of the gas delivery for the next day is done, while the following restrictions apply.

- *Daily contract quantity (DCQ):* Minimum as well as maximum daily volume; typical values are DCQ_{min} 50–90% and DCQ_{max} 100–110% of a given DCQ reference (where DCQ = ACQ / 365).
- *Annual contract quantity (ACQ):* Minimum as well as maximum yearly volume; typical values are ACQ_{min} 80–90% and ACQ_{max} 100–110% of a given ACQ reference.

Owing to these restrictions, a swing option is the same as storage with an initial volume equal to the ACQ_{max} of the swing:

$$v_{min}(0) = v_{max}(0) = ACQ_{max} \tag{6.23}$$

and the following restriction for the final volume:

$$0 = v_{min}(T+1) \leq v(T+1) \leq v_{max}(T+1) = ACQ_{min} \tag{6.24}$$

where only withdrawal is possible:

$$- \text{DCQ}_{\text{max}} = \Delta v_{\text{min}}(t, v(t)) \leq \Delta v(t) \leq \Delta v_{\text{max}}(t, v(t)) = -\text{DCQ}_{\text{min}}. \tag{6.25}$$

Lower and upper bounds for the option value V_S are the intrinsic and ex-post value of the option, as defined in Section 5.6.1. The ex-post value V_S^{expost}, which gives the upper bound, can easily be obtained by subtracting the withdrawal costs, sorting the scenarios in descending order and exercising at least the first ACQ_{min} rights (even if they are not in-the-money) and up to a maximum of ACQ_{max} rights as far as they are in-the-money. This is done for each scenario and the ex-post value results as the average over all scenarios. Applying this procedure to the daily price forward curve yields the intrinsic value $V_S^{\text{intrinsic}}$ as the lower bound of the value:

$$V_S^{\text{intrinsic}} \leq V_S \leq V_S^{\text{expost}}. \tag{6.26}$$

An American option is again a special case of a swing option:

$$v_{\text{min}}(0) = v_{\text{max}}(0) = 1, \tag{6.27}$$

$$0 = v_{\text{min}}(T + 1) \leq v(T + 1) \leq v_{\text{max}}(T + 1) = 1, \tag{6.28}$$

$$- 1 = \Delta v_{\text{min}}(t, v(t)) \leq \Delta v(t) \leq \Delta v_{\text{max}}(t, v(t)) = 0. \tag{6.29}$$

In this case, withdrawal costs are chosen equal to the strike K of the option, $c_{\text{WD},t} = K$.

Strip of European Options as a Special Case of a Swing Option

If the minimal and maximal yearly restrictions do not limit the daily exercise, the swing option splits up into daily delivery of DCQ_{min} and a strip of European options with volume $\text{DCQ}_{\text{max}} - \text{DCQ}_{\text{min}}$ – one option for each day of the delivery period. In this special case the Black model (5.10) can be applied to value each single European option. If the swing has to be exercised between $T = T_a, \ldots, T_e$, the value of this strip of options is

$$V_{\text{Strip}} = \sum_{T=T_a}^{T_e} e^{-rT}(F(T)N(d_1(T)) - KN(d_2(T))), \tag{6.30}$$

with

$$d_1(T) = \frac{\ln(F(T)/K) + (\sigma^2/2)T}{\sigma\sqrt{T}},$$

$$d_2(t) = d_1(T) - \sigma\sqrt{T}.$$

From this equation it can be seen that the value of the strip is set by five parameters of the Black model, namely the underlying forward curve $F(T)$, the strike price K, the interest rate r, the volatility σ of the underlying and the time to maturity T. Nevertheless, an important limitation

Table 6.1   Valuation for three simple swings option

| | Valuation results | |
Period	Black model	LSMC
1.3.–1.4.	48.9 TEUR	55.3 TEUR
1.4.–1.5.	48.6 TEUR	59.7 TEUR
1.5.–1.6.	69.1 TEUR	70.8 TEUR

of the Black model is that a price dynamic of the underlying is assumed to follow a geometric Brownian motion with constant volatility. This assumption is not completely fulfilled in reality. The advantage is that the value results from an analytical formula and sensitivities to price as well as volatility can easily be calculated.

To illustrate the difference between the Black model and the later introduced LSMC method, the following example is used. For the TTF market three swings with strike price of 29 EUR/MWh, a DCQ_{max} of 2400 MWh and a DCQ_{min} of 0 MWh for the months March, April and May 2013 are examined (see Table 6.1). Each of these swings is nothing but a strip of 30 or 31 European options. As implied volatilities on a daily basis are not available on the market, only a monthly volatility can be used in the valuation with the Black model. In this example a volatility of 22% has been used, which is equal to the spot volatility observed in this time period. Furthermore, the volatility of the spot scenarios used in the LSMC method is the same. Therefore the main difference between the two methods is the assumption of a log-normal distribution in the Black model in contrast to the LSMC method, where a NIG distribution is used for the innovations. This difference in the distribution assumptions is the reason for the resulting 10–20% valuation difference between the Black model and the LSMC method.

Influence of Volatility

Using the Black model, the influence of volatility can be demonstrated as done in Figure 6.19 for an April swing contract, where a volatility of 30% has been chosen as reference (100%

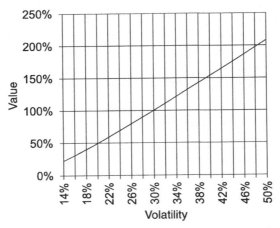

Figure 6.19   Variation of value with volatility.

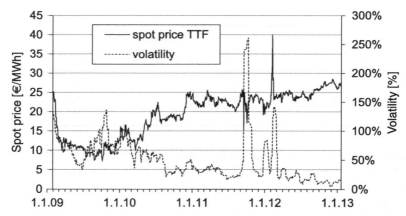

Figure 6.20   Historical volatility derived from TTF spot prices since 2009.

value). As Figure 6.19 shows, the value increases almost linearly with volatility. If the volatility increases from 30% to 48% the value doubles, if the volatility decreases to 20% the value halves.

Figure 6.20 shows that the historical volatility has changed significantly within recent years. Except for spikes in the spot price at the end of 2011 and the beginning of 2012, the spot volatility shows a downward trend. Table 6.2 shows historical volatilities for different periods ending on 31.12.2012. The volatility varies between 14% for a very short period (Q4/2012) and 65% for a long period starting 2009. The fundamental reason for this trend is an increasing availability of flexibility in Germany and the Netherlands due to a significant increase of cavern storage capacity. At the same time the Nord Stream pipeline became operational, which has further increased the security of supply.

Therefore, the question of the correct volatility for valuations as well as hedging of such swing options arises. While options on forwards are occasionally traded, from which implied volatilities can be inferred, there are no options on spot prices available, so that spot volatility can only be deduced from historical prices. Therefore, the calibration should take into account assumptions on the future development of gas price volatility. Neither by dynamic delta hedging nor by a rolling intrinsic hedge strategy can the risk of a volatility change be hedged. This is only possible by including options in the hedge strategy, as these are sensitive to volatility changes. But options are illiquid and often only traded with high premiums.

So far only swing options in special cases can be valued using the Black model and even then the limitations of the Black model are obvious. To overcome the assumption of log-normally

Table 6.2   Historical spot volatility for periods ending 31.12.2012

Start of period	Spot volatility
01.10.2012	14%
01.01.2012	38%
01.01.2011	58%
01.01.2009	65%

distributed innovations and to be able to value complex restrictions on storage, the LSMC method can be used, which is introduced in the following section.

6.3.3   Least-Squares Monte Carlo Method

The storage contract is assumed to be signed at time $t = 0$ and settled at time $t = T + 1$ and the holder is allowed to take action at any discrete date $t = 1, \ldots, T$ after the spot price $S(t)$ is known. Let $v(t)$ denote the volume in storage at the start of day t and $\Delta v(t)$ the volume change during day t, that is

$$v(t + 1) = v(t) + \Delta v(t). \tag{6.31}$$

In case of an injection, $\Delta v > 0$, while $\Delta v < 0$ means withdrawal from storage. By definition the holder cannot take action at time $t = 0$ and therefore $\Delta v(0) := 0$. The payoff on day t is

$$h(S(t), \Delta v(t)) = \begin{cases} (-S(t) - c_{\mathrm{WD},t}) \cdot \Delta v(t) & \Delta v(t) \geq 0, \\ (-S(t) + c_{\mathrm{IN},t}) \cdot \Delta v(t) & \Delta v(t) < 0. \end{cases} \tag{6.32}$$

Here, $c_{\mathrm{WD},t}$ denotes the withdrawal costs and $c_{\mathrm{IN},t}$ the injection costs on day t, which can be different and may include a bid–offer spread. Positive volume changes have to be bought on the spot market and represent costs ($h < 0$), while negative volume changes can be sold on the spot market and represent profits ($h > 0$).

The contract is assumed to settle the day after the last trading date, that is at day $T + 1$. At settlement the holder may have to pay a penalty $q(S(T + 1), v(T + 1))$, which can depend on the volume level of the storage as well as the current spot price. Moreover, two volumetric limitations on the strategy are assumed to exist:

1. The volume in storage is limited by a minimum $v_{\min}(t) \geq 0$ and a maximum level $v_{\max}(t)$ on each day $t = 1, \ldots, T + 1$:

$$v_{\min}(t) \leq v(t) \leq v_{\max}(t). \tag{6.33}$$

Allowing $v_{\min}(t)$ and $v_{\max}(t)$ to be time dependent makes it possible to incorporate physical restrictions. For example, a higher minimum level during a certain period of the year could be required to prevent deformations of the cavern. In a virtual storage contract, $v_{\min}(t)$ and $v_{\max}(t)$ are usually constant.
2. Injection as well as withdrawal rates are limited per day:

$$\Delta v_{\min}(t, v(t)) \leq \Delta v(t) \leq \Delta v_{\max}(t, v(t)), \tag{6.34}$$

where $\Delta v_{\min}(t, v(t))$ and $\Delta v_{\max}(t, v(t))$ are functions of the volume in storage $v(t)$ as well as time t. These functions may be set to a constant for virtual storage. For physical storage they are however relevant, since for low storage volumes the difference between pipeline pressure and pressure in storage is small and maybe even a compressor has to be used to withdraw gas, while for high storage volumes the compressor has to run against the pressure in the storage to inject gas. Usually $\Delta v_{\min}(t, v(t))$ will be negative and restricts withdrawal, while $\Delta v_{\max}(t, v(t))$ will be positive and restricts injection.

The fair value V_S of storage is the expected value of the cumulated future payoffs $h(S(t), \Delta v(t))$ resulting from the optimal strategy π. Thus, the following pricing problem has to be considered:

$$V_S = \sup_\pi \mathbf{E} \left[\sum_{t=1}^{T} e^{-rt} h(S(t), \Delta v(t)) + e^{-r \cdot (T+1)} q(S(T+1), v(T+1)) \right], \qquad (6.35)$$

where $\pi = \{\pi(1, S(1), v(1)), \dots, \pi(T, S(T), v(T))\}$ and $\pi(t, S(t), v(t))$ is the decision rule on day t at spot price $S(t)$ if the volume in storage is $v(t)$.

By exchanging supremum and expectation operator, an upper limit for the fair value – the ex-post value or perfect foresight value $V_S^{\text{expost}} \geq V_S$ – results:

$$V_S^{\text{expost}} = \mathbf{E} \sup_\pi \left[\sum_{t=1}^{T} e^{-rt} h(S(t), \Delta v(t)) + e^{-r \cdot (T+1)} q(S(T+1), v(T+1)) \right]. \qquad (6.36)$$

By passing the expectation operator through the payoff function, a lower limit for the fair value – the intrinsic value $V_S^{\text{intrinsic}} \leq V_S$ – results:

$$V_S^{\text{intrinsic}} = \sup_\pi \left[\sum_{t=1}^{T} e^{-rt} h(\mathbf{E}S(t), \Delta v(t)) + e^{-r \cdot (T+1)} q(\mathbf{E}S(T+1), v(T+1)) \right]. \qquad (6.37)$$

The difference between fair and intrinsic value is the so-called extrinsic value – a measure for the flexibility value contained in the contract:

$$V_S^{\text{extrinsic}} = V_S - V_S^{\text{intrinsic}}. \qquad (6.38)$$

The intrinsic value could be locked in immediately if each single future day were traded as an individual forward contract. From this perspective, the extrinsic value is the part that stays at risk.

Overall, both intrinsic and ex-post value – limit the fair value:

$$V_S^{\text{intrinsic}} \leq V_S \leq V_S^{\text{expost}}. \qquad (6.39)$$

The set of allowed volume levels at day t is denoted by $\mathcal{V}(t)$:

$$\mathcal{V}(t) := \{ v | v_{\min}(t) \leq v \leq v_{\max}(t) \}, \qquad (6.40)$$

and the set of all allowed actions on day t being at volume $v(t)$ by $\mathcal{D}(t, v(t))$:

$$\mathcal{D}(t, v(t)) := \{ \Delta v | v_{\min}(t+1) \leq v(t) + \Delta v(t) \leq v_{\max}(t+1),$$
$$\Delta v_{\min}(t, v(t)) \leq \Delta v(t) \leq \Delta v_{\max}(t, v(t)) \}. \qquad (6.41)$$

Let $U(t, S(t), v(t))$ denote the value of the storage starting at volume level $v(t)$ at time t and let $C(t, S(t), v(t), \Delta v)$ denote the continuation value after taking an allowed action $\Delta v \in D(t, v(t))$, then

$$C(t, S(t), v(t), \Delta v) = \mathbf{E}[e^{-r}U(t+1, S(t+1), v(t) + \Delta v)]. \tag{6.42}$$

As the continuation value only depends on $v(t+1) := v(t) + \Delta v(t)$, from now on it is written as $C(t, S(t), v(t+1))$ for short. With this notation the storage value $U(t, S(t), v(t))$ satisfies the following dynamic programme:

$$U(T+1, S(T+1), v(T+1)) = q(S(T+1), v(T+1)), \tag{6.43}$$

$$U(t, S(t), v(t)) = \max_{\Delta v \in D(t, v(t))} [h(S(t), \Delta v) + C(t, S(t), v(t+1))] \tag{6.44}$$

for all times t. In these equations q is a possible penalty depending on the volume level at time $T+1$ and the spot price at this time $S(T+1)$.

As the continuation value is not exactly known in practice, the LSMC method approximates the continuation value

$$C(t, S(t), v(t+1)) \approx \hat{C}(t, S(t), v(t+1)) = \sum_{l=0}^{m} \beta_{l,t} \cdot \phi_l(t, S(t), v(t+1)) \tag{6.45}$$

using basis functions ϕ_l. If N price scenarios are given, estimates $\hat{\beta}_{l,t}$ for the coefficients $\beta_{l,t}$ result by regression. With these coefficients an approximation $\hat{C}(t, S(t), v(t+1))$ of the continuation value is obtained, which is used to determine the optimal action $\Delta v(t)$ for all volumes $v(t)$.

Moreno and Navas (2003) as well as Boogert and de Jong (2011) have shown that the choice of basis functions is less important. For this reason from now on the easy-to-handle polynomial basis functions $\phi_l(t, S(t)) = S^l$ have been chosen. Calculations show that $m = 3$ is enough to get convergent results. A higher number of basis functions does not significantly improve the obtained results.

Boogert and de Jong use a multi-factor price process and include the factors of the price process in the basis used for regression in the LSMC method. While their factors are unobservable, our price process includes two extrinsic factors that can easily be observed. We include them in the regression by

$$\begin{aligned}
C(t, S(t), \mathrm{HDD}(t), B(t), v(t), \Delta v) &= \sum_{l=0}^{m} \beta_{l,t} \cdot \phi_l(t, S(t), v(t), \Delta v) \\
&+ \alpha_0^B B(t) + \alpha_1^B B^2(t) + \alpha_2^B S(t) \cdot B(t) \\
&+ \alpha_0^T \mathrm{HDD}(t) + \alpha_1^T \mathrm{HDD}(t) \cdot S(t). \tag{6.46}
\end{aligned}$$

Monomials of higher degree in the Brent or temperature components as well as higher mixed terms have also been examined, but do not result in a better fit of the cashflows.

Table 6.3   Gas price paths

Path	$t = 0$	$t = 1$	$t = 2$	$t = 3$
1	30	28.9	28.3	29.1
2	30	29.0	29.3	30.0
3	30	30.3	30.2	29.5
4	30	28.7	29.3	28.1
5	30	30.8	31.0	30.8
6	30	29.2	29.4	30.3
7	30	28.8	28.3	28.0
8	30	34.2	34.0	33.4
9	30	31.5	30.1	32.2
10	30	28.6	30.1	28.6

If the least-squares approximation is omitted and the dynamic programme (6.44) is applied to the whole set of scenarios, the ex-post value V_s^{expost} results. If the daily average of the scenarios is calculated first and the dynamic programme (without least-squares approximation) is applied to the resulting daily price forward curve, the intrinsic value $V_s^{\text{intrinsic}}$ is obtained.

Application of LSMC for an American Option

To illustrate the LSMC algorithm, a simple numerical example with only 10 price paths is presented. Consider an American call option with a strike price of 30 EUR/MWh written on the gas spot price as an underlying. The call option can be exercised at times 1, 2 and 3, where time 3 is the expiration date of the option. The riskless rate is assumed to be 0% for simplification. The sample price paths are shown in Table 6.3. In this example there is no penalty and therefore the algorithm starts with $t = 3$. If the option has not been exercised before the final expiration date, the option holder realises the cashflow from following the optimal strategy given in Table 6.4. These cash flows are identical to the cashflows obtained if the option were European instead of American. This means the fair value of a European call option with strike of 30 EUR/MWh and maturity at $t = 3$ is $V_{\text{European}} = 0.67$ EUR/MWh.

In the next time step $t = 2$, the holder has to decide whether to exercise the option immediately or continue until $t = 3$. This decision is made by comparing the cashflow

Table 6.4   Cashflows at time $t = 3$

Path	$t = 1$	$t = 2$	$t = 3$
1	–	–	0
2	–	–	0
3	–	–	0
4	–	–	0
5	–	–	0.8
6	–	–	0.3
7	–	–	0
8	–	–	3.4
9	–	–	2.2
10	–	–	0

Table 6.5 Exercise decision at time $t = 2$

Path	$S(2)$	$C(3)$	$\hat{C}(3)$	$C(2)$
3	30.2	0	0.59	0.2
5	31.0	0.8	1.01	1.0
8	34.0	3.4	3.39	4.0
9	30.1	2.2	0.54	0.1
10	30.1	0	0.54	0.1

for immediate exercise with the continuation value. To estimate the continuation value, the cashflows $C(3)$ resulting from time step $t = 3$ are approximated by a polynomial $\hat{C}(3) = 51.670 - 3.848 \cdot S(2) + 0.071 \cdot (S(2))^2$. The resulting continuation values $\hat{C}(3)$ are shown in Table 6.5. The option is exercised at $t = 2$ if the cashflow $C(2)$ for immediate exercise is larger than the continuation value $\hat{C}(3)$, which is the case only in scenario 8. In scenarios 3, 5, 9 and 10 the continuation value $\hat{C}(3)$ is larger than the cashflow for immediate exercise and therefore the option is continued until $t = 3$. Thus the cashflow shown in Table 6.6 results. Please note that in scenario 8 the cashflow for $t = 3$ is now zero, as the option is exercised at $t = 2$.

Finally, the algorithm proceeds to $t = 1$, where the spot price $S(1)$ is larger than the strike in scenarios 3, 5, 8 and 9. Now the holder has to decide whether to exercise the option immediately or continue until $t = 2$ (or even $t = 3$). For this purpose the sum of the cashflows at $t = 2$ and $t = 3$, that is $C(2) + C(3)$, is approximated by a polynomial $\hat{C}(2) = 52.088 - 3.976 \cdot S(1) + 0.075 \cdot (S(1))^2$. The resulting continuation values $\hat{C}(2)$ are shown in Table 6.7. In scenarios 8 and 9 the option is exercised at $t = 1$ as $C(1) > \hat{C}(2)$, but in scenarios 3 and 5 the continuation value is larger than the cashflow for immediate exercise and therefore the option is not exercised at $t = 1$ but continued. Finally, the cashflows shown in Table 6.8 result. By summing up the cashflows for all three time steps and averaging over all paths, a fair value of 0.68 EUR/MWh results, which is only slightly larger than the value for the European option.

In contrast to the fair value that results from exercise under uncertainty, the ex-post value can also be calculated by sorting each path and using the cashflow from the resulting largest price in the path. This value can easily be calculated, but in practice it only gives an upper limit for the fair value. In the example, an ex-post value of 0.81 EUR/MWh results, which is much

Table 6.6 Cashflows after exercise at time $t = 2$

Path	$t = 1$	$t = 2$	$t = 3$
1	–	0	0
2	–	0	0
3	–	0	0
4	–	0	0
5	–	0	0.8
6	–	0	0.3
7	–	0	0
8	–	4	0
9	–	0	2.2
10	–	0	0

Table 6.7   Exercise decision at time $t = 1$

Path	$S(1)$	$C(2) + C(3)$	$\hat{C}(2)$	$C(1)$
3	30.3	0	0.68	0.3
5	30.8	0.8	0.99	0.8
8	34.2	4	4.10	4.2
9	31.5	2.2	1.49	1.5

larger than the fair value. However, the intrinsic value is also easily obtained. The expected spot price in each time step is 30 EUR/MWh, which is equal to the strike price. Thus, the intrinsic value is 0 EUR/MWh. In contrast to the fair and ex-post value, this intrinsic value is much lower.

This stylised example can only give an impression of how the algorithm works. Of course, 10 scenarios are not enough to get convergent results.

Valuation Results in the Liquid Horizon

Using this LSMC method in combination with the previously described spot price model, two valuation dates have been chosen: 4 July 2012 and 2 April 2013. Theses dates are characterised by a very different implied volatility observed at the markets – for example, for TTF the long-term volatility has decreased significantly in the 8-month period from 25% to 12%. At the same time, the summer–winter spread between winter 13/14 and summer 13 has gone down from 2.4 EUR/MWh to 1.20 EUR/MWh, whereas the price level has risen from 26.15 EUR/MWh to 27.70 EUR/MWh.

Using this TTF market, prices for slow and fast storage as well as a flexible and an inflexible swing contract have been valued. The parameters for these storage and swings are given in Table 6.9. All valuations have been done using 5000 price scenarios, which results in sufficiently convergent results.

As can clearly be seen by comparing Tables 6.10 and 6.11, the decrease in summer–winter spread results in a lower intrinsic value for the storage. In contrast to this behaviour, the intrinsic value of the flexible swing increases because of the higher price level in 2013 compared with

Table 6.8   Cashflows after exercise at time $t = 1$

Path	$t = 1$	$t = 2$	$t = 3$
1	0	0	0
2	0	0	0
3	0	0	0
4	0	0	0
5	0	0	0.8
6	0	0	0.3
7	0	0	0
8	4.2	0	0
9	1.5	0	0
10	0	0	0

Table 6.9   Parameters for swings and storage

Parameter	Slow storage	Fast storage	Inflexible swing	Flexible swing
Start date			1.4.2013	
End date			1.4.2014	
Minimum volume	0 MWh	0 MWh	0 MWh	0 MWh
Maximum volume	100 MWh	100 MWh	438 MWh	438 MWh
Minimum injection	0 MWh/day	0 MWh/day	–	–
Maximum injection	1 MWh/day	2 MWh/day	–	–
Minimum withdrawal	0 MWh/day	0 MWh/day	0.6 MWh/day	0 MWh/day
Maximum withdrawal	1 MWh/day	5 MWh/day	1.2 MWh/day	1.2 MWh/day
Injection costs	0 EUR/MWh	0 EUR/MWh	–	–
Withdrawal costs	0 EUR/MWh	0 EUR/MWh	27 EUR/MWh	27 EUR/MWh
Start volume	0 MWh	0 MWh	438 MWh	438 MWh
Maximum end volume	0 MWh	0 MWh	146 MWh	146 MWh

Table 6.10   Results for valuation date 4 July 2012 (5000 scenarios)

Case	Factors in regression	Daily intrinsic	Fair value	Extrinsic value
Slow storage	spot	360.8	382.4	21.6
	spot & Brent	360.8	549.5	188.7
	spot and Brent & HDD	360.8	571.2	210.4
Fast storage	spot	517.1	561.8	44.7
	spot & Brent	517.1	1006.6	489.5
	spot and Brent & HDD	517.1	1090.1	572.9
Inflexible swing	spot	−126.2	274.5	400.7
	spot & Brent	−126.2	285.4	411.6
	spot and Brent & HDD	−126.2	286.3	412.4
Flexible swing	spot	−41.6	356.5	398.1
	spot & Brent	−41.6	397.2	438.8
	spot and Brent & HDD	−41.6	959.6	1001.2

Table 6.11   Results for valuation date 2 April 2013 (5000 scenarios)

Case	Factors in regression	Daily intrinsic	Fair value	Extrinsic value
Slow storage	spot	227.3	309.5	82.2
	spot & Brent	227.3	419.1	191.8
	spot and Brent & HDD	227.3	411.7	184.4
Fast storage	spot	353.5	593.4	240.0
	spot & Brent	353.5	855.0	501.6
	spot and Brent & HDD	353.5	877.0	523.5
Inflexible swing	spot	310.0	485.2	175.2
	spot & Brent	310.0	488.0	177.9
	spot and Brent & HDD	310.0	471.9	161.9
Flexible swing	spot	324.1	542.1	218.0
	spot & Brent	324.1	558.5	234.4
	spot and Brent & HDD	324.1	572.2	248.1

2012. Furthermore, the decrease in volatility does not change the extrinsic value of the two types of storage – very much in contrast to the swings.

For storage, these findings correspond very well to what Boogert and de Jong have observed. They also found that a change of volatility in the long-term component does not influence the value of gas storage – it may even decrease the value. An explanation for this behaviour is that it becomes more difficult for traders to decide correctly if today's price is high or low and therefore withdrawal, injection or no action makes most sense. Owing to the decision under uncertainty about the future price development with an increased volatility, more and more wrong decisions are made and this may decrease the value at least of fast storage.

The situation is completely different for swing options. With an increasing volatility their value also increases. This different behaviour can be explained in a special case. If the yearly restriction is not binding, the swing is equivalent to a strip of European options. In this case it is evident that an increase in volatility should go hand in hand with an increase in the extrinsic option value – at least if the Black option price formula with all its restrictions is valid.

Another important difference between swings and storage is their behaviour if the extrinsic components of the spot price process are included in the regression of the LSMC method. For the value of storage, the Brent component is much more important – in contrast to swings. For the inflexible swing both components are irrelevant, while for the flexible swing the temperature component is more important than the Brent component. For storage, the Brent component is a measure of normal long-term levels. As prices revert back to this long-term level mainly defined by the Brent component, a price higher than this level is good for withdrawal while a price lower than this level is good for injection. Therefore, inclusion in the regression is very important for the exercise decision and increases the value.

Another interesting observation is the influence of the two extrinsic components on the less flexible products. While inclusion of the Brent component increases the spot value, a further inclusion of the temperature component decreases the value slightly for valuation date 2 April 2013 – but not for 4 July 2012. This effect can be explained by the construction of the

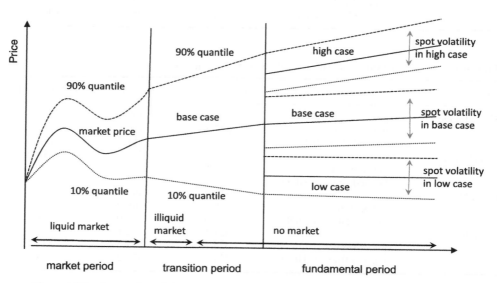

Figure 6.21   Interaction of the three price periods distinguished in long-term valuations.

temperature component NCHDD, which by definition linearly returns to zero during summer (see Section 6.3.1). In April 2013 the end of a long winter has just been exceeded and the linear return to zero is going on. This return to zero results in a decreasing price component contained in all scenarios. In contrast to this situation in April, in July 2012 the return to zero had mostly been finished and the winter was still to come.

Overall, these results indicate that it is very important to include the extrinsic components in the exercise decision for storage as well as swings. This can significantly increase the extrinsic value. So far, gas assets have only been valued in the short term, the problem of long-term valuation has not yet been touched on.

Long-Term Valuation of Gas Assets

In the short term, market prices, spreads and volatilities form the basis for valuation of gas assets. For investment decisions, planning and risk management as well as disinvestment decisions, long-term valuations are important. For this purpose, three periods are distinguished.

- *Market price period:* This period is defined as the time period for which a sufficiently liquid forward and ideally also an options market exists, so that trustworthy forward prices and spreads as well as implied volatilities can be taken from the market. Typically, this period covers around 3–5 years ahead. The price scenarios vary around the price forward curve as an average. All scenarios start at the actual spot price and the implied volatility defines how far scenarios are expected to deviate from the forward curve.
- *Fundamental period:* This period starts after around 7–10 years and may reach out 30 years into the future. In this period equilibrium prices resulting from fundamental market models (see Section 7.6) provide the basis for valuations. Uncertainty is often modelled via a number of consistent fundamental scenarios reflecting different long-term views on the fundamental drivers of the market. These fundamental scenarios can be complemented by assumptions on short-term spot volatility. In Figure 6.21 the situation with three fundamental views (low, base, high) is shown, where the price scenarios for each view are restricted to a constant range that is defined by the spot volatility.
- *Transition period:* As the actual market situation can be far away from a fundamental equilibrium, a third period between market and fundamental model is necessary. This third period depicts the transition from the actual market situation to the equilibrium presumed in the fundamental models. In this period a long-term volatility is necessary to reproduce the growing uncertainty with regard to the price development over the years.

The interaction of the three periods is shown in Figure 6.21. A valuation of gas assets in these three periods can be done using the LSMC method described above. For the fundamental period the valuation is performed separately for each fundamental view combined with the valuation results for the market and transition periods.

Fundamental Market Models

Market prices can be understood as clearing (or equilibrium) prices at the intersection of cumulative bid (demand) and offer (supply) curves (see Figure 7.1). Fundamental market models use cost-based bid and offer curves to derive estimations (or indications) of market prices. They do not necessarily allow forecasting of market prices. These models give insight into fundamental price drivers and market mechanisms. Therefore, fundamental market models can be used for the development of trading strategies as well as for decision support for investments or acquisitions.

This chapter concentrates on fundamental market models for electricity markets. We first describe the most important fundamental price drivers for electricity prices in Section 7.1. The principles of economic power plant dispatch discussed in Section 7.2 are crucial for describing and understanding the supply side of electricity markets. Different methodological modelling approaches are discussed in Section 7.3.

Data quality is critical for a high-quality description of electricity markets. A general overview on the data required for modelling, as well as on information sources, can be found in Section 7.4. Finally, we present examples for the application of fundamental electricity market models in Section 7.5 and describe briefly in Sections 7.6 and 7.7 how fundamental market modelling approaches can be applied to gas markets, other fuel markets and to the market for CO_2 emissions certificates.

7.1 FUNDAMENTAL PRICE DRIVERS IN ELECTRICITY MARKETS

In contrast to other commodities, large quantities of electricity cannot be stored directly.[1] Power generation and demand within an interconnected electric power system have to be in balance at all times. Spot markets have short delivery intervals, commonly 60 or 30 minutes (see Section 1.5). Scheduling periods for physical power delivery are even shorter, with periods as low as 15 minutes in most transmission areas. Deviations of scheduled generation from real-time demand are compensated by balancing power (see Section 1.5.2).

In power markets, spot prices are published for every delivery interval. Each of these interval prices can be understood as an equilibrium price of bid and offer curves for the specific time interval (see Figure 7.1). In most real markets, only part of the total physical demand and supply is traded in the spot market. An exception is compulsory pool markets,

---

[1] For small-scale applications, indirect storage is possible with capacitors, batteries, fly wheels, etc. For large-scale applications, storage is achieved with hydroelectric storage schemes (see Sections 7.1.2 and 7.2.2). With increasing quantities of fluctuating wind energy in Europe, new storage technologies are currently under consideration. Compressed air energy storage (CAES) is the only proven large-scale technology (Crotogino *et al.*, 2001). The main components of a CAES system are an open cycle gas turbine with separated turbine and air compressor and underground caverns for storing compressed air.

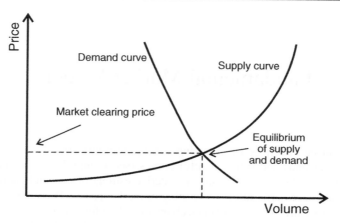

Figure 7.1   Cumulative supply and demand curves.

as in Spain. Most fundamental market models represent the equilibrium price of the whole system considering total physical demand and supply, which are not identical to the bid and offer side in the spot market. The equilibrium prices derived with fundamental market models can explain spot market prices well if economic power plant dispatch for the whole system can be assumed.[2]

Figure 7.2 shows the main price drivers on the demand side and on the supply side. Owing to limited interconnection capacities between different transmission areas of the power system, price differences between market regions occur. Inter-regional transmission flows can have an impact on the demand as well as on the supply situation in any region. The main drivers are analysed in the following subsections.

7.1.1   Demand Side

A sectoral breakdown of the European electricity demand is given in Table 7.1. The main final consumers are industry (33%), households (26%), the services industry (26%) and others (4%). In addition, the consumption of the energy sector (4%) as well as transmission and distribution losses (7%) have to be considered. The regional distribution of electricity demand within Europe is shown in Figure 7.8 later.

Electricity demand fluctuates strongly over time with typical daily, weekly and seasonal patterns and significant regional differences. Electricity demand is also strongly influenced by consumer behaviour. Figure 7.3 depicts the demand or load curves for summer and winter Wednesdays in Germany and France. Differences between these curves are caused by differing consumption patterns and different intensities of activities responsible for electricity demand, such as air-conditioning or electric heating.

Two different approaches are possible to explain and forecast electricity demand (see Section 4.4): a bottom-up approach that analyses load curves at the level of sectors or even single consumers or a top-down approach that analyses aggregated load curves at a country or

---

[2] Fundamental market models based on short-run marginal costs can explain observed spot market prices well in competitive markets as in Germany. In other markets, it might be necessary to consider strategic behaviour of market participants (see Section 7.3.4).

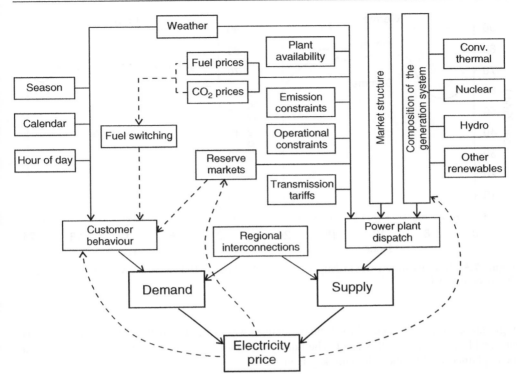

Figure 7.2   Fundamental price drivers in power markets.

Table 7.1   Sectoral breakdown of electricity demand in Europe (EU27) 2011

Sector			TWh
Energy sector (without electricity generation sector)		4%	125
Transmission and distribution losses		7%	201
Industry		33%	1032
Iron and steel industry	12%		*121*
Chemical industry	18%		*188*
Food, drink and tobacco industry	11%		*112*
Paper and printing industry	12%		*124*
Machinery and other metal industry	19%		*191*
Other industries	29%		*296*
Households		26%	803
Services		26%	805
Rail transport		2%	53
Agriculture		2%	48
Other sectors		0%	14
Total consumption (without electricity generation sector)		100%	3082

Source: Eurostat and own calculations; partly provisional values.

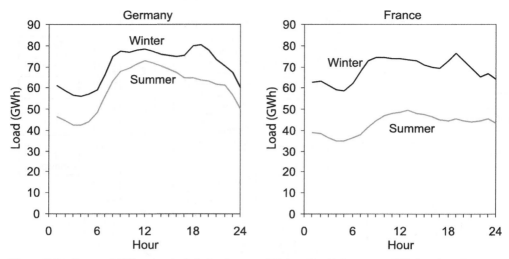

Figure 7.3 Seasonal differences in daily load curves (Wednesday 19 January and Wednesday 17 August 2005). *Source*: UCTE.

regional level. As aggregated load curves exhibit a very regular pattern, load forecasting is preferably performed at this level. The hourly electricity demand of a country or region can be explained well by the following key factors.

1. *Season:* Load patterns show typical seasonal behaviour. This can be explained by the varying duration of day light, seasonal production patterns of some industries, and demand for heating and cooling.
2. *Day of the week:* There are strong differences in the sectoral activities between different weekdays and weekend days.
3. *Irregular sectoral non-work or limited-activity days*: These include public holidays, school holidays, days between public holidays and weekends. On these days, the demand of industry and services is generally lower while household demand might increase.
4. *Hour of the day:* Electricity demand follows typical daily patterns with characteristic differences between different day types (working days, weekends, holidays, etc.).
5. *Weather:* Electricity demand for heating and cooling depends on environmental tempera- tures and, to a smaller extent, on wind speeds. Buildings buffer temperatures to a certain degree and therefore time lags between temperature change and the ensuing electricity demand response can occur. Electricity demand for lighting in most sectors depends on global irradiance.

Using combinations of categories 1 to 3, it is possible to form clusters of days (day types) with distinct load characteristics. Examples for France are shown in Figure 7.4. The differentiation of day types can be used in load forecasting algorithms (see Section 4.4).

 As demand patterns directly impact electricity prices, variables 1 to 4 are generally used for constructing hourly price forward curves (see Section 6.1.2).

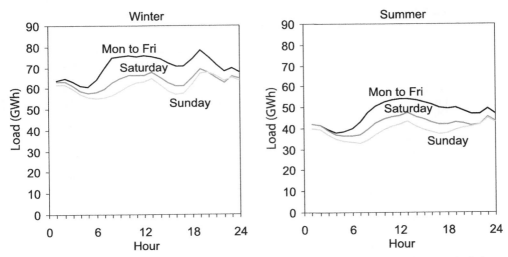

Figure 7.4   Characteristic daily load curves for typical days in France. *Source*: RTE, own calculations.

Besides these exogenous influences, electricity prices also have some impact on electricity demand in the longer term. Electricity prices will have an impact on the penetration of energy-efficient technologies, the extent of substitution by other energy carriers or the relocation of energy-intensive industries to countries with lower electricity costs. In most cases, these longer-term impacts cannot be separated from general consumption trends due to limited availability of disaggregated demand data.

In the short term, the impact of wholesale prices on demand depends strongly on pricing signals in electricity contracts with final customers. Up-to-date real-time pricing is not common in the electricity sector in Europe. There are, however, a large variety of contracts that impact customer behaviour to a certain degree and cause demand elasticity. The main types include the following.

- *Interruptible contracts:* The supplier can interrupt the contract for a certain number of hours each year with or without the payment of compensation for electricity not supplied.
- *Capacity payments:* Contracts containing a price component that depends on the customer's peak load within a defined time interval (e.g., one year). As a statistical correlation between individual customer load, total system load and prices exists, these contracts may cause a slight price elasticity of demand.
- *Spot market indexed contracts:* Contracts with a variable price component indexed to spot market prices in the wholesale market. These types of contracts are common in some sectors in Scandinavia (Bye, 2003).
- *Short-term price adjustments:* Most Scandinavian utilities have standard contracts that allow price adjustments with two weeks' notice. These standard contracts are the most common types of contract in the residential sector. In combination with spot-indexed contracts, they did have a significant demand impact during a period of high prices in the Nord Pool in 2003 (von der Fehr et al., 2005). Price adjustments with short notice can also be found in the UK.

Table 7.2   Breakdown of electricity generation in Europe (EU27) 2010

Technology			TWh
Conventional thermal		50.0%	1604
Coal	29.2%		468
Natural gas	46.6%		748
Lignite	19.4%		311
Oil	4.8%		77
Nuclear		27.2%	872
Renewables		20.0%	642
Hydropower (non-pumped storage)	53.7%		345
Biomass	10.3%		66
Biogas	4.0%		26
Renewable waste	4.7%		30
Solar	3.7%		24
Geothermal	0.8%		5
Wind	22.7%		146
Hydropower (pumped storage)		1.40%	45
Derived gas		0.9%	28
Other		0.5%	15
Total net electricity generation including pumped storage hydropower		100.0%	3206

Source: Eurelectric (2012) and own calculations.

- *Flexible price tariffs:* With one or two days' notice, the supply company can increase electricity tariffs for a limited number of days during the winter period to a predefined higher level. Peak day prices generally exceed normal prices by more than 200%. This pricing element is common for industrial as well as residential consumers in France. Load reduction of up to 20% can be achieved at peak load times (International Energy Agency, 2003).

In spite of these measures, the extent of demand responses to prices is generally considered small. It is strongly dependent on pricing strategies in different countries. Clear statistical quantification of the impact is generally not possible. Hence, in fundamental market models the price elasticity of demand is usually only reflected by the use of observed historical load patterns that already contain price responses of the demand. In this case, the demand curve is a vertical line.

7.1.2   Supply Side

Electricity is generated by a wide variety of different technologies. This variety is caused by regional differences in availability of resources, different or changing political preferences and incentive patterns for specific technologies. A breakdown of generation in Europe is listed in Table 7.2. As a uniform classification of generation technologies does not exist, statistical data from different sources is often inconsistent.[3]

---

[3] Reasons for inconsistencies include: thermal power plants using more than one fuel, generation from waste sometimes counted as renewable and sometimes not, and statistics not differentiating between generation in hydro plants from natural inflow (renewable) and from pumped storage (not renewable).

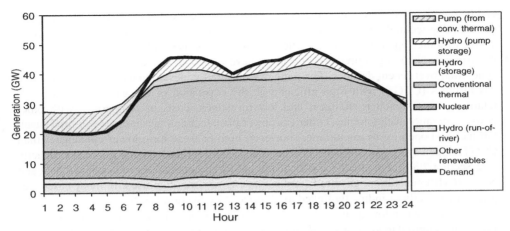

Figure 7.5   Typical daily dispatch patterns for different generation technologies.

Figure 7.5 shows a typical demand curve and the corresponding generation (or dispatch) pattern for different plant types. Nuclear power plants are operated in baseload with constant output. Conventional thermal plants are operated at more or less constant power. To meet the variable changes in demand, conventional thermal, hydro storage and hydro pumped storage plants are used. During the night when demand is low, the pumps of hydro storage schemes are operated to raise water from lower into upper reservoirs. This creates additional demand. During the day changes in demand are compensated using storage and pumped storage plants. Run-of-river hydro plants, geothermal, wind and solar power plants produce in correspondence to the current resource availability (water flow rates, sunshine, wind, etc.). The actual dispatch pattern varies from country to country due to different load patterns and generation system configurations. It is generally a result of economic power plant dispatch. The mathematical description for modelling power plant dispatch will be discussed in Section 7.2. The following sections give a short overview of the main characteristics of the technologies that have relevance for electricity markets.

Conventional Thermal Power Plants

Conventional thermal power plants have the largest share of electricity generation in Europe. Their energy sources are fossil fuels or in some cases biomass. Conversion to electricity occurs by means of a steam turbine (Rankine cycle), a gas turbine (Joules cycle) or an internal combustion engine (diesel cycle). The main fuels are listed below.

- *Coal:* Coal fired power plants have a long tradition in electricity systems due to the availability of indigenous resources in Europe. The share of coal in electricity generation has been declining due to fuel costs. Coal mining in Europe is no longer competitive on the world market and is highly subsidised. Increasing quantities of imported coal are used in European power stations; however, transportation costs for imported coal can be high. Other reasons for the declining generation share of coal power plants are environmental constraints and associated costs. European countries have introduced limits for dust, SO_2

and NO_x emissions. For compliance, coal power plant operators either have to invest in flue gas cleaning technologies or reduce the generation output. Coal composition varies from source to source and not all coal qualities are suitable for use in all power stations.

- *Natural gas:* Natural gas-fired power stations have gained an increasing share of electricity generation over recent decades. The main reasons are the development of combined cycle gas turbines (CCGT) with high efficiencies, the expansion of the gas pipeline system, relative environmental friendliness and low investment costs in comparison with other power generation technologies. Other gas power plant technologies include gas-fired steam turbines and open cycle gas turbines; however, both of these have lower efficiencies than CCGTs. Open cycle gas turbines (GTs) are mainly used for peak load or as reserve capacity (see Section 7.3.1). For small-scale local and industrial applications of combined heat and power (CHP) generation, gas-fired combustion engines are often used. In many cases, gas prices are directly or indirectly linked to oil prices (see Section 1.3.2).
- *Lignite:* Lignite is a low-quality coal with high moisture and ash content and low calorific value, also referred to as *brown coal*. In Europe, lignite resources are predominantly located in Germany, Poland, Greece, Romania, Hungary and Slovakia. Owing to the low calorific value of lignite, lignite-fired power plants are generally located close to the mine to avoid high transport costs. Lignite-fired plants have low fuel costs compared with other conventional thermal power stations. Disadvantages are higher investment costs and higher specific CO_2 emissions.
- *Oil:* The role of oil in power generation in Europe is relatively small due to environmental legislation that limits the use of heavy fuel oil. In most countries, only low-sulphur gasoil is used. As gasoil prices are generally higher than prices for other fossil fuels, oil fired power plants are primarily used as peak or reserve capacity or in local applications. Italy is the only country in Europe where oil-fired power plants play a significant role. Steam turbines, gas turbines as well as combustion engines are common technologies.
- *Other fuels:* A large variety of other fuels are used in conventional thermal power stations either as primary fuel or as auxiliary fuel. Examples are: peat (in Finland and Iceland), derived gas (e.g., coke oven gas or coal-derived synthesis gas), petroleum coke, Orimulsion[4] (an emulsion of natural bitumen suspended in water produced in Venezuela – used in Italy), industrial and municipal waste and different types of biomass (e.g., wood, straw, olive cake residue or sewage sludge). These fuels play a minor role in power generation and have little impact on wholesale market prices.

Nuclear Power Plants

Nuclear power plants play an important role in electricity generation in Europe. Nuclear power plants are thermal power plants with a Rankine cycle. A nuclear fission reaction in the reactor provides the required heat. Nuclear power plants are characterised by low variable operation costs (fuel costs) and zero CO_2 emissions but high operation and maintenance costs, high investment costs and long planning and construction times. Nuclear plants are generally used for baseload electricity generation.

The future development of nuclear power in Europe is currently under debate. In several European countries, a nuclear phase-out has been introduced: Sweden (1980), Italy (1987),

---

[4] Orimulsion is a registered trademark of Petroleos de Venezuela SA.

Belgium (1999) and Germany (2000 and 2011). The nuclear phase-out limits the remaining operation time or generation of existing nuclear power plants. In Germany, the last nuclear reactor is expected to close in 2021. Austria, the Netherlands and Spain have enacted laws not to build new nuclear power stations. France and Finland have decided to build a new nuclear reactor and governments in other countries, including the UK, are considering this option as well.

Hydropower Plants

The use of hydropower for electricity generation in Europe started in the 19th century. The potential energy of dammed water is converted into electricity by use of a turbine and a generator. Hydroelectricity is classified as renewable energy with the exception of pumped storage. Different types of hydropower plants exist and are listed below.

- *Run-of-river power plants:* These hydroelectric power plants are located at rivers and utilise height differences at weirs. They can be found all over Europe with a wide range of installed capacities. The turbine flow rate and generation output depends on the natural flow rate of the river. In some cases, generation output can be slightly adjusted on a short-term basis (hours to days) by modulation of the headwater level.
- *Storage power plants:* These hydropower plants consist of a reservoir, a turbine located below the reservoir and a generator. The turbine is connected to the reservoir by a pipe (see Figure 7.6(a)). The reservoir is filled by natural inflow. The water is released through the turbine at times of peak demand or peak electricity price.
- *Pumped storage power plants:* These hydropower plants consist of an upper and a lower reservoir connected by a turbine as well as a pump (see Figure 7.6(b)). The upper reservoir is filled by water pumped uphill from the lower reservoir at times of low electricity demand or price. In addition, there may be natural inflows to the upper reservoir. During times of

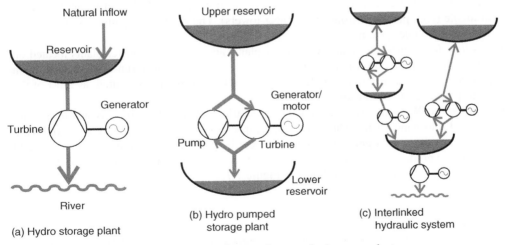

Figure 7.6   Storage and pumped storage hydropower plants.

peak demand or price, the water is released from the upper reservoir. It flows through the turbine, generates electricity and is received in the lower reservoir.

- *Tidal power plants:* The only large-scale tidal power plant in operation in Europe is located in La Rance, France. It utilises the tidal range. A barrage (dam) blocks the incoming and outgoing tides of a coastal basin. A tidal power plant is operated similar to a run-of-river power plant, but with changing flow directions.

Storage and pumped storage plants often form complex interlinked hydraulic systems (see Figure 7.6(c)). Their operation may also impact the generation of run-of-river power plants located on a river below these storage schemes. External constraints such as minimum flow rates in original river beds have to be respected.

Other Renewables

The main characteristics of different sources of renewable energy relevant for fundamental market models are described in the following.

- *Biomass:* Biomass can be categorised into solid, liquid and gaseous forms. There are several technologies for conversion into electricity: use as auxiliary fuels in conventional thermal power stations, conventional steam turbines (especially for solid biomass) or internal combustion engines (biogas and bioliquids). CHP is possible. With the exception of co-firing, the production pattern is generally flat.
- *Photovoltaic (PV):* The installed capacity of PV is growing rapidly, with capacity additions of approximately 3000 MW per year. End of 2012, the installed capacity worldwide was over 100 000 MW, of which almost one-third was located in Germany. The generation pattern depends on solar radiation (daylight hours only, summer peak) and is characterised by a low annual load factor[5] (approximately 10% in Central Europe and up to 20% in regions with high sunshine).
- *Solar thermal power:* Solar thermal power systems use concentrated solar radiation as a high-temperature energy source to produce electrical power. Different technologies are available (e.g., parabolic troughs or power towers). The production pattern is comparable with photovoltaic systems.
- *Small hydro:* Generally, small hydropower plants are run-of-river power plants located on small rivers. These power plants generate electricity with a typical run-of-river production pattern. The expansion of hydroelectricity generation in Europe is limited, as most of the hydropower resources are already utilised.
- *Wind power:* Wind energy is converted into electricity by use of turbines. Wind turbines are grouped into wind farms, which can reach capacities as large as 100 MW or more. Wind energy has the most significant impact on electricity wholesale markets in Europe due to fluctuating production patterns and high cumulative installed capacity. A production pattern for Germany for one month is shown in Figure 7.7.

---

[5] The load factor *LF* is defined as $LF = \sum_{t=1}^{T} P_t/(Pmax \cdot T)$, where P_t is the generation output during time interval t, $Pmax$ is the installed peak capacity and T is the number of time intervals t. A similar measure is the number of full-load hours *FLH* defined as $FLH = \sum_{t=1}^{T} P_t/Pmax$.

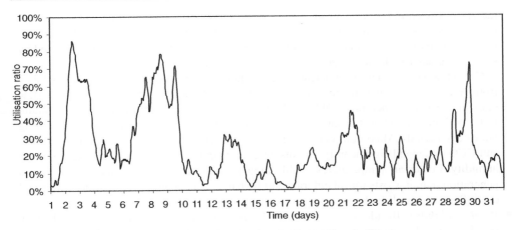

Figure 7.7   Variability in wind production pattern in Germany.

- *Geothermal energy:* Instead of fossil fuels, hot geothermal fluids can be utilised as heat source in thermal power plants with Rankine cycle. Geothermal energy is utilised for electricity generation in Iceland and Italy. The production pattern is flat.
- *Ocean energy:* Besides the tidal power plants mentioned above, the utilisation of ocean energy is still in the prototype stage with a large variety of different technologies.

For more details on renewable energy, see Chapter 2.

Price Drivers on the Supply Side

Figure 7.2 shows the main price drivers on the supply side. The most important one is the composition of the generation system. It is not static but changes and develops over time. Old, uneconomic plants are closed and new ones are opened. The long-term development of a generation system is influenced by multiple factors including resource availability, load development, electricity and fuel prices, technological development, development of investment and operational costs, politics and market structure.

In an existing generation system, the supply curve can be influenced by the market structure and the behaviour of single market participants. In markets with perfect competition, all players will bid on the basis of short-run marginal costs. In oligopolic or monopolic markets, strategic behaviour can be rational instead. This can lead to offers above or below short-run marginal costs. Strategic behaviour can have a broad variety of motivations and therefore it is difficult to assess or reflect in a model. Game theory is one approach (see Section 7.3.4), but strategic behaviour is only considered on a purely economic basis and assumes more or less perfect information. Another modelling approach that does reflect strategic decisions is system dynamics (see Section 7.3.3).

Additional price drivers on the supply side, which have to be considered in fundamental market models, are as follows.

- *Weather:* Weather has several impacts on the available generation output and to a lesser extent on generation costs. The output of photovoltaic systems depends directly on solar radiation. The output of wind turbines depends on wind speeds. The production from run-of-river plants depends on river flow rates, which are influenced by precipitation. The natural inflow into hydro storage plants depends on precipitation as well, but is also influenced by snow and glacier melt and evaporation and seepage rates.

Conventional thermal and nuclear plants require cooling water. If this water is taken from rivers, maximum generation output as well as efficiency can depend on river flow rates and water temperatures. Where there are environmental restrictions on maximum water withdrawal and heat discharge to rivers, this can restrict the generation output during hot or dry periods. Maximum generation output and efficiency of open cycle gas turbines and CCGTs depend significantly on outside air temperatures and to a lesser degree on air humidity. Lower air temperatures enable higher efficiencies and increase the maximum generation output. Costs for inland transport by barge can depend on river water levels and can influence overall fuel costs.

- *Plant availability:* Besides the environmental conditions mentioned above, plant availability is reduced by planned outages for maintenance and by unplanned outages. Where possible, planned outages are scheduled to occur during times with low electricity demand and low market prices. Unplanned outages are stochastic events distributed uniformly over the year. The probability of unplanned outages is slightly higher after longer shut-downs and might also depend on environmental conditions and authorisation constraints.

- *Fuel prices:* Under the assumption of perfect markets every power plant will offer electricity in the spot market at short-run marginal cost. For conventional thermal power plants, fuel costs are the primary factor in these short-run variable costs. Fuel costs can be derived from world market fuel prices (e.g., coal prices in ARA; see Section 1.4.2) plus costs for transport to the power station. There are many exceptions. Gas-fired power plants may have individual long-term supply contracts including take-or-pay quantities. Lignite or coal mines can be owned by the generation company. In these cases, variable fuel costs can be a result of internal cost calculations.

Operators of nuclear plants often have long-term fuel contracts lasting several years. Therefore, uranium world market prices might not be relevant for individual operators.

- *CO_2 prices:* Since the introduction of the European Emissions Trading Scheme (EU ETS) in 2005, CO_2 emission allowances have become a new production factor (see Section 1.6). Other countries and regions have also introduced trading systems for greenhouse gas emissions or taxes on these emissions. Specific emission factors depend on the fuel type and plant efficiency.

- *Emission constraints:* In certain European countries (e.g., the UK, France and Italy), emission constraints, especially on SO_2 emissions, impact power plant dispatch and therefore wholesale market prices.

- *Operational constraints:* Minimum up- and downtimes, restrictions on load change rates, start-up costs and other technical constraints impact plant dispatch (see Section 7.2). Further constraints can be imposed by the grid operator. Some plants have to be dispatched for network stability reasons. CHP plants are another type of plant with operational constraints. In this case, commitments for serving heat demands impact electricity generation. Supply alternatives (e.g., heat-only boilers) have to be considered.

- *Reserve markets:* For system stability reasons, generation reserves in different qualities are required to balance short deviations between generation and demand (see Section 1.5.2). In many countries, there are markets for these system services. Generation capacity allocated for reserve provision cannot take part in the energy market. This has an important impact on the dispatch of these power plants. Owing to their ability to change generation output with high gradients, hydropower plants are often used for reserve provision, which significantly changes their dispatch pattern. Often, storage and pumped storage hydropower plants are also dispatched at times of low demand to a certain degree to provide negative reserve capacity. In Figure 7.5, these impacts are not depicted.

Positive tertiary reserve can also be provided by interruptible loads on the demand side, but generally the fraction of reserves provided by the demand side is small compared with those provided by the supply side. In Figure 7.2, the interaction between demand side and reserve markets is indicated by a dotted line.

- *Transmission tariffs:* In some European countries, power plant operators have to pay transmission tariffs for generation or for consumption in hydro storage pumps. These tariffs in some cases have an energy (i.e., production-related) component and they might vary over time (ETSO, 2005).

7.1.3 Interconnections

The European electricity market is a non-uniform market that is composed of different regional markets with different delivery points or zones for which different prices are recorded (see Section 1.5). Market regions are physically interconnected by transmission lines. Consequently, market prices in different regions can influence each other. The interconnected European network is divided into regional balancing zones, which cover in most cases the geographical areas of individual transmission system operators (TSOs). Physical network constraints within one balancing zone are generally handled by the TSO via redispatching measures and do not affect trading activities. Between some neighbouring balancing zones (e.g., in Germany) there are no transmission limits that would restrict trading activities. In most cases, a transmission restriction occurs at borders between countries. If a transmission restriction between zones exists, transmission rights are generally auctioned by the TSOs to the market participants. Capacity limits and the design of capacity allocation procedures impact the demand and supply side and therefore wholesale electricity market prices in affected zones. Physical energy flows between countries in Europe during 2005 are depicted in Figure 7.8.

7.2 ECONOMIC POWER PLANT DISPATCH

To build fundamental market models, it is necessary to understand how power plants are dispatched and which parameters are considered in dispatch decisions. In this section, we discuss how economic power plant dispatch can be modelled.

Economic power plant dispatch can have two different objectives.

- *Minimisation of total operating costs:* In a situation where a given load has to be met (e.g., after the closure of the spot market to serve the customer load or other electricity sales), the total variable generation costs have to be minimised. Costs in this sense include all direct costs as well as opportunity costs, for example for CO_2 certificates or for the use of water from hydro reservoirs.
- *Maximisation of profit margins in the electricity wholesale market:* This is the normal framework for a producer with a small market share in the mid term where he optimises and hedges his generation revenues by trading on the forward markets for electricity and fuels (see Section 3.2.2).

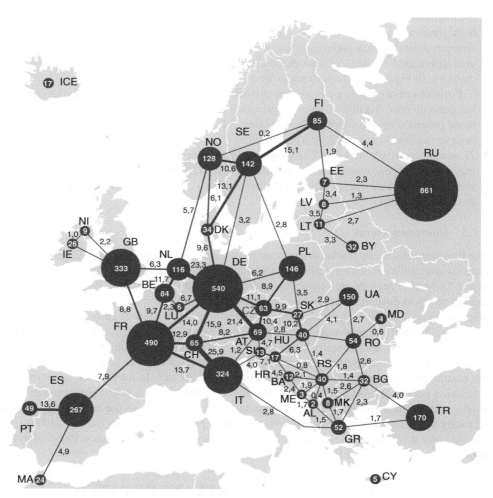

Figure 7.8 Consumption and international electricity exchange in Europe 2012 in TWh. *Source*: ENTSO-E, EIA and own calculations.

The mathematical depiction of plant characteristics is similar in both cases. However, the objective function is different. In the second situation with profit margin maximisation, units can generally be modelled independently unless there are overall constraints (e.g., emission limits, reserve requirements or connections between generation units in interlinked hydro systems). In the following subsections, we both consider planning objectives and describe appropriate optimisation methods.

Economic dispatch has been the main issue in the electric power industry since the establishment of interconnected networks and is covered by many textbooks and scientific publications (see, e.g., Sheble and Fahd (1994); Sen and Kothari (1998); Bhattacharya *et al.* (2001); Stoft (2002); Weber (2005)). In this section, the focus is to give an overview of the most important aspects relevant to understanding electricity market fundamentals.

7.2.1 Thermal Power Plants

In this section, we describe the main constraints for modelling of thermal power plants including load-dependent heat rates, variable start-up costs, minimum load, maximum up- and downtimes, maximum load change rates and reserve requirements. Other restrictions like emission limits, take-or-pay quantities or additional operational constraints for combined heat and power (CHP) plants will be considered briefly. The formulation below does not cover all technical, operational and financial constraints at a single plant level, but from a market perspective it is sufficient for most practical applications. One further simplification is the (piecewise) linear approximation of non-linear constraints, which is generally sufficient as well. The linear approximation increases problem solvability and allows the use of standard optimisation methods including mixed integer programming (MIP).

Indices, Parameters and Variables

In terms of notation we use the following conventions: parameters and indices are printed in italic font (e.g., parameter $Pmax_g$ or index t). Variables are printed in roman font (e.g., $P_{g,t}$). Discrete variables are printed in overlined font (e.g., $\overline{B}_{g,t}$). The index $t^{\leftarrow 1}$ refers to the time interval previous to t and the index $t^{\rightarrow 1}$ refers to the time interval after t. Here we assume hourly time intervals t. All values for variable costs and time durations are in hourly values.[6] For simplicity, marginal effects at the beginning and end of the modelling horizon are neglected here. In reality they often have to be considered carefully.

Thermal power plants are modelled as single generation units g. The smallest element we consider is one unit. A power plant can consist of several units, which might have different characteristics. Sometimes it is possible to depict units with similar characteristics by one modelled unit. The state of one unit g during time interval t is described by the following variables:

- $\overline{B}_{g,t}$ is the binary operation variable. It has the value 1 if the unit g is running and otherwise the value 0.
- $\overline{A}_{g,t}$ is the binary start-up variable. For the time interval t during which the state of a unit changes from off-line to on-line, it has the value 1 and for all other time intervals the value 0.
- $P_{g,t}$ is the electric power output of the unit g during the interval t.

Capacity Constraints and Start-Up Variables

The main constraint of a thermal unit is its capacity constraint (equation (7.1)). This limits the electric power $P_{g,t}$ to the maximum power $Pmax_g$ if the unit is turned on ($\overline{B}_{g,t} = 1$) and otherwise to 0. Thermal units further have a minimum output $Pmin_g$ below which stable operation is not possible. This constraint is reflected by equation (7.2). The unit has to run at least with the electric power $Pmin_g$ or it has to be switched off ($\overline{B}_{g,t} = 0$):

$$P_{g,t} \leq \overline{B}_{g,t} \cdot Pmax_g \qquad \forall (g,t)^7, \tag{7.1}$$

$$P_{g,t} \geq \overline{B}_{g,t} \cdot Pmin_g \qquad \forall (g,t). \tag{7.2}$$

---

[6] For short-term optimisation, quarter hourly, half hourly or hourly time intervals are chosen. For mid-term optimisation and market models, several hours can be combined into one modelled time section. To appropriately reflect load shapes one might choose non-equidistant time sections as well as representative days instead of a complete chronological hourly time scale.

The start-up variable $\overline{A}_{g,t}$ must have the value 1 if the status of a unit g changes from off-line in time interval $t^{\leftarrow 1}$ to on-line in time t as defined in equation (7.3). As in most cases, plant start-up is associated with start-up costs (see equation (7.8)); generally no further constraints are required to ensure that $\overline{A}_{g,t}$ has the value 0 in all other time intervals:[7]

$$\overline{A}_{g,t} \geq \overline{B}_{g,t} - \overline{B}_{g,t^{\leftarrow 1}} \qquad \forall(g,t). \qquad (7.3)$$

Minimum Up- and Downtimes

Many thermal plants have restrictions on the frequency of start-ups and shut-downs introduced to prevent risks of system failure or damage or for other technological reasons. These restrictions are modelled with minimum uptimes Tup_g and minimum downtimes $Tdown_g$ and the two constraints

$$\overline{A}_{g,t} \cdot Tup_g \leq \sum_{\tau=t}^{t+Tup_g-1} \overline{B}_{g,\tau} \qquad \forall(g,t) \qquad (7.4)$$

and

$$\overline{A}_{g,t} \cdot Tdown_g \leq \sum_{\tau=t-Tdown_g}^{t-1} (1 - \overline{B}_{g,\tau}) \qquad \forall(g,t). \qquad (7.5)$$

If the start-up variable $\overline{A}_{g,t}$ has the value 1 in time interval t (i.e., the unit was off-line in time interval $t^{\leftarrow 1}$ and changed its status to on-line in time interval t) then the sum of the operation variables $\overline{B}_{g,\tau}$ over the duration of the minimum uptime Tup_g after t has to be equivalent to Tup_g. Corresponding considerations are valid for the minimum downtime: the operation variable $\overline{B}_{g,\tau}$ has to be 0 for the time period of $Tdown_g$ before a start-up.

Maximum Ramp Rates

To avoid wear due to thermal stress for most thermal power plants, restrictions for load changes apply. These restrictions can be different for different operation points between minimum and maximum load $Pmin_g$ and $Pmax_g$ and different for increasing and decreasing the load. Here we consider one constant maximum ramp rate DP_g. The load $P_{g,t}$ (i.e., the generation output or power) in time interval t cannot differ by more than $\pm DP_g$ from the load $P_{g,t^{\leftarrow 1}}$ in the previous time interval $t^{\leftarrow 1}$ (i.e., $P_{g,t} \leq P_{g,t^{\leftarrow 1}} + DP_g$ and $P_{g,t} \geq P_{g,t^{\leftarrow 1}} - DP_g$). It has to be ensured that a unit can be started or switched off even if DP_g is smaller than the minimum power $Pmin$. In these situations where $\overline{B}_{g,t^{\leftarrow 1}} = 0$ or $\overline{B}_{g,t} = 0$, respectively, the maximum load change is not DP_g but rather $\max(DP_g, Pmin_g)$. This potentially higher load change than DP_g is enabled by the expressions $+(1 - \overline{B}_{g,t^{\leftarrow 1}}) \cdot \max(0, Pmin_g - DP_g)$ and $-(1 - \overline{B}_{g,t}) \cdot \max(0, Pmin_g - DP_g)$

---

[7] $\forall(g,t)$: for all generation units g that are part of the economic dispatch problem and for all time intervals t in the optimisation period.

in equations (7.6) and (7.7), respectively:

$$P_{g,t} \leq P_{g,t-1} + DP_g + (1 - \overline{B}_{g,t-1}) \cdot \max(0, Pmin_g - DP_g) \qquad \forall(g,t), \qquad (7.6)$$

$$P_{g,t} \geq P_{g,t-1} - DP_g - (1 - \overline{B}_{g,t}) \cdot \max(0, Pmin_g - DP_g) \qquad \forall(g,t). \qquad (7.7)$$

In economic dispatch models with high time resolution, it might be necessary to consider generation curves for the start-up process before the minimum stable load $Pmin_g$ is reached as the generation output of a unit in reality does not jump from 0 to $Pmin_g$ instantaneously. The same consideration holds for the shutdown process.

Variable Operation Cost

The aim of economic plant dispatch is the minimisation of the operation costs or the maximisation of the profit margin. In both cases, the variable operation costs C have to be determined. In practice, many components and aspects have to be considered to derive good estimates for variable operation costs and their dependence on plant dispatch. For modelling purposes, we consider two cost components: start-up costs $CA_{g,t}$ and variable operation costs $CP_{g,t} = f_g(P_{g,t})$, which depend on generation output $P_{g,t}$. It is not easy for plant operators to calculate the start-up costs and the operation cost function. It is even more difficult to estimate these costs for generation units of other operators participating in the market for modelling purposes (see Section 7.4). The main aspects that have to be considered are fuel and CO_2 costs, heat rate (i.e., efficiency) and variable maintenance costs. Here we assume that variable start-up costs and the operation cost function $f_g(P_{g,t})$ are known.

In the easiest case, start-up costs are considered to have a constant value cA_g. In this case,

$$CA_{g,t} = cA_g \cdot \overline{A}_{g,t} \qquad \forall(g,t). \qquad (7.8)$$

Generally, the operation cost function $f_g(P_{g,t})$ is a non-linear curve. In most cases, the approximation by a linear function is possible (see Figure 7.9), with

$$CP_{g,t} = cB_g \cdot \overline{B}_{g,t} + cV_g \cdot P_{g,t} \qquad \forall(g,t). \qquad (7.9)$$

The parameter cV_g is the slope of the linear approximation k of the cost function $\mathbf{f}$ in Figure 7.9. Generally, the parameters cA_g, cB_g and cV_g are time dependent. The time dependency is neglected here.

The total operation cost for the modelling horizon can now be derived as

$$C = \sum_{g,t}(CA_{g,t} + CP_{g,t}) \qquad (7.10)$$

or

$$C = \sum_{g,t}(cA_g \cdot \overline{A}_{g,t} + cB_g \cdot \overline{B}_{g,t} + cV_g \cdot P_{g,t}). \qquad (7.11)$$

If the approximation of the operation cost function $f_g(P_{g,t})$ with one single straight line is not sufficient, a piecewise linear approximation is possible to improve accuracy.

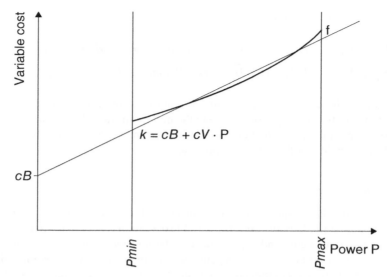

Figure 7.9   Linear approximation of the operation cost function.

Idle Time-Dependent Start-Up Costs

Start-up costs may be dependent on the duration of idleness before the start-up. With longer duration of idleness, the start-up costs increase as the boiler cools down further and more heat is required to warm it up again. Therefore, the approximation equation (7.8) might not be adequate but a more precise depiction is possible with only a few additional equations. Figure 7.10 shows a start-up cost curve.

For every start-up, costs of at least *cAmin* are incurred. For long idle times prior to the start-up, the start-up costs reach *cAmax* asymptotically. After an idle time *Tm* the start-up costs can be considered as constant. If the idle time is increased from $i - 1$ to i time intervals, the start-up costs increase by ΔC_i. For an idle time of τ before a start-up ($Tdown + 1 \leq \tau \leq Tm$), the total costs CAn for this start-up are

$$CAn = cAmin + \sum_{i=Tdown+1}^{\tau} \Delta C_i. \tag{7.12}$$

The fixed component *cAmin* of the start-up costs is allocated to the time interval in which the start-up takes place, the additional component $\sum_{i=Tdown+1}^{\tau} \Delta C_i$ to time intervals prior to the start-up:

- The variable $CA_{g,t}$ is defined as a positive variable (see equation (7.13)). It does not reflect the total costs for one start-up but only the part of the start-up costs allocated to interval t.
- The minimum start-up cost $cAmin_g$ is allocated to the time interval in which the start-up takes place (see equation (7.14)).
- All remaining start-up costs are allocated to the time intervals of the idle time ($\overline{B}_{g,t} = 0$) prior to the start-up that are more than $Tdown_g$ before the start-up and not more than Tm_g before the start-up (see equation (7.15)).

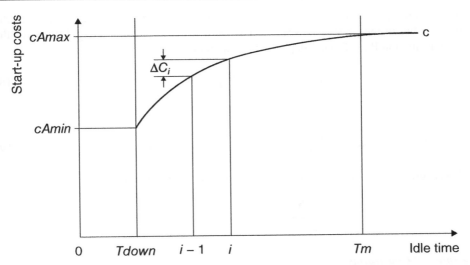

Figure 7.10   Dependence of start-up costs on previous idle time.

- If the unit g is idle in time interval t ($\overline{B}_{g,t} = 0$) and τ time intervals later a start-up occurs for the first time ($Tdown_g \le \tau \le Tm_g$), the variable $CA_{g,t}$ will have the value $\Delta C_{g,\tau}$ of the incremental start-up costs (see equation (7.15)). The term $-\overline{B}_{g,t} \cdot cAmax_g$ in equation (7.15) ensures that the right part of the equation is negative if the unit g is in operation in time interval t ($\overline{B}_{g,t} = 1$). These equations apply if incremental start-up costs $\Delta C_{g,i}$ are decreasing with increasing idle time (see equation (7.16)):

$$CA_{g,t} \ge 0 \qquad \forall(g,t), \tag{7.13}$$

$$CA_{g,t} \ge A_{g,t} \cdot cAmin_g \qquad \forall(g,t), \tag{7.14}$$

$$CA_{g,t} \ge \overline{A}_{g,t+i} \cdot \Delta C_{g,i} - \overline{B}_{g,t} \cdot cAmax_g \qquad \forall(g,t,i)|Tdown_g < i \le Tm_g, \tag{7.15}$$

$$\Delta C_{g,i+1} \le \Delta C_{g,i} \qquad \forall(g,i)|Tdown_g < i < Tm_g. \tag{7.16}$$

Equation (7.11) for total variable costs is now replaced by

$$C = \sum_{g,t}(CA_{g,t} + cB_g \cdot \overline{B}_{g,t} + cV_g \cdot P_{g,t}). \tag{7.17}$$

Reserve Constraints

For system stability reasons, the provision of positive and negative reserve capacity in different qualities is required (see Section 1.5.2). For simplicity reasons, we consider one positive reserve quality with the capacity $Rtotal_t$. An idle unit g ($\overline{B}_{g,t} = 0$) can contribute with a maximum value of RS_g to the reserve. For nuclear power stations and other large thermal power stations, this value is 0. If a unit g is in operation ($\overline{B}_{g,t} = 1$), the maximum reserve contribution is

RB_g as the ramp rate limits the flexibility. Further, the reserve contribution is limited to the difference between the present power $P_{g,t}$ and the maximum power $Pmax_g$. Limits for the reserve contribution $R_{g,t}$ of unit g depend on its operation state:

$$R_{g,t} \leq Pmax_g - P_{g,t} \qquad \forall(g,t) \tag{7.18}$$

and

$$R_{g,t} \leq \overline{B}_{g,t} \cdot RB_g + (1 - \overline{B}_{g,t}) \cdot RS_g \qquad \forall(g,t). \tag{7.19}$$

We also ensure that the sum of all reserve contributions is sufficient by

$$\sum_g R_{g,t} \geq Rtotal \qquad \forall t. \tag{7.20}$$

Time-Integral Constraints

Besides the time-integral constraints imposed by minimum up- and downtimes (equations (7.4) and (7.5)), further time-integral constraints are relevant including annual emission or heat discharge limits to rivers, or take-or-pay contracts for fuels. As an example, we consider upper fuel limits $Fmax_g$ and lower fuel limits $Fmin_g$. We assume that the fuel consumption depends linearly on the number of start-ups, the number of operation hours and the energy produced. To describe this dependency, we introduce linear parameters fA_g, fB_g and fV_g, respectively, and receive as approximation for the cumulative fuel consumption F_g

$$F_g = \sum_t (fA_g \cdot \overline{A}_{g,t} + fB_g \cdot \overline{B}_{g,t} + fV_g \cdot P_{g,t}) \qquad \forall g. \tag{7.21}$$

Upper and lower limits can be formulated as

$$F_g \leq Fmax_g \qquad \forall g \tag{7.22}$$

and

$$F_g \geq Fmin_g \qquad \forall g. \tag{7.23}$$

CHP Constraints

For economic dispatch of CHP plants, not only the electricity generation $P_{g,t}$ but also the heat flow $Q_{g,t}$ have to be considered. In most cases, the ratio between electricity generation and heat flow can be varied to a certain degree. For short-term optimisation, the complete range of possible operation points in a P–Q chart and associated variable costs for each point generally has to be taken into account. Further, there may be a variety of other heat supply and heat storage options that have to be considered. For market models, it is often difficult to find detailed information on CHP systems. The most significant impact of CHP is a reduction of maximum electric power by $PredCHP_{g,t}$, which, in most cases, can be considered dependent on season and weather or, more generally, time dependent (equation (7.24)). Further, a minimum forced generation output might apply, which is also time dependent (equation (7.25)):

$$P_{g,t} \leq Pmax_g - PredCHP_{g,t} \qquad \forall(g,t), \tag{7.24}$$
$$P_{g,t} \geq PminCHP_{g,t} \qquad \forall(g,t). \tag{7.25}$$

For mid-term planning, these approximations may be sufficient as well. If time-integral fuel or emission restrictions exist, additional fuel consumption or emissions due to heat generation $Q_{g,t}$ have to be taken into account.

Objective Functions

The objective of short-term planning after the closure of the day-ahead market is to meet the load L_t at minimum total variable cost C derived by equations (7.11) or (7.17). The load balance equation is

$$\sum_g P_{g,t} \geq L_t \qquad \forall t \tag{7.26}$$

and the objective function[8] is

$$C = \sum_{g,t} (CA_{g,t} + cB_g \cdot \overline{B}_{g,t} + cV_g \cdot P_{g,t}) \stackrel{!}{=} \min. \tag{7.27}$$

The load balance equation (7.26) could be formulated as well as an equality constraint, but the formulation as an inequality constraint is more common as it helps to avoid infeasibility.

For mid-term planning in liquid markets, the objective is to maximise profit margins M between variable generation cost and generation revenues at expected spot market prices S_t. In this case, the load balance equation (7.26) does not apply and the objective function is

$$M = \sum_t \left(S_t \cdot \sum_g P_{g,t} \right) - C \stackrel{!}{=} \max. \tag{7.28}$$

If no reserve constraints (see equation (7.20)) or other constraints affecting more than one power plant apply, the optimisation problem can be decomposed by plant and formulated and solved for each plant separately. This has implications for the optimisation methods that can be used (see Section 7.2.3).

---

[8] To reflect the time value of money, a discount factor d_t can be introduced in the objective function. In this case, equation (7.27) has to be modified to

$$C = \sum_{g,t} \left(d_t \cdot (CA_{g,t} + cB_g \cdot \overline{B}_{g,t} + cV_g \cdot P_{g,t}) \right) \stackrel{!}{=} \min.$$

For simplicity, we neglect the discount factor in all equations in this chapter. If required it can be inserted in the same way into the other objective functions (7.28) and (7.35).

7.2.2 Hydropower Plants

Hydro storage and hydro pumped storage power plants can be dispatched freely within certain technical constraints.[9] While the dispatch of thermal power plants is mainly influenced by specific variable generation costs, the main criteria for the dispatch of hydropower plants is the optimal use of limited reservoir contents.

Here we present a general formulation of the economic dispatch problem for interlinked hydraulic systems (see Figure 7.6). This formulation is also applicable for standalone hydro storage or pumped storage power plants as they can be interpreted as specific (simple) cases of an interlinked hydraulic system. First, we have to describe the topology of the hydraulic system and the main characteristics of its elements.

- Reservoirs r: For modelling purposes we can describe reservoirs by the following parameters and variables:
  - $Vmax_r$: Maximum volume of the reservoir r that can be utilised. For simplicity, we assume that this parameter and most other technical parameters do not depend on time t.
  - $Qin_{r,t}$: Natural inflow into reservoir r in time interval t. In most cases, expected values are used. But for some applications it is necessary to reflect the stochastic nature of this parameter by the use of scenarios (see also Section 2.6.3).
  - $V_{r,t}$: Reservoir content at the end of time interval t (positive variable).
  - $Qr_{r,t}$: Race water flow rate (positive variable). This variable is needed to allow an overflow when the reservoir exceeds the maximum level. There may be restrictions for race water flow rates; however, these restrictions are neglected here.
- Hydropower stations h: These elements in the model can contain pumps as well as turbines. One power station can consist of several separate units, but it is often possible to depict all hydro turbines in one hydropower station as one single model element. Hydropower stations h can be described by:
  - $PTmax_{h,t}$: Maximum available cumulative electric power of the turbines in power station h.
  - $PPmax_{h,t}$: Maximum available cumulative electric power of the pumps in power station h.
  - QT_h: Specific flow rate per electric turbine power output.
  - QP_h: Specific flow rate per electric pump power input.
  - $PT_{h,t}$: Electric turbine power output (positive variable).
  - $PP_{h,t}$: Electric pump power input (positive variable).[10]
- Hydraulic connections between reservoirs r and power stations h: In the following equations, we will use the index $hup(r)$ for all power stations that are located directly above reservoir r and the index $hdown(r)$ for all power stations that are located directly below reservoir r.

Figure 7.11 summarises all variables and parameters for modelling hydropower plants.

In general, maximum power $PTmax_{h,t}$ and specific flow rates QT_h and QP_h depend on the reservoir levels $V_{r,t}$ of the upper and lower reservoir. Further, specific flow rates of turbines

---

[9] Run-of-river hydropower plants are not considered here as their production patterns are only determined by the river flow rates and are not influenced by economic power plant dispatch.

[10] In most cases, pumps can only be switched on or off but not freely regulated to a certain power input. This restriction can be modelled by the introduction of discrete variables. As this restriction is generally not relevant for market models it is neglected here for simplicity reasons.

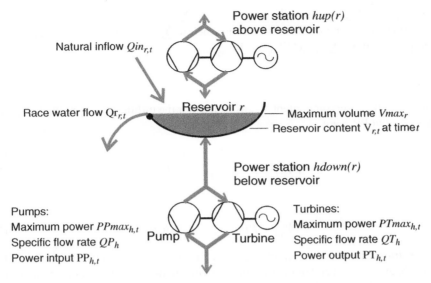

Figure 7.11   Variables and parameters for modelling hydropower plants.

QT_h also depend on the power output $PT_{h,t}$ and the number of turbines in operation (i.e., $QT_h = f(PT_{h,t})$). A similar consideration is valid for pumps. To keep the model formulation linear, we assume constant parameters. While this approximation is generally appropriate for market models, it may be necessary to consider more accurate approximations of these functions (e.g., piecewise linear approximations and operation states of single turbines or pumps) for short-term planning models. Water travel time between reservoirs is also assumed to be negligible. They might be relevant for hydraulic systems with several reservoirs on one river and can be included in a linear model formulation (see Graeber, 2002).

Volume units for the reservoir content and the flow rates (e.g., m^3 and m^3/h) are commonly used, although the use of energy units (e.g., MWh and MW) is also common but can be slightly confusing.

Reservoir Balance

The main equation for hydropower plants is the reservoir balance equation

$$
\begin{aligned}
V_{r,t} = {}& V_{r,t-1} + Qin_{r,t} - Qr_{r,t} \\
& + \sum_{hup(r)} (QT_{hup(r)} \cdot PT_{hup(r),t}) + \sum_{hdown(r)} (QP_{hdown(r)} \cdot PP_{hdown(r),t}) \\
& - \sum_{hdown(r)} (QT_{hdown(r)} \cdot PT_{hdown(r),t}) - \sum_{hup(r)} (QP_{hup(r)} \cdot PP_{hup(r),t}) \\
& \hspace{8cm} \forall (r,t). \quad (7.29)
\end{aligned}
$$

The reservoir content $V_{r,t}$ at the end of time interval t is equivalent to the content at the end of the previous interval $t-1$ plus the natural inflows $Qin_{r,t}$ and inflows from turbines above

$\sum_{hup(r)}(QT_{hup(r)} \cdot PT_{hup(r),t})$ as well as pumps below $\sum_{hdown(r)}(QP_{hdown(r)} \cdot PP_{hdown(r),t})$ minus race water flows $Qr_{r,t}$ and outflows to turbines below $\sum_{hdown(r)}(QT_{hdown(r)} \cdot PT_{hdown(r),t})$ as well as to pumps above $\sum_{hup(r)}(QP_{hup(r)} \cdot PP_{hup(r),t})$.

Constraints

Upper limits for the reservoir content $V_{r,t}$ as well as for the turbine power output $PT_{h,t}$ and the pump power input $PP_{h,t}$ are

$$V_{r,t} \leq Vmax_r \qquad \forall(r,t), \tag{7.30}$$

$$PT_{h,t} \leq PTmax_{h,t} \qquad \forall(h,t) \tag{7.31}$$

and

$$PP_{h,t} \leq PPmax_{h,t} \qquad \forall(h,t). \tag{7.32}$$

Further constraints have to be formulated to fix the reservoir content to its initial and final value at the beginning and end of the modelling period. In the case of daily or weekly reservoir cycles, it is possible to introduce an equation that forces the initial and final reservoir content to be equal instead of fixing it to explicit values. For simplicity reasons, we do not include these constraints for initial and final reservoir contents here.

Not only thermal power plants but also hydropower plants can participate in the provision of positive and negative reserve capacity. Again, for simplicity reasons we consider only one positive reserve quality with the capacity $Rtotal_t$ and assume that all turbines and pumps are flexible enough to contribute to the total free turbine capacity $PTmax_h t - PT_{h,t}$ and the present pump power $PP_{h,t}$ in providing this reserve quality. If thermal as well as hydro units participate in the reserve provision, equation (7.20) is enhanced to

$$\sum_g R_{g,t} + \sum_h (PTmax_h t - PT_{h,t} + PP_{h,t}) \geq Rtotal \qquad \forall t. \tag{7.33}$$

Objective Functions

The objective of short-term planning after the closure of the day-ahead market is to meet the load L_t at minimum total variable cost C of the thermal generation units derived in Section 7.2.1. In the case of a system with thermal and hydro units, these costs remain the same. Therefore, the objective function (7.27) itself remains unchanged. In the load balance equation of the thermal system (7.26), net hydro generation $\sum_h (PT_{h,t} - PP_{h,t})$ has to be added to receive

$$\sum_g P_{g,t} + \sum_h (PT_{h,t} - PP_{h,t}) \geq L_t \qquad \forall t. \tag{7.34}$$

If the objective is to maximise profit margins M, net hydro generation $\sum_h (PT_{h,t} - PP_{h,t})$ has to be added to the objective function (7.28) for the thermal system. We obtain

$$M = \sum_t \left[S_t \cdot \left(\sum_g P_{g,t} + \sum_h (PT_{h,t} - PP_{h,t}) \right) \right] - C \stackrel{!}{=} \max. \tag{7.35}$$

It is possible to decompose this optimisation problem into several smaller problems representing parts of the generation system that can be optimised independently from the rest of the system if no overlapping constraints exist.

7.2.3 Optimisation Methods

To solve the economic power plant dispatch problem, different optimisation methods can be applied. Here we concentrate on the most common methods including linear and mixed integer programming, dynamic programming and decomposition approaches. More comprehensive descriptions can be found in standard operations research or optimisation textbooks (e.g., Chong and Zak (2001); Winston (2003); Hillier and Lieberman (2004)). Examples of the application of optimisation methods for swing option and virtual storage pricing are described in Sections 5.6.1 and 6.3.2.

Linear and Mixed Integer Programming

Linear optimisation problems (LP-problems[11]) consist of a linear objective function and linear constraints. The profit maximisation problem for hydropower plants formulated above is an example of a linear programming problem.

In matrix form with the vector $\mathbf{x}$ of all variables, the parameter vectors $\mathbf{c}$ and $\mathbf{b}$ and the parameter matrix $\mathbf{A}$, the problem can be expressed as

$$\mathbf{c}^T \mathbf{x} \overset{!}{=} \max,$$
$$\mathbf{A}\mathbf{x} \leq \mathbf{b},$$
$$\mathbf{x} \geq 0.$$

To solve LP-problems, several algorithms have been developed. The most common one is the simplex algorithm. Faster but often less robust methods include interior point algorithms. With these algorithms, LP-problems with several million variables can be solved efficiently. Generally, the time required for solving a problem can be predicted reasonably well.

If some of the variables $\mathbf{x}$ are required to be integer values the problem is a *mixed integer programming* (MIP) problem. The problem formulation for our thermal power plants includes binary operation and start-up variables and therefore it is an MIP problem.

MIP problems are generally solved with branch-and-bound or branch-and-cut algorithms. Large-scale MIP problems with a large number of integer variables are difficult to solve. Solver time can increase almost exponentially with the number of binary variables. Slight changes in the data can result in huge changes in required solver time (e.g., a few minutes versus several hours). Therefore, it is very difficult to predict solver times. For this reason, MIP problems are often not solved until a proven optimum is reached. Often, only a feasible solution that is reached within a given time limit or that is within defined distance from the optimum is generated.

Several commercial development environments are available for the efficient formulation and solution of LP or MIP problems.[12] Within these environments, several optimisation algorithms and solvers can be selected.

---

[11] LP: linear programming.
[12] Common development environments include AIMMS, AMPL, GAMS, Ilog OPL Studio, Lindo, Xpress-MP (Dash).

Dynamic Programming

Often, it is not possible to solve large-scale optimisation problems within an acceptable time with standard algorithms. If the problem structure allows decomposition into smaller subproblems which can be solved sequentially, solution times can be reduced significantly. One approach that can be used for power plant dispatch problems is dynamic programming.

An optimisation problem can be solved by dynamic programming algorithms if it has the following characteristics:

- The optimisation problem can be divided into several stages n. In economic power plant dispatch problems, for every time interval a new dispatch decision can be taken. Therefore, every time interval can be considered as a separate stage.
- In every stage n, a finite number of discrete states s_n can be reached. For example, for thermal power plants there could be three relevant operation states: *switched off*, *running at minimum power output* and *running at maximum power output*.
- If the system is at state s_n in stage n a discrete number of decisions $x_{n,s}$ is possible. Every decision will transform the system into a new state s_{n+1} in the next stage $n + 1$. A transition function T can be introduced to link the new state s_{n+1} to the previous state s_n and the decision $x_{n,s}$: $s_{n+1} = T(s_n, x_{n,s})$. For example, if a thermal plant is in the state *running at minimum load* and the decision *shutdown* is taken, then the new state in the next time interval will be *switched off*.
- In all stages n, the optimal sequence of decisions $x_{m,s}$ for this and all later stages ($m \geq n$) does depend on the state s_n in stage n but not on the sequence of decisions $x_{o,s}$ with $o \leq m$ that led to the state s_n. This criterion is called the Bellman principle. If we neglect minumum up- and downtimes and if there are no time-integral constraints, this criterion is satisfied for our dispatch problem. But if there are, for instance, time-integral upper fuel limits for a power plant, the optimal dispatch decision for future time intervals will depend on the remaining fuel and therefore on the path chosen to reach a certain operation state. In this case, the Bellman principle would not be satisfied.

If the contribution of decision $x_{n,s}$ to the global objective is $M(s_n, x_{n,s})$ then the global objective function is $f = \sum_n M(s_n, x_{n,s})$. If we are in stage n at state s_n and we consider all further stages as a subproblem then we have a new objective function $f_{n,s} = \sum_m M(s_m, x_{m,s})$ with $m \geq n$. If the Bellman principle is satisfied then the objective value $f_{n,s}^\star$ of this objective function and the optimal decision $x_{n,s}^\star$ does not depend on decisions in earlier stages. We can formulate

$$f_{n,s}^\star = \max_{x_{m,s}} \left[f_{n,s} \right] \qquad \text{with} \quad m \geq n$$

$$= \max_{x_{n,s}} \left[M(s_n, x_{n,s}) + f_{n+1,s'}^\star \right] \qquad \text{with} \quad s' = T(s_n, x_{n,s})$$

$$= M(s_n, x_{n,s}^\star) + f_{n+1,s'^\star}^\star \qquad \text{with} \quad s'^\star = T(s_n, x_{n,s}^\star).$$

This formulation of the Bellman equation can be used for backward recursively solving a dynamic programming problem.

The following adapted travelling salesman example will illustrate the backward recursive approach of dynamic programming algorithms.

Suppose that a salesman has to travel in five days from town A to town J along the road network shown in Figure 7.12. His profit margins M depend on the towns he visits and on the

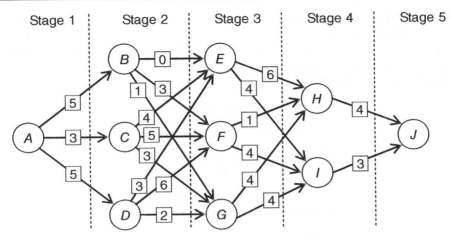

Figure 7.12   Dynamic programming example: road network.

travel expenses to get from one town to the next town. The numbers on the arrows in Figure 7.12 represent the margins he can achieve if he decides to choose one specific path. Owing to the special structure of the problem, we can break it up into five stages n. Stage 1 contains node A, stage 2 contains nodes B, C and D, stage 3 contains node E, F and G, stage 4 contains node H and I, and stage 5 contains node J. The states s in each stage correspond to the names of the nodes. For instance, stage 3 contains states E, F and G. The decisions $x_{n,s}$ that can be taken are to go to the next town along one of the arrows, for example in the first stage *go to B*. The transition matrix $T(s_n, x_{n,s})$ which links a decision $x_{n,s}$ taken in stage n and state s_n with the reached state s_{n+1} in the next stage $n+1$ is straight forward as the name of the decision already contains the state in the next stage. For example if the salesman is in stage $n = 2$ at node $S_2 = C$ and he takes the decision $x_{2,C} = go\ to\ F$, he will end up at node $s_3 = F$. Therefore $T(C, go\ to\ F) = F$.

If we let s denote a node in stage n and z a node in the next stage $n+1$ and let $f_{n,s}^{\star}$ be the maximum profit that can be obtained on a path from node s to the destination node J, we can write

$$f_{n,s}^{\star} = \max_{z} \left[M_{s,z} + f_{n+1,z}^{\star} \right]$$

where $M_{s,z}$ is the profit that can be achieved by the decision to go from s to z. This equation gives us the recursion we need to solve this specific problem. We start at stage 5 where no decision is taken with $f_{5,J}^{\star} = 0$.

For the other stages, we obtain the following.

- *Stage 4:* During stage 4, there are no real decisions to make. The salesman has to go to destination J. So we derive:

  $f_{4,H}^{\star} = 4$ \qquad by going to J,

  $f_{4,I}^{\star} = 3$ \qquad by going to J.

- *Stage 3:* In this stage, there are more choices. To calculate $f_{3,E}^{\star}$, we have to make the following considerations. From E it is possible to go to H or I. The immediate profit of going to H is $M_{E,H} = 6$ and the maximum profit in stage 4 at state H is $f_{4,H}^{\star} = 4$, adding up to a total of 10. The immediate profit of going to I is $M_{E,I} = 4$ and the maximum profit in stage 4 at state I is $f_{4,I}^{\star} = 3$, adding up to a total of 7. Therefore, from E the best decision is to go to H to obtain a total maximum profit of $f_{3,E}^{\star} = 10$.

The following table displays all results:

s_3	$M_{s_3,z_3} + f_{4,z_3}^{\star}$		$f_{3,s_3}^{\star}$	Decision:
	H	I		go to
E	10	7	10	H
F	5	7	7	I
G	8	7	8	H

The same calculations have to be done for the remaining stages.

- *Stage 2:* The following table displays all results for stage 2:

s_2	$M_{s_2,z_2} + f_{3,z_2}^{\star}$			$f_{2,s_2}^{\star}$	Decision:
	E	F	G		go to
B	10	10	9	10	E or F
C	14	12	11	14	E
D	13	13	10	13	E or F

If we are in node B or D in stage 2 it is possible to take two decisions that lead to the same maximum profit. In many cases, only one best solution is required and therefore, most implementations of dynamic programming algorithms record only one of several decisions that lead to identical objective values.

- *Stage 1:* The following table displays all results for stage 1:

s_1	$M_{s_1,z_1} + f_{2,z_1}^{\star}$			$f_{1,s_1}^{\star}$	Decision:
	B	C	D		go to
A	15	17	18	18	D

The optimal value f for this small salesman problem is $f = f_{1,A}^{\star} = 18$ and there are two paths that lead to this result: $A \rightarrow D \rightarrow E \rightarrow H \rightarrow J$ and $A \rightarrow D \rightarrow F \rightarrow I \rightarrow J$.

This small problem could have been solved without more effort by complete enumeration. But for larger problems with discrete decisions, complete enumeration is often not feasible and the benefit of dynamic programming algorithms is significant.

Dynamic programming algorithms can be very efficient at solving economic dispatch problems for single plants with profit maximisation against market prices as objective if they can be formulated without stage-integral constraints. As mentioned above, time intervals can be considered as stages. As time-integral constraints exist for thermal as well as for hydropower plants we have to discuss these constraints and have to find an appropriate definition of states that avoids stage-integral constraints violating the Bellman principle.

To apply dynamic programming to a single thermal power plant g, the following constraints have to be considered.

- *Time-integral fuel or emission constraints:* For example, equations (7.22) or (7.23). If these kinds of constraint exist, the efficient application of dynamic programming algorithms is not straightforward and not necessarily faster than standard LP or MIP algorithms. Therefore, we assume that no such constraints exist.
- *Maximum ramp rates:* Constraints (7.6) and (7.7) introduced by maximum ramp rates can be reflected by defining several reasonable power output levels as separate states but it is not common to consider them in dynamic programming algorithms. If ramp rates are neglected, three relevant power output levels have to be considered: no generation ($P = 0$), generation at minimum load ($P = Pmin$) and generation at maximum load ($P = Pmax$). All other power output levels between minimum and maximum load would lead to identical or lower objective values. Identical objective values occur in the case that market prices S_t are identical with incremental variable costs cV.
- *Minimum up- and downtimes:* Constraints (7.4) and (7.5) can be considered by defining states not only by the power output level but as second characteristic also by the time a plant is already in one of the two operation states *on* or *off*.

With these considerations we can define a dynamic programming problem for the profit optimisation of a thermal power plant in the following way.

- *Stages:* Every time interval t is one stage.
- *States:* A state is defined by the power level and the number of time intervals the plant is already in one of the two operation states *on* or *off*. Let's consider a minimum uptime of $Tup = 2$ and a minumum downtime of $Tdown = 3$. If a continuous operation time of Tup is reached or exceeded, future decisions do not depend on the duration by which Tup is exceeded. Therefore, all these states can be summarised to one state. Similar considerations apply to $Tdown$. Therefore, in our example, we have to consider only the following seven states s at the end of each time interval:

$s_{0/1}$	the plant is switched off for 1 time interval
$s_{0/2}$	the plant is switched off for 2 time intervals
$s_{0/2+}$	the plant is switched off for 3 or more time intervals
$s_{min/1}$	the plant is running at minimum power and is switched on 1 time interval
$s_{min/1+}$	the plant is running at minimum power and is switched on 2 or more time intervals
$s_{max/1}$	the plant is running at maximum power and is switched on 1 time interval
$s_{max/1+}$	the plant is running at maximum power and is switched on 2 or more time intervals.

- *Decision variables:* Generally, in each stage three decisions x have to be considered:

x_0	change to or remain at $P = 0$
x_{min}	change to or remain at $P = Pmin$
x_{max}	change to or remain at $P = Pmax$.

Table 7.3 Dynamic programming transition matrix for thermal power plants

State	Decision x_t					
	x_0		x_{min}		x_{max}	
s_t	$M(t,x_t)$	s_{t+1}	$M(t,x_t)$	s_{t+1}	$M(t,x_t)$	s_{t+1}
$s_{0/1}$	0	$s_{0/2}$	—	—	—	—
$s_{0/2}$	0	$s_{0/2+}$	—	—	—	—
$s_{0/2+}$	0	$s_{0/2+}$	$M1_{t+1} - cA$	$s_{min/1}$	$M2_{t+1} - cA$	$s_{max/1}$
$s_{min/1}$	—	—	$M1_{t+1} +$	$s_{min/1+}$	$M2_{t+1}$	$s_{max/1+}$
$s_{min/1+}$	0	$s_{0/1}$	$M1_{t+1} +$	$s_{min/1+}$	$M2_{t+1}$	$s_{max/1+}$
$s_{max/1}$	—	—	$M1_{t+1} +$	$s_{min/1+}$	$M2_{t+1}$	$s_{max/1+}$
$s_{max/1+}$	0	$s_{0/1}$	$M1_{t+1} +$	$s_{min/1+}$	$M2_{t+1}$	$s_{max/1+}$

But it has to be ensured that only decisions are possible that do not violate minimum up- or downtime constraints as shown in Table 7.3.

- *Profit margins:* The profit $M(t, x_t)$ generated in the stage $t + 1$ depends on the decision x taken in stage t and on the current state s_t. The same cost and profit components as in the objective function (7.28) have to be considered here for every stage t.[13] We can summarise these components in the following way: start-up costs cA; profit margin at minimum load $M1_t = Pmin \cdot (S_t - cV) - cB$; profit margin at maximum load $M2_t = Pmax \cdot (S_t - cV) - cB$.
- *Transition matrix:* The transition matrix shown in Table 7.3 describes the new state s_{t+1} in the next stage reached by decision x_t.

Possible decisions x_t (— indicates an infeasible decision), profit margins $M(t, x_t)$ and the new state s_{t+1} reached are shown in Table 7.3 and illustrated by Figure 7.13. These definitions describe all parameters required to formulate a dynamic programming algorithm for a single thermal power plant.

The economic dispatch problem for single hydropower plants can also be formulated as a dynamic programming problem. In the case of a linear problem formulation as shown in Section 7.2.2, only small performance gains compared with LP algorithms can be expected. But in the case of the depiction of non-linearities, dynamic programming algorithms can exhibit significant advantages compared with standard algorithms. The following considerations can be used.

- *Stages:* For hydropower plants operated on a daily or weekly cycle, every time interval t is one stage. For seasonal reservoirs, it might be appropriate to model one day or one week as one stage. In this case, separate subproblems have to be formulated for every stage, which can be solved, for example with LP algorithms.
- *States:* Water levels of the upper reservoir can be used to describe states. This continuous variable has to be discretised by identifying relevant discrete levels. For daily or weekly reservoir cycles, it is possible to identify water levels by considering possible changes caused by natural inflow and three reasonable decisions: *no generation, generation at maximum load* and *pumping at maximum load* (see below). Beginning at the initial reservoir level it is

---

[13] The time value of money can be considered by optimising discounted profits $d_t \cdot M(t, x_t)$ with d_t representing the discount factor instead of undiscounted profits $M(t, x_t)$.

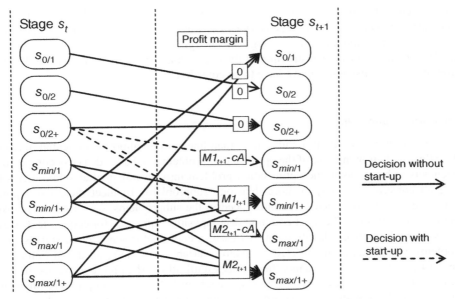

Figure 7.13   Definition of states for thermal power plants.

possible to build a tree to identify all possible states. Upper and lower reservoir levels have to be respected in this process as well as possible race water flows. It is possible to depict the dependency of turbine and pump flow rates on reservoir levels. If a certain number of states (e.g., 20 to 50) are reached in one stage, reservoir levels that are very close to each other are combined to one modelled state to limit the number of states. The resulting approximation is generally small compared with other approximations. The optimal number of modelled states has to be determined by trade-off considerations between computational resources and accuracy. For hydropower plants with seasonal reservoir cycles and daily or weekly stages, states can be formulated by dividing the possible reservoir range into a certain number (e.g., 50 to 100) equidistant stages. Once again this is an approximation.

- *Decision variables:* In the case of daily or weekly reservoir cycles, three decision variables have to be considered:
  - *no generation*
  - *generation at maximum load*
  - *pumping at maximum load.*

In cases where generation or pumping at maximum load would lead to a violation of upper or lower reservoir levels, these decisions have to be interpreted as pumping or generation at maximum possible part-load not to exceed reservoir levels. Maximum generation and pumping load as well as specific flow rates depend on reservoir levels and therefore on the state of the system. This can be depicted in the model formulation.

In the case of seasonal reservoir cycles, decision variables that have to be considered are to reach each of the states possible in the next stage. Possible stages must be within the range of reservoir levels that can be reached by generating or pumping at maximum load for all time intervals between these stages. In each case, the decision would be to choose the optimal path to reach the specific state in the next stage. This small subproblem could be formulated as an LP-problem and solved with standard solvers.

- *Profit margins:* The profit margins for each decision can be calculated equivalent to the hydro part of equation (7.35) as net electricity generation times wholesale market prices. In the case of several time intervals per stage, this margin has to be optimised.
- *Transition matrix:* For the construction of the decision matrix, approximations in the definition of nodes as discussed above have to be considered.

Decomposition Approaches

As most optimisation algorithms exhibit more than linear, often almost exponential, increase of solver time with growing size of the optimisation problem, the basic idea of decomposition approaches is to break down the optimisation problem into several smaller subproblems by relaxing all constraints that span more than one subproblem. To meet these overlapping constraints, additional parameters are introduced in the subproblems, which give incentives to meet these constraints. The most common decomposition approach for economic dispatch problems is the Lagrange relaxation. In this case, a coordinator sends price signals to all subproblems, which can be interpreted as shadow variables for the relaxed constraints (see Figure 7.14). The coordinator adapts these prices until all overlapping constraints are met. While for continuous convex problems this approach leads to a proven optimum, this is not the case for problems with integer constraints, which occur in economic dispatch problems including thermal plants. Therefore, the iteration approach has to be designed carefully to avoid suboptimal solutions as well as convergence problems. For decreasing solution time, it is possible to solve subproblems in parallel on several CPUs. But due to the required coordination effort, the performance gains are often less than expected.

For decomposition approaches, it is necessary to decide carefully where the problem can be divided into subproblems most efficiently. For economic dispatch problems, it is often possible to decompose the problem into several subproblems with reduced number of time intervals (e.g., hours or days) or into sub problems considering only single plants.

If a good approximation of the optimal solution is sufficient, it is possible in some cases to avoid iterative approaches by applying heuristical approaches for fixing variables affected by overlapping constraints. For example, one could divide the dispatch optimisation problem for one thermal power plant with the aim of optimising market revenues into separate monthly subproblems and neglect the small differences to the optimal solution that might occur at the transition from one month to another.

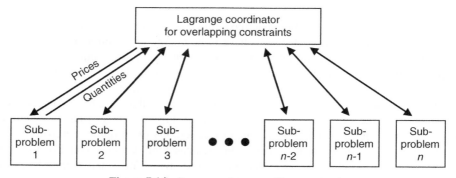

Figure 7.14   Lagrange decomposition approach.

Heuristics

Heuristics are optimisation algorithms that solve optimisation problems quickly but there is no proof that the solution obtained is the optimal solution or that the solution is within a defined distance from the optimal solution for all possible combinations of parameters. Often, heuristics are based on specific structures of an optimisation problem and have to be adapted or abandoned if the problem structure changes. Most decomposition approaches can be considered as heuristics as well.

Heuristics can often be applied to reduce the problem size by fixing variables for which an easy heuristic solution can be derived. The remaining smaller problem can be solved with standard algorithms. For the economic power plant dispatch problem with cost minimisation as objective, one heuristical approach could be the following:

1. Formulate a linear dispatch problem *LDP* that neglects minimum up- and downtimes (constraints (7.4) and (7.5)) as well as start-up costs cA_g and the minimum output constraint (7.2).
2. Solve the *LDP* with a standard LP algorithm. The result can be considered as an approximation of the more complex mixed integer problem *MIDP* without negligence of binary constraints.
3. Analyse the resulting dispatch pattern for every thermal power plant chronologically. If one plant g is continuously in operation for n time intervals before the next shutdown, then if n exceeds the minimum uptime Tup_g by at least x time intervals, one could assume that the power plant would also be dispatched in the precise problem *MIDP* for a number of $n - x$ time intervals in the middle of these n intervals. The operation variables $\overline{B}_{g,t}$ for these $n - x$ time intervals t could be fixed to $\overline{B}_{g,t} = 1$ for step 4. The same consideration could be made for times with continuous power output of 0 that exceed the minimum downtime $Tdown_g$ by at least y time intervals to fix additional binary variables to $\overline{B}_{g,t} = 0$. The parameters x and y would have to be chosen appropriately in such a way that differences between the exact solution of the mixed integer problem *MIDP* and the heuristical solution can be tolerated.
4. Solve the complete mixed integer problem *MIDP* that was simplified by the fixation of binary variables in step 3.

This example algorithm does not result in proven optimal solutions but might be significantly faster than the complete mixed integer problem *MIDP* as the computing times for mixed integer problems depend strongly on the number of binary variables. In Section 7.3.1 the calculation of shadow prices or water values for hydro reservoirs based on price duration curves is explained. This is another example of a heuristical approach.

For economic dispatch problems, it is also possible to apply more general heuristical approaches like simulated annealing or generic algorithms. But in any case, methodological approaches have to be adapted to the specific problem structure to exhibit full performance advantages.

Selecting Appropriate Methods

For practical applications, it is very important to consider carefully all requirements before starting to implement one optimisation approach for the economic power plant dispatch problem. Advantages and disadvantages have to be considered against many, often conflicting aims. The most important aspects are as follows.

- *Level of detail:* It is possible to develop very detailed dispatch models, which consider many features, for example non-linear efficiency curves or time-dependent start-up costs. Higher levels of detail will result in more effort for model development and maintenance as well as longer solution times but also more effort to keep all parameters accurate and correct when the model is applied. Practical experience shows that the last aspect limits the value of very detailed models. For example, efficiencies depend on outside temperature and humidity conditions and on fuel quality. Further, the exact marginal fuel costs are very difficult to determine. Considering these uncertainties, a linear approximation of the efficiency curve might be adequate.

  Appropriate depiction of stochastic parameters, like reservoir inflows or load, is a challenge for many economic dispatch problems. Scenario analysis, that is solving the problem independently for every scenario, can be a first approach. Stochastic programming models, which derive an optimal solution simultaneously considering a large number of scenarios, are more complex. While these approaches are appropriate in some cases, the danger is that certain stochastic aspects are modelled with a very high level of detail while other aspects with similar impacts on the results are modelled with much less detail. Further, uncertainties in the estimation of probability distributions for stochastic parameters have to be considered. As stochastic programming models require more resources for model development and maintenance, and as they are often difficult to solve, it is advisable to analyse potential benefits compared with deterministic approaches carefully. The number of scenarios that can be used for describing stochastic parameters is often very limited due to computational resource limits. Therefore, scenario reduction algorithms are often applied (see Heitsch and Römisch (2003)).

- *Optimality of results:* While standard algorithms often guarantee the optimality of the results, heuristics and decomposition approaches often do not allow us to find the exact optimum. Keeping the uncertainty of several input parameters in mind, the added value of an optimal solution against a good approximation may be minimal in many cases.

- *Solution times:* Decomposition approaches and heuristical approaches can often reduce the solution time dramatically compared with standard algorithms. It is also possible to reduce solution times by using faster commercial solvers, better hardware or by solving several problems in parallel. Heuristical approaches and branch and bound algorithms sometimes have very unpredictable solution times. While a standard algorithm solves a problem predictably within 40 to 60 minutes, a heuristic approach may solve the problem 95% of the time within 15 minutes but require more than 3 hours in a few cases. In this case, the standard algorithm with good predictability of the solution time might be favourable even if the average solution time is much longer.

- *Robustness:* Some optimisation algorithms, especially decomposition approaches or heuristics, are not very robust, that is for certain input parameters the solver does not manage to find a solution although a solution exists that can be found by using another solver. Reasons for this behaviour can be numerical as well as convergency problems. Often, this behaviour is not acceptable. In many cases, even extensive tests with different sets of input parameters do not reveal this behaviour, but in operation it suddenly appears. For critical applications, it may be advisable to develop two different optimisation algorithms to provide a backup for these rare events. Commercial optimisation packages often allow the use of different solvers and can easily provide this kind of algorithmic backup solution.

- *Development resources:* With optimisation packages and standard algorithms it is often possible to implement economic dispatch models within days or weeks by one or two experts. The development resources required for dynamic programming, heuristics and especially decomposition approaches are much higher. For heuristical approaches, it is very difficult to estimate the time needed for development and to judge if the algorithm will lead to the expected results.

- *Flexibility:* In practical application, it is often necessary to modify and adapt economic dispatch models to meet new requirements as electricity markets and regulatory requirements change. While models implemented with optimisation packages can be adapted quickly, it requires a longer time with all other approaches. In the case of heuristics or dynamic programming, it is possible that the algorithm cannot be adapted at all and totally new algorithms have to be developed. One example is the use of dynamic programming algorithms for thermal power plants, which cannot handle time-integral fuel constraints. Therefore, the introduction of these kinds of constraints would require new approaches.

In view of all these aspects, it is advisable to discuss operational requirements as well as advantages and disadvantages of different optimisation approaches intensively before starting the development of a model.

7.3 METHODOLOGICAL APPROACHES

Economic power plant dispatch is the main fundamental aspect for understanding the supply side of electricity markets. Under the common assumption of inelastic demand, it is all we need to simulate wholesale electricity market prices in a competitive market.

There are two main differences between the economic power plant dispatch problem and market models: data availability and model size. While within a company good information is available about the company's own power plants, this information is only partly available for the whole market being modelled. The number of power plants of one company is generally significantly smaller than the total number of power plants participating in the market. Therefore, building market models can be similar to solving economic power plant dispatch problems but is not identical. In this section, we discuss different methodological approaches that can be applied for electricity market modelling.

7.3.1 Merit Order Curve

A merit order curve is a cost-based description of the fundamental supply curve in a market as depicted in Figure 7.1. We first want to consider the basic principles of applying merit order curves for market models[14] and then we will discuss how additional constraints and influencing factors can be reflected.

---

[14] Market models based on merit order curves are also called *stack models.*

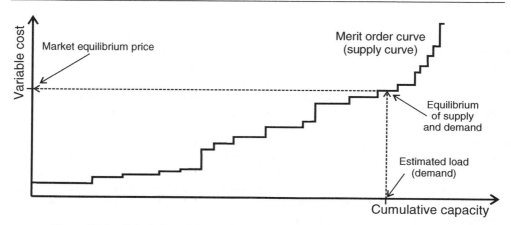

Figure 7.15 Calculation of the market equilibrium price with the merit order curve.

Construction Principles

The merit order curve can be constructed and applied for modelling electricity markets in the following six steps:

1. Estimate the variable operation costs c_i for every power plant i available for electricity generation in a specific market.[15]
2. Estimate the maximum available capacity $Pmax_i$ for every power plant i.
3. Rank all power plants i by variable cost c_i and plot the variable costs over the cumulative available capacity (e.g., see Figure 7.15). This curve is called the *merit order curve* or *supply curve*.
4. Estimate the load (demand) that has to be met in this specific market during a specific time interval.
5. Plot the demand curve as a vertical line at the estimated load on the capacity axis.
6. The position of the intersection of the vertical demand curve with the merit order curve indicates the market equilibrium price, which can be read on the variable cost axis.

   This method generates an estimation for the market equilibrium price for one specific time interval. The repeated application allows the calculation of hourly price curves or average prices for longer periods (e.g., annual base and peak prices). In addition to prices, it is also possible to calculate electricity production, fuel consumption and CO_2 emissions for every power plant, by assuming that all plants with variable costs below the equilibrium price are in operation at maximum available capacity $Pmax_h$, that all plants above equilibrium price are not in operation and that the plant at the equilibrium price is in operation at part load at a level required to meet the remaining gap of the load.

---

[15] Theoretically, it is not the question to estimate variable operation costs but rather to estimate the minimum price at which the dispatcher of a plant is willing to produce electricity for a specific time interval with a specific plant. A dispatcher will have to consider many constraints, although for thermal power plants variable operation costs are a good estimate for this price.

Time Aggregation

Time aggregation is one measure to reduce computation time. Variable costs c_i and available capacity Pmx_i change with time. Therefore, the shape of the merit order curve also changes with time. If no detailed information is available with hourly or daily resolution, the merit order curve can be considered as constant within a longer time period (e.g., one month). In this case, time aggregation based on a load duration curve is possible. The load duration curve is constructed out of a chronological load curve by sorting the load values in descending order. The load duration curve can be approximated by calculating average values for load levels representing several time intervals in the load duration curve (see Figure 7.16). These load levels can all represent an identical number of time intervals or different numbers. In sections where the load duration curve is steeper, more load levels can be introduced to improve the accuracy of results. As a next step all load levels can be intersected with the merit order curve to obtain a price duration curve or an average price for the whole time period. It is also possible to reconstruct chronological load curves by remembering which load level represents which chronological time interval.

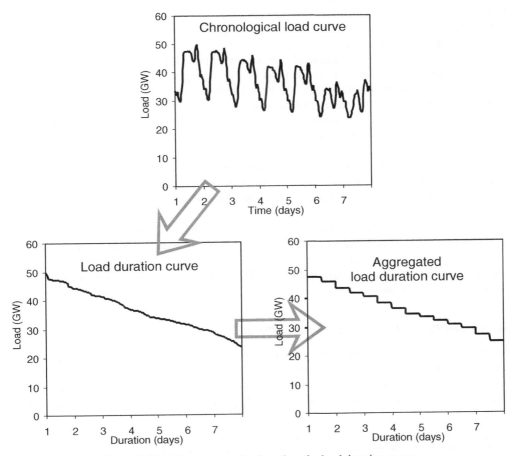

Figure 7.16   Time aggregation based on the load duration curve.

The aggregation of time intervals based on the load duration curves allows depiction of the full range of load levels including extreme peaks by a relatively small number of load levels. Capturing the extreme peaks is quite important as the merit order curve usually becomes very steep at high load levels.

Must-Run Power Plants

Not all power plants are freely dispatchable. Run-of-river hydropower plants and wind turbines produce at zero variable cost only depending on resource availability. There are two approaches for modelling these type of plants.

- *Integration into the merit order curve:* The available capacity of run-of-river hydropower plants, wind turbines and PV plants, which is equivalent to their generation output, can be integrated into merit order curves at zero variable cost. As wind and PV generation is strongly fluctuating, in systems with a substantial amount of wind or PV energy, it is not adequate to use average generation levels for these plants.[16] Therefore, the merit order curve would have to be reconstructed for every individual time interval.
- *Subtraction from the load:* Instead of depicting run-of-river hydropower plants, wind turbines and PV plants in the merit order curve (supply side), their generation can also be considered as reduction of the demand. In this case, chronological generation patterns can be subtracted from chronological load values. Furthermore, it is possible to apply one merit order curve valid for longer time intervals and to aggregate time intervals based on the duration curve of the residual load. Figure 7.17 shows the construction of this duration curve for a system with a substantial amount of fluctuating wind energy generation. The shape of the residual load duration curve is significantly different from the load duration curve. Minimum load levels are lower.

Besides wind and PV energy, there are other renewable generation sources which are dispatched independently of market prices. Most of these technologies have more or less uniform production patterns. Therefore, it is adequate to assume a flat production pattern and apply one of the two methods explained above.

A further category includes CHP plants and must-run plants for network stability. These plants produce at a certain minimum output level, but can increase output up to the full available capacity. They are best depicted by generally two intervals in the merit order curve: one segment for the must-run part at zero variable cost and one segment for the additional available capacity at variable cost.

Storage and Pumped Storage Hydropower Plants

Storage and pumped storage hydropower plants have negligible variable costs, but they cannot simply be depicted at the left-hand side of the merit order curve with full capacity due to limited reservoir capacity and natural inflows. Economic power plant dispatch considers these limits. Generation will be allocated to times with high prices and pumping will occur at times

---

[16] It is adequate to model average generation levels as long as the merit order curve can be considered as linear in the range of wind and PV generation fluctuations. However, close to the maximum cumulative capacity the merit order curve becomes steep and non-linear; an approximation with average generation levels might result in different, less volatile prices.

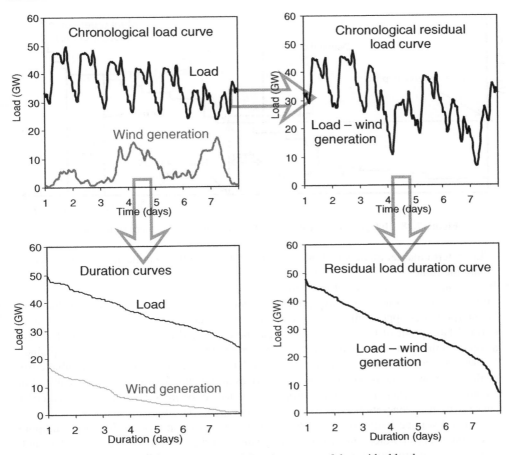

Figure 7.17   Construction of duration curves of the residual load.

of low prices, generally at night or during weekends. Depending on the system being modelled, the reservoir sizes and the time frame under consideration, there are two main approaches for integrating hydropower plants into the merit order approach.

- *Typical generation patterns:* The generation of storage and pumped storage plants has typical daily, weekly and seasonal patterns. Therefore, it is possible to use historical production patterns to derive expected hydro generation patterns. With these production patterns, storage and pumped storage plants can be considered as must-run plants, as described above. Their generation can be subtracted from the load or integrated at zero variable cost into the merit order curve. In the case of huge annual differences in hydro production due to meteorological impacts, it might be necessary to consider different hydrological scenarios.
  This simple approach is suitable for the following purposes:
  - Electricity markets with a small amount of hydro generation from storage and pumped storage.
  - Storage and pumped storage plants with small reservoirs, which are operated in daily or weekly cycles.

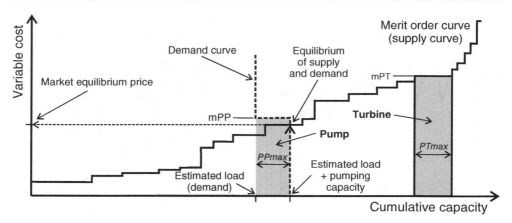

Figure 7.18   Integration of hydro generation capacity into the merit order curve.

– Long-term market models with low time resolution and their application for many years
  into the future.
• *Water values:* Operators of storage hydropower plants have to decide when to use the
  limited reservoir content. For this purpose, water values are calculated. Water values can
  be interpreted as opportunity costs of using reservoir water at a specific time and not at an
  optimal later point of time. Water values can be calculated for reservoir content but also
  as opportunity costs $mPT_{h,t}$ for electricity generated in a hydropower station as explained
  in the next section. These opportunity costs $mPT_{h,t}$ can be compared with variable costs
  of thermal power plants and determine the prices at which a hydropower plant will bid in
  a competitive market. Therefore, hydropower plants can be integrated into the merit order
  curve with their generation capacity $PTmax_{h,t}$ and their opportunity costs $mPT_{h,t}$.
  Pumped storage hydropower plants will pump if market prices are low. For pumping
  based on reservoir water values, opportunity values $mPP_{h,t}$ for pumping can be calculated.
  With these opportunity values the maximum pumping capacity $PPmax_{h,t}$ can be integrated
  into the demand curve. Figure 7.18 depicts the integration of hydro generation capacity into
  the supply curve as well as the integration of pumping capacity into the demand curve.
  This water-value-based approach is suitable for the following purposes:
– Electricity markets with a large amount of hydro generation from storage and pumped
  storage.
– Storage and pumped storage plants with large reservoirs, which are operated in seasonal
  cycles.
– Short-term market models, which focus on several months or weeks, as for this modelling
  horizon electricity prices on the futures market and present reservoir levels can strongly
  influence water values and therefore opportunity costs of hydro generation.

Water Values for Hydropower Plants

Water values are important for calculating the prices at which a hydropower plant bids in a
competitive market. Therefore, we want to consider in more detail how they can be derived.
  Linear optimisation models for economic power plant dispatch can be used for calculating
water values. Most commercial solvers calculate not only optimal values for all variables but

also marginal values for all constraints.[17] In our case, we use the marginal values $mV_{r,t}$ of the reservoir balance equation (7.29), which are the water values of reservoir r at time t.[18] Water values $mV_{r,t}$ stay constant over time unless the reservoir content reaches upper or lower limits. For market offers, the water values have to be converted into opportunity costs $mPT_{h,t}$ for electricity generated in a power station h[19] as

$$mPT_{h,t} = \frac{mV_{rup(h),t} - mV_{rdown(h),t}}{QT_h} \tag{7.36}$$

where $rup(h)$ is the reservoir directly above hydropower plant h, $rdown(h)$ is the reservoir directly below hydropower plant h and QT_h is the specific flow rate per electric turbine power output.

For pumped storage hydropower plants, the calculation of an opportunity value $mPT_{h,t}$ for pumping can be calculated as well using the specific pump flow rate QP_h as

$$mPP_{h,t} = \frac{mV_{rup(h),t} - mV_{rdown(h),t}}{QP_h}. \tag{7.37}$$

For large standalone reservoirs with an annual reservoir cycle, it is possible to derive opportunity costs $mPT_{h,t}$ for turbine generation with a heuristical approach using price duration curves. Assuming the same reservoir level at the beginning and the end of a long time period (e.g., one year), we first calculate the number n_h of full load hours of electricity generation as

$$n_h = \frac{\sum_t Qin_{rup(h),t}}{QT_h \cdot PTmax_h} \tag{7.38}$$

where $Qin_{rup(h),t}$ is the natural inflow and $PTmax_h$ is the maximum generation output.

A price duration curve can be constructed from an hourly price forward curve (see Section 6.1.2) or from hourly stochastic price paths (see Section 6.2) by sorting price values in descending order. The construction principle is the same as for the load duration curves shown in Figure 7.16. As shown in Figure 7.19, a hydropower plant with $n_h = 2000$ full load hours per year will aim to produce in the hours with the 2000 highest prices out of the 8760 hourly prices of one year. The lowest of these prices represents the opportunity costs mPT_h for turbine generation. In the remaining price segments with prices below mPT_h, the hydropower plant will not generate.

The size of the shaded area in Figure 7.19 multiplied by the generation capacity $PTmax_h$ is equivalent to the market revenue M_h of the hydropower plant. We obtain

$$M_h = \sum_{t|S_t > mPT_{h,t}} S_t \cdot PTmax_h. \tag{7.39}$$

---

[17] In the case of mixed integer linear dispatch models, marginal values can be calculated as well. Most solvers fix all integer variables and solve the resulting LP-problem for deriving marginal values. For calculating water values, these marginal values can be used in most cases, while remaining aware of the fact that integer constraints are not reflected.
[18] If a discount factor is used in the objective function the marginal values of the reservoir balance equation are discounted water values.
[19] Often, the opportunity costs $mPT_{h,t}$ for electricity generation are also called water values.

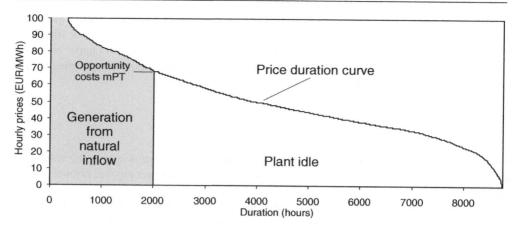

Figure 7.19   Deriving water values from a price duration curve.

This heuristical approach is applicable if the hydro reservoir is large and if no reservoir limits are reached. But it can also be applied for a time period at the end of which a reservoir limit is reached. Most large-scale reservoirs in Europe reach their minimum levels before the snow melt in spring. Therefore, the existing usable reservoir content and the expected inflows before the minimum level is reached determine the quantity of electricity that can be generated in the time before the snow melt.

For pumped storage hydropower plants, it is possible to calculate opportunity costs mPT_h for generating and opportunity values mPP_h for pumping based on price duration curves. Figure 7.20 shows the construction principle under the assumption of identical generation and pumping capacity ($PPmax_h = PTmax_h$), cycle efficiency of $\eta^{\circlearrowleft} = \frac{QP_h}{QT_h} = 75\%$ and $n_h = 2000$ full load hours generation from natural inflow as in the example above. In this case, for every 3 additional hours of generation, 4 hours of pumping are required. The price difference between

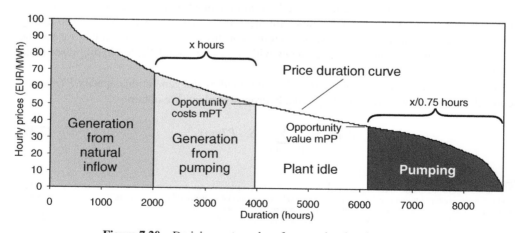

Figure 7.20   Deriving water values from a price duration curve.

the lowest price hour with generation and the highest price hour with pumping has to be 25% to cover cycle losses ($mPP_h = \eta^{\circlearrowleft} \cdot mPT_h$).

In this case, market revenues M_h can be calculated as the difference between the size of the two light shaded areas for generation in Figure 7.20 multiplied by the generation capacity $PTmax_h$ and the dark shaded area for pumping multiplied by the pumping capacity $PPmax_h$. We obtain

$$M_h = \sum_{t|S_t > mPT_{h,t}} S_t \cdot PTmax_h - \sum_{t|S_t < mPP_{h,t}} S_t \cdot PPmax_h. \tag{7.40}$$

Reserve Constraints

Reserve requirements constrain the operation of power plants and therefore impact electricity markets. Quality requirements for reserves vary between grid operators and it is difficult to obtain detailed information on means of reserve provision in different markets. Therefore, we will concentrate here only on the characteristic impacts of reserve provision and differentiate by type.

- *Primary reserve:* This type of reserve has the task of keeping the frequency of the interconnected synchronised AC[20] electricity network at a constant level. As fast reaction times are required it can only be provided by generators in synchronised operation, that is as *spinning reserve*. It is shared in the whole interconnected network, for example in the UCTE network, 3000 MW positive and 3000 MW negative primary reserve are available. Within UCTE the primary reserve capacity is relatively small compared with other reserves and primary reserve can be provided to a certain degree by some thermal or hydropower plants from technically available short-term reserves without imposing any constraints on the longer-term maximum output level. Therefore, it can be neglected for market modelling within UCTE. In smaller synchronised networks such as in England, Scotland and Wales, the primary reserve capacity exceeds the provision potential with no impact and should be considered in the same way as secondary reserve.
- *Secondary reserve:* This type of reserve has the task of keeping the sum of all exchanges of one network control area with all neighbouring areas at the planned level. If generation is too low within one control area, net exports of this area would be lower than planned (or net imports higher than planned) and positive secondary reserve will be requested. With too much generation within a control area, negative reserve will be called for. Most network operators ask for secondary reserve provision with synchronised generators, that is as *spinning reserve* like primary reserve. This means that some of the generating plants cannot operate at full capacity to provide positive reserve and that some of the plants have to operate above minimum generation level to provide negative reserve. If it is known which plants are used for positive secondary reserve provision, the available power reflected in the merit order curve of these plants can be reduced by their contribution to the positive reserve capacity. Part of the available capacity of plants providing negative secondary reserve can be considered as must-run. Therefore, it can be depicted at the left-hand side of the merit order curve with zero variable cost. This zero cost part consists of the minimum power plus

---

[20] Alternating current.

the negative reserve capacity. Hydropower plants are often used for provision of secondary reserves. If hydropower generation is modelled with typical generation patterns based on historical values as described above, one has to consider that they already reflect the impact of reserve provision.

If no information is available on which plants are used for providing secondary reserve, one possible approach is to add the total positive secondary reserve to the load and neglect the negative secondary reserve.

- *Tertiary reserve:* This type of reserve compensates for deviations from planned exchanges between control areas and assists secondary reserve. It has longer activation times and is not provided as spinning reserve. Positive tertiary reserve is often provided with open cycle gas turbines (GTs). These plants have high variable costs and therefore they can normally be found at the right-hand side of the merit order curve. Part of the positive tertiary reserve can also be provided from the demand side by interruptible load. In both cases, positive tertiary reserve has no direct impact on the merit order approach.

If supply capacity limits are reached within a system, positive tertiary reserve capacity has to be considered as reduction of available generation capacity. If no other information on tertiary reserve provision is available, tertiary reserve provided by thermal power plants and hydropower plants within the merit order curve can be allocated to power plants with the highest variable costs on the right side of the merit order curve. It has to be considered that part of the positive tertiary reserve can be provided by interruptible load or by hydro generation depicted by typical production curves.

Negative tertiary reserve can be provided by most synchronised power plants by load reduction or by switching on pumps of pumped storage hydropower plants. In some cases, increasing the load on the demand side is also possible to a certain degree. Like negative secondary reserve it is either possible to neglect negative tertiary reserve in the merit order approach or to reflect it as additional must-run generation.

Time-Integral Constraints

Time-integral constraints cannot be depicted directly in the merit order approach. However, it is possible to estimate their impact and to adjust variable costs c_i of power plants accordingly. Start-up costs and minimum up- and downtimes have the following effects.

During peak load times, when marginal thermal plants are dispatched only for a short period of time, these plants are only dispatched if electricity prices are high enough to cover variable costs as well as start-up costs. This can be reflected by estimating relevant variable costs $c_{i_{peak}}$ of thermal peaking power plants i_{peak} as

$$c_{i_{peak}} = cV_{i_{peak}} + \frac{cB_{i_{peak}}}{Pmax_{i_{peak}}} + \frac{cA_{i_{peak}}}{Tup_{i_{peak}} \cdot Pmax_{i_{peak}}}, \tag{7.41}$$

where $cV_{i_{peak}}$ are incremental variable costs, $cB_{i_{peak}}$ are hourly operation costs, $cA_{i_{peak}}$ are start-up costs and $Tup_{i_{peak}}$ is the minimum uptime.

During low load periods thermal plants are only shut off for short times if this is more economic than operating them at minimum load under consideration of required start-up costs in the case of shutting down. Therefore, baseload thermal plants bid into electricity markets during these periods below their incremental variable costs cV_i. This can be reflected by estimating *for low load periods* relevant variable costs $c_{i_{base}}$ of thermal baseload power plants i_{base} as

$$c_{i_{base}} = cV_{i_{base}} + \frac{cB_{i_{base}}}{Pmin_{i_{base}}} - \frac{cA_{i_{base}}}{Tdown_{i_{base}} \cdot Pmin_{i_{base}}},$$ (7.42)

where $Pmin_{i_{base}}$ is the minimum load of power plant i_{base} and $Tdown_{i_{base}}$ is the minimum down time.

Time-integral minimum or maximum fuel or emission constraints (equations (7.22) and (7.23)) can cause thermal power plants to bid below or above variable costs. A common example in this respect are combined cycle gas turbine (CCGT) power plants with take-or-pay gas contracts. Similar to water values of hydropower plants, opportunity costs for fuel usage are the relevant criteria. They can be derived as marginal values of equations (7.22) or (7.23) or from a price duration curve as described above for hydropower plants.

International Exchange

International exchange can influence electricity prices significantly. It is important to depict them in merit order curve models. The easiest approach is to estimate chronological net import time series, which are subtracted from the load or integrated into the supply curve with zero variable cost. These approaches are equivalent to the one described above for renewable must-run generation.

A more sophisticated approach would be to estimate bid and offer curves of neighbouring market areas and integrate them into the supply and demand curve.

It is also possible to build multi-regional merit order curve models for calculating regional prices using a market splitting or implicit auction approach similar to the algorithm used at Nord Pool, the Scandinavian electricity exchange. For multi-regional or nodal markets, linear programming optimisation approaches as described in Section 7.3.2 should be considered as well. A detailed mathematical description of market splitting can be found in Bompard *et al.* (2003).

Price Peaks Caused by Supply Scarcity

As it is very difficult to estimate available capacity and load exactly, it is also often necessary to extend the merit order curve with virtual capacity to the left to ensure that in the model a match of supply and demand is always possible. For this virtual capacity variable, costs higher than variable costs of the last real power plant in the merit order curve should be assumed.

Variable generation costs even under consideration of start-up costs do not exceed approximately 200 EUR/MWh. However, spot market prices in many markets do exceed this level for several hours every year. In these hours, market participants do not offer all available capacity at short-run marginal costs. This market behaviour can be reflected in the merit order approach by adding a scarcity premium cS_i to the variable costs c_i. There are two approaches for estimating the level of this scarcity premium.

- *Historical price fit:* By comparing historical price duration curves on the spot market with simulation results based on variable costs, it is possible to estimate scarcity premiums cS_i.

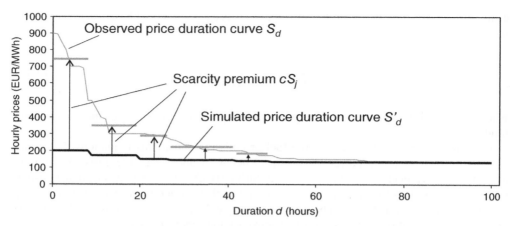

Figure 7.21 Deriving scarcity premiums from historical price duration curves.

It is necessary to determine the marginal plant i_d that is responsible for each simulated price S'_d at duration d in the duration curve. With observed historical prices S_d we can estimate a scarcity premium cS_j for every plant j as

$$cS_j = \frac{\sum_{d|i_d=j} (S_d - S'_d)}{\sum_{d|i_d=j} 1}. \qquad (7.43)$$

Figure 7.21 depicts this approach for the 100 highest hours of an annual price duration curve. To obtain robust results, it is advisable to use several years of historical data. This approach is not only suitable for estimating scarcity premiums but also for adjusting variable costs of the merit order curve in general to historically observed prices.

• *Merit order curve fit to published bid and offer curves at electricity exchanges:* Several electricity exchanges publish hourly cumulative bid and offer curves for the spot market. Figure 7.22(a) depicts one example for bid and offer curves as they can be observed in the spot market. The elasticity of physical supply and possibly also physical demand is reflected in both cumulative offer and bid curves, as generation companies have commitments for physical delivery (short position) when they enter into the spot market. Therefore, incremental physical generation capacity can be reflected in the bid as well as in the offer curve. With our assumption of inelastic demand we can calculate a residual cumulative offer curve in Figure 7.22(b) by adding all decremental bids as incremental offers to the offer curve. If all physical supply capacity was entered into the spot market strictly at variable cost, this residual cumulative offer curve would have exactly the same shape as the merit order curve. In reality this is not the case, as shown in Figure 7.22(c). There can be several reasons for the differences.

– Inaccuracies and uncertainties regarding data and assumptions when deriving the merit order curve.

– Market players with generation assets generally offer capacity only in the expected price range but not all available capacity. This explains the deviation at the left-hand side of Figure 7.22(c).

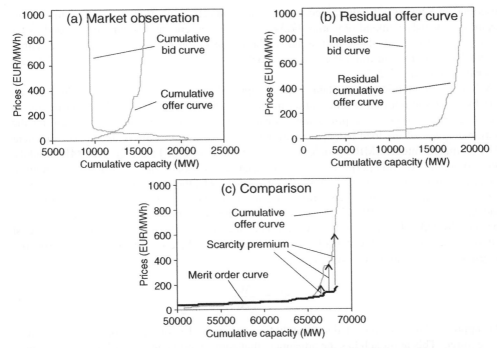

Figure 7.22   Deriving scarcity premiums from observed spot market bid and offer curves.

- Block offers (combined offers for several hours) are not completely reflected in published cumulative bid and offer curves of electricity exchanges.
- Scarcity premiums.
   Scarcity premiums can be estimated from differences between the merit order curve and the cumulative residual offer curve in Figure 7.22(c). It is advisable to use several observed bid and offer curves of carefully selected hours for which high prices have been expected and for which it can be assumed that all available physical supply capacity is reflected.

7.3.2 Optimisation Models

Optimisation models describe the whole market as an economic power plant dispatch problem (see Section 7.2). The optimisation objective is to minimise total system costs for satisfying electricity demand. Market prices can be derived as hourly marginal costs. In this section, we discuss single and multi-regional approaches, possibilities for reducing computation time and how system expansion can be included for long-term analysis.

Single-Region Models

In general, a market model formulated as an optimisation problem for one single region without any transmission constraints is identical to the economic power plant dispatch problem described in Section 7.2 with the cost-minimising objective function (7.27). The main constraint is to satisfy demand (equation (7.34)). All relevant constraints can be included as far as sufficient data is available and as far as the optimisation problem stays solvable within acceptable computation time. Possible approaches for solving the optimisation problem are described in Section 7.2.3.

While for economic power plant dispatch optimal decisions (i.e., optimal values for all variables) are the relevant result, market models try to derive fundamental market prices. In a competitive market, these prices are equivalent to system marginal costs, which are the marginal values of the load balance equation (7.34). Most optimisation algorithms for linear (LP) or mixed integer (MIP) problems compute these values. In the case of MIP models, most solvers fix for this purpose all integer variables and solve the resulting LP-problem to derive marginal values. To calculate system marginal costs, these marginal values can be used, remaining aware that integer constraints are not reflected. Another approach is to vary the load L_t by $\pm\Delta L$ (e.g., ± 100 MW) for a time period τ (e.g., peak or off-peak periods within one month) and solve the optimisation problem for these two cases to obtain the total cost difference ΔC between the two objective values of the objective function (7.27). Specific marginal costs S'_τ can be derived as

$$S'_\tau = \frac{\Delta C}{2\Delta L}. \tag{7.44}$$

This approach has to be repeated separately for every period τ for which marginal cost values are required. This approach has the advantage that start-up costs and other integer constraints are reflected.

Multi-Regional Models

Transmission capacity limits within an interconnected network can create different market areas with different market prices.[21] A nodal model topology is suitable to depict interlinked electricity markets with transmission constraints. Figure 7.23 depicts an example with all relevant system elements.

To build a multi-regional market model, the economic dispatch problem has to be enhanced by regional differentiation for load and generation as well as by modelling transmission capacities. The load balance equation (7.34) has to be formulated for every node n and has to take into account transmission flows $PF_{n,m,t}$ from node n to node m during time interval t. $PF_{n,m,t}$ is a positive variable ($PF_{n,m,t} \geq 0$). We obtain as the nodal load balance equation

$$\sum_{g(n)} P_{g(n),t} + \sum_{h(n)} (PT_{h(n),t} - PP_{h(n),t}) + \sum_m (PF_{m,n,t} - PF_{n,m,t}) \geq L_{n,t} \qquad \forall (n,t), \quad (7.45)$$

where $g(n)$ and $h(n)$ are thermal or hydropower plants located at node n, respectively. $P_{g,t}$ is the power output of a thermal power plant g. $PT_{h,t}$ and $PP_{h,t}$ are the turbine power generation or pumping power consumption of a hydropower plant h, respectively. $L_{n,t}$ is the load at node n during time interval t.

---

[21] Minor transmission constraints within one market area are in many cases solved by redispatching measures paid for by the transmission system operators.

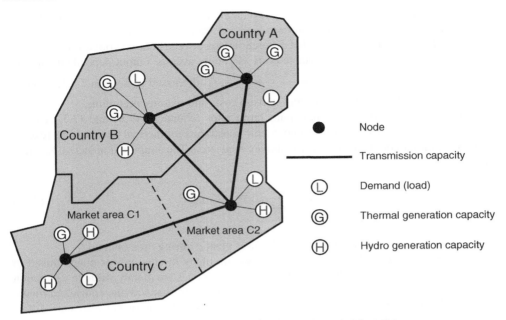

Figure 7.23   Topology example for a multi-regional model.

Transmission flows $PF_{n,m,t}$ are constrained to available transmission capacity $PFmax_{n,m}$ by

$$PF_{n,m,t} \leq PFmax_{n,m} \qquad \forall(n, m, t). \tag{7.46}$$

Transmission capacity is published by grid operators as net transfer capacity (*NTC values*). These values depend on the overall load flow situation as well as on the availability of network elements. Therefore, these values vary with time.

All remaining equations of the economic power plant dispatch problem described in Section 7.2 remain unchanged, including the objective function (7.27). In the same way as for a single regional model, market prices (marginal system costs) at every node n can be derived as marginal values of the nodal load balance equation (7.45).

Model Simplification and Aggregation

Large-scale market models with several hundreds of power plants, with a time horizon of several months or years, with hourly time resolution and with detailed depiction of all elements including integer constraints resemble a huge and complex optimisation problem, which cannot be solved within acceptable time. Therefore, it is necessary to reduce model size and complexity. The possible steps are as follows.

1. *Reducing model detail:* As data quality is generally a limiting factor in market models, model detail can often be reduced without significantly reducing result quality. Integer constraints cause most difficulties while solving the optimisation problem. Therefore, a

first step would be to neglect start-up costs (equation (7.3)), minimum up- and downtimes (equations (7.4) and (7.5)) and minimum load constraints (equation (7.2)). Start-up costs cA_g would be neglected and instead of differentiating between hourly variable costs cB_g and output-dependent incremental variable costs cV_g, only average output-dependent variable costs c_g would be considered: $c_g = \frac{cA_g + cV_g \cdot Pmax_g}{Pmax_g}$. As discussed in Section 7.3.1, variable costs could be adjusted by considering start-up costs and scarcity premiums.

With these simplifications, maximum ramp rates (equations (7.6) and (7.7)) can be neglected as well. This means that all dynamic constraints for thermal power plants (except time-integral fuel or emission constraints) are neglected. The simplified objective function is

$$C = \sum_{g,t} c_g \cdot P_{g,t} \stackrel{!}{=} \min. \tag{7.47}$$

$P_{g,t}$ is the generation output of thermal power plant g during time interval t.

2. *Aggregation of model elements:* In a large system, many thermal power plants linked to one node will have similar characteristics (the relevant ones are mainly variable generation costs). Therefore, it is possible to aggregate several power plants to one equivalent power plant with cumulative capacity and average variable costs. Often, power plants are differentiated by type of fuel and by efficiency (which is derived from the age of a power plant) and aggregated in the resulting clusters. While this is one possible approach, if no detailed data is available it is more advisable to cluster plants by type of fuel and by variable costs as in many cases fuel transport costs vary significantly by plant location.

   Hydro storage and pumped storage power plants with similar ratios between reservoir size and turbine as well as pump capacity can also be aggregated to one equivalent hydropower plant with cumulative capacities. For many systems, it is possible to obtain good results with two to three equivalent hydropower plants (e.g., one hydro storage power plant with annual reservoir cycle, one pumped storage hydropower plant with annual reservoir cycle and one pumped storage hydropower plant with daily or weekly reservoir cycle). Further simplification is possible by depicting hydro generation with typical generation curves, which are derived from historical time series, and by avoiding optimising hydropower dispatch within the market model.

3. *Time aggregation:* Time aggregation is one means of reducing model size. Instead of modelling a long time period in hourly resolution, it is possible to depict different load levels with typical days. Further, it is possible to aggregate hourly time intervals with similar load levels within one day. In the case of a long-term model for several years, it is also possible to model only key years instead of every year. Figure 7.24 depicts an example of a strong aggregation of the time scale used for a long-term model.

   While for long-term modelling strong aggregation of the time scale is adequate, for shorter-term models more detail is required. It is especially important to depict high-load situations and not only medium-load situations. Therefore, it is not adequate to model only one average working day and one average weekend day per month with average wind energy production levels. Instead, it is advisable to include extreme days (e.g., one cold winter day with low wind energy production levels). It is very important to choose the time structure of the model carefully. Cluster analysis or scenario reduction algorithms can be applied to identify similar days, which can be combined into one modelled day.

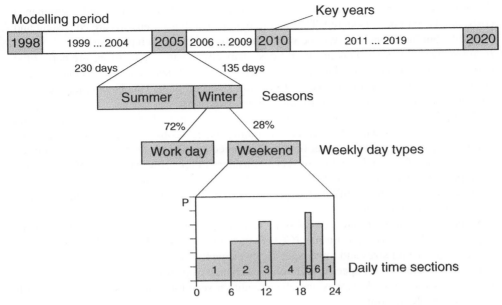

Figure 7.24   Time aggregation example. *Source*: Graeber *et al.* (2005).

4. *Time separation:* Another possibility for reducing model complexity is to separate the problem into smaller subproblems. Besides classical decomposition approaches and iterative,
   coordinated solving of subproblems as described in Section 7.2.3, it is often possible to
   estimate for smaller time periods start and end levels for the time-integral constraints such
   as hydro reservoir levels or emission limits based on historical data. The modelling horizon
   can be, for instance, divided into separate months or seasons. For each of these shorter time
   periods, the optimisation model is solved separately.

System Expansion

So far we have only considered an existing electricity system. This is adequate for modelling
horizons up to a few years into the future. Owing to long lead times for new power plants and
for network capacity expansions, changes in the system can be foreseen for this time period.[22]
For long-term models, it is crucial to have realistic assumptions for capacity additions. There
are two possible approaches for this aspect.

- *Exogeneous capacity expansion:* In this case, capacity expansion is not part of the optimisation problem. Scenarios for system expansion are formulated, for example based on political
  aims for the future fuel mix in the generation system. Development of demand, availability of fuels, availability of sites for new power plants, preferences of single players for

---

[22] This section concentrates on capacity additions. Decommissioning of existing capacity also has to be considered. Generally, technical lifetimes can be estimated. When a power plant reaches this lifetime, it is considered as unavailable thereafter. More detailed considerations would include mothballing of power plants that do not earn their fixed operation and maintenance costs or de-mothballing of power plants. In this section, we will not describe these aspects further, but they can be modelled in a similar way.

different fuels, technological development, investment as well as operation and maintenance costs, etc. have to be considered. The requirement is that these scenarios are consistent and plausible, but in the end they will be very subjective and possibly hard to justify.

- *Indogeneous capacity expansion:* In this case, capacity expansion decisions are part of the optimisation problem. As explained below, additional investment decision variables have to be introduced. The result is a least-cost system expansion plan. This is an objective result but not necessarily a realistic one for the following reasons:
  - The optimisation is based on fixed assumptions about future developments for load, fuel prices, technological development, etc. In reality, expectations for future developments of relevant parameters change over time. For instance, in the year 2000, long-term oil price predictions of \$30/bbl would have been considered high. However, in 2005, long-term oil price predictions of \$40/bbl would have been considered low.
  - Different players have different expectations regarding future developments but also regarding project profitability.
  - Some players have preferences for some technologies, for example small players might prefer combined cycle gas turbine (CCGT) power plants to coal power plants because of their smaller unit sizes and lower specific investment costs.
  - Political incentives for specific technologies change over time.
  - Transmission network expansions often require a very long authorisation process with unpredictable outcome.

To obtain more realistic results, it is common to introduce additional (subjective) constraints that depict minimum requirements for diversity of generation capacity additions.

In the following, we consider basic model enhancements for indogeneous capacity expansion of thermal power plants.[23] For every expansion option, which can be a specific project or just one type of technology with characteristic properties, we introduce as additional model elements new power plants g_{new}. Their installed capacity in year y is described by $\text{Pinst}_{g_{new},y}$.[24] With the availability factor $fa_{g_{new},t}$ we obtain the maximum available capacity $\text{Pmax}_{g_{new},t}$ as

$$\text{Pmax}_{g_{new},t} = fa_{g_{new},t} \cdot \text{Pinst}_{g_{new},y(t)} \qquad \forall (g_{new}, t), \qquad (7.48)$$

where $y(t)$ is the year that belongs to time interval t. For new power plants g_{new}, in equation (7.1) variable $\text{Pmax}_{g_{new},t}$ has to be used instead of parameter $Pmax_g$.

Additional capacity once commissioned is also available in all future years. We introduce

$$\text{Pinst}_{g_{new},t} \geq \text{Pinst}_{g_{new},t'} \qquad \forall (g_{new}, t, t' > t). \qquad (7.49)$$

Besides variable costs $c_{g_{new}}$ (or for more detailed models cost components $cA_{g_{new}}$, $cB_{g_{new}}$ and $cV_{g_{new}}$ as described in Section 7.2.1), we have to consider specific investment costs $cI_{g_{new}}$ as well as specific annual operation and maintenance (O&M) costs $cOM_{g_{new}}$. Both of these parameters are specific values related to installed capacity $\text{Pinst}_{g_{new},t}$. It is important to consider capital costs during the building period and decommissioning costs if they are significant. $cI_{g_{new}}$

---

[23] Expansion of hydropower plants and of transmission capacities can be modelled in a similar way. See Graeber, 2002.
[24] The capacity variable $\text{Pinst}_{g_{new},y}$ can be a discrete variable for given plant sizes or a continuous variable. For reducing model complexity, using continuous variables is recommended.

has to be calculated as net present value of the total investment and decomissioning costs at the time of the commissioning of a new power plant. Specific investment costs $cI_{g_{new}}$ are converted into specific annuities $cY_{g_{new}}$ of the investment costs:

$$cY_{g_{new}} = cI_{g_{new}} \cdot \frac{i \cdot (1+i)^n}{(1+i)^n - 1}. \tag{7.50}$$

In this equation, i is the required rate of return (or capital costs) for the project and n is the technical lifetime of the new power plant. Considering investment costs as annuities $cY_{g_{new}}$ has the advantage that the terminal value at the end of the modelling period for new investments does not have to be considered.

Specific annual O&M costs and annuities have to be added to objective function (7.47) without indogeneous capacity additions. We obtain as new objective function

$$C = \sum_{g,t} c_g \cdot P_{g,t} + \sum_{g_{new},y} \text{Pinst}_{g_{new},y} \cdot (cY_{g_{new}} + cOM_{g_{new}}) \overset{!}{=} \min. \tag{7.51}$$

All other equations of the market model without capacity expansion remain unchanged and have to be applied for existing as well as for new power plants.

For long-term models, one has to decide which currency values to use: *nominal* or *real* values. Nominal values reflect the correct time value of the currency. Real values are inflation-corrected values. Both approaches are possible, but the use of real values has the advantage that some values (e.g., investment costs, O&M costs or fuel costs) can be considered as constant over time.

System marginal costs obtained by market models with indogeneous capacity expansion reflect full costs of new capacity additions. Theoretically, these system marginal costs are the market prices that have to be expected in a competitive market. In the market model results, expansion costs for new peak capacity are allocated to single peak load hours. This leads to very high prices in these hours. As expansion decisions have to be taken many years in advance and future load development stays uncertain, these modelling results are not realistic in current market frameworks. In which way electricity markets will develop further to give efficient incentive for least-cost capacity expansion, especially regarding peaking capacity, is still an open question. Therefore, the main use of long-term models with indogeneous capacity expansion is to derive consistent system expansion scenarios rather than market prices with high time resolution.

7.3.3 System Dynamics

System dynamics is a modelling approach for analysing the behaviour of complex dynamic systems over time. The basic elements of a system dynamics model are stocks, flows and feedback loops. Within feedback loops time delays can occur. Mathematically, a system dynamics model is a set of non-linear coupled differential equations solved as an approximation with discrete time steps. System dynamics models can be implemented in a spreadsheet program but more convenient is the use of special commercial software tools.[25] The aim of

---

[25] Commercial systems dynamics software packages include AnyLogic, CONSIDEO, MapSys, Powersim Studio, Stella and iThink, and Vansim.

system dynamics models is not to provide precise forecasts of future developments, rather, they provide insight into dynamic interdependencies taking into account socio-economic, environmental and technical aspects. They are often used for studying possible impacts of political measures.

System dynamics was developed in the 1960s by Jay W. Forrester at the MIT Sloan School of Management. Its application for energy economical studies has long tradition. One popular example is *The Limits of Growth: A report for the Club of Rome's project on the predicament of mankind* (Meadows *et al.*, 1972).

Long-term electricity market models with indogeneous system expansion based on optimisation approaches as described in Section 7.3.2 depict a long-term steady state of the system. Dynamics that can cause deviations from this steady state, for example overcapacity after a period of high market prices, are not reflected. Studying such long-term dynamic behaviour is the strength of market models based on system dynamics. It allows depiction of a decision-making process for investments in new power plants, but as it is not possible to estimate all required parameters reliably from historical data, most modelling results rely strongly on subjective estimation of required input parameters.

Figure 7.25 depicts the basic structure of a simplified system dynamics electricity market model. The main elements of a system dynamics model are stocks, which are associated with state variables. In our example, we have on the supply side generation capacity under construction Gc and available installed capacity Ga. The demand side consists of the demand variable L. Further elements are flows, which are characterised by flow rates (decision variables). On the demand side, we have the demand growth Lr. Demand and demand growth rate are linked with one feedback loop in the following way:

$$Lr_t = \alpha \cdot L_t, \tag{7.52}$$

$$L_t = L_{t-1} + Lr_{t-1}, \tag{7.53}$$

where α is the load growth rate (e.g., 3% p.a.). Installed generation capacity Ga changes by generation capacity being comissioned Gs and generation capacity being decomissioned Gx:

$$Ga_t = Ga_{t-1} + Gs_{t-1} - Gx_{t-1}, \tag{7.54}$$

$$Gd_t = \beta \cdot Ga_t, \tag{7.55}$$

where β is the decomissioning factor (e.g., 3% of the installed capacity p.a.). Capacity under construction Gc is increased by investment decisions Gd and decreased by comissioned capacity Gs:

$$Gc_t = Gc_{t-1} + Gd_{t-1} - Gs_{t-1}. \tag{7.56}$$

Generation capacity being comissioned Gs depends on investment decisions of past years:

$$Gs_t = Gd_{t-\tau}, \tag{7.57}$$

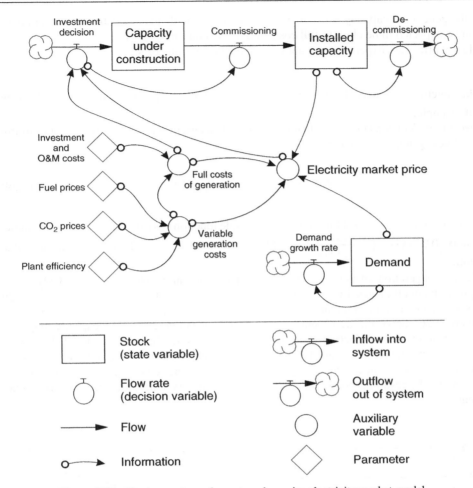

Figure 7.25 Basic structure of a system dynamics electricity market model.

where τ is the construction time, for example 4 years. Electricity market prices S depend on the ratio of demand L to installed capacity Ga as well as on variable generation costs Cv and full costs of generation Cf:

$$S_t = f_1 \left(\frac{L_t}{Ga_t}, Cv, Cf \right).$$

(7.58)

There is no correct function f_1. A plausible function has to be found that considers the following aspects:

- If the ratio of installed capacity to demand increases, electricity market prices can be expected to decrease.

- If the generation capacity is adequate in reference to the demand, electricity market prices can be expected to be close to full costs of new generation capacity.
- Market prices are expected to be above variable generation costs.

The function $f_1 = \max\left[Cf + 3 \cdot \left(\frac{L}{Ga} - 1\right) \cdot (Cf - Cv), Cv\right]$ was used for the following result example.

Investment decisions Gd_t are related to observed electricity market prices as well as to full costs of new generation capacity:

$$Gd_t = f_2(S_t, S_{t-1}, \dots, S_{t-n}, Cf). \tag{7.59}$$

Once again there is no correct function f_2. A plausible function has to be chosen. In our example, $f_2 = \max\left[0.25 \cdot Ga_t \cdot \left(\frac{S_{t-1} + S_{t-2} S_{t-3}}{3 \cdot Cv_t} - 0.8\right), 0\right]$ was used for a model run with annual time resolution.

Variable generation costs Cv can be derived from the parameters fuel prices, CO_2 prices and power plant efficiency. Full costs of generation Cf consist of variable generation costs Cv plus specific operation and maintenance costs as well as capital costs for the investment.

Figure 7.26 shows the development of demand, installed generation capacity, capacity under construction and electricity market prices for this small example model. Phases of high electricity market prices are followed by increased construction activity, which results in overcapacity and reduces electricity prices. Owing to long lead times for new generation investments, the resulting boom and bust cycles have a very long time period of more than 20 years.

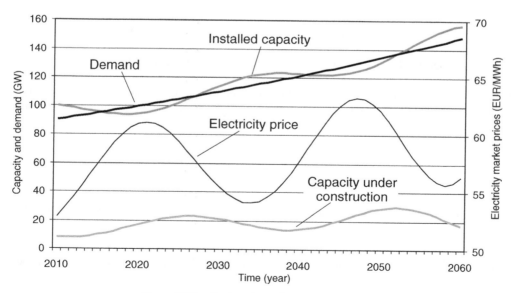

Figure 7.26 System dynamics result example.

A comprehensive review of system dynamics is provided in Sterman (2000). Examples for long-term electricity market models based on system dynamics are Grobbel (1999) and Sanchez *et al.* (2005).

7.3.4 Game Theory

Game theory is a discipline that is used to analyse strategic decision situations, which are characterised by:

- Economic returns of each individual decision maker depend on both their decisions and on the decisions of other decision makers.
- Each decision maker is aware of these interdependencies.
- Each decision maker takes these interdependencies into consideration for their individual decisions.

Game theory can be considered as a generalisation of decision theory which includes multiple decision makers and interdependencies. It is a formal framework for analysing strategic decision situations and provides methods for deriving optimal decisions within this framework.

Similar to system dynamic models, fundamental market models based on game theory do not focus on forecasting, rather, they allow the study of market power and can assist market design and the development of regulatory measures.

The aim of this section is to describe strategic decisions in power markets, provide a short introduction to game theory and explain with some examples how the concepts of game theory can be applied to analyse electricity markets.

Market Power in Electricity Markets

In Section 7.3.1, we assumed independent players that offer their complete generation capacity at short-run marginal costs (variable costs). In reality, generation companies can own more than one power plant and there are situations where it is possible to increase revenues by withholding generation capacity or offering it at prices above short-run marginal costs. In Figure 7.27, all generation capacity of company A is indicated. Under the assumption that company A sells all its capacity at the spot market, based on a merit order curve approach spot market profits M_A can be calculated as the difference between spot market price S and variable generation costs c_{i_A} multiplied by dispatched generation capacities P_{i_A} of all generation assets i_A as

$$M_A = d \cdot \sum P_{i_A} \cdot (S - c_{i_A}) \overset{!}{=} \max$$

$$\text{subject to} \quad \sum_{i_A} P_{i_A} = Ptotal_A$$

$$P_{i_A} \leq Pmax_{i_A}, \tag{7.60}$$

where d is the duration of the time interval under consideration, $Ptotal_A$ is the total generation capacity sold by company A and $Pmax_{i_A}$ is the available generation capacity of power plant i_A.

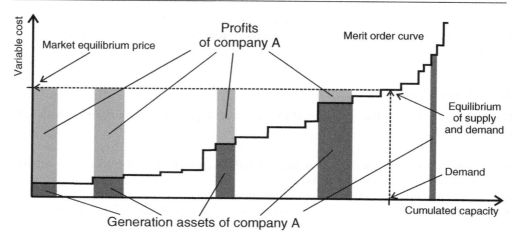

Figure 7.27   Spot market revenues achieved by offering all capacity at variable cost.

Company A's aim is to optimise these revenues M_A. They depend on the chosen offer strategy $\mathcal{O}_A$ ($M_A = f(\mathcal{O}_A)$). If company A assumes that its offers have no impact on market prices S, the optimal strategy is to offer all generation capacity at marginal cost. In this case, all power plants with variable generation costs c_{i_A} below the spot market price S will be dispatched.

In reality, market prices are not inelastic and do depend on strategy $\mathcal{O}_A$. If company A decides to withhold part of its capacity with variable costs below market prices, market prices will increase. As depicted in Figure 7.28, the right part of the merit order curve is shifted to the left-hand side. The new equilibrium of supply and demand moves towards higher prices. The change in revenues for company A is indicated in Figure 7.28: the losses incurred by withholding part of the capacity are outweighed by additional profits generated by plants further left in the merit order. To achieve this impact, it is not necessary to withhold capacity completely. Company A could also offer part of its capacity at prices above spot market so

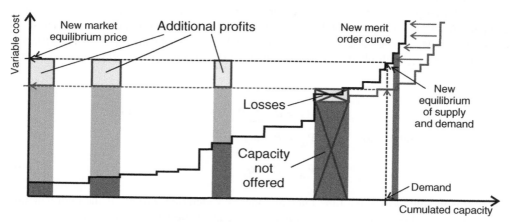

Figure 7.28   Increased spot market profits by withholding capacity.

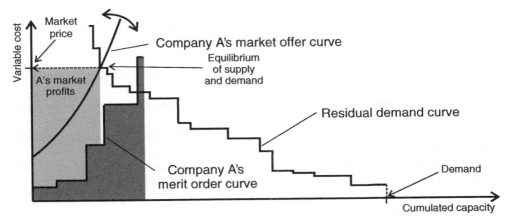

Figure 7.29   Market equilibrium derived from a residual demand curve.

that this capacity moves to the right in the merit order above the intersection of supply and demand.

To analyse the potential for optimising company A's offer strategy $\mathcal{O}_A$, we can draw supply and demand curves from company A's perspective (Figure 7.29). The part of the supply side that can be influenced by company A is characterised by the merit order curve of its generation capacity. The rest of the market is characterised by the residual demand curve. This residual demand curve can be derived by subtracting the merit order curve of all other generation assets in the market from the demand. Company A's profits are the grey area. Its strategy $\mathcal{O}_A$ is expressed by the market offer curve. In a situation of complete information about the residual demand curve in the market, the shape of this offer curve does not play any role as long as it intersects at the same point with the residual demand curve, that is it could also be a vertical line (fixed capacity offer) or a horizontal line (fixed price offer). The optimal strategy $\mathcal{O}_A$ maximises company A's profits. In Figure 7.29, this optimisation problem would be unconstrained as we have assumed inelastic demand and company A's generation capacity is required to meet the assumed demand.

The potential for exerting market power depends on the shape of company A's merit order curve and on the shape of the residual demand curve. The steeper the slope of the residual demand curve at the intersection of supply and demand, the higher the potential for exerting market power. Also, the lower the slope of company A's merit order curve at the intersection of supply and demand, the higher the potential for exerting market power as well. In extreme peak load situations, the potential for increasing profits through exertion of market power is high.

In our example, it is possible for company A to exert market power independently of all other players. Price fixing or quantity fixing together with other companies as in a cartel is not required.

In real electricity markets, exertion of market power and deriving optimal offer strategies are not as easy as in this example, because:

- Only incomplete information is available in the market. This transforms the optimisation of strategy $\mathcal{O}$ into a complex stochastic optimisation problem.

- Most generation companies do not sell all of their electricity generation in the spot market. Part of it is also sold in the forward market or futures to other market participants or is needed for satisfying the final demand of direct customers. This reduces market power, as shown in an example below.
- Spot market prices have additional impact on profits in the case of futures contracts or physical sales or purchase agreements that are indexed to the spot market.
- Spot market prices indirectly impact futures market prices, which impact the longer-term profits of a generation company.
- While electricity demand can be considered as inelastic in the short term, elasticities have to be considered in the longer term.
- Spot market prices above full costs of new generation capacity create investment incentives for new market participants. This reduces market power in the long run.

So far we have only considered the strategic behaviour of one company. Game theory analyses optimal bidding strategies for all market participants. In the following, we will explain the basic concepts of game theory.

Representation of Games

Decision situations (games) studied by game theory are exactly defined mathematical objects consisting of a set of players, a set of strategies available to these players and a specification of profits for each combination of strategies. There are two common ways to represent games.

- *Normal form:* The normal or strategic form usually represents a game by a matrix that shows players, strategies and profits for each combination of strategies. In Table 7.4, we have two generation companies A and B. Each of them has one coal power plant with 100 MW capacity and variable generation costs of 30 EUR/MWh and one gas-fired power plant with 50 MW capacity and variable generation costs of 50 EUR/MWh. For both companies, we consider three strategy options: to generate $P_1 = 50$ MW with the gas power plant, to generate $P_2 = 100$ MW with the coal power plant or to generate $P_3 = 150$ MW with the coal and the gas power plant. These strategies are represented by rows and columns in Table 7.4. The rest of the market consists of competitive players. Market prices $S = f(P_A + P_B)$ are characterised by the residual demand curve depicted in Figure 7.30. The resulting profits for one hour for company A and B are shown as pairs (M_A, M_B) inside the matrix. When a game is represented in nominal form, it is assumed that all players act simultaneously or without knowledge of the decisions of the others.

Table 7.4   Normal form of profit matrix for a two-player, three-strategy game: profits (M_A, M_B) in EUR 1000

		Strategy company B		
		50 MW	100 MW	150 MW
Strategy company A	50 MW	(10,10)	(5,12)	(3,11)
	100 MW	(12,5)	(8,8)	(4,5)
	150 MW	(11,3)	(5,4)	(2,2)

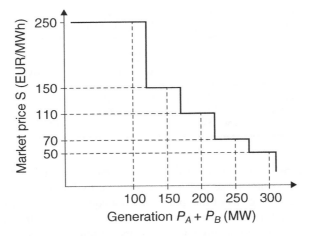

Figure 7.30   Residual demand function for deriving profit matrix.

• *Extensive form:* If a game of several stages exists and players have information about the decisions of other players, a game is usually represented in extensive form. The game is often represented as a tree. Figure 7.31 depicts an example with two stages and two decision options for each stage. Each node (or vertex) represents one point of a decision by one player. Lines out of a node represent possible decisions. Profits are represented at the right of the tree.

   The extensive form can also capture simultaneous decisions or games with incomplete information. A dotted line between two nodes indicates that they are part of the same information set, that is the players do not know at which of these linked nodes they are. In example Figure 7.31, this is the case for nodes N2 and N3.

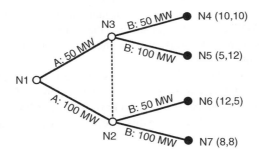

Figure 7.31   Extensive form for a two-player, three-strategy game.

Nash Equilibrium

Game theory can be classified into two areas: *cooperative* and *non-cooperative*. A prerequisite for cooperative game theory is that it is possible for companies to make binding agreements about price fixing or quantity fixing and that these agreements can be enforced. As this is not the case in most real-world situations, we only consider non-cooperative game theory here.

Table 7.5   Nash equilibrium in a two-player,
three-strategy game: profits (M_A, M_B) in EUR 1000

		Strategy company B		
		50 MW	100 MW	150 MW
Strategy	50 MW	(10,10)	(5,12)	(3,11)
company	100 MW	(12,5)	(**8,8**)	(4,5)
A	150 MW	(11,3)	(5,4)	(2,2)

Non-cooperative games can be classified into *zero-sum games* and *non-zero-sum games*. In zero-sum games, the gains of one player are equivalent to the losses of the other players. In non-zero-sum games, the gains of one player are not equivalent to the losses of the other players. As this is the case in most economic situations, we will concentrate on non-zero-sum games. The solution for non-zero-sum games was first formulated by John Nash. The *Nash equilibrium* is the most common solution concept for non-zero-sum non-cooperative games.

In the example described above, the Nash equilibrium is reached when both companies offer 100 MW (see Table 7.5). In a cooperative game, both players would choose 50 MW as this leads to higher profits. But in a non-cooperative situation, this is not a stable situation as each company has an incentive to offer 100 MW regardless of what the other player chooses to offer. A Nash equilibrium is reached if, for a given set of chosen strategies by other players, each player's strategy is an optimal response to those strategies. At a Nash equilibrium it is not possible for one player to increase his profit by changing his strategy assuming that all other players' strategies remain the same.

Mitigation of Market Power through Futures Contracts

Table 7.6 shows the impact of company A and B's strategies on electricity market prices in our example above. If both companies were to offer all their capacity at variable cost the market price would be 50 EUR/MWh, which is equivalent to the competitive equilibrium price. In the oligopoly case where companies A and B optimise their profits, the market price reaches 110 EUR/MWh at the Nash equilibrium.

In most electricity markets, generation companies sell part of their electricity production in advance on the futures or forward markets or to final customers for a fixed price. As an example, we assume that both companies A and B have sold 120 MW of futures contracts for 70 EUR/MWh settled at spot market prices. In this case, they have to pay the difference between

Table 7.6   Electricity market prices depending on
strategies: market prices in EUR/MWh

		Strategy company B		
		50 MW	100 MW	150 MW
Strategy	50 MW	250	150	110
company	100 MW	150	110	70
A	150 MW	110	70	50

Table 7.7 Nash equilibrium with 120 MW futures contracts: profits (M_A, M_B) in EUR 1000

		Strategy company B		
		50 MW	100 MW	150 MW
Strategy	50 MW	(−11.6,−11.6)	(−4.6,0.4)	(1.8,6.5)
company	100 MW	(0.4,4.6)	(3.2,3.2)	(4,5)
A	150 MW	(6.8,−1.8)	(5,4)	**(4.4,4.4)**

the spot market price and the contract price to their counterparts (contract for difference). The resulting profits generated on the spot and on the futures market are shown in Table 7.7. The Nash equilibrium is reached if both companies produce 150 MW, which leads to the competitive market price of 50 EUR/MWh. Similar impacts are seen in the case of forward contracts or other physical sales at fixed prices.

The establishment of liquid futures markets is an effective measure for mitigating market power.

Duopolies

Many electricity markets have an oligopolistic structure with a small number of dominant players. Market strategies in oligopolies can be described as non-cooperative games. As a special case, duopolies with only two strategic players are a common starting point for modelling.

A *Bertrand model* describes a duopoly game in which each company chooses the price S for an identical product at which it is willing to produce. Neglecting output limits, we can assume that the company with lower prices will gain market share and that both companies will have equal output at equal price. If $L = L(S)$ describes how the demand L depends on the market price S and uniform production costs are c, the market profits of company A can be calculated as

$$M_A(S_A, S_B) = \begin{cases} L_A \cdot (S_A - c_A) & \text{if } S_A < S_B \\ \frac{1}{2} \cdot L_A \cdot (S_A - c_A) & \text{if } S_A = S_B \\ 0 & \text{if } S_A > S_B. \end{cases} \tag{7.61}$$

A Bertrand game has a similar structure to our example in Table 7.4. If both companies decide to cooperate, they are able to charge the monopoly price. But each company has an incentive to reduce the price slightly to gain market share and to increase his profit even though he knows that both companies will be worse off if both decide to reduce their price.

A *Cournot model* describes a duopoly game in which each company has to decide on the production quantity for an identical product without knowing the decision of the other player. We assume that P_A and P_B are the output decisions and that $S(P)$ is the inverse demand curve with S being the market price. The profit M_A of company A is

$$M_A(P_A, P_B) = P_A \cdot \left[S(P_A + P_B) - c_A \right]. \tag{7.62}$$

The strategy of each company is to choose his output P_A or P_B to maximise its profits without knowing the output decision of the other company. If both companies have no potential for increasing their profits by unilaterally adjusting their production, the Nash equilibrium is reached.

Nash Equilibrium for Continuous Strategies

In the profit matrices above, we have considered a discrete set of strategies. In economic analysis, it is often more realistic to consider a continuous set $\mathcal{O}$ of strategies like the decision how much to produce in the Cournot model above. As an example, we consider two generation companies $i \in \{A, B\}$. We approximate the merit order curves of both companies with the continuously differentiable function $C_i = P_i^2$ and neglect generation capacity limits. All other market participants are competitive. The residual demand function, which considers the supply and demand of all other market participants without companies A and B, can be described as $P = 180 - 0.5S$. The corresponding inverse demand function is $S = 360 - 2P$. The profit M_i for each company is described as $M_i = S(P_A + P_B) \cdot P_i - P_i^2$. In this equation, the profits of one company depend on the output decision of the other company. Therefore, company A has to conjecture the output decisions P_B of company B in order to optimise its profits and vice versa. If company A takes the conjectured output decision P_B as given, it optimises its profit $M_A(P_A, P_B)$ by adjusting output P_A to reach the first-order condition $\frac{\partial M_A(P_A, P_B)}{\partial P_A} = 0$. This behaviour is called *Cournot behaviour*.

How can company A derive a realistic forecast for P_B? For every output P_B, there is an optimal response $P_A = r_A(P_B)$ for company A and vica versa $P_B = r_B(P_A)$. An equilibrium $(P_A^\star, P_B^\star)$ is reached if $P_A^\star = r_A(P_B^\star)$ and $P_B^\star = r_B(P_A^\star)$. This equilibrium is a Nash equilibrium. It is also called a *Cournot equilibrium* or *Cournot–Nash equilibrium*.

For our example, we first calculate the response functions r_A and r_B. The profit functions are

$$
\begin{aligned}
M_A &= \left[360 - 2(P_A + P_B)\right] \cdot P_A - P_A^2, \\
M_B &= \left[360 - 2(P_A + P_B)\right] \cdot P_B - P_B^2.
\end{aligned}
\tag{7.63}
$$

The first-order conditions under which the profits M_A and M_B are maximised are

$$
\begin{aligned}
\frac{\partial M_A(P_A, P_B)}{\partial P_A} &= 360 - 6P_A - 2P_B = 0, \\
\frac{\partial M_B(P_A, P_B)}{\partial P_B} &= 360 - 6P_B - 2P_A = 0.
\end{aligned}
\tag{7.64}
$$

We obtain as response functions r_A and r_B the following system of equations:

$$
\begin{aligned}
P_A &= r_A(P_B) = 60 - \tfrac{1}{3}P_B, \\
P_B &= r_B(P_A) = 60 - \tfrac{1}{3}P_A.
\end{aligned}
\tag{7.65}
$$

These response functions r_A and r_B are plotted in Figure 7.32. The equilibrium $(P_A^\star, P_B^\star)$ can be derived by solving the system of equations (7.65). In Figure 7.32, it can be derived as

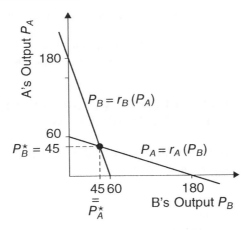

Figure 7.32 Cournot–Nash equilibrium in a duopoly.

the intersection of the two response functions. In our example, we obtain $P_A^\star = P_B^\star = 45$ and $S^\star = 180$. Profits are $M_A^\star = M_B^\star = S^\star \cdot P_i^\star - (P_i^\star)^2 = 180 \cdot 45 - 45^2 = 6075$.

Implementation of Game Theory Models

Electricity market models based on game theory for studying oligopolies can be implemented as a *mixed complementary problem (MCP)*. The supply side can be described by monotonically increasing polynomial costs functions $C_i(P_i)$ for every generation company i as an approximation of their merit order curves (equation (7.66)). Further, maximum output limits have to be respected (equation (7.67)):

$$C_i = c_{i,n}P_i^n + c_{i,n-1}P_i^{n-1} + \cdots + c_{i,2}P_i^2 + c_{i,1}P_i + c_{i,0}, \tag{7.66}$$
$$P_i \le Pmax_i. \tag{7.67}$$

The demand side can be modelled as an inverse linear demand function (7.68) or inverse constant elasticity demand function (7.69), where the dependence of the market price S on the total generation output P is described as

$$S = a - b \cdot P \tag{7.68}$$

or

$$S = \alpha \cdot P^{\frac{1}{\varepsilon}}, \tag{7.69}$$

respectively, where a and b are positive coefficients of the inverse linear demand function, α is a positive coefficient and ε is the demand elasticity, which is negative. As demand elasticities are difficult to derive from historical data, it is suggested to use the residual demand curve instead, which incorporates the supply of all market participants with competitive behaviour.

Based on these continuous supply and demand functions, it is possible to calculate Cournot equilibria with standard solvers for MCP optimisation problems. An example of the application of game theory for analysing electricity markets is presented by Ellersdorfer (2005). General introductions can be found in a number of textbooks, for example Osborne (2003).

7.4 RELEVANT SYSTEM INFORMATION FOR ELECTRICITY MARKET MODELLING

Modelling results are never better than the input data they are based on. Practical modelling experience shows that finding adequate system information is often a crucial point. Key challenges are:

- Attainment of high-quality data.
- Correct interpretation of information.
- Focus on relevant details.
- Good estimates and assumptions for missing or contradictory information.
- Building models with adequate detail with regard to available information.

In this section, we want to describe what type of data is needed for modelling and what additional information can be used for deriving unavailable details. Further, potential sources of information are listed.

7.4.1 Demand Side

Relevant for modelling of the demand side is the load for the whole modelling period with appropriate time resolution. In the case of game-theory-based models, price elasticities of the demand are required.

TSOs, associations of grid operators like UCTE or ENTSO-E, and statistical offices publish load data as historical time series with high time resolutions and, in some cases, also load forecasts. This data, in general, does not describe final customer demand (since it is not metered for all customers in high time resolution); rather, it is derived from generation data of central power stations and from measured transmission flows at the boundaries of transmission areas. Consequently, transmission and distribution losses are included and decentralised generation as well as industrial autogeneration are not included in published load data. Some data sources publish average values, for example hourly values, while other data sources publish real-time data, for example for every full hour. Time stamps associated with metered data for a period can be the beginning or the end of this period. Many grid operators publish data with the end of a period as time stamp, for example an hourly value published for 07:00 is in this case the average value for the period from 06:00 to 07:00. Information about the precise content of published data should be taken into account.

It is important to have consistent model boundaries on the supply and demand side. For example, if load data does not include generation from industrial power plants, these plants must not be included on the supply side of the model either.

Load forecasting is required to derive load values for future time periods. For short-term models, these forecasts can be based on weather forecasts (see Section 4.4). For long-term models with low time resolution, historical load patterns can be used. As load depends strongly on weather conditions, especially in countries where electric heating or air-conditioning are common, scenarios for different weather conditions might be appropriate. One further input parameter is long-term load growth. It might be estimated based on an extrapolation of historical load growth rates or based on forecasts for economic growth and its correlation with load growth. Definition of several scenarios might be adequate.

Price elasticities of electricity demand needed for game-theory-based models are very difficult to obtain. In most countries, real-time pricing is not common and demand can be considered as very inelastic in the short term. In the longer term, elasticities certainly exist as the extent of energy-efficiency measures implemented depends on electricity prices to a certain degree. However, compared with other determinants of electricity demand, price elasticity certainly plays a minor role.

7.4.2 Supply Side

For modelling the supply side of an electricity market, it is necessary to estimate the generation capacity that is offered at a particular price by market participants. As explained in the following sections, different aspects have to be considered for different types of power plants.

In the case of market models based on game theory, it is also necessary to find out who is economically responsible for the dispatch of every power plant. This is not necessarily the owner or operator of a power plant, especially in the case of independent power producers (IPPs) or plants with shared ownership. Based on tolling agreements or similar agreements, contract partners might be in charge of power plant dispatch and exposed to economic results of these decisions.

Conventional Thermal Power Plants

The main required parameters for conventional thermal power plants are available capacity $Pmax_g$ and variable generation costs c_g.

Available generation capacity $Pmax_g$ depends on the following parameters.

- *Nominal net generation capacity:* Unfortunately this figure is not clearly defined, but in most cases it is the maximum electric output of the plant that can be fed into the grid under optimal environmental conditions at the time of commissioning of the plant or after a plant retrofit. In many publications, the gross capacity value can be found. This value is the maximum generator output and does not consider own use within the power plant, for example for coal mills or flue gas cleaning.
- *Age of the power plant:* With increasing age of a power plant, maximum generation output decreases slightly due to wear.
- *Environmental conditions:* Maximum generation output as well as plant efficiency depends on outside conditions, especially on air temperature and humidity, as well as on river temperatures. Maximum generation output increases at lower temperatures. Open cycle gas turbines (GTs) and combined cycle gas turbines (CCGTs) are very sensitive to air temperatures. In summer, their maximum generation output can be several percentage points less than in winter. Many thermal power plants rely on cooling water from rivers and have to respect water usage limits. In summer, flow rates of rivers might be low and river temperatures high. In this case, power plants often face restrictions regarding water withdrawal or heat discharge into rivers. Water withdrawal restrictions are relevant for

power plants with cooling towers, which evaporate substantial amounts of water. Heat discharge restrictions are relevant for power plants with direct cooling. In hot and dry summers, maximum generation output can be restricted severely for days or weeks. In extreme conditions, some power plants cannot be operated at all.

- *Heat demand in combined heat and power plants:* Maximum electricity output of combined heat and power plants depends on the heat demand. Higher heat demand in winter reduces available electrical output and conversely in summer.
- *Power plant maintenance:* Power plants have to be shut down at regular intervals for maintenance. Maintenance intervals depend on plant type, age of the power plant and maintenance strategy of the plant operator. Often, maintenance periods are scheduled several months in advance. Preferred times for maintenance are periods of low demand. Peak demand periods are generally avoided for scheduled maintenance. Owing to a limited number of maintenance groups and incentives to adapt available capacity to system load, most plant operators avoid too many scheduled plant outages for maintenance at the same time. Commonly there are annual maintenance intervals with durations of three to six weeks.

  For market models, it is common to depict power plant maintenance with seasonal patterns unless more detailed information about maintenance schedules is available.
- *Unplanned outages:* Besides planned outages for maintenance, unplanned outages due to failures have to be considered. These outages occur stochastically during the whole year. For market models, it it common to reduce the generation capacity for the whole year by average values for unplanned outages.

Considering all of these aspects, the average available generation capacity of thermal power plants is often only between 80% and 85% of the nominal net generation capacity.

Variable generation costs c_g consist of several components. They can be calculated as

$$
c_g = \frac{(cfuel_f + ctx_f + ctransp_{f,g} + fCO_{2f} \cdot cCO_2) \cdot fc_f}{\eta_g} + cOM_g. \tag{7.70}
$$

The parameters of equation (7.70) are explained below.

- *Fuel prices $cfuel_f$:* In the case of gas and imported coal, fuel prices at trading hubs can be obtained for historical periods as well as for future periods covered by a futures market. In the case of fuels that are traded in other currencies, foreign exchange rates have to be considered. For other fuels like indigenous coal or lignite, it might be more difficult to obtain detailed information and estimates might be required.

  For gas-fired power plants, long-term integrated contracts for fuel and transport are common. Significant deviations from market prices can occur. With further liberalisation of energy markets these differences are likely to disappear.
- *Fuel taxes ctx_f:* In some countries, taxes or other duties apply for fuels used in power stations.
- *Fuel transport costs $ctrans_{f,g}$:* Specific transport costs for fuels f to power station g depend on transport distance and means of transport. In case of coal, the main means are transport by barge or rail. Additional harbour costs and handling costs might apply. In the case of barge transport, water levels on rivers might have an important impact on transport costs as low river levels reduce transport capacity of barges. In the case of gas, fuel transport

costs might have fixed and variable components. Only variable components are relevant for calculating variable generation costs.

- *Calorific value fc_f:* As electric generation output is generally measured in other energy units than fuels, the calorific value of the fuel has to be considered as a conversion factor. In the case of gas, it is important to notice that gas prices are generally related to the higher heating value while power plant efficiencies are sometimes related to the lower heating value. In this case, the difference of approximately 10% between higher and lower heating value has to be considered.
- *Specific CO_2 emissions fCO_{2f} per unit of fuel.*
- *CO_2 emission allowance price cCO_2.*
- *Power plant efficiency η_g:* Relevant for market modelling is the average net efficiency. It can be several percentage points lower than published nominal net efficiencies, which are only achieved by new power plants under optimal environmental conditions and do not reflect aging effects, real environmental conditions and part-load efficiencies. Relevant average efficiencies are often 2–3% lower in absolute terms than nominal net efficiencies. If no detailed information on power plant efficiencies is available, values can be estimated based on power plant age, size and technology.
- *Variable operation and maintenance costs cOM_g:* While labour costs are generally fixed costs, part of the maintenance cost can be allocated to plant operation, which causes wear. Which part of total operation and maintenance costs are considered as variable costs varies from plant operator to operator and can depend on maintenance contracts with external service companies. Auxiliary costs (e.g., for chemicals, ash disposal, water withdrawal or emissions) might apply and have to be considered as well. Transmission tariffs can have a variable component, which has to be considered as variable operation cost.

In the case of aggregated depiction of power plants, cumulative capacities and average cost values can to be used.

Besides available generation capacity $Pmax_g$ and variable generation costs c_g, the following parameters can be relevant for more detailed market models.

- *Time-integral fuel or emission constraints:* For example, take-or-pay quantities in gas contracts.
- *Start-up costs:* Start-up costs consist of fuel costs and operation and maintenance costs allocated to start-ups. Fuel needed for one start-up depends on the idle time before the start-up. Required emission allowances related to fuel usage have to be considered as well. Start-up costs are significant and generally of the same order of magnitude as variable costs for one hour of full-load operation.
- *Minimum up- and downtimes:* These depend on power plant type and power plant size. Smaller plants and more flexible plants generally have lower minimum up- and downtimes. Often, no strict technical constraints exist, rather these constraints are introduced to reduce operational risks. Two to eight hours are common values used for market models.
- *Minimum load constraints:* This parameter depends on power plant type and power plant size. 20% to 40% of the maximum capacity are typical values.
- *Ramp rates:* For models with hourly or lower time resolution, ramp rates can be neglected.
- *Must-run constraints:* For the dispatch of some thermal power plants, must-run constraints due to grid requirements or heat requirements in case of combined heat and power plants have to be considered.

Nuclear Power Plants

The main parameter for nuclear power plants is the available capacity. To derive this parameter, the same considerations as for conventional thermal power plants are valid. Maintenance periods for nuclear power plants are generally longer than for conventional thermal power plants.

Variable costs of nuclear power plants do not play an important role in most electricity markets as they are generally lower than variable costs of thermal power plants and as nuclear power plants are price setting in the market only for a few hours of the year. Depending on the operation and maintenance strategy of plant operators, relevant variable costs range from zero in the case of fixed maintenance intervals with fixed exchange of fuel rods to consideration of opportunity costs in the case of limited remaining fuel quantities until the next scheduled maintenance period. In the latter case, operation patterns are similar to those of a storage hydropower plant with limited reservoir content.

Hydropower Plants

Data required for depicting hydropower plants in electricity market models depends on the modelling approach. In the case of depiction by typical production patterns, historical production patterns and forecasted production patterns are required. In some cases, the consideration of scenarios is adequate to depict fluctuations.

For more detailed modelling approaches, installed pump and turbine capacities, hydrological interconnections of power plants and reservoirs, reservoir volumes, specific pump and turbine flow rates as well as inflows are required. Power plant availabilities have to be considered as expected values. For inflows, a scenario approach might be adequate. In some cases, variable transmission tariffs need to be considered for pumping.

As it is often not possible to depict all hydropower plants in detail, they are commonly depicted as a small number of aggregated hydropower plants.

Renewables

The production of electricity from renewable energy source plants, except storage and pumped storage hydropower plants, depends on resource availability. Therefore, historical production patterns as well as forecasts are required for renewable electricity generation. For short-term modelling, that is for time horizons of several days, generation forecasts based on weather forecasts can be used. For long-term market models, the main challenge is to estimate long-term development of installed capacities of different technologies. Scenarios might be adequate.

Waste-to-energy power plants are considered in some statistics as renewable power plants as well. Their generation pattern is generally a baseload pattern.

7.4.3 Transmission System

The transmission system has two main impacts on electricity markets: transmission capacities between different transmission regions are provided and create interdependencies between these regions, and reserve requirements impact power plant dispatch.

Transfer Capacities

In the case of single-region models, historical exchange patterns and forecasts for future time periods are required to describe exchanges with adjacent regions. For multi-regional market models, net transfer capacities (NTC values) between regions are relevant. NTC values depend on transmission system availability as well as on load flow conditions. Values published by grid operators generally do not include transmission capacity of independently owned and operated DC-links.[26]

Reserve Capacity Requirements

To depict reserve capacity requirements adequately, values for the required capacity in positive and negative directions as well as information on typical means of reserve provision are required. Part of the required reserves may be provided by the supply side.

7.4.4 Historical Data for Backtesting

Backtesting is an important step for market model development. To identify shortcomings of a market model, it is very useful to compare market modelling results for historical time periods with available historical data. Besides electricity market prices, generation by type of fuel as well as CO_2 emission figures are valuable data for this purpose.

7.4.5 Information Sources

Information sources and data availability vary strongly from country to country. Therefore, it is necessary to systematically search for available data. Common information sources are the following.

- *Transmission system operators:* Internet publications, annual reports, statistical yearbooks, press releases, etc.
- *Associations of grid operators:* National associations as well as international associations of grid operators publish data in different ways. In Europe, for instance, ENTSO-E, UCTE and NORDEL publish relevant information on the Internet.
- *Generation companies:* Internet publications, annual reports, environmental reports, power plant brochures, press releases, etc.
- *Energy regulators:* Internet publications and statistical reports.
- *Ministries for energy and environment:* Ministries often publish a political programme for the future development of the electricity system. This information can be relevant for long-term models.
- *Statistical offices:* National and international statistical offices publish different relevant details regarding generation capacity and historical electricity production by fuel. Sometimes statistics on power plant availability, fuel and electricity prices, transport costs, etc. are available.
- *Emissions registries:* National emissions registries or the Community Independent Transaction Log (CITL) publish historical emission data on installation level. This can be useful for backtesting.

---

[26] DC: direct current.

- *Energy exchanges:* Energy exchanges like the EEX or Nord Pool publish relevant system information, for example on power plant availability as well as market results. Fuels and CO_2 emission allowances are traded at exchanges, which publish spot as well as futures market results (see Sections 1.2.2, 1.2.3, 1.3.2, 1.4.2 and 1.6.4).
- *Energy brokers:* Besides price data for electricity, fuels and CO_2 emission allowances, brokers can provide other market information, for example in the form of newsletters or load and wind energy production forecasts.
- *Meteorological offices and private weather services:* Historical weather data as well as forecasts can be obtained by these institutions. In some cases, weather services provide special products like load forecasts and wind energy production forecasts as well.
- *Water authorities:* In some cases, these authorities publish relevant information not only in respect to hydropower generation but also in respect to production constraints of thermal power plants and transport restrictions on rivers.
- *Research institutes:* Many private and public research institutes analyse electricity markets or relevant aspects like renewable energy and can provide research results as well as data. However, it is important to mention that many research institutes have a strong focus on methodological issues and do not necessarily pay attention to data accuracy.
- *Consulting companies:* Specialised consulting companies have detailed knowledge about electricity markets and can provide information, assist market model development and sometimes even sell complete market models including data updates.
- *Financial institutions:* Many investment banks publish reports and other information regarding electricity markets and market participants.
- *Financial data providers:* Besides relevant financial information like exchange rates, these companies also provide market data for electricity and fuel markets.
- *Real-time data providers:* Real-time data about production of large power plants as well as physical electricity flows at major interconnections can be obtained from specialised information providers.
- *Journals and newspapers:* Some relevant information, for example regarding power plant development, can be found in journals specialising in energy or in general newspapers.

A good overview on the European electricity system and relevant companies as well as institutions is provided in Meller *et al.* (2006).

As information content changes rapidly it is important to keep well informed about information availability so as to keep market models as up-to-date and precise as possible.

7.5 APPLICATION OF ELECTRICITY MARKET MODELS

Fundamental electricity market models are widely used in middle offices of energy trading companies, in strategy departments of utilities, in energy consulting companies and at research institutes. Typical areas for the application of market models are the following.

- *Spot markets:* Fundamental market models can assist spot market trading decisions by quantifying price effects of exogenous impacts. Many electricity trading companies use market models for short-term price forecasts up to seven days into the future. Based on these price forecasts it is possible to take short-term trading positions, for example to buy electricity for the next day OTC and sell it later at the auction of the electricity exchange if

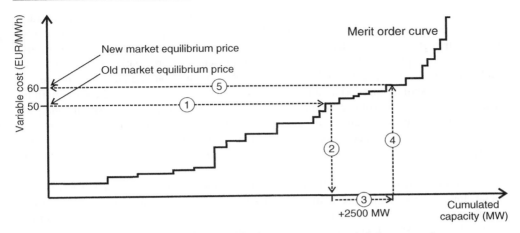

Figure 7.33   Spot market delta analysis based on a merit order approach.

OTC prices are below the expected auction price. To derive good short-term price forecasts, it is important to use all available information for the relevant time period. The main focus should be on load forecasts, forecasts for renewable energy production, especially wind and solar energy production, as well as changes in power plant availability. Significant changes of spot market fuel prices and futures market electricity prices have to be considered as well. The latter impact influences opportunity costs for generation of storage hydropower plants. Rather than deriving absolute prices directly, it is more appropriate to derive price changes that are caused by changes of fundamental factors.

Figure 7.33 shows an illustrative example based on a merit order approach. If the market price for one hour was 50 EUR/MWh, then this value can be used as a starting point to forecast the market price for the same hour of the following day. In the merit order diagram, we can backtrack the load associated with this price following arrows 1 and 2. This load is not necessarily identical to the load forecast for this hour due to model inaccuracies. We consider three changes in fundamental influencing factors from one day to the next:

– Increase of system load by 2000 MW. The forecasts are relevant.
– Increase of wind energy generation by 1000 MW. Again forecasts are relevant.
– Unplanned outage of one nuclear power plant with 1500 MW capacity.

In total, we have a resulting change of +2500 MW (arrow 3). Finally, we can read the new price as forecast for the second day in the merit order diagram. Following arrows 4 and 5 we obtain the value 60 EUR/MWh.

For spot market trading, market models can be used to quantify price risks. If it is possible to quantify uncertainties, for example if there is news that one specific large power plant in the market might be back to service after maintenance the next day or not, it is possible to analyse resulting price impacts. This kind of risk analysis is especially valuable in situations where total demand comes close to available generation capacity and therefore high price peaks could occur.

• *Futures markets:* Electricity market models can provide price forecasts for the time horizon covered by futures markets for electricity and fuels. These forecasts can be used as a basis for the development of trading strategies. While for the spot market fuel and CO_2 prices can be considered as constant from one day to the next, over several months or years significant changes occur. Fundamental market models can be used to quantify the impact of fuel and CO_2 price changes. This consideration leads to the development of multi-commodity trading strategies. If, for instance, market model results indicate that present electricity forward market prices are too high considering present forward market prices for fuels and CO_2, a multi-commodity trading strategy might consist of buying electricity futures or forwards and selling appropriate amounts of coal, gas, oil and CO_2 for the same period. The required estimation of these *appropriate* amounts can be based on a sensitivity analysis using market models to quantify the impact of fuel and CO_2 price changes on electricity market prices. If different commodities are traded in different currencies, foreign exchange contracts should be included in the multi-commodity trading strategy to exclude currency risks.

• *Long-term scenarios*: For long-term decisions, for example the construction of a new power plant, long-term scenarios are required for project evaluation.[27] For long-term scenarios, the focus is not on correct scenarios as there are no correct scenarios as such, but rather on plausible and consistent scenarios. Consistency can be achieved by considering fundamental relations between fuel, CO_2 and electricity prices as shown in Figure 7.2. Fundamental electricity market models can assist in creating consistent scenarios for long-term scenarios. Besides fuel and CO_2 prices, changes in the electricity system, for example the expansion of renewable generation capacity, have to be considered. Often, it is important to build several consistent sets of scenarios to reflect uncertainty in the future development of key influencing factors.

If historical market data is available, this information should be used for calibrating market models. However, the application of electricity market models is not restricted to established electricity markets. For emerging markets without liquid electricity markets, market models can be especially valuable in simulating a future market. However, it is important to note that electricity market models rely on implicit assumptions with regard to electricity market design. If these assumptions are not adequate, for example in the case of regulated electricity prices or oligopolistic market structures, additional approaches might be required for scenario generation.

Electricity market models can provide decision support for the development of trading strategies and for strategic long-term decisions. However, it is important to check the plausibility of market modelling results carefully as inadequate assumptions regarding input data or market design might lead to inadequate results.

7.6   GAS MARKET MODELS

Fundamental gas market models are used for natural gas market analysis with short- to long-term perspectives. While the basic modelling approaches are similar to electricity market models, there are significant differences on the demand as well as on the supply side. Furthermore, transmission and storage of gas play an important role. A clear separation into different market regions, for example on a country-by-country basis, which can then be modelled independently from adjacent regions, is more difficult than in electricity markets. Many market

---

[27] Asset investment decisions are described in more detail in Section 7.8.

regions cannot be modelled separately, as gas import capacities are very significant compared with domestic production capacities. With increasing LNG capacities, even a global gas market is emerging (see Section 1.3.3). Another difference between gas and electricity markets is the impact of regulation. Especially regarding transmission and storage, regulations have significant market impact and differ strongly from country to country. It is necessary to adapt modelling approaches accordingly.

The optimisation of a gas portfolio consisting of delivery contracts, supply contracts, transmission capacities and storage facilities is a task comparable to economic power plant dispatch in the electricity sector. Understanding gas portfolio optimisation is a prerequisite for understanding gas markets. Furthermore, it provides a good starting point for developing gas market models. In the following sections, we describe how these portfolio components can be described for both portfolio optimisation and gas market modelling.

While balancing periods of 15 or 30 minutes are common in electricity markets, balancing periods of one day are common in gas markets.[28] Load fluctuations within one day are compensated by the network operators, which can modulate pipeline pressures within certain ranges (line packing). This flexibility can be used to balance intra-day fluctuations. The delivery period of spot market trades is generally also one day. Therefore, portfolio optimisation is conducted with daily time resolution.

As unit for gas flows, either volume per time or energy per time is used. For modelling, the use of energy units is recommended, as heat rates of gas vary between different parts of the system.

7.6.1 Demand Side

In Europe, natural gas demand has a strong seasonal pattern and is very temperature sensitive in winter. Figure 7.34 shows the cumulative gas demand of most regions in France. Winter peak demand is more than five times the demand of an average summer day. A regular weekly pattern can be observed in summer. In winter, demand is negatively correlated with outside temperature as gas is used predominantly for heating. The weekly demand pattern also exists in winter, but is much less obvious due to the strong temperature sensitivity. This temperature sensitivity results in significant differences in cumulative winter demand between years. Forecast uncertainty, for example on a monthly basis, is much higher for gas demand than for electricity demand. To capture this uncertainty, scenario approaches can be applied.

The gas demand $L_{n,t}$ in region n during time interval t can be modelled as a function of outside temperature τ_t and day type D_t:

$$L_{n,t} = f(\tau_t, D_t). \tag{7.71}$$

Gas supply contracts with large industrial customers often contain interruption clauses. The gas supplier can interrupt the supply with prior notice (e.g., one day in advance). Contracts specifying temperatures below which the supply can be interrupted or specifying a maximum number of days with interruption during the winter period are common. Short-term price elasticity of gas demand has to be considered for portfolio optimisation as well. In industrial

---

[28] In Germany, hourly balancing periods are common. While in some markets the balancing periods are calendar days, in other markets daily periods start at 6 a.m. and last until 6 a.m. the following day.

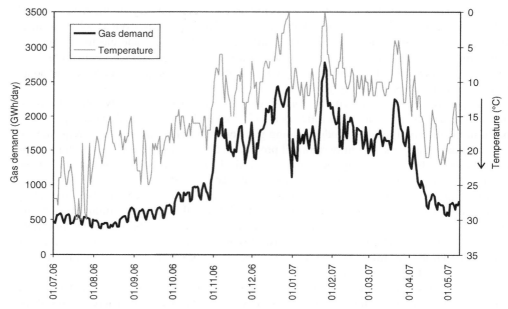

Figure 7.34   Gas demand in France (GDF Network). *Source*: GDF and own calculations.

sectors, fuel oil can be used to substitute natural gas in many applications. In the electricity sector, gas demand depends on the price differential between variable generation costs of coal and gas power plants. The extent of this fuel-switching potential in the electricity sector depends on installed coal and gas generation capacities. In the UK, this potential is very significant for example. Final customer gas demand with or without interruptibility and with or without price elasticity can be part of a gas portfolio. For simplicity reasons, we assume that gas demand $L_{n,t}$ is given.

7.6.2   Supply Side

There are three main sources for natural gas supply.

- *Domestic gas supply:* In Europe, domestic gas sources are mainly located in the North Sea (UK and Norway) and in the Netherlands. Production rates have been declining in recent years with declining remaining resources in the gas fields.
- *Pipeline gas:* Long-distance pipelines are used for the delivery of gas to Europe from Russia and Algeria.
- *Liquified natural gas (LNG):* Pipeline transport is only economically efficient for large quantities and moderate distances. Pipeline construction offshore is much more cost inten-sive than onshore. LNG is transported by ship on routes that would not be economically efficient for pipeline transport. LNG terminals with regasification facilities exist in Europe in several countries including Belgium, France, Italy, Spain and the UK. With declining domestic gas production and technological progress reducing LNG transport costs, LNG is gaining market share.

Natural gas is not a uniform commodity as gas qualities differ from source to source. Domestic gas in the Netherlands and in Germany has a lower calorific value than gas from Norway or Russia. For different gas distributions networks, different gas specifications apply. Most common are L-gas with a calorific value of approximately 10 kWh/m^3 and H-gas with approximately 12 kWh/m^3. The conversion of H-gas to L-gas is possible, but not vice versa. For portfolio optimisation, regions with different gas qualities can be considered as separate portfolios unless conversion capacities from H-gas to L-gas are part of the portfolio. Accordingly, for simplicity, we consider a gas portfolio or gas supply system with only one gas quality.

Economically, gas supply is characterised by high investment costs and negligible variable production costs. The same holds for long-distance gas transport. Variable costs occur only in the form of gas used for transport. For pipeline transport, gas is needed for the operation of compressors. For LNG transport, gas is needed for the liquefaction process and for the regasification process. Furthermore, during sea transport, part of the LNG evaporises (boils off) and part is used as fuel for the ship's engine. In total, approximately 20% losses occur throughout the LNG chain.

While in many electricity markets wholesale market prices are based on short-run marginal system costs, this cannot be the case in gas markets as short-run marginal production costs are negligible. Instead of variable production costs, gas import conditions have to be considered to understand market prices. Gas imports are based predominantly on long-term contracts with oil indexation. Oil indexation was introduced to ensure economic viability of gas in comparison with gasoil or fuel oil. Final customer gas prices are calculated to ensure that the use of gas is slightly cheaper than oil for the same application. In some cases, coal-indexed prices are also found. With this direct or indirect indexation on the supply and demand side, gas import companies remain without any major price or volume risks. Gas producers bear the price risk but no major volume risk. For more details on indexed gas contracts, see Section 1.3.2.

Import contracts c are characterised by the following parameters.

- *Contract price:* The contract price $p_{c,t}$ is generally variable and indexed to different oil product or other commodity prices $p_{i,t}$. Often, a time lag Δt and averaging of price indices over several months applies (see Section 1.3.2). The indexed price can be expressed as

$$p_{c,t} = p_{oc} + \sum_i \left(a_{i,c} \cdot (p_{i,t-\Delta t} - p_{i,t_o}) \right), \qquad (7.72)$$

where t_o is the reference time, p_{oc} is the reference price at time t_o and $a_{i,c}$ are weights for different price indices $p_{i,t}$.
- *Contract duration:* In Europe, contract durations between 10 and 40 years are common for long-term import contracts.
- *Contract volume:* The contract volume Q_c is generally defined as annual maximum quantity.
- *Take-or-pay volume:* Many import contracts are flexible with regard to the annual volume. The take-or-pay volume $Qmin_c$ is the minimum volume that has to be paid for, for example 80% of the contract volume. In addition, some contracts define take-or-pay volumes for the summer period. Carry-forward clauses are also common. They allow the importer to shift a limited volume of gas to be used to the following year if he falls below the take-or-pay limit in one year.

- *Swing:* Within one year, the import can be flexible within certain ranges. This flexibility is called *swing*. The maximum daily volume $Qmaxd_c$ is generally limited. For example, a swing of 20% would allow the importing company to receive up to $Qmaxd_c = 1.20 \cdot Q_c/365$ of gas per day.

We introduce the positive flow variable $QC_{c,t}$ for long-term contracts. Assuming daily time resolution and an annual modelling period, we can formulate the following constraints for imports:

The daily flow $QC_{c,t}$ is limited by the maximum swing to

$$QC_{c,t} \leq Qmaxd_c \qquad \forall(c,t).^{29} \tag{7.73}$$

The annual volume is constrained to the contract volume Q_c. We obtain

$$\sum_t QC_{c,t} \leq Q_c \qquad \forall c. \tag{7.74}$$

The lower limit for the annual volume is given by the take-or-pay volume $Qmin_c$. We obtain

$$\sum_t QC_{c,t} \geq Qmin_c \qquad \forall c, \tag{7.75}$$

assuming that no carry forward is possible.[30]

Long-term gas supply is delivered to a delivery point n specified in the contract. We denote by the index $c(n)$ all long-term contracts c that have node n as their delivery point.

As an additional supply option we assume a liquid spot market in some regions or at some trading hubs or balancing points n. Relevant for modelling is the spot market price $S_{n,t}$. For future time periods, it can be derived from a price forward curve or scenario. The volume traded at the spot market is described by variable $QSp_{n,t}$. In the case of spot market purchases, $QSp_{n,t}$ is positive; in the case of sales, it is negative. To reflect limited market liquidity in some regions, the parameter $QSpmax_{n,t}$ is introduced as an upper limit for sales and purchases. As constraints we obtain

$$QSp_{n,t} \leq QSpmax_{n,t} \qquad \forall(n,t) \tag{7.76}$$

and

$$QSp_{n,t} \geq -QSpmax_{n,t} \qquad \forall(n,t). \tag{7.77}$$

In most cases, the import of LNG is also based on long-term contracts, but in some cases LNG imports are more flexible and transport can be diverted to regions with higher gas prices. With increasing LNG volumes and sufficient flexibility in the LNG chain, regional gas markets

---

[29] $\forall(c,t)$: for all long-term contracts c in the gas portfolio and for all time intervals t in the optimisation period.
[30] It would also be possible to take less volume than the take-or-pay volume and still pay for this minimum volume. To reflect this theoretical possibility, we formulate the node balance equation (7.85) as a lower bound for gas arriving at a node.

will become more and more linked to each other. LNG imports can either be modelled as long-term contracts c or, in the case of flexible destinations, as sources with variable volume and prices. These prices can be derived from the price forward curve at alternative destinations under consideration of differences in transport costs.

7.6.3 Transport

Transmission is regulated in different ways in different countries. Most relevant for portfolio optimisation and market model development are the rules for capacity allocation to market participants. Most common are entry/exit systems. Different entry and exit points are defined for every market area. Entry capacity is required for gas flows entering a market region and exit capacity is required for gas flows exiting a market region. Within the region, gas can be transported freely. Physical bottlenecks within a region which might occur are resolved by the system operator, for example by purchasing load flow commitments. There are two predominant means for allocating entry and exit capacities to market participants: auctions and allocations based on a first-come, first-served basis with fixed published tariffs. Capacity allocation is possible for different time frames. Part of the capacity allocation can be long term, that is for several years, part of it on an annual, quarterly or monthly basis and part of it day ahead. Use-it-or-lose-it rules may apply. These allow system operators to offer to the market once again capacity not nominated the day ahead. In some markets, a secondary transport capacity market starts to develop. Capacity can be allocated as firm or as interruptible capacity. Generally, different tariffs apply to firm and to interruptible capacity. In the case of interruptible tariffs, a priority order is established on a first-come, first-serve basis. Modelling interruptible capacity in portfolio optimisation or in a risk-control context requires estimation of the probability of interruptions, which proves difficult.

We use a nodal model structure to depict the gas supply system's topology. Figure 7.35 shows an example of the representation of a gas transport network. Every market area contains one node. Trading hubs that are adjacent to several market areas have to be considered as separate nodes.

We introduce the flow variable $\text{QF}_{n,m,t}$ for flows from node n to node m during time interval t. $\text{QF}_{n,m,t}$ is a positive variable.

As an example, we assume that firm transport capacity (exit and entry capacity) from node n to node m is available on an annual basis. The combined entry and exit tariffs are $TC_{n,m}$. The flow $\text{QF}_{n,m,t}$ is constrained by the capacity variable $\text{CF}_{n,m}$:

$$\text{QF}_{n,m,t} \leq \text{CF}_{n,m} \qquad \forall(n, m, t). \tag{7.78}$$

7.6.4 Storage

As the flexibility provided by the swing of import contracts is limited, gas storage facilities are used to compensate changes in gas demand. There are four main types of gas storage facility

- *Depleted gas or oil fields or aquifers:* These storage facilities have small injection and withdrawal rates in relation to the storage volume. They are used mainly for seasonal storage.
- *Underground caverns:* These are constructed predominantly in underground salt domes by washing out part of the salt to create a cavern. Specific injection and withdrawal rates are

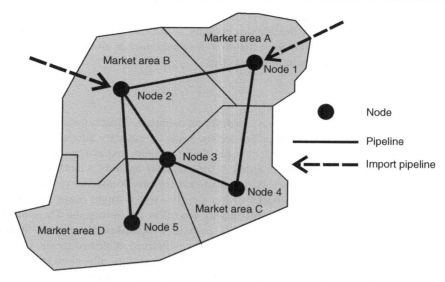

Figure 7.35   Nodal gas transport system topology.

higher than for depleted oil or gas fields or aquifers. Underground caverns are used for weekly or monthly storage rather than for seasonal storage.

- *LNG storage facilities:* Liquefied natural gas can be stored in tanks. LNG storage facilities are predominantly located at LNG terminals.
- *Pipeline storage facilities:* The pipeline system itself can be used as a storage facility to a certain degree by pressure variation (line packing). Additional flexibility can be created by increasing pipeline diameters or by additional pipelines, often arranged in a square pattern. Pipeline storage is predominantly used in the distribution system for intra-day balancing.

Access to storage facilities is regulated in some markets. Tariffs and conditions differ significantly. Besides using physical storage facilities, virtual storage products can be obtained in the gas market. Virtual gas storage is a complex product that allows the buyer to inject gas into and withdraw gas from a virtual gas account. He delivers gas to the seller or receives gas from the seller, respectively, based on daily nominations. For physical storage facilities, many constraints have to be considered, including the volume dependency of injection and withdrawal rates, the gas required for operation of the compressor, maintenance and unplanned outages. Virtual storage products have fewer constraints.

Physical storage facilities have many non-linear constraints. Here we consider constraints relevant for underground gas storage facilities (depleted oil or gas fields, aquifers or caverns). To reduce complexity, we describe a linear approximation to these constraints and neglect maintenance and other causes of unavailability. We introduce the following parameters and variables.

- $Vmax_s$: Maximum gas content of the storage s. The minimum content is assumed to be 0.
- $V_{s,t}$: Storage content at the end of time interval t (positive variable).
- $QImax_s$: Maximum injection rate.

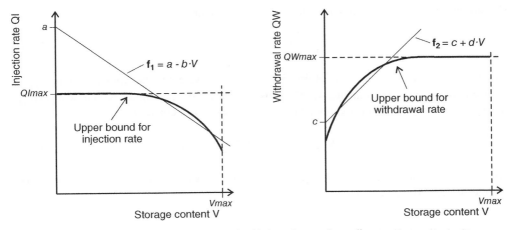

Figure 7.36   Gas storage injection and withdrawal rates depending on storage content.

- $QWmax_s$: Maximum withdrawal rate.
- $QI_{s,t}$: Injection rate during time interval t (positive variable).
- $QW_{s,t}$: Withdrawal rate during time interval t (positive variable).
- fI_s: Specific compressor gas consumption in relation to the injection rate. To keep the model linear, we assume a constant parameter. In practice, this parameter depends on the pressure difference between the storage and the connecting pipeline. Besides gas-fuelled compressors, electric compressors are used. In these cases, electricity prices have to be taken into account.

Gas storage facilities are linked to a specific node n of the system. In the following equations, we will use the index $s(n)$ for storage facilities connected to node n.

Possible injection and withdrawal rates depend on the storage content $V_{s,t}$. Possible injection rates decrease with increasing storage content and possible withdrawal rates increase. These constraints are depicted schematically in Figure 7.36. The non-linear part of these curves can be approximated by lines f_1 and f_2 that are defined by parameters a, b, c and d where $-b$ and d are the slopes of the lines f_1 and f_2, respectively.

Injection rates $QI_{s,t}$ are constrained by the maximum injection rate $QImax_s$ and by line f_1. We obtain

$$QI_{s,t} \leq QImax_s \qquad \forall (s,t) \tag{7.79}$$

and

$$QI_{s,t} \leq a - b \cdot V_{s,t} \qquad \forall (s,t). \tag{7.80}$$

Withdrawal rates $QW_{s,t}$ are constrained by

$$QW_{s,t} \leq QWmax_s \qquad \forall (s,t) \tag{7.81}$$

and

$$QW_{s,t} \leq c + d \cdot V_{s,t} \qquad \forall (s,t). \tag{7.82}$$

The storage content $V_{s,t}$ is limited by the maximum content $Vmax_s$:

$$V_{s,t} \leq Vmax_s \qquad \forall(s,t). \tag{7.83}$$

The storage content $V_{s,t}$ at the end of time interval t is equivalent to the storage content $V_{s,t\leftarrow 1}$ at the end of the previous time interval $t^{\leftarrow 1}$ plus injections $QI_{s,t}$ and minus withdrawals $QW_{s,t}$ during time interval t. This is expressed by the storage balance equation

$$V_{s,t} = V_{s,t\leftarrow 1} + QI_{s,t} - QW_{s,t} \qquad \forall(s,t). \tag{7.84}$$

Additional constraints are required to define start and end values for the storage content. For simplicity, they are neglected here.

7.6.5 Portfolio Optimisation

Portfolio optimisation aims to maximise revenues utilising the flexibility inherent in a gas portfolio. Its primary constraint is the node balance equation (7.85), which ensures that demand does not exceed supply at any node n at any time t. Considering all flows from and to a node, we obtain

$$
\sum_{c(n)} QC_{c,t} + QSp_{n,t}
$$
$$
+ \sum_m (QF_{m,n,t} - QF_{n,m,t})
$$
$$
+ \sum_{s(n)} (QW_{s,t} - (1 + fl_s) \cdot QI_{s,t}) \geq L_{n,t} \qquad \forall(n,t), \tag{7.85}
$$

where $QC_{c,t}$ is the long-term contract flow, $QSp_{n,t}$ is the flow of gas purchased in the spot market, $QF_{m,n,t}$ is the transport flow from node m to node n, $QW_{s,t}$ is the gas flow out of storage s, $QI_{s,t}$ is the gas flow into storage s, fl_s is the specific gas consumption of the compressor for the storage and $L_{n,t}$ is the customer demand.

The objective of portfolio optimisation is to maximise revenues or to minimise costs. We choose to use a cost-minimising formulation, as we have defined all prices on the cost side. Revenues from spot market sales $QSp_{n,t} < 0$ result in negative costs $QSp_{n,t} \cdot S_{n,t}$. We have to consider costs for long-term gas contracts $QC_{c,t} \cdot p_{c,t}$, costs for spot market purchases $QSp_{n,t} \cdot S_{n,t}$ and transmission capacity costs $CF_{n,m} \cdot TC_{n,m}$ to obtain the total cost C for the whole optimisation period:

$$C = \sum_{c,t} (QC_{c,t} \cdot p_{c,t}) + \sum_{n,t} (QSp_{n,t} \cdot S_{n,t}) + \sum_{n,m} (CF_{n,m} \cdot TC_{n,m}) \overset{!}{=} \min. \tag{7.86}$$

Equation (7.86) is the objective function of the portfolio optimisation problem. It is a linear programming (LP) problem, which can be solved with standard solvers. If final customer demand is a significant part of the gas portfolio, scenario approaches are required to reflect demand uncertainty. In this case, a decomposition approach might be required to solve the resulting stochastic programming problem. Different optimisation approaches are discussed in more detail in Section 7.2.3.

7.6.6   Formulation of the Market Model

In contrast to gas portfolio optimisation, gas market models have to consider the whole market consisting of the sum of the portfolios of all market participants. There are significant differences between models for short-term and long-term market models. As short-term market models are closer to gas portfolio optimisation and as they are more suitable for explaining observed market prices, we will concentrate first on short-term models with a modelling horizon of one to five years.

Short-Term Market Models

We assume that none of the market participants exerts market power. In this case, a short-term gas market model can be considered as a portfolio optimisation problem for the whole system under consideration. While the main approach is identical to the mathematical description of the portfolio optimisation problem above, some differences apply.

- *Scope of the market model:* It is necessary to define the scope of the market model carefully. In addition to market areas for which model results are required, all connected market areas might have to be considered as well. It is possible to exclude market areas from the scope of the model if the gas flows between the modelled system and these external areas can be considered as inelastic with respect to market prices.
- *Demand:* As relevant demand $L_{n,t}$, we have to consider the complete demand in all market areas n. Besides final customer demand, the demand required for the operation of the gas transport and distribution system (gas demand for compressors) has to be included.
- *Supply:* Besides supply based on long-term import contracts described in Section 7.6.2, we have to consider domestic supply and flexible imports on a short-term basis via pipeline or LNG. In many cases, domestic supply can be considered exogenous with predefined flows $QD_{n,t}$ following typical seasonal production patterns. Alternatively, they can be described similarly to long-term contracts with minimum and maximum daily and annual volumes.

     Imports on a short-term basis can be considered as spot market purchases $QSp_{n,t}$ at defined prices $S_{n,t}$ and with maximum volumes $QSpmax_{n,t}$ entering the system from external areas. Assuming that spot market exports are not relevant, $QSp_{n,t}$ has to be defined as a positive variable. Spot market trades within the scope of the market model need not be considered, as the complementary deals are also within the scope of the model.
- *Transport:* The gas transport system can be modelled with a nodal topology as explained in Section 7.6.3. Maximum transport capacities $QFmax_{n,m,t}$ have to be introduced to limit pipeline flows $QF_{n,m,t}$. As constraint we obtain

$$QF_{n,m,t} \le QFmax_{n,m,t} \qquad \forall (n, m, t). \tag{7.87}$$

In the case of auction-based capacity allocation for entry and exit capacities, transport prices can be assumed to be equal to 0 in the model. In the case of transport bottlenecks, price differences between nodes in the modelling results can be interpreted as expected values for capacity prices. In the case of tariff-based capacity allocation, these tariffs will have to be reflected in the model. If they are entered into an LP model as capacity prices for longer time periods, they will be reflected in the modelling results as market price differences between nodes only in time intervals t with maximum capacity utilisation. To avoid these unrealistic results, capacity tariffs can be broken down into daily tariffs based on estimates for capacity utilisation factors. We assume that daily specific transport costs $TC_{n,m,t}$ can be estimated for this purpose.

In addition, exogenous gas flows $QFx_{n,t}$ from and to external regions have to be considered. In the case of positive flows to node n, $QFx_{n,t}$ is positive.

• *Storage:* In addition to underground storage facilities s described in Section 7.6.4, LNG storage might have to be considered separately. The dependence of injection and withdrawal rates on storage content (equations (7.80) and (7.82)) can be neglected in many cases. In markets with regulated access to storage facilities, storage tariffs also need to be included in the model.

The gas market model can be formulated as an LP problem with constraints (7.73), (7.74) and (7.75) on long-term contract flows $QC_{c,t}$, constraint (7.76) on spot market import flows $QSp_{n,t}$, constraint (7.87) on pipeline flows $QF_{n,m,t}$ and constraints (7.79), (7.81), (7.83) and (7.84) on storage injection flows $QI_{s,t}$ and storage withdrawal flows $QW_{s,t}$. We have to add exogenous domestic production $QD_{n,t}$ and exogenous transmission flows $QFx_{n,t}$ to equation (7.85) to obtain the node balance equation of the market model:

$$\sum_{c(n)} QC_{c,t} + QSp_{n,t}$$
$$+ \sum_{m} (QF_{m,n,t} - QF_{n,m,t})$$
$$+ \sum_{s(n)} (QW_{s,t} - (1 + fl_s) \cdot QI_{s,t})$$
$$+ QD_{n,t} + QFx_{n,t} \geq L_{n,t} \qquad \forall (n, t). \tag{7.88}$$

In the objective function (7.86), the representation of transport tariffs has to be modified accordingly to receive the objective function of the market model

$$C = \sum_{c,t} (QC_{c,t} \cdot p_{c,t}) + \sum_{n,t} (QSp_{n,t} \cdot S_{n,t}) + \sum_{n,m,t} (QF_{n,m,t} \cdot TC_{n,m,t}) \overset{!}{=} \min. \tag{7.89}$$

Market prices can be derived as marginal costs of the node balance equation (7.88). In addition, especially pipeline flows $QF_{m,n,t}$ can be modelling results relevant for market analysis. Pipeline flow results help to identify bottlenecks which can lead to significant price differences between nodes.

Long-Term Market Models

Long-term gas market models include the whole supply chain from gas production to final customer demand. The following system expansion options have to be considered and described by discrete expansion variables:

- *production capacity expansion*
- *construction of new pipelines*
- *construction of new LNG regasification terminals*
- *LNG transport capacity expansion*
- *construction of new LNG liquefaction terminals*
- *storage capacity expansion.*

For all of these system expansion options, lead times, capital investment costs, economic lifetimes and annual operation and maintenance costs have to be considered.

The scope of long-term market models is generally a whole-world region, for example Europe together with Northern Africa and Russia as supply regions. With increasing importance of LNG, global models might be required to reflect the interdependency of different regional markets. Monthly time resolution is adequate if storage is considered, otherwise annual time resolution is sufficient.

An example for a European long-term gas market model is explained by Perner (2002). A worldwide model with specific focus on the emerging LNG market is described by Seeliger (2006).

Methodological Modelling Approaches

The application of linear programming (LP) or mixed integer programming (MIP) is most common for simulating competitive gas markets. If market power is relevant, approaches based on system dynamics or on game theory can be applied (see Sections 7.3.3 and 7.3.4).

7.6.7 Application of Gas Market Models

Short-term gas market models can be used to support the gas market analysis of an energy trading company. In comparison with electricity market models, it is more difficult to use gas market models to derive actual market prices, as gas market prices are not based on short-term marginal production costs. However, gas market models can be used to identify bottlenecks in the transport system and to derive price differences between trading hubs. Furthermore, they can be used to analyse the impact of system modifications, such as the expansion of pipeline capacities or the commissioning of new pipelines or new LNG terminals. Gas market models can be used for the development of trading strategies.

Another application for short-term market models is in analysing the impact of regulatory changes. One example is the application of a regional gas market model by Scheib *et al.* (2006) to analyse the impact of different numbers of market areas in Germany.

Long-term gas market models are more common than short-term models. Long-term market models can be used for system expansion planning in general or for decision support in more specific areas, including:

- *gas supply infrastructure projects*
- *gas storage projects*
- *gas fired power plant projects*
- *long-term gas contracts*
- *national energy security considerations.*

The level of detail, the time resolution and the geographical coverage of long-term market models might have to be adapted for different applications.

7.7 MARKET MODELS FOR OIL, COAL AND CO_2 MARKETS

Fundamental market models are not restricted to electricity and gas markets. Similar modelling approaches can also be applied to other fuel markets and to emissions markets. For these markets, it is also possible to derive cost-based supply and demand curves and market clearing prices.

Oil market models can be developed for crude oil or for oil products. For crude oil, worldwide supply and demand has to be considered. A multi-regional model is generally not required, as transport costs are small in comparison with oil prices. Compared with electricity markets, oil markets are less transparent and purely cost-based approaches might not be adequate. Oil prices cannot be explained directly by short- or long-term marginal production costs. Therefore, price mechanisms have to be analysed in detail. Modelling approaches based on game theory can be applied to reflect the market power of OPEC. Even if it is not possible to use fundamental oil market models for price forecasting, they can assist market analysis in a structured way. They can be used to identify key influencing factors on the supply and demand side and for supporting risk analysis.

Market models for oil products focus on oil refining capacities as supply side and on demand for different oil products. Transport costs might have to be considered.

Market models for coal can either depict regional markets or the global coal market. Steam coal and coking coal are different products in the world coal market. However, as some steam coal qualities can also be used as coking coal, it might be appropriate to consider the interdependence of these markets. Transport costs are significant in comparison with coal prices. Therefore, a multi-regional nodal model structure similar to the structure of multi-regional electricity market models discussed in Section 7.3.2 can be applied. Besides transport restrictions, transport costs have to be considered.

Fundamental market models for CO_2 certificates are widely used to describe the EU ETS. On the supply side, NAPs as well as international supply by CERs and ERUs are relevant. On the demand side, all emissions within the trading scheme have to be depicted. The most important sector is the electricity generation sector, which may be covered by electricity market models. The electricity sector is also the sector with the highest potential for short-term CO_2 price-driven emission reductions. In many countries, electricity generation from coal as well as gas power plants is possible. As variable fuel costs in gas power plants are generally higher than in coal power plants, the utilisation factors of gas-fired power plants are lower. Specific CO_2 emissions from gas power plants are lower than from coal power plants. With increasing CO_2 prices, utilisation factors of gas power plants increase and those of coal power plants decrease. This fuel-switching potential is the main mechanism that creates short-term price elasticity in the CO_2 market. But overall, the total price elasticity on the demand side is very low. For all other sectors in the EU emissions trading scheme, production quantities and technological improvements are the key drivers for the development of CO_2 emissions. The development of production quantities and decisions about technical improvements can currently be considered as almost independent of CO_2 prices.

CO_2 market models will not be able to forecast CO_2 prices reliably. The main reasons are the price-inelastic demand in combination with fixed supply by the NAPs and many exogeneous impacts like economic development, weather impacts (which influence electricity demand as well as hydropower generation) and politics. Nevertheless, fundamental CO_2 market models can be used as decision support tool for trading decisions as well as for long-term investment decisions.

7.8   ASSET INVESTMENT DECISIONS

Fundamental market models can generate scenarios which can be used for asset investment decisions. Derivatives pricing theory can be applied to valuing options inherent in real assets, such as power plants or gas storage (see Chapter 6). Virtual power plants or gas swing options are examples of specific derivatives products structured in a way to match the optionality of the respective real asset. They can be used to transfer financial asset risks to other market participants who can risk-manage financial positions, but are not required to own the underlying asset. However, virtual asset derivatives generally cover only a time period up to a few years ahead, for which a liquid futures market exists. This time period is therefore much shorter than the typical lifetime of the underlying assets. Since risk-neutral derivatives pricing theory assumes that liquid market instruments are available for hedging, the theory fails for long-term assets beyond the tenor of the liquid futures market. Instead, risk premia investors impose when valuing long-term assets need to be modelled explicitly. One standard approach to deal with this is the *discounted cashflow (DCF) method*, where future cashflows are discounted with a risk-adjusted discount rate.

7.8.1   The Discounted Cashflow Method

We assume a utility considers investing in a new power plant which would require an initial investment of CF_0 and is expected to generate annual cashflows CF_i over the following years $1, \ldots, N$. All expenditures including CF_0 are negative values, all revenues are positive values. In the risk-neutral setup of derivative pricing, future cashflows would be based on commodity forward prices and discounted with the risk-free rate R_f, so that the net present value (NPV) V is given by

$$V = \sum_{i=0}^{N} \frac{CF_i}{(1 + R_f)^i}.$$

In such a derivatives pricing framework, the commodity price risk of cashflows (prices for electricity and fuels) can be hedged via forward contracts, so that the NPV value V is indeed an arbitrage price, in the sense that deviating prices would lead to arbitrage opportunities.

For an investment in a power plant with a lifetime of multiple decades, there is no forward market available to hedge commodity price risk. Without available forward market prices, the utility needs to rely on its own estimates on future cashflows, which could be based on fundamental market models. However, as there are substantial risks attached to these future cashflow estimates (also beyond commodity price risks), the utility will attach a lower present value to this cashflow compared with a fixed cashflow (e.g., from a government bond). One way to account for this is to use a higher *risk-adjusted discount rate* R_a that reflects the risk of the investment project. Now, the discounted cashflow V is

$$V = \sum_{i=0}^{N} \frac{CF_i}{(1 + R_a)^i} \,. \tag{7.90}$$

When valuing financial instruments, taxes are often not considered explicitly. This is appropriate if the financial instruments are valued on a mark-to-market basis for tax purposes. Then the present value without considering taxes is the pre-tax profit or loss. The after-tax profit can be derived through multiplying by $(1 - T_c)$, where T_c is the applicable corporate tax rate. For real assets or other tax treatments, taxes should be modelled explicitly as cashflows, so that CF_i in equation (7.90) denotes the after-tax cashflow in period i. V can then be interpreted as the true value contribution (after taxes) to the company. In a simple case of an asset, the tax payment is given by

$$\text{tax payment} = T_c \cdot (\text{revenue} - \text{expenses} - \text{depreciation})$$

A consistent way to apply the DCF method is to use the *weighted average cost of capital (WACC)* (see Section 7.8.2 below) as discount rate combined with after-tax cashflows generated by the asset. Cashflows from financing (e.g., interest rate payments from loans) are not considered explicitly, since the financing structure is already taken into account by the WACC.

Example (valuation of a gas power plant): Consider a CCGT plant with the following specification.

- Capacity: $Pmax = 800$ MW
- Efficiency: $\eta = 56\%$
- CO_2 intensity: $\lambda = 0.37$ t/MWh
- Lifetime: $T = 30$ years.

It is further assumed that the investment amount is EUR 500 m. to be paid in year $i = 0$ and operation starts in year $i = 1$ with operational costs of EUR 16 m. p.a. inflated at 2% p.a. The applicable tax rate is assumed as $T_c = 30\%$.

The gross margin per MWh from running the plant at year i is $S(i) - (1/\eta)G(i) - \lambda CO_2(i)$, where $S(i)$ is the electricity spot price, $G(i)$ the gas spot price and $CO_2(i)$ the spot price for carbon emissions at year i. Neglecting technical restrictions, the power plant will only run if the gross margin is positive. For simplicity, we assume that the plant runs 3000 hours per year and achieves on average a power price of 65 EUR/MWh, a gas price of 25 EUR/MWh and a CO_2 price of 5 EUR/t inflated at 2% p.a. The resulting average gross margin is therefore 18.51 EUR/MWh inflated at 2% p.a. If we further assume linear depreciation over 30 years, the taxable income will be reduced by EUR 16.67 m. each year.

The corresponding DCF scheme is the following.

- $i = 0$: $CF_0 = -500$ m. EUR.
- $i = 1, \ldots, 30$:

$$CF_i = (1 - T_c) \cdot (\text{gross margin} - \text{opex}) + T_c \cdot (\text{depreciation})$$

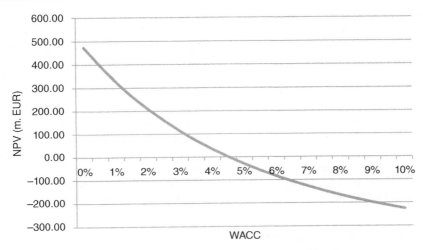

Figure 7.37 DCF valuation of a CGGT as a function of the discount rate.

where

$$\begin{aligned}
\text{gross margin} &= 3000 \cdot 800 \cdot 18.51 \cdot 1.02^i \text{ EUR} \\
\text{opex} &= 16 \cdot 1.02^i \text{ m. EUR} \\
\text{depreciation} &= 16.67 \text{ m. EUR.}
\end{aligned}$$

Figure 7.37 shows the result of the DCF valuation as a function of the WACC. As a result, the investment would only generate positive value for the company if the WACC were below 4.5%.

7.8.2 Weighted Average Cost of Capital

One way to derive the discount rate for the DCF method (7.90) is to relate it to the cost of capital for the company. The rationale is that the company needs to provide the capital for the investment either in the form of debt or equity, for which the debt and equity investors require a certain return. The *weighted average cost of capital (WACC)* is defined as

$$\text{WACC} = w_e R_E + w_d R_d (1 - T_c),$$

where w_d and w_e denote the ratio of debt and equity and R_d and R_e denote the expected returns on debt and equity. If E denotes the market value of equity and D the market value of debt, then

$$w_e = \frac{E}{E+D}, \quad w_d = \frac{D}{E+D}.$$

The cost of debt is multiplied by $(1 - T_c)$, since usually costs of debt can be deducted from corporate taxes (*tax shield*).

In practice, the weights w_d and w_e can also be derived from the target capital structure instead of using current values. The (pre-tax) cost of debt R_d is typically set to the yield to maturity of the company's debt, neglecting the company's default risk. Since equity investors are exposed directly to the risk and return of the asset,[31] the cost of equity R_e needs to reflect the risk structure of the project. Further, R_e needs to reflect the leverage, since a high debt ratio R_d amplifies the asset risk (and chances) for the equity investor. One standard approach to derive R_e is the CAPM model (see below).

Since the WACC is typically evaluated at company level, additional considerations need to be made in case the company has different business lines with different risk structures or in case a certain project is evaluated that has a significantly different risk structure compared with the rest of the company. In such cases the WACC should be determined specifically for the business line or project. This is consistent with the theoretical argument that the relevant measure should be the marginal cost of capital rather than the current total cost of capital.

7.8.3   The Capital Asset Pricing Model

The capital asset pricing model (CAPM) gives an answer to the question of what return an investor should expect for an investment that implies taking over a certain risk. A starting assumption is that investors are typically *risk-averse*, that is they require to earn a premium for assuming risk. However, large investors do not hold a single asset, but a diversified portfolio of assets. Within such a large portfolio, risks specific to a single asset will be well diversified and have a minor impact on the overall portfolio risk. Therefore, in the CAPM framework, those risks will not lead to a risk premium in the market. *Systematic risks* (e.g., general economic cycles) which affect the whole market, however, cannot be mitigated through portfolio diversification. As a consequence, the market will demand a premium for such risks.

Let R_a be the return of a specific asset and R_M the return of the *market portfolio*, for which a proxy could be a broad stockmarket index. It is further assumed that there is a risk-free asset (e.g., government bond) available for investors with return R_f. According to CAPM, the expected return $\mathbb{E}[R_a]$ of any asset is given by

$$\mathbb{E}[R_a] = R_f + \beta_a(\mathbb{E}[R_m] - R_f), \tag{7.91}$$

where β_a is a factor that represents the sensitivity of the asset with respect to systematic risk of the market portfolio,

$$\beta_a = \frac{\text{Cov}[R_a, R_m]}{\text{Var}[R_m]}. \tag{7.92}$$

The market premium $\mathbb{E}[R_m] - R_f$ can be estimated from historical data of a broad market index, where the risk-free rate R_f is typically set to the return of a government bond. If an asset is liquidly traded, that is historical prices are available, then β can be estimated as the regression coefficient of R_a against R_m corresponding to equation (7.92).

Usually, such historical data is not available for a single asset, but only for shares of a listed company. A common approach therefore is to derive β from the stock price information

---

[31] As opposed to debt holders who only share the risk in case of insolvency.

of a company with a comparable business. However, the risk structure of the equity of a company is additionally influenced by its capital structure—a highly leveraged company (i.e., low equity ratio) has a higher equity risk compared with a company with low leverage. To analyse this effect we assume two companies owning the same assets, one of which is 100% equity financed and the other partly debt financed. Let β_a (*asset beta*) denote the beta of the 100% equity financed company, since the company just holds assets. The beta of the partly debt financed company shall be denoted by β_e (*equity beta*). The *Hamada model* can be used to relate asset beta and equity beta:

$$\beta_e = \left[1 + (1 - T_c)\frac{D}{E} \right] \beta_a. \tag{7.93}$$

If one wants to compare the betas of two companies with similar business model but different capital structure, one can first "unleverage" the beta of one of the companies by calculating its asset beta from equation (7.93) and then "releverage" it using the same formula but a different D/E ratio. This leads to a typical approach for calculating the equity beta β_e to be used for the WACC (see Section 7.8.2):

1. Define a number of peer companies with similar business model.
2. Calculate their equity betas from a regression using equation (7.91).
3. Calculate the corresponding asset betas using equation (7.93) with the respective D/E ratios.
4. Define a suitable average asset beta β_a.
5. Calculate the equity beta β_e using equation (7.93) with the actual or target D/E ratio of the company.

It remains to be noted that the CAPM is derived under very idealistic assumptions on the market that are only partially fulfilled in practice. Besides assuming a frictionless market, one limiting assumption is that the expected return is only explained by one factor, which is the overall market return. An alternative approach is the *arbitrage pricing theory*, which assumes multiple common factors to explain asset returns (e.g., including company size).

Appendix

Mathematical Background

This appendix reviews some important mathematical concepts that are used throughout the book. We do not give mathematically exact formulations or proofs, but refer the reader to specialised books on econometrics, stochastic analysis or financial mathematics for these.

A.1 ECONOMETRIC METHODS

A.1.1 Linear Regression

A *linear regression* models a linear relationship between a dependent variable y and a number of independent variables (*regressors*) $x_1, \ldots, x_n$ of the form

$$y = \beta_1 x_1 + \beta_2 x_2 + \cdots + \beta_n x_n + \epsilon, \qquad (A.1)$$

where ϵ is an error term. Setting $x_1 = 1$, a constant term can be included in the model. The linear regression is used to find the coefficients of such a relationship based on a number of observations on y and x_i. If these observations are made at different times t, the given data is y_t and x_{ti} for $i = 1, \ldots, n$ and $t = 1, \ldots, N$ and the linear relation becomes

$$y_t = \beta_1 x_{t1} + \beta_2 x_{t2} + \cdots + \beta_n x_{tn} + \epsilon_t.$$

In vector notation, using $\mathbf{y} = (y_1, \ldots, y_N)^T$, $\beta = (\beta_1, \ldots, \beta_n)^T$, $\epsilon = (\epsilon_1, \ldots, \epsilon_N)^T$ and $\mathbf{X}$ for the $N \times n$ matrix (x_{ti}), this is written as

$$\mathbf{y} = \mathbf{X}\beta + \epsilon.$$

The *ordinary least squares (OLS)* estimator for β minimises the quadratic error

$$\min_{\beta} \|\mathbf{y} - \mathbf{X}\beta\|^2.$$

The solution to this problem is given by

$$\hat{\beta} = (\mathbf{X}^T \mathbf{X})^{-1} \mathbf{X}^T \mathbf{y}. \qquad (A.2)$$

In many numerical libraries or statistical software packages there are methods available to solve this least-squares problem efficiently.

We now make the following general assumptions:

1. The regressors x_{ti} are non-stochastic.
2. The error terms ϵ_t are independent and normally distributed with mean zero and standard deviation σ. The covariance matrix of ϵ is then given by

$$\text{Cov}[\epsilon] = \mathbb{E}[\epsilon\epsilon^T] = \sigma^2 I_{N \times N}.$$

The standard error σ can be estimated from the residual sum of squares (RSS) as

$$\hat{\sigma}^2 = s^2 = \frac{\text{RSS}}{N - n},$$

where

$$\text{RSS} = (\mathbf{y} - \mathbf{X}\hat{\beta})^T(\mathbf{y} - \mathbf{X}\hat{\beta}) = \mathbf{y}^T\mathbf{y} - \hat{\beta}^T\mathbf{X}^T\mathbf{y}.$$

One typical measure of the goodness of fit of the model is the squared correlation coefficient

$$R^2 = \frac{\hat{\beta}^T\mathbf{X}^T\mathbf{X}\hat{\beta}}{\mathbf{y}^T\mathbf{y}} = \frac{\sum_{t=1}^{N}\left(\sum_{i=1}^{n}\hat{\beta}_i x_{ti}\right)^2}{\sum_{t=1}^{N} y_t^2}.$$

Even if the true value of the model parameter β has a fixed (non-stochastic) value, the OLS estimator $\hat{\beta}$ is a random variable due to the randomness of $\mathbf{y}$. Estimating β from a different sample with different values of ϵ will give a different estimation of $\hat{\beta}$. It can be shown that the covariance matrix for $\hat{\beta}$ is

$$\text{Cov}[\hat{\beta}] = \sigma^2(\mathbf{X}^T\mathbf{X})^{-1}$$

with estimator

$$\hat{\mathbf{v}}^\beta = s^2(\mathbf{X}^T\mathbf{X})^{-1}.$$

The estimated standard error of β_i is denoted by $\hat{\sigma}_i^\beta = \sqrt{\hat{v}_{ii}^\beta}$. To get confidence bounds for β, one can build the t-ratio

$$t = \frac{\hat{\beta}_i - \beta_i}{\hat{\sigma}_i^\beta} \tag{A.3}$$

that is t-distributed with $v = N - n$ degrees of freedom. A 95% confidence interval for β_i is given by

$$\hat{\beta}_i - t_{v,0.025}\,\hat{\sigma}_i^\beta < \beta_i < \hat{\beta}_i + t_{v,0.025}\,\hat{\sigma}_i^\beta,$$

where $t_{v,0.025}$ denotes the 2.5% percentile for the t-distribution with v degrees of freedom.

When testing a regressor for significance, one can set $\beta = 0$ in (A.3) and compare the t-ratio $t = \hat{\beta}_i/\hat{\sigma}_i^{\beta}$ to the critical value $t_{v,\alpha}$. If the t-ratio exceeds the critical value, the regressor is significant for the given confidence level.

More details on regression methods can be found in Alexander (2001) or Hamilton (1994).

A.1.2 Stationary Time Series and Unit Root Tests

Stochastic models for time series often have a deterministic component, such as a trend or a periodicity, and a stochastic component. In simple cases, the stochastic properties of the stochastic component do not change over time in which case the component is called *stationary*. The more exact definition is:

Definition A.1 *A stochastic process $X(t)$ is* covariance-stationary *or simply* stationary *if*

1. *The expectation $\mathbb{E}[X(t)]$ and variance $\mathrm{Var}[X(t)]$ are finite and constant over time.*
2. *The autocovariance $\mathrm{Cov}[X(t), X(t-s)]$ depends only on the lag s.*

The process $X(t)$ is called strict stationary *if the whole joint distribution of $X(t)$ and $X(t-s)$ depends only on s.*

A time series with trend $x_t = at + \epsilon_t$, where the ϵ_t are independent normally distributed random numbers, is not stationary since $\mathbb{E}[x_t] = at$ depends on t. A random walk model $x_t = x_{t-1} + \epsilon_t$ is also not stationary since the variance $\mathrm{Var}[x_t] = t$ increases with time t.

The following classes of time series models give examples of stationary processes.

AR(p) models: The *autoregressive* model is given by

$$x_t = \mu + \alpha_1 x_{t-1} + \alpha_2 x_{t-2} + \cdots + \alpha_p x_{t-p} + \epsilon_t,$$

where $\epsilon_t \sim N(0, \sigma)$ are independent normally distributed random numbers with variance σ^2. The expectation value of x_t is

$$\mathbb{E}[x_t] = \mu(1 - \alpha_1 - \alpha_2 - \cdots - \alpha_p)^{-1}.$$

It can be shown that the time series is stationary if all roots of the polynomial

$$1 - \alpha_1 x - \alpha_2 x^2 - \cdots - \alpha_p x^p$$

lie outside the unit circle.

MA(q) models: The *moving average* model is given by

$$x_t = \mu + \epsilon_t + \beta_1 \epsilon_{t-1} + \beta_2 \epsilon_{t-2} + \cdots + \beta_q \epsilon_{t-q},$$

where $\epsilon_t \sim N(0,\sigma)$ are independent normally distributed random numbers with variance σ^2. The expectation value of x_t is $\mathbb{E}[x_t] = \mu$ and the process is always stationary.

ARMA(*p,q*) models: The *autoregressive moving average* model is given by

$$x_t = \mu + \alpha_1 x_{t-1} + \cdots + \alpha_p x_{t-p} + \epsilon_t + \beta_1 \epsilon_{t-1} + \cdots + \beta_q \epsilon_{t-q}.$$

The ARMA(*p,q*) model is stationary under the same conditions as the AR(*p*) model.

To identify which model is appropriate for a given time series, the following two indicators are useful.

1. **Correlograms:** The empirical autocorrelation function

$$\rho(s) = \frac{\mathrm{Cov}[x_t, x_{t-s}]}{\mathrm{Var}[x_t]}$$

should match the theoretical one, which can be calculated for any ARMA process. If a model specification is appropriate, the autocorrelation function of the (empirical) residuals ϵ_t should be near zero. There are also statistical tests available for the autocorrelation (see, e.g., Alexander (2001) or Hamilton (1994)).
2. **Significance test:** Using a regression approach for the model parameters of an AR(*p,q*) process, the *t*-ratio shows whether all of the parameters are significant. In this way the model can be reduced to lower parameters.

Financial time series are often not stationary, but have trends or increasing variance. From a non-stationary process one can build the differentiated process

$$\Delta x_t = x_t - x_{t-1}.$$

If the process Δx_t is stationary, the process is called an *integrated process* of order 1, denoted by $I(1)$. A stationary process is also denoted $I(0)$. As an example, the random walk

$$x_t = x_{t-1} + \epsilon_t$$

is not stationary because of increasing variance. Applying the difference operator yields

$$\Delta x_t = \epsilon_t,$$

which is a stationary white noise process, so the random walk is $I(1)$.

If a time series exhibits a trend, but then deviates from the fitted trend form a stationary process, then it is also called a *trend-stationary process*.

A statistical test for stationarity is the *Dickey–Fuller (DF) test*. The idea is to take first differences and regress on the first lag:

$$\Delta x_t = c + \alpha x_{t-1} + \epsilon_t.$$

The equation is an equivalent reformulation of $x_t = c + (1 + \alpha)x_{t-1} + \epsilon_t$. If α is significantly less than zero, the time series is stationary. For this purpose one can use the t-ratio described in Section A.1.1. The critical values for the t-ratio in the DF test differ from the standard t-test of the OLS because of a bias in the estimator. As an extension to the DF test, the *augmented Dickey–Fuller (ADF) test* takes into account more time lags of x_t. The DF and ADF tests are available in most statistical software packages.

A.1.3   Principal Component Analysis

Let $\mathbf{x}_t = (x_{t1}, \dots, x_{tn}) \in \mathbb{R}^n, t = 1, \dots, N$ be a stationary vector process. Then in general the ith and jth component series $(x_{ti})_t$ and $(x_{tj})_t$ are correlated. The aim of the PCA is to decompose $\mathbf{x}_t$ into independent factors

$$\mathbf{x}_t = w_{t1}\mathbf{p}_1 + \cdots + w_{tn}\mathbf{p}_n, \tag{A.4}$$

where $\mathbf{p}_i$ are the principal component factors ordered by their significance to explain the variance of $\mathbf{x}_t$ and w_{ti} are the *factor loads*.

To carry out PCA, the vector series $\mathbf{x}_t$ is written as a matrix

$$X = (x_{ti}) \in \mathbb{R}^{N \times n}.$$

As a first step, X is assumed to be normalised such that all columns have mean zero and standard deviation one. This is achieved by replacing x_{ti} with $(x_{ti} - \bar{x}_i)/\sigma_i$, where $\bar{x}_i$ and σ_i are the mean and standard deviation of the ith column of X. In the following it is assumed that X is already normalised.

Let $V = X^T X/N$ be the covariance matrix of $\mathbf{x}_t$ and P the $n \times n$ matrix of eigenvectors of V, that is

$$VP = P\Lambda,$$

where $\Lambda = diag(\lambda_1, \dots, \lambda_n)$ is the diagonal matrix of eigenvalues. The factors $\mathbf{p}_i$ in (A.4) are now defined as the columns of P.

The matrix notation of (A.4) is

$$X = WP^T.$$

Since P as a matrix of eigenvectors is orthogonal ($P^T = P^{-1}$), the matrix W of factor loads is calculated as

$$W = XP.$$

The factor loads are indeed uncorrelated, since their covariance matrix is

$$W^T W = P^T X^T XP = NP^T VP = NP^T P\Lambda = N\Lambda$$

and the variance of the ith factor load is the ith eigenvalue λ_i.

A.1.4 Kalman Filtering Method

The Kalman filter (Kalman, 1960) is a flexible algorithm to forecast and calibrate stochastic dynamical systems. It can be used in those cases where not all stochatic processes (states) can be observed directly. Details of the Kalman filtering method can be found in Hamilton (1994) or Harvey (1991).

The State Space Representation

The state-space representation of a dynamic model for $\mathbf{y}_t \in \mathbb{R}^n$ is given by the following system of equations:

$$
\begin{aligned}
\mathbf{a}_{t+1} &= \mathbf{T}_t\mathbf{a}_t + \mathbf{c}_t + \mathbf{v}_{t+1} \quad &\textit{(state equation)} \\
\mathbf{y}_t &= \mathbf{H}_t\mathbf{a}_t + \mathbf{d}_t + \mathbf{w}_t \quad &\textit{(measurement equation),}
\end{aligned}
\tag{A.5}
$$

where $\mathbf{a}_t \in \mathbb{R}^r$ is the (possibly) unobservable state vector, $\mathbf{c}_t \in \mathbb{R}^r$, $\mathbf{d}_t \in \mathbb{R}^n$ are displacement vectors and $\mathbf{T}_t \in \mathbb{R}^{r \times r}$, $\mathbf{H}_t \in \mathbb{R}^{n \times r}$ are matrices. The vectors $\mathbf{v}_t$ and $\mathbf{w}_t$ are uncorrelated white noise processes with covariance matrices

$$
\text{Cov}[\mathbf{v}_t] = \mathbf{Q}_t, \quad \text{Cov}[\mathbf{w}_t] = \mathbf{R}_t.
\tag{A.6}
$$

Example: Every ARMA process can be written in state-space form. This state-space representation, however, is not unique. Consider an ARMA(p, q) process of the form

$$
\begin{aligned}
y_t - \mu = {}& \phi_1(y_{t-1} - \mu) + \cdots + \phi_r(y_{t-r} - \mu) \tag{A.7} \\
& + \epsilon_t + \theta_1\epsilon_{t-1} + \cdots + \theta_{r-1}\epsilon_{t-r+1} \tag{A.8}
\end{aligned}
$$

with $r = \max(p, q+1)$. In this equation the additional coefficients not needed for the ARMA(p, q) process are understood to be zero, that is $\phi_{p+1} = \cdots = \phi_r = 0$ and $\theta_{q+1} = \cdots = \theta_{r-1} = 0$. The state equation and observation equation are given by

$$
\mathbf{a}_{t+1} =
\begin{bmatrix}
\phi_1 & \phi_2 & \cdots & \phi_{r-1} & \phi_r \\
1 & 0 & \cdots & 0 & 0 \\
0 & 1 & \cdots & 0 & 0 \\
\vdots & \vdots & \cdots & \vdots & \vdots \\
0 & 0 & \cdots & 1 & 0
\end{bmatrix}
\mathbf{a}_t +
\begin{bmatrix}
\epsilon_{t+1} \\
0 \\
\vdots \\
0
\end{bmatrix},
$$

$$
y_t = \mu + [1 \quad \theta_1 \quad \theta_2 \quad \cdots \quad \theta_{r-1}]\mathbf{a}_t.
$$

The Kalman Iterations

Given observations $\mathbf{x}_0, \ldots, \mathbf{x}_T$ and $\mathbf{y}_0, \ldots, \mathbf{y}_T$ the Kalman filtering algorithm iteratively calculates forecasts $\hat{\mathbf{a}}_{t+1|t}$ of the unobservable state $\mathbf{a}_{t+1}$ based on all observations up to time t and the associated mean square error

$$
\mathbf{P}_{t+1|t} = \mathbb{E}\left[(\mathbf{a}_{t+1} - \hat{\mathbf{a}}_{t+1|t})^T(\mathbf{a}_{t+1} - \hat{\mathbf{a}}_{t+1|t})\right].
$$

Furthermore, it yields a maximum likelihood function for the observations. The results can be used to calibrate unknown parameters in (A.5) and forecast values $y_{T+1}, y_{T+2}, \ldots$ The iteration steps are as follows.

1. **Iteration start:** The iteration starts with

$$\hat{a}_{1|0} = \mathbb{E}[a_1],$$
$$P_{1|0} = \mathbb{E}\left[(a_1 - \mathbb{E}[a_1])^T(a_1 - \mathbb{E}[a_1])\right].$$

In many cases the initial values can be calculated as $\hat{a}_{1|0} = 0$ (for $c_t = 0$) and $\text{vec}(P_{1|0}) = \left(I_{r^2} - T \otimes T\right)^{-1} \cdot \text{vec}(Q)$, where $T \otimes T$ is the $r^2 \times r^2$ Kronecker product matrix consisting of the submatrices $F_{ij}T$ and $\text{vec}(Q) \in \mathbb{R}^{r^2}$ (similarly $\text{vec}(P_{1|0})$) is the vector of stacked columns of Q, that is $\text{vec}(Q) = (Q_{11}, \ldots, Q_{r1}, Q_{21}, \ldots, Q_{rr})^T$. In this way $P_{1|0}$ solves the matrix equation $P_{1|0} = T P_{1|0} T^T + Q$.

2. **Updating a:** Given $\hat{a}_{t|t-1}$ and $P_{t|t-1}$, the next forecast for a is calculated as

$$\hat{a}_{t+1|t} = T_{t+1}\hat{a}_{t|t-1} + c_t + K_t(y_t - d_t - H_t\hat{a}_{t|t-1}) \tag{A.9}$$

where

$$K_t = T_{t+1}P_{t|t-1} H_t^T (H_t P_{t|t-1}H_t^T + R_t)^{-1}.$$

3. **Updating P:** Given $P_{t|t-1}$, the next forecast for P is calculated as

$$P_{t+1|t} = \left(T_{t+1}P_{t|t-1} - K_t H_t P_{t|t-1}\right) T_{t+1}^T + Q_{t+1}. \tag{A.10}$$

A.1.5   Regime-Switching Models

For many financial markets it can be observed that longer time series of prices or interest rates exhibit structural breaks at certain times. These breaks can be caused by changes in the general market conditions such as changes in government policies or wars or by the behaviour of market participants. Regime-switching models can also be used to model price spikes occuring, for example, in electricity markets.

To model regime-dependent time series one can introduce a *regime* or *state* process $s_t \in \{1, \ldots, N\}$ and make the parameters in the time series equation depend on the current state. One further needs a law for s_t that governs the stochastic regime changes. Regime-switching models and calibration methods are described in detail by Hamilton (1994, pp. 677–703) and we follow his notation to describe the basic methods.

Markov Chains

The simplest model for the integer-valued regime variable s_t is a Markov chain, where the probabilities of switching to a certain different regime depend only on the current regime and not on its history. We define

$$p_{ij} = P(s_t = j \mid s_{t-1} = i) = P(s_t = j \mid s_{t-1} = i, s_{t-2} = \ldots).$$

All transition probabilities put together define the *transition matrix* of the Markov chain

$$
\mathbf{P} = \begin{pmatrix}
p_{11} & p_{21} & \cdots & p_{N1} \\
p_{12} & p_{22} & \cdots & p_{N2} \\
\vdots & \vdots & \vdots & \vdots \\
p_{1N} & p_{2N} & \cdots & p_{NN}
\end{pmatrix}.
$$

We must have $\sum_{j=1}^{N} p_{ij} = 1$, since the entries in one column represent all possibilities of change to the next time step.

A convenient way to represent a Markov chain is to use a vector-valued process $\xi_t = e_{s_t}$, where e_i is the ith unit vector $(0, \ldots, 1, \ldots, 0)$. In other words, we have $\xi_t = (1, 0, \ldots, 0)$ when $s_t = 1$, $\xi_t = (0, 1, 0, \ldots, 0)$ when $s_t = 2$ and so on. We have $\mathbb{E}[\xi_{t+1} \mid \xi_t] = \mathbf{P}\xi_t$ and, by iteration, $\mathbb{E}[\xi_{t+m} \mid \xi_t] = \mathbf{P}^m \xi_t$. The jth entry of the left-hand side can be interpreted as the probability that $s_{t+m} = j$ conditional on ξ_t. Thus, we get

$$
\mathbf{P}^m e_i = \begin{pmatrix}
P(s_{t+m} = 1 \mid s_t = i) \\
\vdots \\
P(s_{t+m} = N \mid s_t = i)
\end{pmatrix}.
$$

A Markov chain is called *reducible* if the states can be relabelled (i.e., we set $\tilde{s}_t = \sigma(s_t)$ for a permutation σ) in such a way that the new transition matrix $\tilde{P}$ (given by $\tilde{p}_{ij} = p_{\sigma(i)\sigma(j)}$) has a block structure

$$
\tilde{P} = \left(\begin{array}{c|c}
\mathbf{B} & \mathbf{C} \\
\hline
\mathbf{0} & \mathbf{D}
\end{array} \right).
$$

Once one of the first states $\tilde{s}$ corresponding to the matrix $\mathbf{B}$ is attained, the process will never again leave those states and the dynamic is reduced to a lower number of states with transition matrix $\mathbf{B}$. If a Markov chain is not reducible it is called *irreducible*.

We have seen that using $\mathbf{P}^m e_i$, we can calculate the conditional probabilities that s_{t+m} is at a certain state j. For a certain class of Markov chains the *ergodic* Markov chains $\mathbf{P}^m e_i$ converge to a vector π for $m \to \infty$. This limit vector π, called the *ergodic probability vector*, is independent of the state i at time t and gives the unconditional probabilities that the system is in a certain state.

Mathematically, a Markov chain is called *ergodic* if the transition matrix $\mathbf{P}$ has one eigenvalue of 1 and all other eigenvalues within the unit circle. We note that from the property of transition matrices that the column elements add up to 1, we have $\mathbf{P}^T \mathbf{1} = \mathbf{1}$, where $\mathbf{1} = (1, \ldots, 1)^T \in \mathbb{R}^N$. This implies that 1 is always an eigenvalue of $\mathbf{P}$. The vector π of ergodic probabilities must satisfy $\mathbf{P}\pi = \pi$ and $\mathbf{1}^T \pi = 1$. In practice, π can be calculated from the linear system

$$
\mathbf{A}^T \mathbf{A} \pi = e_{N+1},
$$

where e_{N+1} is the $(N+1)$th unit vector and

$$
\mathbf{A} = \begin{pmatrix} I_N - \mathbf{P} \\ \mathbf{1}^T \end{pmatrix} \in \mathbb{R}^{(N+1) \times N}.
$$

The Hamilton Filter Algorithm

We assume that we are given an observable time series $(\mathbf{y}_t)_{t=0,1,2,\ldots}$ of vectors $\mathbf{y}_t \in \mathbb{R}^n$. If $(\mathbf{y}_t)$ is governed by a regime-switching model, we have transition probabilities

$$f(\mathbf{y}_t \mid s_t = j, \mathbf{y}_{t-1}, \mathbf{y}_{t-2}, \ldots).$$

To calibrate such a regime-switching model knowing only the observables $(\mathbf{y}_t)$ we cannot immediately use a maximum likelihood optimisation since we do not know the regime state (s_t) at each time.

To overcome this problem, the Hamilton filter can be used since it generates estimates for the probabilities that the system is in a certain regime j at a given time t using only information from the observable process $(\mathbf{y}_t)$. More specifically, it generates estimates $\hat{\xi}_{t|t}$ (*optimal inference*) for the vector of conditional probabilities

$$P(s_t = j \mid \mathbf{y}_t, \mathbf{y}_{t-1}, \ldots), \quad j = 1, \ldots, N$$

and estimates $\hat{\xi}_{t+1|t}$ (*forecast*) for the vector of conditional probabilities

$$P(s_{t+1} = j \mid \mathbf{y}_t, \mathbf{y}_{t-1}, \ldots), \quad j = 1, \ldots, N.$$

The optimal inference and forecast can be calculated iteratively from the equations

$$\hat{\xi}_{t|t} = \frac{\left(\hat{\xi}_{t|t-1} \odot \eta_t\right)}{\mathbf{1}^T \left(\hat{\xi}_{t|t-1} \odot \eta_t\right)}, \tag{A.11}$$

$$\hat{\xi}_{t+1|t} = \mathbf{P} \cdot \hat{\xi}_{t|t}. \tag{A.12}$$

Here, $\odot$ denotes element-by-element multiplication and

$$\eta_t = \begin{pmatrix} f(\mathbf{y}_t \mid s_t = 1, \mathbf{y}_{t-1}, \mathbf{y}_{t-2}, \ldots) \\ \vdots \\ f(\mathbf{y}_t \mid s_t = N, \mathbf{y}_{t-1}, \mathbf{y}_{t-2}, \ldots) \end{pmatrix}$$

denotes the vector of conditional probability densities. If no further information is given, the iteration can be started with $\hat{\xi}_{1|0} = \pi$, where π is the ergodic probability vector.

From the calculations done within the Hamilton filter, one can immediately infer the value of the log-likelihood function

$$\mathcal{L} = \sum_{t=1}^{T} \ln f \left(\mathbf{y}_t \mid \mathbf{y}_{t-1}, \mathbf{y}_{t-2}, \ldots\right)$$

using

$$f \left(\mathbf{y}_t \mid \mathbf{y}_{t-1}, \mathbf{y}_{t-2}, \ldots\right) = \mathbf{1}^T \left(\hat{\xi}_{t|t-1} \odot \eta_t\right).$$

A.2 STOCHASTIC PROCESSES

A *stochastic process* $(X(t))_{t \in I}$ is a family of random variables, where I usually represents some time interval or a discrete set of times. One of the main examples is a price process $S(t)$ that represents the market price of some asset. Other examples are the temperature at a given place or the total load in a power grid. A stochastic process is *discrete* if I is a discrete set, usually a set of integer numbers (e.g., $t = 0, 1, \ldots, T$) representing days or hours. If I is a subinterval of the real line $\mathbb{R}$, the process is said to be *continuous* (e.g., $I = [0, \infty)$).

A.2.1 Conditional Expectation and Martingales

A typical task in financial mathematics is to calculate the expected value of a stochastic process at a future time T given all information up to today's time $t < T$. This quantity is denoted by the *conditional expectation* $\mathbb{E}_t [X(T)]$. Viewed as a function of t, the conditional expectation $Y(t) = \mathbb{E}_t[X(T)]$ is itself a stochastic process, since with increasing time t the randomly incoming information changes the expectation of $X(T)$.

Formally, conditional expectations can be defined by means of the *Radon–Nikodým theorem*, which we do not discuss here. To carry out calculations with conditional expectations, we have the following rules:

1. $\mathbb{E}_s[X(s)Y(t)] = X(s)\mathbb{E}_s[Y(t)]$ for $s \leq t$
2. $\mathbb{E}_s[\mathbb{E}_t[X(T)]] = \mathbb{E}_s[X(T)]$ for $s \leq t \leq T$
3. $\mathbb{E}_t[\mathbb{E}_s[X(T)]] = \mathbb{E}_s[X(T)]$ for $s \leq t \leq T$.

The first identity follows from the fact that, knowing all information up to time s, the value $X(s)$ is not stochastic any more and can be pulled out of the expectation operator. The second identity says that the expectation at time s about the expectation at a later time t of $X(T)$ is just the expectation at time s of $X(T)$. The third identity is due to the fact that $\mathbb{E}_s[X(T)]$ is a deterministic quantity at a later time t, since it uses only information up to time s. Therefore, it is equal to its expectation at time s.

An important class of stochastic processes is defined by the property that their future expected value equals today's value. If a process is known to have this property, it is easy to state analytical results about their expectations. The formal definition is:

Definition A.2   *A stochastic process $M(t)$ is called a* martingale *if*

$$M(s) = \mathbb{E}_s[M(t)] \quad for \; s \leq t.$$

Example: By the second rule above, the stochastic process $M(t) = \mathbb{E}_t[X(T)]$ is a martingale. This fact is used extensively in option pricing theory. For example, if we model a futures price as $F(t, T) = \mathbb{E}_t[S(T)]$ then we know that the futures price is a martingale. For other examples see Section A.3.

A.2.2 Brownian Motion

Since the work of Bachelier (1900), Brownian motion has been utilised as a main ingredient for modelling security prices. It is defined as follows:

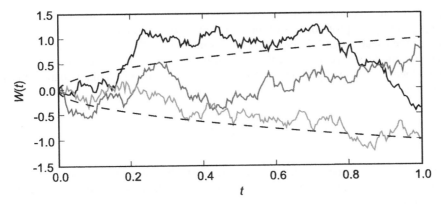

Figure A.1   Brownian motion sample paths.

Definition A.3   *A stochastic process* $W = (W(t))_{t \geq 0}$ *is a* (standard) *Brownian motion if*

1. $W(0) = 0$.
2. $W(t)$ *has continuous paths*.
3. $W(t)$ *has independent, stationary, normally distributed increments, that is for* $0 = t_0 < t_1 < \ldots < t_n$ *the increments* $Y_1 = W(t_1) - W(t_0), \ldots, Y_n = W(t_n) - W(t_{n-1})$ *are independent and normally distributed with mean zero and variance* $\text{Var}[Y_j] = t_j - t_{j-1}$ *for all* $j = 1, \ldots, n$.

The last property means that the increment from t to $t + u$ does not depend on the history of the process up to time t, but only on the time interval u. In particular, the process is therefore *Markovian*, meaning that the process after time t depends only on the value at time t and not on the history before t. Since all increments have mean of zero, another immediate conclusion is that $W(s) = \mathbb{E}_s[W(t)]$ for $s < t$, thus $W(t)$ is a martingale. See Figure A.1 for sample Brownian paths.

In practice, Brownian motion can be simulated numerically using normal random variables. If one is only interested in $W(T)$ for some time T, the simulated values are just normally distributed random numbers with mean zero $(= W(0))$ and standard deviation $\sqrt{T}$. If one needs a whole simulation path $W(t_1), \ldots, W(t_n)$, the iterative scheme is

- $W(0) = 0$;
- $W(t_i) = W(t_{i-1}) + \sqrt{\Delta t_i} \epsilon_i$, where $\epsilon_1, \ldots, \epsilon_n$ are independent normally distributed random numbers.

A.2.3   Stochastic Integration and Itô's Lemma

To give some motivation for stochastic integration we start with an example. Assume that a Brownian motion $W(t)$ models the price of a security and, at time t_0, we hold a number ξ_0 of that security. Then our profit or loss up to time t_1 is given by $\xi_0(W(t_1) - W(t_0))$. If we rebalance the portfolio at each time t_i, such that we hold a number ξ_i of the security at time t_i, then our profit or loss up to time t_n is given by the sum $\sum_{i=0}^{n-1} \xi_i(W(t_{i+1}) - W(t_i))$. If we make the time intervals between the portfolio rebalancings shorter and shorter, such that in the limit

$X(t)$ denotes the number of securities we hold in our portfolio at time t, then the sum we had before representing the profit or loss of the portfolio becomes an integral $\int_0^t X(s)\,dW(s)$.

However, the usual integral (Lebesgue–Stieltjes integral) $\int X\,dW(t)$ with Brownian motion $W(t)$ as integrator does not exist, since the paths of $W(t)$ are not of bounded variation. A special integration theory, initiated by Itô (*Itô calculus*), can be used to give a mathematical meaning to expressions such as

$$\int_0^t X(s)\,dW(s),$$

where $X(t)$ may be another stochastic process. First, the integral is defined for the special case where $X(t)$ is a piecewise constant function that takes the value ξ_i on the interval $[t_i, t_{i+1})$, that is

$$X(t) = \sum_{i=0}^{n-1} \xi_i \mathbf{1}_{[t_i, t_{i+1})}(t)$$

with $0 = t_0 < t_1 < \ldots < t_n = t$. In this case the integral is defined by

$$\int_0^t X(s)\,dW(s) = \sum_{i=0}^{n-1} \xi_i \left(W(t_{i+1}) - W(t_i) \right).$$

Note that in the sum on the right-hand side, the integrand is evaluated at the left boundary of each interval $[t_i, t_{i+1})$. For financial applications this is consistent with the fact that decisions for the next period have to be made at the beginning of each period using information up to that point of time. A formal definition of stochastic integrals for more general integrands $X(t)$ can be given using approximations of $X(t)$ by piecewise constant functions.

The following properties of stochastic integrals will often be used:

Theorem A.1   *Let a stochastic process be given by* $Z(t) = \int_0^t b(t)\,dW(t)$*, where $b(t)$ is a deterministic function. Then*

1. $Z(t)$ *is normally distributed with mean zero and variance* $\mathrm{Var}[Z(t)] = \int_0^t b^2(s)\,ds$.
2. $Z(t)$ *is a martingale.*

In this theorem the martingale property is even true if $b(t)$ is a stochastic process instead of a deterministic function.

Many stochastic processes used to model financial data are constructed via stochastic integrals. These processes, also called Itô processes, are defined as follows:

Definition A.4   *A process $X(t)$ is called an* Itô process *if it is of the form*

$$X(t) = X_0 + \int_0^t a(s)\,ds + \int_0^t b(s)\,dW(s), \tag{A.13}$$

where $a(t)$ and $b(t)$ are functions or, more generally, stochastic processes. A shorthand notation for such an Itô process is

$$dX(t) = a(t)\,dt + b(t)\,dW(t). \tag{A.14}$$

The last expression is also called the stochastic differential equation *describing $X(t)$.*

For stochastic processes we have the following generalisation of the chain rule:

Theorem A.2   (Itô's lemma or Itô's formula) *Let $X(t)$ be an Itô process given by (A.14) and $f(t, X)$ a smooth function. Then $f(t, X(t))$ has the differential*

$$df(t, X(t)) = \frac{\partial f(t, X(t))}{\partial t}\,dt + a\frac{\partial f(t, X(t))}{\partial X}\,dX(t) + \frac{1}{2}\frac{\partial^2 f(t, X(t))}{\partial X^2}b^2(t)\,dt \tag{A.15}$$

$$= \left(\frac{\partial f}{\partial t} + a\frac{\partial f}{\partial X} + \frac{1}{2}b^2\frac{\partial^2 f}{\partial X^2}\right)dt + b\frac{\partial f}{\partial X}\,dW(t).$$

Example: In many financial applications we model a price $S(t)$ as the exponential $S = \exp(X(t))$, where $X(t)$ is a Brownian motion with drift given by the Itô process

$$dX(t) = \tilde{\mu}\,dt + \sigma\,dW(t).$$

Now we can use Itô's lemma to find the stochastic differential equation describing $S(t)$:

$$dS(t) = de^{X(t)} = e^{X(t)}\,dX(t) + \tfrac{1}{2}\sigma^2 e^{X(t)}\,dt = \left(\tilde{\mu} + \tfrac{1}{2}\sigma^2\right)S(t)\,dt + \sigma S(t)\,dW(t).$$

Thus, writing $\mu = \tilde{\mu} + \tfrac{1}{2}\sigma^2$ we find the well-known Black–Scholes model

$$\frac{dS(t)}{S(t)} = \mu\,dt + \sigma\,dW(t).$$

Itô's lemma can be generalised to multiple dimensions.

A.3   OPTION PRICING THEORY

It is beyond the scope of this book to give a rigorous account of the mathematical theory of derivatives pricing. There are many specialised books on this subject available (e.g., Bingham and Kiesel (2004), Hull (2011)). Here we describe only the basic principles.

A.3.1   Pricing Under the Risk-Neutral Measure

In option pricing theory, one assumes that the market is governed by a number of risk factors $X_1(t), \ldots, X_n(t)$. These risk factors do not need to be tradable assets but can rather be general.

Examples of the types of risk factors for energy markets are the environmental temperature or the total system load, or future electricity prices for a given future delivery period. By assumption, the risk factors follow a stochastic model of the form

$$dX_i(t) = m_i(t) \, dt + s_i(t) \, dW_i(t),$$

where $W_1(t), \ldots, W_n(t)$ are Brownian motions and $m_i(t)$ and $s_i(t)$ can be rather general (depending on $W_i(t)$), allowing mean-reverting or fat-tail behaviour. Thus, one can think of $W_1(t), \ldots, W_n(t)$ as true, but non-observable, risk factors. Classical option pricing theory assumes a *complete market*, meaning that there are enough tradable contracts available to hedge each risk factor separately. In this case there would be at least n tradable contracts $Z_1(t), \ldots, Z_n(t)$ depending on the corresponding risk factors. From Itô's lemma, the tradable contract prices also follow some stochastic differential equation of the form

$$dZ_i(t) = \mu_i(t) \, dt + \sum_{j=1}^{n} \sigma_{i,j}(t) \, dW_j(t), \quad i = 1, \ldots, n.$$

It is assumed that tradable contracts have no yield or cash flow up to the expiry date. Because of convenience yield and storage costs, the commodity itself does not qualify as such a contract, but forward contracts do. Assume that a derivative at its maturity date T has a payoff of the form $h(X_1(T), \ldots, X_n(T))$. Mathematical theory identifies a replicating hedge portfolio consisting only of the tradable contracts that has the same payoff as the derivative and therefore can be used to hedge all risk. Under those assumptions the value of the derivative is independent of any risk preferences in the market and the derivative price (*fair value*) is uniquely determined by the hedging costs. Any other derivative price would lead to an arbitrage opportunity. As the derivative price does not depend on the risk preferences it should be the same in a totally risk-indifferent (*risk-neutral*) world. In such a world there should on average be no excess return of a risky tradable contract relative to a riskless money market account. The value of a riskless money market account is given by $\beta(t) = e^{rt}$ and, for non-constant interest rates, by $\beta(t) = \exp\left(\int_0^t r(s) \, ds\right)$. We have the following rule. In the risk-neutral world (denoted by Q), the discounted price process $\tilde{Z}(t) = Z(t)/\beta(t)$ of a tradable contract Z is a *martingale*, that is the following holds for all $t \leq T$:

$$\tilde{Z}(t) = \mathbb{E}_t^Q[\tilde{Z}(T)].$$

For constant interest rates this is equivalent to

$$Z(t) = e^{-r(T-t)} \mathbb{E}_t^Q[Z(T)].$$

The martingale property holds only for tradable contracts that have no yield or cashflow for the holder of the contract. This is true for a forward contract, but not necessarily for a holder of the commodity itself due to storage costs or convenience yield. Therefore, the spot price of a commodity in general has no martingale property, so that mean reversion is for example a possible characteristic of a spot price process but not a forward price under the risk-neutral measure.

Example: (forward–spot price relation): Let $K = F(t, T)$ be the forward price (not the value of the forward contract) and $S(t)$ the spot price at time t. By definition of the forward price, the fair value at time t of a forward contract with contract price K and expiry date T is zero. Since a forward contract is a tradable asset, its discounted value is a martingale under the risk-neutral measure Q. Consequently, the discounted value of the forward contract at time t (which is zero) must be equal to the expectation of the discounted value of the forward contract at time T. Assuming constant interest rates, we get

$$0 = e^{-r(T-t)}\mathbb{E}_t^Q[S(T) - K].$$

Substituting $K = F(t, T)$, we arrive at the important formula for the forward price

$$F(t, T) = \mathbb{E}_t^Q[S(T)], \tag{A.16}$$

that is the forward price is the expected spot price under the risk-neutral measure. More generally, the process $F(t, T)$ as a function of t is a martingale.

Since the discounted prices of tradable contracts $Z_1, \ldots, Z_n$ are martingales and the derivative can be replicated exactly by a portfolio of tradable contracts, the discounted value of the derivative must also be a martingale. This argument leads to the option pricing formula

$$U(t) = e^{-r(T-t)}\mathbb{E}_t^Q[h(X_1(T), \ldots, X_n(T))]. \tag{A.17}$$

Switching from the "true" world to the "risk-neutral" world in mathematical terms means choosing an appropriate equivalent probability measure under which the discounted price processes of all tradable contracts are martingales (in particular of $Z_1, \ldots, Z_n$). This probability measure is called the *risk-neutral measure* or the *equivalent martingale measure*. It is *equivalent* in the sense that it leaves the possible paths for the risk factors $W_i(t)$ the same but assigns different probabilities. We denote the risk-neutral measure by Q and the original statistical measure by P. Under Q, the processes $W_i(t)$ are no longer standard Brownian motions but have a drift. However, according to *Girsanov's theorem*, the processes

$$\tilde{W}_i(t) = W_i(t) + \int_0^t \gamma_i(s)\,ds$$

are standard Brownian motions under Q for some (drift) function γ_i. Taking the differential, we get (under Q)

$$dW_i(t) = d\tilde{W}_i(t) - \gamma_i(t)\,dt.$$

Substituting $\tilde{W}_t$ back into the equations for $Z_i(t)$ and $X_i(t)$ we get under Q:

$$dX_i(t) = \tilde{m}_i(t)\,dt + s_i(t)\,d\tilde{W}_i(t),$$

$$dZ_i(t) = \tilde{\mu}_i(t)\,dt + \sum_{j=1}^n \sigma_{i,j}(t)\,d\tilde{W}_j(t),$$

with new drift constants $\tilde{m}_i = m_i - s_i\gamma_i$ and $\tilde{\mu}_i = \mu_i - \sum_{j=1}^n \sigma_{i,j}(t)\gamma_j$.

To price derivatives, we have the following steps:

1. Take a stochastic model for the risk factors $X_1(t), \ldots, X_n(t)$.
2. Identify the risk-neutral measure Q under which the discounted price processes of the tradable contracts $Z_1(t), \ldots, Z_n(t)$ are martingales. This changes the drift coefficients in the model equations for the risk factors.
3. Calculate the derivatives price from the discounted expected value of the derivatives payoff under the risk-neutral measure according to equation (A.17).

The *fundamental theorem of asset pricing* gives some more information about the risk-neutral measure:

1. If a market admits no arbitrage (riskless gains above the riskless money market rate), then there always exists a risk-neutral measure (equivalent martingale measure).
2. If a market is complete (all relevant risk factors can be hedged by tradable contracts), then the risk-neutral measure is unique.

As a consequence, option prices in a complete arbitrage-free market are uniquely determined and do not depend on risk preferences of the market participants. However, in typical energy markets the assumptions of no arbitrage and a complete market can be far from the reality. Since many markets are not yet fully transparent to market participants, there may be more arbitrage opportunities available than in classical financial markets. Market incompleteness arises in situations where for some risks there are no tradable hedge contracts available. In incomplete markets not all risk can be hedged and risk-minimising hedging strategies can be considered instead (Carr *et al.*, 2001). An example from electricity markets is the risk of a change in the hourly shape of the forward curve when selling or buying an individual load schedule. Hedging instruments typically are standardised products such as baseload or peakload contracts that do not hedge all risk on an hourly granularity. Compared with many financial markets, the classical derivative pricing theory in complete markets may be less accurate, but is nevertheless of value to find a basis for trading decisions and make adjustments to take into account individual risk preferences.

A.3.2   The Feynman–Kac Theorem

By equation (A.17) the fair value of an option with one risk factor X is given as the conditional expectation of the discounted payoff $h(X(T))$:

$$U = e^{-r(T-t)}\mathbb{E}_t[h(X(T))].$$

Therefore, a typical task is to evaluate such a conditional expectation either analytically or numerically. An important tool for this purpose is the following theorem:

Theorem A.3   (Feynman–Kac) *Let $u(t, x)$ be defined as the conditional expectation*

$$u(t, x) = \mathbb{E}_t[h(X(T)) \mid X(t) = x],$$

where X(t) is an Itô process of the form

$$dX(t) = a(X(t)) dt + b(X(t)) dW(t)$$

with $X(t) = x$. Then $u(t, x)$ satisfies the partial differential equation

$$\frac{\partial u(t, x)}{\partial t} + a\frac{\partial u(t, x)}{\partial x} + \frac{1}{2}b^2\frac{\partial^2 u(t, x)}{\partial x^2} = 0$$

with terminal value

$$u(T, x) = h(x) \quad \text{for all } x.$$

The terminal value problem given in Theorem A.1 can be solved numerically using standard finite-difference methods (explicit, implicit, Crank–Nicolson) for parabolic partial differential equations.

Example: An example of the Feynman–Kac theorem is the Black–Scholes equation, where the spot price with risk-neutral drift is given by the stochastic model

$$dS(t) = rS(t) dt + \sigma S(t) dW(t).$$

The price of a European option is given by the conditional expectation

$$u(t, S) = e^{-r(T-t)}\mathbb{E}_t[h(S(T))].$$

By the Feynman theorem, the conditional expectation $v(t, S) = \mathbb{E}_t[h(S(T))]$ satisfies the partial differential equation

$$\frac{\partial v(t, S)}{\partial t} + rS\frac{\partial v(t, S)}{\partial S} + \frac{1}{2}\sigma^2 S^2\frac{\partial^2 v(t, S)}{\partial S^2} = 0$$

with terminal value $v(T, S) = h(S)$. Now we use the relation $v(t, S) = e^{r(T-t)}u(t, S)$ to make the substitutions

$$\frac{\partial v(t, S)}{\partial t} = -re^{r(T-t)}u(t, S) + e^{r(T-t)}\frac{\partial u(t, S)}{\partial t},$$

$$\frac{\partial v(t, S)}{\partial S} = e^{r(T-t)}\frac{\partial u(t, S)}{\partial S},$$

$$\frac{\partial^2 v(t, S)}{\partial S^2} = e^{r(T-t)}\frac{\partial^2 u(t, S)}{\partial S^2}$$

and arrive at the Black–Scholes equation

$$\frac{\partial u(t, S)}{\partial t} + rS\frac{\partial u(t, S)}{\partial S} + \frac{1}{2}\sigma^2 S^2\frac{\partial^2 u(t, S)}{\partial S^2} - ru(t, S) = 0$$

with terminal value $u(T, S) = h(S)$.

A.3.3   Monte Carlo Simulation

The Monte Carlo method can be used to calculate numerical approximations of an expectation value $\mathbb{E}[X]$. Since, according to equation (A.17), the fair value U of an option is given as the conditional expectation of the discounted payoff, the Monte Carlo method has an immediate application to option pricing problems. Monte Carlo methods in their basic form are easy to implement and mainly used in the following situations:

- The stochastic model for the underlying is complex such that analytical or other numerical methods (tree, PDE) are not available or not efficient.
- The payoff H depends on underlying prices at different times. Examples of such path-dependent options are Asian options.
- The option has multiple risk factors $X_1(t), \ldots, X_n(t)$. For $n > 3$ other numerical methods, such as tree or PDE methods, become quickly inefficient.

To use a Monte Carlo approach for options with early exercise rights (American options) one needs extensions to the classical Monte Carlo method. One example of such an extension is given in Longstaff and Schwartz (2001).

The basic Monte Carlo method for an option with maturity T and payoff function h depending on a risk factor X at different times,

$$H = h(X(T_1), \ldots, X(T_n)),$$

consists of the following steps:

1. Compute N sample paths $X^{(1)}(t), \ldots, X^{(N)}(t)$ evaluated at times $T_1, \ldots, T_n$ to evaluate the option payoff. For the ith path, we have the values $X^{(i)}(T_1), \ldots, X^{(i)}(T_n)$. In total, these are $N \times n$ values.
2. Compute the sample option payoffs discounted to time t:

$$U^{(i)} = e^{-r(T-t)} H(X^{(i)}(T_1), \ldots, X^{(i)}(T_n)).$$

3. The Monte Carlo estimate of the option price at time t is the average

$$\hat{U} = \frac{1}{N} \sum_{i=1}^{N} U^{(i)}.$$

The standard estimation error can be calculated as follows. Let

$$s_U^2 = \frac{1}{N-1} \sum_{i=1}^{N} (U^{(i)} - \hat{U})^2$$

be the variance estimator of the sample option values. Then the standard pricing error of the Monte Carlo approximation is

$$\epsilon_U = \frac{s_U}{\sqrt{N}}. \tag{A.18}$$

Asymptotically, the error is of order $1/\sqrt{N}$ meaning that to reduce the error by a factor $1/2$, the number of sample paths has to increase by a factor 4. Compared with other numerical methods (e.g., PDE solvers), the convergence with $1/\sqrt{N}$ is rather slow and achieving a good accuracy may require a large number of sample paths. An approach to reduce the number of samples needed and thereby to reduce the the computing time is to reduce the variance of the sample option values s_U^2. The following two *variance reduction* methods are frequently used.

- *Antithetic paths:* Let the sample value $U_+^{(i)}$ be generated by the normally distributed random numbers $\epsilon_1^{(i)}, \ldots, \epsilon_n^{(i)}$. Then $-\epsilon_1^{(i)}, \ldots, -\epsilon_n^{(i)}$ give rise to a different sample path (the *antithetic path*) with sample value $U_-^{(i)}$. Using $U_+^{(i)}$ and $U_-^{(i)}$ as sample paths doubles the number of sample paths without having to generate new random numbers. Additionally, the use of antithetic paths often decreases the variance s_U^2 of the sample option values. By equation (A.18) this reduces the approximation error for a given number of sample paths.
- *Control variates:* A very efficient way to reduce the variance s_U^2 in equation (A.18) is to use the Monte Carlo method not for the option itself but for the difference between the option and a similar option (the *control variate*) for which an exact analytical solution is known. Let V be such a control variate and $Z = U - V$ be the difference for which the Monte Carlo method yields an estimate $\hat{Z}$. Then the option price approximation is given by

$$\hat{U} = V + \hat{Z}.$$

A typical example is to use a geometric average Asian option, for which an analytical solution is known, as a control variate to the arithmetic average Asian option (see Section 5.4.2).

References

Alexander, C. *Market Models: A Guide to Financial Data Analysis*. Wiley, Chichester, UK, 2001.

Bachelier, L. Théorie de la spéculation. *Annales Scientifiques de l'École Normale Supérieure*, 17:21–86, 1900.

Bank for International Settlements. *Insolvency Arrangements and Contract Enforceability*, 2002.

Barlow, M. T. A diffusion model for electricity prices. *Mathematical Finance*, 12:287–298, 2002.

Barndorff-Nielsen, O. E. Hyperbolic distributions and distributions on hyperbolae. *Scandinavian Journal of Statistics*, 5(3):151–157, 1978.

Basel Committee on Banking Supervision. *Principles for Sound Liquidity Risk Management*, 2008.

Basel Committee on Banking Supervision. *International Framework for Liquidity Risk Measurement, Standards and Monitoring*, 2009.

Basel Committee on Banking Supervision. *Principles for Enhancing Corporate Governance*, 2010a.

Basel Committee on Banking Supervision. *Revisions to the Basel II Market Risk Framework*, 2010b.

Basel Committee on Banking Supervision. *Principles for the Sound Management of Operational Risk*, 2011.

Benth, F. E. and Benth, J. S. The volatility of temperature and pricing of weather derivatives. *Quantitative Finance*, 7:553–561, 2007.

Benth, F. E., Lange, N., and Myklebust, T. A. Pricing and hedging quanto options in energy markets, 2012. Working paper available at http://papers.ssrn.com/sol3/papers.cfm?abstract_id=2133935.

Bessembinder, H. Systematic risk, hedging pressure, and risk premiums in futures markets. *The Review of Financial Studies*, 5(4):637–667, 1992.

Bessembinder, H. and Lemmon, M. L. Equilibrium pricing and optimal hedging in electricity forward markets. *Journal of Finance*, 57(3):1347–1382, 2002.

BFE. *Schweizerische Elektrizitätsstatistik 2012*. Bundesamt für Energie, Bern, Switzerland, 2013. http://www.bfe.admin.ch.

BGR. Energy Study 2012. Federal Institute for Geosciences and Natural Resources (BGR) on behalf of German Mineral Resources Agency (DERA), 2011.

Bhattacharya, K., Bollen, M. H., and Daalder, J. E. *Operation of Restructured Power Systems*. Kluwer, Boston, 2001.

Bingham, N. H. and Kiesel, R. *Risk-Neutral Valuation. Pricing and Hedging of Financial Derivatives*. Springer Finance. Springer, Berlin, 2nd edn, 2004.

Black, F. The pricing of commodity contracts. *Journal of Financial Economics*, 3, 1976.

Black, F. and Scholes, M. The pricing of options and corporate liabilities. *Journal of Political Economy*, 81:637–659, 1973.

BMU. *Zeitreihen zur Entwicklung der erneuerbaren Energien in Deutschland*. Bundesministerium für Umwelt, Naturschutz und Reaktorsicherheit, Berlin, 2013. http://www.erneuerbare-energien.de/die-themen/datenservice/zeitreihen-entwicklung-ab-1990/.

Böcker, K. and Klüppelberg, C. Operational VAR: A closed-form approximation. *Risk Magazine*, December:90–93, 2005.

Bollerslev, T. Generalized autoregressive conditional heteroskedasticity. *Journal of Econometrics*, 31:307–327, 1986.

Bompard, E., Correia, P., Gross, G., and Amelin, M. Congestion-management schemes: A comparative analysis under a unified framework. *IEE Transactions on Power Systems*, 18:346–352, 2003.

Boogert, A. and de Jong, C. Gas storage valuation using a Monte Carlo method, Birkbeck Working Papers in Economics & Finance, 2006.

Boogert, A. and de Jong, C. Gas storage valuation using a multifactor price process. *The Journal of Energy Markets*, 4(4):29–52, 2011.

BP. Statistical review of world energy. http://www.bp.com/statisticalreview, 2013.

Brockwell, P. J. and Davis, R. A. *Introduction to Time Series and Forecasting*. Springer Series in Statistics. Springer, Berlin, 2nd edn, 2002.

Burger, M., Klar, B., Müller, A., and Schindlmayr, G. A spot market model for pricing derivatives in electricity markets. *Quantitative Finance*, 4:109–122, 2004.

Burger, M. and Müller, J. Risk-adequate pricing of retail power contracts. *The Journal of Energy Markets*, 4(4):53–74, 2011.

Bye, T. A. Nordic energy market under stress. *Economic Survey from Statistics Norway*, 2003(4):26–37, 2003. http://www.ssb.no/english/subjects/08/05/10/es/200304/bye.pdf.

Carmona, R. and Durrleman, V. Pricing and hedging spread options. *SIAM Review*, 2003.

Carr, P., Geman, H., and Madan, D. Pricing and hedging in incomplete markets. *Journal of Financial Economics*, 62:131–169, 2001.

Cartea, A. and Williams, T. UK gas markets: The market price of risk and applications to multiple interruptible supply contracts. *Energy Economics*, 30(3):829–846, 2008.

Chen, Z. and Forsyth, P. A. Implications of a regime-switching model on natural gas storage valuation and optimal operation. *Quantitative Finance*, 10(2):159–176, 2010.

Chong, E. K. P. and Zak, S. H. *An Introduction to Optimization*. Wiley, New York, 2nd edn, 2001.

Cortazar, G. and Schwartz, E. S. Implementing a stochastic model for oil futures prices. *Energy Economics*, 25(3):215–238, 2003.

Cox, J. C., Ingersoll, J. E., and Ross, S. A. The relation between forward prices and futures prices. *Journal of Financial Economics*, 9:321–346, 1981.

Cox, J. C., Ingersoll, J. E., and Ross, S. A. A theory of the term structure of interest rates. *Econometrica*, 385–407, 1985.

Crotogino, F., Mohmeyer, K.-U., and Scharf, R. Huntorf CAES: More than 20 years of successful operation. In *SMRI Spring Meeting 2001, Orlando, 23.-24.04.2001*, pp. 351–357, 2001. http://www.kbbnet.de.

de Jong, C., van Dijken, H., and Enev, E. Wie erneuerbare Energien die (Preis-)Zukunft gestalten. *Energiewirtschaftliche Tagesfragen*, 5, 2013.

De Laurentis, G. D., Maino, R., and Molteni, L. *Developing, Validating and Using Internal Ratings: Methodologies and Case Studies*. Wiley, Chichester, UK, 2010.

Deng, S. Stochastic models of energy commodity prices and their applications: Mean-reversion with jumps and spikes, Working paper, 2000.

Deng, S.-J., Li, M., and Zhou, J. Closed-form approximations for spread option prices and greeks, 2006. http://ssrn.com/abstract=952747.

Deutsche WindGuard. *Status des Windenergieausbaus in Deutschland – Jahr 2012*. Deutsche WindGuard GmbH, Varel, 2013. http://www.wind-energie.de/infocenter/statistiken.

EIA. Annual Energy Outlook 2013. US Energy Information Administration, 2013.

Ellersdorfer, I. A multi-regional two-stage Cournot model for analyzing competition in the German electricity market. In *Proceedings of the 7th IAEE European Energy Conference, Bergen, 28–30 August 2005*, 2005. http://elib.uni-stuttgart.de/opus/volltexte/2005/2450/.

ETSO. *Comparison on transmission pricing in Europe: Synthesis 2004*. ETSO Tariffs Task Force, Brussels, 2005. http://www.etso-net.org/activities/tariff_benchmarking/e_default.asp.

Eurelectric. *Power Statistic & Trends 2012*. Brussels, 2012. http://www.eurelectric.org/media/113657/power_statistics_2012_hr-2012-180-0002-01-e.pdf.

European Commission. *Environmental fact sheet: Climate change*. Brussels, 2013. http://ec.europa.eu/clima/publications/docs/factsheet_climate_change_en.pdf.

European Photovoltaic Industry Association. *Global Market Outlook for Photovoltaics 2013–2017*. Brusseles, 2013. http://www.epia.org.

Fleten, S.-E. and Lemming, J. Constructing forward prices in electricity markets. *Energy Economics*, 25:409–424, 2003.

Fleten, S.-E., Paraschiv, F., and Schürle, M. Spot forward model for electricity prices. Working papers on finance 2013/11, Institute of Operational Research and Computational Finance, 2013.

Franzen, D. *Design of Master Agreements for OTC Derivatives*. Springer-Verlag, Berlin, 2001.

FS – UNEP-Centre. *Global Trends in Renewable Energy Investment 2013*. Frankfurt School – UNEP Collaborating Centre for Climate & Sustainable Energy and Bloomberg New Energy Finance, Frankfurt, 2013. http://fs-unep-centre.org.

Geman, H. and Vasicek, O. Forwards and futures on non storable commodities: The case of electricity. *RISK*, 14, 2001.

Global Wind Energy Council. *Global Wind Report 2012*. Brussels, 2013. http://www.gwec.net.

Graeber, B. *Grenzübergreifende integrierte Elektrizitätsplanung im südlichen Afrika (PhD thesis)*. Universität Stuttgart, Stuttgart, 2002. http://elib.uni-stuttgart.de/opus/volltexte/2002/1132/.

Graeber, B., Spalding-Fecher, R., and Gonah, B. Optimising trans-national power generation and transmission investments: A Southern African example. *Energy Policy*, 33:2337–2349, 2005.

Grobbel, C. *Competition in electricity generation in Germany and neighboring countries from a system dynamics perspective. Outlook until 2012*. Peter Lang, Frankfurt, 1999.

Guldimann, T. M. RiskMetrics-Technical Document. Technical report, Morgan Guaranty, 1995.

Hamilton, J. D. *Time Series Analysis*. Princeton University Press, Princeton, NJ, 1994.

Hamisultane, H. Which method for pricing weather derivatives?, 2008. Working paper available at http://halshs.archives-ouvertes.fr/halshs-00355856/PDF/wpaper0801.pdf.

Harding, P. *Mastering the ISDA Master Agreements: A Practical Guide for Negotiation*. Financial Times/Prentice Hall, 3rd edn, 2010.

Harvey, A. C. *Forecasting, Structural Time Series Models and the Kalman Filter*. Cambridge University Press, Cambridge, 1991.

Heath, D. and Jara, D. Term structure models based on futures prices, Working paper, 2000.

Heath, D., Jarrow, R. A., and Morton, A. Bond pricing and the term structure of interest rates: A new methodology. *Econometrica*, 60(1):77–105, 1992.

Heitsch, H. and Römisch, W. Scenario reduction algorithms in stochastic programming. *Computational Optimization and Applications*, 24(2&3):187–206, 2003.

Heren. Icis heren coal swaps daily methodology. Available at http://www.icis.com/staticpages/ICISHerenCoalMethodology.htm.

Heston, S. L. A closed form solution for options with stochastic volatility with applications to bond and currency options. *Review of Financial Studies*, 6:327–343, 1993.

Hildemann, M., Herzog, F., Stokic, D., Cornel, J., and Andersson, G. Robust calculation and parameter estimation of the hourly price forward curve. In *17th Power Systems Computation Conference*, Stockholm, Sweden, 2011.

Hillier, F. S. and Lieberman, G. J. *Introduction to Operations Research*. McGraw-Hill, New York, 2004.

Hirsch, G., Müller, A., and Müller, J. Modeling the price of natural gas with temperature and oil price as exogenous factors, 2013. Preprint of University of Siegen.

Holden, L., Loland, A., and Lindqvist, O. Valuation of long-term flexible gas contracts. *Journal of Derivatives*, 3:75–85, 2011.

Holton, G. A. *Value-at-Risk, Theory and Practice*. Academic Press, New York, 2nd edn, 2009.

Hull, J. C. *Options, Futures and Other Derivatives*. Prentice Hall International, New York, 8th edn, 2011.

International Energy Agency. *Power to Choose – Demand Response in Liberalised Electricity Markets*. Paris, 2003.

International Energy Agency. *Energy Technology Perspectives 2010*. Paris, 2010.

International Energy Agency. *Technology Roadmap. Biofuels for Transport*. Paris, 2011. http://www.iea.org.

International Energy Agency. *World Energy Outlook 2012*. IEA/Organization for Economic Cooperation and Development, 2012.

International Organization for Standardization. *ISO Guide 73, Risk Management-Vocabulary*, 2009.

International Panel on Climate Change. *Climate Change 1995, The Science of Climate Change: Summary for Policymakers and Technical Summary of the Working Group I Report*. Geneva, 2005.

IRENA. *Renewable Energy Auctions in Developing Countries*. International Renewable Energy Agency (IRENA), Abu Dhabi, 2013. http://www.irena.org/Publications.

Jaillet, P., Ronn, E. I., and Tompaidis, S. Valuation of commodity-based swing options. *Management Science*, 50(7):909–921, 2004.

Jordan, D. C. and Kurtz, S. R. Photovoltaic degradation rates – an analytical review. *Progress in Photovoltaics: Research and Applications*, 2012.

Jorion, P. *Value-at-Risk, The New Benchmark for Managing Financial Risk*. Mc-Graw-Hill, New York, 3rd edn, 2006.

J.P. Morgan. *RiskMetrics Monitor*, 1995.

Kalman, R. E. A new approach to linear filtering and prediction problems. *Journal of Basic Engineering, Transactions of the ASME Series D*, 82:35–45, 1960.

Kaltschmitt, M., Streicher, W., and Wiese, A. (eds). *Renewable Energy: Technology, Economics and Environment*. Springer, Berlin, 2007.

Kiesel, R., Schindlmayr, G., and Börger, R. H. A two-factor model for the electricity forward market. *Quantitative Finance*, 9(3):279–287, 2009.

Kirk, E. Correlation in the energy markets. In *Managing Energy Price Risk*. Risk Publications and Enron, 1995.

KPMG. *Taxes and incentives for renewable energy 2013*. KPMG International, Zug, Switzerland, 2013. http://www.kpmg.com/energytax.

Longstaff, F. A. and Schwartz, E. S. Valuing American options by simulation: A simple least-squares approach. *The Review of Financial Studies*, 14(1):113–147, 2001.

Margrabe, W. The value of an option to exchange one asset for another. *Journal of Finance*, 33:177–186, 1978.

Meadows, D. H., Meadows, D. L., Randers, J., and Behrens, W. W. *The Limits of Growth: A report for the Club of Rome's project on the predicament of mankind*. Universe Books, New York, 1972.

Meinshausen, N. and Hambly, B. Monte Carlo methods for the valuation of multiple-exercise options. *Mathematical Finance*, 14:557–583, 2004.

Meller, E., Milojcic, G., Wodopia, F.-J., and Schöning, G. (eds). *Jahrbuch der europäischen Energie- und Rohstoffwirtschaft 2007*. VGE Verlag, Essen, 114th edn, 2006.

Mengle, D. The importance of close-out netting. Technical report, International Swaps and Derivatives Association (ISDA) Research Notes, 2010.

Merton, R. C. Option pricing when underlying stock returns are discontinuous. *Journal of Financial Economics*, 3:125–144, 1976.

Moreno, M. and Navas, J. On the robustness of least-squares Monte Carlo for pricing American derivatives. *Review of Derivatives Research*, 6:107–128, 2003.

Müller, A. and Grandi, D. M. Weather derivatives for protection against weather risks, 2000. Munich Re ART Solutions.

Müller, J. Stochastic modeling of the spot price of electricity incorporating commodities and renewables as exogenous factors, 2013. Preprint from University of Siegen.

Musiela, M. and Rutkowski, M. *Martingale Methods in Financial Modelling*. Stochastic Modelling and Applied Probability. Springer, Berlin, 2004.

OFGEM. *Renewables Obligation: Guidance for Generators 2013*. OFGEM, London, 2013. https://www.ofgem.gov.uk/environmental-programmes/renewables-obligation-ro.

Osborne, M. J. *An Introduction to Game Theory*. Oxford University Press, New York, 2003.

Pearson, N. D. An efficient approach for pricing spread options. *Journal of Derivatives*, 3:76–91, 1995.

Perner, J. *Die langfristige Erdgasversorgung Europas: Analysen und Simulationen mit dem Angebotsmodell EUGAS (PhD thesis)*, vol. 60 of *Schriften des Energiewirtschaftlichen Instituts*. Oldenbourg Industrieverlag, München, 2002.

Pindyck, R. S. The dynamics of commodity spot and futures markets: A primer, Working paper, 2001.

Pindyck, R. S. Volatility and commodity price dynamics, Working paper, 2002.

Poitras, G. Spread options, exchange options, and arithmetic Brownian motion. *The Journal of Futures Markets*, 1998.

Prokopczuk, M., Rachev, S., Schindlmayr, G., and Trück, S. Quantifying risk in the electricity business: A RAROC-based approach. *Energy Economics*, 29(5):1029–1033, 2007.

Qu, D. Pricing basket options with skew. *Wilmott magazine*, 2010.

Sanchez, J. J., Centeno, E., and Barquin, J. System dynamics for electricity generation expansion analysis. In *15th PSCC, Liege, 22–26 August 2005*, 2005.

Sawin, J. L. *Renewables 2013 Global Status Report*. Renewable Energy Policy Network for the 21st Century (REN21), Paris, 2013. http://www.ren21.net.

Scheib, P., Kalisch, F., and Graeber, B. *Analysis of a liberalised German gas market. CNI Working Paper 2006-11.* Center for Network Industries and Infrastructure, Technische Universität Berlin, 2006.

Schindlmayr, G. A regime-switching model for electricity spot prices, 10th Symposium on Banking, Finance and Insurance, University of Karlsruhe, 2005.

Schwartz, E. and Smith, J. E. Short-term variations and long-term dynamics in commodity prices. *Management Science*, 46:893–911, 2000.

Schwartz, E. S. The stochastic behavior of commodity prices: Implications for valuation and hedging. *Journal of Finance*, 52(3):923–973, 1997.

Seeliger, A. *Entwicklung des weltweiten Erdgasangebots bis 2030 (PhD thesis)*, vol. 61 of *Schriften des Energiewirtschaftlichen Instituts*. Oldenbourg Industrieverlag, München, 2006.

SEIA. *Solar Net Metering by State.* Solar Energy Industries Association, Washington, DC, 2012. http://www.seia.org.

Sen, S. and Kothari, D. P. Optimal thermal generation unit commitment – a review. *Electric Power & Energy Systems*, 20:443–451, 1998.

Sheble, G. and Fahd, G. Unit commitment literature synopsis. *IEE Transaction on Power Systems*, 9:128–135, 1994.

Skantze, P., Gubina, A., and Ilic, M. Bid-based stochastic model for electricity prices: The impact of fundamental drivers on market dynamics, Report, MIT Energy Laboratory (2000), 2000.

Sørensen, B. *Renewable Energy: Physics, Engineering, Environmental Impacts, Economics & Planning.* Academic Press, Oxford, 4th edn, 2010.

Sterman, J. D. *Business Dynamics: System thinking and modeling for a complex world.* McGraw-Hill, Boston, 2000.

Stoft, S. *Power System Economics.* Wiley, New York, 2002.

Stoll, S.-O. and Wiebauer, K. A spot price model for natural gas considering temperature as an exogenous factor and applications. *The Journal of Energy Markets*, 3(3):113–128, 2010.

Talberg, A. and Swoboda, K. *Emissions trading schemes around the world.* Parliamentary Library, Parliament of Australia, Melborne, 2013. http://www.aph.gov.au/About_Parliament/Parliamentary_Departments/Parliamentary_Library/pubs/.

UNFCCC. *National greenhouse gas inventory data for the period 1990–2010.* UNFCCC Subsidiary Body for Implementation, Bonn, 2012.

US Energy Information Agency. *International Energy Outlook 2013*, Washington, DC, 2013. http://www.eia.gov.

Verein der Kohlenimporteure. Annual Report 2012, 2012.

von der Fehr, N.-H. M., Amundsen, E. S., and Bergman, L. The Nordic market: Signs of stress? *The Energy Journal*, 26(Special Issue):71–98, 2005.

Vorst, T. Prices and hedge ratios of average exchange rate options. *International Review of Financial Analysis*, 1(3):179–194, 1992.

Wagner, A. Residual demand modeling and application to electricity pricing. Technical report, Fraunhofer ITWM, 2012.

Weber, C. *Uncertainty in the Electric Power Industry: Methods and models for decission support.* Springer, New York, 2005.

Weron, R. *Modeling and Forecasting Electricity Loads and Prices: A statistical approach.* Wiley, Chichester, UK, 2006.

Wilmott, P. *Paul Wilmott Introduces Quantitative Finance.* Wiley, Chichester, UK, 2nd edn, 2007.

Winston, W. L. *Operations Research. Applications and Algorithms.* Duxbury Press, Pacific Grove, CA, 2003.

Wissel, S., Fahl, U., Blesl, M., and Voss, A. *Erzeugungskosten zur bereitstellung elektrischer energie von kraftwerks- optionen in 2015.* Technical report, University Stuttgart, Institute of Energy Economics and the Rational Use of Energy. Available at http://www.ier.uni-stuttgart.de/publikationen/arbeitsberichte/Arbeitsbericht_08.pdf.

Xu, Z. *Stochastic models for gas prices.* Master's thesis, University of Calgary, 2004. http://math.ucalgary.ca/sites/finance.math.ucalgary.ca/files/u22/JamesXuMSc.pdf.

Index

25-day forward market trades 11

AAUs *see* Assigned Amount Units
accounting standards 140, 144, 148–9
ACCUs *see* Australian Carbon Credit Units
Acid Rain Program 51–2
actuarial pricing of weather derivatives 170
afforestation 52–3
Africa 8–10, 13–15, 22–4, 27–8, 385
Agency for the Cooperation of Energy Regulators
    (ACER) 103
agriculture 5, 44–5, 52–3, 60–1
air pollution 55
Alberta 53–4
Algeria 9, 17–20
All Publication Index (API) 25
Alpha Ventus offshore wind-farm 78
American options 200–1, 212–13, 294–9, 410
    see also options
Amsterdam–Rotterdam–Antwerp delivery point
    (ARA) 7, 24–5
anaerobic digester facilities (biogas plants) 73, 75–6,
    84, 96–9, 306–13
analytical VaR, computational method 115
Angola 9
annual contract quantity (ACQ) 18–19, 287–99
antithetic paths, variance reduction methods 411
appendix 393–411
APX (Amsterdam Power Exchange) 41
aquifers, gas storage methods 379–86
Aquila Energy 168
ARA refined oil market 12, 312
arbitrage-free pricing of weather derivatives 170–1
Argus Media Ltd 25
Argus oil pricing reporting agency 10
Argus Sour Crude Index (ASCI) 10–11
artificial neural networks (ANNs), load forecasts
    163–5
Asia & Pacific 7–10, 13–15, 19–20, 22–4, 27–8
Asian options 213–16, 410, 411
asset investments 194, 387–91, 408–9

Assigned Amount Units (AAUs) 48–54
at-the-money options 206, 218
auctions 4, 38, 40–2, 85–6, 229, 278–81
audits, corporate governance 103–4
augmented Dickey–Fuller test (ADF) 397
Australia 15, 19–20, 22–5, 44, 48–49, 52–4
Australian Carbon Credit Units (ACCUs) 49, 52–4
Austria 5, 29, 44, 309
autocorrelation 268–81, 396
autocovariance 395–6
autoregression 268–81, 395–6, 398–9
autoregressive moving averages time series models
    (ARMA) 268–81, 396, 398–9
autoregressive time series models (AR) 395–6

back-to-back risks 131–4
backtesting 114, 123–5, 164–5, 171–2, 371–2
backwardation, forward curves 192–6, 234–7, 239–41
Bacton hub, UK 18
balancing energy 33–4, 37–42, 159–60, 175–6, 375
Baltic Dry Index (BDI), freight rates 26
Bank for International Settlements 134
bankruptcies 133–5, 140–4, 173, 176–7, 193–4
barge transport 368–9
Basel Committee on Banking Supervision 101–3,
    113–14, 134, 144–7
Basel II 113–14
baseload electricity contracts 36, 105–30, 141–4,
    152–83, 190–1, 254–65, 278–81, 307–13
basic price, retail markets 155–83
basis risks 190, 196–7
basket options 216–19
Belarus 44
Belgium 17–18, 29, 38, 41, 44, 84–5, 278–9, 309,
    376–86
Bellman principle 326–35
Belpex 41
benchmark oils 10–11
Bermudan options, definition 212–13
Bernoulli's equation, fluid dynamics 62–3
Bertrand duopoly model 363–4

beta values, CAPM 390–1
BFOE crude oil (Brent Forties, Oseberg and Ekofisk) 10–11
bid–offer spreads 144–6, 173, 263–5
binomial trees 212–16
biodiesel biofuels 60–1, 76–7
biodiversity 61
bioethanol biofuels 60–1
biofuels 1–3, 55, 60–1, 69, 73–7, 97–100, 306–13, 320–1
    definition 60, 73
    statistics 1–3, 60–1, 306–13
    technologies 60–1, 73–7
biomass renewable energy 55–8, 59–61, 69, 73–7, 84, 87, 90–1, 96–9, 264–5, 306–13
    anaerobic digester facilities (biogas plants) 73, 75–6, 84, 96–9, 306–13
    definition 73, 310
    market risks 97–100
    power plants 73–5, 97–100, 310
    statistics 55–8, 59–61, 73–7, 97–9, 306–13
    storage problems 98–9
    technologies 60–1, 73–7, 90–1, 96–9, 310
bitumen 12, 308
Black–Scholes equation
    see also partial differential equations
    definition 409
Black–Scholes model 175, 200–2, 208–9, 213–24, 235–7, 240–1, 244, 279, 288–99, 405
    see also options pricing theory
    definition 405
Black's formula for swaptions 211–12
Black's Futures Price Model (1976) 116, 200, 208–9, 211–12, 224, 231–2, 247–51, 269, 288–99
block electricity contracts 36, 263–5, 347
BlueNext 49
board of directors 102–3
bonds 146, 387–91
BP 21, 56
Brazil 44, 48, 60–1
Brent benchmark oil 10–11, 196–7, 209–10, 286, 293–9
British Energy 144–5
brokers 24–6, 372
brown coal 21–6, 308
    see also coal; lignite . . . ; sub-bituminous . . .
Brownian motion 116–18, 182, 200, 211–12, 213–24, 225–45, 246–51, 268–81, 402–5, 406–7
    see also geometric . . .
    definition 402–3
Bulgaria 29, 44
business plan 147–8
business-to-business customer (B2B) 155–61, 173, 177, 305–13
business-to-consumers customer (B2C) 155–60, 162–3, 175–6, 183, 305–13
butane 13

California 31, 42, 53–4, 58, 81–2
call options 6, 120, 185, 197–212, 235–7, 294–9

Canada 13, 15, 43–4, 53–4, 83, 168
cap-and-trade systems, emissions market 51–4
capacity expansion, optimisation methods 351–3
capacity remunerations, electricity markets 30, 305–6, 388–91
Cape-sized vessels, coal freight 26
capital adequacy requirements 101–3, 112–14, 144–6
capital asset pricing model (CAPM) 390–1
caps 185, 226–9
carbon dioxide (CO_2) 42–54, 131–4, 216–18, 307–8, 312–35, 355–7, 369–74, 386–7
carbon emission certificates 3–4, 5, 28–9, 46–54, 312–35, 372, 386–7
    see also EU Emissions Trading Scheme
carbon emissions 3–4, 5, 23, 28–9, 42–54, 131–4, 216–24, 307–8, 312–35, 355–7, 369–74, 386–7, 388–91
    see also emissions market; greenhouse effect
Carbon Farming Initiative (CFI) 53–4
Carbon Price Mechanism (CPM) 52–4
carry forward terms, gas contracts 18–19, 377–86
cascading procedures, futures 34–6
cash flow models, project developers 89
cash-and-carry arbitrage 194
Cashflow-at-Risk (CFaR) 127–30
cashflows 89, 127–30, 387–91
caverns 379–86
Central America 7–10, 13–15, 27–8
Central Appalachianin delivery point 24–5
central counterparties, futures 189–91
Central Western Europe (CWE) 38
Certified Emissions Reductions (CERs) 47–54, 386–7
CFaR see Cashflow-at-Risk
characteristics of electricity 31–3
Chicago Board of Trade (CBOT) 5
chief risk officers (CROs) 103
China 1–2, 7–10, 13–15, 21–5, 27–8, 44–5, 48, 54, 57–8, 60–1
    biofuels 60–1
    coal 21–5
    electricity markets 27–8, 57–8
    emissions market 54
    energy demands 1–2, 7–10, 22–4, 27–8
    greenhouse gas emissions 44, 48, 54
    renewable energy 57–8, 60–1
CHPs see combined heat and power biofuel plants
clean dark/spark spread 219, 278–81
Clean Development Kyoto Protocol flexible mechanism (CDM) 45, 47–8, 53–4
clearinghouses, futures 189–91
cluster analysis 349–53
CME Group 2, 5, 11, 15–16, 26, 42, 168, 169
coal 1–4, 6–7, 12, 15, 21–9, 31, 51–2, 98, 100, 118–20, 131–4, 145–6, 154, 157–60, 188–9, 216–18, 269–81, 306–13, 368–72, 376, 386–7
    see also hard . . . ; lignite . . . ; sub-bituminous . . .
    classification 21, 307–8
    consumption, production and reserves 21–4
    freight 26
    fundamental market models 386–7

price determinants 21, 24–5, 26, 51, 118–19,
    157–60, 216–17, 269–81, 306–13, 368–72,
    386–7
  statistics 1–2, 21–6, 31, 306–13
  transportation and storage considerations 24–6,
    307–8, 368–72
  uses 21–4, 27–9, 31, 100, 306–13, 386–7
Coal India 24
coalbed methane 15, 16
Coface 137
coking coal 21–6, 386
  see also coal; hard . . .
collateral 3–4, 142–4
Colombia, coal 23–4
Colorado, renewable energy 58
combined cycle gas turbines (CCGT) 308, 312–13,
    345–7, 352–3, 367–72, 388–91
combined heat and power biofuel plants (CHPs) 76–7,
    98, 308, 310–13, 320–1, 338, 369–72
combined load and spot price model for
    electricity/natural-gas 180–1
commercial operation date (COD) 93
Commodity Exchange Bratislava (CEB) 49
Commodity Futures Trading Commission (CFTC)
    104
Community Independent Transaction Log (CITL) 46,
    371–2
compensation schemes, corporate governance 103–4
complete markets 228–31, 406–9
compliance checks, corporate governance 103–4,
    148–9
composite options 221–4
compressed air energy storage (CAES) 301
compressors, gas storage methods 380–6
concentrated solar power (CSP) 70–1
conditional expectations 275–81, 402, 408–9
conditional VaR, definition 113
Conferences of the Parties (COPs) 43–4
confidence intervals 93–5, 112–20, 142–4, 171–2,
    394–5
Consolidated Edison Co. 168
construction risks 88–9, 93
consumption assets, definition 194–6
contango, forward curves 192–7, 234–7, 239–41
continuous stochastic processes, definition 402
contracts-for-differences (CFDs) 11, 39–40
control variates, variance reduction methods 213–16,
    411
convenience yield 194–6, 221–2, 234–5, 406–7
cooling degree days (CDDs) 166–72
cooperative game theory 361–2
copulas 140–4, 218
Cornish–Fisher expansion 120
corporate bonds 146
corporate governance principles 102–4, 143–4, 148–9
correlation coefficient 118–19, 120–3, 177–81,
    218–24, 394–5
correlation matrices 118–19, 218
correlograms 396
cost of capital 388–91

Cost, Insurance and Freight Incoterms (CIF) 7, 24–5
cost-based purchase prices, feed-in renewable energy
    tariffs 81–3
cost-efficiency risk-mitigation approaches 92–3
counterparty analysis 136–44, 148–9
countertrades, credit risks 144
country risks 88–9, 100
coupled electricity markets 38
Cournot duopoly model 363–6
covariance 123, 178–81, 245, 246–51, 390–1, 394,
    395–7
covariance matrices 245, 394, 397
covered call strategy, definition 199–200
Cox–Ingersoll–Ross interest rate model 248–9
Cplex 280
CPM see Carbon Price Mechanism
crack spread 219
cracking refinery processes, definition 12
Crank–Nicolson method 409
credit rating agencies 136–44
  see also Fitch; Moody's; Standard & Poor's
credit ratings 133–44
credit risk exposure 136
credit risks 3, 5–6, 102–4, 130–44, 147, 173, 176–7,
    183, 187–9, 192
  definition 3, 135–7, 173, 176–7
  quantification methods 139–44
  risk management 135–44, 173, 176–7, 183
credit sleeves 143–4
Credit VaR 137, 140–2
Creditform 137
Croatia 29, 44, 46
crude oil (petroleum) 1–12, 13, 15, 25, 27, 61, 98,
    106–10, 135–6, 145–6, 154, 186–9, 192–7,
    386–7
  see also oil
cumulated cooling degree days (CCDDs) 166–72
cumulated heating degree days (CHDDs) 165–72
cumulative normal distribution function 202
customer types, retail markets 155–60, 305–13
Czech Republic 29, 44

daily contract quantity (DCQ) 18–19, 287–99
daily electricity demands 253–65, 283–99, 302–13,
    350–3
daily and hourly forward curve models 253–65,
    304–13
daily price forward curves (DPFCs) 253–65, 283–99
dark/spark spread 216, 218–24, 278–81
Dated Brent, definition 11
day-ahead electricity spot markets 34–6, 39–42,
    270–81
DCF see discounted cashflow method
debt finance 78–90, 389–91
debt service coverage ratio (DSCR) 90
debt/equity ratios 388–91
decision theory, game theory 311–13, 357–66
decommissioning costs 352–5
decomposition optimisation methods 325, 332–5,
    351–3

default probabilities, credit risks 136–40, 142–4, 177
deforestation 52–3
delayed-sourcing risks 182
Delivered-At-Place Incoterms (DAP) 7
Delivered-ex-Ship Incoterms (DES) 7
delivery terms, energy trading 6–7, 33–42, 313,
    378–86
delta
    see also gamma
    definition 203–4
delta hedging 203–4, 206, 208, 281, 290–9
delta neutrality 204
delta position of the portfolio 104–30, 152–5, 160–1
delta position of power schedules 108–30, 152–5,
    160–1, 373–4
delta-gamma VaR, computational method 115,
    119–20
delta-neutral position 105–30
delta-normal VaR, computational method 114–19
demand charges, retail markets 156–83
demand curves 301–2, 336–47, 357–66, 373–4
demonstration projects, renewable energy 78–9
Denmark 29, 38–9, 44, 83, 278–9
depleted oil/gas fields, gas storage methods 379–86
depreciation 388–91
deregulated markets 2–3, 17–18, 28–31, 134–5, 151–5
derivatives see energy derivatives
derived gas 306–13
Dickey–Fuller test (DF), definition 396–7
diesel oil product 12
diffusion 408–9
discounted cashflow method (DCF) 387–91
discounts
    forwards 105–30, 186–9, 190–1, 225–6, 407–8
    time value of money 330
discrete stochastic processes 266–7, 402
distribution losses 302–35
diversification risk-mitigation approaches 92–3,
    159–60, 173, 390–1
Dodds–Frank Act 2010 104, 143–4
Dong Energy 279
downstream portfolios, retail markets 153–83
drift 116–18, 222–3, 234–7, 242–5, 246–51, 272–99,
    405, 407–8
    see also Itô's lemma
Dubai benchmark oil 10–11
due diligence activities 136
Dun and Bradstreet 137
dynamic hedging strategies 206, 281, 290–9
dynamic programming optimisation method (DP)
    281, 325–35

Earnings-at-Risk (EaR) 127–30
Eastern Europe, greenhouse gas emissions 45
EBITDA 89
econometric methods 393–401
economic capital, RAROC 174
economic power plant dispatch 301, 313–35, 338–53,
    357–66, 371–2
Ecuador 9

EDF 278–81
EFA calendar 41–2
EFET see European Federation of Energy Traders
efficiency factors, energy markets 1–2, 9, 305–13,
    325–35, 341–7, 369–72, 388–91
EFP (exchange for physical) 41
Ekofisk, Brent benchmark 11
elasticity of demand 50–1, 357–66, 367–72, 375–86
Elbas intra-day electricity spot markets 39–40
election sheets 131–4
electric utility quota obligations, renewable energy
    support schemes 83–5, 99
Electricity Market Directives of 1996 and 2003 28–9
electricity markets 1–7, 12–13, 21–42, 50–100,
    151–83, 186–91, 220, 253–99, 301–74, 406–7
    application of electricity market models 372–4, 385
    auctioning 38, 40–2, 85–6, 278–81
    balancing periods 33–4, 37–42, 159–60, 173–83,
        301–13, 348–53
    barriers to entry 28, 83, 140
    capacity 30, 305–6, 388–91
    categories 33–8
    characteristics of electricity 31–3
    consumption and production 27–31
    coupled markets 38
    daily and hourly forward curve models 253–65,
        304–13
    deregulated markets 2–3, 28–31, 36–42, 134–5,
        151–5
    economic power plant dispatch 301, 313–35,
        338–53, 357–66
    energy trading 3–7, 31–42, 151–83, 313–14,
        345–7, 348–53, 370–2
    exchanges 38–42, 313–14, 345–7, 348–53, 370–2
    forwards 33–6, 39–40, 186–9, 197, 253–65, 304–13
    fundamental market models 301–74
    fundamental price drivers 301–13, 336–47, 357–66
    futures 33–6, 39–40, 42, 190–1, 253–65, 360–6,
        373–4
    game theory 311–13, 357–66, 367
    granularity concepts 33–6, 155–83, 253–65,
        272–99
    grid infrastructures 28, 62–5, 98, 100, 151–83,
        271–81, 366–72
    load forecasts 158, 160–1, 163–5, 266–81, 282–99,
        302–74
    market power 357–60, 362–6, 374
    market risks 97–100
    merit order curves 265–81, 335–47, 357–74
    methodological model approaches 335–66
    monopolies 28–9, 311–13, 357–66
    oligopolies 311–13, 357–66, 374
    optimisation methods 280–1, 315, 325–35, 341–53,
        359–66, 371–2, 375
    options 39–40, 278–9
    physical energy flows 313–14, 345, 348–53, 370–2
    price determinants 27–42, 144, 151–83, 220,
        253–99, 301–74, 406–8
    price spikes 29–31, 253–99
    products 33–42, 155–60, 182–3, 253–65, 305–13

retail markets 151–83
settlement periods 151–83
spot markets 3–6, 29–30, 34–42, 151–83, 301–74
statistics 1–3, 12–13, 27–42, 56–100, 302–74
stochastic models 253–99
storage methods 64–5, 301, 306, 309–10, 313,
    322–5, 338–47
storage problems 31–4, 98, 151–83, 225–6,
    253–99, 301–13, 338–47
structural electricity price models 253, 265–81,
    335–47
system dynamics 311–13, 353–7
system information for electricity market
    modelling 366–72
TSOs 33–8, 312–13, 366–72
uses 27–8
weather risks 165–72
wholesale markets 27–42, 135, 151–5, 278–81,
    305–35
Elspot day-ahead electricity spot markets 39–40
EMIR Directive 103–4, 143
Emission Performance Credits (EPCs) 53–4
Emission Reduction Purchase Agreements (ERPAs)
    49–54
Emission Reduction Units (ERUs) 47–54, 386
emissions market 3–4, 5, 28–9, 42–54, 60, 118–20,
    131–4, 154, 157, 269, 302–13, 369–72, 386–7
    see also carbon . . . ; EU Emissions Trading
    Scheme; greenhouse effect;
    hydrofluorocarbons . . . ; methane . . . ; nitrous
    oxide . . . ; perfluorocarbons . . . ; sulphur . . .
    AAUs 48–54
    ACCUs 49, 52–4
    cap-and-trade systems 51–4
    carbon emission certificates 3–4, 5, 28–9, 46–54,
        312–35, 372, 386–7
    CERs 47–54, 386–7
    concepts 42–54, 157, 269, 312–13, 371–2, 386–7
    energy derivatives 48–50
    ERUs 47–54, 386
    EUAs 3–4, 5, 28–30, 46–54, 118–20, 386–7
    exchanges 49–54
    fundamental market models 386–7
    limits 43–8, 312–13, 371
    list of greenhouse gases 42–4
    NZUs 49, 52–4
    prices 50–4, 269, 302–13, 373–4, 386–7
    products and marketplaces 3–5, 28–9, 46–54
    statistics 49–54, 371–2, 386–7
    Swiss ETS 53
Emissions Trading Directive (2003/87/EC) 45–6
empirical merit order curves 267–81, 335–47
ENDEX 18, 41
energetic portfolio position 104–30
energy derivatives 3–7, 11–12, 15–20, 26, 33–42,
    48–50, 99, 103–4, 117–18, 132–4, 144–6,
    168–72, 185–251, 253, 313–35, 387–91, 402–11
    see also forwards; futures; options . . . ; swaps;
    weather . . .
    definition 185–6

statistics 11, 15–20
    terminology 4–7, 11, 185–6, 191–2, 197–8, 212–16
Energy Information Agency (EIA), US 56, 59–60,
    313–14
energy markets 1–54, 97–149, 151–83, 194–7,
    265–99, 301–91, 405–8
    see also coal; electricity . . . ; gas; market risks;
    nuclear . . . ; oil; renewable . . . ; retail . . . ;
    wholesale . . .
    demands 1–2, 7–10, 12–13, 15–20, 22–4, 27–42,
        97–100, 151–83, 194–7, 265–99, 301–13,
        336–72, 374–86
    deregulated markets 2–3, 17–18, 28–31, 134–5,
        151–5
    efficiency factors 1–2, 9, 305–13, 325–35, 341–7,
        369–72, 388–91
    fundamental market models 13, 27, 89–90, 185,
        253, 280–1, 301–91
    statistics 1–54, 151–83, 302–91
    supply 1–2, 7–10, 12–13, 15–24, 27–42, 97–100,
        151–83, 194–7, 265–99, 301–72, 374–86
    types 2–6, 151–5, 305–13
Energy Policy Act 1992, US 31
energy trading 2–7, 10–12, 15–21, 23–6, 31–42,
    118–19, 131–49, 151–83, 377–86
    delivery terms 6–7, 33–42, 313, 378–86
    exchanges 5–6, 38–42, 313–14, 345–7, 348–53
Enron 135, 168
Environmental Protection Agency (EPA) 51–2
EPEX 40–1, 264–5
equilibrium prices 301–2, 336–47, 357–66, 373–4
equity finance 78–90, 389–91
equivalent martingale measure 246–51, 407–8
ergodic Markov chains, definition 400
ergodic probability vector, definition 400
error terms, linear regression 393–5
ERUs see Emission Reduction Units
Estonia 29, 39, 44
ethane 13
ETS Directive (2009/29/EC) 46
EU Emissions Trading Scheme (EU ETS) 28–9,
    45–54, 386–7
    see also Certified Emissions Reductions; European
        Emission Allowances
EUAs see European Emission Allowances
Euler discretisation 240–1
Euler Hermes 137
Eurasia 7–10, 13–15, 17–20, 22–4, 27–8
Europe 2–5, 7–10, 12–15, 17–20, 22–5, 27–54,
    57–100, 103–4, 259–99, 302–91
    see also individual countries
    biofuels 60–1
    carbon emission certificates 3–5, 28–9, 46–54,
        312–13, 372, 386–7
    coal 22–5, 306–13
    deregulated markets 2–3, 17–18, 28–31
    Electricity Market Directives of 1996 and 2003
        28–9
    electricity markets 27–42, 57–100, 259–99, 302–74
    EMIR Directive 103–4, 143

Europe (*Continued*)
  emissions market 48–54
  Emissions Trading Directive (2003/87/EC) 45–6
  energy trading 2–3, 17–20
  ETS Directive (2009/29/EC) 46
  gas 13–15, 17–20, 284–99, 306–13, 376–86
  governance principles and market regulations
    103–4, 143–4
  greenhouse gas emissions 43–54, 312–13
  Kyoto Protocol 43–54
  Linking Directive (2009/27/EC) 48
  MiFID Directives 103
  National Renewable Energy Action Plan of 2010
    58
  oil 7–10, 306–13
  physical energy flows 313–14, 345, 348–53, 370–2
  refined oil products 12
  REMIT Directive 103–4
  renewable energy 57–100, 306–13
  renewable sources Directive (2009/28/EC) 58,
    84–5
European Banking Federation 132–4
European Climate Exchange 5
European Commission 28–9, 45–6, 50–1
European Commodity Clearing AG (ECG) 40–1
European Council 45–6
European Electricity Index (ELIX) 41
European Emission Allowances (EUAs) 3–5, 28–30,
    46–54, 118–20, 132, 154, 216–18, 269, 312–13,
    386–7
European Energy Certificate System – Guarantee of
    Origin (EECS-GoO) 84–5
European Energy Exchange (EEX) 5, 30, 40–1,
    49–54, 253–5, 267–81, 372
European Federation of Energy Traders (EFET)
    131–4, 142–3, 148–9
European Master Agreement (EMA) 132–4
European Network of Transmission System Operators
    for Electricity (ENTSO-E) 36–8, 313–14, 366–7,
    370–2
European options 40, 169–72, 201–12, 217–24,
    240–1, 288–99, 409
  see also options
European Union Transaction Log (EUTL) 46
EWMA *see* exponentially weighted moving averages
exchange-traded markets 3–6, 26, 34–6, 186, 189–91
exchanges
  electricity markets 38–42, 313–14, 345–53, 370–2
  emissions market 49–54
exercise strategies, American options 212–13
expectation values 410–11
expected additional costs, risk premiums 173, 182–3
expected losses, measure of credit risk 140–4
expert systems, load forecasts 163–5
explicit finite-difference methods 409
exponentially weighted moving averages (EWMA)
    121–2, 257
extensive forms, game theory 360–1
extra heavy oils 9–10
extrinsic values, structural gas price models 292–9

factor loads, principal component analysis 397
failed projects 91–100
fair value derivative prices 185–251, 254–65, 291–9,
    406–7, 410–11
fat-tailed distributions 406
Federal Energy Regulatory Commission (FERC)
    36
feed-in renewable energy tariffs 80–5, 97–100
Feynman–Kac theorem 408–9
finance sources 78–90, 389–91
financial crisis from 2007 3, 7–8, 15–18, 29–30, 45,
    51, 102–3
financial information, system information 372
finite-difference methods 212–16, 409
Finland 29, 38–9, 44, 308, 309
Fitch 136–40
fixed leg of a swap, definition 191–2
fixed-price retail contracts 155–6, 160–3, 178–9
fixing issues, indexed contracts 156–62, 305–6
'flexible mechanisms', Kyoto Protocol 45–9
flexible price tariffs 306–13
floating leg of a swap 191–2, 211
floating price indexes, swaps 6, 11–12, 191–2,
    211–12
floors 185, 226–9
fluid dynamics, Bernoulli's equation 62–3
Force Majeure contract clauses 131–4
Forties, Brent benchmark 10–11
forward curves 108–10, 173, 192–7, 229, 234–7,
    239–41, 244–51, 253–65, 288–99, 304–13,
    408–9
  backwardation 192–6, 234–7, 239–41
  contango 192–7, 234–7, 239–41
  definition 192–4
forward–spot price relations 187–9, 194–7, 407–8
forwards 4–5, 11, 33–40, 49–50, 99, 105–30, 135–45,
    151–83, 185–9, 190–7, 199–200, 204–12,
    216–25, 236–51, 253–65, 313–35, 379–91,
    406–11
  definition 4–5, 11, 34, 39, 185–93
  delivery 34–5, 188–9, 192–7, 253–99
  pricing 107–30, 185–9, 190–7, 216–25, 234–7,
    239–41, 243–5, 253–99, 379–91, 407–8
  profits 4–5, 186–9, 194–7
  uses 187–97, 199–200, 253–65, 313–35
fossil-energy subsidies 60
France 5, 28–31, 40–1, 44, 47, 77, 132–4, 278–9,
    302–6, 309, 312–13, 376–86
  electricity markets 28–31, 40–1, 132–4, 278–9,
    302–6, 309, 312–13
  gas 376–86
  greenhouse gas emissions 44, 47, 312–13
  tidal renewable energy 77, 310
Francis reaction turbines, hydropower 63–5
Free-On-Board Incoterms (FOB) 7, 24–5
freight, coal 26
fuel costs 312, 368–74
fuel oil 7–12
  see also oil
full service retail contracts 157–60, 182–3

fundamental market models 13, 27, 89–90, 185, 253, 265–81, 301–91
  application of electricity market models 372–4, 385
  application of gas market models 385–6
  asset investment decisions 194, 387–91, 408–9
  coal 386–7
  definition 301
  economic power plant dispatch 301, 313–35, 338–53, 357–66
  electricity markets 301–74
  emissions market 386–7
  game theory 311–13, 357–66, 385–6
  gas market models 253, 281–99, 374–86
  merit order curves 265–81, 335–47, 357–74
  methodological approaches 335–66, 385–6
  oil 386–7
  optimisation methods 280–1, 315, 320–1, 325–35, 347–53, 359–66, 371–2, 375, 382–6
  system dynamics 311–13, 353–7, 385–6
  system information 366–72
fundamental theorem of asset pricing 408–9
funding liquidity risk, definition 144–5
futures contract 3–6, 11–20, 26, 33–6, 39–40, 42, 48–50, 104, 106–30, 143–4, 157–83, 185–6, 189–91, 196–7, 199–200, 202–25, 246–51, 253–65, 269, 360–6, 373–4, 402
  definition 4–5, 11, 34, 39, 185–6, 189–90
  delivery 34–6, 190–1, 253–65, 406–7
  margins 34–6, 142–5, 170–2, 189–91, 202–3
  pricing 116, 169–72, 190–1, 196–7, 200, 202–12, 224–5, 246–51, 253–65, 269, 360–6
  profits 4–5, 190–1, 197–8
  uses 189–91, 199–200, 373–4
FX 154, 194, 221–4, 374

game theory 311–13, 357–66, 367, 385–6
  cooperative/non-cooperative classifications 361–2, 363–6
  definition 357, 360–2
  duopolies 363–6
  extensive forms 360–1
  implementation of game theory models 365–6
  market power 357–60, 362–6
  Nash equilibrium 361–6
  normal forms 360–1
gamma 115, 119–20, 206, 208
  see also delta . . .
GARCH models, definition 122–3
gas 1–7, 12–21, 25, 28–9, 31, 51–2, 75–6, 98, 106–10, 131–6, 145–6, 151–83, 186–9, 193–7, 220, 253–99, 306–13, 368–72, 374–86
  application of gas market models 385–6
  balancing periods 375
  consumption, production and reserves 13–15, 21, 376–86
  daily and hourly forward curve models 253–65
  demand models 375–84
  deregulated markets 2–3, 17–18, 151–5
  derivatives 15–20

energy trading 2–7, 15–20, 131–6, 151–83, 377–86
  formulation of the market model 383–6
  forwards 188–9, 193–7, 253–65
  fundamental market models 253, 281–99, 374–86
  futures 15–20, 253–65
  HDDs 165–72
  hubs 15–20, 131–4, 368–72, 379–86
  imports 15–20, 131–4, 368–72, 377–86
  LNG 13–20, 131–4, 375–86
  long-term market models 374–5, 384–6
  market power 385–6
  networks 15–20, 131–4, 368–72, 379–86
  oil prices 3, 106–10, 281–99, 308, 377–8
  optimisation methods 375, 382–6
  portfolio optimisation 382–6
  price determinants 15–17, 31, 51, 106–10, 151–83, 186–9, 193–7, 220, 253–99, 368–72, 374–86, 388–91
  product types 13, 15, 155–60, 182–3, 253–65, 376–86
  quality factors 15–16, 308
  reserves-to-production ratios 14–15
  retail markets 151–83
  short-term market models 374–5, 383–6
  sources 376–7
  spot prices 4, 15–20, 151–83, 253–99, 388–91
  statistics 1–2, 12–20, 306–13, 374–86
  stochastic models 253–99
  storage 379–86
  structural gas price models 253, 281–99
  supply models 375–86
  system dynamics 385–6
  temperatures 151, 255–65, 281–99, 375–86
  transportation and storage 13–14, 19–20, 151–83, 193–4, 225–6, 253–99, 368–72, 374–86
  uses 12–15, 21, 28–9, 31, 51–2, 306–13, 374–86
  weather risks 165–72, 375–86
  wholesale markets 15–20, 151–5, 306–13
gasoil 12, 106–10, 186–9, 308–13
gasoline 7–12
  see also oil
Gaspool Hub in Germany (GPL) 17–18, 131–4
Gaussian copula model of time to default 140–4
geological risks 93
geometric Brownian motion (GBM) 200, 211–16, 221, 225–51, 269–81, 285–99
  see also Black–Scholes model; Brownian motion; stochastic processes
geometric means, Asian options 213–16
geothermal heat renewable energy 55–60, 71–2, 87, 91, 306–13
Germany 2, 5, 12, 17–18, 28–31, 33, 38, 40–1, 44, 46–7, 56–8, 78, 82–3, 94–5, 97–8, 100, 132–4, 151, 176, 259–65, 278–9, 290–1, 302–6, 308–11, 377–86
  electricity markets 2, 5, 28–31, 33, 38, 40–1, 56–8, 82–3, 94–5, 97–8, 100, 132–4, 151, 176, 259–65, 278–9, 302–6, 308–11
  gas 17–18, 290–1, 377–86

Germany (*Continued*)
  greenhouse gas emissions 44, 46–7
  renewable energy 56–8, 78, 82–3, 94–5, 97–8, 100,
    260–5, 310–11
Girsanov's theorem 407–8
global warming 42, 55, 95–6, 307–8
  see also emissions market; greenhouse effect
globalCOAL 24–5, 132–4
goodness of fit 394–5
government policies 1–2
grants and subsidies, renewable energy support
    schemes 86–7, 91, 99–100
granularity concepts, electricity markets 33–6,
    155–83, 253–65, 272–99
Greece 308
The 'Greeks' 202–8, 218, 281
  see also delta . . . ; gamma; theta; vega
greenhouse effect 13, 42–55, 60, 95–6, 307–8, 312–13
  see also emissions market
grid infrastructures, electricity markets 28, 62–5, 98,
    100, 151–83, 271–81, 366–72
grids 6–7, 28, 62–5, 98, 100, 151–83, 271–81,
    366–72, 402
gross calorific values (GCVs) 21–6, 369, 377
Growian demonstration project 78
guaranteed grid access, feed-in renewable energy
    tariffs 81–3
Gulf Wars 7–8

half-life period, EWMA method 122
Hamada model 391
Hamilton filter algorithm 275–6, 401
Handy-sized vessels 26
hard coal 21–6
  see also coal; coking . . . ; steam . . .
HDDs *see* heating degree days
heat 1, 13, 165–72, 282–99, 320–1, 367–72
Heath–Jarrow–Morton interest rate model 246–51
heating degree days (HDDs) 165–72, 282–99
heating oils 12
heavy oils 9–10
heavy tailed distributions 127, 147–9
hedge ratios, forwards/futures 190–1
hedging 5–6, 11, 33–6, 105–30, 145, 152–3, 168–72,
    179–83, 190–2, 194–7, 198–200, 202–12, 216,
    225–45, 290–9, 313–35, 387, 406–9
Henry Hub gas in the Gulf of Mexico 15–17
Heston's stochastic volatility model 209–10
heuristics, optimisation methods 333–5, 341–3
HFCs *see* hydrofluorocarbons
high tariff prices, retail markets 155–83
historical calibration 235–6, 240–1, 244–5, 256–65,
    267–81, 290–9, 345–7, 371–2
historical pricing of weather derivatives (burn
    analysis) 170
historical simulation VaR computational method
    114–15
hot dry rock geothermal technology 72
hourly electricity contracts 36, 180–1, 183, 253–65,
    302–13

hourly price forward curves (HPFCs) 253–65,
    274–81, 304–13
hubs, gas 15–20, 131–4, 368–72, 379–86
Hungary 29, 44, 308
hurdle rates, returns 174–81
hydraulic fracturing, shale gas 15
hydrocarbons 7, 12, 13, 43–4
hydrofluorocarbons (HFCs) 43–4, 48
hydropower 27–9, 31, 48, 55–65, 69, 72, 79–80, 82,
    88–91, 93–100, 264–5, 280–1, 301, 303, 306–35,
    338–53, 370–2
  Northumberland (UK) station of 1880 62
  pumped storage hydropower plants 64–5, 306,
    309–10, 313, 322–5, 338–53, 370–2
  statistics 28–9, 31, 55–6, 59–60, 82, 94–5, 306–13,
    370–2
  system information 370–2
  technologies 61–5, 79, 90–1, 93–5, 301, 309–10,
    322–5, 338–47, 350–3
  types of station 64–5, 309–10, 338–47, 350–3
  water values 240–7
hydropower plants 61–5, 79, 90–1, 93–5, 264–5, 301,
    306–35, 338–53, 370–2

ICE *see* IntercontinentalExchange
ICE Brent futures 5, 11
ICE ENDEX 18, 41
ICE gasoil futures 12, 17
ICE UK Natural Gas Futures 18
Iceland 308, 311
ICIS Heren 279
idle time-dependent start-up costs 318–21, 342–7
IFRS accounting standards 140
IHS McCloskey 25
imperfect competition 311–13, 348, 357–66
implicit auctioning, electricity markets 38
implicit finite-difference methods 409
implied volatilities 175, 208–10, 237, 246–51, 288–99
in-the-money options 201–2
incomplete markets 228–31
Incoterms (international commerce terms), definition
    7
indexed contracts 3, 17–18, 105–10, 156–62, 183,
    305–6
India 1–2, 7–10, 21–4, 27–8, 44, 48
Indonesia 19–20, 22–4
industrial sector energy demands 1–3, 9, 21–4, 44–6,
    58–100, 140, 302–13
ineligible firms, operational risks 148
information
  sources 371–2
  system information for electricity market
    modelling 366–72
initial margin, futures 34–6, 189–91
initial-screening risk-mitigation processes 91–3
injections, gas 291–9, 380–6
insider dealing 103–4
insurance 89, 100–2, 170, 199–200
integrated process of order 1 396–7
Interconnector gas pipeline 18, 313–14

IntercontinentalExchange (ICE) 5, 26, 41–2, 49–54, 270–81
interest rates 5, 104–30, 136–46, 188–9, 190–1, 194–7, 203–12, 237–41, 246–51, 279–81, 288–99, 399–400, 406–7
Intergovernmental Panel on Climate Change (IPCC), concepts 42–4
Interim Tight Volume Coupling (ITVC) 38
intermediate crudes, definition 9–10
internal credit ratings 138–40
internal rate of return (IRR) 89–90
International Emissions Trading (IET) Protocol flexible mechanism 45, 47–8, 132–4
International Energy Agency (IEA) 21–2, 27, 59–61
International Energy Outlook (IEO) 59–60
international exchanges 38–42, 313–14, 345–53, 370–2
International Petroleum Exchange (IPE) 5, 11, 17
International Renewable Energy Agency (IRENA) 58
International Swaps and Derivatives Association (ISDA) 131–4, 142–3
Internet 149
Internet information sources 371–2
interruptible retail contracts 160, 305–6
intra-day electricity spot markets 34–6, 39–40
intrinsic values, options 200–2, 204–12, 218, 227–31, 280–1, 288–99
investment assets 194, 387–91, 408–9
investors 79–80, 83, 86–100, 194, 299, 387–91, 408–9
IPCC see Intergovernmental Panel on Climate Change
Iran 9, 13–15
Iraq 8, 9
Ireland 29, 44, 46
iron ore 26
irreducible Markov chains, definition 400
ISDA see International Swaps and Derivatives Association
ISO 31000 risk/risk-management definitions 101–2
IT systems, risk management 148–9
Italy 28–31, 44, 46–7, 83–5, 308–9, 311, 376–86
Itô's lemma (formula) 202–3, 222–3, 232–41, 403–6, 409
   see also stochastic processes

Japan 16–17, 19–20, 23–4, 43–4, 54, 83, 168
jet fuel 12
Joint Implementation (JI) Kyoto Protocol flexible mechanism 45, 47–8
JP Morgan's RiskMetrics 112, 122
jump-diffusion model 209–10

Kalman filtering method 244–5, 398–9
Kaplan reaction turbines, hydropower 65
Kazakhstan 22, 44, 53
kerogen oil product 9
kerosine oil product 12
Keynes, John Maynard 197
kinetic energy, turbines 37, 63–5
Kirk's approximation 220–1, 279–81
know your customer processes (KYC) 148–9

KYC see know your customer processes
Kyoto offsets 47–8, 53
Kyoto Protocol 42–54

Lagrange relaxation 332
Land-Use, Land-Use Change and Forestry (LULUCF) 44
landfill sites 97
Latvia 29, 39, 44
least-squares Monte Carlo (LSMC) 281–99
Lebesgue–Stieltjes integral 404–5
legal risks 17–18, 102, 130–4, 146, 148–9
Lehman Brothers 7–8, 102, 135, 193–4
Libya 9
Liechtenstein 46
light crudes, definition 9–11
light distillates, definition 12
light tight oil 9
lignite coal 21–6, 306–13
   see also coal
linear programming optimisation method (LP) 325–35, 341, 348–53, 382–6
linear regression 256–65, 267–81, 393–6
Linking Directive (2009/27/EC) 48
liquefied natural gases (LNG) 13–20, 131–4, 375–86
   see also gas
   definition 19–20
   statistics 19–20, 375–86
   storage methods 380–2, 384
liquefied petroleum gases (LPGs) 12
liquidity coverage ratio 145–6
liquidity risks 102, 144–6
liquidity-adjusted VaR (LVaR) 123–6, 144
Lithuania 29, 39, 44
LNG see liquefied natural gas
load duration curves 337–47
load forecasts 158, 160–1, 163–5, 173, 176–83, 266–99, 302–74, 375–86, 402
loading schedules
   LNG 19–20, 375–86
   oil 11
locally affected parties, renewable energy stakeholders 80
location spread 219
locational marginal price (LMP) 42
log-likelihood functions 401
log-normal approximation Asian option pricing method 213, 215–18
log-normal distributions 114–20, 127, 182, 213–16, 239–41, 243, 272–81, 290–1
long positions 4, 6, 105–30, 187–9, 195–7, 199, 204–5
Long-Term Capital Management (LTCM) 144
long-term fuel supply contracts 98, 281–99
long-term gas market models 374–5, 384–6
long-term load forecasts 163–5, 266–81, 372–4
long-term purchase price guarantee, feed-in renewable energy tariffs 81–3
long-term scenarios, application of electricity market models 374

long-term valuations of gas assets, structural gas price models 298–9
Longstaff and Schwartz Monte Carlo method 212–16, 228–31, 281–99, 410
low tariff prices, retail markets 156–83
LP *see* linear programming optimisation method
lubricating oils 12
Luxembourg 29, 38, 44
LVaR *see* liquidity-adjusted VaR

maintenance, power plants 159–60, 185, 312–13, 368–72
Malaysia, LNG 19–20
Malta 29, 44
manufacturers 79–80, 93, 96–7
marginal cost of production 265, 311–13, 335–53, 357–66
margins 34–6, 142–5, 152–83, 189–91, 202–3, 301, 313–35, 347–53, 357–66, 388–91
Margrabe formula 219–21
mark-to-market settlements, futures 39–40
mark-to-market valuations 185, 187–9
market clearing prices 4
market liquidity risk 144–5
market power 357–60, 362–6, 374, 385–6
market price period, long-term valuations of gas assets 298–9
market price of risk 196–7, 200, 243–5
market risks 88–9, 97–100, 102, 104–30, 140, 146–7, 152–83, 405–6
    definition 104, 146–7
    risk management 98–9, 104–30, 152–83
Markov chains 246–51, 265–81, 399–400
martingales 200, 225–6, 246–51, 402–3, 406–7
master agreements 24–5, 45–8, 131–4, 137, 144
mathematical concepts 393–411
Matlab 268
maturity (expiration) date
    definition 197–8
maximum likelihood function 241, 271–81, 399, 401
maximum ramp rates, thermal power plants 316–21, 329–35, 350–3, 369–72
MCP *see* mixed complementary problem
mean reversion 209–10, 224–5, 226–45, 253, 265–81, 406–7
media providers, system information 372
Mediterranean refined oil market 12
medium-term load forecasts 163–5
merit order curves 265–81, 335–47, 357–74
    see also supply curves; variable costs
Merton, Robert C. 144
metals 5
meteorological offices 43, 372
    see also weather . . .
methane (CH4) 13–20, 42–54, 75–6
middle distillates 12
Middle East 7–10, 13–15, 17–20, 27–8
MiFID Directives 103
MIP *see* mixed integer programming optimisation method

mixed complementary problem (MCP), game theory 365–6
mixed integer programming optimisation method (MIP) 280–1, 315, 325–35, 341, 348–53, 385
monopolies, electricity markets 28–9, 311–13, 357–66
Monte Carlo simulations 116, 126, 140–1, 212–16, 218, 231, 237, 241, 245, 280–99, 410–11
    definition 410
Moody's 136–41
moving averages time series models (MA) 395–6
multi-commodity SMaPS model 269–81
multi-factor exponential model 251
multi-region models, optimisation methods 347–53, 371–2, 374–5, 385–6
multi-underlying options 216–24
    see also basket . . . ; composite . . . ; quantos . . . ; spread . . .
must-run power plants 338, 369–72

N2EX 39, 40
NAG 268
naphtha oil product 12
NAPs *see* national allocation plans
NASDAQ OMX Commodities Europe 5
NASDAQ OMX Commodities Europe financial market 39–40, 49–54
Nash equilibrium, game theory 361–6
national allocation plans (NAPs) 46–54, 386
National Balancing Point (NBP) 17–18, 131–4
National Energy Act, US 81–2
national implementation measures (NIMs) 46–54
National Renewable Energy Action Plan of 2010, Europe 58
natural gas 1–7, 12–20, 28–9, 31, 52, 131–4, 145–6, 151–83, 281–99, 306–91
    see also gas
natural greenhouse effect 42
net present value (NPV) 89–90, 188–9, 387–91
net stable funding ratio 145–6
net worth 139–40
net-metering/billing renewable energy support schemes 83
NetConnect Germany (NCG) 17–18, 176
Netherlands 17–20, 28–31, 38, 41, 44, 48, 278–9, 285–6, 290–1, 309, 377–86
netting agreements 131–4, 137, 144
New York Mercantile Exchange (NYMEX) 5, 11, 15, 42, 49–54
New Zealand 44, 48, 49, 52–4
New Zealand Units (NZUs) 49, 52–4
Newcastle, Australia delivery point 24–5
Nigeria 9, 20
nitrous oxide (N2O) 42–3, 45–54, 308
nominal currency values 353
non-cooperative game theory 361–6
non-zero-sum games, non-cooperative game theory 362
Nord Pool electricity spot exchange 5, 38–40, 305–6, 345, 372
    see also Elbas . . . ; Elspot . . .

Nord Stream pipeline 290–1
NORDEL 371–2
Nordic Region (NWE) 38
normal distributions 93–5, 113–30, 202–12, 233, 237,
        240–1, 394–5, 403
normal forms, game theory 360–1
normal-inverse Gaussian (NIG) 285–99
normalised cumulated heating degree days
        (NCHDDs) 166–72, 282–99
North America 7–11, 13–20, 21–4, 27–8, 49–54, 58
    see also Canada; US
North Sea 10–11, 376–7
Northumberland (UK) hydropower station of 1880 62
Norway 5, 13–15, 17–20, 28–9, 38–9, 44, 46, 376–86
NPV see net present value
nuclear power 27–31, 48, 154, 269, 271–81, 303,
        306–13, 319–20, 370–2
    definition 308–9
    statistics 1–2, 28–31, 306–13, 370–2
numerical methods 212–16, 228–31, 410–11
    see also Monte Carlo simulations; partial
        differential equations; tree . . .
NYMEX see New York Mercantile Exchange
NZUs see New Zealand Units

ocean thermal energy conversion (OTEC) 77, 311
off-standard contracts 263–5
oil 1–13, 15, 27, 61, 98, 106–10, 135–6, 145–6, 154,
        186–9, 192–7, 281–99, 306–91
    see also diesel; fuel . . . ; gasoline; liquefied
        petroleum gases
    benchmark oils 10–11
    consumption, production and reserves 7–10, 15
    derivatives 11, 12
    energy trading 5–6, 7, 10–12, 135–6
    forwards 11, 186–9, 192–7
    fundamental market models 386–7
    futures 11, 12
    gas prices 3, 281–99, 308, 377–8
    loading schedules 11
    physical market structure 11
    price determinants 7–10, 12, 51, 61, 106–10,
        186–9, 192–7, 281–99, 386–7
    product types 7, 9, 11–12, 386–7
    quality factors 9–12
    refined oil products 11–12, 386–7
    reserves-to-production ratios 9, 15
    spot prices 7–12
    statistics 1–2, 7–12, 306–13
    sulphur contents 9–12
    swaps 11–12, 191–2
    uses 7–12, 27, 306–13, 386–7
    viscosity 9–12
oil sands 9
oil-indexed supply contracts 3, 17–18, 105–10, 377
oligopolies 311–13, 357–66, 374
OLS see ordinary least squares
one-factor Schwartz model 237–45, 282–99
one-factor spot price models 226, 237–45, 282–99
one-factor stochastic forward curve models 247–51

OPEC 9–10, 386
open cycle gas turbines (GTs) 308, 344–7, 367–72
open retail contracts 158
operating costs 301, 313–35, 347–53
operational risks 88–9, 93–7, 102, 136, 146–9, 173,
        181–3
    see also construction . . . ; legal . . . ; market . . . ;
        regulatory . . . ; resource . . . ; technical . . .
    definition 146–8, 173, 181–2
operational VaR 147–9
opportunity costs 313–35, 341–7, 373–4
optimisation methods 280–1, 315, 325–35, 341–53,
        359–66, 371–2, 375, 382–6
    see also decomposition . . . ; dynamic
        programming . . . ; heuristics; linear
        programming . . . ; mixed integer . . .
    economic power plant dispatch 320–1, 325–35,
        341, 347–53, 359–66
    electricity markets 280–1, 315, 325–35, 341–53,
        359–66, 371–2, 375
    gas markets 375, 382–6
    multi-region models 347–53, 371–2, 374–5, 385–6
    selection considerations 333–5, 349–53
    single-region models 347–8
option premiums, definition 6
options 3, 5–6, 11, 15–20, 39–40, 49–50, 99, 105–6,
        117–18, 120, 159–60, 168–72, 175, 185–6,
        197–212, 221–51, 278–9, 387–91, 402–11
    see also American . . . ; Asian . . . ; Bermudan . . . ;
        call . . . ; caps; European . . . ; floors;
        multi-underlying . . . ; put . . . ; swaptions;
        swing . . .
    definition 6, 40, 185–6, 197–8
    hedging 198–200, 202–12, 216, 225–6, 290–9
    premiums 197–212
    profits 6, 197–8
    strategies 198–200
    terminology 197–8, 212–16
    types 40, 185, 197–8, 212–16, 409–10
    uses 198–200, 387–91
options pricing theory 105–6, 117–18, 159–60,
        169–72, 175, 199–212, 226–45, 253, 279–81,
        298–9, 387–91, 402–11
    see also Black–Scholes model; Monte Carlo
        simulations; risk-neutral measures
    assumptions 159, 200–12, 290–1, 406
ordinary least squares (OLS) 241, 256–65, 269–81,
        393–4, 397
Orimulsion 308
Ornstein–Uhlenbeck process 241–5, 251, 265–6
Oseberg, Brent benchmark 11
out-of-the-money options 200–2
over-the-counter transactions (OTCs) 3–6, 11, 12, 26,
        34–6, 39–41, 103–4, 136–46, 168–9, 186–9, 197,
        263–5, 372–4
    see also forwards; swaps
ozone (O3) 42

Panamax-sized vessels, coal freight 26
PaR see Profit-at-Risk

paraffin wax oil products 12
partial delivery retail contracts 157–60
partial differential equations (PDEs) 203–16,
    409–11
path-dependent options 212–16, 410
payer swaps, definition 191–2, 210–11
Peabody Energy 24
peakload electricity contracts 34–6, 105–30, 141–4,
    151–83, 261–5, 345–7
peat fuel 308
Pelton impulse turbines, hydropower 63–5
perfect competition 311–13, 348, 357–66
perfluorocarbons (PFCs) 43–54, 258
petroleum coke 12, 308
PFCs see perfluorocarbons
photovoltaics (PV) 57–8, 69–71, 77–80, 82, 84,
    88–90, 94–7, 99–100, 260–1, 310–13, 338–9
    see also solar renewable energy
physical energy flows 313–14, 345, 348–53,
    370–2
physical market structure, oil 11
PJM Western Hub 42
'plain vanillas' see options
Planta Solar, Seville 78
Platts oil pricing reporting agency 10, 12
Poland 28–31, 44, 46–7, 84–5, 308
political goals 55, 58–60, 78–87, 266–7, 371–2
polynomial basis functions 293–9
portfolio compression 143–4
portfolio concepts 153–5, 158–60, 375–86, 390–1
portfolio management retail contracts 158–60, 183
portfolio optimisation, gas market models 382–6
Portugal 44
potential exposure measure of credit risk 140–4
power generation sector demands 9, 12–13, 21–6,
    44–6, 48, 51–2, 58–100, 302–13
power plants 64–5, 73–7, 97–100, 157–60, 185–251,
    278–81, 286–99, 301, 306–35, 338–72,
    387–91
    see also hydropower . . . ; technologies;
        thermal . . .
    economic power plant dispatch 301, 313–35,
        338–53, 357–66
    system information 366–72
power purchase agreements (PPAs), renewable energy
    support schemes 85–6
power schedule electricity 34–6, 108–30, 152–5
power systems, fundamental market models 301–74
Powernext 40–1
precipitation 307–13
premiums, options 197–212
Price Coupling of Regions (PCR) 38
price fixing 359–66
price profile risks 157–60, 171–3, 177–81,
    183
price spikes 29–31, 224–6, 253–99
price validity period risk premium 173–5, 183
price–volume correlation risk premium 177–81, 183
primary reserves, electricity markets 37–8, 312–13,
    319–20, 343–7

principal component analysis (PCA) 272–81, 397
private equity 79–80
probability of default (PD) 136–40, 142–4, 177
production tax credit (PTC), renewable energy
    support schemes 87
products
    electricity markets 33–42, 155–60
    emissions market 3–5, 28–9, 46–54
    retail markets 155–60
Profit-at-Risk (PaR) 102, 124, 127–30, 174
project developers 78–9, 83, 85–100
project schedules, risk-mitigation processes 92–3
propane 13
protective put strategy, definition 199–200, 228
Public Utility Regulatory Policies Act 1978 (PURPA),
    US 81–2
pumped storage hydropower plants 64–5, 306,
    309–10, 313, 322–5, 338–47, 348–53, 370–2
put options 6, 185, 197–212, 228–9, 235–7
put–call parity 198–212

Q-Flex, LNG carriers 20
Q-Max, LNG carriers 20
Qatar 9, 13–15, 17–20
QQ-plots 115
quality factors
    coal 21, 307–8
    gas 15–16
    oil 9–12
quantos (quantity-adjusting options) 169–72, 221–4
Quebec Cap-and-Trade System 53–4

Radon–Nikodym theorem 402
rail transport 368–9
rain forests 61
ramp rates, thermal power plants 316–21, 329–35,
    350–3, 369–72
random walks 268–81, 395–7
Rankine cycle 308, 311
RAROC see risk-adjusted return on capital
real currency values 353
real options 387–91
real-time data providers, system information 372
receiver swaps, definition 191–2, 210–11
reduced-form models 253
reducible Markov chains 400
refined oil products 11–12, 386–7
    see also oil
regasification terminals, LNG 20
regime-switching models 265–81, 399–401
Regional Greenhouse Gas Initiative (RGGI) 53
regional interconnections 301–35, 345–6, 370–2,
    374–5
regression model load forecasts 163–5
regressors, concepts 393–5
regulations 7, 28–9, 31, 36–42, 79–83, 85–6, 87,
    99–104, 132–4, 143–4, 148–9, 312–13, 371–2,
    375–86, 399–401
regulatory risks 88–9, 99–100
REMIT Directive 103–4

renewable energy 1–3, 27–31, 55–100, 260–7, 303, 306–91
  see also bio . . . ; geothermal . . . ; hydropower . . . ; solar . . . ; tidal . . . ; wave . . . ; wind . . .
  auctioning 85–6
  barriers 59–61, 83
  benefits 55
  costs 59–60, 63–5, 68, 70, 77–100
  definition 55–8
  demonstration projects 78–9
  economic factors 55, 59, 78–80, 87–90
  electric utility quota obligations 83–5, 99
  feed-in tariffs 80–5, 97–100
  finance sources 78–90
  forecasts 59–60, 260–5
  grants and subsidies 86–7, 91, 99–100
  historical background 55–60, 61–3, 66, 68, 71, 77, 81–2, 309–10
  net-metering/billing support schemes 83
  political goals 55, 58–60, 78–87, 266–7, 371–2
  returns 78–90
  risk factors 55, 79–100
  risk mitigation 55, 89–100
  stakeholders 78–80, 83, 85–7
  statistics 1–2, 28–31, 55–100, 260–5, 306–13, 370–2
  support schemes 55–6, 58, 60–1, 78–87, 266–7
  taxes 80, 86–7, 89, 99–100, 312–13
  technologies 55, 59–79, 84, 87–100, 260–5, 309–11
  tradable certificates 83–5, 99, 312–13, 372
  trends 55–61
  types 55–8, 264–5, 306–13
  value chains 87–90
Renewable Energy Certificates (RECs), US 84–5
Renewable Obligation Certificates (ROCs) 84–5
Renewable Obligations (ROs) 83–5
Renewable Portfolio Standard (RPS) 83–4
renewable sources Directive (2009/28/EC) 58, 84–5
replacement risks 136, 144, 176–7
reputational risks 146
research institutes, system information 372
reserve capacity needs, system information 370–2
reserve constraints, thermal power plants 319–21, 343–7
reserve contracts for electricity 159–60
reserve electricity markets 34–8, 302–13, 319–21, 370–2
reserves-to-production ratios 9, 14–15, 22–4
reservoir balance equation, hydropower plants 323–5, 339–47, 350–3
reservoir/storage hydropower plants 64–5, 309–10, 313–35, 339–47, 350–3
residual sum of squares (RSS) 394
resource risks 88–90, 93–6
retail markets 151–83, 302–91
  customer types 155–60, 305–13
  load forecasts 158, 160–1, 163–5, 173, 176–7, 302–91
  product types 155–60, 182–3

risk management 151–83
risk premiums 153–70, 172–83
sourcing of contracts 153–63, 181–2
wholesale markets 151–5, 172–3, 305–13
return on capital 159–60, 174, 176, 182, 353, 390–1
return on equity 139–40
returns 78–93, 111–30, 139–40, 153–70, 172–83, 196–7, 271–99, 353, 387–91
RGGI *see* Regional Greenhouse Gas Initiative
Richards Bay, South Africa delivery point 6–7, 24–6
rights of cancellation of the supply contract 160, 183
risk appetite 147–9
risk assessments 91–102, 147–9, 182, 225–6, 373–4, 387–91
risk committees 103
risk factors 3, 5–7, 55, 79–149, 151–83, 225–6, 299, 387–91, 405–8
  see also construction . . . ; credit . . . ; legal . . . ; liquidity . . . ; market . . . ; operational . . . ; regulatory . . . ; resource . . . ; technical . . . ; volume . . .
risk identification 97–102, 147
risk management 55, 89–149, 151–83, 191–2, 225–6, 299, 387–91
  avoidance/reduction/transference/acceptance strategies 101–3, 168–72, 387–91
  Basel Committee on Banking Supervision 101–3
  credit risks 135–44, 173, 176–7, 183
  definitions 101–2
  governance principles and market regulations 101–4, 143–4, 148–9
  ISO 31000 risk/risk-management definitions 101–2
  legal risks 130–4, 148–9
  market risks 98–9, 104–30, 152–83
  operational risks 146–9
risk maps, risk identification 101–2
risk mitigation 55, 89, 90–149, 153–5, 362–3
risk premiums 153–70, 172–83, 196–7, 390–1
risk-adjusted discount rate 388–91
risk-adjusted return on capital (RAROC) 159–60, 174, 176, 182
risk-adjusted returns 89–93, 159–60, 174, 387–91
risk-at-default measure of credit risk 140–4
risk-aversion 390–1
risk-free rates 203–12, 387–91
risk-neutral measures 200, 216–51, 387, 405–9
Romania 29, 44, 308
run-of-river hydropower plants 64–5, 264–5, 307–13, 322, 338–9
Russia 13–15, 17–24, 44, 376–86
  coal 21–4
  gas 13–15, 17–20, 376–86
  greenhouse gas emissions 44
  LNG 20

S-PLUS 268–9
Saitama, emissions market 54
SARIMA processes 181, 266–81
Saudi Arabia 9, 13–15
scarcity premiums, merit order curves 345–7, 350–3

scenario analysis 89, 91–3, 114–15, 180–1, 334–5,
    350–3, 366–7, 374–86
scheduled outages 159–60, 185, 312–13, 368–72
Scholes, Myron S. 144
    see also Black . . .
Schwartz one-factor model *see* one-factor Schwartz
    model
Schwartz–Smith two-factor model *see* two-factor
    Schwartz–Smith model
seasonal load forecasts 164–5, 224–6, 253, 255–65,
    282–99, 302–91
secondary forms of energy 1, 9, 27–42
secondary reserves, electricity markets 37–8, 312–13,
    343–7
sensitivity analysis 89, 91–3
services sector energy demands 302–13
settlement periods, electricity markets 151–83
settlement risks 135–6, 144, 176–7
shale gas 9, 13–20, 31
short positions 4, 105–30, 187–9, 194–7, 199, 204–5,
    372–4
short-term gas market models 374–5, 383–6
short-term load forecasts 163–5, 266–81, 372–4
short-term price adjustments, Scandinavian countries
    305–6
sigmoid functions 166–7
significance tests 396
single-region models, optimisation methods 347–8
Slovakia 29, 44, 308
Slovenia 29, 44
SMaPS (spot market price simulation) model 111,
    129–30, 178–81, 266–81
smoothing, calibration improvements 263–5
SO_2 emissions 51–3, 307–8, 312–13
solar chimney power plants 77
solar constant 69
solar renewable energy 28–30, 55–60, 69–73, 77–80,
    82, 84, 88–90, 93–100, 260–5, 306–13, 373–4
    statistics 56–60, 69–71, 78, 94–5, 306–13
    technologies 69–71, 77–80, 90, 93–7, 260–1, 310
sour oils 10
sourcing of contracts 153–63, 181–2
South America 7–10, 13–15, 23–4, 27–8
South Korea 19–20, 23–5, 77
Spain 28–31, 44, 47, 78, 99–100, 278–9, 309, 376–86
speculation 187–9, 190–1, 197
spinning reserves 343–4
spot markets 3–12, 15–26, 29–30, 34–42, 127–30,
    151–83, 187–9, 194–212, 224–45, 301–91,
    406–8
    application of electricity market models 372–4
    definition 3–4
spot price models 224–51, 253, 256–65, 267–99,
    345–7, 371–2
    historical calibration 235–6, 240–1, 244–5,
    256–65, 267–81, 290–9, 345–7, 371–2
    one-factor spot price models 226, 237–45, 282–99
    two-factor spot price models 226, 241–5, 249–51,
    272–81, 282–99
spot price options, pricing 226–31

spot prices 6, 7–20, 127–30, 151–83, 187–9, 194–212,
    224–45, 253–99, 345–7, 388–91, 406–8
    forward–spot price relations 187–9, 194–7, 407–8
    price spikes 29–31, 224–6, 253–99
spread options 218–21, 279–81
squared correlation coefficient 394–5
stack models 334–47
stakeholders
    see also investors; manufacturers; project
    developers; regulations
    renewable energy 78–80, 83, 85–100
Standard & Poor's (S&P) 136–40
Standard Coal Trading Agreement (SCoTA) 24–5,
    131–4
standard deviations 113–20, 235–7, 240–1, 394–5,
    403
standard error 394, 410–11
start-up costs 308–9, 317–35, 342–7, 350–3
state-space representation, Kalman filtering methods
    244–5, 398–9
stationary time series, concepts 395–7
stationary white noise processes 396–7
statistic learning algorithms, load forecasts 163–5
statistical offices 371–2
steam coal 21–6, 386
    see also coal; hard . . . ; sub-bituminous . . .
steel production 21
stochastic differential equations (SDEs) 216–24,
    232–51, 405, 406
stochastic forward curve models 246–51, 253–65,
    274–81
stochastic integration 403–5
stochastic models 111, 129–30, 178–81, 246–51,
    253–99
stochastic processes 111–20, 164–5, 170–2, 178–81,
    199, 209–10, 225–6, 228–9, 231–45, 246–51,
    253–99, 334–5, 395–7, 398–400, 402–5
    see also Brownian motion; geometric Brownian
    motion; Itô's lemma; martingales
    definition 284–5, 402–3
stochastic volatility models 209–10
stop-loss strategies 124
storage costs 307–13, 406–7
storage
    electricity 64–5, 301, 306, 309–10, 313, 322–5,
    338–47
    gas 379–86
storage problems, electricity markets 31–4, 98,
    151–83, 225–6, 253–99, 301–13, 338–47
strategic-partnership, risk-mitigation approaches
    92–3
strict risk premiums 173
strict stationary processes, concepts 395–7
strike prices, definition 6, 197–8
strips 288–99
structural models 111, 129–30, 178–81, 253–99,
    335–47
structuring fee and balancing energy risk premium
    173, 175–6
student *t*-distributions 181, 271–2

sub-bituminous coal 21–6
  see also coal; steam . . .
sulphur contents 9–13, 21–6, 51–4, 307–8, 312–13
sulphur hexafluoride (SF6) 43–4
supplementary retail products 159–60
supply 1–2, 7–10, 12–13, 15–24, 27–42, 97–100,
      151–83, 194–7, 265–99, 301–72, 374–86
  economic power plant dispatch 301, 313–35,
      338–47
  fundamental price drivers 301–13, 336–47,
      357–66, 374–86
supply curves 301–2, 335–47, 357–66, 373–4
support schemes, renewable energy 55–6, 58, 60–1,
      78–87, 266–7
Supramax-sized vessels 26
swaps 6, 11–12, 25–6, 131–4, 185–6, 191–2, 210–12
swaptions 210–12
Sweden 28–9, 38–9, 44, 84–5, 308–9
sweet oil, definition 10, 11
swing 185, 229–32, 286–99, 325, 378–86, 387–91
Switzerland 5, 29, 44, 53, 94–6
system dynamics 311–13, 353–7, 385–6
system expansion, optimisation methods 351–3
system information for electricity market modelling
      366–72
systematic risks 173, 177–81, 197, 390–1

t-ratio 394–7
Taiwan, LNG 20
take-or-pay volume, gas contract terms 18–20, 345–7,
      377–86
tariffs 80–5, 97–100, 155–83, 306–13, 380–6
taxes 12, 80, 86–7, 89, 99–100, 148–9, 312–13,
      368–72, 389–90
Taylor series expansion 120, 208
technical risks 96–7
technologies
  biofuels 60–1, 73–7
  biomass renewable energy 60–1, 73–7, 90–1, 96–9,
      310
  economic power plant dispatch 315–35
  electricity storage methods 64–5, 301, 306,
      309–10, 313, 322–5, 338–47
  gas 308, 379–86
  geothermal heat renewable energy 71–2, 91, 311
  hydropower 61–5, 79, 90–5, 301, 309–10, 322–5,
      338–47, 350–3
  renewable energy 55, 59–79, 84, 87–100, 260–5,
      309–11
  solar energy 69–71, 77–80, 90, 93–7, 260–1, 310
  wind power generation 66–9, 78–80, 90–1, 93–5,
      310
temperatures 151, 255–65, 281–99, 375–86, 402, 406
term structure of interest rates 246–51
tertiary reserves, electricity markets 37–8, 313, 344–7
thermal power plants 306–8, 315–21, 329–66, 367–72
theta, definition 204–6
three-factor Cortazar and Schwartz model 282–3
tidal renewable energy 55–8, 77, 310
Tier 1,2 capital 146

tight gas 15–16
time aggregation, optimisation methods 350–3
time horizons 113–20, 123–30, 155–83, 204–6,
      337–47, 373–4
time series 155–83, 266–81, 366–72, 395–7, 399–400
time spread 219
time value of money 330
time value of the option 204–5
time-integral constraints, thermal power plants 320–1,
      329–35, 337–8, 344–7, 351–3, 369–72
Title Transfer Facility (TTF) 17–18, 131–4, 171–2,
      284–99
Tokyo, emissions market 54
total system load, risk factors 406–7
tradable certificates, renewable energy support
      schemes 83–5, 99, 312–13, 372
transfer capacities, system information 370–2
transition matrices, definition 327–8, 330, 400
transition period, long-term valuations of gas assets
      298–9
transition probability matrices 274–81
transmission system operators (TSOs) 33, 34–8,
      155–60, 173, 175–6, 183, 312–13, 366–7,
      370–2
transport sector energy demands 1–3, 9, 12–13, 44–6,
      58–100, 302–13
transportation and storage considerations
  coal 24–6, 307–8, 368–72
  gas 13–14, 19–20, 151–83, 193–4, 225–6, 253–99,
      368–72, 374–86
tree numerical methods 212–16, 410
trend-stationary process 396
trifluoromethane 48
Trinidad & Tobago, LNG 19–20
trinomial trees 212–16
TSOs *see* transmission system operators
turbines 37, 63–9, 78–80, 306–35, 339–47, 348–53,
      367–72
Turkey 28–31, 44, 100
two-factor Schwartz–Smith model 241–5, 249–51,
      272–99
two-factor spot price models 226, 241–5, 272–99
two-factor stochastic forward curve models 249–51

UK 2–3, 16–20, 28–42, 44, 46–7, 58, 83–5, 151,
      193–7, 305–6, 309, 312–13, 376–86
  deregulated markets 2–3, 17–18, 28–31, 151
  electric utility quota obligations 83–5
  electricity markets 28–42, 58, 83–5, 151, 305–6,
      309, 312–13
  energy trading 2–3, 16–20, 28–42, 151, 312–13
  gas 16–20, 193–7, 376–86
  greenhouse gas emissions 44, 46–7, 312–13
  net-metering/billing renewable energy support
      schemes 83
  nuclear power options 309
  renewable energy 58, 83–5, 312–13
  Renewable Obligation Certificates (ROCs) 84–5
  Renewable Obligations (ROs) 83–5
Ukraine 22, 44

ultra-short-term load forecasts 163–5
unconventional gases 15
unconventional oils 9
underlying assets 4, 11, 25, 185, 197–216, 224–45, 288–99, 387–91
unit root tests 395–7
United Arab Emirates 9
United Nations Conference on Environment and Development (UNCED) 43–4
United Nations Environment Programme (UNEP) 42–3
United Nations Framework Convention on Climate Change (UNFCCC) 43–4, 47–8
United Nations General Assembly (UNGA) 43–4
unscheduled outages 160, 312–13, 368–72
unsystematic risks 173, 177–81, 390–1
unsystematic volume risks 177–81
up-and-downtimes, thermal power plants 316–21, 329–35, 344–7, 369–72
upstream portfolios 153–83
US 2–3, 5–11, 13–24, 27–8, 31, 36–7, 42–4, 49–54, 58, 60–1, 81–5, 87, 104, 148–9, 166–8, 197, 255–65, 278–9
   Acid Rain Program 51–2
   air conditioning demands 166–8, 255–65
   biofuels 60–1
   California electricity crisis of 2000 31, 42
   coal 21–4
   deregulated markets 2–3, 31
   Dodd–Frank Act 2010 104, 143–4
   electricity markets 27–8, 31, 36–7, 42, 58, 81–4, 87, 197, 278–9
   emissions market 43–4, 49–54
   energy trading 2, 5–6, 10–11, 15–20
   gas 13–20
   governance principles and market regulations 104, 143–4, 148–9
   greenhouse gas emissions 43–4, 51–4
   Kyoto Protocol 43–4
   oil 7–11
   production tax credit 87
   renewable energy 58, 60–1, 81–4, 87
   shale gas 13–17, 31
US-GAAP accounting standards 140

value chains 87–90, 135, 383–6
Value-at-Risk (VaR) 102, 111–30, 140–4, 170, 174, 182
   see also Credit . . . ; liquidity-adjusted . . .
   definition 112–13
value-equivalent hedging 109–10
VaR see Value-at-Risk
variable costs 265–81, 308–9, 313–53, 357–66, 368–72, 377–86

variance 110–20, 202–16, 233, 390–1, 394–7, 403, 411
variance minimising hedging 110–11, 152–3, 411
variation margins, futures 34–6, 189–91
Vasicek model 237–41
VAT 87
vega 153–5, 206–7, 208
Venezuela 9, 308
venture capital 79–80
verification checks, operational risks 149
virtual gas storage 380–6
virtual power plants (VPPs) 157–60, 185–251, 278–81, 286–99, 325, 345–7, 387–91
viscosity issues, oil 9–12
volatilities 116–30, 145–6, 160–1, 175, 182, 202–12, 225–45, 246–51, 273–99
   see also implied . . . ; stochastic . . . ; vega
volatility skew 209
volatility smile 208–10, 250–1
volatility of volatility 209–10
volume risks 102, 157–60, 173, 177–81, 183, 291–2, 377–86
Vorst Asian option pricing method 213–15

WACC see weighted average cost of capital
waste handling and disposal 44–5, 48, 306–13
water authorities, system information 372
water values, hydropower plants 240–7
water vapour 42
wave renewable energy 55–8, 77
weather derivatives 168–72
weather forecasts 164–72, 255–65, 281–99, 302–91
weather risks 165–72, 225, 255–65, 281–99, 302–91
weighted average cost of capital (WACC) 388–91
West Texas Intermediate benchmark oil (WTI) 10–11
Western Climate Initiative (WCI) 53
wholesale markets 15–20, 27–42, 135, 151–5, 172–3, 278–81, 305–35
wind power generation 29–30, 55–60, 66–9, 72, 78–80, 82, 84, 87–91, 93–100, 264–5, 306–13, 338–47, 350–3, 373–4
   statistics 55–8, 59–60, 66–9, 78, 93–5, 306–13
   technologies 66–9, 78–80, 90–1, 93–5, 310, 338–47
withdrawals, gas 291–9, 380–6
World Climate Conference of 1979 42–3
World Climate Programme 42–3
World Commission on Dams 48
World Energy Outlook (WEO) 59–60
World Meteorological Organization (WMO) 43
Worldbank 148
WTI futures 11

Zeebrugge Hub (ZEE) 17–18, 131–4
zero-sum games, non-cooperative game theory 362

Index compiled by Terry Halliday

Printed and bound by CPI Group (UK) Ltd, Croydon, CR0 4YY

23/04/2025

14660970-0004